1994

INTEREST GROUP
POLITICS

INTEREST GROUP POLITICS

Fourth Edition

Edited by
Allan J. Cigler
Burdett A. Loomis
University of Kansas

A Division of Congressional Quarterly Inc.
Washington, D.C.

Copyright © 1995 Congressional Quarterly Inc.
1414 22nd Street, N.W., Washington, D.C. 20037

Printed in the United States of America

Cover design: Paula Anderson

Library of Congress Cataloging-in-Publication Data

Interest group politics / edited by Allan J. Cigler, Burdett A.
Loomis. -- 4th ed.
    p.   cm.
    Includes bibliographical references (p.   ) and index.
    ISBN 0-87187-801-1
    1. Pressure groups--United States. I. Cigler, Allan J., 1943- .
II. Loomis, Burdett A., 1945- .
JK1118.I565 1995
322.4'3'0973--dc20   94-33764
                                                                             CIP

Contents

Preface

We write this preface as the often-fractious debate over health care reform comes to a head. In hundreds of ways, hundreds of organized interests have sought to shape the ultimate results. The explosion of advocacy advertisements, grassroots mobilizations, and public relations campaigns have provided scholars, politicians, and citizens with a remarkably public set of confrontations over the kind of health care system that will emerge. The assorted machinations have often made mud wrestling look tame in comparison.

The health care struggle reminds us that organized interests remain central to both the theory and practice of politics in the United States. In previous editions, we noted the resurgence of academic attention in interest group politics; that attention continues, hampered somewhat by the difficulties inherent in collecting data from large numbers of organized interests. At the same time, the practice of interest group politics continues to evolve, offering new opportunities to explore both how groups organize and how interests seek to affect policies and election results.

We hope that the first three editions of *Interest Group Politics* have played some role in increasing the attention paid to understanding organized interests. Moving from an emphasis on the proliferation of groups in the first edition (1983), we looked at new roles for interests in the second edition (1986) and their continuing evolution in the third edition (1991). As in our previous volumes, this collection begins with an introductory essay, followed by sections on internal group development (Chapters 2-6), electoral politics (Chapters 7-8), and attempts to influence a wide range of policies (Chapters 9-17). Finally, we conclude with an essay that suggests that American politics is experiencing some fundamental changes in the conduct of interest group politics.

Such changes are apparent in many of the articles; in particular, we would alert readers to Chris Foreman's study of so-called "Grassroots Victim Organizations," the Guth, et al., piece on the religious right, two articles on interests and regulatory politics, and Frank Sorauf's examination of adaptation by political action committees.

Once again we have tested the capacity of the folks at CQ Press to deal with the terminally disorganized; once again, against all odds, they have prevailed. Wonders never cease. Our great thanks go to Brenda Carter and Shana Wagger. Steve Kennedy did yeoman service in his copyediting work. As always, our contributors provided us with first-rate material; occasionally it arrived on time.

Finally, we dedicate this book to Bob Salisbury, who has labored so long and with such insight in the vineyards of interest group politics.

Allan J. Cigler
Burdett A. Loomis

Contributors

Jeffrey M. Berry is a professor of political science at Tufts University. Most of his research has been on interest groups and citizen participation. He is currently working on a project on the growing influence of citizen groups in national politics.

Christopher J. Bosso is an associate professor of political science at Northeastern University. His teaching and research interests include American politics and policy processes, particularly environmental policy making.

William P. Browne is a professor of political science at Central Michigan University. Most of his research has been in agricultural policy or interest groups, including work with the National Center for Food and Agricultural Policy and the Economic Research Service of the U.S. Department of Agriculture.

Loree Bykerk is an associate professor of political science at the University of Nebraska at Omaha. Her research interests include interest groups and public policy. She has recently been publishing in the area of consumer interest group behavior.

Allan J. Cigler is Chancellors Club Teaching Professor of Political Science. His research focuses on parties and interest groups, and particularly the interrelationship between the two groups.

Beverly A. Cigler is Professor of Public Policy and Administration at Pennsylvania State University, Harrisburg. Her teaching and research interests focus broadly on state and local politics, policies, and management. She is currently conducting a three-year study of multicommunity collaboration in the United States, funded by the USDA.

M. Margaret Conway teaches at the University of Florida. She received her Ph.D. from Indiana University in 1965. She has written or co-written several books focusing on political participation and political parties. She also has published a number of articles in academic journals.

Christine DeGregorio is an assistant professor at the School of Public Affairs at The American University. She studies the elaborate partnerships that form in the business of lawmaking. She is currently writing a book on congressional leadership that details the role of three sets of players—officeholders, aides, and advocates.

Christopher H. Foreman, Jr., is a senior fellow in the governmental studies program at the Brookings Institution. His research interests include legislative-executive relations, regulatory politics, and public health policy.

Joanne Connor Green is an assistant professor of political science at Texas Christian University. Her research interests include the dynamics of open seat elections for the U.S. House of Representatives, potential for issue voting, and the role of parties in the political process.

John C. Green is the director of the Ray Bliss Institute of Applied Politics and is a professor of political science at the University of Akron. His research interests include religion and politics.

James L. Guth is a professor of political science at Furman University. His research interests include religion and politics and political finance.

Ronald J. Hrebenar is a professor of political science at the University of Utah. With Clive S. Thomas, he is coeditor of a series of books on interest group politics in the states. He specializes in interest groups and political party politics.

Kevin Hula is an assistant professor of political science at Loyola College in Baltimore, Maryland. His research interests include interest groups and the presidency. He is currently a doctoral candidate at Harvard University.

Lyman A. Kellstedt is a professor of political science at Wheaton College. His research interests include religion and politics and American political behavior.

Burdett A. Loomis is a professor of political science at the University of Kansas. His research interests include legislatures, political careers, interest groups, and policy making.

Ardith Maney is an associate professor at Iowa State University, Ames. Her research interests include comparative bureaucracy, business/government relations, and food and agricultural policy.

Anthony J. Nownes is an assistant professor of political science at the University of Tennessee. His research interests include public interest groups and group formation.

Kent E. Portney is a professor of political science at Tufts University. His research interests are in citizen participation, environmental politics, and the NIMBY (not-in-my-backyard) Syndrome.

Jack E. Rossotti is an assistant professor of political science at The American University. His research interests include interest groups and the judicial process, as well as behavioral patterns of political action committees.

Lawrence S. Rothenberg is an associate professor of political science and public policy at the University of Rochester. His research interests revolve around organized groups and bureaucratic politics. He is currently writing a book on the politics of campaign contributions and on the economic foundations of public policy.

Eric Sexton is a Ph.D. student in political science at the University of Kansas. His research interests are interest groups and bureaucracy and their effect on public policy.

Corwin E. Smidt is a professor of political science at Calvin College. His research interests are in the relationship between religion and politics, focusing on evangelical political involvement.

Frank J. Sorauf is Regent's Professor of Political Science at the University of Minnesota. His research for the last fifteen years has chiefly been on American campaign finance, and he has recently published two books about money in elections.

Clive S. Thomas is a professor of political science at the University of Alaska in Juneau. He is coeditor with Ronald J. Hrebenar of a series of books on interest group politics in the states. He also has worked as a lobbyist in Alaskan state politics.

Eric M. Uslaner is a professor of government and politics at the University of Maryland—College Park. In 1981-1982 he was a Fulbright professor of American studies at the Hebrew University in Jerusalem. His interests focus on Congress, elections, energy policy, and Canadian politics.

1

Introduction: The Changing Nature of Interest Group Politics

Burdett A. Loomis and Allan J. Cigler

From James Madison to Madison Avenue, political interests have played a central role in American politics. But this great continuity in our political experience has been matched by the ambivalence with which citizens, politicians, and scholars have approached interest groups. James Madison's warnings on the dangers of faction echo in the rhetoric of reformers ranging from Populists and Progressives near the turn of the century to the so-called public-interest advocates of today.

If organized special interests are nothing new in American politics, can today's group politics nevertheless be seen as having undergone some fundamental changes? Acknowledging that many important, continuing trends do exist, we seek to place in perspective a broad series of changes in the nature of modern interest group politics. Among the most substantial of these developments are:

1. a great proliferation of interest groups since the early 1960s;
2. a centralization of group headquarters in Washington, D.C., rather than in New York City or elsewhere;
3. major technological developments in information processing that promote more sophisticated, more timely, and more specialized grassroots lobbying;
4. the rise of single-issue groups;
5. changes in campaign finance laws (1971, 1974) and the ensuing growth of political action committees (PACs);
6. the increased formal penetration of political and economic interests into the bureaucracy (advisory committees), the presidency (White House group representatives), and the Congress (caucuses of members);
7. the continuing decline of political parties' abilities to perform key electoral and policy-related activities;
8. the increased number, activity, and visibility of public-interest groups, such as Common Cause and the Ralph Nader-inspired public interest research organizations;

9. the growth of activity and impact by institutions, including corporations, universities, state and local governments, and foreign interests; and
10. a continuing rise in the amount and sophistication of group activity in state capitals.

All these developments have their antecedents in previous eras of American political life; there is little genuinely new under the interest group sun. Political action committees have replaced (or complemented) other forms of special interest campaign financing. Group-generated mail directed at Congress has existed as a tactic since at least the early 1900s.[1] Many organizations have long been centered in Washington, members of Congress traditionally have represented local interests, and so on.

At the same time, however, the level of group activity, coupled with growing numbers of organized interests, distinguishes contemporary group politics from the politics of earlier eras. Current trends of group involvement lend credence to the fears of scholars such as political scientist Theodore Lowi and economist Mancur Olson, who view interest-based politics as contributing to governmental stalemate and reduced accountability.[2] If accurate, these analyses point to a fundamentally different role for interest groups than those suggested by Madison and later group theorists.

Several contemporary studies, such as those by Olson and political scientists Robert Salisbury and Terry Moe, illustrate the weakness of much interest group analysis that does not account adequately for the reasons groups form and persist.[3] Only during the last thirty years, in the wake of Olson's path-breaking research, have scholars begun to examine realistically why people join and become active in groups. It is by no means self-evident that citizens should naturally become group members—quite the contrary in most instances. We are faced, then, with the paradoxical and complex question of why groups have proliferated, as they certainly have, when usually it is economically unwise for individuals to join them.

Interest Groups in American Politics

Practical politicians and scholars alike generally have concurred that interest groups (also known as factions, pressure groups, and special interests) are natural phenomena in a democratic regime—that is, individuals will band together to protect their interests.[4] In Madison's words, "the causes of faction ... are sown in the nature of man," but controversy continues as to whether groups and group politics are benign or malignant forces in American politics. "By a faction," Madison wrote, "I understand a number of citizens, whether amounting to a majority or minority of the whole, who are united and actuated by some common impulse of passion, or of interest, adverse to the rights of other citizens, or to the permanent and aggregate interests of the community."[5]

Although Madison rejected the remedy of direct controls over factions as "worse than the disease," he saw the need to limit their negative effects by promoting competition among them and by devising an elaborate system of procedural "checks and balances" to reduce the potential power of any single, strong group, whether that group represented a majority or minority position.

Hostility toward interest groups became more virulent in industrialized America, where the great concentrations of power that developed far outstripped anything Madison might have imagined. After the turn of the century many Progressives railed at various monopolistic "trusts" and intimate connections between interests and corrupt politicians. Later, in 1935, Hugo Black, then a senator (and later a Supreme Court justice), painted a grim picture of group malevolence: "Contrary to tradition, against the public morals, and hostile to good government, the lobby has reached such a position of power that it threatens government itself. Its size, its power, its capacity for evil, its greed, trickery, deception and fraud condemn it to the death it deserves."[6]

Similar suspicions are expressed today, especially in light of the substantial growth of PACs since 1974. PAC contributions to congressional candidates rose from less than $23 million in 1976 to $178 million in 1992, which amounted to almost a third of the candidates' campaign funds. Still, the number of PACs has leveled off at just over four thousand, only a fraction of which are major players in electoral politics. Reformers in and out of Congress have sought to limit purported PAC influence, but as of 1994 legislators could not agree on major changes in laws regulating campaign spending or group activity. PACs continue to be an attractive target for reformers. One typical expression of dismay came from Common Cause, the self-styled public interest lobby:

> The Special Interest State is a system in which interest groups dominate the making of government policy. These interests legitimately concentrate on pursuing their own immediate—usually economic—agendas, but in so doing they pay little attention to the impact of their agendas on the nation as a whole.[7]

Despite the considerable popular distrust of interest group politics, political scientists and other observers often have viewed groups in a much more positive light. This perspective also draws upon Madison's *Federalist* writings, but it is tied more closely to the growth of the modern state. Political science scholars such as Arthur Bentley, circa 1910, and David Truman, forty years later, placed groups at the heart of politics and policy making in a complex, large, and increasingly specialized governmental system. The interest group becomes an element of continuity in a changing political world. Truman noted the "multiplicity of co-ordinate or nearly co-ordinate points of access to governmental decisions" and concluded that "the significance of these many points of access and of the complicated texture of relationships among them is great. This diversity assures various ways for interest groups to participate in the formation of policy, and this variety is a flexible, stabilizing element."[8]

Derived from Truman's work, and that of other group-oriented scholars, is the notion of the pluralist state in which competition among interests, in and out of government, will produce policies roughly responsive to public desires, and no single set of interests will dominate. As one student of group politics summarized:

> Pluralist theory assumes that within the public arena there will be countervailing centers of power within governmental institutions and among outsiders. Competition is implicit in the notion that groups, as surrogates for individuals, will produce products representing the diversity of opinions that might have been possible in the individual decision days of democratic Athens.[9]

In many ways the pluralist vision of American politics corresponds to the basic realities of policy making and the distribution of policy outcomes, but a host of scholars, politicians, and other observers have roundly criticized this perspective. Two broad (although sometimes contradictory) critiques have special merit.

The first critique argues that some interests systematically lose in the policy process; others habitually win. Without endorsing the contentions of elite theorists that a small number of interests and individuals conspire together to dominate societal policies, one can make a strong case that those interests with more resources (money, access, information, and so forth) usually will obtain better results than those that possess fewer assets and employ them less effectively. The numerically small, cohesive, well-heeled tobacco industry, for example, does well year in and year out in the policy-making process; marginal farmers and the urban poor produce a much less successful track record. Based on the continuing unequal results, critics of the pluralist model argue that interests are still represented unevenly and unfairly.

A second important line of criticism generally agrees that inequality of results remains an important aspect of group politics. But this perspective, most forcefully set out by Theodore Lowi, sees interests as generally succeeding in their goals of influencing government—to the point that the government itself, in one form or another, provides a measure of protection to almost all societal interests. Everyone thus retains some vested interest in the ongoing structure of government and array of public policies. This does not mean that all interests obtain just what they desire from governmental policies; rather, all interests get at least some rewards. From this point of view the tobacco industry surely wishes to see its crop subsidies maintained, but the small farmer and the urban poor also have pet programs, such as guaranteed loans and food stamps, which they seek to protect.

Lowi labels the proliferation of groups and their growing access to government "interest-group liberalism," and he sees this phenomenon as pathological for a democratic government:

> Interest-group liberal solutions to the problem of power [who will exercise it] provide the system with stability by spreading a *sense* of representation at the expense of genuine flexibility, at the expense of democratic forms, and ultimately at the expense of legitimacy.[10]

Interest group liberalism is pluralism, but it is *sponsored* pluralism, and the government is the chief sponsor.

On the surface, it appears that the "unequal results" and "interest-group liberalism" critiques of pluralism are at odds. Reconciliation, however, is relatively straightforward. Lowi does not suggest that all interests are effectively represented. Rather, there exists in many instances only the appearance of representation. Political scientist Murray Edelman pointed out that a single set of policies can provide two related types of rewards: tangible benefits for the few and symbolic reassurances for the many.[11] Such a combination encourages groups to form, become active, and claim success.

The Climate for Group Proliferation

Substantial cleavages among a society's citizens are essential for interest group development. American culture and the constitutional arrangements of the U.S. government have encouraged the emergence of multiple political interests. In the pre-Revolutionary period, sharp conflicts existed between commercial and landed interests, debtor and creditor classes, coastal residents and those in the hinterlands, and citizens with either Tory or Whig political preferences. As the new nation developed, its vastness, characterized by geographical regions varying in climate, economic potential, culture, and tradition, contributed to a great heterogeneity. Open immigration policies further led to a diverse cultural mix with a wide variety of racial, ethnic, and religious backgrounds represented among the populace. Symbolically, the notion of the United States as a "melting pot," emphasizing group assimilation, has received much attention, but a more appropriate image may be a "tossed salad."[12]

The Constitution also contributes to a favorable environment for group development. Guarantees of free speech, association, and the right to petition the government for redress of grievances are basic to group formation. Because political organization often parallels government structure, federalism and the separation of powers—principles embodied in the Constitution—have greatly influenced the existence of large numbers of interest groups in the United States.

The decentralized political power structure in the United States allows important decisions to be made at the national, state, or local levels. Within each level of government there are multiple points of access. For example, business-related policies such as taxes are acted upon at each level, and interest groups may affect these policies in the legislative, executive, or judicial arenas. In the case of federated organizations such as the U.S. Chamber of Commerce, state and local affiliates often act independently of the national organization. Numerous business organizations thus focus on the varied channels of access.

In addition, the decentralized political parties found in the United States are less unified and disciplined than parties in many other nations. The resulting power vacuum in the decision-making process offers great potential for alternative political organizations such as interest groups to influence policy.

Finally, American cultural values may well encourage group development. As Alexis de Tocqueville observed in the 1830s, values such as individualism and the need for personal achievement underlie the propensity of citizens to join groups. Moreover, the number of access points—local, state, and national—contributes to Americans' strong sense of political efficacy when compared to that expressed by citizens of other nations.[13] Not only do Americans see themselves as joiners, but they actually tend to belong to more political groups than do people of other countries.[14]

Theories of Group Development

A climate favorable to group proliferation does little to explain how interests are organized. Whatever interests are latent in society and however favorable the context for group development may be, groups do not arise spontaneously. Farmers and a landed interest existed long before farm organizations first appeared; laborers and craftsmen were on the job before the formation of unions. In a simple society, even though distinct interests exist, there is little need for interest group formation. Farmers have no political or economic reason to organize when they work only for their families. In the early history of the country before the industrial revolution, workers were craftsmen, often laboring in small family enterprises. Broad-based political organizations were not needed, although local guilds often existed to train apprentices and to protect jobs.

David Truman has suggested that increasing societal complexity, characterized by economic specialization and social differentiation, is fundamental to group proliferation.[15] In addition, technological changes and the increasing interdependence of economic sectors often create new interests and redefine old ones. Salisbury's discussion of American farming is instructive:

> The full scale commercialization of agriculture, beginning largely with the Civil War, led to the differentiation of farmers into specialized interests, each increasingly different from the next.... The interdependence which accompanied the specialization process meant potential conflicts of interests or values both across the bargaining encounter and among the competing farmers themselves as each struggled to secure his own position.[16]

Many political scientists assume that an expansion of the interest group universe is a natural consequence of growing societal complexity. According to Truman, however, group formation "tends to occur in waves" and is greater in some periods than in others.[17] Groups organize politically when the existing order is disturbed and certain interests are, in turn, helped or hurt.

Not surprisingly, economic interests develop both to improve their position and to protect existing advantages. For example, the National Association of Manufacturers (NAM) originally was created to further the expansion of business opportunities in foreign trade, but it became a more powerful organization largely in response to the rise of organized labor.[18] Mobilization of business interests since the 1960s often has resulted from threats posed by consumer advocates and environmentalists, as well as requirements imposed by the steadily growing role of the federal government.

Disturbances that act to trigger group formation need not be strictly economic or technological. Wars, for example, place extreme burdens on draft-age men. Thus, organized resistance to U.S. defense policy arose during the Vietnam era. Likewise, broad societal changes may disturb the status quo. The origin of the Ku Klux Klan, for example, was based on the fear that increased numbers of ethnic and racial minorities threatened white, Christian America.

Truman's theory of group proliferation suggests that the interest group universe is inherently unstable. Groups formed from an imbalance of interests in one area induce a subsequent disequilibrium, which acts as a catalyst for individuals to form groups as counterweights to the new perceptions of inequity. Group politics thus is characterized by successive waves of mobilization and countermobilization. The liberalism of one era may prompt the resurgence of conservative groups in the next. Similarly, periods of business domination often are followed by eras of reform group ascendancy. In the 1990s, health care reform proposals have raised the stakes for almost all segments of society. Interest group politicking has reached historic proportions, as would-be reformers, the medical community, and business interests have sought to influence the direction of change in line with their own preferences.

Personal Motivations and Group Formation

Central to theories of group proliferation are the pluralist notions that elements of society possess common needs and share a group identity or consciousness, and that these are sufficient conditions for the formation of effective political organizations. Although the perception of common needs may be necessary for political organization, whether it is sufficient for group formation and effectiveness is open to question. Historical evidence documents many instances in which groups have not emerged spontaneously even when circumstances such as poverty or discrimination would seem, in retrospect, to have required it.

Mancur Olson effectively challenged many pluralist tenets in *The Logic of Collective Action*, first published in 1965. Basing his analysis on a model of the "rational economic man," Olson posited that even individuals who have common interests are not inclined to join organizations that attempt to address their concerns. The major barrier to group participation is the "free-rider" problem: "rational" individuals choose not to bear the participation costs (time, membership) because they can enjoy the group benefits (such as favorable legislation) whether or not they join. Groups that pursue "collective" benefits, which accrue to all members of a class or segment of society regardless of membership status, will have great difficulty forming and surviving. According to Olson, it would be economically irrational for individual farmers to join a group seeking higher farm prices when benefits from price increases would be enjoyed by all farmers, even those who contribute nothing to the group. Similarly, it would be irrational for an individual consumer to become part of organized attempts to lower consumer prices, when all consumers, members or not, would reap the benefits. The free-rider problem is especially serious for large groups because the larger the group the less likely an individual will perceive his or her contribution as having any impact on group success.

For Olson, a key to group formation—and especially group survival—is the provision of "selective" benefits. These rewards, such as travel discounts, informative publications, and cheap insurance, go only to members. Organizations in the best positions to offer such benefits are those initially formed for some nonpolitical purpose and that ordinarily provide material benefits to their clientele. In the case of unions, for example, membership may be a condition of employment. For farmers, the American Farm Bureau Federation (AFBF) offers inexpensive insurance, which induces individuals to join, even if they disagree with AFBF goals. In professional circles, membership in professional societies may be a prerequisite for occupational advancement and opportunity.

Olson's notions have sparked several extensions of the rational man model, and a reasonably coherent body of "incentive theory" literature now exists.[19] Incentive theorists view individuals as rational decision makers interested in making the most of their time and money by choosing to participate in those groups that offer benefits greater than or equal to the costs they incur by participation.

Three types of benefits are available. As an economist, Olson emphasized *material* benefits—tangible rewards of participation, such as income or services that have monetary value. *Solidary* incentives—the socially derived, intangible rewards created by the act of association, such as fun, camaraderie, status, or prestige—also are significant. Finally, *expressive* (also known as *purposive*) rewards—those derived from advancing a particular cause or ideology—clearly are important in explaining individual actions.[20] Groups formed on both sides of issues such as abortion or gun control illustrate the strength of such expressive incentives.

The examination of group members' motivations, and in particular the focus on nonmaterial incentives, allows for some reconciliation between the traditional group theorists' expectations of group development and the recent rational-actor studies, which emphasize the barriers to group formation. Nonmaterial incentives, such as fellowship and self-satisfaction, may encourage the proliferation of highly politicized groups and, according to Terry Moe, "have the potential for producing a more dynamic group context in which politics, political preferences, and group goals are more centrally determining factors than in material associations, linking political considerations more directly to associational size, structure, and internal processes."[21] Indeed, pure political benefits may attract potential members as well, and even collective benefits can prove decisive in inducing individuals to join large groups. Like elected officials, groups may find it possible to take credit for widely approved government actions, such as higher farm prices, stronger environmental regulations, or the protection of Social Security.[22]

Finally, several recent studies indicate that the free-rider problem may not be quite the obstacle to participation that it was once thought to be, especially in an affluent society. Albert Hirschman, for example, has argued that the costs and benefits of group activity are not always clear; in fact, some costs of participation for some individuals, such as time and effort expended, might be regarded as benefits, in terms of personal satisfaction, by others.[23] Other researchers have questioned whether individuals even engage in rational, cost-benefit thinking as they make membership decisions. Michael McCann noted that "there seems to be a general threshold level of involvement below which free rider calculations pose few inhibitions for ... commitment from moderately affluent citizen supporters."[24] In short, there is increasing evidence that in the modern era individuals may join and participate in groups for reasons beyond narrow economic self-interest or the availability of selective benefits.[25]

Contemporary Interest Group Politics

Several notable developments mark the modern age of interest group politics. Of primary importance is the large and growing number of active groups and other interests. The data here are sketchy, but one major study found that most current groups came into existence after World War II and that group formation has accelerated substantially since the early 1960s.[26] Also since the 1960s groups have increasingly directed their attention toward the center of power in Washington, D.C., as the scope of federal policy making has grown, and groups seeking influence have determined to "hunt where the ducks are." As a result, the 1960s and 1970s marked a veritable explosion in the number of groups lobbying in Washington.

A second key change is evident in the composition of the interest group universe. Beginning in the late 1950s political participation patterns underwent some significant transformations. Conventional activities such as voting declined, and political parties, the traditional aggregators and articulators of mass interests, became weaker. Yet at all levels of government, evidence of citizen involvement has been apparent, often in the form of new or revived groups. Particularly impressive has been the growth of citizens' groups—those organized around an idea or cause (at times a single issue) with no occupational basis for membership. Fully 30 percent of such groups have formed since 1975, and in 1980 they made up more than one-fifth of all groups represented in Washington.[27]

In fact, a participation revolution has occurred in the country as large numbers of citizens have become active in an ever-increasing number of protest groups, citizens' organizations, and special interest groups. These groups often comprise issue-oriented activists or individuals who seek collective material benefits. The free-rider problem has proven not to be an insurmountable barrier to group formation, and many new interest groups do not use selective material benefits to gain support.

Third, government itself has had a profound effect on the growth and activity of interest groups. Early in this century, workers found organizing difficult because business and industry used government-backed injunctions to prevent strikes. By the 1930s, however, with the prohibition of injunctions in private labor disputes and the rights of collective bargaining established, most governmental actions directly promoted labor union growth. In recent years changes in the campaign finance laws have led to an explosion in the number of PACs, especially among business, industry, and issue-oriented groups. Laws facilitating group formation certainly have contributed to group proliferation, but government policy in a broader sense has been equally responsible.

Fourth, not only has the number of membership groups grown in recent decades, but a similar expansion has occurred in the political activity of many other interests such as individual corporations, universities, churches, governmental units, foundations, and think tanks.[28] Historically, most of these interests have been satisfied with representation by trade or professional associations. Since the mid-1960s, however, many have chosen to employ their own Washington representatives. Between 1961 and 1982, for example, the number of corporations with Washington offices increased tenfold.[29] The chief beneficiaries of this trend are Washington-based lawyers, lobbyists, and public relations firms. The number of attorneys in the nation's capital, taken as a rough indicator of lobbyist strength, tripled between 1973 and 1983, and the growth of public relations firms was dramatic. The lobbying community of the 1990s is large, increasingly diverse, and part of the expansion of policy domain participation, whether in agriculture, the environment, or industrial development. As of 1993, the *Encyclopedia of Associations* listed approximately twenty-three thousand organizations, up more than 50 percent since 1980 and almost 400 percent since 1955.[30]

Governmental Growth

Since the 1930s the federal government has become an increasingly active and important spur to group formation. A major aim of the New Deal was to use government as an agent in balancing the relationship between contending forces in society, particularly industry and labor. One goal was to create greater equality of opportunity, including the "guarantee of identical liberties to all individuals, especially with regard to their pursuit of economic success."[31] For example, the Wagner Act (1935), which established collective bargaining rights, attempted to equalize workers' rights with those of their employers. Some New Deal programs did have real redistributive qualities, but most, even Social Security, sought only to ensure minimum standards of citizen welfare. Workers were clearly better off, but "the kind of redistribution that took priority in the public philosophy of the New Deal was not of wealth, but a redistribution of power."[32]

The expansion of federal programs has accelerated since 1960. In what political scientist Hugh Heclo termed an "Age of Improvement," the federal budget has grown rapidly (from nearly $100 billion in 1961 to well over a trillion dollars in 1991) and has widened the sweep of federal regulations.[33] Lyndon Johnson's Great Society—a multitude of federal initiatives in education, welfare, health care, civil rights, housing, and urban affairs—created a new array of federal responsibilities and program beneficiaries. The growth of many of these programs has continued, although that growth was slowed markedly by the Reagan administration. In the 1970s the federal government further expanded its activities in the areas of consumer affairs, environmental protection, and energy regulation. It also redefined some policies, such as affirmative action, to seek greater equality of results.

Many of the government policies adopted early in the Age of Improvement did not result from interest group activity by potential beneficiaries. Several targeted groups, such as the poor, were not effectively organized in the period of policy development. Initiatives typically came from elected officials responding to a variety of private and public sources, such as task forces composed of academics and policy professionals.[34]

The proliferation of government activities led to a mushrooming of groups around the affected policy areas. Newly enacted programs provided benefit packages that served to encourage interest group formation. Consider group activity in the field of policy toward the aging. The radical Townsend Movement, based on age grievances, received much attention during the 1930s, but organized political activity focused on age-based concerns had virtually no influence in national politics. Social Security legislation won approval without the involvement of age-based interest groups. Four decades later, by 1978, roughly $112 billion (approximately 24 percent of total federal expenditures) went to the elderly, and it was projected that in fifty years the outlay would amount to 40 percent of the total budget.[35] By 1991, however, the elderly already received one-third of federal outlays, and long-term projections had been revised upward. The existence of such massive benefits has spawned a variety of special interest groups and has encouraged other organizations, often formed for nonpolitical reasons, to redirect their attention to the politics of the aging.

Across policy areas two types of groups develop in response to governmental policy initiatives: *recipients* and *service deliverers*. In the sector devoted to policies affecting the elderly, recipient groups are mass-based organizations concerned with protecting—and if possible expanding—old-age benefits. The largest of these groups—indeed, the largest voluntary association represented in Washington—is the American Association of Retired Persons (AARP).

The AARP is well over twice the size of the AFL-CIO and, after the Roman Catholic church, is the nation's largest organization. In 1994 it counted thirty-two million members, an increase of twenty-two million in fifteen years. Approximately one-half of Americans over fifty, or one-fifth of all voters, belong to the group, in part because membership is cheap—$5 for the first year, $8 thereafter. Much of the organization's revenue is derived from advertising in its bimonthly magazine, *Modern Maturity*. The organization's headquarters in Washington has its own zip code, a legislative/policy staff of 165, 28 registered, in-house lobbyists, and more than 1,200 staff members in the field. Charles Peters, the editor of *Washington Monthly*, observed that the "AARP is becoming the most dangerous lobby in America," given its vigorous defense of the elderly's interests.[36]

Federal program growth also has generated substantial growth among service delivery groups. In the health care sector, for example, these range from professional associations of doctors and nurses to hospital groups to the insurance industry to suppliers of drugs and medical equipment. Not only is there enhanced group activity, but hundreds of individual corporations (Johnson & Johnson, Prudential, Humana, among many others) have strengthened their lobbying capacities by opening Washington offices or hiring professional representatives from the capital's many lobbying firms.[37]

Federal government policy toward the aging is probably typical of the tendency to "greatly increase the incentives for groups to form around the differential effects of these policies, each refusing to allow any other group to speak in its name."[38] The complexity of government decision making increases under such conditions, and priorities are hard to set. Particularly troublesome for decision makers concerned with national policy is the role played by service delivery groups. In the area of the aging, some groups are largely organizational middlemen concerned with their status as vendors for the elderly. The trade associations, for example, are most interested in the conditions surrounding the payment of funds to the elderly. The major concern of the Gerontological Society, an organization of professionals, is to obtain funds for research on problems of the aged.

Middleman organizations do not usually evaluate government programs according to the criteria used by recipient groups; rather, what is important to them is the relationship between the program and the well-being of their organizations. Because many service delivery groups offer their members vitally important selective material incentives (financial advantages and job opportunities), they are usually far better organized than most recipient groups (the elderly in this case, the AARP notwithstanding). As a result, they sometimes speak for the recipients. This is particularly true when recipient groups represent disadvantaged people, such as the poor or the mentally ill.

Middleman groups have accounted for a large share of total group growth since 1960, and many of them are state and local government organizations. Since the late 1950s the federal government has grown in expenditures and regulations more than in personnel. Employment in the federal government has risen only 20 percent since 1955, while that of states and localities has climbed more than 250 percent. Contemporary federal activism largely involves overseeing and regulating state and local governmental units, which seek funding for a wide range of purposes. The intergovernmental lobby, composed of such groups as the National League of Cities, the International City Manager Association, the National Association of Counties, the National Governors' Association, and the U.S. Conference of Mayors, has grown to become one of the most important in Washington. In addition, many local officials such as transportation or public works directors are represented by groups, and even single cities and state boards of regents have established Washington offices.

Not only do public policies contribute to group proliferation, but government often directly intervenes in group creation. This is not an entirely new activity. In the early twentieth century, relevant governmental officials in the agriculture and commerce departments encouraged the formation of the American Farm Bureau Federation and the U.S. Chamber of Commerce, respectively. Since the 1960s the federal government has been especially active in providing start-up funds and sponsoring groups. One study found that government agencies have concentrated on sponsoring organizations of public service professions:

> Federal agencies have an interest in encouraging coordination among the elements of these complex service delivery systems and in improving the diffusion of new ideas and techniques. Groups like the American Public Transit Association or the American Council on Education ... serve as centers of professional development and informal channels for administrative coordination in an otherwise unwieldy governmental system.[39]

Government sponsorship also helps explain the recent rise of citizens' groups. Most federal domestic legislation has included provisions requiring some citizen participation, which has spurred the development of various citizen action groups, including grassroots neighborhood associations, environmental action councils, legal defense coalitions, health care organizations, and senior citizens' groups. Such group sponsorship evolved for two reasons:

> First, there is the ever-present danger that administrative agencies may exceed or abuse their discretionary power. In this sense, the regulators need regulating. Although legislatures have responsibility for doing this ... the administrative bureaucracy has grown too large for them to monitor. Therefore, citizen participation has developed as an alternative means of monitoring government agencies. Second, government agencies are not entirely comfortable with their discretionary power ... . [T]o reduce the potential of unpopular or questionable decisions, agencies frequently use citizen participation as a means for improving, justifying, and developing support for their decisions.[40]

Participation by citizens' groups thus has two often inconsistent missions: to oversee an agency and to act as an advocate for the groups' programs.

Government funding of citizens' groups takes numerous forms. Several federal agencies—including the Federal Trade Commission (FTC), Food and Drug Administration (FDA), and Environmental Protection Agency (EPA)—have reimbursed groups for participation in agency proceedings.[41] At other times the government makes available seed money or outright grants. Interest group scholar Jack Walker found that 89 percent of citizens' groups received outside funding in their initial stages of development.[42] Not all the money was from federal sources, but much did come from government grants or contracts. Government can take away as well as give, however, and the Reagan administration made a major effort to "defund" interests on the political Left, especially citizens' groups. But once established, groups have strong instincts for survival. Indeed, the Reagan administration provided an attractive target for many citizens' groups in their recruiting efforts.

Citizens' groups, numbering in the thousands, continually confront the free-rider problem because they are largely concerned with collective goods and rarely can offer the selective material incentives so important for expanding and maintaining membership. With government funding, however, the development of a stable group membership is not crucial. Increasingly, groups have appeared that are essentially staff organizations with little or no membership base.

Government policies contribute to group formation in many *unintended* ways as well. Policy failures can impel groups to form, as happened with the rise of the American Agriculture Movement in the wake of the Nixon administration's grain export policies. An important factor in the establishment of the Moral Majority was the perceived harassment of church-run schools by government officials. As for abortion, the 1973 Supreme Court decision in *Roe v. Wade* played a major role in right-to-life group mobilization, as did the 1989 *Webster* decision in the growth of pro-choice groups.

Finally, the expansion of government activity itself often *inadvertently* contributes to group development and the resulting complexity of politics. Here a rather obscure example may prove most instructive: the development of the Bass Anglers Sportsman Society (yes, the acronym is BASS).

It all began with the Army Corps of Engineers, which dammed enough southern and midwestern streams to create a host of lakes, thereby providing an inviting habitat for largemouth bass. Anglers arrived in droves to catch their limits, and the fishing industry responded by creating expensive boats filled with specialized and esoteric equipment. The number and affluence of bass aficionados did not escape the attention of Ray Scott, an enterprising soul who began BASS in 1967. In 1990, with its membership approaching one million (up from four hundred thousand in 1982), BASS remained privately organized, offering its members selective benefits such as a slick magazine filled with tips on how to catch their favorite fish, packages of lures and line in return for joining or renewing their memberships, instant information about fishing hot spots, and boat owners' insurance. BASS also provided a number of solidary benefits, such as the camaraderie of fishing with fellow members in specially sanctioned fishing tournaments and the vicarious excitement of fishing with "BASS pros," whose financial livelihood revolved around competitive tournament fishing. The organization is an excellent example of Robert Salisbury's exchange theory approach to interest groups, as it provides benefits to both members and organizers in a "mutually satisfactory exchange."[43]

In fact, "members" may be a misnomer, in that the nominal members have no effective role in group decision making. In 1993 a federal district judge dismissed a $75 million suit filed against Scott by some BASS members. The judge reasoned that the organization was and always had been a for-profit corporation; its "members" thus had no standing to sue.

Although Scott sold the organization to a private corporation in 1986 (the ultimate expression of entrepreneurial success), he remains active in much of its work and writes a column for the monthly publication, *BassMaster*. Never denying that the organization was anything but a profit-making entity, Scott stated, "Every time I see one of those BASS stickers I get a lump, right in my wallet."[44]

Like most groups, BASS did not originate as a political organization, and, for the most part, it remains a sportsman's organization. Yet, BASS has entered politics. *BassMaster* has published political commentary and in both 1980 and 1988 endorsed George Bush for president. It also has called for easing travel restrictions to Cuba, where world-record catches may lurk.

Most groups claim that access is their major goal within the lobbying process, and here BASS has succeeded beyond its wildest dreams. President George Bush has been a life member of BASS since 1978 and has labeled *BassMaster* his favorite magazine. Scott has used his relationship with Bush to lobby for a number of goals of the fishing community in general and BASS in particular. In March 1989 Scott visited the White House and, during a horseshoe match, indicated his concern about rumors that the Office of Management and Budget (OMB) planned to limit the disbursement of $100 million in trust funds for various fishery-management projects. The next morning Bush informed Scott that "all of *our* monies are secure from OMB or anyone else."[45]

Scott and BASS have increased their political activities in other ways as well. The group now sponsors VOTE (Voice of the Environment), which lobbies on water quality issues, and the group has filed class-action lawsuits on behalf of fishermen against environmental polluters. While the organization can point to a number of conservation and environmental activities, it is distrusted by much of the mainstream environmental movement. BASS's connections to the boating industry often put it at odds with groups seeking to preserve a pristine natural environment or elite angling organizations whose members fish for trout in free-flowing streams rather than for the bass that swim behind federally funded dams.

Indeed, regardless of the entrepreneurial skills of Ray Scott, there would probably be no BASS if it were not for the federal government and the Army Corps of Engineers. (Moreover, there would be far fewer large-mouth bass.) Fifty years of dam building by the Corps and the U.S. Bureau of Reclamation have altered the nature of fish populations. Damming of rivers and streams has reduced the quality of fishing for cold-water species such as trout and pike and has enhanced the habitat for largemouth bass, a game fish that can tolerate the warmer waters and mud bottoms of manmade lakes. Finally, because many of these lakes are located close to cities, the government has made bass fishing accessible to a large number of anglers. From angling to air traffic control, the federal government has affected, and sometimes dominated, group formation. Governmental activity does not, however, exist in a vacuum, and many other forces have contributed to group proliferation, often in concert with increased public sector involvement.

The Decline of Political Parties

In a diverse political culture characterized by divided power, political parties emerged early in our history as instruments to structure conflict and facilitate mass participation. Parties function as intermediaries between the public and formal government institutions, as they reduce and combine citizen demands into a manageable number of issues and enable the system to focus upon the society's most important problems.

The party performs its mediating function primarily through coalition building—"the process of constructing majorities from the broad sentiments and interests that can be found to bridge the narrower needs and hopes of separate individuals and communities."[46] The New Deal coalition, forged in the 1930s, illustrates how this works. Generally speaking, socioeconomic divisions dominated politics from the 1930s through the 1960s. Less affluent citizens tended to support government provisions for social and economic security and the regulation of private enterprise. Those better off economically usually took the opposite position. The Democratic coalition, by and large, represented disadvantaged urban workers, Catholics, Jews, Italians, eastern Europeans, and blacks. On a variety of issues, southerners joined the coalition along with smatterings of academics and urban liberals. The Republicans were concentrated in the rural and suburban areas outside the South; the party was made up of established ethnic groups, businessmen, and farmers; it was largely Protestant. Party organizations dominated electoral politics through the New Deal period, and interest group influence was felt primarily through the party apparatus.

Patterns of partisan conflict are never permanent, however, and since the 1940s various social forces have contributed to the creation of new interests and the redefinition of older ones. This has had the effect of destroying the New Deal coalition without putting a new partisan structure in its place and has provided opportunities for the creation of large numbers of political groups—many that are narrowly focused and opposed to the bargaining and compromise patterns of coalition politics.

Taken as a whole, the changes of recent decades reflect the societal transformation that scholars have labeled "postindustrial society."

Postindustrial society is centered on several interrelated developments:

> [A]ffluence, advanced technological development, the central im-
> portance of knowledge, national communication processes, the grow-
> ing prominence and independence of the culture, new occupational
> structures, and with them new life styles and expectations, which is to
> say new social classes and new centers of power.[47]

At the base is the role of affluence. Between 1947 and 1972 median
family income doubled, even after controlling for the effects of inflation.
During that same period the percentage of families earning $10,000 and
more, in constant dollars, grew from 15 percent to 60 percent of the population.[48] A large proportion of the population thus enjoys substantial discretionary income and has moved beyond subsistence concerns.

The consequences of spreading abundance did not reduce conflict,
as some observers had predicted.[49] Instead, conflict heightened, as affluence increased dissatisfaction by contributing to a "mentality of demand,
a vastly expanded set of expectations concerning what is one's due, a
diminished tolerance of conditions less than ideal."[50] By the 1960s the
democratizing impact of affluence had become apparent, as an extraordinary number of people enrolled in institutions of higher education. Not
surprisingly, the government was under tremendous pressure to satisfy
expectations, and it too contributed to increasing demands both in rhetoric and through many of its own Age of Improvement initiatives.

With the rise in individual expectations, class divisions and conflicts
did not disappear, but they were drastically transformed. Political parties
scholar Walter Dean Burnham noted that the New Deal's class structure
changed, and by the late 1960s the industrial class pattern of upper, middle, and working class had been "supplanted by one which is relevant to a
system dominated by advanced postindustrial technology."[51] At the top
of the new class structure was a "professional-managerial-technical elite
... closely connected with the university and research centers and significant parts of it have been drawn—both out of ideology and interest—to
the federal government's social activism."[52] This growing group tended
to be cosmopolitan and more socially permissive than the rest of society.
The spread of affluence in postindustrial society was uneven, however,
and certain groups were disadvantaged by the changes. At the bottom of
the new class structure were the victims of changes, those "whose economic functions had been undermined or terminated by the technical
revolution of the past generation ... people, black and white, who tend to
be in hard core poverty areas."[53] The focus of the War on Poverty was to
be on this class.

The traditional political party system found it difficult to deal effectively with citizens' high expectations and a changing class structure. The
economic, ethnic, and ideological positions that had developed during the
New Deal became less relevant to parties, elections, and voter prefer-

ences. The strains were particularly evident among working-class Democrats. New Deal policies had been particularly beneficial to the white working class, enabling that group to earn incomes and adopt lifestyles that resembled those of the middle class. And although Age of Improvement policies initiated by Democratic politicians often benefited minorities, many white workers viewed these policies as attempts to aid lower-class blacks at whites' expense. By the late 1960s the white working class had taken on trappings of the middle class and conservatism, both economically and culturally.

At the same time, such New Deal divisions as ethnicity also had lost their cutting edge because of social and geographic mobility. One analyst observed in 1973 that

> it does not seem inaccurate to portray the current situation as one in which the basic coalitions and many of the political symbols and relationships, which were developed around one set of political issues and problems, are confronted with new issues and new cleavages for which these traditional relationships and associations are not particularly relevant. Given these conditions, the widespread confusion, frustration, and mistrust are not surprising.[54]

Various conditions led to the party system's inability to adapt to the changing societal divisions by "realigning"—building coalitions of groups to address new concerns. For example, consider the difficulty of coalition building around the kinds of issues that have emerged over the past fifteen or twenty years.

"Valence" issues—general evaluations of the goodness or badness of the times—have become important, especially when related to the cost of living. Yet most such issues do not divide the country politically. Everyone is against inflation and crime. A second set of increasingly important issues are those that are highly emotional, cultural, or moral in character such as abortion, the "right to die," AIDS, the death penalty, and drug laws. These subjects divide the electorate but elicit intense feelings from only a relatively few citizens. Opinion on such issues often is unrelated to traditional group identifications. Moreover, public opinion is generally disorganized or in disarray—that is, opinions often are unrelated or weakly related to one another on major issues, further retarding efforts to build coalitions.

There is some question about whether parties retain the capacity to shape political debate even on issues that lend themselves to coalition building. Although the decline of political parties began well before the 1960s, the weakening of the party organization has accelerated in the postindustrial age. The emergence of a highly educated electorate, less dependent upon party as an electoral cue, has produced a body of citizens that seeks out independent sources of information. Technological developments—such as television, computer-based direct mail, and political polling—have enabled candidates to virtually bypass political parties in their quest for public office. The rise of political consultants has reduced even further the need for party expertise in running for office. The recruitment function of parties also has been largely lost to the mass media, as journalists now "act out the part of talent scouts, conveying the judgment that some contenders are promising, while dismissing others as of no real talent."[55]

Evidence does suggest that parties are finally starting to adapt to this new political environment, but party organizations no longer dominate the electoral process. The weakness of political parties has helped to create a vacuum in electoral politics since 1960, and in recent years interest groups have moved aggressively to fill it.

The Growth of Interest Groups

Although it may be premature to formulate a theory that accounts for spurts of growth, we can identify several factors fundamental to group proliferation in contemporary politics. Rapid social and economic changes, powerful catalysts for group formation, have developed new interests (for example, the recreation industry) and redefined traditional ones (for example, higher education). The spread of affluence and education, coupled with advanced communication technologies, further contributes to the translation of interests into formal group organizations. Postindustrial changes have generated a large number of new interests, particularly among occupational and professional groups in the scientific and technological arenas. For instance, genetic engineering associations have sprung up in the wake of recent DNA discoveries.

Perhaps more important, postindustrial changes have altered the pattern of conflict in society and created an intensely emotional setting in which groups rise or fall in status. Ascending groups, such as members of the new professional-managerial-technical elite, have both benefited from and supported government activism; they represent the new cultural liberalism, politically cosmopolitan and socially permissive. At the same time, rising expectations and feelings of entitlement have increased pressures on government by aspiring groups and the disadvantaged. The 1960s and early 1970s witnessed wave after wave of group mobilization based on causes ranging from civil rights to women's issues to the environment to consumer protection.

Abrupt changes and alterations in status, however, threaten many citizens. Middle America, perceiving itself as downwardly mobile, has grown alienated from the social, economic, and cultural dominance of the postindustrial elites, on one hand, and resentful of government attempts to aid minorities and other aspiring groups, on the other. The conditions of a modern, technologically based culture also are disturbing to more traditional elements in society. Industrialization and urbanization can uproot people, cutting them loose from familiar life patterns and values and depriving them of meaningful personal associations. Fundamentalist elements feel threatened by various technological advances (such as use of fetal tissue for medical research) as well as by the more general secular liberalism and moral permissiveness of contemporary life. And the growth of bureaucracy, both in and out of government, antagonizes everyone at one time or another.

Postindustrial threats are felt by elites as well. The nuclear arms race and its potential for mass destruction fostered the revived peace movement of the 1980s and its goal of a freeze on nuclear weapons. In addition, the excesses and errors of technology, such as oil spills and toxic waste disposal, have led to group formation among some of the most advantaged and ascending elements of society.

Illustrating the possibilities here is the growth since the mid-1980s of the animal rights movement. Although traditional animal protection organizations such as the Humane Society have existed for decades, the last fifteen years have "spawned a colorful menagerie of pro-animal offspring" such as People for Ethical Treatment of Animals (PETA), Progressive Animal Welfare Society (PAWS), Committee to Abolish Sport Hunting (CASH), and the Animal Rights Network (ARN). Reminiscent of the 1960s, there is even the Animal Liberation Front, an extremist group.[56] Membership in the animal rights movement has increased rapidly; founded in 1980, PETA grew from 20,000 in 1984 to 250,000 in 1988 and 370,000 by 1994.[57] One estimate places the number of animal rights organizations at 400, representing approximately 10 million members.[58]

One major goal of these groups is to stop, or greatly retard, scientific experimentation on animals. Using a mix of protest, lobbying, and litigation, the movement has contributed to the closing of several animal labs, including the Defense Department's Wound Laboratory and a University of Pennsylvania facility involved in research on head injuries. In 1988 Trans-Species, a recent addition to the animal rights movement, forced the Cornell University Medical College to give up a $600,000 grant, which left unfinished a fourteen-year research project in which cats had to ingest barbiturates.[59]

As the most visible of the animal rights groups, PETA embarked on an intensive campaign in the early 1990s to influence children's attitudes and values toward society's treatment of animals. Using a seven-foot mascot, Chris P. Carrot, to spread its message, PETA organizers have sought to visit public schools throughout the Midwest. Although some of their message is noncontroversial (e.g., children should eat their vegetables), they also argue aggressively against consuming meat. Chris P. Carrot thus carries a placard stating "Eat your veggies, not your friends." More prosaically, PETA produces publications denouncing hunting, trapping, and other practices that abuse animals; PETA's *Kids Can Save Animals* even encourages students to call the toll-free numbers of department stores to protest furs and animal-test cosmetics, to call sponsors and object to rodeos, circulate petitions for 'violence-free' schools that do not use frog corpses for biology lab, and to boycott zoos and aquariums, and marine parks.[60]

Not surprisingly, threats to those involved in activities under attack by PETA have spawned countermobilizations, as, for instance, in the growth of an anti-animal rights movement. In the forefront of such actions are organizations that support hunting as a sport. They must contend with a public that has become increasingly hostile to hunting; a 1993 survey reported that 54 percent of Americans were opposed to hunting, with the youngest respondents (ages 18 to 29) expressing the most negative sentiments.[61] In addition, farm and medical groups have mobilized against the animal rights movements, and a number of new organizations have been formed. Such groups range from the incurably ill for Animal Research (iiFAR), representing those who hope for medical breakthroughs in biomedical research, to the Foundation for Animal Health, organized by the American Medical Association in hopes of diverting funds away from animal rights groups.

The most visible group in the animal rights countermobilization, Putting People First (PPF), claimed more than 35,000 members and 100 local chapters within one year of its formation. As well as its individual members, PPF counted hunting clubs, trapping associations, rodeos, zoos, circuses, veterinary hospitals, kennels/stables, and carriage horse companies among its membership. Taking a page from animal rights' public relations activities, PPF has begun a "Hunters for the Hungry" campaign that has provided 160,000 pounds of venison to the needy in the South. To PPF, the animal rights movement has declared war on much of America and is "seeking to destroy a way of life—to tell us we can no longer believe in the Judeo-Christian principles this country was founded on. They insist every form of life is equal: humans and dogs and slugs and cockroaches." PPF leaders see the organization as speaking for "the average American who eats meat and drinks milk, benefits from medical research, wears leather, wool, and fur, hunts and fishes, and owns a pet and goes to the zoo." [62]

The intensity of conflict between the animal rights advocates and their opponents typifies the deep cultural divisions of the postindustrial era. Similar differences affect many other key issues, from gun control to education (school choice) to immigration policy. Moreover, many of these conflicts do not lend themselves to compromise, whether because of vast policy differences or group leaders' desire to keep "hot" issues alive as a way to increase membership.

While postindustrial conflicts generate the issues for group development, the spread of affluence also systematically contributes to group formation and maintenance. In fact, affluence creates a large potential for "checkbook" membership. Issue-based groups have done especially well. Membership in such groups as PETA and Common Cause might once have been considered a luxury, but the growth in discretionary income has placed the cost of modest dues within the reach of most citizens. For a $15-$25 membership fee, people can make an "expressive" statement without incurring other organizational obligations. Increasing education also has been a factor in that "organizations become more numerous as ideas become more important."[63]

Reform groups and citizens' groups depend heavily upon the educated, suburban/urban, white middle class for their membership and financial base. A 1982 Common Cause poll, for example, found that members' mean family income was $17,000 above the national average and that 43 percent of members had an advanced degree.[64] Animal rights groups display a similar membership profile, although they are disproportionately composed of college-educated, urban, professional women.[65] Other expressive groups, including those on the political Right, have been aided as well by the increased wealth of constituents and the community activism that result from education and occupational advancement.

Groups can overcome the free-rider problem by finding a sponsor who will support the organization and reduce its reliance upon membership contributions. During the 1960s and 1970s private sources (often foundations) backed various groups. Jeffrey Berry's 1977 study of eighty-three public interest organizations found that at least one-third received more than half of their funds from private foundations, while one in ten received more than 90 percent of its operating expenses from such sources.[66] Jack Walker's 1981 study of Washington-based interest groups confirmed many of Berry's earlier findings, indicating that foundation support and individual grants provide 30 percent of all citizens' group funding.[67] Such patterns produce many staff organizations with no members, raising major questions about the representativeness of the new interest group universe. Finally, groups themselves can sponsor other groups. The National Council of Senior Citizens (NCSC), for example, was founded by the AFL-CIO, which helped recruit members from the ranks of organized labor and still pays part of NCSC's expenses.

Patrons often are more than just passive sponsors who respond to group requests for funds. In many instances, group mobilization comes from the top down, rather than the reverse. The patron—whether an individual such as General Motors' heir Stewart Mott or Adolph Coors, an institution, another group, or a government entity—may serve as the initiator of group development, to the point of seeking entrepreneurs and providing a forum for group pronouncements.

Postindustrial affluence and the spread of education also have contributed to group formation and maintenance through the development of a large pool of potential group organizers. This group tends to be young, well educated, and from the middle class, caught up in a movement for change and inspired by ideas or doctrine. The 1960s was a period of opportunity for entrepreneurs, as college enrollments skyrocketed and powerful forces such as civil rights and the antiwar movement contributed to an idea-orientation in both education and politics. Communications-based professions—from religion to law to university teaching—attracted social activists, many of whom became involved in the formation of groups. The government itself became a major source of what James Q. Wilson called "organizing cadres." Government employees of the local Community Action Agencies of the War on Poverty and numerous VISTA volunteers were active in the formation of voluntary associations, some created to oppose government actions.[68]

Compounding the effects of the growing number of increasingly active groups are changes in what organizations can do, largely as a result of contemporary technology. On a grand scale, technological change produces new interests, such as cable television and the silicon chip industry, which organize to protect themselves as interests historically have done. Beyond this, communications breakthroughs make group politics much more visible than in the past. Civil rights activists in the South understood this, as did many protesters against the Vietnam War. Of equal importance, however, is the fact that much of what contemporary interest groups do derives directly from developments in information-related technology. Many group activities, whether fund raising or grassroots lobbying or sampling members' opinions, rely heavily on computer-based operations that can target and send messages and process the responses.

Although satellite television links and survey research are important tools, the technology of direct mail has had by far the greatest impact on interest group politics. With a minimum initial investment and a reasonably good list of potential contributors, any individual can become a group entrepreneur. These activists literally create organizations, often based on emotion-laden appeals about specific issues, from Sarah Brady's Handgun Control to Randall Terry's Operation Rescue.[69] To the extent that an entrepreneur can attract members and continue to pay the costs of direct mail, he or she can claim—with substantial legitimacy—to articulate the organization's positions on the issues, positions probably defined initially by the entrepreneur.

In addition to helping entrepreneurs develop organizations that require few (if any) active members, information technology also allows many organizations to exert considerable pressure on elected officials. The Washington-based interests increasingly are turning to grassroots techniques to influence legislators. Indeed, after the mid-1980s these tactics had become the norm in many lobbying efforts, to the point that they were sometimes discounted as routine and "manufactured" by groups and consultants.

Communications technology is widely available but expensive. In the health care debate, most mobilized opinion has come from the best-financed interests, such as insurance companies, the drug industry, and the medical profession. Money remains the mother's milk of politics. Indeed, one of the major impacts of technology may be to inflate the costs of political action, whether for candidates engaged in increasingly expensive election campaigns or in public lobbying efforts that employ specifically targeted advertisements and highly sophisticated grassroots efforts.

Group Impact on Policy and Process

Assessing the policy impact of interest group actions has never been an easy task. We may, however, gain some insights by looking at two different levels of analysis: a broad, societal overview and a middle-range search for relatively specific patterns of influence (for example, the role of direct mail or PAC funding). Considering impact at the level of individual lobbying efforts is also possible, but here even the best work relies heavily on nuance and individualistic explanations.

Although the public at large often views lobbying and special interest campaigning with distrust, political scientists have not produced much evidence to support this perspective. Academic studies of interest groups have demonstrated few conclusive links between campaign or lobbying efforts and actual patterns of influence. *This does not mean that such patterns or individual instances do not exist.* Rather, the question of determining impact is exceedingly difficult to answer. The difficulty is, in fact, compounded by groups' claims of impact and decision makers' equally vociferous claims of freedom from any outside influence.

The major studies of lobbying in the 1960s generated a most benign view of this activity. Lester Milbrath, in his portrait of Washington lobbyists, painted a Boy Scout-like picture, depicting them as patient contributors to the policy-making process.[70] Rarely stepping over the limits of propriety, lobbyists had only a marginal impact at best. Similarly, Raymond Bauer, Ithiel de Sola Pool, and Lewis Dexter's lengthy analysis of foreign trade policy, published in 1963, found the business community to be largely incapable of influencing Congress in its lobbying attempts.[71] Given the many internal divisions within the private sector over trade matters, this was not an ideal issue to illustrate business cooperation, but the research stood as the central work on lobbying for more than a decade—ironically, in the very period when groups proliferated and became more sophisticated in their tactics. Lewis Dexter, in his 1969 treatment of Washington representatives as an emerging professional group, suggested that lobbyists would play an increasingly important role in complex policy making, but he provided few details.[72]

The picture of benevolent lobbyists who seek to engender trust and convey information, although accurate in a limited way, does not provide a complete account of the options open to any interest group that seeks to exert influence. Lyndon Johnson's long-term relationship with the

103, 114

Texas-based construction firm of Brown & Root illustrates the depth of some ties between private interests and public officeholders. The Washington representative for Brown & Root claimed that he never went to Capitol Hill for any legislative help because "people would resent political influence."[73] But Johnson, first as a representative and later as a senator, systematically dealt directly with the top management (the Brown family) and aided the firm by passing along crucial information and watching over key government-sponsored construction projects.

> [The Johnson-Brown & Root link] was, indeed, a partnership, the campaign contributions, the congressional look-out, the contracts, the appropriations, the telegrams, the investment advice, the gifts and the hunts and the free airplane rides—it was an alliance of mutual reinforcement between a politician and a corporation. If Lyndon was Brown & Root's kept politician, Brown & Root was Lyndon's kept corporation. Whether he concluded that they were public-spirited partners or corrupt ones, "political allies" or cooperating predators, in its dimensions and its implications for the structure of society, their arrangement was a new phenomenon on its way to becoming the new pattern for American society.[74]

Subsequent events, like the 1980s' savings and loan scandal, demonstrate that legislators can be easily approached with unethical and illegal propositions; such access is one price of an open system. More broadly, the growth of interest representation has raised long-term questions about the ethics of ex-government officials acting as lobbyists. Despite some modest reforms, many executive-branch officials, members of Congress, and high-level bureaucrats leave office and eventually return to lobby their friends and associates who have remained. Access is still important, and its price is often high.

Contemporary Practices

Modern lobbying emphasizes information, often on complex and difficult subjects. Determining actual influence is, as one lobbyist noted, "like finding a black cat in the coal bin at midnight,"[75] but we can make some assessments about the overall impact of group proliferation and increased activity.

First, more groups are engaged in more forms of lobbying than ever before—both classic forms, such as offering legislative testimony, and newer forms, such as mounting computer-based direct mail campaigns to stir up grassroots support.[76] As the number of new groups rises and existing groups become more active, the pressure on decision makers—especially legislators—mounts at a corresponding rate. Thus, a second general point can be made: congressional reforms that opened up the legislative process during the 1970s have provided a much larger number of access points for today's lobbyists. Most committee (and subcommittee) sessions, including the mark-ups at which legislation is written, remain open to the public, as do many conference committee meetings. More roll-call votes are taken, and congressional floor action is televised. Thus, interests can monitor the performance of individual members of Congress as never before. This does nothing, however, to facilitate disinterested decision making or foster statesmanlike compromises on most issues.

In fact, monitoring the legions of Washington policy actors has become the central activity of many groups. As Robert Salisbury recently observed, "Before [organized interests] can advocate a policy, they must determine what position they wish to embrace. Before they do this, they must find out not only what technical policy analysis can tell them but what relevant others, inside and outside the government, are thinking and planning."[77] Given the volume of policy making, just keeping up can represent a major undertaking.

The government itself has encouraged many interests to organize and articulate their demands. The rise of group activity thus leads us to another level of analysis: the impact of contemporary interest group politics on society. Harking back to Lowi's description of interest group liberalism, we see the eventual result to be an immobilized society, trapped by its willingness to allow interests to help fashion self-serving policies that embody no firm criteria of success or failure. For example, even in the midst of the savings and loan debacle, the government continues to offer guarantees to various sectors, based not on future promise but on past bargains and continuing pressures.

The notion advanced by Olson that some such group-related stagnation affects all stable democracies makes the prognosis all the more serious. In summary form, Olson argued that the longer societies are politically stable, the more interest groups they develop; the more interest groups they develop, the worse they work economically.[78] The United Automobile Workers' protectionist leanings, the American Medical Association's fight against FTC intervention into physicians' business affairs, and the insurance industry's successful prevention of FTC investigations all illustrate the possible linkage between self-centered group action and poor economic performance—that is, higher automobile prices, doctors' fees, and insurance premiums for no better product or service.[79]

Conclusion

The ultimate consequences of the growing number of groups, their expanding activities both in Washington and in state capitals, and the growth of citizens' groups remain unclear. From one perspective, such changes have made politics more representative than ever before. While most occupation-based groups traditionally have been well organized in American politics, many other interests have not. Population groupings such as blacks, Hispanics, and women have mobilized since the 1950s and 1960s; even animals and the unborn are well represented in the interest group arena, as is the broader "public interest," however defined.

Broadening the base of interest group participation may have truly opened up the political process, thus curbing the influence of special interests. For example, agricultural policy making in the postwar era was almost exclusively the prerogative of a tight "iron triangle" composed of congressional committee and subcommittee members from farm states, government officials representing the agriculture bureaucracy, and major agriculture groups such as the American Farm Bureau. Activity in the 1970s by consumer and environmental interest groups changed agricultural politics, making it more visible and lengthening the agenda to consider such questions as how farm subsidies affect consumer purchasing power and how various fertilizers, herbicides, and pesticides affect public health.

From another perspective, more interest groups and more openness do not necessarily mean better policies or ones that genuinely represent the national interest. "Sunshine" and more participants may generate greater complexity and too many demands for decision makers to process effectively. Moreover, the content of demands may be ambiguous and priorities difficult to set. Finally, elected leaders may find it practically impossible to build the kinds of political coalitions necessary to govern effectively, especially in an era of divided government.

This second perspective suggests that the American constitutional system is extraordinarily susceptible to the excesses of minority faction—in an ironic way a potential victim of the Madisonian solution of dealing with the tyranny of the majority. Decentralized government, especially one that wields considerable power, provides no adequate controls over the excessive demands of special interest politics. Decision makers feel obliged to respond to many of these demands, and "the cumulative effect of this pressure has been the relentless and extraordinary rise of government spending and inflationary deficits, as well as the frustration of efforts to enact effective national policies on most major issues."[80]

In sum, the problem of contemporary interest group politics is one of representation. For particular interests, especially those that are well defined and adequately funded, the government is responsive to the issues of their greatest concern. But representation is not just a matter of responding to specific interests or citizens; the government also must respond to the collective needs of a society, and here the success of individual interests reduces the possibility of overall responsiveness. The very vibrancy and success of contemporary groups contribute to a society that finds it increasingly difficult to formulate solutions to complex policy questions.

Notes

1. Kay Lehman Schlozman and John T. Tierney, "More of the Same: Washington Pressure Group Activity in a Decade of Change," *Journal of Politics* 45 (May 1983): 351-377. For an earlier era, see Margaret S. Thompson, *The Spider's Web* (Ithaca: Cornell University Press, 1985).
2. Theodore J. Lowi, *The End of Liberalism*, 2d ed. (New York: Norton, 1979); and Mancur Olson, *The Rise and Decline of Nations* (New Haven, Conn.: Yale University Press, 1982).
3. Mancur Olson, *The Logic of Collective Action* (Cambridge, Mass.: Harvard University Press, 1971); Robert Salisbury, "An Exchange Theory of Interest Groups," *Midwest Journal of Political Science* 13 (February 1969): 1-32; and Terry M. Moe, *The Organization of Interests* (Chicago: University of Chicago Press, 1980).
4. David Truman's widely used definition of interest groups is "any group that, on the basis of one or more shared attitudes, makes certain claims upon other groups in the society for the establishment, maintenance or enhancement of forms of behavior that are implied by the shared attitudes." Truman, *The Governmental Process*, 2d ed. (New York: Knopf, 1971).
5. James Madison, "Federalist 10," in *The Federalist Papers*, 2d ed., ed. Roy P. Fairfield (Baltimore: Johns Hopkins University Press, 1981), 16.
6. L. Harmon Ziegler and Wayne Peak, *Interest Groups in American Society*, 2d ed. (Englewood Cliffs, N.J.: Prentice-Hall, 1972), 35.
7. Common Cause, *The Government Subsidy Squeeze* (Washington, D.C.: Common Cause, 1980), 11.
8. Truman, *Governmental Process*, 519.
9. Carole Greenwald, *Group Power* (New York: Praeger, 1977), 305.
10. Lowi, *End of Liberalism*, 62.
11. Murray Edelman, *The Politics of Symbolic Action* (Chicago: Markham Press, 1971).
12. Theodore J. Lowi, *Incomplete Conquest: Governing America* (New York: Holt, Rinehart & Winston, 1976), 47.
13. Gabriel Almond and Sidney Verba, *The Civic Culture* (Boston: Little, Brown, 1963), chaps. 8 and 10.
14. Ibid., 246-247.
15. Truman, *Governmental Process*, 57.
16. Salisbury, "Exchange Theory of Interest Groups," 3-4.
17. Truman, *Governmental Process*, 59.
18. James Q. Wilson, *Political Organizations* (New York: Basic Books, 1973), 154.
19. Major works include: Olson, *Logic of Collective Action;* Peter Clark and James Q. Wilson, "Incentive Systems: A Theory of Organizations," *Administrative Science Quarterly* 6 (September 1961): 126-166; Wilson, *Political Organizations;* Terry Moe, "A Calculus of Group Membership," *American Journal of Political Science* 24 (November 1980): 593-632; and Moe, *Organization of Interests*. The notion of group organizers as political entrepreneurs is best represented by Salisbury, "Exchange Theory of Interest Groups," 1-15.
20. See Clark and Wilson, "Incentive Systems: A Theory of Organizations," 129-166; and Wilson, *Political Organizations*, 30-51. In recent years researchers have preferred the term *expressive* to *purposive*, since, as Salisbury notes, the term purposive includes what we call collective material benefits. Material, solidary, and expressive would seem to be mutually exclusive conceptual categories. See Salisbury, "Exchange Theory of Interest Groups," 16-17.
21. Moe, *Organization of Interests*, 144.
22. John Mark Hansen, "The Political Economy of Group Membership," *American Political Science Review* 79 (March 1985): 79-96.

23. Albert O. Hirschman, *Shifting Involvements* (Princeton, N.J.: Princeton University Press, 1982).
24. Michael W. McCann, "Public Interest Liberalism and the Modern Regulatory State," *Polity* 21 (Winter 1988): 385.
25. See, for example, R. Kenneth Godwin and R. C. Mitchell, "Rational Models, Collective Goods, and Non-Electoral Political Behavior," *Western Political Quarterly* 35 (June 1982): 161-180; and Larry Rothenberg, "Choosing among Public Interest Groups: Membership, Activism and Retention in Political Organizations," *American Political Science Review* 82 (December 1988): 1129-1152.
26. Jack L. Walker, "The Origins and Maintenance of Interest Groups in America," *American Political Science Review* 77 (June 1983): 390-406; for a conservative critique of this trend, see James T. Bennett and Thomas Di Lorenzo, *Destroying Democracy* (Washington, D.C.: Cato Institute, 1986). See also many of the articles in *The Politics of Interests*, Mark P. Petracca, ed. (Boulder: Westview, 1992).
27. Walker, "Origins and Maintenance of Interest Groups," 16.
28. Robert H. Salisbury, "Interest Representation and the Dominance of Institutions," *American Political Science Review* 78 (March 1984): 64-77.
29. Gregory Colgate (ed.), *National Trade and Professional Associations of the United States 1982* (Washington, D.C.: Columbia Books, 1984).
30. Jonathan Rausch, *Democlerosis* (New York: Times Books, 1994), 39.
31. Samuel H. Beer, "In Search of a New Public Philosophy," in *The New American Political System*, ed. Anthony King (Washington, D.C.: American Enterprise Institute, 1978), 12.
32. Ibid., 10.
33. Hugh Heclo, "Issue Networks and the Executive Establishment," in King, *New American Political System*, 89.
34. Beer, "In Search of a New Public Philosophy," 16.
35. Allan J. Cigler and Cheryl Swanson, "Politics and Older Americans," in *The Dynamics of Aging*, ed. Forrest J. Berghorn, Donna E. Schafer, and Associates (Boulder, Colo.: Westview Press, 1981), 171.
36. See John Tierney, "Old Money, New Power," *New York Times Magazine*, October 23, 1988; and "The Big Gray Money Machine," *Newsweek*, August 15, 1988.
37. Tierney, "Old Money, New Power."
38. Heclo, "Issue Networks and the Executive Establishment," 96.
39. Walker, "Origins and Maintenance of Interest Groups," 401.
40. Stuart Langton, "Citizen Participation in America: Current Reflections on the State of the Art," in *Citizen Participation in America*, ed. Stuart Langton (Lexington, Mass.: Lexington Books, 1978), 7.
41. Ibid., 4.
42. Walker, "Origins and Maintenance of Interest Groups," 398.
43. Salisbury, "Exchange Theory of Interest Groups," 25.
44. Quoted in Ted Williams, "River Retrieval," *Fly Rod and Reel* 15 (January/February, 1994), 17.
45. Ray Scott, "Presidential Promises," *BassMaster*, May 1989, 7 (emphasis added).
46. David S. Broder, "Introduction," in *Emerging Coalitions in American Politics*, ed. Seymour Martin Lipset (San Francisco: Institute for Contemporary Studies, 1978), 3.
47. Everett Carll Ladd, Jr., with Charles D. Hadley, *Transformations of the American Party System*, 2d ed. (New York: Norton, 1978), 182.
48. Ibid., 196.
49. See, for example, Daniel Bell, *The End of Ideology* (New York: Free Press, 1960).
50. Ladd and Hadley, *Transformations of the American Party System*, 203.
51. Walter Dean Burnham, *Critical Elections and the Mainsprings of American Politics* (New York: Norton, 1970), 139.

52. Ibid.
53. Ibid.
54. Richard E. Dawson, *Public Opinion and Contemporary Disarray* (New York: Harper and Row, 1973), 194.
55. Everett Carll Ladd, *Where Have All the Voters Gone?* 2d ed. (New York: Norton, 1982), 56.
56. Kevin Kasowski, "Showdown on the Hunting Ground," *Outdoor America*, 51 (Winter 1986): 9.
57. Sarah Lyall, "Scientist Gives Up Grant to Do Research on Cats," *New York Times*, November 21, 1988.
58. Lauristan R. King and Kimberly Stephens, "Politics and the Animal Rights Movement" (Paper presented at the annual meeting of the Southern Political Science Association, Tampa, Florida, 1991).
59. Lyall, "Scientist Gives Up Grant."
60. John Balzar, quoted in Kit Harrison, "Animal 'Rightists' Target Children," *Sports Afield* 211, June 1994, 12.
61. "Americans Divided on Animal Rights," *Los Angeles Times*, December 17, 1993. This national survey of 1,612 adults also found that 50 percent opposed the wearing of fur.
62. Phil McCombs, "Attack of the Omnivore," *Washington Post*, March 27, 1992, B1, B4.
63. Wilson, *Political Organizations*, 201.
64. Andrew S. McFarland, *Common Cause* (Chatham, N.J.: Chatham House, 1984), 48-49.
65. King and Stephens, "Politics and the Animal Rights Movement," 15.
66. Jeffrey M. Berry, *Lobbying for the People* (Princeton, N.J.: Princeton University Press, 1977), 72.
67. Walker, "Origins and Maintenance of Interest Groups," 400.
68. Wilson, *Political Organizations*, 203.
69. Sarah Brady, wife of former White House press secretary James Brady, organized Handgun Control after her husband was wounded in John Hinckley's 1981 attack on Ronald Reagan. Randall Terry formed Operation Rescue, which seeks to shut down abortion clinics through direct action (for example, blocking entrances), after concluding that other pro-life groups were not effective in halting abortions.
70. Lester Milbrath, *The Washington Lobbyists* (Chicago: Rand-McNally, 1963).
71. Raymond Bauer, Ithiel de Sola Pool, and Lewis Dexter, *American Business and Public Policy* (New York: Atherton Press, 1963).
72. Lewis A. Dexter, *How Organizations Are Represented in Washington* (Indianapolis: Bobbs-Merrill, 1969), chap. 9.
73. See Ronnie Dugger, *The Politician* (New York: Norton, 1982), 273; and Robert A. Caro, *The Years of Lyndon Johnson: The Path to Power* and *The Years of Lyndon Johnson: Means of Ascent* (New York: Knopf, 1982 and 1990, respectively).
74. Dugger, *Politician*, 286.
75. Quoted in "A New Era: Groups and the Grass Roots," by Burdett A. Loomis, in *Interest Group Politics*, ed. Allan J. Cigler and Burdett A. Loomis (Washington, D.C.: CQ Press, 1983), 184.
76. Schlozman and Tierney, "Washington Pressure Group Activity," 18.
77. Robert H. Salisbury, "The Paradox of Interest Groups in Washington—More Groups and Less Clout," in *The New American Political System*, 2d ed., ed. Anthony King (Washington, D.C.: American Enterprise Institute, 1990), 225-226.
78. For an expansion of this argument, see Rausch, *Democlerosis*.
79. Robert J. Samuelson's description in *National Journal*, September 25, 1982, 1642.
80. Everett Carll Ladd, "How to Tame the Special Interest Groups," *Fortune*, October 1980, 6.

I. GROUP FORMATION AND MEMBERSHIP

2

Grassroots Victim Organizations: Mobilizing for Personal and Public Health

Christopher H. Foreman, Jr.

Over the past thirty years, interests have organized at an increasing pace. This has meant, among other things, that new types of interests have entered the pluralist mix. For example, many environmental groups and consumer organizations sprouted up during the 1960s and 1970s. These groups struggled with the "free rider" problem that Mancur Olson had pointed out in 1965. The large number of group members and the broadly inclusive (collective) benefits the groups pursued meant that it was rational for an individual not to become a member, since he or she could reap the benefits (e.g., clean air) without joining. Many of the new groups prospered as group "entrepreneurs" offered both selective benefits and intangible, expressive rewards to lure prospective members.

In this chapter, Christopher Foreman explores a type of group that became prominent in the 1980s, although some had been started earlier. He identifies populations of individuals with a common bond of victimization who have banded together to obtain group benefits and to offer mutual support. Some victims' groups coalesce in discrete geographic settings, such as New York's Love Canal area, but many others engage in the national airing of a problem or affliction that many potential members will recognize in themselves or their family members. Substantial media coverage is often essential for the formation of these groups. Indeed, Foreman reports that the same television reporter covered stories that led to the creation of two separate organizations. Entrepreneurs provide various membership incentives, including information that may be crucial for the members of some groups, especially those that organize around a disease (for example, chronic fatigue syndrome or Lyme disease). At the same time, leaders of victims' groups frequently must cope with factional conflict; the status of members as victims does not produce unanimous support for given courses of action, as the AIDS movement has demonstrated since the early 1980s.

The author thanks Kevin Hula, Allen Schick, and John T. Tierney for their helpful comments.

I n the 1970s and earlier, organized victims of illness and injury were seldom very visible in health and safety policy debates. Three types of interest groups were particularly prominent: (1) economic stakeholders, such as the American Medical Association and the Pharmaceutical Manufacturers Association, which were blessed with large staffs and substantial budgets, national memberships, and mainstream legitimacy; (2) the traditional disease lobbies, which included the American Cancer Society and American Heart Association; and (3) ideological advocacy organizations committed especially to strong health and safety regulations and tough enforcement. The Ralph Nader-affiliated Health Research Group, the Food and Drug Administration's most zealous and best known watchdog, is a prime example of this third type.[1] This chapter profiles a fourth kind of group that has become prominent since about 1980: the grassroots victim organization (GVO).[2] While closely resembling ideological advocacy groups in some respects, the GVO is nonetheless distinct.

I am concerned here not with the political influence of GVOs, but rather with their structure and dynamics. How are GVOs created and maintained? What strategies and tactics do they adopt, and what hurdles must they overcome, to pursue political advocacy? To answer these questions I consulted published sources and conducted informal telephone interviews with organization founders and staff. This essay is exploratory and suggestive; careful surveys and longitudinal studies will be needed to confirm the findings presented here.

A GVO consists of persons directly affected, often quite suddenly and tragically, by a health hazard. Persons who form, join, or contribute to such groups include mainly victims, their relatives or friends, and persons who fear imminent victimization of themselves or others to whom they feel a personal attachment. Such organizations are not necessarily, or even primarily, composed of persons with an illness. To serve as a basis for GVO creation, a problem must be neither so fleeting nor so immediately catastrophic as to make organization unsustainable. An inherently transient problem (influenza, for example) is unlikely to inspire a GVO. On the other hand, if infection with the human immunodeficiency virus that triggers AIDS caused death within hours or days, the AIDS Coalition to Unleash Power (ACT-UP) could not exist and might have been unnecessary because the disease immediately would have seized a commanding position on the public agenda.[3]

Depending on the kind of hazard that propels it, a GVO may be either community-directed or condition-directed. The community-directed GVO emerges out of a threat to individuals sharing a common and defined public space. For example, the leakage of toxic material onto residential property or into groundwater, and attendant concern over perceived injury to persons in a particular neighborhood or town, can provide the occasion for such organization. Two particularly well documented examples of community-directed victim groups include the Love Canal Homeowners Association, which sought government help to escape a leaking deposit of hazardous wastes in Niagara Falls, New York, and For a Cleaner Environment (FACE), which was spawned by the discovery of a cluster of childhood leukemia cases in Woburn, Massachusetts.[4]

A condition-directed GVO arises out of victimization that is not place-specific. Instead, a particular hazardous product or disease provides organizational focus. Breast cancer, AIDS, vaccine injuries, and nutritionally deficient infant formulas have all triggered grassroots organizing. ACT-UP is currently the best-known condition-directed group, and one whose example has inspired others.[5]

Community-directed and condition-directed groups confront somewhat different problems of creation and maintenance, and significant variation occurs within each type. Variety also exists in the way GVOs select and pursue their goals. Many groups will concentrate solely on the information and personal support that are crucial membership incentives. To the extent that they eschew public-policy advocacy such groups are less interesting to students of interest-group politics.

Organizational Creation

Until the mid-1960s, scholars were generally inclined to the view, most often associated with David B. Truman, that formal voluntary organization tended naturally to emerge from broad social forces and interaction among persons (such as factory workers or farmers) who shared similar attitudes and common economic interests in a complex society.[6] But in *The Logic of Collective Action* Mancur Olson argued that organizational existence was actually far more problematic. Whereas Truman had envisioned people as drawn to organization as a natural consequence of social interaction, Olson held that a rational individual seeking to maximize personal welfare would ordinarily fail to join or actively support a group. Olson reasoned that because any individual's contribution would not visibly affect a large organization's fortunes and that a nonmember could in many cases enjoy "free rider" status, reaping the collective benefits achieved by the group (for example, higher wheat prices or significant research breakthroughs) without joining. The solution to these problems, suggested Olson, lay either in: (a) having the group remain small, so that each member's contribution made a manifest difference, (b) coercing potential members to join (that is, transforming the "voluntary" nature of association), or, most likely, (c) offering selective inducements, available solely as a benefit of group membership.[7]

Organizational Entrepreneurs

Olson's theory addresses the maintenance of organizations without explaining how those organizations are created in the first place.[8] To explain group origins several theorists have embraced the concept of the organizational entrepreneur.[9] For Robert H. Salisbury, among the earliest proponents of an explicitly entrepreneurial theory of organizational creation, the "entrepreneur/organizer" resembles entrepreneurs in the business world. He or she will "invest capital to create a set of benefits" that are available "to a market of potential customers at a price."[10] What benefits might these be? Salisbury adapts an earlier typology of Peter B. Clark and James Q. Wilson to suggest that such benefits are of three kinds: material, solidary, and expressive.[11] Material benefits include tangible goods and services or the means (for example, a job) to attain them. Solidary benefits are the various intangible emotional and social rewards that individual members may derive from interacting with others or being perceived favorably by them. Expressive benefits derive from the opportunity the organization offers to support policy goals or values of significance to the member.

For the GVO entrepreneur to begin supplying such incentives, at least three prior conditions must exist. First, the entrepreneur must already have at least a modest stock of information. Second, she must also have become motivated to pursue organizational creation. Since she cannot in most cases have any reasonable expectation of earning a living from the enterprise (at least not right away) the prospect of employment or personal subsidy from organizational resources is unlikely, by itself, to spur the potential entrepreneur into action. Jeffrey M. Berry observed in his study of the origins of public interest groups that "financial self-sacrifice on the part of entrepreneurs" appeared common.[12] The entrepreneur must also have at her disposal some reasonably efficient means of communicating with potential contributors to the organization.

Meeting the motivational condition requires that the GVO entrepreneur have a very strong, even consuming, personal stake in a health- or safety-related issue. Such a stake may derive from an immediate threat to one's own health or safety, or to the health or safety of one's family and close friends. The threat will often be relatively new or newly recognized; recently revealed, rare, unfamiliar, or involuntarily borne risks tend to strike us as more threatening than those we bear willingly or to which we are accustomed.[13] The pack-a-day smoker, long complacent about the dangers of his habit, will feel much differently about a sudden and unwanted exposure to toxic waste, even if the actual level of risk associated with the latter is much lower than that of his chosen habit.[14]

The entrepreneur will be someone who has learned the harmful nature of a threat at first hand, or who becomes convinced (possibly through media coverage of the threat or of problems similar to it) that she has reason to fear imminent harm to herself or her loved ones. Moreover, the threat must extend plausibly to a wider potential audience whose assistance can be enlisted. In brief the entrepreneur must be: (a) informed about an immediate threat, (b) driven by a combination of fear, outrage, and hunger for useable knowledge, and (c) able to share perceptions and a promise of organizational incentives with others afflicted or at risk. Recent history offers many examples of such entrepreneurs, several of whom will be discussed in the paragraphs that follow.

AIDS Activists. New York writer Larry Kramer was alarmed about AIDS well before it even had a name; his friends were falling ill and dying. Remarkably, Kramer would play the role of organizational entrepreneur twice. He first helped organize what became the service organization Gay Men's Health Crisis (GMHC). After considerable feuding with GMHC leadership over the organization's unwillingness to pursue lobbying and protest, Kramer launched ACT-UP, which is now renowned for aggressively protesting both governmental and corporate responses to AIDS.[15] Kramer later tested positive for the human immunodeficiency virus (HIV).

On the West Coast a gay business consultant named Martin Delaney watched his lover suffer with AIDS. Delaney began making trips to Mexico to bring back unapproved drugs that he believed might help his lover and others with his condition. In October 1985, frustrated with government's failure to test and approve drugs more rapidly, Delaney and a few associates conceived Project Inform, a novel effort to design and conduct community-based research that was more responsive to the epidemic.[16] As head of Project Inform, Delaney became a vocal and articulate critic of government AIDS policy. Indeed, the epidemic would spawn numerous and varied grassroots organizations, including a lively and well informed alternative press.[17]

Lois Gibbs and Love Canal. In June 1978 homemaker Lois Gibbs was upset to learn from a news report that chemicals present in New York State's Love Canal dump site were associated with respiratory and neurophysiological disorders. Although she was already mildly interested in the problem—a local newspaper had begun running stories about the site in late 1976—Gibbs now realized to her horror that there might be a direct connection between her young son's attendance at a school built over the dump and his recent development of "severe asthmatic symptoms and convulsions." The realization sparked a one-woman campaign of neighborhood door-knocking to try, as she later stated, "to get some sort of a cleanup in the school area, and in general to form a parents' action committee for whatever might need to be done to make the school safe for the children."[18] Thus were planted the seeds of what became the Love Canal Homeowners Association, whose primary goal would be the government-subsidized relocation of neighborhood residents.

Infant Formula Mothers. In the summer of 1979 the Food and Drug Administration learned that Syntex Laboratories had marketed soy-based infant formula lacking salt, a crucial nutrient, causing a debilitating failure to thrive in many children nourished on the product.[19] Two Washington-area mothers whose children had been fed the formula, Carol Laskin and Lynne Pilot, discovered that the product could still be found on store shelves even after the FDA had asked Syntex to recall it.[20] The angry women contacted Lea Thompson, a consumer affairs reporter at WRC-TV, a Washington, D.C., television station. The station's report on the incomplete recall launched a congressional investigation that led to the Infant Formula Act of 1980. Because the two women were also featured on the program, it helped launch Formula, the organization that Laskin and Pilot still operate. When the local story was replayed the following morning on NBC's "Today" show, as Pilot recalled in an interview, "the phone rang until midnight and it has kept ringing ever since."[21]

Dissatisfied Parents Together. The same consumer reporter who broke the infant formula story would prove instrumental in the creation of yet another GVO nearly three years later.[22] In April 1982 Lea Thompson hosted a documentary entitled "DPT: Vaccine Roulette" that highlighted possibly serious side-effects from the pertussis component of the combined diphtheria-pertussis-tetanus (DPT) shot given to millions of American children. Two affected nephews of Rep. Dan Mica (D-Fla.) appeared on the program, which generated a huge viewer response. Hundreds of concerned and angry parents contacted the station, which began putting the parents in touch with one another. This enabled a core group to meet in Representative Mica's office barely ten days after the documentary had aired. The organization that emerged from that meeting gave itself the name Dissatisfied Parents Together, or DPT.

Breast Cancer Activists. A New York breast cancer GVO calling itself "1 in 9" originated in 1987 when school teacher Francine Kritchek and a colleague, Marie Quinn, told one another of their diagnoses.[23] In the wake of a state-sponsored study of Long Island breast cancer rates that had downplayed environmental factors and suggested that no further inquiry was warranted, the women decided to hold a meeting, placing an ad in the local paper and mailing hundreds of announcements. "Fifty-seven angry, frustrated women showed up," recalled Kritchek.[24] Formally established in 1991, the group later helped lobby for increased federal funding for breast cancer research. In January 1993 it demanded that the federal government reconsider findings that no environmental factors peculiar to Long Island had triggered an increase in breast cancer there.

Lyme Disease Advocates. The Lyme Borelliosis Foundation (later renamed the Lyme Disease Foundation) in Tolland, Connecticut, was begun in 1988 by Tom Forschner and his wife, Karen Vanderhoof-

Forschner, after Karen contracted the disease. Four years later the organization had a $350,000 budget and a four-person staff. Not only was it handling some sixty thousand calls annually, but it also had begun making small research grants.[25]

GVO entrepreneurs such as those profiled above have been personally affected by a health threat and thus inspired to outrage against an "establishment" (business firms, health professionals, government officials) perceived as performing inadequately. Unlike multi-issue policy entrepreneur Ralph Nader and his kindred Naderites, who exhibit a long-standing suspicion of a wide variety of institutions (including corporations, legislatures, and universities), GVO entrepreneurs often have little prior interest in ideology or activism. They have been thrust suddenly by circumstances into situations in which they conclude that important health and safety concerns have not been addressed, at least not with sufficient alacrity or resources, and that the establishment must be pressured to act. Lyme Disease Foundation chairman Tom Forschner, for example, complains that the federal Centers for Disease Control and Prevention originally claimed that Lyme disease was "a self-limiting disease." "They didn't know what they were talking about," concludes Forschner. Moreover, he adds, the "state epidemiologist said the tick [that transmits the Lyme spirochete] didn't go beyond the Connecticut River." He "fought us," not wanting "to expand the boundaries of the problem."

Defining a condition as a public-policy problem is a crucial first step for many GVOs. Several years after its founding in 1987, the CFIDS Association, the largest grassroots organization of persons affected by chronic fatigue syndrome (more recently dubbed "chronic fatigue immune dysfunction syndrome" by activists), continues to combat physicians' dismissive image of the condition as a psychosomatic "yuppie flu."[26] In a similar vein, AIDS activists have long complained of the limits imposed by the definition of their disease, arguing that because AIDS in the United States has affected mostly gay men and intravenous drug users (along with their sexual partners and offspring) the response of government has been unconscionably slow.[27]

Women make up a high proportion of GVO entrepreneurs, particularly in cases of community mobilization against toxic exposure.[28] The social networks women maintain, and their generally greater responsibility for, and sensitivity to, the health of a family doubtless help explain their disproportionate role. Historically, from the temperance and consumer movements of the Progressive Era to the advent of Mothers Against Drunk Driving (MADD) in the early 1980s, women have been conspicuous in their roles on the cutting edge of practical health and welfare problems.[29] In addition, women may be less willing than men "to rationalize risks as necessary for economic well-being."[30] The prominent role of women in breast cancer advocacy requires no explanation.

Media Exposure and Support from Experts

As Allan Cigler and Anthony Nownes suggest elsewhere in this volume, entrepreneurs often need help getting started. One key resource is the media, which perform two crucial functions. First, they help potential entrepreneurs and members learn of a hazard. Second, they facilitate contact among potential entrepreneurs and between entrepreneurs and potential members or contributors. The latter resource is particularly vital for condition-directed groups that lack any geographic or neighborhood cohesiveness. At the extreme, the DPT and infant formula groups both grew out of reports by a single television station.[31]

A second important resource is the sympathetic expert. Lois Gibbs knew nothing about toxic chemicals at the outset of her struggle at Love Canal, but she recruited invaluable interpretive help through her brother-in-law, then a biologist at the Buffalo campus of the State University of New York who put her in touch with environmentalists and offered crucial advice on how to organize and what to read.[32] The FACE group in Woburn enticed biostatisticians at the Harvard School of Public Health into conducting an epidemiological study that produced results at variance with official conclusions.[33]

Some group founders may themselves possess vital expertise (such as legal, business, or medical training) or career experience that facilitates effective organizing. As one might expect, the national capital area is especially rich in such talent. Formula cofounder Pilot had worked on Capitol Hill, and her husband in the FDA's bureau of medical devices, while cofounder Carol Laskin had been a health-care consultant.[34] Jeff Schwartz, a cofounder and first president of DPT, had served as a staff attorney for the House Interstate and Foreign Commerce Committee and in health-related federal agencies over which the committee wielded jurisdiction.[35] To persons with such backgrounds, activism at the junction of health and politics is unforbidding. For example, one cofounder of the National Breast Cancer Coalition, an umbrella organization of more than 180 advocacy groups, is Dr. Susan M. Love, director of the UCLA Breast Center.[36] Before his untimely death from AIDS, physician Andrew S. Zysman "encouraged hundreds of doctors to support ACT-UP ... at fundraising events he sponsored." Energizing a network of health professionals to fight the disease provided significant assistance to the AIDS-focused GVO.[37]

Communication with Members

The GVO entrepreneur typically offers a blend of benefits to potential members, including information and personal support. By producing a modest newsletter, hardly an obstacle in an era of desktop publishing, the entrepreneur can promise the potential member regular access to "news

you can use." Practical information about potential therapies and pallia-
tives, pending legislation, planned protests, relevant court rulings, and
agency decisions make up the standard fare of most such organs.[38] As
Terry M. Moe observes, the organizational entrepreneur can use such
communications not only to present selective and collective benefits, but
also to manipulate members' perceptions of both:

> He can acquaint members with the various selective incentives,
> explain their value, and try to increase the perceived value of group
> membership. In the process, he might be able to create a market for
> some selective incentives where none existed before—by advertising
> new services, for example, or by arguing on behalf of new techniques or
> methods of production requiring new inputs. His influence on member
> calculations is likely to be particularly important, however, in respect to
> collective goods. While selective incentives can usually be immedi-
> ately purchased, experienced, and evaluated, information on collective
> goods is much more remote and, significantly, *it is difficult to obtain
> except through the entrepreneur.* By emphasizing the number, value, and
> type of political goals he seeks, the effectiveness of his political meth-
> ods, and the need for funds (none of which is necessarily close to the
> truth), he can endeavor to increase the levels of contributions and
> political support. He is especially likely to be successful with low-
> information members who depend heavily upon him for "the facts." [39]

Other things being equal, the community-directed organization depends less on refined communication approaches to get organized and
operating than does a condition-directed group. When an organization's
target audience resides in a discrete and manageable locale the entrepreneur can rely much more on personal contact, such as door-to-door visits
or blanketing a neighborhood with flyers and posters. Communities affected by toxic exposures and neighborhoods with notably large gay
populations concerned about AIDS have proved fertile ground. Where
affected persons live in close proximity to one another, it will naturally be
somewhat easier to induce membership through solidary benefits.

In the absence of a small or close-knit community, the entrepreneur
must be more energetic about arranging and communicating opportunities for useful or enjoyable interaction. One vehicle for entrepreneurial
communication lies in the growing use of personal computers. The vast
and growing system of computer networks and bulletin boards known as
the Internet makes it easy for persons with an endless variety of narrow
interests, including specific health problems, to find and communicate
with one another.[40]

Organizational Maintenance and Methods

The most powerful and common selective incentives for involvement in a GVO are information and personal support of a quality and

quantity not otherwise readily available. Present and potential members crave concrete and up-to-date knowledge on how best to cope with difficult and personally unprecedented circumstances. While some relevant information may surface in the mass media or become available through individual research and monitoring, membership in an active group provides a far more efficient means for obtaining it. For example, the National Vaccine Information Center, an outgrowth of the DPT group, charges annual dues of $25, entitling one to receive both a newsletter and a law firm directory listing plaintiff's attorneys around the country who will accept vaccine injury cases.[41]

Group membership may also provide a solidary benefit by addressing a hunger for personal validation and by offering an emotional outlet. The residents of communities with a toxic exposure problem may feel beleaguered and perhaps abandoned by officials who seem distant and unresponsive. In a study of community response to such problems Michael R. Edelstein argues that "when victims turn to government, disappointment is the norm."[42] Similarly, persons with AIDS, breast cancer, or chronic fatigue immune dysfunction syndrome (CFIDS) may have had extremely unsatisfactory encounters with a medical establishment perceived as unhelpful, insensitive, or even disbelieving. An individual with CFIDS may well have been told repeatedly that nothing (or at least nothing definitively physical) could be found wrong.[43] Anger, a potent though volatile organizational fuel, is one natural outcome of such experiences.

Translating Cohesion into Action

Two fundamental challenges facing any GVO are, first, to sustain itself by offering the kinds of incentives described above and, second, to translate group bonds into action while avoiding internal and external threats to the group's existence. The most obvious way to resolve this tension is simply by concentrating on providing selective incentives to the near (or even complete) exclusion of public-policy pursuits. Where a group seeks a political role, however, it may avoid potential conflict by keeping its policy forays modest in scope or reasonably conventional.

The CFIDS Association must maintain harmony and loyalty among twenty-three thousand dues-paying members across the country while pursuing effective advocacy. As the group's executive director explains: "Unlike the AIDS movement, there is nothing these people have in common except the disease."[44] The group's agenda—the dissemination of information, direct funding of research, and lobbying for more government resources—must not disturb significant portions of its diverse clientele. The leadership nurtures an advocacy image that combines mainstream respectability with an aggressive focus on the practical. Cofounder and president Marc M. Iverson is clearly anxious to win over skeptical health professionals and researchers rather than alienate them. "There is only one way," he counselled members in 1991, "to drive the medical establishment to come to grips with CFIDS: scientific research. Period. Nothing else will validate the existence and seriousness of the disease." On the other hand, he argues, "We are not militant."[45] A program of sit-ins or noisy street protests might satisfy some but would likely risk serious disruption of group life; many persons with the disease and their organizational allies would surely feel uncomfortable and might withdraw support. In any case, as the group's executive director observes, "people with the illness just physically can't do these sorts of things."[46]

In pursuing their policy agendas GVO leaders are constrained to embrace strategies and tactics that they and their members find acceptable. Conventional lobbying of both politicians and bureaucrats is an attractive way for groups to reconcile goal pursuit with organizational imperatives. The directness and flexibility of lobbying are important attributes. Group leaders can lobby selectively and with adjustable visibility and militancy, depending on what appears to be called for. In addition, to the extent that pure knowledge is a factor in lobbying effectiveness, the relatively small size of any particular GVO may actually work to its advantage. The specialized information entrepreneurs provide to their members can be served up to busy legislators at little additional cost.

Even a small or new group can cultivate friends in high places, and it does not take many such friends to have a discernible impact. A single congressional advocate can offer visibility for the group agenda and sometimes more tangible victories. For a community-directed GVO one obvious source of help is the community's House member and senators. Love Canal activists received a boost and gained legitimacy from the sympathetic attention of Rep. John LaFalce (D-N.Y.). During the community meeting at which the homeowners association was established, LaFalce received a standing ovation when he "brought the news that President Jimmy Carter was backing an amendment to the Resource Conservation and Recovery Act to use $4 million for remedies at the dump site."[47]

Condition-directed GVOs may similarly enjoy leverage derived from access to a congressional sponsor. In 1992 Sen. Tom Harkin (D-Iowa), chair of the health appropriations subcommittee, helped the National Breast Cancer Coalition win $210 million for Army-sponsored breast cancer research.[48] Dissatisfied Parents Together had not yet formally convened when Kathi Williams, who would serve as a vice president, testified before a hearing on vaccine issues chaired by Sen. Paula Hawkins (R-Fla).[49] The CFIDS Association counts Democratic Sen. Harry Reid of Nevada (where the first cluster of cases was discovered) among its champions in Congress, along with Rep. Mike Synar (D-Okla.) and Rep. John Edward Porter (R-Ill.), who has made the disease a prominent aspect of his work on the powerful appropriations subcommittee that oversees the federal health budget.[50] Not surprisingly, Lyme disease activists won help from members of Congress representing areas where the disease is particularly prevalent, such as Rep. George J. Hochbrueckner (D-N.Y.), whose constituency spans the eastern half of Long Island.[51]

Organizations may use quiet lobbying or more aggressive tactics. Lyme Disease Foundation chairman Tom Forschner says that his organization shuns not only confrontational protest but also adversarial committee hearings. Although some other Lyme activists have favored a more aggressive posture, Forschner calculates that his group can best gain and retain credibility with members of Congress and other officials through quiet, low-keyed lobbying rather than theatrics and "extreme" demands. Like the CFIDS Association, the Lyme group has directly funded research, an appealingly practical use of organizational resources.

In contrast, ACT-UP has become virtually synonymous with "in-your-face" protest, which is exactly the kind of identity Larry Kramer envisioned for the organization. In a now famous speech to the Lesbian and Gay Community Services Center in New York's Greenwich Village in March 1987, Kramer blasted both the Gay Men's Health Crisis and his audience for political timidity in the face of an epidemic—"plague" would become Kramer's preferred term—that he believed was costing lives. "If what you're hearing doesn't rouse you to anger, fury, rage, and action," declared Kramer, "gay men will have no future here on earth."[52] In the days that followed, Kramer found listeners willing to respond. Adopting the slogan that "Silence=Death," accompanied by an upright pink triangle logo resembling those worn by homosexual prisoners in Nazi death camps, ACT-UP "halted trading on the floor of the New York Stock Exchange, delayed for two hours the opening of an international AIDS conference in Montreal, [and] bolted and chained themselves to the offices of pharmaceutical companies" before setting off a firestorm of controversy in December 1989 with the disruption of a mass by John Cardinal O'Connor in Saint Patrick's Cathedral in New York.[53]

For ACT-UP, protest would become both a means to an end (more attention and resources devoted to AIDS) and a mobilizing inducement. This approach set it apart from other AIDS organizations and allowed members, many of them HIV-positive, to wring a sense of personal affirmation and empowerment from their own desperate circumstances.[54] In a 1985 essay, published two years before the founding of ACT-UP, Kramer articulated his vision, later embodied in the organization, for mobilizing the gay community along lines that transcended the more conventional and bureaucratized service focus of GMHC.[55] Kramer wanted to keep his readers viscerally and continually in touch with their victimization without allowing them to become immobilized by it. He proposed a kind of mantra: "Each and every minute of my life, I must act as if I already have AIDS and am fighting for my life." For some with HIV and for those close to them, ACT-UP's enthusiasm for militant protest offers a measure of personal redemption, giving the group some of the flavor of a religious sect.[56] ACT-UP's rhetoric reinforces that impression through its professed indifference to hostile external opinion and by commonly portraying adversaries (such as drug companies and government officials) as fundamentally evil.[57]

Unlike the classic sect, however, ACT-UP has assiduously pursued practical policy goals. Its treatment and data committee successfully spearheaded unprecedented change in AIDS-related biomedical research and drug evaluation.[58] In addition to being gratifying to members, ACT-UP's protests have been carefully "groomed for the media" and designed to further the goals of AIDS awareness, education, and treatment.[59]

ACT-UP's protest prowess and policy successes fired the imagination of other GVOs, including breast cancer groups and HIV-positive hemophiliacs who have demanded a fuller accounting of the clotting factor contamination that left a majority of severe hemophiliacs infected.[60] By serving as a model for other groups, ACT-UP performed a function similar to that of Ralph Nader, whose example stimulated a wave of public-interest organizing in the late 1960s and 1970s.

Magnifying Action through the Media and in the Courts

Through protest and more conventional public relations efforts GVOs try to generate media interest, which helps expand the scope of conflict by attracting the involvement of sympathetic parties.[61] Media coverage may be vital to keeping key elites attentive and target institutions on the defensive. It can also directly serve the cause of organizational maintenance by increasing the excitement, even glamour, of an organizational endeavor. In their study of events in Woburn, Phil Brown and Edwin J. Mikkelsen quote Gretchen Latowsky, a FACE organizer, on why residents were willing to become involved:

> It was all new, and I think this sounds kind of crazy, but there was a tremendous amount of excitement. As awful as that sounds, I think part of the reason people got so involved was that it was fascinating, the whole thing—the technology, the illness, the statistics, the government relations, the publicity, the media involvement—all of that.[62]

Lois Gibbs, currently executive director of the Citizens Clearing House for Hazardous Wastes (which offers advice and support to community groups), observes that media coverage can serve organizational maintenance in another way—by publicizing and celebrating victories. "People need to know that the group is winning," she says. "Nobody wants to be part of something that's losing all the time."[63] In her view such publicity (which can occur more reliably on a smaller scale through internal celebratory events) is a vital tool for inspiring new recruits and generating enthusiasm among the largest possible number of members. Otherwise, she says, a small subgroup may bear too much of the organizational burden, resulting in personal burnout.

Finally, media coverage offers a particularly significant advantage for small or fledgling organizations—it is a cheap and therefore remarkably efficient way to mobilize interest. One need not already have enlisted broad mass support to entice the attention of a newspaper reporter or television crew. The entrepreneur need only present a good story (and for television, good pictures), apparently reliable factual information, and plausible interpretive claims.[64]

The potential payoff of national television exposure can be huge. In the wake of a January 1981 segment on ABC's "20/20," Formula received some sixty-five thousand letters of interest within a few weeks.[65] Small but colorful protests, compelling accounts of victimization, and well-informed criticism of institutional performance offer ammunition that can compensate for a lack of raw organizational size, as the public interest movement discovered long ago.[66]

The same is true of access to the courts. Even a small and somewhat informal group like Formula, heavily reliant on an unpredictable pool of volunteer labor, may file suit, or attach itself (at little or no cost) to actions brought by stronger and better-heeled plaintiffs.[67] While court action is in a general sense more conventional than protest, there is no guarantee that all group members will feel entirely comfortable going to court. In May 1979 a dissident faction of the Love Canal Homeowners Association voted to seek an injunction to prevent completion of remedial construction work because of a possible danger to some residents, but Gibbs and others feared that the action "would alienate the moderate association members and destroy the fragile working relations that still existed with many of the state personnel."[68]

As implied in much of the foregoing, small size alone does not mean failure. Indeed, small groups may enjoy maintenance advantages over large ones. First, as Mancur Olson indicates, the smaller the group, the less likely the need for selective inducements; each member perceives that he or she truly makes a difference. Second, all other things being equal, small size makes a group more cohesive and easier to lead. Small-group leadership is spared the worries associated with monitoring and coordinating far-flung chapters. Moreover, crucial incentives of interpersonal support and information are often available at the community level. Small size may also mean that a group can lie dormant or adopt a low public profile for long periods and with little strain, as one or a few persons collect data and monitor the policy environment until the next agency decision, congressional hearing, or flurry of media interest makes a revival appropriate. Even a small group can maintain a very large mailing list or telephone file of supportive individuals and groups that can be activated when the need arises.

One well known way for a group to sustain itself in a changing environment is by adapting its agenda, moving beyond the concerns that animated its creation and early life, much as the National Foundation for

Infantile Paralysis (The March of Dimes) sought out the new territory of birth defects in the wake of its successful conquest of polio.[69] In 1986 Dissatisfied Parents Together formally expanded its franchise beyond pertussis vaccine and created the National Vaccine Information Center to address more general policy questions, including those stemming from the creation of a national vaccine injury compensation program.[70] Formula did not die once the original scare had yielded legislation. Instead it carved out a role as watchdog of the law's implementation, promoter of more stringent formula safety standards, and spokesman for the continuing interests of the twenty thousand or more children estimated to be at continued risk of impairment from their earlier exposure to unsalted formula.[71]

Organizational Failure and Demise

Like any other kind of organization, a GVO may fail to gel or may collapse over time. To the extent that a threat is familiar, its apparent adverse effects minor, and official response competent grassroots organization becomes less sustainable.[72]

Other forces can threaten group existence. Ironically, goal attainment is one of them. The Love Canal Homeowners Association, for example, became moribund around 1982, once its prime goal of relocation was achieved.[73] Unstable leadership or the erosion of financial resources may also undermine an organization, as they did the CFIDS Society International in Portland, Oregon, prior to the group's 1991 dissolution.[74] Larry Kramer's portrait of GMHC as a relatively tame and bureaucratic service organization highlighted precisely those characteristics that helped it thrive after his departure.[75] On the other hand a group like ACT-UP, zealously antibureaucratic and painstakingly participatory, risks fragmentation and exhaustion over the long run, developments that Kramer was openly lamenting by 1993.[76] The group's treatment and data committee, for example, became a focus of some internal resentment, and dissidents within it later withdrew to form a separate organization, the Treatment Action Group.[77]

Perhaps the most fundamental impediment to GVO durability in the political realm is the inability of group leaders to contain conflict and sustain a sense of shared purpose. The Love Canal organization faced both suspicion by area renters, who believed the organization did not speak for them, and an insurgent Action Group that wanted a more aggressively confrontational style. Gibbs and her colleagues pursued a generally tolerant course, anxious to incorporate the latter group's energy and commitment. This succeeded temporarily, but by the fall of 1979 the dissidents had largely withdrawn.[78] On the other hand, the Citizens Committee that formed in 1981 in response to the contamination of a state office building in Binghamton, New York, failed to endure, at least partly because it "lacked a mechanism that would develop and exploit a network of ties that would have given the association some organizational coherence." Unlike Love Canal, where "the physical proximity of the residents to each other was a kind of social lubricant that increased the likelihood of collective consciousness, in Binghamton members of the Committee had to rely on those who perceived themselves aggrieved to come to them."[79] Finally, unless recruits find organizational activity gratifying, the enterprise is in jeopardy over the long run. Writing about local environmental activism, Nicholas Freudenberg describes how a destructive stratification can infect even highly participatory groups:

> It is all too common for a few activists to do most of the work.... New people who join are often less knowledgeable and experienced, and so are given routine work: typing, answering phones, handing out leaflets. As the group gains recognition the founders inevitably talk to the press and television and speak at public meetings—after all, they can do it best, and they "deserve" the recognition for their hard work. After a while the typists and telephone answerers stop coming around. They begin to suspect the motives of the leaders or doubt their own ability to make a meaningful contribution. Soon the organization falls apart.[80]

GVOs and the New Political Environment

Why have grassroots victim organizations grown more visible since the late 1970s? Much of the answer may lie in a transformation of the national political landscape in recent decades. Although Americans have long displayed a much-noted propensity for voluntary association, developments in postwar America have created conditions quite unlike anything Alexis de Tocqueville might have imagined in the 1830s.[81] An educated and technically sophisticated middle class is both larger and less politically deferential than ever before. By 1980 this segment of society had experienced at least a decade of the environmental movement, some fifteen years of Naderism and feminism, a quarter-century of civil rights struggle, and political upheavals over both the Vietnam War and the Watergate scandal.[82] The wide penetration of the news media, and the increased skepticism of journalists, provide leverage for organizers. So does the judiciary, which has widened access to persons challenging administrative decisions and displayed diminished deference to those decisions in its opinions.[83] Although the decentralized character of Congress can be overstated, individual subcommittees clearly remain more numerous, and their chairs generally more autonomous, than they were half a century ago.[84] Congress is therefore a more likely resource for, and target of, GVO activity. In addition to these institutional changes, the AIDS epidemic has generated conspicuously effective GVO mobilization from which advocates for other health issues have learned much. In sum, the incentives and opportunities for grassroots activism are now greater than ever. Situations in which ordinary citizens might once have remained silent or largely compliant are today more likely to produce cries like that of Howard Beale, a fictional television newscaster in the 1976 film, *Network*: "We're mad as hell, and we're not going to take it anymore!" He might well have added: "We're going to organize!"

Notes

1. Susan Okie, "Running on Outrage," *Washington Post Health*, December 5, 1989, 12-15 and Susan Gross, "The Nader Network," *Business and Society Review*, No. 13 (Spring 1975): 12.
2. Many disease activists currently eschew the term "victim" as implying a passive and even demeaning status. The preferred term in contemporary discourse is "person with …," as in "person with AIDS" or "persons with chronic fatigue immune dysfunction syndrome." This reflects activists' effort to influence the way society regards persons with a given condition and the way those persons regard themselves. In keeping with traditional usage, this essay regards any formal organization initiated by such persons as a GVO, the antithesis of passivity.
3. Stephen C. Joseph, *Dragon Within the Gates: The Once and Future AIDS Epidemic* (New York: Carroll & Graf, 1992), 87-89.
4. On Love Canal see Adeline Gordon Levine, *Love Canal: Science, Politics, People* (Lexington, Mass.: Lexington Books, 1982); Lois Marie Gibbs as told to Murray Levine, *Love Canal: My Story* (Albany, N.Y.: State University of New York Press, 1982); and Martha R. Fowlkes and Patricia Y. Miller, "Chemicals and Community at Love Canal," in *The Social and Cultural Construction of Risk: Essays on Risk Selection and Perception*, ed. Branden B. Johnson and Vincent T. Covello (Boston: D. Reidel, 1987), 55-78. On the Woburn, Massachusetts, case see Phil Brown and Edwin J. Mikkelsen, *No Safe Place: Toxic Waste, Leukemia, and Community Action* (Berkeley and Los Angeles: University of California Press, 1990).
5. Jason DeParle, "Rude, Rash, Effective, Act-Up Shifts AIDS Policy," New York Times, January 3, 1990, B1, B4. When a large number of persons with an identified condition happen to live in close proximity to one another, as do persons with AIDS in the Castro neighborhood of San Francisco, for example, the community/condition distinction will be less meaningful.
6. David B. Truman, *The Governmental Process: Political Interests and Public Opinion* (New York: Alfred A. Knopf, 1951).
7. Mancur Olson, *The Logic of Collective Action* (Cambridge: Harvard University Press, 1965).
8. James Q. Wilson, *Political Organizations* (New York: Basic Books, 1973), 195-196.
9. Robert H. Salisbury, "An Exchange Theory of Interest Groups," *Midwest Journal of Political Science* 13 (February 1969): 1-32. See also Wilson, *Political Organizations*, chap. 10, and Terry M. Moe, *The Organization of Interests: Incentives and the Internal Dynamics of Political Interest Groups* (Chicago: University of Chicago Press, 1980), chap. 3. Some literature on grassroots organizations contains possibly confusing references to groups as a whole performing as "issue entrepreneurs." See Lee Clarke, "The Political Ecology of Local Protest Groups," in *Communities at Risk: Collective Responses to Technological Hazards*, ed. Stephen Robert Couch and J. Stephen Kroll-Smith (New York: Peter Lang, 1991), 83.
10. Salisbury, "Exchange Theory," 11.
11. For the earlier typology, see Peter B. Clark and James Q. Wilson, "Incentive

Systems: A Theory of Organizations," *Administrative Science Quarterly* 6 (September 1961): 129-166. Wilson later elaborated the argument alone in *Political Organizations*. Clark and Wilson use the term "purposive incentive." Salisbury explains his departure from their terminology at 16-17.

12. Jeffrey M. Berry, "On the Origins of Public Interest Groups: A Test of Two Theories," *Polity* 10 (Spring 1978): 392-393.

13. Peter M. Sandman, "Hazard versus Outrage in the Public Perception of Risk," in *Effective Risk Communication: The Role and Responsibility of Government and Nongovernment Organizations*, ed. Vincent T. Covello, David B. McCallum and Maria T. Pavlova (New York: Plenum, 1989), 45-49.

14. Similarly, in prior eras, diseases that generated sudden and unpredictably recurring epidemics—examples include cholera, plague, and yellow fever—were viewed differently from those, such as tuberculosis, that were routinely endemic, quite apart from the actual levels of morbidity and mortality associated with them. See John Duffy, *The Sanitarians: A History of American Public Health* (Urbana and Chicago: University of Illinois Press, 1990).

15. Larry Kramer, *Reports from the holocaust: The Making of an AIDS Activist* (New York: St. Martin's Press, 1989). "Holocaust" is lower-cased in the title of the work.

16. Jonathan Kwitny, *Acceptable Risks* (New York: Poseidon Press, 1992), chap. 18.

17. Charles Perrow and Mauro F. Guillén, *The AIDS Disaster: The Failure of Organizations in New York and the Nation* (New Haven: Yale University Press, 1990), chap. 7. See also Katherine Bishop, "Underground Press Leads Way on AIDS Advice," *New York Times*, December 16, 1991, A16. A thorough discussion of knowledge dissemination by grassroots AIDS groups appears in Debbie Indyk and David A. Rier, "Grassroots AIDS Knowledge: Implications for the Boundaries of Science and Collective Action," *Knowledge* 15 (September 1993): 3-43.

18. Levine, *Love Canal: Science, Politics, People*, 30-31.

19. Christopher H. Foreman, Jr., *Signals from the Hill: Congressional Oversight and the Challenge of Social Regulation* (New Haven: Yale University Press, 1988), 47-48.

20. Contrary to common belief, and unlike some other regulatory agencies, the FDA's legislative mandate does not empower the agency to order product recalls. The FDA may request a manufacturer to initiate a recall and threaten a court-ordered seizure or adverse publicity should the firm not comply.

21. Telephone interview with Lynne Pilot, September 29, 1993.

22. This account relies on a telephone interview with Kathi Williams, National Vaccine Information Center, September 29, 1993, and on *Dissatisfied Parents Together News* 1 (Fall 1983). See also Harris L. Coulter and Barbara Loe Fisher, *A Shot in the Dark: Why the P in the DPT Vaccination May Be Hazardous to Your Child's Health* (Garden City Park, N.Y.: Avery Publishing Group, 1991), 138.

23. The group's formal name is 1 in 9: The Long Island Breast Cancer Action Coalition. The name derives from a widely cited though controversial statistic promoted by the American Cancer Society, suggesting that one of every nine American women will develop breast cancer. To understand why this may be a misleading ratio see Lisa Davis, "One in Nine," *Health* 7 (January/February 1993): 40-49.

24. Susan Ferraro, "The Anguished Politics of Breast Cancer," *New York Times Magazine*, August 15, 1993, 61; Thomas J. Lueck, "New Studies on Breast Cancer Sought by D'Amato and Women," *New York Times*, January 8, 1993, B5.

25. Telephone interview with Tom Forschner, chairman, Lyme Disease Foundation, September 11, 1992.

26. Telephone interview with K. Kimberly Kenney, executive director of the CFIDS Association, Charlotte, North Carolina, October 20, 1993.

27. Randy Shilts, *And the Band Played On: Politics, People, and the AIDS Epidemic* (New York: St. Martin's Press, 1987).

28. See Brown and Mikkelsen, *No Safe Place*, 45 and Michael R. Edelstein, *Contami-*

nated Communities: The Social and Psychological Impacts of Residential Toxic Exposure (Boulder, Colo.: Westview, 1988), 141.

29. Mothers Against Drunk Driving (MADD) was founded by Candy Lightner in 1980 after her thirteen-year-old daughter was killed by a drunk driver. By 1984 the group claimed a half-million members in 44 states; that year MADD helped spearhead passage of a federal law (P.L. 98-363) designed to encourage states to raise the legal drinking age to twenty-one and establish mandatory minimum sentences for drunk drivers. See "Congress Encourages 21-Year Drinking Age," *Congressional Quarterly Almanac--1984* (Washington, D.C.: Congressional Quarterly, 1985), 283-284. On the historical role of women in the early consumer protection movement see James Harvey Young, *Pure Food: Securing the Federal Food and Drugs Act of 1906* (Princeton, N.J.: Princeton University Press, 1989), 183-186.

30. Edelstein, *Contaminated Communities*, 141.

31. A similar episode led to an organization of persons interested in a genetic abnormality known as Klinefelter's syndrome, caused by the presence of more than one X chromosome in the male genetic profile. Nationally syndicated columnist Ann Landers published a desperate letter from a California woman seeking information about the condition, generating more than a thousand letters from men with the condition and from parents of affected children. See Jane E. Brody, "Personal Health" (column), *New York Times*, December 15, 1993, C17.

32. Gibbs and Levine, *Love Canal: My Story*, 10-17 and Levine, *Love Canal: Science, Politics, People*, 30-32.

33. Brown and Mikkelsen, *No Safe Place*, 14-17.

34. Telephone interview with Lynne Pilot.

35. *Dissatisfied Parents Together News* 1 (Spring 1983): 6. In 1981, at the beginning of the Ninety-Seventh Congress, the House Committee on Interstate and Foreign Commerce was renamed the Committee on Energy and Commerce.

36. Ferraro, "Anguished Politics," 27.

37. "Andrew S. Zysman, 38; Pushed AIDS Research" (obituary), *New York Times*, October 15, 1993, B10.

38. As Terry Moe points out, there is no reason necessarily to believe that the information the entrepreneur doles out is accurate. Indeed, it may well be in the entrepreneur's interest to provide "false, misleading or ambiguous information." See Moe, *Organization of Interests*, 39.

39. Ibid., 41. Emphasis added.

40. Robert Wright, "Voice of America," *The New Republic*, September 13, 1993, 20-21, 24-27.

41. Telephone interview with Kathi Williams.

42. Edelstein, *Contaminated Communities*, 138.

43. Katrina H. Berne, *Running on Empty: Chronic Fatigue Immune Dysfunction Syndrome (CFIDS)* (Alameda, Calif.: Hunter House, 1992), 28-32. See also Marc M. Iverson, "Letter from the President and Annual Report to Members," *CFIDS Chronicle* (Fall 1991): iii.

44. Telephone interview with K. Kimberly Kenney.

45. Iverson, "Letter from the President," iv.

46. Telephone interview with K. Kimberly Kenney.

47. Levine, *Love Canal: Science, Politics, People*, 42.

48. Ferraro, "Anguished Politics," 27 and Eliot Marshall, "The Politics of Breast Cancer," *Science* 259 (January 29, 1993): 616-617.

49. U.S. Senate, Committee on Labor and Human Resources, *Immunization and Preventive Medicine, 1982*, hearing before the Subcommittee on Investigations and General Oversight, 97th Cong., 2d sess., May 7, 1982, 44-85.

50. For an example of Rep. Porter's activity see House of Representatives, Committee on Appropriations, *Departments of Labor, Health and Human Services, Education,*

and Related Agencies for 1993, Part 2, 102d Cong., 2d sess., 1992, 1619-1627. According to Washington lobbyist Tom Sheridan, who represents the CFIDS Association, representatives Synar and Porter were each drawn to the issue by the entreaties of aggressive constituents.

51. In the 101st Congress Rep. Hochbrueckner introduced H.R. 5245 ("The Lyme Disease Research and Education Act of 1990") and H.J. Res. 138 to declare "Lyme Disease Awareness Week."

52. For an account of this meeting see DeParle, "Rude, Rash, Effective," and Peter S. Arno and Karyn L. Feiden, *Against the Odds: The Story of AIDS Drug Development, Politics and Profits* (New York: Harper Collins, 1992), pp. 73-75.

53. DeParle, "Rude, Rash, Effective," B1. See also the account of the disrupted mass in Jason DeParle, "111 Held in St. Patrick's AIDS Protest," *New York Times,* December 11, 1989, B3. ACT-UP raised money through the sale of merchandise imprinted with its logo. See Paul Taylor, "AIDS Guerrillas," *New York,* November 12, 1990, 63.

54. See for example Andrew Sullivan, "Gay Life, Gay Death," *New Republic,* December 17, 1990, 24-25.

55. See Kramer's "We Can Be Together: How To Organize the Gay Community," reprinted in Kramer, *Reports from the holocaust,* 78-91.

56. On redemptive organizations see Wilson, *Political Organizations,* 47-48.

57. Ibid., 208.

58. See generally Arno and Feiden, *Against the Odds.*

59. Taylor, "AIDS Guerrillas," 70. See also Valeria Fabj and Matthew J. Sobnosky, "Responses from the Street: ACT UP and Community Organizing Against AIDS," in *AIDS: Effective Health Communication for the 90s,* ed. Scott C. Ratzan (Washington, D.C.: Taylor & Francis, 1993), 91-109.

60. On ACT-UP as a model for breast cancer advocacy see Ferraro, "Anguished Politics," 61 and Jane Gross, "Turning Disease into Political Cause: First AIDS, and Now Breast Cancer," *New York Times,* January 7, 1991, A12. On grassroots advocacy among HIV-infected hemophiliacs see Gina Kolata, "Hit Hard by AIDS Virus, Hemophiliacs Speak Up," *New York Times,* December 25, 1991, 7; Mireya Navarro, "Hemophiliacs Demand Answers as AIDS Toll Rises," *New York Times,* May 10, 1993, A1; and Elizabeth Kastor, "Blood Feud: Hemophiliacs and AIDS," *Washington Post,* May 10, 1993, B1.

61. The classic explication of the "socialization of conflict" is that of E.E. Schattschneider, *The Semi-Sovereign People* (New York: Holt, Rinehart and Winston, 1960).

62. Brown and Mikkelsen, *No Safe Place,* 47.

63. Telephone interview with Lois Gibbs, October 28, 1993.

64. For an analysis of the processes by which political actors try to shape "difficulties" into "stories" worthy of attention and preferred action see Deborah A. Stone, "Causal Stories and the Formation of Policy Agendas," *Political Science Quarterly* 104 (1989): 281-300.

65. Telephone interview with Carol Laskin, Formula executive director, November 5, 1993. The January 15, 1981, broadcast was the second one that had featured the group. The first, aired March 13, 1980, did not result in the same outpouring of mail, a difference apparently resulting from the broadcasting of the group's address at the end of the second program.

66. Mark V. Nadel, *The Politics of Consumer Protection* (Indianapolis: Bobbs-Merrill, 1971), 208-210.

67. Philip J. Hilts, "FDA Sued Over New Infant Formula Rules," *Washington Post,* December 2, 1982, A7, and Susan Okie, "Baby-Formula Rules Foster Long Struggle," *Washington Post,* February 20, 1986, A17, and *Formula, et al. Appellants v.*

Margaret M. Heckler, Secretary of Health and Human Services, et al., 779 F. 2d 743, December 31, 1985.

68. Levine, *Love Canal: Science, Politics, People*, 203.

69. Wilson, *Political Organizations*, 206.

70. National Childhood Vaccine Injury Act of 1986 (P.L. 99-660).

71. Susan Okie, "NIH Study Links Faulty Baby Food to Permanent Brain Impairment," *Washington Post*, June 9, 1987, A4.

72. Janet M. Fitchen, Jenifer S. Heath, and June Fessenden-Raden, "Risk Perception in Community Context: A Case Study," in *The Social and Cultural Construction of Risk*, ed. Johnson and Covello, 31-54.

73. Interview with Lois Gibbs. See also Clarke, "Local Protest Groups," 89.

74. See the letter to members of the CFIDS Society International in *CFIDS Chronicle* (Fall 1991): 53. Similarly the CFIDS Action Campaign for the United States (CACTUS), an umbrella group of CFIDS leaders intended to concentrate on political advocacy, expired in early 1992, little more than a year after getting started, due to an inability to raise necessary funds. The demise of CACTUS left the CFIDS Association with a much greater advocacy burden. See *CFIDS Chronicle* (Winter 1993).

75. Perrow and Guillén, *AIDS Disaster*, 107-113.

76. See "Playboy Interview: Larry Kramer," *Playboy*, September 1993, 64.

77. On resentment of the treatment and data committee see David Handelman, "ACT UP in Anger," *Rolling Stone*, March 8, 1990, 86.

78. Levine, *Love Canal: Science, Politics, People*, chap. 7.

79. Clarke, "Local Protest Groups," 105.

80. Nicholas Freudenberg, *Not in Our Backyards! Community Action for Health and the Environment* (New York: Monthly Review Press, 1984), 128.

81. Alexis de Tocqueville, *Democracy in America*, 2 vols. (New York: Vintage, 1945).

82. Diana B. Dutton, *Worse than the Disease: Pitfalls of Medical Progress* (Cambridge and New York: Cambridge University Press, 1988), chap. 10.

83. Richard B. Stewart, "The Reformation of American Administrative Law," *Harvard Law Review* 88 (June 1975): 1669-1813.

84. An excellent brief statement of the various ways that majority-party leadership in Congress can combat decentralization is Barbara Sinclair, "House Majority Party Leadership in an Era of Legislative Constraint," in *The Postreform Congress*, ed. Roger H. Davidson (New York: St. Martin's, 1992), pp. 91-111.

3

Onward Christian Soldiers:
Religious Activist Groups in American Politics

James L. Guth, John C. Green,
Lyman A. Kellstedt, and Corwin E. Smidt

The religious community has a long history of involvement in American politics. Issues such as civil rights, prohibition, slavery, abortion, and many others have had deep, church-based roots. Since the 1970s religious interests, particularly on the political right, have again become highly visible forces in American politics. Such involvement has been extraordinarily controversial, raising fears among secular interests that the separation of church and state was being threatened by attempts to impose religious values through the political process.

In this chapter, James Guth, John Green, Lyman Kellstedt, and Corwin Smidt first discuss the factors underlying the proliferation of religious groups active in politics in recent decades. They suggest that contemporary religious activism represents a departure from the past, in which denominations were the "basic building blocks of religious life and the institutional connection to national politics." Today, large numbers of religious citizens groups mobilize like-minded Christians across denominational boundaries.

The authors next turn their attention to the results of their 1990 survey of religious activists from five prominent religious citizens groups, three considered as representative of the "Christian Right" and two representing the less-publicized "Christian Left." On the surface, religious activists look a lot like typical political activists: they tend to be older and predominantly white, are better educated, have higher-status occupations and incomes than the population at large, and communicate frequently with public officials. But they differ markedly in their willingness to engage in activities such as demonstrating or boycotting. The authors conclude that, ideologically, both "Christian conservatives and liberals meld into contemporary alignments." The moral traditionalism of the former and the social justice concerns and environmental orientation of the latter correspond nicely to the broader ideological patterns that separate Republicans and Democrats on the national political spectrum.

R eligious organizations have always been enmeshed in American politics, from the days when colonial clergy blessed the American Revolution to the 1960s when Protestant, Catholic, and Jewish leaders fought for civil rights. Throughout most of American history, according to many historians, the interlocked dimensions of ethnicity and faith have been the main ingredients of party politics.[1]

Although God's people were not strangers in the lobbies of Caesar, the advent of the Moral Majority in 1979 stunned scholars and pundits alike. Historically apolitical, evangelical Protestants were entering the political arena, and doing so in a fashion more reminiscent of secular interest groups than other religious organizations. When the Moral Majority folded a decade later, a host of larger and more sophisticated successors remained on the scene.[2] These organizations were part of broader institutional changes taking place in American politics and religion.

The Rise of Religious Citizen Groups

The last thirty years have witnessed a remarkable profusion of citizen groups of all kinds. The rapid expansion of the middle class generated a large pool of activists with the interests, resources, and opportunities to pursue public-policy goals independent of political parties and economic interest groups. Many of these activists were less concerned with New Deal economic issues than with new questions such as minority rights, women's rights, environmental policy, and consumer protection. The continued nationalization of economic and cultural life, as well as government's growing penetration into matters once left to local communities, heightened interest in organizing. At the same time, new tools for mobilization—such as computerized direct mail and radio and television solicitation—became available. These could reach millions of like-minded people across the country. The combination of novel issues and new techniques enabled political entrepreneurs to mobilize members, financial resources, and expertise into citizen groups. Religious constituencies were no exception to the general trend.[3]

Two important changes in American religion furthered the rise of religious citizen groups. These were the decline of centralized denominations and the shifting balance of power within Protestantism. For most of American history, denominations were the basic building blocks of religious life and the institutional connection to national politics. Ethnic ties, lifestyle concerns, and philosophical worldviews generated social and political ideologies that bound the denominations to one political party or another. During the twentieth century, white mainline Protestants—Congregationalists, Episcopalians, Presbyterians, and Methodists—constituted the religious core of the Republican party. Members of the mainline denominations shared a common northern European ancestry, a nineteenth-century impulse for moral and social reform (as revealed, for example, in the abolition and temperance movements), and support for unfettered capitalism, at least among more affluent church members.

In contrast, Catholics were the backbone of the Democratic party in the North. The Democratic party better accommodated their more mixed European heritages and expressed their philosophical preference for "personal liberty" during Prohibition and for New Deal social welfare programs. White southern Protestants, another element of the Democratic coalition, were tied to the party of the former Confederacy by Civil War memories and racial attitudes. Despite some convergence with their northern Protestant kin on moral questions, the oft-impoverished southern Protestants' economic interests were better represented by Roosevelt's New Deal than by Republican business conservatism. So most Southern Baptists, many Southern Methodists, and other theologically conservative Protestants were yoked with their religious arch-enemies, the Catholics, in the Democratic coalition, along with Jews and other cultural "outgroups."[4]

More recently, however, these historic alliances began to break up. First, major denominations experienced deep divisions, over theology and politics.[5] Just as general farm organizations, labor federations, and peak associations in the business world (such as the U.S. Chamber of Commerce) lost influence to specialized commodity groups, unions, and trade associations, denominations have often failed in aggregating the religious views and policy interests of diverse constituencies. For example, mainline Protestant elites who endorsed liberal Democratic domestic programs and dovish foreign policies often became "generals without armies," with little supporting fire from their predominantly conservative Republican laity. Similarly, in the 1980s, the Catholic bishops' policies on nuclear war, the economy, and abortion elicited vocal dissent from both liberal and conservative Catholics, depending on the issue. Such conflicts often led the warring forces to seek other avenues for political expression.[6]

Shifts in the balance of power within Protestantism also fostered citizen-group politics. By the 1960s the numerical and cultural dominance of mainline Protestant churches was fading as steep membership losses beset their high-status congregations, further undermining the "progressive" political witness of these theologically liberal denominations and their umbrella organization, the National Council of Churches. At the same time, theologically conservative evangelical Protestants prospered, both in numbers and, especially, in social status. In the process, their own umbrella organization, the National Association of Evangelicals, gained in visibility and prestige.[7]

This new prominence confronted evangelicals with hard choices. Traditionally dedicated to "soul winning," they were now tempted to "go political," as school prayer, abortion, gay rights, and other moral issues hit the national agenda. For those so inclined, however, there were limits to the political utility of existing agencies. Local evangelical clergy often refused to add political dimensions to their ministry, as did many national leaders. The evangelical community was still divided into distinct theological camps, including fundamentalists, charismatics, Pentecostals, and neo-evangelicals, who often found cooperation difficult. Evangelicals were scattered in dozens of denominations, movements, and nondenominational churches, often with little or no national organization.[8] Thus, the new political vitality of a self-confident evangelical community struggled to find an effective outlet.

By the 1970s, ready constituencies of religious activists sought new vehicles for political action. Like members of other middle-class citizen groups, liberal and conservative Christians had formulated rival ideologies containing competing critiques of American society, programs for action, and rationales for collective effort.[9] For liberal Christians (primarily mainline Protestants and Catholics), the key issues were disarmament, world hunger, and social justice, while for conservatives (including many evangelicals), school prayer, abortion, and gay rights were crucial. Emulating the founders of other citizen groups, ambitious entrepreneurs used new techniques to exploit salient issues and mobilize preexisting religious networks, producing a rich variety of organizations. Although liberal Christians were not unrepresented, most of the new citizen groups were conservative.[10]

Most of the new citizen groups of the 1970s faced resistance from established political organizations. The new religious groups aroused extraordinary controversy. Secular (and culturally liberal) interests attacked any overt expression of religious values in politics, while other critics expressed narrower concerns, worrying that the new groups might violate the "separation of church and state" by imposing sectarian views on policy or some sort of "religious test" for public office. Even some who welcomed religious people into the public square worried about "undemocratic" traits such as political intolerance.[11] Finally, religious leaders themselves feared that politics would dilute the churches' spirituality, destroy their internal harmony, and debase their moral authority.[12]

Resistance to the new religious groups was intensified by recognition of their potential power. Their greatest strength lay in their large membership, which not only supplied money for lobbying and campaign work by group leaders, but also constituted a vast reservoir of potential activists. Religious beliefs provide many citizens with a powerful source of direction; clear priorities and policy stances orient them in the political process. Religious people are enmeshed in webs of local churches, channels of religious information, and networks of religious associations that make them readily accessible for mobilization. Finally, active churchgoers often have organizational experiences—such as speaking in public, leading committees, and managing budgets—that are almost directly transferrable to politics.[13] Thus equipped, the new groups brought formidable institutional and personal resources into the political fray.

A Profile of the Organizations

Our 1990-91 Religious Activist Survey included 5,002 members of eight religious interest groups. In this chapter, we report the results of our study of members of five organizations: Concerned Women for America (CWA), Americans for the Republic (AFR), Focus on the Family (Focus), JustLife, and Bread for the World (BFW). Although these constitute a fair cross section of citizen religious lobbies, and the factors that influence their members also shape many other religious organizations, we make no claim that they are strictly representative of the range of such groups.[14] The first three groups are conservative to varying degrees and are often considered part of the so-called Christian Right, whereas the last two organizations are liberal, representing a less-publicized "Christian Left." As we shall see, Right and Left groups differ sharply in their theologies, social philosophies, political ideology, and public activities.

Concerned Women for America (CWA)

Founded in 1979 by Beverly LaHaye, wife of fundamentalist minister and author Tim LaHaye, CWA is a staunchly antifeminist women's group that concentrates on "profamily" issues. CWA began as groups of neighborhood church women who met to pray for the country, and its one thousand local units in forty-nine states are still called "Prayer Action Chapters." While CWA claims almost six hundred thousand members— far more than its feminist rival, the National Organization for Women (NOW)—its active membership is probably only modestly larger than that of NOW. CWA publishes the monthly *Family Voice*, has a daily radio program broadcast on Christian stations across the country, and maintains a well-staffed lobbying and legal affairs office in Washington, D.C.

Americans for the Republic (AFR)

Modeled on Ronald Reagan's "Citizens for the Republic," AFR was created as a political action committee (PAC) to support religious broadcaster Marion "Pat" Robertson's 1988 GOP presidential bid by attracting hundreds of thousands of small contributors, primarily from among Pentecostal and charismatic Christians. Although in a sense AFR was nothing more than a list of Robertson donors, it was also a repository for activists from previous Robertson organizations (such as the Freedom Council and the Committee for Freedom) and the base from which he created the Christian Coalition in 1989. The Coalition is a grassroots organization with more than 450,000 members and almost one thousand chapters located in all fifty states. The Coalition staff, led by executive director Ralph Reed, organizes local chapters, trains activists and potential candidates, and supplies materials for mobilizing voters, such as candidate "score cards." Many observers credited the Coalition with a key role in writing the 1992 GOP platform and in getting conservative Christians to the polls in support of Republican candidates. The Coalition participated in the purported "capture" of some state and local Republican parties by Christian Right forces. Headquartered in Virginia Beach, the Coalition also maintains a Washington lobbying office and publishes a monthly paper, the *Christian American*. A related Robertson group, the American Center for Law and Justice, litigates for conservative causes, and Robertson still uses his "700 Club" TV program to advance his political agenda.

Focus on the Family (Focus)

Founded and led by popular radio psychologist and evangelical layman James Dobson, Focus has several hundred thousand members and is headquartered in a mammoth, well-equipped office complex in Colorado Springs. Dobson's radio program is broadcast on eighteen hundred stations throughout the country and has the third largest daily audience of any radio program, ranking behind only Paul Harvey and Rush Limbaugh. Focus receives more than two hundred thousand letters from listeners monthly and twelve hundred phone calls each day. The group publishes several magazines for segments of its membership; more than 267,000 members pay $15 a year for the political monthly, *Citizen*. Political training seminars are routinely offered to interested subscribers, but few local chapters have appeared. Focus is associated with several state-level research units on family policy and for a time had a Washington lobbying arm, the Family Research Council, headed by former Reagan staffer Gary Bauer. Focus later dropped the tie because of tax concerns. Although Dobson tries to keep his distance from the Christian Right, Focus has been embroiled in local battles over school curricula and gay rights. California, Colorado, Texas, Michigan, Pennsylvania, and North Carolina have especially strong state units.

JustLife PAC

Formed in 1986 by seminary professor and best-selling author Ron Sider and other "progressive" evangelical leaders, JustLife PAC promoted a "seamless garment of life ethic." The group backed antiabortion candidates but only if they also took liberal "prolife" stances on social justice and militarism issues. Recruited by direct mail appeals, donors numbered more than five thousand by 1990, when JustLife assisted fifty-four candidates. It also produced a newsletter, compiled candidate score cards, and lobbied on Capitol Hill. As anticipated by JustLife's founders, contributors were primarily evangelical Protestants and Catholics. JustLife tried to develop local chapters but with little success, and in 1993, as a result of increasing financial difficulties, the group disbanded.

Bread for the World (BFW)

Founded in 1973 by Arthur Simon, a Lutheran pastor and brother of U.S. senator Paul Simon, BFW focuses on national hunger policy. BFW's forty thousand members live in virtually every congressional district and receive a monthly newsletter to keep them abreast of Washington policy issues. BFW members engage in grassroots lobbying, such as calling, writing, or visiting public officials. Besides its large Washington office, BFW's hundreds of local chapters are often connected to Catholic parishes and Methodist and other mainline Protestant churches, which in effect serve as sponsors. BFW has a reputation for particular clout on hunger issues.

On the surface, members of these groups look like typical political activists: they are older, predominantly white, better educated, and have higher-status occupations and incomes than the population at large.[15] Their religious interests aside, they are just the sort of people who participate regularly and exercise influence in American politics. Nevertheless, there are important differences among them. The conservatives are not as highly educated as their liberal rivals: fewer than one-half of the members of CWA, AFR, and Focus have college degrees, whereas nearly nine-tenths of BFW and JustLife members do. Educational differences are reflected in occupation as well, with the conservatives including more business managers, clerical and skilled workers, and homemakers, whereas the liberals draw heavily from traditional professions such as law, medicine, education, and the clergy. CWA, AFR, and Focus members tend to live in the South and West; JustLife and BFW members are concentrated in the Northeast and Midwest. All groups draw disproportionately from rural areas, small towns, and suburbs, rather than major metropolitan areas. Women are numerous in all five groups but are the majority in the conservative organizations.

The Religious Basis: Beliefs, Denominations, Networks

As their histories suggest, all five groups are rooted in religious communities, but in different ones. CWA, AFR, and Focus are composed almost entirely of evangelical Protestants (Table 3-1). In contrast, JustLife drew a majority from among Catholics, with evangelical and mainline Protestants constituting substantial minorities. BFW is predominantly mainline Protestant, with a significant Catholic minority.

Even more revealing are specific denominational patterns (for which the data are not shown in the table). In all three conservative groups, nondenominational evangelicals are most numerous, followed by Baptists, Pentecostals and, at a distance, by Holiness denominations, such as the Nazarenes. Thus, all three recruit from movements with strong local churches but minimal national organization (and a history of eschewing politics). On the liberal side, Protestants in JustLife and Bread differ. Those in JustLife come from Reformed (Calvinistic) backgrounds, such as conservative Presbyterians and the Christian Reformed Church, as well as from Anabaptist churches like the Mennonites. (Calvinists differ from other evangelicals in their historic affinity for politics, while Anabaptist pacifism sometimes generates antiwar and foreign policy involvement.) BFW's Protestants are mostly mainline: Lutherans (perhaps reflecting founder Simon's role), Presbyterians, United Methodists, and Episcopalians, in that order. Thus, BFW typifies the religious coalition on the liberal side of the civil rights, nuclear freeze, and environmental movements.

The religious beliefs and identifications of group members vary greatly. CWA, AFR, and Focus members hold very orthodox Christian beliefs (such as the deity of Jesus, His virgin birth, and His resurrection), while JustLife and BFW adherents are less orthodox. The same pattern appears on a scale of fundamentalism (including items on Biblical literalism, the second coming of Christ, and the historicity of Adam and Eve, among others).

Most conservatives have entered the Christian community by a sudden "born-again" experience, whereas most JustLife and BFW members eschew the term or see it as representing gradual nurture in the church. Asked to select shorthand religious labels, majorities in the conservative groups think of themselves as both "evangelical" and "fundamentalist" Christians. But they differ significantly on two other identifications: most AFR members are either "charismatic" or "Pentecostal" (or both), whereas the proportion of both is much lower in CWA and, especially, Focus. Thus, the religious similarity of the three groups must be sharply qualified: the AFR's reliance on charismatics and Pentecostals divides the Robertson movement from the wider evangelical constituency, which is better represented in groups such as Focus. Although significant minorities in JustLife and BFW are also "evangelicals," most prefer "mainline," "liberal," or "ecumenical" labels.

Not surprisingly, general religious measures do not differentiate the groups very well. Almost all activists are church members, attend services regularly, and regard religion as very important. About half of each group also report that all or most of their friends attend their own church, suggesting intense social ties to the congregation. Many are also members of other religious entities (often called "parachurch groups"), including devotional organizations, mission societies, and charities. Although faith may be a little more central psychologically to conservatives, their advantage in actual involvement is not very large.

Table 3-1   Religious Characteristics of Group Activists (in percent)

	CWA	AFR	FOCUS	JL	BFW
Religious tradition					
Evangelical Protestant	86	79	81	28	13
Mainline Protestant	10	16	12	18	54
Roman Catholic	3	4	7	52	32
Other	1	1	0	2	2
Religious beliefs					
High doctrinal orthodoxy	81	79	80	28	15
High fundamentalist	67	63	59	5	1
Self-identification					
Evangelical	77	69	68	40	29
Fundamentalist	62	52	51	4	3
Charismatic/Pentecostal	37	75	27	16	7
Mainline/liberal/ecumen'l	9	14	17	72	88
Religious involvement					
Church attendance					
Attend more than weekly	69	61	59	47	35
Attend once a week	26	27	31	42	47
"Very active" in church	43	34	41	42	43
Religion at center of life	80	66	67	63	49
All/most friends in same church	53	45	48	33	40
Member of parachurch group	59	57	45	52	40

Source: 1990 Religious Activist Survey conducted by authors.

On the whole, Christian conservatives and Christian liberals inhabit different religious worlds, sharing little but commitment to faith and church—and the dense social and organizational networks that facilitate political mobilization.

The Role of Religion in Politics

If historians are correct, these religious differences have shaped the way activists connect their faith and public policy. Perhaps the fundamental question has been that of religion's role in transforming society. Evangelicals long ago adopted an individualistic theory of social change. Because evil springs from the depravity of the human heart, society can be improved only by the religious conversion and reform of the individual, rather than by altering social and governmental institutions. In contrast, both Catholics, with a communitarian social theology, and mainline Protestants, influenced by the social gospel of the Progressive Era, have held a more optimistic view of human nature, one that admits the possibility of bettering society by reforming institutions.[16]

These varying "social theologies" have had clear implications for politics. As evangelicals emphasized salvation in the next world, the priority of converting sinners, and the separation of true Christians from corrupt worldly institutions (including most churches), they rejected "getting involved in politics."[17] Catholics, mainline Protestants, and the Reformed churches, on the other hand, remained open to politics as an avenue for social betterment.

Of course, the Christian Right's growth suggests some change in contemporary evangelical attitudes, at least among activists. To discover how our respondents see those issues, we asked several questions about the political roles of religion, churches and clergy, and grassroots Christians (Table 3-2). Conservatives remain staunchly individualistic in theory, arguing that the church should inculcate personal morality rather than fight for social justice and should strive to change human hearts rather than social institutions. In this view, social problems such as poverty result from personal inadequacies and will disappear if enough people are converted to true faith. JustLife and BFW members, though still hoping for individual transformation, are more sympathetic to communitarian views and institutional solutions, understandings justified by the historic social theologies of their traditions.

Despite the continuing individualism of evangelical social theology, important changes have occurred in attitudes about politics. Large majorities in all organizations think Christians ought to cooperate in politics, even if they differ in theology. At least some of the distaste that evangelicals historically have felt for other religious traditions (and sometimes for each other) has clearly dissipated. Less surprising is the willingness of "ecumenical" Christians in JustLife and BFW to cooperate. All five groups also have a solid consensus concerning the clergy's involvement in political campaigns and lobbying by churches. Indeed, if national polls are correct, activists approve such activity far more often than do average Americans.[18]

On the linkage between religious beliefs and political choices, however, activists differ. Conservatives now see a strong connection between their faith and political activities, whereas liberals mix religious motivations with other considerations. Conservatives deny that political success inevitably requires compromise of principle, whereas many liberals admit the possibility. In a similar vein, CWA, AFR, and Focus members often see only one "Christian" view on most issues, while JustLife and BFW members sense more religious ambiguity in politics. Finally, many conservatives think the United States needs a Christian party, although some disagreed with the question's premise, arguing that the nation already had one—the GOP! Few JustLife or BFW members want a religious party system.

These last findings suggest that some conservative activists may, in fact, be intolerant of political rivals. Table 3-2 concludes with direct evi-

Table 3-2   Social and Political Theology of Group Activists (in percent)

	CWA	AFR	FOCUS	JL	BFW
Percentage agreeing with assertion					
Role of church					
The church should...					
Focus on individual morality	57	72	63	12	11
Focus on morality and justice	39	25	30	51	45
Focus on social justice	4	3	7	37	44
Change hearts	84	90	86	42	33
Change hearts and institutions	13	5	10	38	39
Change social institutions	3	5	4	20	28
If people were converted, social ills would disappear	71	82	69	32	28
Cause of poverty					
Poverty is due to ...					
Individual inadequacies	36	45	27	3	3
Inadequacies and social factors	41	34	36	21	18
Social factors	23	21	37	76	79
Christians in politics					
Cooperate even if theology differs	91	89	82	94	91
Approve clergy in campaigns	76	75	59	65	68
Churches should be free to lobby	69	59	62	73	73
Religion has "great deal" of influence on my politics	84	73	59	56	43
Religious views of candidates very important to me	77	65	72	25	25
Christians need not compromise	81	84	80	57	59
There is only one correct Christian view	65	69	53	20	10
U.S. needs Christian party	39	53	46	13	12
Position on "political tolerance scale"					
High political tolerance	43	36	41	68	64

Source: 1990 Religious Activist Survey conducted by authors.

dence on this point. Using a technique developed by political scientist John Sullivan and others,[19] we asked respondents to name the "most dangerous group" in America, and then asked if members of that group should be allowed to speak in public, demonstrate, teach in public schools, and run for office. We also asked if the government should outlaw the group or tap their telephones. Combining answers into a single scale produces a strong test of tolerance. As expected, activists usually saw political foes as "most dangerous": conservatives typically named the American Civil Liberties Union, the feminist movement, or prochoice groups, while liberals mentioned neo-Nazis, the Ku Klux Klan, or pro-lifers. And although activists in each group are more tolerant than the mass public, there are significant variations between conservatives and liberals. Half or fewer of the conservative groups' members scored in the top quarter of the tolerance scale, compared with two-thirds of the liberals. These results reflect both the higher education level among liberals—which encourages tolerance—and the impact of fundamentalism among conservatives—which has the opposite effect.[20]

Competing Agendas: Priorities and Issues

Although all five organizations are based in religious communities, their members have different perspectives on social reform and Christian politics. They also have very distinctive ideas about national priorities. We first asked respondents to list "the two or three most important problems confronting the United States" (Table 3-3). Most CWA members, AFR contributors, and Focus members mentioned at least one spiritual or religious problem. The same pattern reappears on "moral" issues, such as abortion, gay rights, and prayer in schools. Not surprisingly, BFW and JustLife members worry more about defense spending, social welfare, and the environment. Mentions of economic issues, public order problems, and the political process are fairly uniform, although Focus members have a special interest in economics and AFR contributors complain more about politics. These responses are validated by activists' reasons for entering politics: conservatives cite anger or concern over a moral issue, whereas liberals often want to alter social welfare or regulatory programs (data not shown).

We also tapped deep-seated views about the public agenda, using a modified version of political scientist Ronald Inglehart's "Postmaterial Values" battery to determine what activists thought were the most important government functions in the 1990s.[21] Table 3-3 is instructive: CWA, AFR, and Focus members all stress "raising moral standards," followed by the related goal of "maintaining public order." Surprisingly, JustLife and BFW members also give morality a fairly high ranking, although their responses to another set of questions (not shown) confirms that by morality they often mean something quite different than preserving traditional sexual and social mores. JustLife and BFW members emphasize "protecting the environment," which conservative activists put close to the bottom of their lists. Finally, conservatives and liberals differ little on "protecting freedom of speech" or "giving people more say in government." Nor does any group put a high priority on "maintaining a high rate of economic growth." Regardless of ideological stripe, religious activists are not motivated primarily by economic issues.

Quite clearly, activists of the Right and Left disagree over what government should do: shape personal and social morality, on the one hand, or address environmental and social justice issues, on the other. This

Table 3-3   Political Agendas of Group Activists (in percent)

	CWA	AFR	FOCUS	JL	BFW
Percentage mentioning each category					
Most important problems					
Religious/spiritual	74	70	62	27	19
Morality problems	58	40	45	43	27
Public order	28	28	30	31	38
Political process	19	25	18	14	14
Defense, military spending	16	15	6	31	30
Economic issues	28	34	44	32	38
Environment	5	6	10	33	42
Social welfare	8	8	19	44	49
Priorities for government					
Raising moral standards	97	94	94	65	54
Maintaining public order	41	45	43	15	18
Maintaining free speech	32	35	28	36	39
Giving people more say	21	20	20	27	21
Promoting economic growth	5	6	9	7	7
Protecting the environment	6	12	15	59	65

Source: 1990 Religious Activist Survey conducted by authors.

helps us understand how evangelicals justify their departure from a traditional individualistic, antipolitical social theology: When government abandons traditional morality or, worse yet, protects "deviant" behavior, political action must be taken.[22] In contrast, Christian liberals see political involvement as intrinsic to the churches' role and have simply incorporated new issues and needs into an established social theology, stressing government action in pursuit of social justice.

Ideology, Issues, and Alliances

The interest group literature predicts that active members of purposive or expressive organizations such as these should share the policy preferences of group leaders.[23] Is this the case here? To locate activists politically, we asked about their attitudes on specific political issues, ideological and partisan self-identifications, and proximity to prominent political organizations and leaders. The findings in Table 3-4 confirm that activists generally agree with the group's founders. CWA, AFR, and Focus members are very conservative on touchstones of the Christian Right agenda: pornography, teaching of evolution in public schools, capital punishment, abortion, gay rights, sex education, and support for traditional morality. On the other hand, JustLife and BFW members favor a modern-day social gospel: the Equal Rights Amendment, national health insurance, racial justice, and environmental protection, as well as tax hikes to

Table 3-4 Political Attitudes and Identifications of Group Activists (in percent)

	CWA	AFR	FOCUS	JL	BFW
"Conservative" agenda issues					
Favor strong pornography laws	98	99	95	78	66
Teach creationism with evolution	97	96	95	41	34
Support capital punishment	93	90	80	27	18
Abortion: only mother's life	91	66	74	51	22
Not allow gay teachers	90	90	78	21	13
No birth control info in school	88	74	68	34	14
Highly traditional moral views	77	63	57	10	4
"Liberal" agenda issues					
Adopt Equal Rights Amendment	5	8	14	51	68
Raise taxes to help needy	12	16	27	84	87
Adopt national health insurance	13	20	31	72	75
Raise taxes for world hunger	14	20	25	83	90
Help minorities more	21	22	28	81	87
Save environment despite costs	27	39	41	89	93
Raise taxes to cut deficit	30	47	35	77	82
Ideological self-identification					
Conservative	97	93	83	18	10
Moderate	3	7	14	23	26
Liberal	0	0	3	59	64
Party identification					
Republican	93	85	78	18	16
Independent	5	11	15	24	20
Democrat	2	4	7	58	65
1988 presidential vote					
Bush	99	99	96	31	22
Dukakis	1	1	4	69	78

Source: 1990 Religious Activist Survey conducted by authors.

address world hunger, aid the needy, and cut the budget deficit. Note, however, that JustLife members are less liberal on moral issues, such as abortion, reflecting Ron Sider's "seamless garment" ideology.

The ideological gaps between groups are also clear from members' political self-identifications and 1988 vote choices. Ideological self-identification encapsulates the activists' policy preferences, with CWA the most conservative group and BFW the most liberal. Partisanship is a little less polarized: CWA members are overwhelmingly Republican; AFR and Focus members slightly less so. JustLife and BFW are dominated by independents and Democrats. The liberals' Democratic propensities are weaker than the corresponding Republican bias among conservatives. Activists' current partisanship has often resulted from personal migrations. Many conservatives were raised as Democrats but have moved toward the

GOP, whereas many JustLife and BFW members have abandoned a Republican family heritage for the Democratic party. Finally, 1988 presidential choices range from a Bush monopoly in CWA, AFR, and Focus to the strong preference of JustLife and BFW members for Dukakis. Observe once again the greater political consensus among the three conservative organizations.

A slightly different picture is provided by activists' reports of how close they feel to interest groups and political leaders. Table 3-5 shows "net proximities" of activists to certain groups, calculated by subtracting the percentage of respondents who felt "far" from the group from the percentage feeling "close." Positive numbers indicate more members of a group feel close to an organization or leader; negative ones indicate the reverse. As expected, conservatives feel very close to the National Right to Life Committee, but less close to the more militant Operation Rescue and the American Family Association, an anti-pornography group. Once again, however, some significant differences exist among the three conservative groups, and JustLife's moderation falls short of BFW's consistent liberalism. Similar patterns appear in ratings of liberal organizations. Conservatives reserve special ire for enemies of traditional values: the American Civil Liberties Union (ACLU), a foe on many church-state issues; People for the American Way (PAW), formed to oppose Christian Right politics; NOW, a venerable feminist and prochoice group; and the gay rights movement. The NAACP does poorly with the conservatives, and although liberal activists feel warmly toward this mainstream civil rights group, they are hardly admirers of the ACLU, PAW, NOW, or the gay rights movement. Thus, conservatives may be a better fit with potential conservative allies than liberals are with some possible coalition partners on the left.

Among recent presidents and presidential candidates, George Bush does well with the conservative groups, splits JustLife, and has negative ratings only from BFW, while disapproval of Ronald Reagan becomes a factor among Focus members and rises to overwhelming proportions among the liberals. Not surprisingly, Pat Robertson gets almost unanimous support from AFR members, warm ratings from CWA, but mixed assessments from Focus, and matches Reagan in unpopularity among the liberals. On the other hand, Jimmy Carter is disliked by CWA and AFR activists, gets better reviews from Focus members, and is warmly regarded by JustLife and BFW members. Jesse Jackson is even more unpopular than Carter with conservatives but has a comfortable positive margin among liberals.

To summarize the dominant ideological tendencies in each organization, we assigned activists to ideological "clusters," based on responses to all our questions on issues, political self-identifications, and proximities, including many not reported here.[24] The most satisfying solution appor-

Table 3-5   Ideology: Proximities and Ideological Clusters of Group Activists (in percent)

	CWA	AFR	FOCUS	JL	BFW
Net proximity to other groups and political leaders					
National Right to Life	+93	+83	+71	+30	(–23)
Operation Rescue	+62	+54	+26	(– 9)	(–36)
American Family Association	+61	+54	+21	(–18)	(–54)
George Bush	+76	+66	+60	+ 1	(–29)
Ronald Reagan	+67	+69	+29	(–73)	(–78)
Pat Robertson	+57	+93	+17	(–70)	(–78)
Jimmy Carter	(–69)	(–50)	(–25)	+74	+75
Jesse Jackson	(–86)	(–90)	(–73)	+15	+21
NAACP	(–71)	(–68)	(–63)	+41	+53
American Civil Liberties Union	(–97)	(–96)	(–86)	(–35)	(– 0)
People for the American Way	(–99)	(–79)	(–81)	(–45)	(–28)
National Organization for Women	(–98)	(–88)	(–84)	(–52)	+ 6
Gay Rights Movement	(–99)	(–99)	(–97)	(–38)	(– 9)
Political cluster					
Christian Right	73	51	39	2	0
Traditional conservatives	25	44	45	9	6
Christian moderates	2	6	15	33	25
Seamless garment liberals	0	0	1	48	34
Christian Left	0	0	1	7	36

Source: 1990 Religious Activist Survey conducted by authors.

Note: Proximities with (+) signs indicate net positive evaluation; those in brackets (–), net negative ones.

tioned activists into five groups, which we labeled "Christian Right," "traditional conservatives," "Christian moderates," "seamless garment liberals," and "Christian Left" (Table 3-5).

Despite many commonalities, each group has its own ideological center of gravity, accurately embodying the political preferences of the organizations' entrepreneurs and other officials.

Political Activity

To this point, we have learned that our activists come from different religious communities, have distinctive orientations on religion's political role, and espouse divergent ideologies. What about their political activity? Do they learn about the political world from different sources? Do they specialize in different kinds of political activity? Are conservatives or liberals more active?

Table 3-6   Sources of Information for Group Activists (in percent)

	CWA	AFR	FOCUS	JL	BFW
Conservative sources					
Religious radio	76	49	67	10	6
Direct mail	62	41	28	24	22
Religious TV	44	73	28	3	3
Liberal sources					
Newspapers	59	57	70	86	89
TV news	50	61	68	66	72
News magazines	37	32	35	61	63
Radio news	35	27	47	50	54
Opinion journals	28	17	15	46	39
Coworkers/colleagues	13	11	16	29	31
Both use equally					
Religious magazines	74	56	55	60	51
Family/friends	39	29	41	39	37
Clergy/church	28	26	35	24	28

Source: 1990 Religious Activist Survey conducted by authors.

Mechanisms of Communication and Mobilization

Activists are mobilized politically by means as varied as the people themselves, but several sources of contact and information are especially relevant to religious activists: churches and clergy, religious publications and media, the intense personal networks common to church loyalists, and direct mail from special purpose groups (Table 3-6).[25] Christian conservatives and Christian liberals nevertheless have distinct patterns of information acquisition. CWA, AFR, and Focus members regard religious TV or radio as their most important sources. Not surprisingly, AFR members, presumably fans of Pat Robertson's "700 Club," see religious television as very important, while Focus members, probably recruited by James Dobson's program, favor religious radio over religious TV. CWA members rely on both. The conservatives use direct mail more often than liberals, perhaps reflecting the American Right's pioneering use of this technique. Both ideological communities read religious magazines—though probably not the same ones.

Whereas conservatives prefer specialized religious sources not familiar to most Americans, liberals absorb the "public" media, using network TV, secular radio news, newspapers, news magazines, and opinion journals. If one sums mentions of these secular sources, the liberal preference for secular news sources is even more noticeable. Thus, we see two disparate communities of political discourse. Conservatives rely on a few sources dominated by a clear ideological message, which surely fosters issue consistency, a certain militancy, and sense of political direction. Religious TV and radio, along with direct mail, mobilize conservatives directly for Christian Right causes and recruit them into specific organizations. Liberals, on the other hand, participate in a wider national community of discourse, encountering (and perhaps assimilating) a range of perspectives, especially liberal ones. These sources may produce more political sophistication and, ultimately, greater effectiveness, but they are not useful for direct mobilization and seldom produce the intense enthusiasm which makes the Christian Right a potent force.

The role of clergy as a source of information and mobilization is not altogether obvious. Local clergy do command substantial personal and institutional resources, but they encounter many constraints.[26] Table 3-6 shows that ministers and priests are not cited as a source of information by a majority in any group. Perhaps clergy abstain from preaching about political issues, or perhaps many activists want clergy to "stay out of politics" and therefore do not seek their views. We asked respondents if they approved of clergy addressing specific political issues, and whether their minister or priest actually did so. The results were straightforward: Religious activists endorse preaching on politics and say that their clergy often does so—but on different issues. Members of BFW and JustLife hear sermons addressing "social justice," but usually not abortion, prayer in schools, and sexual morality, while conservatives report the reverse pattern. Nevertheless, all the activists want more pulpit politics than they get—especially pronouncements on candidates for public office! Of course, their own ministers and less enthusiastic coparishioners might not concur—and survey data suggest they do not.[27] In any event, interest groups provide a political vehicle not matched by local churches, no matter how successfully they fulfill activists' spiritual needs.

Forms of Activism

Finally, we assessed the political activities of interest group members. We gave respondents a checklist for activities undertaken during "the past two years," a period including the 1988 elections. It was hardly a surprise to find them far more active than the average citizen (Table 3-7).[28] Virtually all reported voting in the 1988 presidential primaries and the general election. Most signed petitions and large numbers reported participating in a boycott of a company or product, contacting public officials, making political donations, demonstrating, and writing letters to the editor. CWA and AFR members, however, excelled in electoral politics: attending rallies, campaigning door to door, and running for public or party office. Focus members were the least active, suggesting that many joined for James Dobson's pronouncements on child rearing, not on partisan politics.

Overall, the results are easily summarized. Religious activists invari-

Table 3-7   Political Activities Undertaken by Group Activists
(in percent)

	CWA	AFR	FOCUS	JL	BFW
Voted in 1988 presidential election	98	97	92	86	88
Voted in 1988 presidential primaries	93	94	82	86	88
Signed or circulated petition	93	85	79	87	85
Contacted public official	74	44	37	53	52
Wrote letter to editor	47	23	19	36	29
Boycotted company or product	77	40	45	56	47
Participated in demonstration	53	20	23	38	30
Made financial contribution	59	84	26	49	51
Attended political rally	44	44	14	24	22
Door-to-door campaigning	25	18	7	11	10
Served as party official	12	14	1	3	1
Ran for public office	6	4	1	3	1
Average number of acts of political participation per activist	6.79	5.64	4.16	5.44	5.12

Source: 1990 Religious Activist Survey conducted by authors.

ably vote, engage at unusually high levels in unconventional activities such as boycotting and demonstrating, and frequently communicate with public officials. They are not as involved in other kinds of activity, such as partisan campaigns, but nevertheless represent potent resources for both parties if mobilized. Although our survey showed that CWA and AFR adherents performed the highest average number of acts of political participation, we should not make too much of the difference. The late 1980s were a period in which conservative elites were more effective in mobilization than their liberal counterparts and, in any event, a slightly varied list of activities might well have produced different totals.

Conclusions

Our examination of these five interest groups leads to some broader conclusions about religion's role in American politics. The first is the striking extent to which Christian conservatives and liberals meld into contemporary alignments. Although the former emphasize moral traditionalism and the latter social justice and environmental causes, their positions on most issues correspond to broader ideological and partisan patterns. In other words, these groups and similar ones are expressions of a new "two-party system" in American religion, in which theological conservatives are being absorbed by the political Right and theological liberals by the political Left.[29]

Both conservative and liberal activists represent potential sources of personnel, money, and talent for the Republican and Democratic alliances, but each presents a very different mix of assets and liabilities to its secular allies. The conservatives are far more numerous, have several organizations mobilizing varied religious constituencies, and possess greater enthusiasm for political combat. Some, however, may eventually be tempted back into the political quietism that is consistent with their social theology and typical of theological conservatives since the 1920s—especially if their political crusades are unsuccessful. Their political liabilities include espousal of some unpopular views, a certain political and intellectual rigidity, and the unwillingness of some to compromise—whether with political opponents or potential allies. The frequent tension between the Christian Right and other Republicans testifies to these characteristics.

Ironically, the strengths and weaknesses of Christian liberals are almost mirror images of the Right's. Although considerably less numerous—and drawn from a shrinking religious base—liberal activists share the same community of political discourse as their secular counterparts, appeal to powerful themes in the social theologies of mainline Protestant and Catholic traditions, and draw upon a history of successful activism. To the extent that they use religious language, however, they may find themselves outside the secularist intellectual frames of reference dominant among Democrats and activists in other liberal movements. Indeed, their coolness toward prominent organizations such as the ACLU and NOW reveals the tension that religious liberals feel when dealing with potential allies hostile to religious values.

What of the future? Will religious citizen groups grow in size and importance? In religion, like politics, prediction is hazardous, but the forces stimulating such groups are not likely to disappear and may intensify. The theological and political polarizations within religious traditions, the growing individualism of American religious expression, the declining efficacy of older organizational forms, the expanding social and economic resources of many religious citizens, the availability of organizing techniques and leaders willing to use them—all these combine with the heightened role of government in policies vital to religious people to ensure that this brand of citizen-group politics will have a future.

Notes

1. For essays on religious influence in American political history, see Mark A. Noll, ed., *Religion and American Politics* (Oxford: Oxford University Press, 1990).
2. James L. Guth, "The Politics of the Christian Right," in *Interest Group Politics*, ed. Allan J. Cigler and Burdett A. Loomis (Washington, D.C.: CQ Press, 1983), 60-83; Matthew C. Moen, *The Transformation of the Christian Right* (Tuscaloosa: University of Alabama Press, 1992).
3. Jeffrey Berry, *Lobbying for the People* (Princeton, N.J.: Princeton University Press, 1977); R. Kenneth Godwin, *One Billion Dollars of Influence* (Chatham, N.J.: Chatham House, 1988).

4. Lyman A. Kellstedt and Mark A. Noll, "Religion, Voting for President, and Party Identification," in *Religion and American Politics*, ed. Noll, 355-379.
5. Robert Wuthnow, *The Restructuring of American Religion* (Princeton, N.J.: Princeton University Press, 1988).
6. James F. Findlay, Jr., *Church People in the Struggle* (Oxford: Oxford University Press, 1993); Timothy A. Byrnes, *Catholic Bishops in American Politics* (Princeton, N.J.: Princeton University Press, 1991).
7. Wade Clark Roof and William McKinney, *American Mainline Religion* (New Brunswick, N.J.: Rutgers University Press, 1987); William R. Hutchison, ed., *Between the Times* (Cambridge: Cambridge University Press, 1989).
8. The evangelical community includes a variety of overlapping theological groups, including "fundamentalists," "pentecostals," "charismatics," and "evangelicals." Fundamentalists stress Biblical inerrancy, historic Christian orthodoxy, and separation from "the world." Pentecostals share many doctrinal views with fundamentalists but practice "gifts of the Spirit," such as speaking in tongues and faith healing. "Charismatic" usually refers to mainline Protestants and Catholics who practice such gifts, without joining a pentecostal denomination. "Evangelical" can refer to any of these or, more specifically, to the moderate wing of the fundamentalist movement. The National Association of Evangelicals, founded in 1942, represents many (but by no means all) of these groups. For a good overview of the varied elements of the evangelical community, see Donald W. Dayton and Robert K. Johnson, eds., *The Variety of American Evangelicalism* (Downers Grove, Ill.: Intervarsity Press, 1991).
9. For the ideology of an earlier middle-class citizen group, see Andrew S. McFarland, *Common Cause* (Chatham, N.J.: Chatham House, 1984).
10. Moen, *Transformation of the Christian Right*.
11. For a widely read discussion (and critique) of the hostile reaction to religious group politics, see Stephen L. Carter, *The Culture of Disbelief* (New York: Basic Books, 1993).
12. A representative caution about political activism from a prominent evangelical is Charles Colson, *Kingdoms in Conflict* (New York: William Morrow, 1987).
13. For the political resources provided by church involvement, see Sidney Verba, Kay Lehman Schlozman, Henry Brady, and Norman H. Nie, "Race, Ethnicity and Political Resources: Participation in the United States," *British Journal of Political Science* 23 (October 1993): 453-497.
14. This study is based on a 1990-91 national survey of a stratified random sample of the membership of eight religious interest groups. Six of the organizations cooperated by making membership lists available; a subsample for Concerned Women for America was drawn from CWA's monthly magazine, and for Americans for Robertson, from the public records of the Federal Election Commission in Washington. We sent questionnaires to well over nine thousand group members and, after four mailings, received 5,002 completed forms, a response rate of 56 percent. More details on the study and many of the measures used here can be found in James L. Guth, Corwin E. Smidt, Lyman A. Kellstedt, and John C. Green, "The Sources of Antiabortion Attitudes: The Case of Religious Political Activists," *American Politics Quarterly* 21 (January 1993): 65-80.
15. Steven J. Rosenstone and John Mark Hansen, *Mobilization, Participation, and Democracy in America* (New York: Macmillan, 1993); John C. Green and James L. Guth, "Big Bucks and Petty Cash: Party and Interest Group Activists in American Politics," in *Interest Group Politics*, 2d ed., ed. Allan J. Cigler and Burdett A. Loomis (Washington, D.C.: CQ Press, 1986).
16. For more on individualistic and communitarian perspectives, see David C. Leege and Lyman A. Kellstedt, "Religious Worldviews and Political Philosophies," in *Rediscovering the Religious Factor in American Politics*, ed. David C. Leege and

Lyman A. Kellstedt (Armonk, N.Y.: M.E. Sharpe, 1993).

17. Timothy P. Weber, *Living in the Shadow of the Second Coming* (Chicago, Ill.: University of Chicago Press, 1987).
18. For data on public approval of clergy involvement, see Michael R. Welch, David C. Leege, Kenneth D. Wald, and Lyman A. Kellstedt, "Are the Sheep Hearing the Shepherds?" in *Rediscovering the Religious Factor*, ed. Leege and Kellstedt, 235-254.
19. John L. Sullivan, James Piereson, and George E. Marcus, *Political Tolerance and American Democracy* (Chicago: University of Chicago Press, 1982).
20. For comparisons with the mass public and other political activists, see James L. Guth and John C. Green, "An Ideology of Rights: Support for Civil Liberties Among Political Activists," *Political Behavior* 13 (December 1991): 321-344.
21. Ronald Inglehart, *Culture Shift* (Princeton, N.J.: Princeton University Press, 1990).
22. Clyde Wilcox, *God's Warriors* (Baltimore: Johns Hopkins, 1992); Steve Bruce, *The Rise and Fall of the New Christian Right* (Oxford: Oxford University Press, 1988).
23. Terry M. Moe, *The Organization of Interests* (Chicago: University of Chicago Press, 1980).
24. For a brief description of cluster analysis, see Mark S. Aldenderfer and Roger K. Blashfield, *Cluster Analysis* (Newbury Park, Calif.: Sage, 1984).
25. Leege and Kellstedt, *Rediscovering the Religious Factor*, chaps. 6, 12, and 13.
26. Harold Quinley, *The Prophetic Clergy* (New York: Wiley, 1974); James L. Guth, John C. Green, Corwin E. Smidt, and Margaret M. Poloma, "Pulpits and Politics: Protestant Clergy in the 1988 Presidential Campaign," in *The Bible and the Ballot Box*, ed. James L. Guth and John C. Green (Boulder, Colo.: Westview, 1991).
27. Welch, Leege, Wald, and Kellstedt, "Are the Sheep Hearing the Shepherds?"
28. Rosenstone and Hansen, *Mobilization*, chap. 3.
29. Guth and Green, *The Bible and the Ballot Box*, chap. 12.

4

Public Interest Entrepreneurs and Group Patrons

Allan J. Cigler and Anthony J. Nownes

The growth of public interest representation has been a central feature of the interest group universe over the past quarter of a century. More than 2,500 public interest organizations were in existence by the beginning of the current decade. They represent a spectrum of political perspectives, and each seeks to advance its version of the public interest. Many are large membership organizations with budgets well into the tens of millions of dollars, whereas others have no members at all; some are wholly funded by a single foundation, corporation, or individual.

Competition for funds among public interest groups is fierce. In recent years several groups, eager to expand their resource base, have accepted money from financial patrons whose goals and political objectives have appeared to observers to be in conflict with those of the group. Some believe that the imperative of financial survival faced by public interest groups, coupled with reliance upon institutional sources of revenue, will make it difficult for such groups to continue to challenge establishment interests in the policy arena.

In this chapter Allan Cigler and Anthony Nownes examine the process by which public interest groups raise money from patrons, especially foundations, corporations, the federal government, and wealthy individual donors. Using the results of in-depth interviews from a sample of group fund-raising officers as the basis for their analysis, they find that such officers are extremely conscious of the cost-benefit tradeoffs that typically accompany the solicitation or acceptance of funds from outside sources. Although group officials are strongly motivated to obtain the resources necessary for group survival and are attracted to patrons' money, "those impulses are tempered by desires to retain decision-making autonomy and to influence public policy in particular directions." The authors found little evidence that raising funds from patrons compromises the mission and political goals of the groups they examined.

This research project was partially funded by a grant from the General Research Fund of the University of Kansas.

T he expansion of the public interest sector of the interest group universe in the late 1960s and 1970s was greeted by many political scientists with genuine surprise and enthusiastic support. The tremendous growth in the number of such groups appeared to challenge much of the conventional wisdom on group formation and survival. Many scholars had feared that social and political interests representing broad constituencies would have great difficulty organizing and surviving as permanent actors in the political process.[1] The surprising expansion of the public interest sector was applauded by many with a pluralist perspective, who believed that public interest groups could act as healthy "countervailing forces" in American politics, protecting citizens-at-large from the excesses of dominant economic interests.[2]

The reasons for the proliferation of public interest groups are now no longer a mystery, but the impact of such groups as countervailing forces is less clear. Interest group theorists initially deemed it unlikely that groups seeking collective benefits would develop. Such groups would have to face the formidable obstacle of the "free-rider problem": the tendency of "rational" individuals to choose not to bear the costs of group involvement (time, dues) because they could enjoy the fruits of the group's efforts even if they were not members. Why, for example, would a consumer join a consumer protection group when he or she would benefit from group successes without participating in or helping to fund the organization as a member?

Subsequent research has found, however, that the free-rider problem can be overcome in various circumstances.[3] Skillful group leaders or entrepreneurs can often attract members by providing "selective" benefits such as informative publications, travel discounts, and inexpensive insurance that nonmembers cannot receive. Moreover, some individuals will join organizations even though it is "nonrational" in an economic sense: intangible factors such as notions of fairness, rightness, duty, and moral obligation override rational economic calculations in some individuals and cause them not to "free ride."[4] One can point to a number of public interest groups (Greenpeace comes to mind) composed of members motivated by collective concerns who provide virtually all of the group's funding yet receive few tangible benefits in return.

Such groups are more the exception than the rule. The proliferation of public interest groups may well be due less to the ability of group entrepreneurs to attract members than to their abilities to bypass or substantially reduce the free-rider problem by locating a patron to sponsor the organization, thus reducing its reliance on membership dues. The patron—be it an individual, a corporation, the government, another interest group, or a private foundation—may even be the initiator of group development, not merely by contributing funds but by seeking out group entrepreneurs and perhaps creating groups for the patron's own purposes. Political scientist Jeffrey Berry found that at least one-third of public interest groups received more than half of their funds from private foundations, while one in ten received more than 90 percent of its operating expenses from such sources.[5] More generally, Jack Walker's study in the early 1980s revealed that foundation support and large individual grants provided 30 percent of all citizens' group funding.[6]

One thing is clear. Members are only one source of the resources that are crucial to the survival of virtually all public interest groups.

Such reliance raises a number of questions about the nature of public interest representation. In particular, can public interest groups be effective countervailing forces in the policy process? Outside patronage can be intrusive and distort public interest representation. There is some evidence, for example, that patronage has affected the composition of the public interest sector by channeling funds to "professional" rather than "activist" organizations.[7] Individual group strategies and choices of what types of influence techniques to utilize may be conditioned by patrons' money.[8] In some cases funding by patrons has apparently been designed primarily to control the turbulence of system-challenging groups, such as organizations concerned with expanding civil rights for minorities.[9] Moreover, the withdrawal of patronage may not only lead to the demise of groups; it may substantially alter the mission and focus of those groups that survive.[10]

If we accept the assumptions that money leads to influence and that patrons are not neutral actors, then the potential for patrons to affect group agendas, priorities, and activities is real indeed. Patrons have reasons for giving money, presumably "because they [the group] are effective advocates for a cause or because they do a good job of representing the interests of the constituency that the patron wishes to see protected or promoted."[11] Patron money can be used as an incentive not only to encourage a group to act on the patron's behalf, but as an incentive to demobilize opposition. Attempts by oil companies in recent years to offer support to various environmental groups, or efforts by companies like Philip Morris to contribute to civil rights and women's rights organizations, may reflect attempts to preempt opposition.

Although patronage offers obvious benefits for public interest groups needing funds, it presents potential costs as well. Groups that take money from outside sources may be regarded by important political actors as agents of the patron rather than as representatives of broader interests. Group members may find themselves at odds with their leaders' decisions. A good example is the recent experience of the American Civil Liberties Union (ACLU), an organization with a long tradition of protecting citizens from government encroachment upon First Amendment freedoms. In the late 1980s the ACLU's executive director approached tobacco giant Philip Morris about possible funding for the American Civil Liberties Union Foundation, the tax-exempt wing of the ACLU. (Though legally separate, both organizations have the same officers and board of directors.) The ACLU Foundation received a half-million dollars in annual grants from Philip Morris between 1987 and 1992, and during that period its parent organization allied itself with the tobacco industry to fight congressional legislation aimed at banning or restricting tobacco advertising and promotion.[12] When the Philip Morris connection became public in 1993, many of ACLU's three hundred thousand members expressed outrage that the leadership had not informed them about the tobacco money. The seeming inconsistency between the leadership's stance that the First Amendment protected the "commercial free speech" of the tobacco industry and the ACLU's explicit "approval of consumer-protection laws empowering the government to control the content of ads for lawful products, including prescription drugs and securities," did not go unnoticed by the press, by politicians, or by the dues-paying members of the organization.[13]

In this chapter, we explore the impact of patronage on public interest representation from the perspective of those who seek resources for groups. In particular, we focus on the process of acquiring patronage and whether acceptance of patronage compromises the ability of public interest groups to advance the priorities of the interests they claim to represent. What we find, generally speaking, is that group entrepreneurs are keenly aware of both the costs and benefits of taking money from outside sources. Seeking and accepting outside money can have the effect of modifying public interest group agendas, but even resource-strained groups do not typically seek or accept funds that would cause them to engage in activities beyond their mission or in conflict with their stated political goals.

Theoretical Considerations: Group Entrepreneurs as Public Interest Group "Guardians"

One useful way to conceptualize the impact of patronage upon public interest groups is through the analytical framework that has come to been known as "exchange theory."[14] From this perspective, groups do not form spontaneously even if a need for collective action exists. Certain individuals or "entrepreneurs" must come forward to secure the resources necessary for collective action, prospect for potential members and other sources of support, and design an organization to provide benefits to members, as well as to manage the affairs of the group. In essence, group creation and development can be viewed as an "exchange" process in which group entrepreneurs offer a package of incentives to potential members in return for their support. Group entrepreneurs and members alike must obtain a net benefit from the exchange if the group is to succeed.

As noted earlier, public interest groups face particularly difficult problems in attracting and retaining members, because many of the incentives they offer are collective in nature and cannot be excluded from nonmembers. One consequence is that many have had to turn to alternative means to acquire the resources necessary to organize and maintain themselves. As a result, group entrepreneurs often find themselves in another type of exchange relationship, this time with potential patrons, who also have certain wants and needs.

From the perspective of the group entrepreneur, survival of the group is the primary goal, in the same sense that reelection must be the primary goal of members of Congress.[15] A group entrepreneur must ensure group survival to achieve his or her other goals. A patron's money may have the advantage of providing a group with more reliable and stable funding than membership dues can provide. After all, people may assess the costs and benefits of group membership differently under different circumstances.[16] People can bear certain costs, such as dues, better in some economic contexts than in others (membership in public interest groups appears to suffer particularly in recessions), and they are more willing to take risks under certain circumstances than in others, especially when threatened. (There is nothing like an oil spill or an ecological disaster to spark interest in an environmental group.) Soliciting money from patrons may actually be more cost-efficient than fund raising from members. Raising money from a few large donors may be far less time-consuming and require far fewer resources than an expensive direct mail campaign. Furthermore, entrepreneurs and their staffs may find that patrons may even give them opportunities to focus upon their own pet projects, using discretionary money that does not have to be defended to the membership.

Pure economic survival, however, should not be viewed as the singular aim of group entrepreneurs. The very notion of entrepreneurship implies a desire to exercise personal control over an organization and to retain as much authority as possible over internal decision making. Often the group entrepreneur has made a considerable investment (in capital or time) in the group. We can assume, with the exchange theorists, that the entrepreneur has certain ideas about how the organization should be run. Many probably take pride in what they are doing and value highly the organization's credibility and regard in the political arena and among the membership. Group entrepreneurs probably wish to avoid delegating much authority to people outside the organization. They seek instead to retain decision-making power and, as a consequence, are particularly sensitive to accepting resources with "strings attached."

The group entrepreneur typically is at least partially motivated by a desire to influence public policy. In some public interest groups—although this is less common today than previously—the group entrepreneur is "a person willing to forgo monetary gratification entirely or defer it indefinitely."[17] The spirit of voluntarism is expressed in compensation patterns. Among groups that pay their employees, salaries usually are not

Table 4-1   Average Percentage of Revenue Obtained by Groups
from Various Sources in Budget Year 1990

Contribution source	Percentage
Contributions from members/associates	
Dues	36.0
Publications	6.0
Conferences	2.5
Subtotal	44.5
Nonrecurring contributions from patrons	
Individual gifts	13.0
Foundations	26.0
Government	1.7
Corporations	4.0
Other associations or groups	<1.0
Subtotal	44.7
Miscellaneous	
Investment, endowment, sales, fees	8.3
Loans	2.0
Other	0.5
Subtotal	10.8
Total	100.0

Note: N=53. Some data needed to construct this table were missing from nine of the sample groups.

comparable to those paid in private-sector groups. Thus it seems reasonable to assume that public interest group entrepreneurs have some desire to influence public policy in directions compatible with their values.

Our guiding hypothesis is that although public interest entrepreneurs are motivated to obtain the resources necessary for group survival and are attracted to patronage money, those impulses are tempered by desires to retain decision-making autonomy and to influence public policy in particular directions. Group entrepreneurs can be seen as rational actors who calculate the costs and benefits of each "exchange" with group patrons, who themselves may represent a complex set of motives, ranging from an altruistic desire to contribute to a good cause to controlling or manipulating the group for their own purposes. Unless the benefits for group entrepreneurs outweigh the costs, we would hypothesize that patrons' money will not be sought or taken.

The Study

To examine this general proposition, we conducted a series of phone interviews with sixty-two randomly chosen public interest group offi-

Table 4-2   Budgetary Dependence on Patrons, 1990

Percentage of group budget obtained from patrons	Number of groups	Percentage of groups
Less than 1%	3	6
1-9	3	6
10-19	4	8
20-29	8	15
30-39	4	7
40-49	8	15
50-59	5	9
60-69	6	11
70-79	4	8
80-89	4	8
90-99	4	8
100	0	0
Total	55	101[a]

Note: Complete data needed to construct this table were missing from seven sample groups.

[a] Percentages in the table were rounded to the nearest whole number.

cials.[18] Typically we talked to the person responsible for making final decisions about how to attract funding. That individual was either the development director or, on occasion, the executive director.

The interviews were intensive and varied in length from twenty minutes to over two hours. Most responses came from a set of structured but open-ended questions. Typically we asked respondents to respond generally to questions and then to give us examples from their own experience. We believed (and this belief was confirmed by our interviewees) that only by promising anonymity could we get the kind of candid information we were seeking on sensitive financial matters. As a result, none of the comments quoted below were made for attribution.

The Findings

Using data from our interviews, as well as written material such as annual reports sent to us by respondents, it was possible to compile information about the revenue sources of most groups in our sample. A summary of this information is presented in Table 4-1. The average group in our sample received roughly equal proportions of its income from members and patrons, about 45 percent each. But averages can distort variation and a much clearer picture of the impact of patrons on group revenues is presented in Table 4-2.

The data in Table 4-2 suggest that although almost all groups for which we have information received some patronage, that patronage was for some no doubt critical. Four of the groups for which we had complete information received more than 90 percent of their 1990 revenue from patrons, while another four received more than 80 percent from such sources. Groups highly reliant upon patronage tended to be groups such as public interest legal organizations that made no attempt to develop a membership base (for example, the Women's Legal Defense Fund). On the other hand, six groups reported receiving less than 10 percent of their income from patrons; typically such groups were well-known, mass-membership organizations such as the National Wildlife Federation. Overall, patronage was an important source of income for many groups: thirty-five of the fifty-five groups for which we obtained information received between one-fifth and four-fifths of their revenues from patrons. Twenty-three groups in our sample received at least half of their income from such sources. Clearly, many groups would be out of business or would have diminished programs without the aid of patrons.

The importance of patrons' money has led over the past quarter-century to the development of an extensive "infrastructure" which has made it easier for groups to locate, solicit, apply for, and obtain money of all kinds. The solicitation process has been routinized. Virtually all of the studied groups that receive outside support referred to the large variety of publications and services that now exist to aid grant-seeking organizations. The cornerstones of this infrastructure are regular publications such as the *Foundation Giving Watch* and *Corporate Giving Watch*, monthly publications that report on donation trends, provide helpful hints on grant seeking, and list available grants. The *Taft Corporate Giving Directory*, which includes detailed information on more than five hundred of the largest corporate giving programs, is a particularly important source for group revenue-seekers according to our respondents.

Perhaps the single most useful resource available to grant-seeking organizations is the Foundation Center, a nonprofit educational institution founded in 1956 to act as a clearinghouse on grant-seeking information. The Foundation Center publishes a variety of indices, directories, and guidebooks, and its Washington office and library, according to a number of our respondents, are the first stop for groups seeking money from patrons. *The Foundation Directory*, an annual source of information about more than seven thousand private, community, and corporate foundations and their funding priorities, is the organization's most widely known publication.

For government grants and contracts, there are government publications such as the annual *Catalog of Federal Domestic Assistance*, *Federal Grants and Contracts Weekly*, and the *Federal Register*. Specialized areas have evolved their own sources dealing with grant availability. For example, the American Youth Work Center makes grant information available to groups concerned with children. An organization called The Environmental Grantseekers informs the environmental community of trends in environmental giving. There is even a formal organization to help public interest organizations learn how to raise money from outside sources. The Advocacy Institute, funded primary by many of the public interest groups themselves, exists to train group activists, including fund raisers. Advocacy Institute staff also advise and counsel public interest groups on the potential costs of patronage, the focus of our study. The many resource groups and their publications and networks mean that the information costs of nonmembership fund raising are lower than at any time in recent history. Even small groups can afford to identify donors and apply for grants.

The Group Entrepreneur/Foundation Patron Exchange: The Potential of High Rewards at Little Cost

Foundations are motivated primarily by a desire to help like-minded political advocates. They exist to give away money and have well-articulated funding priorities. In most cases, foundations have broad ideological outlooks, within which they adumbrate specific programs they would like to fund. Typically they decide which projects they would like to fund, solicit proposals, and select the applicant they think will do the best job. Foundations decide on program priorities independent of interest groups and almost always make restricted grants. Formally, foundations make their funding priorities known via the infrastructure described earlier. But there is much more to the grant process. As one group leader put it:

> We do research at the Foundation Center and, of course, we rely heavily upon their publications. But I guess I've been at this long enough to know that what's in the book is very much skeletal and often misleading ... nothing more than bread crumbs on the trail. I have a lengthy relationship with a lot of foundation people because of some of the work I have done in the past. So a lot of it is through personal contact, either through me, or board members.

The main "grantsman" at a mid-sized environmental group put it even more explicitly:

> There's a network. You know, we're sitting around with the Board of Directors and the chairman of the board says, you ought to talk to so and so at the Packard Foundation, or the Rockefellers are doing this ... I mean, these people have been at this [working for the group] for years. We have a president, and he has a past ... and he knows all these foundation people. So he calls somebody up and says, "Hey, I'm going to be in the area, can I stop by and talk to you about your plans for giving in the next five years?" There is a core group of foundations which gives in our issue area. And there's no secret about it ... they're all right there.

Allusions to a funding network in the foundation world were numerous. Two points were emphasized by interviewees. First, the number of foundations that give within the scope of any group is limited. Most foundations have narrowly defined missions and are regional in nature. Groups know this and approach the foundations most likely to fund them. Second, many interviewees noted that their personal relationships with people in the foundation world were determining. As one interviewee put it:

> It's almost strictly informal, I would say. For one thing ... out of approximately 55,000 foundations in the United States, there are only about fifty that give in this field. So you're talking about one tenth of one percent, and they've pretty much remained constant since 1980. So you're dealing with the same group of people and it's not expanding. I know all of these people, and for four years I was the executive director of one of the foundations, so I have a collegial relationship with most of those folks.

Most established groups rely heavily on an informal network of contacts in the foundation world, cultivated over years of social and business interaction. The development director of a large membership group pointed out the bottom line for groups seeking grants:

> When I first started to do this many years ago, the man I was working for, who is a brilliant grantsman, said, "Foundations don't fund projects, they fund people." And that has been my experience. Building ... confidence in your work, that's most important.

Groups that lack the relationships with funders necessary to give them an edge are clearly disadvantaged. They must rely on the formal grant process, which is costly in terms of time, money, and labor. Building relationships with funders allows groups to save resources, because they can apply only for those grants they are likely to get. Moreover, groups with personal contacts in the foundation world undoubtedly have an advantage when funding decisions are made. Foundations are likely to have many applicants for the funds earmarked for a given project and they are likely to fund people they know and trust.

We can think of the foundation-interest group network as the occasional intersection of two communities that are vastly different, yet interdependent. As the assistant director of a group that monitors government behavior told us:

> I don't look upon them [foundation people] as part of my community.... They're funders, they're part of the philanthropic community.... They really don't know that much about the work I do and they shouldn't, their job is to give away money.... It isn't to know what I'm doing. They look at the quality of work I've done, [and] they trust that.

Personal relationships with others within the public interest group sector are enormously helpful as well. As one group leader put it:

> We [also] learn about grants through a network of public interest fund

raisers. You talk to staff people from other organizations. I am thinking about one foundation in particular that we never would have approached ... but the man whose money it was had a very personal interest in [our issue]. We found out about it through a group that he's affiliated with.

Foundations set broad priorities, and then watch the proposals come in. Decisions, according to development staff, hinge on personal relations and whether foundations believe recipient groups will use the foundation's money responsibly for the intended purposes.

Foundation oversight is potentially a major cost for group entrepreneurs, to the extent that it could decrease their autonomy and flexibility. According to a number of our respondents, however, formal foundation oversight generally is very loose; often the only requirements are periodic updates and a final research report (in the case of a restricted grant) or simply keeping the foundation updated on group activity through the annual report (in the case of unrestricted grants). Foundations stay out of groups' business, and the autonomy of group entrepreneurs is not threatened.

A bigger potential cost to group entrepreneurs can be the risk of relying on foundation funds as a stable source of group revenue. Patrons can be fickle and "trendy ... they change their priorities all the time." Foundations are highly responsive to political stimuli, in particular. The development director of a peace group notes:

> In 1980 our issue [nuclear disarmament] was the number one issue on the public agenda.... In 1980, if you came up with a good idea, it might be two weeks until you had the money to do it. Now, it can be like two years.

The most obvious disadvantage of foundation money is that it is almost always given for specific projects and purposes: groups that would like to build their general support cannot rely on foundations. Does this compromise group goals? Probably not, although it may influence the contents of a group's agenda. We found not one case of a group accepting foundation money to do something that radically departed from its mission. However, foundation support may subtly channel group activity in certain directions. Typically groups have large lists of programs and projects they would like to see funded; foundations choose programs from this list. A development director for a large liberal group told us:

> This is a big enough organization, that operates in enough different areas, that ... I wouldn't say our program is distorted. But it does mean that there are probably some areas where we probably have a higher level of activity than we otherwise might have. For example, we have one foundation that provides a very large grant every year for [a specific project]. I think we have eight lawyers working on it. If we didn't have that grant, we might have a lawyer or two working [on that] issue ... If

anything ever happened to that grant, we'd probably have to cut [the program] back.... Foundation priorities ... enable us to do more than we might otherwise do in some areas.

Foundation money is not cost free, but group entrepreneurs apparently see few threats to their autonomy or to the group's mission. Most eagerly seek and accept foundation money.

The Group Patron/Corporate Patron Exchange: Danger Lurking

Corporations are in business to make money. Nonetheless, corporate philanthropy in America is quite extensive. Nearly half (twenty-seven out of fifty-five) of the groups for which we had financial data reported receiving at least some corporate funds. As Table 4-1 indicates, however, the average percentage of budgetary revenues received from corporate patrons was just four percent. As a source of public interest group income, corporate contributions are dwarfed by membership contributions and foundation grants. Still, corporate funds are eagerly sought by many public interest groups.

One reason, according to a number of our interviewees, is that corporate donors often allow more flexibility in the use of funds than do members or foundations.

Most corporate money is unrestricted, and, because amounts are usually not crucial to group survival, entrepreneurs can be discriminating about the corporations from which they will accept grants. For this reason, much corporate giving poses no real dilemmas for group fund raisers. Corporations often fund groups closely related to their business specialties. For example, environmental, hunting, fishing, and gun groups have a natural corporate constituency. Group leaders often try to exploit these constituencies. As the development director of a mid-size environmental group that often works on water issues related to us:

These are people [corporate sponsors] who are tied into the recreational business so they have a vested interest in keeping the rivers open.... It's a symbiotic relationship.

Some groups find that they may even develop corporate constituencies through their advocacy work, even if they are not always able to take advantage of the relationship. The leader of an environmental group observes:

There are basically two different pesticides that are being marketed for killing gypsy moths. And essentially, one is significantly more toxic than the other ... so we promote one of the pesticides over the other. And of course, there's a company out there that produces the one that we're basically "lobbying for"—and they have in the past said ... "Here's a check." Support like that, it's hard to come by ... but we have for the past several years sent those checks back.

Some groups are so controversial that it is difficult to imagine any corporations supporting them. The most obvious examples are pro- and antiabortion groups. Groups on the far right and far left are also pariahs to the corporate world. But even many of these succeed in finding some corporate funding.

The most "fundable" groups—apart from those with built-in corporate constituencies—are those easily identified with a cause that everyone, at least in the abstract, supports. Examples of such causes include children's rights, the homeless, humane treatment of animals, civil rights, and "good government." The leader of a small group working on behalf of the homeless told us:

> We get a lot of calls. Tons and tons of calls. Not only from companies wanting to promote their products, but also D grade celebrities and sometimes O.K. ones too ... people wanting to write songs for us, put out an album for the homeless, and give us some money.

In short, the nature of a group's issue tends to affect its potential for receiving corporate money. This is not to say that groups focusing on noncontroversial issues eagerly seek or even accept corporate money. Our interviews reveal that public interest entrepreneurs are careful to assess the costs and benefits of taking corporate money—especially money from certain corporations or corporate sectors.

Some groups staunchly refuse to solicit or take corporate money of any kind. Few corporations meet their ideological litmus tests. One environmental group leader told us:

> I'd be surprised if any *really* progressive environmental group got *any* corporate money. Well, I guess there are some [corporations] we would consider.... Patagonia has a corporate giving program, and Ben and Jerry's Ice Cream. But we're very cautious about who we take money from.... Very few corporations have [our] stamp of approval.

The development director of a medium-sized group, which often deals with issues of interest to the gay and lesbian communities, commented that:

> We're talking about Philip Morris trying to buy off the gay community ... and making all this money available to people doing AIDS service work. They're doing it for PR, the gay market is a huge market for them, and they want to make nice with the community so people will keep buying their shit.... We're having a hard year just like everybody else ... but, you know, they dangled some serious money ... and we had to develop a policy about ... such offers. But here they are, Philip Morris ... and they've helped keep the scourge of the HIV epidemic [Jesse Helms] in Congress.... There's just no way we can justify that.

The biggest fear of fund raisers is that taking money from a certain company or corporate sector will alienate group members and other supporters. Development personnel told us repeatedly that taking corporate money could backfire and become a losing proposition. True believers may become cynical, bad publicity may scare away potential members and supporters, and the group's reputation for integrity may suffer. One group leader repeated an oft-cited example of the disadvantages of taking money from "unnatural allies":

> What you hear over and over again from people who have been around for a long time is that in the long run, taking the money ... is going to hurt you. The National Coalition Against Domestic Violence took Johnson & Johnson money, and did their shelter aid campaign, when [Johnson & Johnson] weren't even doing the Sullivan principles in South Africa, and it caused a huge problem. They have not recovered from that, and that was five years ago.... The ... damage you are going to sustain by taking money that runs counter to your group ... you're going to pay heavy.

Virtually all of the group officials we talked to recognized that corporate philanthropy is "bottom line" oriented. As the exchange theory perspective suggests, there is often an explicit quid pro quo with corporate relationships. For example, a development director told us, "A car company came to us a couple of years ago about giving us X dollars for every model they sold." In exchange for the contribution, the company requested permission to mention that a portion of company profits went to support the group in question. This type of "cause-related marketing" is not at all uncommon. Most of the groups we talked to that received corporate money had been approached, at one point or another, by a corporation that wished to engage in this sort of exchange. Groups often do agree to take part in cause-related marketing. The development director of a mid-sized environmental group commented:

> One of the corporate sponsors of [another environmental group] realized that they were not doing much in [our issue area] ... so they contacted us. They were interested in putting some money into protecting some rivers.... So we have just started discussions on how they can do that. What's in it for us; what's in it for them? They haven't really ever said, "We want this." But we know what they would like; you know, when we have a stream project, they want to erect a sign that says, "This is a cooperative effort ... [between the group and the corporation]." They like that, because as fishermen go by and see these signs, they know the company is doing something for the resource.

There are a wide variety of benefits groups can provide corporate sponsors. Corporations may simply wish to be identified with a certain cause that they perceive as "good for business." They often ask permission to use their group beneficiaries' names in advertisements.

Economic advantage is not the only motivation for corporate support. For example, many corporate donors, like interest groups that contribute money to legislators, do so for the access it may give them to adversaries. The development director of a large environmental group gave us a good example.

> They are definitely looking for public relations when they make a straight gift. But often ... they are, in effect, paying for access; a sort of forum to be talking in a nonconfrontational way ... with some environmental folks. It's not so much a question of once a dispute has really arisen, it's more a question of knowing them before it gets to the point of where we're throwing bombs at each other on the six o'clock news. When the *Exxon Valdez* hits, there ain't nothing that's going to help our relationship with Exxon. On the other hand, if you're talking with Exxon about ways to come up with a reformulated gasoline that would not screw up the air so much ... or different alternatives to fuel-efficiency standards ... You know, in that kind of situation, it's very valuable to have an idea of who you're talking to and to have some relationship ... some level of trust.

Corporate altruism is often hard to separate from corporate self-interest. The motivation of those in the recreation industry who contribute to environmental groups provides a good example. As the executive director of a small environmental group told us:

> I am convinced that there is a strong level of altruism in these people. That's one reason they got into the recreation business in the first place ... they have fun, they enjoy the outdoors, they have a desire for beauty and challenge. And as I have talked to these people ... I get the real strong sense that they care very deeply that [we] succeed. They think it's important. And they have less of a tendency to be cold dollars and cents about it. They're willing to fund something because they think it's right, and they may or may not get something direct out of it.

In the real world, the motives of corporate donors are virtually impossible to identify specifically. The point to be made is that with every donation an exchange takes place, and that exchange usually is explicit. Corporations that give to advocacy groups usually make it clear to their beneficiaries why they are giving and what they expect in return.

Corporate money presents interest groups with their most difficult dilemma. Unlike those of foundations, members, the government, and large individual donors, the motivations of corporations are almost always called into question by public interest groups. Most development personnel are predisposed to be somewhat suspicious of offers of corporate support—taking corporate money, while working to convince others that you represent a nonprofit group that is working for the "public interest," *is* problematic. Because groups engage in so many types of activities, they may debate the option of taking corporate money for certain purposes but not others. For example, some groups that otherwise eschew corporate money, actively solicit or accept corporate support for "special" events. The leader of a small women's group told us:

> Our grant activity is very low ... but recently, one of the beer companies sponsored one of our receptions. They covered the expenses, and the only strings attached were that we serve their brand of beer. We didn't really debate it, because we had intended to have beer available anyhow, and we figured, well, it's a very well known brand of beer, so ... why not?

The group entrepreneur/corporate patron exchange is initiated in several different ways. Corporations initiate contact with groups they think can help them in some way. For special events, however, groups tend to contact corporations. As in the case of procuring foundation funds, a network based on personal relations is often crucial. The executive director of a group that works extensively on women's issues related to us:

> You have to know somebody really, to get decent money. You might get $5,000 here or there if you have a lot of good projects. But to get any decent money you have to know someone and it's either an old boy network or an old girl network. I know there's one in Washington; there's a national one too.... If you were having, for example, a very important strategy meeting, or a very important social function, you certainly would invite the ... old girl network. There's a lot of intermingling on boards, too.

With respect to their impact on group autonomy, corporations seem to be even less demanding than foundations in monitoring how their funds are spent once they are given, and our interviewees gave us no examples of groups that had lost control of their agenda to outside interests. But a number pointed to "illusions of impropriety" created when groups accepted money from corporations and then appeared to involve corporate officials in group activities. The most frequently cited examples were those of the National Audubon Society and the National Wildlife Federation, which received funds from, and then welcomed to their governing boards, officials from Waste Management, Inc., a firm that had been fined numerous times for violating environmental laws at its incinerator sites. Public interest organizations that take large sums of money, even unrestricted money, from "bad" corporations potentially alienate themselves from the rest of the public interest community. One example given several times by our interviewees was that of the Food Research and Action Center (FRAC), an organization concerned with the Federal Food Stamp Program, which accepted a $1 million unrestricted grant from Kraft Foods, a division of Philip Morris. The reputational costs of taking corporate patronage in this case were high indeed among FRAC's public interest peers.

The Group Entrepreneur/Government Patron Exchange: Minimal Funding, Too Much Hassle

Overall, the public interest groups in our sample did not rely heavily on government funding. On average, according to Table 4-1, sample groups relied on the government for only 1.7 percent of their revenues. Only eleven groups received any money at all from this source. Properly speaking, the government does not give to public interest groups the way other patrons do. The federal government awards grants and contracts for a variety of programs and purposes. In our sample, six of the eleven groups that received government grants were environmental groups. The government often pays environmental and other groups to take part in regulatory proceedings. In addition, environmental groups are often called upon to provide technical assistance to government regulators (in the EPA for instance), perform research on policy proposals, and conduct training and demonstration projects.

The other five groups in our sample that received government money utilized it for a wide variety of purposes, ranging from providing legal help to the elderly to helping low-income families become eligible for federal food assistance programs.

Two major factors apparently determine whether a group seeks or receives government funding. The first is group ideology. There are many groups for which taking government money is simply not an option. For example, numerous political reform, taxpayers', and civil liberties groups have a strict prohibition against accepting government grants or contracts. The development director of a large broad-based liberal group emphatically told us: "We watch government ... it's generally not a good idea to take their money." The perception among many group leaders is that taking government money would seriously compromise the group's mission and perhaps alienate members and other supporters. Again, an explicit cost-benefit calculus is applied.

The second factor is the group's mission. Environmental groups, for example, are perfectly suited for government funding. Environmental laws are complex, and regulatory proceedings are common. Moreover, most large environmental groups employ scientists and other experts in environmental matters. Thus, government is very likely to call upon them to participate in regulatory activities. On the other hand, the interests of some groups do not overlap with those of government; such groups are therefore very unlikely to apply for or receive government funding. Gun control or animal rights groups, for example, are unlikely to perform any services the government would be interested in funding.

Without question, the federal government is the most demanding of all patrons, and a number of the group entrepreneurs we talked to would not seek government funds even though they would probably be successful. Our respondents were virtually unanimous in the opinion that the government requires the most in terms of formal accountability, and often attaches onerous strings to grants. The development director of a civil liberties group gave us a vivid example:

> We don't accept government grants.... Government grants come with very onerous reporting requirements which we feel violate privacy rights. One thing that's a problem right now is that some government grants are conditioned upon the grantee certifying that they conduct urine testing.

Some groups refuse to solicit government money simply because doing so requires a tremendous amount of effort that many groups believe could be put to better use elsewhere. Most government grants are secured through a very formal and lengthy process by which groups apply for grants made public through various government publications.

Even when it comes to government grants, however, an informal network helps grantseekers. As is so often the case, "knowing someone" can significantly increase a group's probability of securing government funding. The development director of a medium-sized environmental group that often works on water issues told us:

> We often help with state assessments. They will say, "Here's the state assessment stuff, now go help organize it." It really helps that the former executive director here now runs the department in the Park Service [from which the group often gets money].... Everybody knows everybody.... But we're pretty limited in who we can approach because of what we do, so we're not real active. But we do have people we go to on a regular basis.

Overall, government patronage was not a high priority for the group development officers we interviewed. Almost by definition most public interest groups, on both ends of the political spectrum, view government as inadequate or flawed in some way. The credibility costs of taking funds from such a source far outweigh the benefits.

The Group Entrepreneur/Individual Benefactor Exchange: Money from a Friend

On average, 13 percent of the 1990 budgetary revenues of the groups in our sample came from individual donors, and every group reported receiving at least some money from such sources. Generally speaking, most groups consider individuals who give $100 a year or more to be large donors. Membership and nonmembership groups alike reported to us that a small number of individuals met this criterion, but some reported very large contributions by a select group of individuals. As the executive director of a large conservative group explained:

We do have some individuals who are big hitters for us, who may give $25,000 in one year. They're in our membership, but what basically happens is that they ... see through the press or through our newsletter or by talking to us that we're involved and that we're doing a good job in certain areas that are near and dear to their hearts. So they express an interest, and we will write them a letter and tell them what we're doing and how we're doing it and so on ... and we'll ask them to give us a little extra.

Virtually all of the membership groups in our sample have some kind of large donor program. The cornerstone of such a program is usually an active research regimen that seeks to identify those within the membership who are capable of giving large sums of money by concentrating on their giving histories. Networking is also a popular strategy. As the development director of a large conservative group related to us:

If we have reason to believe that a certain guy has a lot of money and has given to other groups and seems to like what we're doing, we'll write and tell him about us. We find out [about large donors] by word of mouth usually. We network with other conservative groups.

Networking is a popular strategy among groups of all political stripes. Contributions of more than $1,000 typically are generated by asking wealthy, long-time members to contribute to special projects. Groups cultivate smaller donations through direct-mail "upgrades" of members. This strategy—which entails asking long-time members for more and more money—appears to be quite successful for many groups. As the development director of a mid-size good government group told us:

We solicit these people pretty much the same way we do other members; through direct mail. (M)any of them worked their way up through direct mail ... eventually giving more and more and more. We'd send out letters asking for $25, and receive letters giving $5,000.

Most of the groups that receive large donations from individuals have a variety of inducements and perquisites for large donors. Such "perks" include more personal attention, greater access to group personnel (often including the executive director), and recognition in group publications and events. A smaller number of groups go further by placing large donors on their board of directors. Although large donors are seldom motivated to give by such perks alone, they usually expect some type of special treatment. As the development director of a large liberal-leaning group indicated:

We make phone calls, we treat these people like friends. If you know they've had a loss in the family, or a new grandchild, or whatever, you acknowledge it the way you would any good friend. We let them know they are appreciated. The correspondence is highly personalized. We put a tremendous effort into it. It's a very labor-intensive job. But in a tough market, it's the only way to hold on to people.

Although many groups have very active large-donor programs, it is not exceedingly unusual for public interest groups to receive large individual donations "out of the blue." As the executive director of a small environmental group told us:

> It could be somebody who, for example, has a bad experience with a pesticide and who all of a sudden becomes aware.... They've called us and we've helped them, and they send us an unsolicited check. Often, many of the people who send anything over $100 do it out of the blue.... We're not really sure why. We really need to look into that more closely.

Large donors are the least demanding patrons, hence the most desirable from the perspective of group developmental directors. Money is seldom given with onerous or obvious strings attached, and most donors are typically enthusiastic supporters of the group's cause. As the executive director of a small group that deals with population issues told us:

> Most [large donors] just get our annual report and they really don't ask for anything more. Larger donors really don't ask that many questions.

Since large donors are usually very familiar with groups' activities and are frequently long-time group members, they generally are unconcerned with accountability. Large donors know and trust the groups to which they contribute.

We did uncover a few instances in which large donors were viewed as challengers for organizational control. As the executive director of a small humane organization related to us:

> Part of my donors [sic] are like the power hitter: whoever they are, whatever community they're in, they want to have more control over the organization. And we really do a good job of not allowing people to buy power.

Such occasional situations do not deter group development officers. Over half of the officials we talked to indicated they were seriously looking into expanding their large-donor programs, because of the advantages inherent in doing so.

Conclusion

Overall, our findings support the notion that those responsible for fund raising in public interest groups eagerly seek money from outside sources, through both formal and informal means. Several groups in our survey were nearly totally dependent on patronage for their existence, and four-fifths of the organizations received at least a quarter of their revenues from such sources. Many public interest organizations would not be active at all or would have greatly curtailed programs if patronage were not available. Public interest groups totally reliant upon members for financial support are rather rare in American politics.

It would be a mistake, however, to conclude that the importance of patronage alters the goals of such groups. Public interest group entrepreneurs seek and approach funding sources that are compatible with group goals: liberal groups generally receive money from liberal funding sources, and more conservative groups receive funding from like-minded patrons. Even in the case of corporate money, which constitutes a surprisingly small portion of overall outside funding for most groups, patrons typically support groups with which they share either a constituency or value perspectives. Companies like Philip Morris, in tempting public interest groups whose values seem very different, are the exception rather than the rule.

Patrons' money is not free of costs, however. Our findings also indicate that group entrepreneurs are well aware of potential encroachments on group agendas and autonomy, including the risks to the group's reputation that are incurred by accepting patronage from outside sources. Some patrons are more problematic than others. Foundation money is especially attractive to groups, because it promises relatively large amounts of money with little in the way of control or oversight, although group priorities may be altered through the acceptance of a foundation grant. Money from large individual donors also is largely cost free: such donors are often a group's strongest issue supporters. Government patronage, on the other hand, apparently poses large acquisition costs, provides relatively small amounts of money, and compromises a group's autonomy because of the stringent oversight provisions of most grants and contracts. For public interest groups that view government as an adversary, government patronage is often incompatible with ideology.

Corporate money clearly creates the biggest dilemma for group fund raisers, due to the potentially high credibility costs of taking money from sources motivated by bottom-line concerns. Many groups simply eschew corporate funding altogether and others refuse to accept support from specific corporate sectors or individual companies.

Despite highly publicized examples of public interest groups accepting money from sources that conflict with group goals—or appear to do so—our study would seem to indicate that group fund raisers are careful in protecting group images and autonomy. By and large, public interest groups remain true to their missions even while soliciting and receiving money from outside patrons.

Notes

1. Mancur Olson, *The Logic of Collective Action* (Cambridge: Harvard University Press, 1971).

2. See, for example, Andrew S. McFarland, *Public Interest Lobbies* (Washington, D.C.: American Enterprise Institute, 1976).

3. A major research area in political science deals with why people join and remain in political groups. For a summary of the major research findings on the "collective action problem," see Allan J. Cigler, "Interest Groups: A Subfield in Search of an Identity," in *Political Science: Looking to the Future*, vol. 4, ed. William Crotty (Evanston, Ill.: Northwestern, 1991), particularly 105-112.

4. See, for example, Russell Hardin, *Collective Action* (Baltimore: Johns Hopkins University Press, 1982); Jack H. Nagel, *Participation* (Englewood Cliffs, N.J.: Prentice-Hall, 1987); R. Kenneth Godwin and Robert Cameron Michael, "Rational Models, Collective Goods, and Non-electoral Political Behavior," *Western Political Quarterly* 35 (May 1982): 160-180; Terry M. Moe, *The Organization of Interests* (Chicago: University of Chicago Press, 1980).

5. Jeffrey M. Berry, *Lobbying for the People* (Princeton, N.J.: Princeton University Press, 1977).

6. Jack L. Walker, "The Origins and Maintenance of Interest Groups in America," *American Political Science Review* 77 (June 1983): 390-406.

7. See Craig J. Jenkins, *The Politics of Insurgency* (New York: Columbia University Press, 1985); Craig J. Jenkins and Craig M. Eckert, "Channelling Black Insurgency: Elite Patronage and Professional Social Movement Organizations in the Development of the Black Movement," *American Sociological Review* 51 (June 1986): 812-829.

8. David C. King and Jack L. Walker, "The Provision of Benefits by Interest Groups in the United States," *Journal of Politics* 54 (May 1992): 394-426.

9. Douglas McAdam, *Political Process and the Development of Black Insurgency* (Chicago: University of Chicago Press, 1982).

10. Douglas Imig, "Resource Mobilization and Survival Tactics of Poverty Advocacy Groups," *Western Political Quarterly* 45 (June 1992): 501-520.

11. King and Walker, "The Provision of Benefits," 423.

12. Morton Mintz, *Allies: The ACLU and the Tobacco Industry* (Washington: The Advocacy Institute, 1993).

13. Ibid., 15.

14. Robert H. Salisbury, "An Exchange Theory of Interest Groups," *Midwest Journal of Political Science* 13 (February 1969): 1-32.

15. See, for example, David Mayhew, *Congress: The Electoral Connection* (New Haven: Yale University Press, 1974).

16. John Mark Hansen, "The Political Economy of Group Membership," *American Political Science Review* 82 (March 1985): 79-96.

17. James Q. Wilson, *Political Organizations* (New York: Basic Books), 196.

18. In designing our sample, we utilized Jeffrey Berry's working definition of a public interest group: "One that seeks a collective good, the achievement of which will not selectively and materially benefit the membership or activists of the organization." To construct a population of nationally active public interest groups that met this test, we compiled a list of 270 groups from the following sources: *Washington Representatives*, Congressional Quarterly's *Washington Information Directory*, and *The Encyclopedia of Associations*. All were organizations that had an office in Washington and were "national" in orientation. Professional and occupational groups were not included, nor were charities. One hundred organizations were randomly selected and initially contacted by mail, and then by telephone, and asked if they

would be interested in participating in a research project dealing with the maintenance problems of public interest groups. Sixty-two groups agreed to participate. The interviews were conducted from early fall 1991 through the following spring. The groups ranged in size from small, nonmembership organizations funded by one or two outside patrons and having one or two staff members to prominent, mass-membership groups with large staffs and budgets well into the millions of dollars.

5

The Color of Money: Environmental Groups and the Pathologies of Fund Raising

Christopher J. Bosso

The environmental movement has undergone great change over the past three decades. From a handful of groups staffed by largely self-sufficient and part-time cadres of amateurs dedicated to wildlife protection and land conservation, the movement has evolved into a diverse collection of highly professional organizations that sometimes conflict as they engage in advocacy on policy concerns ranging from domestic agriculture to foreign trade. Environmental organizations involved in contemporary Washington politics are characterized by their extensive technical and scientific expertise, deep legal talent, professional management, state-of-the-art communications and fundraising technologies, and sophisticated educational and public relations campaigns, as well as by their use of direct lobbying.

The transformation of the environmental movement into one of professionalized interest representation has made it necessary for environmental groups to pay increasing attention to fund raising. In this chapter, Christopher Bosso explores the dilemma environmental groups face in attempting "to manage big, expensive, professional advocacy operations while retaining the commitment and financial support of a heterogeneous and frequently restive membership." The early 1990s have proved to be especially challenging, because of the stagnation in membership and revenues that accompanied economic recession.

Bosso finds that most groups today "rely far less on institutional patrons than critics claim or than might have been true a decade ago." Many are diversifying their revenue sources; others are attempting to create membership bases to reduce their dependence on foundation money. Unlike foundation and corporation money, which comes with "strings attached," money raised from large numbers of small contributors provides a group "some freedom to maneuver," giving the group "the numbers and resources they need to carry the battle onward without putting a lot of limits on how and where that money is spent."

The Green Malaise

These should be salad days for the environmental community in the United States. After years of sparring with presidents considered hostile to their goals, the coming of the Clinton Administration offered prospects of greater executive-level receptivity. Environmental leaders certainly were happy to see at least two dozen of their colleagues get key positions in the new administration, beginning with interior secretary (and former League of Conservation Voters president) Bruce Babbitt. They also must have been gratified that "greener" perspectives were starting to percolate more openly in niches of the federal establishment where such views had seemed marginal only months before.

For its part, the organized environmental community in the United States never seemed bigger, richer, stronger. The nation's largest environmental groups had seen memberships and revenues swell into the millions in the previous decade: in 1990, by one account, the environmental community as a whole took in some $2.9 billion—almost double 1987 revenues.[1] The sheer number of environmental groups throughout the nation—by one estimate, more than ten thousand different organizations—implied how widely and deeply green values had permeated the society.[2]

Yet in the mid-1990s there is a noticeable sense of unease within the nation's organized environmental community. For one thing, American environmentalism seems more internally fragmented than ever over goals, strategies, and tactics. Such heterogeneity has virtues; for example, there arguably is an identifiable group for every issue or "shade of green" imaginable. Nonetheless, it raises serious questions about whether the term "environmental movement" continues to make any ideological, conceptual, or operational sense.[3]

More practically, activists worry that a gaggle of often overlapping groups, compounded by sharp ideological and tactical cleavages within environmentalism, only confuses the public and creates opportunities for opposing interests to make mischief by playing environmentalists against one another. Further, despite often amazing growth, for most environmental organizations the 1980s also were years of intense internal turmoil. Many groups went through wrenching and sometimes frequent changes in leadership, and almost all were forced to retool organizational capacities and governance structures as they mobilized to blunt the initiatives of their industrial and political foes. The energy and money spent fighting successive Republican administrations left lingering scars in terms of opportunities lost and resources wasted to defend previous gains. It was no surprise that the "green vote" in 1992 sided strongly with the Democratic ticket.

Even with Clinton and Gore in office, life for environmental groups will not suddenly become easy, nor will relations with the new administration always be smooth or even amicable. Frictions over ratification of the North American Free Trade Agreement (NAFTA), logging of old-growth timber, raising grazing fees and mining royalties on public lands, and the future of the Council for Environmental Quality were but the most apparent examples of strain in the administration's first year. In most cases the strains grew out of conflicts between the president's need to nurture an inchoate governing coalition and the contrary needs of environmental groups to promote their own, arguably narrower agendas. Former allies criticized one another openly. More often than not, their stated positions depended on whether they hailed from the headquarters of an environmental organization or had a job in a federal office building. Such strains echoed those that existed between environmentalists and Jimmy Carter, their last ostensible friend in the White House.

The 1993 debate over NAFTA underscored the sense of uncertainty now felt within the environmental community. The acrimonious battle over the trade pact pitted the Clinton administration and one collection of environmental groups against a coalition led by organized labor and supported by another set of environmentalists, exactly the kind of rift that activists worry about. Support for NAFTA tended to come from the older and larger national titans of "mainstream" environmentalism such as the National Wildlife Federation and the National Audubon Society, or from groups such as the Environmental Defense Fund that are likelier to advocate free-market answers to pollution problems. Those opposing the agreement were either coalitions of grassroots "environmental justice" groups such as the Citizens Clearinghouse for Hazardous Wastes, or groups such as the Sierra Club, Greenpeace, and Friends of the Earth whose ideological stances are warier of corporate capitalism. Supporters accused opponents of fear-mongering, nativism, and ideological hostility to business; opponents charged backers with being the useful dupes of an administration whose favor they were loath to lose or, worse, captive to their corporate sponsors and middle-class Baby Boomer members.[4] Nuggets of truth lay in the muck of charges and countercharges.

Indeed, the 1990s have not been kind to the segment of American environmentalism that comprises the nation's largest and most well-established membership organizations. For these groups the 1980s meant membership increases that in some cases more than doubled group size (Table 5-1) and revenues that in many cases more than tripled (Table 5-2). The 1990s, by contrast, brought recession-fueled stagnation in membership and revenues—and, in some cases, real decreases. These setbacks, in turn, produced widespread retrenchment. The National Wildlife Federation, whose budget had tripled in less than a decade, in 1991 laid off staff and froze salaries as revenue growth stalled.[5] The Sierra Club also cut its payroll despite modest membership increases, and the Wilderness Society, which saw a 5 percent drop in revenues in 1991 after years of

Table 5-1 Membership Trends Among Selected National Groups, 1970-1992

Group	1970	1980	1985	1990	1992
Sierra Club (1892)	113,000	181,000	364,000	630,000	650,000
National Audubon Society (1905)	105,000	400,000	550,000	575,000	600,000
Izaak Walton League (1922)	54,000	52,000	47,000	50,000	53,000
Wilderness Society (1935)	54,000	45,000	147,000	350,000	313,000
National Wildlife Federation (1936)[a]	540,000	818,000	900,000	997,000	975,000
Defenders of Wildlife (1947)	13,000	50,000	65,000	75,000	80,000
Nature Conservancy (1951)	22,000	n/a	400,000	600,000	690,000
World Wildlife Fund (1961)	n/a	n/a	130,000	400,000	940,000
Environmental Defense Fund (1967)	11,000	46,000	50,000	150,000	150,000
Friends of the Earth (1969)[b]	6,000	n/a	30,000	9,000	50,000
Environmental Action (1970)	10,000	20,000	15,000	20,000	16,000
Greenpeace USA (1972)	n/a	n/a	800,000	2.35 million	1.8 million

Notes: All figures rounded.

[a] Full members only. The Federation in 1992 also had affiliated memberships (e.g., schoolchildren) of 5.3 million.

[b] Merged in 1990 with the 30,000-member Oceanic Society and the non-member Environmental Policy Institute.

Sources: Annual reports; *The Encyclopedia of Associations*, various editions (Detroit: Gale Research Company); "1990 Directory of Environmental Organizations," *Buzzworm: The Environmental Journal* 2, 3 (May/June 1990): 65-77; Margaret E. Kriz, "Shades of Green," *National Journal*, July 28, 1990, 1828; George Hager, "For Industry and Opponents, A Showdown is in the Air," *Congressional Quarterly Weekly Report*, January 20, 1990, 144; Robert Cameron Mitchell, "Public Opinion and the Green Lobby: Poised for the 1990s?" in *Environmental Policy in the 1990s*, ed. Norman J. Vig and Michael E. Kraft (Washington, D.C.: CQ Press, 1990), 92; Environmental Protection Section, Congressional Research Service, *Selected Environmental and Related Interest Groups: Summary Guide*, CRS Report 91-295 ENR (March 22, 1991), *passim*; *National Journal*, January 4, 1992, 30; *Chronicle of Philanthropy*, March 24, 1992, 31.

Table 5-2   Budgetary Trends among Selected National Groups, 1970-1992 (in millions of dollars)

Group	1970	1980	1985	1990	1992
Sierra Club	3.0	9.5	22.0	40.0	41.0
National Wildlife Federation	13.0	34.5	46.0	89.5	90.0
Defenders of Wildlife	n/a	n/a	3.0	4.3	4.4
Nature Conservancy	n/a	n/a	156.0	200.0	216.0
Environmental Defense Fund	n/a	2.0	3.5	16.0	20.8
Friends of the Earth	0.36	1.0	1.0	3.0	3.3
Environmental Action	n/a	0.55	0.6	1.1	1.3
Greenpeace USA	n/a	n/a	24.0	35.0	50.0

Note: All figures are rounded.

Sources: Annual reports; *The Encyclopedia of Associations,* various editions (Detroit: Gale Research Company); "1990 Directory of Environmental Organizations," *Buzzworm: The Environmental Journal* 2, 3 (May/June 1990): 65-77; Margaret E. Kriz, "Shades of Green," *National Journal,* July 28, 1990, 1828; George Hager, "For Industry and Opponents, A Showdown is in the Air," *Congressional Quarterly Weekly Report,* January 20, 1990, 144; Robert Cameron Mitchell, "Public Opinion and the Green Lobby: Poised for the 1990s?" in *Environmental Policy in the 1990s,* ed. Norman J. Vig and Michael E. Kraft (Washington, D.C.: CQ Press, 1990), 92; Environmental Protection Section, Congressional Research Service, *Selected Environmental and Related Interest Groups: Summary Guide,* CRS Report 91-295 ENR (March 22, 1991), *passim; National Journal,* January 4, 1992, 30; *Chronicle of Philanthropy,* March 24, 1992, 31.

often spectacular growth, instituted stringent cost-cutting measures to eliminate a sudden operating deficit.[6] Even Greenpeace, whose phenomenal expansion in the 1980s outpaced almost all others, fell upon sober times as slumping revenues forced it to cut staff, close offices, and trim operations. Such conditions cropped up in other advanced industrial nations—Greenpeace Canada, for example, suffered an almost 30 percent drop in donations in the early 1990s—even as pleas for assistance mounted throughout the world.[7]

For many groups the new austerity also means yet another period of leadership instability, intramural disputes over goals and tactics, and, most palpably, intensified drives to recruit more members and generate new revenues. If the past is a guide, however, even successful organization-building efforts will create their own strains, particularly in terms of governance, group identity, and core beliefs. This chapter examines the kinds of dilemmas facing the major national environmental membership groups as they struggle to maintain fiscal health without sacrificing key goals and values. A cynic might argue that you cannot seek gold without compromising virtue: the cynic probably is right. The question is whether these groups—or their counterparts within the broader public interest community—have much of a choice.

It's Money That Matters

Why money matters must seem obvious. Without it a group cannot really lobby. Thus the group cannot wield influence. End of discussion. But the equation is not so straightforward, particularly in the world of public interest representation. Some history helps to explain why. Environmental activism in the United States once lay squarely in the American tradition of voluntary public service, with largely self-sufficient and part-time cadres of dedicated (and largely affluent) amateurs providing the backbone for the wildlife protection and land conservation groups common prior to the 1960s.[8] Groups like the Sierra Club, National Audubon Society, National Wildlife Federation, and Izaak Walton League tended to restrict "lobbying" to more genteel citizen education and low-key contacts with policy makers. More aggressive advocacy was the exception and often ran contrary to group culture. More directly, it was constrained by a tax exempt status that forbade significant lobbying.[9]

That tradition is long gone within the national environmental community and, for that matter, within the political community at large. In its place we find professionalized interest representation, replete with extensive technical and scientific expertise, deep legal talent, the latest in communications and fund-raising technologies, sophisticated educational and public relations campaigns, and, of course, outright lobbying—especially after changes in the tax code loosened up some of the more onerous restrictions on direct advocacy by tax-exempt groups.

Professional interest representation is not cheap. A full-time staff with policy and managerial expertise is vastly more expensive to recruit and maintain than one comprised of the young volunteers who typified environmentalism in the early 1970s. Professional staff now demand middle-class benefits (health insurance, pensions) in line with their expertise and market demand, the latter the result of a muted but very real competition among groups for the best talent. To direct ever larger and more complicated staff organizations requires big-league managerial skill, and annual compensation packages for executives at the major groups routinely surpass $100,000. Jay Hair, president of the National Wildlife Federation, earned nearly $300,000 in 1991.[10] Critics in and outside the environmental community often point to such figures as proof that the groups have lost their public interest souls, but on average these levels of compensation still fall far below those enjoyed by executives atop major business and trade associations—and even some other public interest groups. Still, top talent in the environmental "industry" is expensive.

Where Money Comes From

Given all of this, money is more nakedly important today than at any other time in the evolution of American environmentalism. Where

Table 5-3   Sources of Revenues for Membership Groups

Source Of Revenue	Mean Percentage
Membership dues	32
Individual contributions	19
Foundation grants	17
Sales	8
Corporate gifts	4
Capital assets	3
Federal grants and contracts	2
State grants and contracts	2
Other contracts	2
User fees	2
Other sources	9

Source: The Conservation Foundation. Data derived from a 1988-89 Foundation survey of 248 conservation and environmental groups, three-fourths of which were classified as membership groups. See Donald Snow, *Inside the Environmental Movement: Meeting the Leadership Challenge* (Washington, D.C.: Island Press, 1992), 63.

environmental groups get their funding thus becomes more than a narrow academic question, especially if one accepts the wisdom that all money has strings attached—even if the strings are not readily visible. At minimum, how a group raises funds must somehow affect its goals, tactics, and internal modes of operation. As the old axiom goes, there is no such thing as a free lunch. True, the equation is not simple: for many environmental groups, as for public interest organizations generally, revenues today come from a much broader array of sources than arguably was true just a decade ago. It thus is useful to examine the relative distribution of sources among a range of major environmental membership organizations before digging deeper into the effects of funding on group dynamics.

The Conservation Foundation, in an effort to improve leadership effectiveness in the environmental community, in 1989 generated survey data from approximately 250 assorted environmental groups on a broad range of dimensions, including funding sources. Table 5-3, derived from these data, indicates the distribution of sources for membership groups only. (Many environmental organizations have no members in the pure sense of the term.) The data are limited by the way all types of membership groups were lumped together, but they do give an idea about the diversity of sources possible. Even so, it is noteworthy that the top two categories—member dues and individual contributions—comprise more than half of all revenues generated. Membership groups, as might be expected, depend more heavily on individuals than on any other single "patron."

Table 5-4 Percentage of Revenues from "Individuals" and "Institutions" for Selected National Environmental Organizations, Fiscal Years 1987 and 1990

	1987		1990	
Group	Individuals	Institutions	Individuals	Institutions
Friends of the Earth[a]	98	0	40	60
Environmental Action	73	22	74	17
Greenpeace USA	98	1	98	1
Defenders of Wildlife	91	0	92	0
League of Conservation Voters	100	0	100	0
Sierra Club	80	0	66	0
Wilderness Society	86	14	81	11
National Audubon Society	74	2	68	0
Environmental Defense Fund	53	35	64	30
Natural Resources Defense Council	44	45	49	42
National Wildlife Federation	38	18	47	0
Izaak Walton League	52	40	39	56
Nature Conservancy	51	49	70	30
World Wildlife Fund	66	12	62	13

Note: "Individuals" includes member dues, individual contributions, gifts, bequests, and legacies. "Institutions" includes foundation, corporate, and government grants and donations. Figures do not add up to 100 percent in many cases because some groups generate revenues from publications, sales of goods and services, and investments, for example. Figures are compiled from annual reports. They are approximate and vary based on differing accounting practices.

[a] Friends of the Earth merged in 1990 with the Environmental Policy Institute, which relied on individual contributions for 23 percent of its fiscal year 1987 budget. The 1990 percentage reflects that merger.

Source: Public Interest Profiles, 1988-1989; 1992-1993 (Washington, D.C.: Foundation for Public Affairs, CQ Press, 1988; 1992).

Individual vs. Institutional Support

We can learn more about this funding profile by looking more closely at a few major membership organizations using data from their annual reports compiled by the Foundation for Public Affairs. Table 5-4 compares the proportion of revenues coming from "individuals" (member dues, individual contributions, bequests, and legacies) with the proportion of revenues coming from "institutions" (government and foundation grants, corporate donations) for two different fiscal years. Many of the major national groups depend extremely heavily on individuals, with the League of Conservation Voters, Greenpeace, Defenders of Wildlife, and the Wilderness Society in both years getting more than 80 percent of their funds from a large number of small contributions. It also is apparent that the national membership groups rely far less on institutional patrons than critics claim or than might have been true a decade ago. For example, both the Environmental Defense Fund and Natural Resources Defense Council were founded as environmental law firms and depended initially on grants (particularly from the Ford Foundation) and legal fees to survive. Neither group had a member base. Today, however, both organizations rely on individual contributions for a significant part of their revenues. This pattern of revenue generation has been common to many environmental groups.[11]

The groups in Table 5-4 are ranked along a crude "pragmatism" scale, with those at the top of the column having reputations as "ideologues" and those at the bottom as "accommodationists."[12] Friends of the Earth, for example, is regarded widely within the environmental community as one of the most reliably "leftist" of the major national groups (though Environmental Action and Greenpeace activists might raise an argument about this), while the World Wildlife Fund is the epitome of the nonconfrontational conservation organization. In the real world these gradations are finer and fuzzier than suggested here, and relative "rankings" certainly are debatable, but the exercise reveals some rough tendencies. For one, the groups that rely most heavily on revenues from member dues and contributions tend to be those considered least willing to compromise with government or industry interests over goals or tactics. Friends of the Earth, Environmental Action, Greenpeace, Defenders of Wildlife, and the Sierra Club stand out in this regard. (The League of Conservation Voters is a political action committee, so its revenues by law come from non-tax deductible individual donations.) At the other end of the spectrum are traditional conservation groups (National Wildlife Federation, Izaak Walton League) and the groups oriented more toward the law, science, or market mechanisms such as the Environmental Defense Fund (EDF) and Natural Resources Defense Council (NRDC). These kinds of groups rely more heavily on monies from institutional patrons if only because their outlooks and tactics are more palatable to corporate sponsors and grant makers. Again, these tendencies are not absolute: both the Nature Conservancy and the World Wildlife Fund rely relatively heavily on individual contributions even though they are both considered "accommodationist" groups that generally take noncontroversial stances. The Nature Conservancy, for example, sticks to buying and managing threatened ecosystems; the World Wildlife Fund to campaigns aimed at protecting easily identifiable (and sympathy provoking) endangered species like the panda bear. These groups also occupy rather distinct ideological and strategic niches where they can appeal to less radical (and less left-leaning) contributors. Neither, it can be safely assumed, competes with Greenpeace or Friends of the Earth for members. The Nature Conservancy does so well, a Sierra Club leader suggested waggishly, because "when corporate America comes to God someone has to take up the collection."[13]

Diversification of Funding

Regardless of ideology or reputation, most groups seem to be diversifying their revenue bases, either seeking to lessen a heavy reliance on individuals (the Sierra Club) or, as noted for the NRDC and EDF, creating member bases to reduce dependence on foundation monies. Those that do not diversify probably have ideology or organizational culture as reasons for sticking with established funding formulae. The history of one group in particular is a good example. Friends of the Earth (FOE), founded by activist David Brower after he left the Sierra Club in 1969, by the 1980s was in serious financial straits in no small part because of Brower's belief that the demands of organizational management and fund raising undercut activism. That belief had led to his ouster as head of the Sierra Club. History repeated itself as Brower fought with his board over FOE's finances, future directions, and a plan, which Brower opposed, to move FOE's headquarters from California to the nation's capital. Brower lost, and left to form the nonmember Earth Island Institute. FOE moved to Washington, where it merged in 1990 with the Oceanic Institute and the Environmental Policy Institute (EPI). The latter, ironically, had been founded in 1972 by FOE dissidents after an earlier spat with Brower over management and funding issues. The new FOE has since found a niche in addressing the environmental problems of developing nations.[14] The merger also altered the new group's funding mix. Whereas FOE once relied on individual contributions and EPI on institutional support, the merged group has a funding mix far less dependent on any single source—a marriage of convenience that might be repeated among other groups in the 1990s.

The relative pathologies of funding are explored in the next two sections. Generally speaking, the biggest trick today for those leading major environmental membership groups is to manage big, expensive, professional advocacy operations while retaining the commitment and financial support of a heterogeneous and frequently restive membership. The dilemmas facing leaders whose groups rely very heavily on individual contributions will differ somewhat from those whose funding bases are more diversified, but the basic challenges of balancing management against issue advocacy are common to all.

Mass Membership Environmentalism

The transformation of organized environmentalism from an odd assortment of conservation groups populated by a rather elite cadre of activists to the staff-run mass-membership behemoths of today is a story worth telling in itself.[15] The surges in mass membership evident since the early 1970s reveal the extent to which environmental concerns have become salient within the society and exemplify the willingness of Americans to subsidize causes they find worthy. Yet this growth did not just happen simply because environmental issues became more important to more people. It also was cultivated as part of a conscious effort by many environmental leaders to build member bases as another tool in their organizational and advocacy armamentarium. To "grow an organization" in this way has practical benefits but nevertheless is a route pursued warily by leaders of most established groups. They know, usually from their own hard experience, that deep dependency on member dues or contributions can produce acute organizational woes, particularly when the flow of donations slows.

A good symbol of both the benefits and the costs of "mass-member environmentalism" is Greenpeace, a group long envied by other environmentalists for its capacity to use its "radical" but nonviolent image to generate staggering levels of contributions through direct mail and door-to-door canvassing. Founded in 1972 as a tiny Quaker-influenced group that engaged in dramatic and well-publicized protests against nuclear weapons tests, whaling, and the dumping of toxic wastes in the world's oceans, by the late 1980s Greenpeace was a Netherlands-based global "green giant" with its own navy, research arm, and sophisticated telecommunications system run by hundreds of professional staff in twenty-three offices worldwide and supported by about $150 million in contributions from about five million people. Greenpeace USA alone in 1990 generated about $60 million from an estimated 2.5 million contributors.[16] The key to Greenpeace's success in fund raising is its often flamboyant style, an image of undiluted advocacy the organization is careful not to undermine by, for example, working openly with the other major membership groups. Being seen as "just another environmental lobby" would not sit well with Greenpeace contributors, for whom "mainstream" is synonymous with accommodation.

Even so, Greenpeace in the early 1990s discovered that its unique image did not shield it from the woes common to mass-membership organizations that rely heavily on individual contributions. Its dependence on direct mail is expensive: by one conservative estimate more than 20 percent of the annual Greenpeace budget is allocated explicitly to fund raising, a figure that is probably low because it does not take into account spending on administrative support or "member communication" that also might be directed at generating publicity and, hence, donations.[17] By one estimate, in fact, forty-eight cents out of every dollar raised through direct mail goes straight back into more fund raising.[18] Reliance on direct mail also leads critics, including other environmentalists, to charge that the Greenpeace agenda is shaped powerfully by whatever new eco-crisis (for example, the killing of dolphins in tuna fishing) it can exploit in the millions of pieces of mail it sends out annually.

The group's size also worries longtime activists, who wonder if the drive toward bigness and the imperatives of organizational maintenance have not dulled Greenpeace's zeal even as more radical direct-action groups like Earth First! and the Sea Shepherds grab public attention. More important, Greenpeace's dependence on millions of small donations makes it acutely sensitive to swings in economic conditions and public attitudes than might be the case for groups with other sources of revenue. The organization was hit hard by the recession of the early 1990s and, to some undefinable extent, by its outspoken opposition to the Persian Gulf War. Only FOE, which like Greenpeace sees itself as an international organization, took a visible ecological position against military action; other groups kept mum on the war itself. In any case, Greenpeace's gross American and worldwide revenues dropped noticeably in 1991, the first such slump in its history. Budgetary woes forced Greenpeace USA to lay off at least fifty of its more than two hundred staffers, close down some regional offices, and cut back *Greenpeace* magazine to a quarterly. The same problems no doubt played a role in the departure of executive director Peter Bahouth.[19] Donations continued to stagnate into 1992, prompting another 25 percent cut in the organization's 1993 budget.[20]

The Cult of Bigness

The story of Greenpeace is not unique. Other mass-membership environmental groups (for example, Defenders of Wildlife and the Sierra Club) have experienced similar kinds of organizational traumas following periods of massive membership growth. Even so, and even though leaders know well the possible dangers of grabbing the mass-membership tiger by the tail, most major environmental groups seem determined to expand their member bases. In this regard, the rationales offered by leaders of the nation's two oldest environmental groups are instructive. The National Audubon Society, for one, intends to increase its current base to 1.2 million members by the end of the decade, "to increase our effectiveness," says Audubon president Peter Berle.[21] How so? Longtime Audubon activist and chronicler Frank Graham explains:

> The membership gives the Society high visibility and much political leverage from coast to coast. This "grass-roots" element will take a more aggressive role in making decisions and in carrying out Audubon programs. If there are great strides to be made in the near future, they must come in this area by expanding both the numbers and the social makeup of the membership.... Numbers imply power in a democracy. But, even more, increased numbers in this case would imply reaching into new sectors of America to bring in people who have been notoriously under-represented in conservation organizations.[22]

A certain critical mass of dues-paying members is seen as essential to effectiveness in today's lobbying climate. The Sierra Club is similarly focused: More members means more resources, argues Carl Pope, the group's executive director. More resources in turn will enable the organization

> to bring a lawsuit, to fight a political candidate, to respond to a legislative crisis. So, in a rough sense, we will be stronger if we can grow from our current 600,000 members to 750,000 or 800,000. If we were to fall back to 300,000 we would be substantially weakened.[23]

Bigger is better.

Direct Mail

But getting bigger is expensive and time consuming in and of itself. The older conservation groups—that is, those founded before the 1960s—usually had stable or slowly growing memberships, with new members usually nominated by old-timers. Commitment, not gross membership numbers, mattered most. But the contemporary world of issue advocacy is one where statistics—length of membership rolls, size of budgets, cost of media campaigns, number of staff—can create a reputation of clout. In this world, being big and rich does matter. It also is no surprise that the most aggressively expansionist groups have been those willing to commit to sophisticated direct-mail campaigns as the backbone of their fund raising.

Using direct mail to generate donations to environmental groups was pioneered in the 1950s by the Defenders of Wildlife and the National Parks and Conservation Association. It was adopted wholeheartedly by the National Audubon Society in the 1960s and today is ubiquitous and, apparently, essential. The reasons seem simple. Computers allow even a small group to communicate with, even "educate," a large audience quickly without having its message diluted by others (namely, the mass media) as it solicits funds. As Robert Mitchell and his collaborators note, direct mail has been a gold mine for environmental groups because the issues they promote

> have a broad scope of appeal, they are extremely visible, they continually recur, they enable individuals to feel a sense of empowerment when engaging in activity on their behalf, and people dread the loss of amenities that environmentalists wish to protect. Direct mail, in addition to the constant media coverage of environmental problems, has combined to keep the public aware of and concerned about such problems.[24]

In short, direct mail has been a lucrative, relatively low-cost way to educate the public about both an issue and a group; it lowers the cost of individual participation to just writing a check. Each new "member" becomes part of an aggregation, the gross size of which itself becomes politically potent. Even the most skeptical member of Congress notes the specter of six hundred thousand Sierra Club members getting excited about an issue, if only because people who write out checks also might care enough to contact policy makers or remember who voted what way on election day.

Direct mail has become part and parcel of the world of environmental advocacy and organizational maintenance. Yet, for its virtues, direct mail imposes real costs. Just inaugurating the initial mailing can cost hundreds of thousands of dollars, even assuming a group already has a mailing list from which to work.[25] Not all groups have either the finances or, perhaps, the desire, to go this route. Relatively smaller membership groups—Environmental Action, for example—have had mixed results with direct mail, as have research-oriented groups such as the Environmental Policy Institute (now merged with FOE), whose appeals cannot easily be "capsulized in a gut-wrenching direct-mail letter."[26] Even Greenpeace, one of the champions of direct mail, relied on a loan from the for-profit firm that does the group's direct-mail campaigns to get started. And, like Greenpeace, most environmental membership groups conservatively spend at least 30 percent of their budgets on "fund raising," "membership communications," and "education," functional categories that may be formally distinct but all of which are aimed ultimately at recruiting new contributors and keeping current ones. Constant membership recruitment is essential just to stay even—never mind get bigger—as attrition rates can average as high as 30 percent annually.[27] Drop-out rates are high in large part because most members are little but passive check writers, with the low cost of participating often translating into an equally low sense of commitment, particularly when most large organizations give members little if any direct input into policy making or governance.

Even so, Mitchell and his collaborators argue that members "possess an indirect voice through their voluntary memberships and contributions, which they can stop at any time."[28] The "exit" option is a serious one. A mass membership of atomistic check writers is highly sensitive to economic conditions and, probably, a bit fickle, shaped in no small way by the vagaries of momentary mass issue saliency. Holding onto such members almost requires that groups maintain a sense of constant crisis, and fund raisers will mine those issues that produce the highest return on the dollars invested. Environmental groups certainly have had no lack of real ecological horror stories to mine, but it does not take a cynic to suggest that Greenpeace, for example, might have overstated its role in fighting for "dolphin-free" tuna in some of its direct mail appeals.[29] Nor must one be a complete cynic to suggest that direct mailers shop for the next eco-crisis to keep the money coming in.

It also helps to have easily typecast enemies, which the Reagan and Bush administrations thoughtfully supplied through the early 1990s. With the arrival of Clinton, however, environmentalists are in much the same quandary as were staunch anticommunists at the end of the Cold War—

their traditional enemy is gone. As a result, environmental direct mail has had to scrounge for new enemies, with several groups training their sights on the conservative "wise use" and "property rights" doctrines that have sprung up in the past decade. For their part, conservative "anti-environmental" groups—including the John Birch Society—have raised the specter of an unshackled Al Gore in much the same way that Dan Quayle once was an environmental fund raiser's dream.[30]

Finally, heavy reliance on direct mail raises the concern that groups may focus less on what is really important than on what appeals most to their contributors. The people who most support major environmental groups, suggests John Judis,

> tend to fit the profile of the Baby Boomer—liberal on social and environmental issues and on foreign policy, but fiscally conservative, often suspicious of unions, indifferent to poverty except in the most melodramatic forms. None of the major organizations that rely on direct mail emphasize the redistribution of income, the rebuilding of cities, the rights of workers to join unions, the need for national health insurance, or the kinds of environmental issues that plague working-class neighborhoods.[31]

Indeed, a profile of the Sierra Club in the late 1980s showed a membership more than twice as likely as the average American to be in a profession, more than twice as likely to earn more than $50,000—and eight times as likely to have an income of more than $100,000.[32] To be fair, environmental leaders are very aware of these disparities, and many groups have programs to reach "nontraditional" constituencies, but such concerns for member diversity and social justice are always weighed against even more proximate worries that existing members may take their loyalties (and checkbooks) elsewhere. With the competition for a limited environmental dollar keener than ever, this is no idle concern.

Effects on Leadership

Defenders of Wildlife, which never capitalized on the membership surge of the 1980s, suffered a severe drop in revenues in the early 1990s. Not coincidentally, in 1991 the group named Rodger Schlickeisen as its fifth president in little over a decade, a turnover rate high by even the turbulent standards of the 1980s.[33] Schlickeisen's appointment is noteworthy for two reasons: First, his background was in economics and budgeting (including a stint at the Office of Management and Budget in the Carter administration), not, as once had been the norm, in science or even law. Second, Schlickeisen's previous positions were not in environmental groups but on Capitol Hill (as chief of staff for Sen. Max Baucus, D-Mont.) and, more telling, as the chief executive officer of Craver, Matthews, Smith & Co., a major direct mail and telemarketing firm that has counted among its clients Greenpeace, the Sierra Club, the NRDC, and, of course, Defenders of Wildlife.[34] Schlickeisen's appointment suggests how the pressures of organizational maintenance and the importance of direct mail may be affecting leadership in the nation's major environmental groups. It also may be no surprise that Defenders of Wildlife almost immediately increased spending on "membership development" and "fund raising" by $300,000 for fiscal year 1991.[35]

Schlickeisen is but a recent example of transformation in the leadership of the national environmental community since the late 1970s, the last period of stagnant memberships and budgetary austerity. "When membership growth slowed after the early 1970s and expected revenues failed to materialize," note Mitchell and his coauthors, "the ensuing financial crunch exposed the weaknesses of some of the organizations' financial planning and control. Since then, the need for professional management and expertise has become more and more urgent."[36] Few argue about those needs, but there are deep concerns that fund raising has become the paramount consideration in executive recruitment and survival, with yesterday's "advocates" replaced by "managers" whose organizational skills count most with the board of directors. The new breed of professional managers, critics lament, have little practical experience as environmentalists.

More nettlesome is the role direct mail in particular has come to play in leadership selection. That Schlickeisen came to Defenders of Wildlife straight from a major direct-mail firm is only the most overt example of the fund-raising tail wagging the environmental group dog. The costs involved in direct-mail fund raising, whether paid to staff members or marketing firms, undoubtedly create conflicts over group direction and emphases. Ultimately, those who can generate the funding find themselves in charge. "At the moment," Sierra Club chairman Michael Mc-Closkey says bluntly,

> groups with little sense of vision are prospering simply because of the fund-raising talents of those working for them and because of the receptivity of the market. The same direct-mail consultants often have contracts with a number of organizations, and their copywriters' skills bring in membership for them all. But this success does not necessarily mean that the organizations are running successful environmental programs.[37]

But what if that "market" hits a recession or reaches a saturation point? The slump of the 1990s only raises the stakes for environmental leaders, particularly those most heavily dependent on raising large sums from hundreds of thousands of small contributors. Perhaps the greatest concern here is the possibility of diminishing returns. One apparent problem, as anybody deluged by mail knows, is "overgrazing," which results when several groups rely on the same mailing lists, often because they use the same direct-mail firm. The torrent of mail can end up turning off many who have donated in the past, a prospect that has led many groups long reliant on direct mail to refocus their approaches.[38] Greenpeace, apparently deciding that it could no longer accept the high annual attrition rates and sheer costs of the more scattershot versions of direct mail, has tried to maximize its efforts by limiting appeals to its most faithful contributors. It also has moved aggressively into door-to-door canvassing, particularly in working-class areas, and into telemarketing. The effects are telling: in 1990 Greenpeace sent out 48 million pieces of mail, but only half that volume in 1992, while the percentage of revenues derived from direct mail dropped from 62 percent in 1990 to 49 percent in 1992.[39] Conservation International went a step further and stopped direct-mail prospecting entirely in 1990, deciding that such campaigns were expensive and wasteful. Indeed, the organization has forsaken "bigger is better" and instead has tried to cultivate stronger ties with its thirty thousand existing members. It also is seeking more funding from corporations and foundations. "We felt that, while it's nice to have large numbers, that was not the way we wanted to do business," said John Heyl, vice president for development.[40]

Not all membership groups will mimic Conservation International, or, for that matter, the Izaak Walton League, which over the decades has avoided bigness and kept its membership constant.[41] Nor should they. For all of the pathologies discussed above, groups that rely on the small donations of many individuals at least have some freedom to maneuver, and may find that an end to economic recession will spur more giving. In a sense, small donations come with fewer strings attached, giving mass-membership groups the numbers and resources they need to carry the battle onward without putting a lot of limits on how and where that money is spent. How this is so can be understood by looking at the alternatives.

Patrons and Priorities

The alternative to member dues is, of course, to generate revenue from other sources, especially foundations and corporations. However, as will become evident, not all groups discussed here are able or willing to seek funding from institutional sources or to generate revenues through various money-making activities. Although environmental groups that rely more heavily on institutional patrons may avoid some of the more troubling practical and normative side-effects of mass membership environmentalism, here too the intersection between funding and organizational soul comes into play. In many ways the implications of dependence on patrons may be more troubling for an advocacy sector that often has to speak up against power.

Foundation Grants

Foundation grants once were a major source of support for environmental groups, especially in contemporary environmentalism's formative years, beginning in the mid-1960s and running through the late 1970s. Both EDF and NRDC began as environmental law firms and were supported by foundation grants in their early years, but both were forced to diversify when the Ford Foundation in particular moved on to other issue concerns and when government funding slowed in the 1980s. Both by necessity have evolved into membership organizations—though certainly not in the same sense as Greenpeace. EDF now gets about 30 percent of its income from foundation and government grants, most targeted to specific programs; NRDC today gets about 42 percent of its annual revenues from grants of all sorts.

For some groups foundation monies have great allure, argues John Judis, because they make "an organization's staff less dependent upon members or constituents for organizational decisions" and, as grants sometimes are directed at organization-building, they "also have encouraged professionalization."[42] For all of these virtues, however, most foundation money comes with very visible strings attached. Grants are targeted on specific programs and goals, rarely toward an organization's general fund. What is more, as both EDF and NRDC learned, changes in foundation priorities can leave an acutely dependent group high and dry, or can cause that group to alter its agenda in line with the grant monies available. This condition is endemic to grant-driven research groups such as the World Resources Institute and may be one more reason why the Environmental Policy Institute merged with FOE or the Conservation Foundation with the World Wildlife Fund. By doing so, both research institutes diversified their funding sources, as did the membership groups with which they merged.

It also is a truism that most American foundations are loath to fund groups with "radical" orientations or tactics, so Greenpeace or Defenders of Wildlife would be unlikely to get much grant money even if they sought it out. One reason for this tendency is that most large foundations are ideologically centrist. Another is that foundations are required by their own tax-exempt status to make grants solely for "exempt purposes," which emphatically precludes lobbying or other overtly "political" activities.[43] In the late 1960s many private foundations found themselves in hot water with the Nixon administration and with many members of Congress over what conservatives saw as a pervasive "funding of the Left"—with the Left defined largely as anybody who challenged the prerogatives of government or business. Although explicit threats to unleash the Internal Revenue Service on the foundations never quite materialized, the experience was enough to warn them away from funding groups or purposes that might raise an eyebrow. "Ideological" environmental groups such FOE can still turn to several liberal foundations (for example, the Charles Stewart Mott Foundation) for general support, but for organized environmentalism overall the foundation dollar seems to play a smaller role today than it did two decades ago.

Corporate Donations

No other single effort to generate revenues is more controversial in the environmental community than the drive by many of the more mainstream groups to seek funding from corporations. For one thing, many of the corporations from which funding is sought often are on some other group's enemies list—few companies, it seems, are perfectly "green." Corporations, for their part, obviously want to improve their always fragile public images and, when real policy changes look unstoppable, are likely to support organizations whose agendas seem more "reasonable" and "pragmatic." The World Wildlife Fund, for example, accepts donations from oil companies and from Philip Morris, the cigarette maker, while the National Wildlife Federation created a "corporate council" with a membership fee of $10,000.[44] The Nature Conservancy may be the most successful reaper of corporate donations among the membership groups, with over 12 percent of its 1992 revenues (around $15 million) coming from the business sector.[45] The Conservancy's "corporate associates" include firms in the extractive industries (forest products, mining, oil), utilities, and waste disposal firms, while hundreds of companies also offer matching funds for employee donations. The more market-oriented law and science groups also tend to cooperate with business, as when EDF worked with McDonald's to distribute coloring books on the rain forest. Both EDF and NRDC relied on corporate monies during their successful capital campaigns in early 1990s.[46]

What does this money buy? Putting aside cynicism—there are at all levels of major American corporations people who care passionately about the environment—corporate money is at least in part public relations, particularly when the company or industry in question might be under public scrutiny. Donations to the Nature Conservancy or the World Wildlife Fund by a forest products firm like Weyerhaeuser or an oil company like Exxon cannot help but burnish an industry's image among some environmental elites. More important, perhaps, the flow of corporate money to receptive environmental groups helps industry get its point of view across in the broader public debate. Corporate executives who sit with environmental leaders on "corporate advisory boards" like that of the National Wildlife Federation become real people, not demonic caricatures. More important, if corporations become important to environmental group budgets, particularly as revenues from other sources tighten, argues Judis, "their voice is now more likely to be heard, and, in Washington, the power to get your opinion heard wins battles."[47]

That reality is what bothers many in the environmental community. Activists in groups like FOE and Greenpeace (not to mention even more "radical" groups such as Earth First!) go further and charge that corporate money is simply a naked bribe. Critics point to Waste Management, Inc., the waste collection and disposal industry giant, as an example of the more egregious effects corporate donations can have on willing recipients. In the late 1980s and early 1990s the fast-growing company spread approximately one million dollars annually among such groups as the World Wildlife Fund, National Wildlife Federation, National Audubon Society, Sierra Club, NRDC, and Izaak Walton League. Such contributions, critics charged, were meant to deflect attention from the millions of dollars in fines levied against the firm for price fixing and illegal dumping, and to give Waste Management a greener reputation when it lobbied for regulatory changes that, in turn, might give it an edge against competitors. In this vein Waste Management allegedly used its position on the National Wildlife Federation corporate advisory board to arrange a meeting with the Bush administration's EPA chief William Reilly, who announced shortly thereafter that he would challenge the rights of states to preempt federal rules on the disposal of hazardous wastes. Reilly expressed surprise when the National Wildlife Federation protested the announcement, because it had "hosted the breakfast at which I was lobbied to do the very thing we are doing." [48] So important is corporate money to many major environmental groups that Waste Management was allowed back into the Environmental Grantmakers Association only a year after it was expelled for "a pattern of abusive corporate conduct." [49] The association's board simply decided that it no longer would monitor members' behavior.

The pathologies of corporate money are clearest when that funding is withdrawn. For one thing, companies are not likely to continue supporting groups that criticize them publicly. Exxon officials, for example, resigned from the National Wildlife Federation's corporate advisory board after the group criticized the company following the 1989 *Exxon Valdez* disaster.[50] But more important potentially is the vulnerability of corporate funding to pressures from countervailing interest groups. The case of the National Audubon Society is telling in this regard. The Society in the early 1990s generated about $2 million annually in corporate donations, less than 5 percent of overall revenues but still a fast-growing portion of the Society's budget.[51] Most of these funds went to relatively "safe" education and recreation programs, among the most popular and sponsor-dependent being the "World of Audubon," a television series aired on PBS and Turner Broadcasting. In December 1991 "World of Audubon" sponsor General Electric announced it would no longer fund the program, citing the recession as the reason. Yet the decision came hard on the heels of a campaign by the National Inholders Association (NIA), a lobbying group for cattlemen, loggers, and others who own property in or near national parks and forests. NIA members were furious about an Audubon special that attacked federally subsidized cattle grazing on public lands. These interests urged a boycott of GE products—a threat that carried some credibility, especially in the Rocky Mountain states—and took credit for GE's subsequent decision. Said NIA president Charles Cushman, "We believe GE is funding propaganda pieces, and we want to make Audubon controversial so that it will be harder for them to get advertisers." Audubon president Peter Berle, calling the NIA "a right-wing group that hires itself out to oppose expansion of public parks and other conservation measures all over the country," expressed fear that such advertiser boycotts could have a chilling effect on issue-oriented programming.[52] GE in fact was only the latest in a line of sponsors to halt funding for "World of Audubon" following one furor or another. Previous advertisers included Stroh's Brewing, Ford, Exxon, and Citicorp.[53] The irony here is that environmental groups themselves made consumer boycotts an effective tool for public persuasion.

What can be concluded about corporate money? In some sense, corporate support for environmental groups is simply part of the broader issue advocacy process; in many ways the influence it buys is probably not much different from the kinds of indefinable influence such donations buy when they go to colleges or charities. Like the colleges or charities, the groups that take corporate money, particularly money from businesses whose products or activities are controversial or run counter to group goals, argue that they never accept money that has strings attached.[54] But in a world of images and perceptions the matter is not that simple. Such money can subtly affect how recipient groups act or the kinds of agendas they pursue. Fear of losing corporate funding, once accepted, may discourage groups from speaking their minds when budgets are tight. What is more, adds Kirkpatrick Sale, corporate money only buttresses the perception that mainstream groups reflect a largely affluent constituency: There is "a practice in some parts of the movement of working with and accepting money from corporate America that seems to compromise its loftier ideals, whether or not this is compensated for by 'pragmatic' working arrangements or increased research and lobbying budgets."[55]

Those perceptions, which are the heart of a real controversy within the environmental community, explain why many groups, even those that could reap significant monies from relationships with major corporations, avoid doing so. After all, a group's reputation is critical. As Cigler and Nownes point out,

> group entrepreneurs are interested in more than simply money. It would be easy, for example, for environmental groups like the Sierra Club, Greenpeace, or Audubon to garner millions in patron support—if they chose to abandon their agendas, cede power to corporate patrons, or back off their policy demands. We believe that group scholars have paid too little attention to entrepreneurial considerations other than

group survival. There is a reason why Greenpeace accepts no corporate contributions, and there are reasons why many groups do not take money from liquor and/or tobacco companies—because this money does not serve non-monetary goals.[56]

In this sense, at least, the cynics are wrong.

Other Revenue Sources

What is a group to do if it will take no corporate money but sees diminishing returns from direct mail? One answer seems to lie in selling things. One of the more intriguing trends in recent years, one that provides incidental evidence of the mass popularity of environmental causes, is the emergence of a virtual industry in environmental goods and services. Groups like the National Audubon Society and Sierra Club always sold books, but in recent years environmental groups have seized the opportunity to trade on their healthy public images with all the fervor of free-marketeers. In the process they have generated increasing and proportionately more important revenues. The reasons are simple: selling calendars, gift books, coffee mugs, "ecotour" packages, and magazines generates money from members without really asking for yet another direct contribution; in fact it is a good way to keep membership dues at a minimum. Selling or licensing goods for sale in retail stores (such as the Nature Company) or through upscale catalogs also is a profitable way of getting revenues from nonmembers, including many who would never give directly to an environmental organization. The Wilderness Society, to cite one example, entered into a licensing agreement with Timberland, the hiking-boot maker, to the tune of about $100,000 per year.[57]

Other ventures reflect even more inventiveness or, some might argue, desperation. Most major groups, having learned well from university development offices, encourage long-time members to remember the group in their wills, and some even offer guaranteed income from gifts made earlier. Many groups, particularly the Nature Conservancy, accept gifts of land, some of which is sold. The National Audubon Society for years even derived income from royalties from oil and gas wells on some of its land.[58] Some groups, such as Greenpeace, have backed "affinity" credit cards; they get a small but cumulatively lucrative percentage of the service charge every time the card is used. Others have taken to renting out their membership lists, which can add a few thousand vital dollars to revenues. Indeed, the National Wildlife Federation ran ads in trade publications calling its mailing list "ideal for reaching responsive, upscale individuals with a social conscience," while the Audubon Society trumpeted: "Here's an affluent, upscale audience it will really pay you to reach."[59] Forty groups even joined together in a quasi-United Way association, Earth Share, to allow government and corporate employees to donate more painlessly through payroll deductions. Earth Share generated $8 million for member groups in 1992.[60]

Other schemes capitalize on connections in the entertainment industry, with groups increasingly using free or subsidized air time in movies, on videos, and in popular music to reach prospective members, particularly among the young. The NRDC sponsored a six-minute message at the beginning of the rental version of the film, "A Few Good Men," in which celebrities Whoopi Goldberg, Tom Cruise, Demi Moore, Billy Crystal, and Warren Beatty praise the group and urge viewers to join. The NRDC reported as many as twenty-five calls per day as a result. The group American Rivers has received fifty calls per day since the release of the video version of Robert Redford's film, "A River Runs Through It," which contains a ninety-second spot complete with an 800 number. The Wilderness Society, which ran a public service spot at the end of the same film, reported receiving more than five hundred calls—and two hundred new members.[61] On the musical side, an operation called Concerts for the Environment sponsors an annual Earth Day concert whose proceeds aid FOE and Greenpeace, among others, while the Wilderness Society in 1993 got frequent on-stage plugs from folk/country singer Mary Chapin Carpenter, the latest in a long line of singers to promote environmental causes and organizations.[62]

Among these sources of nondues revenue, no single "profit center" has become as important, or at least as visible, as the magazine. A group's magazine at once allows it to educate the public, recruit members, and, in many cases, sell advertising to businesses eager to reach a generally educated, active, and affluent readership. Given these factors, and the surge in readership of independent environmental magazines (*Garbage, Earth Journal, E: The Environmental Journal*) in the 1990s, it is no surprise that virtually every major group in recent years has redesigned its magazine for a broader readership, moving beyond the members to general sales at bookstores and newsstands. Some of the makeovers have spawned serious controversies, perhaps none more so than the mid-1991 replacement of the entire editorial staff of *Audubon*, long considered the best magazine in the environmental community. The move was part of an effort by president Peter Berle to recast the Society and meet competition from other groups. The campaign included changing the Society's traditional logo and redirecting *Audubon* toward a younger audience.[63] Critics regarded the changes as an effort by National Audubon Society leaders to rein in what had been a rather independent editorial voice, but the spat was the latest chapter in a long debate over the periodical's role in generating membership and advertising dollars. *Audubon* was a major force during the 1980s, notes Frank Graham, Jr., in

> helping to change the nature of the membership; many of the new members lured into joining the Society because of the magazine's ap-

peal were not deep-dyed conservationists. Thus the turnover in membership approached 25 percent a year, a gap in the ranks that had to be constantly plugged by expensive magazine—and membership—promotion campaigns.[64]

The magazine was an expensive proposition in its own right—costing about $2.5 million a year to produce by the mid-1980s—which made its role even more controversial among longtime members. The Society's leadership, however, had long seen *Audubon* as "the 'premium' attracting the large if passive proportion of the membership that gave the active 20 percent or so the heft to impress legislators."[65]

Such tiffs might be little more than inside baseball were it not for concerns that a magazine's role as member recruiter and revenue enhancer might prompt groups to shrink from issues that would turn readers off. Such concerns arose in 1992 when Defenders of Wildlife president Schlickeisen dismissed *Defenders* columnist Michael Frome as part of a restructuring that gave Schlickeisen editorial control. Frome, known for being controversial, charged publicly that earlier columns had been rejected when he had criticized key Republicans or specific congressional staff members, that the group's board put pressure on the editors to avoid controversy, and that "an organization like Defenders evidently prefers the benign, environmentally politically correct approaches associated with biodiversity, Amazon rain forest, whales and wolves ... catchy issues that appeal to public sentiment without offending potential contributors."[66]

It thus comes back to how the need to generate revenues affects group goals, tactics, and values. Foundation money and corporate donations are the trickiest commodities, if only because they present the appearance of undue influence in decision making within environmental groups. The other sources are small potatoes, comparatively, although they make up an increasingly important percentage of revenues that, for some groups, might alleviate pressures to seek corporate funds. The biggest money and the greatest freedom, it seems, still come from large memberships. The long-term prospects for most of these groups are "dependent not on securing a reliable source of patronage, but rather on building a large and reliable membership base which can be tapped for dues and large contributions."[67] All sources of money affect group agendas and tactics, but revenues derived from thousands of small donors may be the least troublesome money of all.

Conclusions: Prospects for the 1990s

A major theme in the literature on membership groups, Betty Zisk writes, is the tension between "risk taking on behalf of group goals and the caution implicit in maintaining a staff and retaining the support of group members." [68] The push to professionalize and to maintain an organization for the long haul inevitably dulls the sharp edge of militancy. "Increased professionalization," note Mitchell and his collaborators, "also carries with it the dangers of routinization in advocacy, careerism on the part of staff members, and passivity on the part of volunteers, all of which have been detected in the national organizations." [69] Even so, the point of this chapter is not that the major environmental groups have lost their souls in the search for Mammon any more than has any other public interest group, liberal or conservative. If they have sold out, so has everyone else. Whether they have done so depends on the commentator, and one suspects that older and unrepentant activists such as David Brower or Barry Commoner have come to far different conclusions than might contemporary group leaders such as Jay Hair or Carl Pope. The disenchanted and the dissidents will or already have voted with their feet and joined up with more "virtuous" groups—just as Brower did when he left the Sierra Club to form FOE. But, of course, FOE itself eventually "lost its way" in its need to survive.

The larger point here is that all public interest groups will make their respective Faustian bargains if they want to survive and remain as strong counterweights to narrower economic interests whose power is buttressed by the very structure of the American system of governance. [70] Environmental groups, despite everything scholars have written about the disincentives for group mobilization and maintenance, have in fact continued to thrive. The pains described here are the pains of a maturing interest-advocacy sector, one no longer driven by youthful volunteers but inevitably always dependent on the good will of hundreds of thousands of small donors to carry on the fight. That so many of these groups have survived the turbulence of the past two decades is testimony to their capacity to adapt to changing circumstances and challenges.

Undeniably success has come at a price, as most of the mainstream groups quietly or openly have made the commitment to work within the existing political system, to remain a "reformist citizens' lobby, pressured on the fringes by more radical groups but for the most part willing to work within the system and reap the victories, and rewards, therein." [71] Such is "the inherently conservatizing pressure to play by the 'rules of the game' in the compromise world of Washington, D.C." [72] Critics argue that the reformist groups have been coopted by the system, that they traded their souls for organizational power and clout. Yet one wonders whether they had much choice. What happened to the mainstream environmental community always happens to organizations at the vanguard of reasonably successful social movements: their activists become part of the establishment, no longer outsiders but "respectable" representatives of legitimate views. The alternative is to remain permanent outsiders, but American history suggests that no movement has succeeded by remaining entirely out of the mainstream.

For the major national environmental organizations the future lies in expanding memberships while coping with the problems that come with mass-membership environmentalism. The alternatives, for an advocacy community that often alienates powerful interests, are far more problematic. The challenge for membership groups in the 1990s thus will be how to mobilize people to join up and give when the Clinton administration appears sympathetic to their views—even if it is not so "green" as activists might like. Group leaders also must worry about the profile of their members and contributors. The traditional activists may be aging and checkbook members may be harder than ever to motivate to give. Who is going to replace and augment them? "For social and political movements to remain dynamic," Donald Snow argues, "the organizations that comprise them must strive to maintain the spirit and vigor of volunteerism even as they become increasingly professional in their management."[73] The mainstream groups have become, partly by design and partly by the need to fight against often hostile governmental and industry forces, large and technocratic lobbies, in many ways little different from any other major lobby. If members are seen largely as resources to be mined and flaunted, how deep will their commitment be? How does the need to expand membership scope and size affect leadership strategies? Some of the answers are suggested in the analysis offered here, and they present real organizational worries.

As Carl Pope of the Sierra Club notes, the top challenge to the environmental movement in the 1990s is "to speed up the pace of change.... With a new and sympathetic administration, we have the chance to move faster, but we also have the danger that the sense of urgency may fade."[74] Without that sense of urgency memberships may languish, and some groups may find themselves in dire fiscal and organizational trouble. There may yet erupt a spate of cannibalization that will pit groups against one another for members and resources. In the 1980s, "almost every group faced a logical competitor trying to occupy the same market niche and competing for visibility, leadership, membership, and funds," argues McCloskey:

> NRDC competes in this way with the Environmental Defense Fund, the Nature Conservancy with the Trust for Public Lands, the Wilderness Society with the Sierra Club and the National Parks and Conservation Association, Friends of the Earth with Environmental Action, Defenders of Wildlife with the Humane Society of the United States, and the National Wildlife Federation with the National Audubon Society and perhaps increasingly with the World Wildlife Fund.[75]

Mergers may accelerate, creating by decade's end a few mega-organizations each occupying a distinct niche of environmental advocacy. While competition thus far may not have undermined cooperation, one wonders how many different groups the environmental advocacy market can bear.

For all these problems, the environmental mainstream is not static. The National Wildlife Federation of today is not what it was in the 1960s, in large part because the mainstream constantly is being nudged along by new and more radical groups that strike a chord with large chunks of the mass public. If the National Audubon Society once was nudged toward a more broadly palatable version of radicalism by newcomers like Friends of the Earth, and if Friends of the Earth found itself nudged by Greenpeace, Greenpeace by the Sea Shepherds, and so on, then the environmental mainstream has been in constant change as it kept pace with its own members and with those new to the environmental cause. In many ways the center of the environmental mainstream is closer to the radical groups than has been true for a long time, and the constant need to connect with the membership may be the reason. Maybe being bigger is not such a bad idea.

Notes

1. Jay Letto, "One Hundred Years of Compromise," *Buzzworm* 4 (March/April 1992): 28.
2. Donald Snow, *Inside the Environmental Movement: Meeting the Leadership Challenge* (Washington, D.C.: Island Press, 1992), 9.
3. See Christopher Bosso, "Adaptation and Change in the Environmental Movement," in *Interest Group Politics*, 3d ed., ed. Allan J. Cigler and Burdett A. Loomis (Washington, D.C.: CQ Press, 1991), 152-176, and "After the Movement: Environmental Activism in the 1990s," in *Environmental Policy in the 1990s*, 2d ed., ed. Norman J. Vig and Michael E. Kraft (Washington, D.C.: CQ Press, 1993), 31-50.
4. Keith Schneider, "Environmental Groups are Split on Support for Free-Trade Pact," *New York Times*, September 16, 1993; Linda Kanamine, "NAFTA Disturbs Peace in 'Green' Movement," *USA Today*, September 17, 1993, 4A; Michelle Ruess and Tom Diemer, "Environmentalists Split on Trade Policy," *Cleveland Plain Dealer*, July 18, 1993, 4A.
5. John Lancaster, "War and Recession Taking Toll on National Environmental Organizations," *Washington Post*, February 15, 1991, A3; Stephen G. Greene, "Growth Slows for Many Environmental Groups," *Chronicle of Philanthropy* 3 (November 5, 1991): 23-25.
6. Wilderness Society, "Annual Report," *Wilderness* 55 (Spring 1992): 34.
7. Tom Spears, "Other Greens Defend Spending in Wake of Greenpeace Debate," *Ottawa Citizen*, June 10, 1993, A4.
8. On the history of American environmentalism, see Samuel P. Hays, *Conservation and the Gospel of Efficiency* (Cambridge: Harvard University Press, 1958) and *Beauty, Health and Permanence: Environmental Politics in the United States, 1955-1985* (New York: Oxford University Press, 1987); Stephen Fox, *John Muir and His Legacy: The American Conservation Movement* (Boston: Little, Brown, 1981); Robert Paehlke, *Environmentalism and the Future of Progressive Politics* (New Haven: Yale University Press, 1990).
9. On how tax laws affected issue advocacy see, for example, Christopher J. Bosso, *Pesticides and Politics: The Life Cycle of a Public Issue* (Pittsburgh: University of Pittsburgh Press, 1987); and Frank Graham, Jr., *The Audubon Ark: A History of the National Audubon Society* (New York: Knopf, 1990).

10. "Here's What Association Chiefs Are Being Paid," *National Journal*, January 23, 1993, 179.

11. To offer a more recent example, the Rainforest Action Network was founded in 1985 and survived during its early years on foundation support. By 1990, however, RAN was getting over 70 percent of its revenue from member contributions. See *Public Interest Profiles, 1988-1989*, and *1992-1993* (Washington, D.C.: Foundation for Public Affairs, CQ Press, 1988; 1992).

12. See Margaret Kriz, "Shades of Green," *National Journal*, July 28, 1990, 1827; Michael McCloskey, "Twenty Years of Change in the Environmental Movement: An Insider's View," in *American Environmentalism: The U.S. Environmental Movement, 1970-1990*, ed. Riley E. Dunlap and Angela G. Mertig (Philadelphia: Taylor and Francis, 1993), 77-88; Philip Shabecoff, *A Fierce Green Fire: The American Environmental Movement* (New York: Hill and Wang, 1993).

13. Carl Pope, "Want to Climb a Mountain?" (interview), *Sierra* 78, 2 (March/April 1993): 23.

14. See, among others, Robert C. Mitchell, Angela G. Mertig, and Riley E. Dunlap, "Twenty Years of Environmental Mobilization: Trends Among National Environmental Organizations," in *American Environmentalism*, ed. Dunlap and Mertig, 11-26; Cass Peterson, "An Alliance in the War for the World," *Washington Post*, February 10, 1990, 11; Jamie Heard, "Friends of the Earth Give Environmental Interests an Activist Voice," *National Journal*, August 8, 1970, 1711-1718; Shabecoff, *Fierce Green Fire*.

15. See Hays, *Beauty, Health and Permanence* and Robert C. Mitchell, "From Conservation to Environmental Movement: The Development of the Modern Environmental Lobbies," in *Government and Environmental Politics: Essays on Historical Developments Since World War Two*, ed. Michael J. Lacey (Baltimore: Johns Hopkins University Press, 1991), 81-114. See also Barry Commoner, "The Failure of the Environmental Movement," *Current History* 91, 564 (April 1992): 176-181.

16. Tom Horton, "The Green Giant," *Rolling Stone*, September 5, 1991, 44. See also Christopher Manes, *Green Rage: Radical Environmentalism and the Unmaking of Civilization* (Boston: Little, Brown, 1990).

17. "Giving Back," *Changing Times*, November 1990, 107.

18. Horton, "The Green Giant," 48.

19. Eliza Carney and W. John Moore, "From the K Street Corridor," *National Journal*, January 4, 1992, 30.

20. "Greenpeace: Decreased Donations Force Budget Reductions," Greenwire, American Political Network, July 23, 1992.

21. Kirkpatrick Sale, "The U.S. Green Movement Today," *The Nation*, July 19, 1993, 94.

22. Graham, *Audubon Ark*, 311.

23. Pope, "Want to Climb a Mountain?" 23.

24. Mitchell et al., "Twenty Years of Environmental Mobilization," 16.

25. On direct mail, see Kenneth R. Godwin, *One Billion Dollars of Influence* (Chatham, N.J.: Chatham House, 1988).

26. John B. Judis, "The Pressure Elite: Inside the Narrow World of Advocacy Group Politics," *The American Prospect* (Spring 1992), 25.

27. Letto, "One Hundred Years of Compromise," 28.

28. Mitchell et al., "Twenty Years of Environmental Mobilization," 23. On this notion of "checkbook participation" see Michael T. Hayes, "The New Group Universe," in *Interest Group Politics*, 2d ed., ed. Allan J. Cigler and Burdett A. Loomis (Washington, D.C.: CQ Press, 1986), 133-145.

29. On criticism of Greenpeace's use of the dolphin controversy in its fund raising, see Horton, "The Green Giant," 108. See also Clark Norton, "Green Giant," *Washing-*

ton Post Magazine, September 3, 1989, 25-39, and Leslie Spencer, "The Not So Peaceful World of Greenpeace," *Forbes*, November 11, 1991, 174-180.

30. Tim Brown, "Greens Seeking a New Archenemy," *Washington Times*, September 10, 1993, F4.

31. Judis, "The Pressure Elite," 27.

32. Philip A. Mundo, *Interest Groups: Cases and Characteristics* (Chicago: Nelson-Hall, 1990), 178.

33. On the leadership changes in the 1980s, see Rochelle Stanfield, "Environmental Lobby's Changing of the Guard Is Part of Movement's Transition," *National Journal*, June 8, 1985, 1350-1353.

34. *Public Interest Profiles, 1992-1993*, 462.

35. Defenders of Wildlife, "Annual Report," *Defenders* (Summer 1993), 31.

36. Mitchell et al., "Twenty Years of Environmental Mobilization," 22.

37. McCloskey, "Twenty Years of Change," 84.

38. James R. Rosenfield, "In the Mail," *Direct Marketing* 54 (September 1991): 19-21.

39. *Chronicle of Philanthropy*, February 11, 1992, 28.

40. Greene, "Growth Slows for Many Environmental Groups," 23.

41. Mitchell et al., "Twenty Years of Environmental Mobilization," 16.

42. Judis, "The Pressure Elite," 18.

43. Allan J. Cigler and Anthony J. Nownes, "Patrons and Influence: The Impact of Patrons on the Agendas and Activities of Public Interest Groups" (Paper presented at the annual meeting of the Midwest Political Science Association, April 14-17, 1993, Chicago, Illinois), 19.

44. Judis, "The Pressure Elite," 22.

45. "Annual Report," *Nature Conservancy* 43, 1 (January/February 1992), 33.

46. Greene, "Growth Slows for Many Environmental Groups," 25.

47. Judis, "The Pressure Elite," 23.

48. Quoted in Judis, 22.

49. Stephen G. Greene, "Waste-Disposal Company Rejoins Environmental Grantmakers Group," *Chronicle of Philanthropy*, October 8, 1991, 17.

50. Kriz, "Shades of Green," 1827.

51. Keith Schneider, "Natural Foes Bankroll Environmental Group," *New York Times*, December 23, 1991, A12.

52. Jane Hall, "Audubon Specials Are Endangered Species," *Los Angeles Times*, December 17, 1991, F1.

53. Schneider, "Natural Foes Bankroll Environmental Group," A12.

54. Cigler and Nownes, "Patrons and Influence," 24.

55. Sale, "The U.S. Green Movement Today," 93.

56. Cigler and Nownes, "Patrons and Influence," 24.

57. Schneider, "Natural Foes Bankroll Environmental Group," A12.

58. Graham, *The Audubon Ark*.

59. Rosenfield, "In the Mail," 19.

60. Robert Mamis, "Green Giving," *Inc.*, May 1993, 45.

61. "Fund Raising: Hollywood Is Boffo Biz for Enviros," Greenwire, American Political Network, August 26, 1993.

62. Margaret Kriz, "Signing up Stars to Save the Environment," *National Journal*, July 24, 1993, 1876.

63. Anne Raver, "Old Environmental Group Seeks Tough New Image," *New York Times*, June 9, 1991, A1; Roxanne Roberts, "Audubon Fires Editors," *Washington Post*, July 30, 1991, C5. For a review of various environmental magazines, see Paul McClennan, "Magazines That Can Help You Stay in Touch," *Buffalo News*, August 1, 1993, 12.

64. Graham, *Audubon Ark*, 280.

65. Ibid., 291.

66. Michael Frome, "In Defense of Wildlife and Open Expression," *Wild Earth* 3, 1 (Spring 1993): 60-61.
67. Cigler and Nownes, "Patrons and Influence," 25.
68. Betty H. Zisk, *The Politics of Transformation: Local Activism in the Peace and Environmental Movements* (Westport, Conn.: Praeger, 1992), 39.
69. Mitchell et al., "Twenty Years of Environmental Mobilization," 23.
70. See Bosso, *Pesticides and Politics*. See also E. E. Schattschneider, *The Semi-Sovereign People* (Hinsdale, Ill.: Dryden Press, 1960).
71. Sale, "The U.S. Green Movement Today," 9.
72. Mitchell et al., "Twenty Years of Environmental Mobilization," 24.
73. Snow, *Inside the Environmental Movement*, 6.
74. Pope, "Want to Climb a Mountain?" 21.
75. McCloskey, "Twenty Years of Change," 85.

6

Not Just Another Special Interest: Intergovernmental Representation

Beverly A. Cigler

Boundaries between various levels of governmental authority have never been fixed in the United States, and our federal structure has been in a constant state of flux since the nation's founding. Beginning with the New Deal, there has been unmistakable growth in the power of the federal government in intergovernmental relations, growth that has accelerated since the 1960s. State and local governments have come to understand that they must be represented in Washington if they are to take advantage of political opportunities and protect their interests in an increasingly complex policy-making environment.

In this chapter Beverly Cigler examines organized intergovernmental interests in their broad political context. The picture that emerges is one of a growing number of organized interests, many of which compete for members, funding, and policy access. Particularly noteworthy is the growth of "single jurisdictional representation," including individual states, cities, counties, and other governmental units (such as special districts) with a Washington presence. One consequence of such proliferation has been that group and sector cohesion have suffered, posing problems in achieving policy access and influence. In Cigler's view, sector members, in an era of "fend for yourself" federalism, must find new ways to work with each other—blending policy and management concerns and generalist and specialist perspectives—if they want to play a proactive rather than reactive role in Washington decision making.

Governments that lobby other governments are often overlooked when interest groups are studied. States and local governments perform a great deal of lobbying in the American political system, however. The best known organizations are membership-based national associations that represent state and local government "generalists" such as governors, mayors, and legislators.[1]

The so-called intergovernmental lobby does much more than lobby. Its constituent groups monitor and report on governmental actions in the legislative and executive branches, develop and analyze policies, communicate with policy makers, and mobilize political support. Robert Salisbury would describe them as "service organizations" engaged in "interest representation."[2] Other state and local groups do not lobby at all. They are information collectors (but rarely researchers), information disseminators, morale boosters for public service, providers of member services, and facilitators of collaborative linkages among governments and many types of organizations.

An "interest group sector" is a set of organized groups that share broadly similar policy concerns, such as labor, business, or ideologically oriented groups. So-called public interest groups operate in sectors such as civil rights, child welfare, consumer, animal rights, and consumer protection.[3] Intergovernmental associations often label themselves public interest groups because they pursue benefits not limited to their members. Government policy makers sometimes use the acronym "PIGs" to describe the Washington-based intergovernmental organizations that lobby for more federal funds for their communities. Most political scientists embrace the PIGs characterization; they argue that the intergovernmental groups operate in a closed, cozy subsystem or as part of an "iron triangle" in which they and various congressional committees and administrative agencies work out policies of mutual benefit.[4]

More Than Special Interests

Are state and local governments and officials special interests? They are not united in terms of goals or ideology, and they compete with each other and other organized interests for programs and money. They employ lobbying tactics that mirror those of other organized interests, and their actions affect the other groups. The agenda of urban intergovernmental groups often dovetails with the positions set forth by members of the so-called Democratic coalition. All this creates the image of special interest.

Intergovernmental groups often complain that they are treated as "just another special interest," wishing instead to be seen as "intergovernmental partners" with the national government.[5] Public officials join the organizations not only to advance policy positions, but also to promote core political-system values: responsiveness, representativeness, accountability, equity, efficiency, and effectiveness. Their organizations work toward improved intergovernmental partnerships, such as the provision of a sound, balanced, and coordinated national transportation system or manageable environmental and natural resources policies.

The generalist officials' associations pioneered the bipartisan advocacy and reformist ideas essential for collaborative national-state-local activities that contribute to national objectives. On the other hand, those same officials must face the voters and media in their respective jurisdictions. Thus, they seek political flexibility to manage the intergovernmental system for the benefit of their constituents.[6]

Much of the work of making and implementing public policy is inter-governmental.[7] The state and local officials elected to do the business of government enhance their work through their participation in associations of generalists and specialists in state and local government. Although such associations strive to effect policy change, they are strongly oriented toward providing membership services and professionalizing government. Thus they are neither purely special-interest organizations nor purely public-interest organizations.

Political Context and Sector Framework

Social scientists often focus on issue networks to examine the array of actors operating within a policy domain. Such analyses often neglect the broader political context in which networks exist, including how various groups work in harmony or in conflict.[8] This chapter examines the sector comprised of organized intergovernmental interests within the broader political context in which they operate. The focus is on the structural and strategic factors that facilitate or hamper group emergence, development, and decline as these affect the sector's overall roles and performance.

The chapter (1) reviews the emergence and development of Washington-based state and local government interest representation; (2) examines group and sector resources; (3) highlights tactics used to achieve policy and service goals; and (4) summarizes trends affecting the sector.

Emergence and Development of State and Local Representation

Products of the Times

There is a direct linkage between the growth of government and the proliferation of intergovernmental groups. Organized groups of government generalists are a twentieth-century phenomenon. New organizations formed with increasing frequency during the New Deal era in the 1930s and again in the 1960s and early 1970s as programs requiring cooperation among the national, state, and local governments were created to combat an array of public problems.[9]

Beginning with the New Deal, state and local governments grew in their responsibilities, personnel, and budgets, sparking a demand for Washington representation. A special window of opportunity for growth occurred after the mid-1960s when new federal programs established direct links with cities. Urban programs grew rapidly in number and costs, fueled by growing national affluence, heightened concern with social issues, and a Democratic president with an ambitious domestic agenda. By the 1970s, the Washington presence of associations of state and local officials was well established.[10]

Table 6-1   Types of State and Local Interest Representation

The "Big Seven"

Public interest organizations

The intergovernmental information infrastructure

Specialist associations

New and resurgent generalist associations

Single jurisdictional representation

Because cities came to be associated with racial unrest following the urban riots of the late 1960s, public attitudes toward redistributive programs changed quickly, as did congressional and media interest. The state and local associations that had grown up with the federal urban programs were unable to mount a serious defense of programs, and the cities and their associations experienced budget problems during the Reagan years. After 1978, the steady transfer to state and local governments of administrative and fiscal responsibilities for what had begun as federal programs provoked discord within the intergovernmental sector. In the 1990s, local officials have demanded that their national associations deal with state and local issues.[11]

A contemporary examination of state and local interest representation cannot be limited to the handful of organized groups of state and local generalists. The six types of interest representation that comprise the sector are depicted in Table 6-1.

The "Big Seven"

Historically, a small group of well-established associations has dominated the intergovernmental sector. Of the "Big Seven" organizations, five are Washington lobbies for generalist officials. The National League of Cities (NLC), United States Conference of Mayors (USCM), National Association of Counties (NACo), National Governors' Association (NGA), and Council of State Governments (CSG) are known collectively as SLIGs—state and local interest groups. Subsequently the SLIGs were supplemented by two new organizations, the National Conference of State Legislators (NCSL) and the International City Management Association (ICMA), which later added the word "County" to its title. Collectively, all of these are called the "Big Seven." Most academic research on state and local government representation focuses narrowly on these groups.[12] Table 6-2 provides essential information about the "Big Seven."

Table 6-2   The "Big Seven" Intergovernmental Associations

Association (current title)	Date founded	Membership
National Governors' Association (NGA)	1908	Incumbent governors
Council of State Governments (CSG)	1933	Direct membership by states and territories; serves all branches of government; has dozens of affiliate organizations of specialists
National Conference of State Legislatures (NCSL)	1948	State legislators and staff
National League of Cities (NLC)	1924	Direct, by cities and state leagues of cities
National Association of Counties (NACo)	1935	Direct by counties; loosely linked state associations; affiliate membership for county professional specialists
United States Conference of Mayors (USCM)	1933	Direct membership by cities with population over 30,000
International City/County Management Association (ICMA)	1914	Direct membership by appointed city and county managers, and other professionals

Originally called the National Governors Conference, the National Governors' Association was formed during President Theodore Roosevelt's presidency; it is the oldest and most prestigious of the "Big Seven." The NGA meets twice each year and otherwise operates primarily through standing committees and staff activities. Policy positions require the support of three-quarters of the governors present and voting, so a majority vote is difficult to obtain. Governors of large states generally do not play active roles in the NGA.

In 1967, the NGA split from the Council of State Governments (CSG) to become a separate organization. It moved to Washington to focus on building efforts to boost the states' image in American policy making, to showcase the fifty governors, and to promote national policy debates on critical issues. In 1976, NGA moved to a building called the Hall of the States where it remains the most prominent resident.

CSG is an umbrella association that generates information and provides assistance, primarily for legislators in the fifty states; it also serves as the secretariat for many affiliate organizations of state specialists such as the National Association of State Personnel Executives and the National Association of State Treasurers. The association is headquartered in Lexington, Kentucky, although it has a Washington office. The CSG, along with the International City/County Management Association (ICMA), is not a lobbying group, which sets it, and ICMA, apart from the rest of the "Big Seven."

The National Council of State Legislatures (NCSL) provides legislative services to all 50 state legislatures and their staffs, and to commonwealths such as Puerto Rico. Policy positions are taken by a State/Federal Assembly which meets three times a year, with members appointed for two-year terms by the presiding officers of each state's two houses. Policy positions require a three-quarters majority vote of the states, not individual members.

From its main headquarters in Denver, the NCSL staffs the association's committees and conferences. It also provides direct services to member state legislatures and publishes a monthly magazine, *State Legislatures*. Much of the work of its smaller Washington office involves monitoring and publishing information about federal legislation and mandates.

In 1976, NCSL and CSG moved their Washington offices into the Hall of the States, joining the NGA. The move helped facilitate working relationships among the state associations. By the late 1980s, approximately fifty state-oriented organizations, including specialist affiliates of CSG and various single-state offices, had also relocated to the building.

Three local government generalist organizations within the Big Seven have sometimes been called the "urban lobby." The U.S. Conference of Mayors represents the larger cities, the National League of Cities represents medium and small cities, and The National Association of Counties represents rural, suburban, and urban counties.

The remaining generalist group, ICMA, was founded as the International City Managers Association. It represents a large segment of the nation's appointed local chief executives—city and county managers—as well as other local professionals.[13] The word "County" was only recently added to the ICMA title, making it the International City/County Management Association. This is a reflection of the growing influence of counties in the American political system. The ICMA is less active nationally than the other Big Seven groups and tends to focus on technical issues and services. Its publishing program is extensive, and its books are considered "must" reading by local professionals.

CSG and ICMA do not lobby, but they contribute to the overall functioning of the sector in very important ways. They link other organizations together by providing information and other services. They help, in addition, to weaken perceptions that the generalist officials are "just another special interest."

The Big Seven groups often compete with each other, and with other sector members, for resources, including members, government and foundation funding, and policy access. The proliferation of federal grants in the Great Society period of the 1960s fueled that competition. Conflict occurred at many junctures: disagreements between state and local organizations, between generalist and specialist officials, urban and rural officials, large and small governmental jurisdictions, and counties and cities.

Cooperation among the Big Seven splintered further during the Reagan years. The *National Journal, Congressional Quarterly*[14] and political scientists[15] documented their troubled times during President Reagan's first term, although the groups squabbled with each other even before the Reagan presidency. The states accused the local associations of supporting the successful elimination of general revenue sharing funds for states. Federal aid cutbacks and program terminations, such as the elimination of all general revenue sharing and Urban Development Action Grants, were other significant setbacks. The federal government severed direct ties with local governments as federal funds came to be passed through the states.

In the midst of these momentous changes, the government groups complained of being treated as "just another special interest." In the Reagan White House, the cuts in domestic programs were seen as a way to "defund the Left" and reduce subsidies for selfish "special interest groups." Shared goals among the Big Seven and with other sector members were weakened.[16]

The external political environment posed major resource problems for the operations of the "Big Seven" in the Reagan years. Between 1980 and 1990, USCM lost 48.7 percent of its federal funding; NACo lost 67.5 percent; and NLC lost 97.9 percent. ICMA, the nonlobby, lost 74.7 percent of its federal funding.[17] Journalist Jonathan Walters reported that, in the early 1980s, NACo's Washington staff was reduced from 140 to 60; NLC was cut back from about 120 to 65; and the USCM was reduced from 120 to 75. The funding losses caused changes in Washington office operations. Staff resources were shifted from traditional service activities toward raising dues and fees, conducting membership drives, initiating business ventures, and hiring fund raisers. Lobbying operations were relatively insulated from the cutbacks.[18]

Diminished technical service capabilities (for example, tracking state mandates and legislation, computer networking) came to haunt the local government organizations in the early 1990s, as program and fiscal responsibilities continue to shift downward in the federal system. Members of some local associations have criticized their groups for being ill-equipped to deal with the increased importance of the states and of state-local relations.[19]

The state associations provide a wide array of state level services to their members. Because local governments are "creatures of the states," the states and their associations have advantages in dealing with emerging state-local issues. NCSL, for example, has been proactive in efforts to keep state legislatures informed of important state-local issues.

Generalist and Specialist Influence

The views of state and local generalists (governors, mayors, county commissioners, legislators) continue to be important to congressional policy making. Because Congress is specialized in terms of functional policy areas, however, with program and functional specialists providing highly detailed information on Capitol Hill and in executive branch agencies, the specialist associations of state and local officials have relatively easier access in policy-making arenas.[20]

The generalist perspective adds a spatial or "areal" dimension to the national decision-making process. The importance of this dimension was demonstrated recently—in the shaping of welfare reform legislation in 1988 and in strides toward Medicaid reform.[21]

Public Interest Organizations

A second group category important to state and local interest representation in Washington is comprised of some of the more than 2,500 U.S. public interest groups, especially those associated with urban and environmental issues. They compete or cooperate with the major intergovernmental groups, depending on the policy area. The competition is due to ideological and goal differences, as well as the continual quest for federal and foundation support. Unlike the Washington-based generalist officials' associations, many of these groups focus their advocacy on state governments, and even some local governments.

Rates of group formation in the anti-poverty, child welfare, and civil rights sectors declined early in the Reagan Administration. Later in the 1980s, however, there was a resurgence of such groups in reaction to Reagan's perceived hostility. Overall, group formation expanded rapidly from the 1960s; by the mid-1980s public interest groups accounted for 20 percent of the groups active in Washington.[22] This confirms the importance of political context and helps explain patterns of conflict and cooperation among and between sectors.

The Intergovernmental Information Infrastructure

A third category of interest representation within the intergovernmental sector consists of the array of national- and state-level legislative and executive units that facilitate the overall understanding of intergovernmental issues. The national government's institutional capacity for analyzing intergovernmental issues rose in the early 1950s but began to decline again in the 1980s.[23] Beginning in 1953, several institutions were established to analyze and, in some cases, coordinate and manage intergovernmental issues. Key among these were the U.S. Advisory Commission on Intergovernmental Relations (ACIR); intergovernmental divisions in the General Accounting Office (GAO) and in the Office of Management and Budget (OMB); and several congressional subcommittees.

These organizations flourished from the mid-1960s to the mid-1980s. Their analytic capabilities dovetailed with the objectives and tasks of the intergovernmental groups, helping the Big Seven and other organizations to develop and mature. ACIR provides a forum in which officials at all levels may consider common problems and recommend improvements in grant administration and coordination, among other issues. ACIR provides technical advice to Congress and the president on proposed legislation, studies emerging intergovernmental problems, and recommends ways to make the overall policy system function more smoothly.

Through exposure to high-quality information, policy makers at all governmental levels become better informed about intergovernmental issues. The fact that the analytical organizations are governmental units themselves may help defuse the notion of state and local government groups as "just another special interest."

Since 1985, all of the national analytic organizations (ACIR, GAO, OMB, and the intergovernmental congressional committees) have experienced reductions in capacity and, in some cases, their mission has been reoriented or they have been terminated. This has had a major impact on the understanding of intergovernmental issues throughout the American political system. OMB's intergovernmental unit was disbanded by President Reagan, and GAO's and ACIR's capabilities have been diminished through major budget cuts. The House and Senate both demoted the status of intergovernmental concerns, most visibly by reorganizing subcommittees, failing to hire staffers with intergovernmental expertise, and devoting less time to coordinating activities with intergovernmental units.[24] The information infrastructure's decline lessened the analytical abilities and access of the Big Seven and other organizations to executive branch agencies.

The Clinton presidency began with little attention to intergovernmental issues. The ACIR narrowly escaped elimination and suffered major budget cuts. By 1994, there was a rekindling of commitment to ACIR; key appointments were filled and President Clinton was visibly active in the effort. Half of the states have their own versions of advisory commission on intergovernmental relations and other intergovernmental units.

Specialist Associations

Specialist associations represent nearly every identifiable administrative specialty. These were created in response to expanding political opportunities within the intergovernmental sector, such as changes in the U.S. policy-making and service-delivery systems. These specialist organizations share much with the generalist groups, primarily a broad sense of the public interest. Their members are the professionals who staff government bureaucracies at all levels—for example, the finance officers; planners; and human resource, transportation, and housing specialists. During the heyday of the state and local lobbying in the 1960s, the loosely linked specialist associations were dubbed the "Dirty Dozen"; they often clashed with the PIGs.

As early as 1974, Donald Haider observed that the state and local generalist officials faced the rising influence of "functional specialists" across all levels of government. Later writers, however, underrated the importance of the specialist associations, especially in explaining the "decline" of the Big Seven generalist associations during the Reagan years.

Specialists face fewer obstacles to organizing than do generalists. Agency funds, along with individual memberships, help support their associations, which provide a wide variety of professional functions for members besides lobbying.[25] The specialist associations fit well within the functional policy networks at the national level, sharing knowledge and interest with similar professionals at all governmental levels, as well as with nonprofit public interest groups that specialize in particular policy areas. The specialist associations work through vertical and horizontal ties within the political system, including those with private professional organizations. Because so much of their work is concentrated in large and medium-sized cities, they come in frequent contact with the generalist organizations. Some of these associations are affiliates under the Big Seven umbrella.

A classic example of the clash of generalist and specialist perspectives was provided by the debate over general revenue sharing in the early 1970s. Generalist elected officials strongly supported unfettered funds that would be directly under their control; specialists feared the use of funds by governors, mayors, and county commissioners, desiring, instead, that federal dollars be channeled through the intergovernmental bureaucracies they staffed.

New and Resurgent Generalist Associations

Several new generalist organizations were formed in the 1980s and 1990s as some of the established groups experienced a resurgence. Some of the generalist groups think the Big Seven terminology is outdated and urge that the club be expanded to the "Big Eight" or "Big Nine."

The National Association of Towns and Townships (NATaT) is a case in point. This powerful Washington voice represents the views of the tens of thousands of small local jurisdictions in the political system. The impetus for its creation was the perception by many small governments that the NLC and other organizations did not represent their interests well. Created in the 1960s, NATaT achieved some favor during the Reagan administration as a relatively conservative group. Since then, strong membership services and ties to township associations within several states have helped NATaT achieve a number of policy successes. NATaT plays an important role in explaining the special financial and managerial problems confronting small and rural governments in the political system. Such information provided to policy makers throughout the political system replaces some of the information losses that occurred with cutbacks at ACIR and in other research units.

Another emergent organization is the National Association of Regional Councils (NARC). The geographical organization of metropolitan areas does not match the nature of policy problems, which spill over jurisdictional boundaries. Regional organizations, it can be argued, are better equipped to deal with functional policy concerns than are the generalist associations that represent officials from political jurisdictions. NARC recently made the decision to publish a journal and hold an annual conference on regionalism.

The National Civic League, founded in 1894 as part of the "good government" reform movement (and called the National Municipal League), is a good example of a resurgent organization. This nonprofit organization promotes the active involvement of citizens in the governance of their communities. Through conferences, networking, and the *National Civic Review*, the National Civic League has become a leading generalist organization. It provides its dues-paying individual members much of the help in focusing on the state and local levels that elected public official generalists are asking of their national associations.

The National Civic League focuses primarily on making state and local governments more responsive and effective and plays a major leadership role in shaping public dialogue about the future of the federal system. Its directors and activists are a workable blend of public officials from all levels of government and the public, private, and nonprofit sectors, including academics.

An interesting splinter from the "Big Seven" has an explicit ideological focus. In 1983 a group of conservative state legislators, arguing that NCSL had a liberal agenda, worked with several conservative foundations to create the American Legislative Exchange Council (ALEC). ALEC's support is derived from membership dues, foundations, and corporations. About 2,500 state legislators, or approximately 35 percent of the total number in the United States, belong to ALEC. A majority are Republicans, but 40 percent are Democrats. ALEC, with its large membership, hosts four conferences per year, publishes occasional papers, and develops model state legislation.

The ties between ALEC and the Heritage Foundation highlight another trend in state and local interest representation: the emergence of dozens of new think tanks at both the national and state levels. Most of these have explicit ideological concerns and receive funding from like-minded individuals and foundations. Most are conservative.

Single Jurisdictional Representation

Single states, cities, counties, and other governmental units such as special districts that seek Washington representation are also important players in the intergovernmental sector. They can open Washington offices; work with trade or professional associations to pursue interests; establish an intergovernmental liaison office at home; or hire consultants, public relations specialists, lawyers, or lobbyists to pursue specific policies or programs.[26] By 1981, more than a hundred cities had Washington offices. By 1987, two-thirds of U.S. governors had Washington offices; another third of the states had offices connected to other state entities, and only a third had no state lobbying presence. "Going it alone" is often successful.[27]

State governments also have foreign trade offices to represent and promote their economic interests abroad. In 1977, twenty-two states had overseas offices, but by 1990 a total of 163 foreign offices were operated by forty-two American states. Most of these offices are in Japan, which has twice as many as Taiwan, the second most popular location. The economic slowdown of the mid-1970s led business leaders and state officials to seek new foreign markets as a way to supplement waning domestic markets in an interdependent world economy. Another precipitator of state initiatives was the disengagement of federal agencies from foreign trade activities beginning in the 1970s, largely because of the fragmentation of trade responsibilities among agencies.[28]

This review of state and local interest representation has included only the Washington-based organizations. Many parallel associations exist at the state and municipal levels. Examples include statewide associations of municipal and county officials, school boards, tax collectors, sheriffs, and special districts. They lobby state government and provide an array of member services. National associations, meanwhile, are placing greater emphasis on networking with state and local organizations.

Resources

As lobbying organizations, the major state and local groups have less clout than many well-financed private groups. The intergovernmental associations lack resources such as political action committees (PACs) and the opportunity to participate in election campaigns. In varying degrees, however, the intergovernmental associations possess the same types of resources as do other organized interests. These include size, status and prestige, access, organizational structure, leadership skill, organizational cohesion, and intensity.

Size, Prestige, and Access Advantages

The size and prestige of the groups within the sector are impressive. The United States consists of more than 87,000 governments. Only one of those is the national government; the others are state and local governments. Not all governments can afford to be members of the associations that make up the intergovernmental sector, and not all are interested in either the membership services or advocacy provided by the generalists. Still, the NLC has approximately 1,400 member governments, a budget of more than $6.5 million, and a staff of sixty-five. NLC has a large and diverse membership base because cities of any size can join if they are members of their state league of cities or municipalities.

The USCM has 600 members, a budget approaching $4 million, and about fifty staffers. Its membership is limited to cities with a population of 30,000 or more. It has been dominated by very large cities. NACo has 2,100 members and a staff of fifty.

The specialist associations represent professionals working at every level and in every type of government. And, as mentioned earlier, the more than 2,500 public interest groups in the United States engage in activities that represent state and local interests across dozens of issues.

Intergovernmental groups enjoy recognition and a measure of legitimacy with the media and others, which enhance their ability to influence policy. National lawmakers view elected generalists in the political system as having a legitimate right to speak on behalf of their constituents.[29] However, "where you stand is where you sit." Members of the Senate and House are not inclined to accept the policy preferences of state and local officials from their home state when those views conflict with their own. Subnational elected officials assume office on partisan ballots, which gives them additional access through their party connections.

Groups within the sector vary significantly in their status and prestige. The National Governors' Association has a great deal of prestige largely because of the importance of the fifty individual governors. Historically, NACo lacked the prestige and access generally afforded to the USCM and the NLC, in part because counties have been slow to modernize and did not emerge as major human-service providers in the political system until recently. Their future looks bright, however, as local problems are increasingly regional in nature.

Cohesion and Intensity

The intergovernmental associations face significant drawbacks in terms of cohesion and intensity. There are many of them and some are internally fragmented. Their perceptions are shaped by the level of government or policy area in which they operate. Sector associations possess uneven resource bases in terms of their membership size and organizational finances. A few examples are in order.

NACo, a generalist organization, is the most visible example of an a group that lacks internal cohesion. The diversity of American counties in terms of political party control, size, population density, degree of shared responsibility with other local governments, degree of autonomy from state governments, regional and geographic variations in economic base, and cultural attitudes makes the national representation of counties very difficult.[30]

Two-thirds of U.S. counties are rural. Because NACo membership is by individual county, rural counties have tended to dominate NACo's policy and member services agendas. This has meant an emphasis on public works, especially highways, and agricultural issues. As counties have evolved into major providers of human services in our governmental system, NACo's membership has diversified. Its agenda now includes such concerns as public health, social welfare, mass transit, solid waste disposal, and county modernization. The expansion of the agenda has increased conflict among diverse counties. As counties take on more of the responsibilities held by municipalities in the political system and receive additional responsibilities and unfunded mandates, sector conflicts over revenues, responsibilities, and powers increase.

Traditional "urban policy" issues such as poverty, racism, redistribution, and spatial targeting are a tough sell in either the national or the state capitals. Urban problems have rarely generated much sustained and focused interest (intensity) among the state and local associations. Short-term surges of narrow interest have been followed by longer-term indifference. From the national government's perspective, however, the decline of large cities is important for its impacts on the national economy. Even the urban unrest characterized by the Los Angeles riots of 1992 did not result in dramatically increased funding. The USCM, especially, continues to have friction with the national government and in garnering a key resource, "intensity" for dealing with urban issues.

The state groups, in general, have been less active in seeking federal funds for their members as have the local groups. The states have been less critical, also, of national funding priorities. Twenty-five percent of total federal grants went to local governments in 1980 and 75 percent to the states; by 1988, the percentages were 15 and 85 percent, respectively. Local groups are more concerned with federal aid disbursement; the state organizations tend to focus on federal deficit reduction. Differences in ideology and goals explain variations in cohesion between the state and local groups, and thus, within the overall sector.

Some state legislative officials argue that NCSL is ineffective in influencing Congress and too liberal in its views. (Policy positions, however, must be approved by three-quarters of the states, voting as states and not as individual members.) As is the case with so many other groups, NCSL is hampered in achieving policy consensus because of the size and diversity of its membership. NCSL's primary role is thus informational, not political.

ALEC is less active in congressional lobbying than NCSL but can bring formidable resources to bear on particular issues, such as the balanced-budget amendment, largely because of its financial resources and the relative ideological unity of its membership.

Since ALEC's creation, no single organization in Washington has represented all state legislators. ALEC is not housed in the Hall of the States; instead, its offices are with the influential conservative think tank, the Heritage Foundation. Such splintering of the Big Seven highlights, once again, the cohesion problems for the sector.

Organizational Structure and Leadership

The structure created by an organization, and its group leadership capabilities, are additional resources to consider in assessing effectiveness. NACo is a case in point. NACo's diversity mirrors that of its affiliate associations, which are national organizations that represent specialist officials such as county attorneys, administrators, fiscal officers, and parks and recreation personnel. The mix of both generalist and specialist officials under the same umbrella can cause internal policy conflict; it can also lead to success in meshing spatial (rural vs. urban, for example) and functional interests. On the other hand, associations that include only generalists or specialists may be hampered because of a failure to blend differing perspectives.

The local associations possess varying abilities to help their members respond to new political realities, often as a result of their organizational structure. The NLC, for example, with its dues-paying state affiliate organizations, has a relatively strong network in place to forge better linkages with state capitals. Cities of any size can join NLC. There are also statewide associations of counties and county officials, which are the primary legislative lobbyists for counties at that level. Unlike the strong relationship between the state leagues of municipalities and the NLC, the statewide associations of counties traditionally have had weak ties to NACo.[31]

Both NLC and NACo were founded in Chicago and moved to Washington as federal linkages to local governments grew. The USCM's only home, on the other hand, has been Washington. It was founded in 1932, with the encouragement of President Franklin D. Roosevelt. The large-city interests that dominate the group have led to a focus on "big city problems," such as crime and drugs, hunger and homelessness, transportation, housing, education, environment, and AIDS. The mayor of the small city of York, Pennsylvania, recently served as the USCM president, however, demonstrating that "big city problems" no longer affect only large jurisdictions. Such developments open a window of opportunity for coalition building for the association. USCM members, however, claim that the USCM leadership is less willing than other local associations to respond to the changing domestic policy system by turning its interests more to the states.

Financial Resources

The financial resources of the various state and local organizations also affect their successes. As explained earlier, the local associations, like local governments, were hit hard during the Reagan years. As a result, their financial problems are greater than those of the state organizations.

In mid-1993, several states revolted against an NGA plan to increase state membership dues. Annual NGA dues range from $128,000 for large states to $16,000 for the least populous. In addition to receiving nearly $4 million from dues each year, the NGA receives about $7 million in grants, corporate donations, and federal aid. As in the 1980s, staff structure has suffered in the 1990s. Dues were frozen for three years and employees did not receive pay increases in 1993. Six of forty-four staff lobbyists were laid off in the early 1990s and revenues dropped 3 percent because of the dues freeze and partial payments by some states.

Some states argue that they do not get enough for their NCSL membership dues. State legislatures are billed according to population, with the larger states paying $150,000 or more. On the other hand, because ALEC members are individuals, not legislatures, that organization can more easily assess member satisfaction.

In June 1994, at least a half-dozen of CSG's 27 member groups of state specialist officials (for example, National Association of State Purchasing Officials, National Association of State Information Resources Executives, and National Conference of State Fleet Administrators) left the organization. Their departure was the culmination of a two-year internal rift over mission, administration, and money. The disgruntled groups felt that CSG was overcharging them for secretariat services. The CSG has now changed its rules for affiliate status. Prospective members must now apply for membership; membership decisions are made by CSG's administrative and elected leadership.

Tactics and Issues

Congressional and Executive Branch Liaison

Tactics used by the intergovernmental sector to influence congressional policy making often resemble the tactics used by private organized interests. The lobbying groups develop information to support their positions, testify at formal hearings, contact legislators and administrators, and cultivate relations with the media. Prominent members often present their organizations' position. Washington staff maintain contact with appropriate policy makers and their staffs.

The relative advantage of the intergovernmental lobbying groups in gaining access to policy makers is not matched by significant ability to actually influence policy decisions. This is due, in large part, to enormous variations in group resources within the sector, which were discussed earlier, especially the lack of cohesion within the sector and the groups that make it up and the relatively low intensity of issue stands.

The intergovernmental issues on which generalist officials have concentrated in recent years are, first, the cost of unfunded federal mandates to states and communities and the preemption by Congress of state laws and regulations—for product liability, credit reporting, interstate branch banking, and telecommunications, among others. Other concerns are federal intrusions on the states' tax base, such as increases in fuel taxes and a possible tobacco tax or other "sin" taxes to fund health care reform; an inflexible grant system; and restrictive regulations and grant conditions designed to coerce state or local action.

State and local interest representation involves far more than dealing with Congress on program adoption and funding issues. The Washington lobbyists also have close ties to the appropriate executive branch agencies and private sector groups who unite around particular causes. When programs cannot be changed, the task is to try to alter the way they are carried out by influencing the development of bureaucratic rules and regulations.

Because the national government still funnels more than $130 billion per year to states and local governments, USCM, NLC, and NACo must remain very active as Washington lobbyists. New and burdensome mandates, which are often unfunded, continue to be imposed upon the states and localities. Meanwhile, major policy victories by the groups, particularly the local groups, have been few in recent years. One exception was the tax reform bill of 1986, which included a provision on the deductibility of state and local income and property taxes. Local groups increasingly operate at the margins of policy. They attempt, independently and in concert, to avoid the elimination of entire programs and protest delays in the implementation of federal environmental and health mandates.

In an executive order issued October 26, 1993, President Clinton pledged that the national government was ready to work with the state and local governments to reduce the imposition of unfunded mandates, streamline the process of applying for and obtaining waivers from regulations, and establish consultative processes on intergovernmental issues. To date, the most significant effect of the order has been to give states greater flexibility in handling Medicaid. In the months before that pronouncement, however, the Big Seven leadership had been vocal about their disappointment with President Clinton's leadership on intergovernmental matters, including his failure to appoint an intergovernmental adviser and his administration's initial lack of support for ACIR.

Coalition Building

Each of the city organizations has its own base of support in Congress. By combining efforts, a broader base of support can sometimes be developed. For many years, NACo received strong support among suburban and Republican legislators, who were joined by many rural legislators. NACo's alliance with the USCM, with its strong ties to Democratic urban legislators from the Northeast and Midwest, has led to broad congressional support for particular policy objectives such as housing policy and welfare reform.[32]

Through the years, the shared political concerns among the Big Seven encouraged the formation of alliances to enhance policy influence. The executive directors of the various organizations met regularly and their staffs worked together on common strategies for affecting national policy. The organizations jointly sponsored many service activities and, in 1970, the staffs of USCM and NLC were merged, but the merger was dissolved in 1977.

Within-sector collaboration involves both working together for the enactment or defeat of specific legislative policies, the writing of favorable regulations, and the adjustment of deadlines for meeting mandates and other less subtle policy influences. Relations within the sector today range from "ships passing in the night" to "turf wars" to truly collaborative efforts.

The state and local government groups are using a broader range of tactics on a wider range of issues than in the recent past. Collaborative tactics have changed their form. Generalists and specialists, for example, collaborate to provide civic education to the general public, based on their shared professionalism and commitment to public service.

In the Hall of the States, Big Seven association representatives and states meet together each Monday morning with Congressional staffers, state officials, federal agency officials, and even the media, to receive briefings on agency and legislative developments. Such information networks continue to serve a valuable purpose in bringing organizations together to work in an intergovernmental environment.

Perhaps the largest role played by these groups is that of providing member services. Information is developed and distributed in a wide variety of formats: publications such as magazines, bulletins, directories, issue briefs, reports, and books; membership surveys; audio and video tapes; electronic networks; conferences, meetings, orientations, and training sessions; and codes of ethics.

An effective strategy used by the NGA to forge a prominent role in domestic policy making has been to research a single topic each year. Its health-care proposal, for example, is playing a prominent role in the debate over health-care reform. Previous efforts on education and welfare policy were integrated into successful legislation.

Intergovernmental issues are not sexy or exciting; they have low visibility in the daily experiences of the majority of the population. Citizens do not care which level of government delivers services; they just want efficient delivery. But crises can act as focusing events to promote change in a political system. The single issue around which the state and local groups have rallied together in recent years is that of the unfunded mandate, which they collectively believe has deteriorated to crisis proportions. In October 1993, the generalist organizations cosponsored National Unfunded Mandates Day. This was a major effort to educate the public and media.

Groups within the sector are also forging coalitions with private-sector institutions and interests. One example is the public-private partnership developed by the states named as finalists for the location of the supercollider.

Courts

The federal courts condition the problems and policies of the states and local governments. A series of recent cases have eroded state and local protections against the expansion of congressional authority. In effect, subnational governments have been redefined by the courts as interest groups. Their associations contend, in rebuttal, that the Tenth Amendment to the Constitution places a limit on national power. Seemingly endless challenges to subnational authority and capabilities—preemption of their rights and responsibilities, unfunded mandates, unrealistic regulatory deadlines, increased service-delivery and policy-making responsibilities but decreased resources—have led to the creation of a State and Local Legal Center.[33]

A new breed of subnational official is emerging, typified by big city mayors Richard Daley in Chicago and Ed Rendell in Philadelphia. They do not expect any new funding, but they expect the national government to "get out of their way." Other state and local officials send more mixed signals typified by the phrase, "Lead, follow, or get out of the way." Whatever position is taken, it is clear that court actions affect future outcomes.

The Future of Intergovernmental Representation

The American policy-making system today can be described as consisting of "multi-centered policy dominance."[34] The state and local interests must compete with an increasing number of other groups to place their ideas on the public and/or official agenda.

Adjusting to the notion of a "shared power world"—and nurturing the skills to do so—presents major challenges to a sector that lacks a cohesive policy network, whose service network has been diminished by the loss of direct funding, and whose information infrastructure has eroded.

Fragmentation within the intergovernmental policy community from one issue to another is difficult to overcome. Greater interdependence in collecting and sharing information is already evident, however, as is some movement toward rethinking organizational roles in a decentralized intergovernmental system.

Except for federations of local community organizations, which are dispersed among Washington, New York, Chicago, and Philadelphia, the major state and local government presence is in Washington. To be proactive, not simply reactive, sector members must find new ways to work with each other. They must blend policy and management concerns and generalist and specialist perspectives. Common ground must be found within the context of differing ideologies and goals, both within individual organizations and among and between them. Levels of governments, especially, must collaborate more frequently, and policy deliberations and solutions must transcend jurisdictional boundaries.

The intergovernmental associations must also deal with the seemingly endless stream of reform efforts within the political system: government "reinvention," privatization, regionalism, and collaborative governance. Privatization, in particular, poses a challenge. Privatization implies that some issues are no longer government's responsibility, thus undermining much of the agenda of the intergovernmental groups.

On the other hand, some current concerns within the political system create new opportunities for the sector. Societal and governmental attempts to balance citizen and group rights with responsibilities focus attention on the need for sector involvement in civic education. In a society that has in many ways redefined individual and group wants as needs and then redefined those needs as rights, a dialogue that helps citizens in understanding their rights and obligations suggests new roles for the sector.

Based on the notion that organizations must solicit and maintain members by offering the proper supply of incentives, recent demands by generalist officials signal the need for some internal restructuring of their associations to shape a better pattern of organization between national and local affiliates. In the current era of "fend for yourself" federalism, it may be more important for the national organizations representing local governments to be concerned with state-level activities and for increased positive interaction among and between all the state and the local groups.

The jurisdictional nature of representation by the generalist state and local organizations may be their greatest problem. Federal policies have followed the pattern of funding people, not places. Real-world problems seldom occur neatly within jurisdictional boundaries. The interests of specific existing units of local government are not necessarily the same as the interests of the larger metropolitan or regional area. In addition, the American public, with the aid of the media, has lost much of its sense of place.

The types of policies that the local groups deal with are unlike many other policy areas in the American political system. They involve both a governmental function (for example, community development) and a geographic area (such as a city, county, or township). Public policies are usually envisioned and handled in the political system in terms of the clusters of values, objectives, and programs related to basic government functions—for example, education, law enforcement, or transportation. Dealing with the geographic or jurisdictional dimension promoted by the local government groups continues to be problematic. The executive branch and Congress fragment decision making along functional, not spatial, lines. It is, therefore, difficult for the intergovernmental generalists to penetrate the policy process. The specialists (in housing, employment, crime, education) do not consistently deal with these issues in ways that take account of their spatial implications. The sector's most significant role appears to be that of providing information services to members.

Notes

1. Much of the information presented in this chapter is based on formal telephone interviews conducted by the author between fall 1990 and winter 1991 with executive directors of state-level associations of counties and less formal interviews with personnel from the major national associations, plus an additional fifteen telephone interviews with national association officials in 1993. The author also attended or participated in several briefings held in 1993 with representatives of the national associations discussed in the chapter. See Beverly A. Cigler, "The County-State Connection: A National Study of Associations of Counties," *Public Administration Review* 54 (January/February 1994): 3-11. Also see Clive S. Thomas and Ronald J. Hrebenar, "The Integration of Interest Group Activity at the National, State and Local Level in the United States: Extent, Causes and Consequences" (Paper delivered at the Annual Meeting of the American Political Science Association, Chicago, September 3-7, 1992).
2. Robert H. Salisbury, "Interest Representation and the Dominance of Institutions," *American Political Science Review* 78 (March 1984): 64-77.
3. David D. Meyer and Douglas R. Imig, "Political Opportunity and the Rise and Decline of Interest Group Sectors," *The Social Science Journal* 30 (July 1993): 253-270.
4. For representative works, see B. J. Reed, "The Changing Role of Local Advocacy in National Policies," *Journal of Urban Affairs* 5 (Fall 1983), 287-298; George E. Hale and Marian Lief Palley, *The Politics of Federal Grants* (Washington, D.C.: CQ Press, 1981) and H. Charles Levine and James A. Thurber, "Reagan and the Intergovernmental Lobby: Iron Triangles, Cozy Subsystems, and Political Conflict," in *Interest Group Politics*, ed. Allan J. Cigler and Burdett A. Loomis (Washington, D.C.: CQ Press, 1986), 202-220. Also see Clive S. Thomas and Ronald J. Hrebenar, "Government as an Interest and Lobbying Force in the American

152   Cigler

States" (Paper presented at the Annual Meeting of the Western Political Science Association, San Francisco, March 19-21, 1992).

5. See Cigler, "The County-State Connection," 5. This theme has been discussed extensively at meetings of the intergovernmental associations in recent years.

6. See R. Allen Hays, "Intergovernmental Lobbying: Toward an Understanding of Issue Priorities," *The Western Political Quarterly* 44 (December 1991): 1081-1098.

7. See Dale Krane, "American Federalism, State Governments, and Public Policy: Weaving Together Loose Theoretical Threads," *PS: Political Science & Politics* 26 (June 1993), 186-190; Beverly A. Cigler, "Challenges Facing Fiscal Federalism in the 1990s," *PS: Political Science & Politics* 26 (June 1993): 181-186; and Beverly A. Cigler, "State-Local Relations: A Need for Reinvention?" *Intergovernmental Perspective* 19 (Winter 1993): 15-18.

8. Meyer and Imig, "Political Opportunity," 258.

9. Donald Haider, *When Governments Come to Washington: Governors, Mayors and Intergovernmental Lobbying* (New York: Free Press, 1974).

10. See Susanne Farkas, *Urban Lobbying: Mayors in the Federal Arena* (New York: New York University Press, 1971); Haider, *When Governments Come to Washington*; and Samuel H. Beer, "Federalism, Nationalism, and Democracy," *American Political Science Review* 72 (March 1978): 9-21.

11. This is a major theme of Jonathan Walters, "Lobbying for the Past," *Governing* 4 (June 1991), 32-37, and of Cigler, "The County-State Connection."

12. See Haider, *When Governments Come to Washington*, and Levine and Thurber, "Reagan and the Intergovernmental Lobby." On the other hand, David S. Arnold and Jeremy F. Plant, *Public Official Associations and State and Local Government: A Bridge Across One Hundred Years* (Fairfax, Va.: George Mason University Press, 1994) describe many of the member services provided by a wider array of associations.

13. For a review of ICMA's member services, especially publications, see Barbara H. Moore, "Managing Cities and Counties: ICMA Activities and Resources," *Public Administration Review* 54 (January/February 1994): 90-92.

14. These publications have given extensive coverage to the national associations. A newer publication, *Governing*, now also features articles on the state and local interest groups.

15. The best examples are Reed, "The Changing Role of Local Advocacy," and Levine and Thurber, "Reagan and the Intergovernmental Lobby."

16. These points are made by Reed, "The Changing Role of Local Advocacy," and Levine and Thurber, "Reagan and the Intergovernmental Lobby."

17. See Donald C. Menzel, "Collecting, Conveying, and Convincing: The Three C's of Local Government Interest Groups," *Public Administration Review* 50 (May/June 1990): 401-405, and Levine and Thurber, "Reagan and the Intergovernmental Lobby."

18. Walters, "Lobbying for the Past."

19. Walters, "Lobbying for the Past," and Cigler, "The County-State Connection," make these points, based on interviews conducted in 1991.

20. Haider, *When Governments Come to Washington*.

21. The spatial dimension is especially important for dealing with the problems of rural areas.

22. See Douglas R. Imig, "Resource Mobilization, Strategic Action and Poverty Advocacy," *Western Political Quarterly* 45 (June 1992): 501-502. Overall, public-interest-group formation expanded rapidly from the 1960s and public interest groups accounted for 20 percent of groups active in Washington by the mid-1980s.

23. John Kincaid and James A. Stever, "Rise and Decline of the Federal Government's Institutional Capacity for Intergovernmental Analysis: ACIR, OMB, GAO,

and the Congress" (Paper presented at the Annual Meeting of the American Political Science Association, Chicago, Illinois, September 3-6, 1992).

24. Kincaid and Stever make these points in "Rise and Decline."
25. See Haider, *When Governments Come to Washington*; Patrick Donnay, "Professional Administration and Participation in Intergovernmental Organizations" (Paper presented at the Annual Meeting of the Midwest Political Science Association, Chicago, Illinois, April 18-20, 1991); and Arnold and Plant, *Public Official Associations and State and Local Government*.
26. These points are made in Ardith Maney, "What Else Happens When Governments Come to Washington: Intergovernmental Lobbying and the Dominance of Institutions" (Paper presented at the Annual Meeting of the Midwest Political Science Association, Chicago, Illinois, April 5-7, 1990).
27. See Neil Berch, "Why Do Some States Play the Federal Aid Game Better Than Others?" *American Politics Quarterly* 20 (July 1992): 366-377.
28. See J. Kline, *State Government Influence in U.S. International Economic Policy* (Lexington, Mass.: Lexington Books, 1983). Also see Ruth M. Grubel, "Government Efforts to Promote International Trade: State Trade Offices in Japan," in *Economic Development Strategies for State and Local Governments*, ed. Robert P. McGowan and Edward J. Ottensmeyer (Chicago: Nelson-Hall, 1993), 41-53.
29. On this point, see Parris N. Glendening and Mavis Mann Reeves, *Pragmatic Federalism* (Pacific Palisades, Calif.: Palisades Publishers, 1977).
30. Haider, *When Governments Come to Washington*.
31. Cigler, "The County-State Connection."
32. This point is made by Hale and Palley, *The Politics of Federal Grants*.
33. Organized in 1983, the center is housed in the Academy for State and Local Government, within the "Big Seven." It files amicus curiae briefs on cases involving state and local interests with the U.S. Supreme Court. Only cases for which there is a consensus among the "Big Seven" are filed. Also see David E. Nething, "States Must Regain Their Powers," *The Journal of State Government* 63 (January-March 1990): 6-7.
34. This point was recognized by Farkas, *Urban Lobbying*.

II. GROUPS IN THE ELECTION PROCESS

7

Political Action Committees and the Political Process in the 1990s

M. Margaret Conway and Joanne Connor Green

Observers of American political life would be hard pressed to name a feature of contemporary electoral politics that has attracted more attention and aroused more emotion over the past decade than campaign spending by political action committees (PACs). By mid-1993 more than four thousand PACs had registered with the Federal Election Commission, and in the 1991-1992 election cycle they provided 32 percent of the campaign funds received by House candidates and 20 percent of Senate candidates' receipts. The impact of such spending on electoral outcomes and public policy decisions is a matter of widespread debate. Unquestionably, PACs represent a key weapon in the arsenals of influence of many (but not all) interest groups.

In this chapter political scientists Margaret Conway and Joanne Connor Green survey the rise of PACs as potent political forces and assess their effects on electoral and legislative politics. Particular attention is given to PAC contribution strategies and to the conditions and circumstances that may maximize PAC influence. The authors explore the criticisms leveled at PAC politics and evaluate the various reforms that have been suggested to limit PAC influence. Conway and Green conclude that one problem of the possible reforms is that none addresses the "imbalance in the representation of interests through PACs," an imbalance illustrated by the rapid growth in the number of business-related PACs compared to their labor-based counterparts. In their view, despite hostility among reformers and the press, PACs are not likely to be abolished and their role in the political process will continue, as will the many controversies surrounding their activities.

In the two decades since federal laws and Supreme Court decisions conveyed legitimacy on political action committees (PACs), their numbers have increased by 660 percent, growing from 608 in 1974 to 4,210 in 1993 (see Table 7-1). Although the absolute number of PACs declined from 1988 to 1993, their role in the funding of congressional elections remained significant. During the 1991-1992 election cycle,

PACs provided 32 percent of the funds received by House candidates and 20 percent of Senate candidates' receipts.[1]

Many questions about the role of PACs in American politics are addressed in this chapter, including: What laws govern the activities of PACs? Have these laws been effective in achieving their intended aims? What has been the role of PACs in financing congressional campaigns? What types of candidates are favored and what types are disadvantaged by the existing laws? How do PACs make decisions about which candidates should receive contributions and how much to give? What strategies govern contribution decisions by PACs? Do the internal needs of the organization giving the money influence patterns of PAC contributions to congressional candidates?

Two types of political action committees operate at the federal level: independent and affiliated. Independent PACs are officially independent of any existing organization and usually focus on a particular issue or advocate a particular ideology. Affiliated PACs are created by existing organizations such as labor unions, corporations, cooperatives, or trade and professional associations. They serve as a separate, segregated fund to collect money from people affiliated with the organization for contribution to candidates' political campaigns or for use as independent expenditures for or against a particular candidate.

Affiliated PACs obtain funds for use for political purposes through donations made by individuals associated with the group. Corporations and labor unions are not allowed to make direct campaign contributions from their treasuries, but treasury funds may be used to establish and administer a PAC and to communicate with people associated with the organization—such as corporate employees or shareholders and their families or labor union members and their families—for voter registration and get-out-the-vote drives.

Federal Law and the Growth of PACs

Political action committees are governed primarily by the Federal Election Campaign Act of 1971 (FECA) and amendments enacted to it in 1974, 1976, and 1979, as well as the Revenue Act of 1971. Also important are regulations and advisory opinions issued by the Federal Election Commission (FEC) which administers and enforces federal campaign finance laws, as well as several court decisions interpreting federal laws.

To limit the influence of any one group or individual in the funding of campaigns for federal office, individuals and most organizations are restricted in the amount of money that they can give directly to a candidate in any one year. The current limits are $1,000 per election to a candidate for federal office, $20,000 per year to the national political party committees, and $5,000 per election to a campaign committee. No indi-

Table 7-1   PAC Count, Selected Dates and Years, 1974 to 1993

	Corporate	Labor	Trade, member- ship, health	Non- connected	Cooperative	Corporation without stock	Total
1974	89	201	318				608
11/24/75	139	226	357				722
5/10/76	294	246	452				992
12/31/76	433	224	489				1,146
1977	550	234	438	110	8	20	1,360
1978	785	217	453	162	12	24	1,653
1980	1,206	297	576	374	42	56	2,551
1982	1,469	380	649	923	49	103	3,371
1984	1,682	394	698	1,053	52	130	4,009
1986	1,744	384	745	1,077	56	151	4,157
1988	1,816	354	786	1,115	59	138	4,268
1990	1,795	346	774	1,062	59	136	4,172
1991	1,738	338	742	1,083	57	136	4,094
1992	1,735	347	770	1,145	56	142	4,195
1993	1,789	337	761	1,121	56	146	4,210

Source: Federal Election Commission.

Note: For 1974-1976, the figure for Trade/Membership/Health PACs includes Noncommercial, Cooperative, and Corporation without Stock PACs. On November 24, 1975, the FEC issued its "SUNPAC" advisory opinion. On May 11, 1976, the Federal Election Campaign Acts of 1976 (P.L. 94-283) were enacted. All data unless otherwise indicated are as of end of year.

vidual may contribute more than $25,000 to PACs regulated by the Federal Election Commission, national level party organizations, and candidates for federal office in any one year. Federal campaign finance laws give a distinct advantage to multicandidate committees—those contributing to five or more candidates for federal office—whether they are independent or affiliated. A multicandidate committee may contribute as much money as it is able to raise, yet it is restricted to giving no more than $5,000 per candidate in each election. That permits a PAC to give a candidate up to $5,000 for a primary election, $5,000 for a run-off primary election if one is required, and $5,000 for a general election contest. There is no limit on how much a PAC may spend in independent expenditures in behalf of a candidate as long as it does not coordinate its campaign efforts in any way with the candidate, representatives of the candidate, or the candidate's campaign committee. Because PACs are able to raise and funnel large amounts to campaigns for federal office, their numbers have grown; public concern about their influence on members of Congress has grown as well.

The 1974 amendments to FECA permitted government contractors to establish PACs, thus greatly expanding the universe of businesses and labor unions eligible to use this form of political expression. The FEC's April 1975 decision to permit corporations and labor unions to use their treasury funds to create PACs and to administer their activities, including solicitation of funds from employees and stockholders, facilitated the establishment and operation of PACs.[2] Authorization of the use of payroll deductions to channel funds to PACs also stimulated the creation and continuing operations of PACs.

Supreme Court decisions as well played a major role in stimulating the creation of additional PACs. In *Buckley v. Valeo*, the Supreme Court in January 1976 indicated that the 1974 FECA amendments did not limit the number of local or regional PACs that unions or corporations and their subsidiaries could establish.[3] That decision also clarified the right of PACs to make independent expenditures (those not authorized by nor coordinated with a candidate's campaign) on behalf of a candidate. In 1976 further amendments to FECA restricted labor union and corporation PAC contributions to one $5,000 contribution per election, regardless of the number of PACs created by a corporation's divisions or subsidiaries or a labor union's locals. The process of clarifying what is permissible continues, with the FEC and other interested parties proposing amendments to existing laws and advisory opinions being issued by the FEC.

Although PACs had existed prior to 1974, their numbers were limited, and most were affiliated with labor unions. Between 1974 and 1993 the number of labor union PACs increased by just 68 percent, while the number of corporate PACs increased by 1,827 percent.[4] Thus, the first notable effect of changed laws and the FEC's interpretation of the laws was the explosive growth in the number of corporate PACs. Although the number of labor union and corporate PACs has increased significantly, most do not raise and contribute large amounts of money. During the 1991-1992 campaign cycle, only twenty-eight corporate PACs raised more than $500,000, with twenty-four each contributing that much to candidates from funds raised. Thirty-nine labor union PACs raised $500,000 or more, and twenty-seven contributed at least $500,000 to candidates.[5]

After clarification of the campaign finance laws in 1976, other types of PACs were created. The most prominent was the independent or nonconnected PAC. Its numbers increased from 110 in 1977 to 1,121 in 1993; this represents an increase of 919 percent (see Table 7-1). Between 1977 and 1993, another category of PAC, those affiliated with trade associations, membership organizations, or health-related organizations, increased by 139 percent. During the 1991-1992 election cycle, twenty-eight nonconnected PACs raised $500,000 or more, and twenty-seven contributed that much to candidates. Forty-four association- or health-related PACs raised at least $500,000, but fewer than twenty-seven contributed at least that much.[6]

Despite the growth in the number of PACs, a significant proportion of them are relatively inactive. For example, among the more than 4,000 PACs existing during the 1991-1992 election cycle, 910 (23 percent) did not make any contributions to candidates.[7]

Scholars, journalists, and many political leaders have expressed increasing concern about the role of PACs in federal campaign funding. PACs may have enormous influence, affecting who is viewed as a viable candidate, the outcomes of elections, access to the policy-making process, and the content of policy. Because PACs have become a major source of campaign funds for congressional candidates, an inability to obtain PAC support may mean a candidate cannot afford to run an effective campaign. If elected, the successful candidate must be ever mindful of campaign funding sources, both past and future. The escalating costs of congressional and senatorial campaigns force incumbent members of Congress to be watchful of how policy positions taken and votes cast on legislation may affect future fund-raising.

Not all aid from PACs, however, is always welcome. The entry of independent PACs into a contest may be unwelcome, even by the candidate the PACs favor. Moreover, a backlash may develop against independent PACs, particularly those that engage in negative campaigning, and that backlash can extend to the candidate supported by the independent PACs. Some candidates believe that identification with a particular PAC's issue positions, the negative campaign tactics often used by independent PACs, or the fact that a PAC is based outside the constituency hurts rather than helps the candidate's chances for electoral success.

PAC Decision Making

A number of variables influence PAC decision making on campaign contributions. These include the goals of the organization, the expectations of contributors to the PAC, the official positions within the organization of those making the decisions, their physical location (in Washington versus elsewhere), the strategic premises employed by the PAC, and the PAC's competitive position versus those of other organizations. [8]

An organization may follow a "maintaining strategy" and seek simply to continue to ensure access to those members of Congress to whom the sponsoring organization already has access. Or, it may follow an "expanding strategy" and attempt to gain access to additional representatives or senators who would not normally be attuned to the PAC's interests because of the limited presence of the represented interest within the member's electoral constituency. The results of the limited amount of research done on this topic suggest that PACs generally emphasize a maintaining strategy, with only a third of contributions representing an expanding strategy.[9] PACs also tend to be more responsive to the needs of vulnerable representatives and senators who have befriended the PAC's interests.[10]

PAC decision-making patterns vary with the structure of the PAC. If the PAC has staff based in Washington, that staff tends to play a greater role in deciding to whom to contribute and how much to contribute. Contributions are also more likely to occur through the mechanism of a Washington-based fund-raising event.[11] PACs in which substantial funds are raised by local affiliates tend to follow the locals' more parochial concerns. That may not be the most rational allocation strategy to pursue, however. Rationality would require that the PAC allocate funds either to strengthen or broaden access or to replace opponents, but parochialism may require that an already supportive member of Congress receive substantial amounts of locally raised funds.[12] The degree of parochialism appears to vary by type of PAC interest—for example, defense-interest PACs are more locally oriented than labor-interest PACs.[13]

Partisanship and ideology also may influence PAC decision making—for example, defense PACs tend to be less ideological in their contribution decisions than labor, oil, and auto PACs.[14] Business PACs vary in the extent to which they pursue a partisan support strategy; usually this is associated with the vulnerability of a political party's incumbents. When political tides appear to be favoring Republicans, they may contribute more to Republican challengers than when the political climate is less favorable to that party.

Incumbents' voting records on key votes may be a major factor as well in influencing contribution decisions. An incumbent, for example, who voted against legislation the PAC considered of vital importance generally would be unlikely to receive a campaign contribution, but exceptions exist.[15] One study of PACs affiliated with Fortune 500 companies found voting records on key legislation to be the second most frequently cited criterion used in making contribution decisions (the most frequently cited was the candidate's attitudes toward business).[16] Some research suggests that corporate PACs' decisions about whether and to whom to contribute are also influenced by the size of federal contracts held by the company, the corporation's size, and whether or not the company's business is regulated by the federal government.[17] Contribution decisions by both corporate and labor PACs are also influenced by the jurisdictions of the committees on which incumbent members serve,[18] but some research indicates committee jurisdiction is more relevant in decisions regarding contributions to House incumbents than to Senate incumbents.[19]

Some PACs also must be concerned about competition for supporters, and that concern influences contribution patterns. Contributions that would leave the PAC open to criticism sufficiently severe to cost it future support from donors must be avoided. This is a particular problem for nonconnected PACs that raise funds through mass mail solicitations.[20]

Another factor that influences patterns of PAC contributions is concern about relative influence with key holders of power. If other PACs give to a member of Congress and PAC X does not, will that have an impact on relative access? Although some PACs act as though it would, others could pursue a different strategy, gaining the member's attention by giving to his or her challenger. The member of Congress might therefore become more attentive to gain support from the PAC. The effectiveness of that strategy, however, would be limited by the extent to which the PAC's preferred policy outcomes conflict with the strength of a contrary ideology held by the member of Congress or the intensity of support for a different policy position present in that member's constituency.

Role of PACs in Campaign Finance

PAC receipts, expenditures, and contributions to congressional candidates have increased significantly since the early 1970s. PAC receipts grew from $19.2 million in 1972 to $385 million in 1991-1992, while PAC expenditures increased from $19 million to $394 million.[21] PAC contributions to congressional candidates increased from $8.5 million for the 1972 elections to $189 million for the 1992 elections. Congressional candidates' dependence on PAC contributions increased significantly between 1976 and 1992.[22]

The changing technology of campaigns stimulates candidates' perceived needs for PAC funds. Extensive use of professional campaign management firms, surveys, television advertising, and the other requirements of modern campaigns have greatly increased campaign costs. Total spending in contests for the Senate increased by 618 percent between 1974 and 1992, with Senate candidates spending a total of $124.3 million in 1992 compared with $20.1 million in the 1975-1976 election cycle. Candidates for the House of Representatives spent $240 million in 1991-1992, compared with $38 million in 1975-1976. The average campaign cost for a House incumbent seeking reelection in 1992 was $585,000, with forty-four candidates spending more than $1 million in their campaigns. The average general election campaign cost for Senate incumbents was $3.5 million.[23] In 1974 no candidate for the House spent more than $500,000 in a campaign, but in 1992, 224 House candidates spent more than that in general election campaigns, with fifty spending more than $1 million.[24] Total campaign costs in 1992 were affected by the large number of retirements from the House of Representatives and by congressional redistricting, which resulted in more open-seat contests and in the increased need for campaign funds among incumbents seeking reelection.

The dependence on PAC funds to meet the large and ever-increasing costs of campaigns for Congress varies greatly by legislative chamber, incumbency status, and party. In 1992 Democratic House incumbents received 44 percent of their total campaign receipts from PACs, whereas Republican incumbents in the House obtained 40 percent of their funds from that source. Challengers and candidates for open seats received less, with, for example, Republican challengers receiving 10 percent of their funds from PACs and Democratic challengers receiving 29 percent. Senate candidates are less dependent on PAC money; in 1992 Democratic incumbents obtained 38 percent of their funds from PACs, and Republican incumbents received 27 percent from that source. Challengers and open-seat candidates in both parties in the Senate received even less from PACs; neither averaged more than 17 percent.[25]

If candidates obtained a greater share of their funds from other sources, public concern about the role of PACs in American politics would probably lessen. The federal campaign finance laws, however, limit how much political parties may contribute to congressional candidates and spend on their behalf. Although those limits are not met in all contests, they may be met in open-seat contests or in Senate contests, especially by the Republican campaign finance committees. Permitting parties to give more to their candidates and changing the campaign finance laws to permit citizens to give more to political parties would encourage reduced dependence on PAC funding.

To overcome the limits on party funding of congressional campaigns contained within the federal laws, several practices have developed whose effects can only be estimated. In the first practice the political party organizations guide individual or PAC contributions to particular candidates, and especially to those whom the parties believe have a good chance of winning if adequate funding can be made available. A PAC may collect contributions from members in the form of checks made out to a particular candidate and then present the collected checks to the candidate, a practice known as bundling (see Chapter 8). Thus the candidate knows that he or she received a substantial total contribution from the members of the interest group represented by the PAC. The second practice is to guide money—particularly money that may not be given under federal law but is permissible in some states, such as campaign contributions from corporate treasury monies (commonly called "soft money")—to state political party organizations to be used for various campaign purposes such as generic advertising, voter registration drives, and voter mobilization drives on election day. These contributions can be used, of course, for a variety of campaign activities that promote the presidential ticket as well as congressional candidates.

During the 1991-1992 election cycle 70 percent of PAC contributions went to candidates for the House of Representatives.[26] Senate campaigns are much more expensive than House contests, and the $5,000-per-election restriction limits the impact of PAC contributions on Senate contests. Generally, only a finite number of PACs are interested in any one contest, and most PACs do not give to any one candidate the maximum amount of money allowed under the law. Among the factors considered by PACs when determining whether and how much to give are the nature of the state or district and the interests of the PAC within that constituency and, for incumbents, committee assignments, past voting patterns, and help previously provided by the candidate to the PAC in support of its interests. Affiliated PACs tend to be associated with a particular business, industry, or other economic or social entity and may focus on contests in states where the sponsoring interest group is particularly strong. Independent PACs have tended to focus more on Senate than on House contests, particularly in making independent expenditures.

Some members of Congress establish their own PACs. Leadership PACs have been created by party leaders within each chamber, and those who have presidential ambitions have formed PACs as well. These member PACs are used not only to fund research on public issues, speaking trips, and other support-building activity among the general public, but also to make campaign contributions to other candidates for Congress. Contributing to other congressional candidates builds support for the attainment and maintenance of formal positions of power within Congress and may accumulate support for a future presidential campaign. Candidate PACs have been used by former representative Jack Kemp (R-N.Y.), Sen. Robert Dole (R-Kan.), and Sen. Edward Kennedy (D-Mass.). Candidate PACs were also used by presidential candidates Ronald Reagan, Walter Mondale, and George Bush.

Most prominent among the leadership PACs are those sponsored by members of Congress and used to raise and contribute money to other members or to nonincumbent candidates for Congress. In 1988, fifty-five members of Congress (twenty-five Republicans and thirty Democrats) had formed their own PACs; collectively they contributed more than $4.3 million to congressional candidates, with 56 percent going to nonincumbent candidates.[27] In 1992, Sen. Robert Dole's Campaign America PAC contributed $377,000 to congressional candidates, while House Speaker Tom Foley's House Leadership Fund contributed $244,000 to other candidates.[28] Leadership PACs serve as a vehicle for incumbents not facing a significant challenge to raise and contribute campaign funds to others. Not inconsequentially, they serve as mechanisms to foster support and loyalty to the member making the contribution. Some proposals for campaign reform target this type of PAC for elimination.

Strategies: Access and Replacement

Two types of strategy are used by PACs to obtain results from their contributions. One emphasizes contributing to obtain access to members of Congress who are positioned to be most helpful in advancing the policy interests of the PAC. The other focuses on electing people to Congress who will be more helpful to the PAC—that is, the goal is to replace members who are not supportive of the PAC's interests or ideology and to elect people to open seats who are viewed as supportive of the PAC's policy objectives.

The access strategy utilizes contributions to obtain access to members who can be of particular help to the PAC in obtaining its legislative goals. The consequence of this strategy is a disproportionate allocation of funds to incumbents. Those members serving on legislative committees whose jurisdiction includes areas of interest to the PAC are favored in PAC allocations. Also of importance are members who influence budgets for policies relevant to the PAC or who serve on major procedural committees such as the House Rules Committee. PACs also contribute to leaders of the House and Senate whose influence extends over the entire range of legislative policy. PACs are quite aware of a congressional member's voting record on legislation of interest to them, and many PACs make an effort to reward friends in Congress with campaign contributions. Many kinds of PACs appear to pursue an access strategy; indeed, incumbent support is the strategy generally pursued by most types of PACs.[29] In the 1991-1992 election cycle, 72 percent of corporate contributions went to incumbents. The percentage given to incumbents in the past, however, has varied with the situation, with corporate PACs giving to challengers when the electoral tides indicate that incumbents who have been less supportive of corporate interests may be vulnerable. Thus in 1980, 57 percent of corporate contributions went to incumbents, and 28 percent were given to Republicans challenging incumbent Democrats and to open-seat candidates.[30] Other types of business PACs are also highly likely to support incumbents. In contrast, labor union PACs tend to be highly supportive both of incumbent Democrats and of Democratic open-seat and challenger candidates. When Democratic incumbents are more vulnerable, a greater share of labor PAC funds goes to incumbents.

The second strategy of trying to replace members of Congress whose ideology and voting records do not coincide with those preferred by the PAC is more likely to be pursued by nonconnected PACs. The proportion of their contributions going to challengers and open-seat candidates varies, with 72 percent in 1978, 33 percent in 1988, and 41 percent in 1992 being contributed to challengers and open-seat candidates.[31] Incumbents who are perceived as unlikely to be defeated usually have only limited amounts directed against them.

Sometimes, however, other criteria are involved in targeting. In 1982 Sen. Paul Sarbanes (D-Md.) was selected by the National Conservative Political Action Committee (NCPAC) to serve as an object lesson to other members of Congress. NCPAC assumed that other senators and representatives would see the ads run against Sarbanes on the Washington, D.C.-area television stations. The implied threat was that those whose voting records were not sufficiently in accord with NCPAC's preferences also would be the target of negative advertising campaigns. The negative advertising campaign against Sarbanes was not successful, however, and the ads were withdrawn before the general election campaign.[32] Although not effective in the Sarbanes campaign, other independent expenditure efforts have been perceived as successful. In 1984, for example, more than

$1.1 million was spent to influence Illinois voters to cast their votes against Sen. Charles Percy (R-Ill.), who lost his reelection bid by 1 percent of the vote.[33] Independent expenditures also can be important in electing candidates; for example, Sen. Phil Gramm (R-Texas) benefited from more than $500,000 spent on his behalf in the 1984 Senate contest.[34]

Although nonconnected PACs raised $73.9 million in 1991-1992, they contributed only one-fourth of that amount to candidates. In contrast, corporate PACs contributed 61 percent of the $112 million they collected, and labor PACs contributed 46 percent of the $90 million they raised.[35] Nonconnected PACs find it necessary to spend far more to raise money than do affiliated PACs, who have the support of their sponsoring organizations. Nonconnected PACs also allocate more money for direct expenditures in support of or opposition to particular candidates. In 1991-1992, for example, they spent 9 percent of funds raised on expenditures for or against candidates.[36]

Partisan Allocation of PAC Contributions

In 1992 Democratic candidates as a group received 64 percent of campaign contributions made by PACs. The division of PAC money between the two parties' candidates, however, differed greatly by PAC, with 50 percent of corporate PAC contributions and 95 percent of labor union PAC contributions going to Democrats. In elections for the House of Representatives, corporate PACs largely pursued an access strategy, allocating 82 percent of their contributions to incumbents; trade, membership, and health PACs pursued a similar course of action, granting 79 percent of their contributions to incumbents. Labor split its contributions differently, giving 64 percent to incumbents, 15 percent to challengers, and 20 percent to open-seat candidates. Nonconnected PACs also divided their contributions, giving 61 percent to incumbents, 16 percent to challengers, and 23 percent to open-seat candidates. In terms of actual amounts, Democratic Senate candidates received more from PACs than did Republicans ($29 million versus $22 million). Democratic House candidates received substantially more from PACs than did Republicans ($85 million versus $41 million).[37]

PACs and the Policy Process

One way in which PACs affect policy is by influencing who wins House and Senate elections. PAC contributions can affect electoral outcomes in several ways. The first is to help incumbents by inciting reluctance among highly qualified potential candidates to enter the contest. Large sums of money in the incumbent's campaign coffers will intimidate many potential candidates and, in effect, act as a preemptive strike against them. The potential challenger, knowing the incumbent starts with a significant advantage in name recognition and typically with a favorable image with the voters, often concludes that the chance of defeating the incumbent is quite small and thus does not enter the contest.[38]

Large accumulations of campaign funds also permit early campaigning by the incumbent. The objective is to discourage potential opposition, or, if opposition does develop, to control the issue agenda of the campaign. Other goals of early spending include further increasing the incumbent's fund raising and enhancing the popularity of potentially weak incumbents.[39]

After the campaign has begun, do challengers and incumbents benefit equally from campaign expenditures? One point of view is that the challenger benefits more, as higher levels of funding enable the challenger to establish name recognition and create awareness of his or her candidacy. Thus, substantial benefit accrues from initial expenditures. As more potential voters become aware of the challenger, however, the effectiveness of expenditures decreases.[40] Whether incumbents, who already have greater name recognition, benefit as much as challengers from their expenditures is the subject of considerable debate among scholars.[41] Through their expenditures incumbents may increase turnout, or they may prevent loss of support among those previously committed to them. Those incumbents who spend the most may be the most vulnerable, or they may be aiming for "overkill" to discourage future opposition or to gain public acclaim that will help them seek another office such as the governor's office, a U.S. Senate seat, or even the presidency.

The effectiveness of the challenger's expenditures may depend on whether political trends are favorable or unfavorable to the challenger's party.[42] If the challenger is a Democrat and noncandidate factors that influence congressional election outcomes—such as economic conditions and the level of approval of presidential job performance—favor the Republicans, the challenger's expenditures will buy less support than if these noncandidate factors were less favorable to the opposition.

In addition to influencing electoral outcomes, PAC contributions can influence public policy in other ways. For most PACs a primary objective of campaign contributions is to gain access to the member of Congress in order to present policy views and have them heard in the legislative setting. When an issue is not one of primary concern to a senator's or representative's constituency and not in conflict with a strongly held party position or the member's ideology, the recipient of campaign contributions from a particular source may be willing to vote in support of that interest group's issue position. It may be that the effects of campaign contributions are indirect, influencing who is lobbied when legislation of importance to a group is being considered and the receptivity of that legislator to the group's approach and arguments.[43]

Do campaign contributions generally influence legislative outcomes? Unfortunately, insufficient research exists to permit a definitive answer to the question. Studies that examine the relationship between campaign contributions and legislative roll-call votes have reached conflicting conclusions. Some suggest that PAC money affects recipients' support in roll-call votes for legislation. Studies supporting this conclusion analyzed votes on minimum wage legislation;[44] the B-1 bomber;[45] the debt limit, the windfall profits tax, and wage and price controls;[46] trucking deregulation;[47] and legislation of interest to doctors and to auto dealers.[48] A study examining the effects of labor's contributions on both general issues and urban issues concluded that their contributions had a significant impact on five of nine issues relating to urban problems and five of eight general issues, but business contributions were significant in only one issue conflict of each type.[49] One study reports that labor union contributions have an impact on support for labor's preferences on labor legislation only in some congressional sessions and not in others.[50] Other research concluded that contributions influence support for labor's preferred legislation.[51] Still other research, however, suggested that campaign contributions were not important on roll-call votes on such issues as the Chrysler Corporation's loan guarantee and the windfall profits tax[52] and dairy price supports.[53] One study examined a number of PACs and congressional voting behavior over an eight-year period and concluded that contributions rarely are related to congressional voting patterns. When they are, contributions are a surrogate for other support for the member from the interest group.[54] In summary, the evidence on the importance of PAC contributions in influencing congressional voting on roll calls is conflicting, and obviously further research on this topic is needed.

Campaign contributions may be given to reward past support rather than to gain future roll-call support. Furthermore, the most important effects of campaign contributions may not be on roll-call votes but on the various earlier stages of the legislative process such as the introduction and sponsorship of bills, the behind-the-scenes negotiations on legislative provisions, the drafting and proposing of amendments, and the mark-up of bills in subcommittees and committees.

Finally, factors such as constituency interests and ideology and party ties may determine whether campaign contributions influence legislative outcomes. If the issue is important to a significant part of the constituency, for example, constituency interests will likely prevail over PAC policy preferences. Thus, PAC money and the interest group concerns it represents may prevail only on less visible issues where the influences of party, ideology, or constituency are not as important.[55]

Criticisms of Interest Group Activity in Campaign Finance

The increased role of PACs since the early 1970s in funding campaigns for Congress has generated substantial criticism. Certainly PAC funding plays a role in who is elected to Congress, even if the evidence about the impact of PAC contributions on roll-call voting is mixed and the research is too limited to draw firm conclusions about its influence on other stages of the congressional decision-making process.

Organization simplifies the representation of interests in a large and complex society, and PACs are one manifestation of the organized representation of interests. Criticism of the campaign finance system, however, has resulted in a number of suggestions for changes in federal law. One issue underlying the suggested changes is whether the total amount of PAC money a candidate may receive should be limited. Proponents argue that such a limitation will limit PAC influence; opponents point out that limiting PAC contributions will make it more difficult for nonincumbents to seek office.

Two ways to overcome this problem are (1) to permit individuals to make larger contributions to candidates and to political parties and (2) to permit political parties both to give more to candidates of the party and to spend more on behalf of party candidates. Generally, the Democrats have opposed these suggestions as being more likely to favor Republicans, who could both raise more money from larger contributions and have more money to give to the party's candidates.

A means that political parties have used in attempts to skirt the limitations on contributions is to donate money raised by the national party organizations to state party organizations. Such money has been termed "soft" because it falls outside federal regulations on donation limits but the use of it still affects federal elections. In 1991-1992, the Democratic national party organizations raised $37 million in soft money, and contributed $35 million for use by state and local party organizations to fund voter registration efforts, get-out-the-vote drives, and other party-building activities. During this same period the Republicans raised $52 million and contributed $50 million in soft money.[56] In an attempt to address this issue, President Bill Clinton proposed to prohibit state and national parties from spending unregulated money (soft money) to influence federal elections.[57] To replace soft money, an increase in the maximum permitted size of individual contributions was proposed, as well as the creation of a new grassroots fund to be used by state parties to finance generic media and coordinated campaigns. In addition, Clinton's proposal included a provision to increase the level of public funding of presidential elections by $11 million for each candidate, thereby decreasing the necessity for the use of soft money.

Another criticism of PACs is that they weaken the role of the individual citizen in politics, a criticism based on the disparity between the amount an individual may contribute ($1,000) and the amount a PAC may contribute ($5,000). To increase the role of individuals, the maximum individual contribution could be increased or the maximum limit on PAC contributions reduced. Increasing the maximum an individual may give, however, increases the influence of those more affluent. PAC contributions would also be limited under the Clinton proposal. Presidential candidates could receive only $1,000 from any one PAC. Senate and House candidates could receive PAC contributions of $2,500 and $5,000 respectively for both primary and general elections. Some reformers support eliminating PAC donations altogether; however, the constitutionality of such proposals is questionable.

An additional proposal put forth to reduce the dependence on PAC money is to encourage more individuals to give small contributions by permitting them to write off part of the contribution as a deduction from gross income in figuring income taxes or as a deduction from taxes owed. Some proposals would permit the deduction only for contributions to candidates or parties within the state where the contributor resides.

Yet another idea is to establish limits on the amount of money a candidate may spend on Congressional elections. Since the Supreme Court ruled in *Buckley v. Valeo* that limiting the amount spent in congressional elections must be voluntary (the court equated campaign spending with freedom of expression), campaign-limit proposals are typically accompanied by the inducement of public financing. President Clinton proposed a system in which candidates who comply with spending limits would receive partial campaign funding from a government campaign fund.[58] If a candidate accepted the limits but the opponent did not, the candidate would receive more from the fund. But finding the money for such a fund in a very tight federal budget and convincing candidates to limit voluntarily how much they spend are highly unlikely in the present political climate. If spending limits are imposed, one must ensure that the limits are high enough to stimulate competition. If the limits are too low, the better-known incumbents will benefit while the lesser-known challengers will be further disadvantaged.

Discussion of Proposed Reforms

Campaign finance reform efforts focus on several issues. The first stems from concern over the spiraling costs of elections in the United States. More than $678 million was spent in congressional elections in 1991-1992, up from a little more than $342 million a decade previously.[59] Many see this outpouring of money as inappropriate and call for limits on the amount a candidate can spend in an election bid. A second major reform issue relates to the substantial role of PACs in funding congressional elections. PACs donated more than $180 million to candidates for Congress in the 1991-1992 election cycle. Many have proposed to limit PAC influence in congressional elections by eliminating or limiting PAC contributions to candidates.

The essential problem relates to the perception of money's role in congressional elections. The evidence is mixed and the research too limited to draw firm conclusions about money's influence in other stages of the congressional decision making process, but the perception that money buys elections is prevalent in popular culture, some sectors of the academic world, and among the press. Even if money does not buy elections or legislators' loyalty, it appears to have those effects. The *seemingly improper nature* of money in elections is itself of significant consequence. Elections legitimate governmental authority; if elections are biased toward moneyed interests, or appear to be so biased, their legitimacy is questioned. Campaign finance reform is partly motivated by a desire to squash these suspicions of impropriety. Reform is further motivated by a desire to make the electoral races more competitive to address widespread concern over the seemingly noncompetitive nature of congressional elections (especially those for the House of Representatives).

A potential problem that current proposals do not address is the imbalance in the representation of interests through PACs. For example, the rapid increase in the number of business-related PACs and the considerable potential for their future growth, compared to the much more limited potential for the growth of labor-related PACs, suggests that an imbalance in this kind of access/influence mechanism between these two types of interests exists and could become much greater. Although it could be argued that business PACs simply represent a repackaging of activities that occurred previously—free services, for example—the amounts being contributed to candidates are larger than in earlier elections. Of course, it also can be pointed out that labor PACs do much more than contribute money; they are very active in the mobilization of other types of resources as well.

Other types of interests—those less affluent—are not represented through money-based mechanisms of representation such as PACs.

President Clinton proposed a campaign reform bill early in 1993. The bill had many of the essential characteristics of a bill vetoed by former President Bush in 1992. Clinton vowed to sign virtually any bill that dealt with electoral reform to demonstrate his commitment to campaign finance reform. The promise to sign any bill passed by Congress greatly changed the characteristics of the debate. During the previous administration, President Bush had indicated that he would veto campaign finance reform, so the Congress produced a less pragmatic bill. With Clinton's promise to sign any bill passed by the Congress, the task of enacting a reform bill became more difficult.

Also in 1993 the House passed a bill very similar to President Clinton's proposals. The Senate passed quite different legislation, which did not establish public funding of congressional campaigns and which essentially banned PACs. Those campaigns that did not comply with spending limits would be taxed at the highest corporate rate. In contrast, the House bill offered public funding and other benefits to induce compliance with spending limits. In several other ways the two bills differed substantially. As of July 1994, no further progress on the bills had been reported.

Fundamental differences exist between Democrats and Republicans concerning desired campaign finance reform. Democrats advocate limiting expenditures, whereas Republicans want to limit the sources of contributions. However, Democrats are divided over public financing of congressional elections, and Republicans are generally opposed to public funding of congressional campaigns.

These differences between the House and Senate and between Democrats and Republicans in their views on campaign finance reform will continue to make it quite difficult to change laws governing financing of campaigns at the federal level.

The politics of PACs and PAC reform in the funding of campaigns for Congress present many problems. PACs are here and are not likely to be abolished, and their role in the political process will continue, as will the controversies about their role.[60]

Notes

1. FEC press release, March 4, 1993.
2. See Edwin Epstein, "The Emergence of Political Action Committees," in *Political Finance*, ed. Herbert Alexander (Beverly Hills, Calif.: Sage, 1979), 159-179.
3. *Buckley v. Valeo*, 424 U.S. 1 (1976).
4. FEC press release, August 2, 1993.
5. FEC press release, April 29, 1993.
6. Ibid.
7. Ibid.
8. Theodore J. Eismeier and Philip H. Pollock III, "An Organizational Analysis of Political Action Committees," *Political Behavior* 7, 2 (1985): 192-216.
9. John R. Wright, "PAC Contributions, Lobbying, and Representation," *Journal of Politics* 51 (August 1989): 713-729.
10. J. David Gopoian, "What Makes PACs Tick? An Analysis of the Allocation Patterns of Economic Interest Groups," *American Journal of Political Science* 28 (May 1984): 259-281.
11. Larry J. Sabato, *PAC Power: Inside the World of Political Action Committees* (New York: Norton, 1985), 42-43.
12. John R. Wright, "PACs, Contributions, and Roll Calls: An Organizational Perspective," *American Political Science Review* 79 (June 1985): 400-414.
13. Gopoian, "What Makes PACs Tick?" 279.
14. Ibid., 271.
15. Some PACs will contribute to candidates who oppose them in the hope of minimizing the intensity or frequency of the opposition to their interests. Davies found this factor to be statistically significant; Hall and Wayman also suggest some PACs pursue a strategy of attempting to minimize the opposition. See F. L. Davis, "Sophistication in Corporate PAC Contributions: Demobilizing the Opposition," *American Politics Quarterly* 20 (October 1992): 381-410; R. L. Hall and F. W. Wayman, "Buying Time: Moneyed Interests and the Mobilization of Bias in Congressional Committees," *American Political Science Review* 84 (1990): 797-820.
16. Ann B. Matasar, *Corporate PACs and Federal Campaign Financing Laws* (New York: Quorum Books, 1986), Table 13, 58. When incumbents are involved in close contests, voting records may induce contributions for a candidate whose record is favorably assessed by a corporate PAC and against an incumbent whose record is

viewed negatively. See K. T. Poole, Thomas Romer, and H. Rosenthal, "The Revealed Preferences of Political Action Committees," *American Economic Review* 77 (May 1987): 298-302.

17. R. B. Grier and M. C. Munger, "Committee Assignments, Constituent Preferences, and Campaign Contributions," *Economic Inquiry* 29 (January 1991): 24-43.

18. J. W. Endersby and M. C. Munger, "The Impact of Legislator Attributes on Union PAC Campaign Contributions," *Journal of Labor Research* 13 (Winter 1992), 79-97; M. C. Munger, "A Simple Test of the Thesis that Committee Jurisdictions Shape Corporate PAC Contributions," *Public Choice* 62 (1989): 181-186.

19. K. B. Grier, M. C. Munger, and G. M. Torrent, "Allocation Patterns of PAC Monies: The U.S. Senate," *Public Choice* 67 (1990): 111-128.

20. Eismeier and Pollock, "Organizational Analysis," 207-208.

21. FEC press release, April 29, 1993.

22. FEC press release, March, 1993, 3.

23. Calculated from FEC press release, March 4, 1993, table entitled "Financial Activity of Senate and House General Election Campaigns."

24. Ibid. Calculated from table entitled "Financial Data for House General Election Campaigns through December 31, 1992," 23-40.

25. Computed from data contained in the FEC press release, March 4, 1993, 9.

26. Computed from data contained in FEC press release, April 29, 1993, 3.

27. Larry Makinson, *Open Secrets: The Dollar Power of PACs in Congress, Center for Responsive Politics* (Washington, D.C.: CQ Press, 1990), 77.

28. FEC, "PAC Activity Rebounds in the 1991-1992 Election Cycle," *News from the FEC*, March 29, 1993, 25.

29. Frank J. Sorauf, *Money in American Politics* (Glenview, Ill.: Scott, Foresman, 1988), 103.

30. FEC press release, March 2, 1982, and April 29, 1993.

31. FEC press release, May 10, 1979, and April 29, 1993, 3.

32. Polls conducted by the *Baltimore Sun* indicated that the proportion of the public approving of Senator Sarbanes's job performance remained stationary, while the proportion disapproving increased from 20 percent to 29 percent between October 1981 and February 1982. During that period several NCPAC ads critical of Sarbanes's performance were shown on television stations broadcasting to Maryland residents. See Karen Hosler, "Voter Shifts Favor Hughes, Hurt Sarbanes," *Baltimore Sun*, February 22, 1982, A1.

33. FEC press release, October 4, 1985.

34. Ibid.

35. Computed from data in FEC press release, April 29, 1993, 3.

36. FEC press release, April 29, 1993, 3.

37. Computed from data in FEC press release, April 29, 1993, 5.

38. In 1992, eleven members of the House were defeated in primary elections and nineteen lost in the general election.

39. Paul West, "'Early Media' Push '86 Campaign on the Air," *Baltimore Sun*, December 12, 1985, 1A.

40. See Gary C. Jacobson, "Money and Votes Reconsidered: Congressional Elections, 1972-1982," *Public Choice* 47 (1985): 43-46; and Jacobson, "The Effects of Campaign Spending in House Elections: New Evidence for Old Arguments," *American Journal of Political Science* 34 (May 1990): 334-362.

41. See Donald P. Green and Jonathan S. Krasno, "Salvation for the Spendthrift Incumbent: Re-estimating the Effects of Campaign Spending in House Elections," *American Journal of Political Science* 32 (November 1988): 884-907; Jacobson's response in "Effects of Campaign Spending"; and Green and Krasno's response in "Rebuttal to Jacobson's 'New Evidence for Old Arguments,'" *American Journal of Political Science* 34 (May 1990): 363-374. See also J. R. Lott, Jr., "Does Additional

Campaign Spending Really Hurt Incumbents? The Theoretical Importance of Past Investments in Political Brand Name," *Public Choice* 72 (1991): 87-92.

42. Gary C. Jacobson, "Strategic Politicians and the Dynamics of U.S. House Elections, 1946-1986," *American Journal of Political Science* 83 (September 1989): 773-794; C. Wilcox, "Organizational Variables and Contribution Behavior of Large PACs: A Longitudinal Analysis," *Political Behavior* 11 (June 1989): 157-174.

43. J. Wright, "Contributions, Lobbying, and Committee Voting in the U.S. House of Representatives," *American Political Science Review* 84 (June 1990): 417-438.

44. Jonathan I. Silberman and Garey C. Durden, "Determining Legislative Preferences on Minimum Wage: An Economic Approach," *Journal of Political Economy* 94 (April 1986): 317-329.

45. Henry W. Chappel, Jr., "Campaign Contributions and Congressional Voting: A Simultaneous Probit-Tobit Model," *Review of Economics and Statistics* (February 1982): 77-83.

46. James B. Kau and Paul H. Rubin, *Congressmen, Constituents, and Contributors: Determinants of Roll Call Votes* (Boston: Martinus Nijhoff, 1982), Table 7.5, 96-97.

47. John P. Frendreis and Richard W. Waterman, "PAC Contributions and Legislative Behavior: Senate Voting on Trucking Deregulation," *Social Science Quarterly* 66 (June 1985): 401-412.

48. K. F. Brown, "Campaign Contributions and Congressional Voting" (Paper presented at the annual meeting of the American Political Science Association, Chicago, September 1-4, 1983).

49. Kau and Rubin, *Congressmen, Constituents, and Contributors*.

50. A. Wilhite, "Union PAC Contributions and Legislative Voting," *Journal of Labor Research* 9 (Winter 1988): 79-90.

51. Gregory M. Saltzman, "Congressional Voting on Labor Issues: The Role of PACs," *Industrial and Labor Relations Review* 40 (January 1987): 163-179.

52. Diana M. Evans, "PAC Contributions and Roll-Call Voting: Conditional Power," in *Interest Group Politics*, 2d ed., ed. Allan J. Cigler and Burdett A. Loomis (Washington, D.C.: CQ Press, 1986), 114-132.

53. W. P. Welch, "Campaign Contributions and House Voting: Milk Money and Dairy Price Supports," *Western Political Quarterly* 35 (December 1982): 478-495.

54. Janet M. Grenzke, "PACs and the Congressional Supermarket: The Currency Is Complex," *American Journal of Political Science* 33 (February 1989): 1-24.

55. F. L. Davis, "Balancing the Perspective on PAC Contributions: In Search of an Impact on Roll Calls," *American Politics Quarterly* 21 (April 1993): 205-222.

56. FEC press release, March 11, 1993, 1.

57. *CQ Weekly Report*, May 8, 1993, 1121-1122.

58. Ibid.

59. FEC press release, March 4, 1993, 1.

60. For more detailed discussions of the arguments for and against various reform proposals, see David B. Magleby and Candice J. Nelson, *The Money Chase* (Washington, D.C.: Brookings, 1990), chaps. 8-11; Dan Clawson, Alan Neustadtl, and Denise Scott, *Money Talks* (New York: Basic Books, 1992), chap. 7; and Frank J. Sorauf, *Inside Campaign Finance* (New Haven, Conn.: Yale University Press, 1992), chap. 7.

8

Adaptation and Innovation in Political Action Committees

Frank J. Sorauf

Since political action committees (PACs) became major forces in American politics around 1980, various reform efforts have attempted to limit the scope and level of their activities. Ross Perot, Common Cause, and other would-be reformers have argued that too much special interest money has been cast upon American politics, and especially upon congressional elections. Members of the U.S. Congress, most of whom benefit mightily from PAC contributions, have wrestled with many reform proposals. As of 1994, however, they have placed no significant restraints on the PAC prerogatives laid out in 1974 legislation and in a major 1976 Supreme Court case *(Buckley v. Valeo)*. Nevertheless, many politicians, public interest groups, and journalists have continued to attack PACs and the potential influence that their contributions give them.

Political scientist Frank Sorauf has written extensively and dispassionately about PACs and campaign finance, most notably in his prize-winning book, *Inside Campaign Finance*. In this chapter he tracks the considerable adaptation that PACs have undergone in the first twenty years of their modern incarnation and speculates on the possible courses further adaptation might take if and when PACs are further regulated. In particular, Sorauf explores the possibility that PACs might emulate a handful of current groups, such as EMILY's List, that have created sophisticated means for aggregating, or "bundling," large numbers of individual contributions. In conclusion, Sorauf believes PACs will continue to find innovative ways to fund congressional campaigns, although adaptation will exact different costs from different interests.

F or political organizations, too, necessity is the mother of invention. They rarely innovate or adapt except in response to changes in their external environments, whether those are changes in legal regulations or in the competitive politics of organizing influence. Contemporary threats of more stringent limits on political action committees (PACs) in congressional campaign finance now challenge the adaptive resources of PACs once again.

The present era in the federal regulation of PACs and campaign finance generally is now two decades old. Congress completed the Federal Election Campaign Act of 1971 (FECA) with amendments passed in 1974 in the reform-charged aftermath of the Watergate revelations. Although Congress has amended FECA since then, the sections dealing with PACs have remained unchanged since 1974. The contribution limits on PACs—$5,000 per candidate per election, with the primary and general election each counting as an election—have remained fixed at the 1974 level. In the intervening years, therefore, the great reformer has been inflation: the effective $10,000 limit in 1993 buys approximately 35 percent of what it did in 1974.

Innovation and Stability

As the regulatory regime of 1974 aged, the major funders of campaigns discovered the loopholes and interstices of the regulatory structure. They began to see new opportunities for action and new ways of freeing themselves from the limits and constraints of FECA. Party committees, for instance, exploited a number of opportunities in the law to raise great sums of soft money outside of FECA and to channel that money to state parties for party-building, voter mobilization, and state and local campaigns.[1] To take another example, after the Supreme Court, in 1976, struck down FECA's prohibition of "independent spending"— campaign spending carried out without the knowledge or cooperation of a candidate or candidate's campaign committee—some PACs and a few individuals seized the opportunity to urge independently the election or defeat of a candidate via direct mail, billboards, or mass media advertisements.[2]

The most important of the innovations since 1974, however, may well have been "bundling," or the organizing of individual contributions to a candidate in which the organizer—called a "conduit" under the regulations of the Federal Election Commission (FEC)—literally bundles together a number of individual contributions and transmits them to the candidate for whom they are intended. In doing so, the conduit takes credit for organizing the collective generosity. If the conduit is a Charles Keating, he may claim credit for the cause of struggling savings and loan institutions or even for Charles Keating himself. If it is a Washington lobbyist, the indebtedness of a candidate may convert into the access which is the lobbyist's stock in trade. In any event, each of the individual contributions remains exactly that: an individual contribution with a limit of $1,000 per candidate per election.

Beyond generating credit for the conduit, bundling has a second raison d'etre: getting large sums of money to candidates as efficiently as possible. If the conduit, whether an individual or a PAC, brings together ninety-nine other enthusiasts to contribute $500 apiece at a reception for a senatorial incumbent, the fortunate senator receives $50,000. The conduit has helped the candidate of its choice far more than it could by acting as a single PAC or individual, and the candidate has raised a large sum of money with a very modest investment of time and effort.

All of these innovations notwithstanding, most PACs operate pretty much as they did in the early years of FECA. The great majority of them—3,014 of the 4,025 registered with the FEC in mid-1993— have been established by parent groups, especially corporations, labor unions, and membership associations. They act primarily as adjuncts of the interest group activities of their parent organizations and generally contribute relatively small amounts to a large number of candidates, largely incumbent candidates. Such a strategy suits the parent organization's pursuit of legislative goals and influence; above all, it supports the parent's lobbying program. To be sure, labor PACs give much more to nonincumbents and much more consistently to ideologically sympathetic candidates, but with this conspicuous exception, PACs with parents have generally become a part of the broader political strategies of interest groups.[3]

The stability in PAC strategies extends also to their internal organization and governance. Ever since PACs were born in the labor politics of the 1940s, most PACs have been created by parent organizations. Those parents choose the PAC leadership, thus making sure that their PACs serve their political goals. The PAC raises voluntary contributions from its contributing constituency, and the leadership then decides which candidates or party committees will get contributions and in what sums. Although contributors may be consulted, even listened to, they rarely take part in spending decisions, and they rarely complain about the PAC's authoritarian structure. Many, in fact, relish the freedom from political decision-making, just as they happily cede spending control over their charitable contributions to the United Way.

PACs without parent organizations, the so-called nonconnected PACs, have been freer to innovate. The most notorious of them all, the National Conservative Political Action Committee (NCPAC, pronounced "Nick PAC") pioneered big-time independent spending in the senatorial campaigns of 1980. Its spending of $1.1 million to urge the defeat of six liberal Democratic senators in that year brought it to the front pages of the print media and its cheeky young executive director, Terry Dolan, to the nation's talk shows.[4]

It was another of the nonconnected PACs, the Council for a Livable World, that pioneered bundling. The Council was founded in 1962 by nuclear physicist Leo Szilard to promote the causes of arms control and nuclear disarmament. It remains a major PAC contributor, bundling close to $1 million for campaigns in 1992. Still another nonconnected PAC, EMILY's List, caught the nation's attention by raising more than $5.6 million for congressional candidates in 1992. The successes of these PACs make bundling a major alternative to the traditional ways of American PACs.

EMILY's List and the Council for a Livable World

Emily is more than a fictional character; she is an acronym. EMILY stands for Early Money Is Like Yeast. Early money is like yeast because "it makes the dough rise." The organization is the creation of Ellen Malcolm, an experienced Washington political operative who founded it in the mid-1980s and continues to run it in the 1990s. From the beginning EMILY's List had two distinguishing features: it would support only prochoice, Democratic women candidates for the House and Senate, and it would raise and transfer campaign contributions to them by bundling.

Members join EMILY's List by making a contribution of at least $100 to the PAC itself and by pledging to contribute at least $100 to a minimum of two candidates endorsed by EMILY's List. The contributions to the PAC go to its operating and fund-raising expenses, and the contributions to candidates—checks written by members to candidate campaign committees—are sent to EMILY's List for "bundling" and transmittal by the PAC to the campaigns of the recipients. The contributions remain individual contributions, subject to the limit of $2,000 for the primary and general election campaigns in the two-year campaign period.[5] But EMILY's List faces no limit on the total sums it can bundle for any candidate or group of candidates.

The modus operandi is the one pioneered by the Council for a Livable World, but with several refinements. CLW requires no membership contribution to the PAC, nor does it extract a pledge to support any number of endorsed candidates. Rather, CLW simply sends its list of previous and potential contributors a series of flyer-newsletters with profiles of endorsed candidates and fund-raising pitches for them—along with instructions on how to write the check and forward it to CLW. It was Ellen Malcolm's innovation to introduce a more structured sense of participation and commitment into the bundling transaction.

EMILY's List began with modest goals in 1986, the year its $150,000 bundle helped elect Barbara Mikulski (D-Md.) to the Senate. In 1990 it raised $1.5 million for twelve endorsed congressional candidates and two candidates for governorships. Its most visible success that year was the bundling of $400,000 for Ann Richards, the successful Democratic candidate for the governorship of Texas. But those successes pale next to the impact and eclat of 1992. Drawing on a greatly enhanced membership of twenty-four thousand, EMILY's List raised $6.2 million for women candidates. Of the $6.2 million total, $5.63 million went as bundled individual contributions to fifty-five House and Senate candidates, $200,000 went to 171 state and local candidates, and the remainder ($370,000) went in direct contributions from the PAC, most of it in-kind spending on the materials about endorsed candidates sent to members.[6]

The Council for a Livable World and EMILY's List share some strategies and differ on others. They share the strategic outcome inherent in bundling: the sums they channel are the aggregate of hundreds of contributor decisions rather than the result of a PAC leadership's allocation plan. They share also the strategy of supporting only candidates who meet a policy or issue test, in one case support for the prochoice position on abortion and in the other support for arms control and nuclear disarmament. However, whereas EMILY's List supports virtually all viable, prochoice women candidates for Congress, the Council is more selective. It supports chiefly candidates for the Senate, the only ratifier of treaties, and it prefers to concentrate on races in small states where the cost of a campaign is far less and the prize at stake—a single vote in the Senate—is the same as in big-state races.

Finally, CLW and EMILY's List have tapped similar sets of contributors: well educated, politically sophisticated, and comfortably affluent. Although neither has studied the demographics of its supporters, their profiles are not in dispute. EMILY's List has recruited heavily from educated, successful women in business and the professions, women especially involved more broadly in the women's movement and its issues and politics. As for the CLW, its lists of contributors are replete with professional and academic titles. Even a casual inspection reveals Nobel prize winners and other celebrity scientists.

Beyond these two most conspicuous practitioners, bundling is apparently practiced by only a few other PACs. "Apparently" because the Federal Election Commission releases no list of bundlers, nor are they noted in the electronic databases of the Commission. They are required to file as "conduits" under federal law,[7] but they can be located systematically only by searching through the reports of the approximately 3,300 PACs now active in any two-year election cycle. Absent such an arduous search, one relies of necessity on the knowledge of experts on the PAC movement.

Although the two most visible exponents of bundling—EMILY's List and the Council for a Livable World—are PACs without parent organizations, the other long-time bundlers are a few corporate PACs. They deal in far smaller sums and appear to reflect broader, participatory programs of public affairs. In the PAC of the Sundstrand corporation, for example, participants contribute via payroll deduction to accounts in their name; as the campaign approaches they are asked to earmark the funds for specific candidates. The PAC may make recommendations, but the individual donors decide who receives their contributions. Typically, they make their decisions in the context of Sundstrand programs of voter education and candidate visits to Sundstrand plants. The sums are not large; in 1990 Sundstrand's Good Government Support Fund contributed a little more than $17,000 to candidates for Congress. It can and does, therefore, report the earmarked contributions as PAC rather than individual contributions.

The Conditions for Successful Bundling

Bundling has been a conspicuously successful but comparatively rare PAC innovation. Can the kind of bundling with which EMILY's List and CLW have succeeded be exported to other PACs? If not, can it be made more exportable? Those questions prompt another: Considering that the CLW showed that bundling was a viable way of operating a PAC as early as the 1960s, why have more PACs not adopted it?

The answer probably lies in the special nature of the two major bundlers. Both attract, first of all, well-educated, highly motivated, and politicized contributors capable of making the choices that bundling offers them. Second, both focus on a single issue or a single cluster of issues; the PAC and its members agree, therefore, on a small number of readily understood criteria for supporting candidates. The members are comfortable with the limited range of issues and candidates the PAC offers, and the PAC does not risk its purpose or mission by offering them choices. Third, both PACs early found a place on a rising political curve; their early successes rewarded and further motivated a group of contributors committed to the triumph of a policy position. Finally, both PACs began as bundlers; neither had to retrain either contributors or an ensconced group of powerful PAC managers. In neither case, that is, was there the drag of the past, especially among PAC staffers who would see their control of PAC money diminish.

If those are the conditions for successful bundling, it is no surprise that the innovation has not spread widely. Its appeal will be largely limited to issue-oriented PACs pursuing an electoral strategy—that is, trying to increase the like-minded cohort in the Congress. It is a modus operandi ill-suited to most PACs with parent organizations, for the latter most often pursue incumbent-supporting strategies aimed primarily at increasing access for the parent's lobbyists. Whether it is supporting senators in the first four years of their term or giving money to House incumbents without serious competition, their operations are often remote from the excitement of the immediate campaign and election.

Moreover, bundling is not without its inherent operational problems. For example, there is no guarantee that the PAC's members will earmark their contributions collectively in ways that reflect the most efficient possible allocation of the PAC's resources. Although needful big-state senatorial candidates are usually the best known, even the star-quality candidates, the mechanisms of individual choice are less apt to produce rational allocations among endorsed House candidates. Bundling PACs face a second, quite different problem. Because bundled contributions must bear the name of the individual contributor, the recipient candidates may be tempted to add the contributors to their own, personal list of contributors for future solicitations. EMILY's List requires its endorsed candidates to pledge not to do so. The pledge itself would seem to attest to the danger.

So, despite the well-reported success of EMILY's List in recent election cycles, imitators have been scarce. A few state and local PACs, primarily supporting women and minority candidates, reportedly are adopting the model. A few ideological PACs, none of them with parent organizations, seem about to test the waters. Most tangibly, Republican women have established a clone of EMILY's List called WISH List. (The acronym stands for Women in the Senate and House.) WISH List enrolled 1,500 members and raised some $200,000 for ten prochoice Republican women in 1992. Many fell in the Republican primaries, defeated by more conservative, prolife candidates. If there are other aspiring bundlers in the PAC world, they are either not far along in their planning or have not yet found the usual channels of notoriety.

Though it has been little imitated, EMILY's list caught the eye of campaign-finance reformers after the 1992 election. To some, the practice of bundling has always seemed to constitute avoidance of the FECA contribution limits. EMILY's List can contribute only $10,000 to a candidate as a PAC, but bundling allows it to funnel many times that total. That much is beyond dispute. It should be just as clear, however, that in bundling a PAC gives up something of its traditional PAC nature. It permits greater choice and autonomy for the PAC's individual contributors by surrendering some of its discretion over spending. The PAC that bundles is no longer free to make the strategic, last-minute shifts of funds to meet new needs or to help surging, newly viable candidates. The PAC member enjoys new choices and new influence. The result is a very different kind of PAC, one that blurs FECA's basic regulatory distinction between individual and PAC contributions.

The ability of PACs to bundle sums far beyond the limits on PAC contributions is not the only concern of reformers. They are aware also of increased bundling by enterprising political individuals. This is the type of bundling that Charles Keating, his senatorial friends, and the savings and loan crisis brought to public attention. The extent of such bundling is hard to gauge because individuals do not have to make periodic reports to the FEC as PACs do. It is also less clear that the FEC's rules about conduits in fact apply to them.[8]

Reform and the Future of PACs

The PACs that practice bundling now confront reform proposals that would limit their activities. Both EMILY's List and CLW won exemption from the restrictions on bundling contained in the campaign-finance reform bill that George Bush vetoed in 1992. That legislation would have ended bundling by any "political committee with a connected organization" simply by considering the earmarked and bundled contributions they raised as PAC rather than individual contributions.[9] The words, "with a connected organization," exempted the two major PAC bundlers because neither had a parent organization.

The continuing wars over campaign-finance reform in 1993 featured a return to the issue. A new Senate bill contained the same reforms of bundling and the same exemption for PACs without parents that George Bush had vetoed. For much of early 1993, critics of bundling attempted to strike the exemption from the bill. Ellen Malcolm and EMILY's List organized support for the exemption, Common Cause weighed in for a total ban, and the battle raged for a month in the editorial pages of the *New York Times*. That newspaper called the exception, "Emily's Loophole," and deplored PAC bundling as an evasion of the limits on PAC contributions.[10] Malcolm, in response, argued that the best way to reduce the influence of special interests on Congress was to encourage contributions from citizens willing to give to challengers running against entrenched incumbents. She also proposed a simple reform: "Prohibit organizations and individuals that lobby Congress from bundling contributions."[11] As it turned out, the final version of the bill (S. 3), passed on June 17, 1993, banned bundling by all PACs—no exceptions.[12]

Congressional reformers also went to great lengths in 1992 and 1993 to prevent covert bundling by organized interests other than PACs. The bill the Congress passed in 1992 prohibited the bundling of contributions "made or arranged to be made" by any PAC, any labor union or corporation, any party committee, any partnership or sole proprietorship, or lobbyist, or the employee or agent of any of them.[13] It is the phrase, "arranged to be made," that has potentially the broadest sweep. It would appear to prevent a national association from organizing or training its members to organize local membership networks to make contributions or to set up fund-raising events for endorsed candidates. It might come very close to banning much of traditional fund-raising. And it raises major policy and constitutional questions. Is it desirable public policy—is it enforceable public policy?—to discourage all local fund-raising with even indirect organizational auspices? Will the Supreme Court tolerate such burdens on the First Amendment rights of political action and political association?

More important still, the agenda of reform is now replete with proposed restrictions on PACs that go far beyond a reform of bundling. George Bush and others have proposed the ultimate in reform: the prohibition of PAC contributions to candidates for the Congress. The bill that passed the Senate in June 1993 contained a ban on PAC contributions to candidates for the Congress. In case the Supreme Court were to find that provision of the bill unconstitutional, the bill contained a fallback position: a PAC contribution limit of $1,000 per candidate per election (the same as the individual limit) and a receipt limit on a candidate's money from PACs.[14] In the unlikely event such provisions are retained in a bill the Congress passes, many constitutional experts doubt that the Supreme Court, having brought the contribution of campaign funds under the protection of the First Amendment in *Buckley v. Valeo*,[15] would permit the effective abolition of a major set of those contributors.

The more probable reforms—if there will be any—are less draconian. Congress's reform bill of 1992 reduced the contribution limits from $5,000 per candidate per election to $2,500. It also contained FECA's first limit on receipts. Candidates for the House, for example, would have been allowed to accept no more than $200,000 (one-third of the spending limit accepted as a condition of receiving public funds) from PACs collectively.

Any reform of American campaign finance will almost certainly make changes in FECA's treatment of PACs. Although bundling is one of the reformers' targets, PACs have added it to their list of options for adapting to possible future limits on PAC activity. Will PACs turn to bundling as adaptation even though they have been slow to embrace it as useful innovation?

Bundling under Altered Conditions

Bundling as a major, or sole, way of operating seems to have limited appeal or viability for most PACs *within the regulatory regime of 1974's FECA*. If the regulatory system changes, however—if the PAC contribution limits are lowered sharply or if candidates are limited in their aggregate PAC receipts—calculations about the usefulness of bundling will proceed from different premises. The change in the regulatory structure alters both the strategies and benefits of operation.

If PACs Were Pushed out of Congressional Electoral Politics

The hardest case to project involves the most severe change: the prohibition of PAC contributions to candidates for Congress. But we do know something of PAC preferences if that is the scenario. In 1992 the Public Affairs Council surveyed its members for their likely reactions if the Congress should abolish PACs.[16] Because the Council is an association of corporate departments of public or governmental affairs, the respondents represent only one segment of the PAC movement. Their speculations about a threatening future are nonetheless instructive. Almost two-thirds (63 percent) say they will withdraw to state and local politics if they are excluded from congressional campaigns. But 77 percent say that they will remain in federal electoral politics somehow—with educational programs and seminars or by encouraging candidate visits, for instance. Others will begin grass-roots programs such as nonpartisan voter registration

(70 percent), and a substantial 40 percent say they will shift PAC operating funds to lobbying—a choice not surprising in view of the fact that many corporate PACs already make their contributions to cultivate access and entree for the parent's lobbyists.

No fewer than nine of the twenty-five items on the Public Affairs Council's survey suggest adaptations not involving participation of any kind in elections or campaigns. Some 73 percent of the respondents, for example, would look favorably on programs that educated employees about politics and government, and 48 percent react positively to contributing "seed money" to "specific interest/coalition groups/trade associations."

Some large association PACs are reportedly thinking of shifting funds to the kind of grass-roots educational and electoral programs that have for so long characterized the labor movement. Other PACs have talked about becoming, at least in part, "public interest" or ideological groups—nonpartisan advocacy groups of the kind Ralph Nader, and now the conservatives, have used so effectively.[17] As varied as these models are, they have one thing in common: in whole or in part, they would move PACs out of electoral politics.

Alternatively and less radically, the easiest adaptation for many PACs would simply be abandoning congressional campaigns for greater involvement in state and local campaigns. As an adaptation, the state and local option has one great attraction: very few states regulate PAC receipts and contributions with anything approaching the severity of FECA, especially a FECA stiffened as the 1992 bill would have been. Shifting political operations to the states and localities has one great drawback, however—surrendering a perceived avenue of Washington influence. That is a choice a PAC in the soft-drink business might consider with some equanimity, but not one in the health services industry.

If the reform contains not abolition but restrictions resembling those of the 1992 bill—a cutback in contribution limits to $2,500 per candidate per election—many PACs would live within the new restrictions. Few PAC contributions exceed $5,000; in 1990, in fact, only 4.8 percent did. Labor PACs would face the greatest problem. Because they are larger, more centralized, and fewer in number than other types of PACs, a greater proportion of their contributions is made in amounts of more than $5,000. Of all labor PAC contributions in 1990, 13.9 percent exceeded $5,000. No other type of PAC reached 6 percent, and only 2 percent of corporate PAC contributions exceeded $5,000.

For years the PAC movement has had a well-publicized fallback position in the event of tighter limits on contributions: greater independent spending. But in 1994 independent spending looks less viable as an adaptation than it did in 1983. (The Public Affairs Council did not include it as an option in its survey, undoubtedly because corporate PACs had very rarely spent independently heretofore.) Independent spending by

PACs in the 1980s—generally by association or nonconnected PACs—caused a number of problems. Some of the major experimenters encountered intraorganizational resistance; supporters of candidate X reacted with greater displeasure at the PAC's billboards or direct mailings supporting X's opponent than they did when the support was the less visible and much smaller contribution. Candidates also found ways to turn unfriendly independent spending to their own advantage; it was easy to portray it as the work of extremists or out-of-state meddlers. Even the candidates whom the independent spenders wanted to help were uneasy about campaign help over which they had no control. By the 1990s very few PACs of corporations, unions, or membership associations were major independent spenders. The option was largely taken by the ideological PACs, who for lack of a parent organization had greater strategic freedom.[18]

In general the most frequently discussed regulatory changes would force greater adaptive problems for the larger PACs. But with their greater resources, their contributors spread across the nation, and their greater administrative expertise, such PACs have greater capacity to adapt. They may mix the kinds of spending they do, adding some discreet independent spending to their direct contributions. With their greater resources they may also devise mixed adaptive strategies for different groups of their contributors or members. For example, they may develop bundling programs for their more loyal and sophisticated donors, while maintaining regular PAC operations for others less likely to follow PAC cues or endorsements. Or they might allow their donors to choose one or the other method of contributing.

Bundling as Part of the Adaptive Mix

Bundling or some similar form of networking is likely to be a part of the adaptive mix in part because of an absence of alternatives, but also because of the value of bundling. Bundling, or some networking variant of it, suits the populist tenor of contemporary American political life because it empowers and involves the individuals who are the source of the contributions. As the recent successes with bundling have indicated, the number of donors prepared to act on its premises is probably increasing. Bundling is also adaptable, especially in the local networking options, to the large PACs that have federated structures or large numbers of members spread throughout the nation. Finally, it probably also affords the best-protected constitutional position under the First Amendment: a defense resting on the political rights of politically motivated individuals.

Ironically, therefore, bundling may flourish more in new regulatory surroundings than it has under FECA's 1974 status quo. If it does, it will be because it can be transformed into a kind of PAC operation that can more easily escape regulation. The less structured forms of bundling always have in common an element of networking: one or more citizens, perhaps stimulated or trained by a national organization, convince other citizens to support a worthy candidate. Because this form of political action has been with us from the beginning of the republic, it is doubtful that its proscription would withstand a constitutional test, even if the individuals who were persuading others to contribute belonged to an organization that had a PAC.

One other bundling option remains. PAC members or contributors might simply send a contribution directly to an endorsed candidate rather than to the PAC for its bundling and transmission. PACs might send their members duplicate forms and envelopes so that the members could send the original with the check to the candidate—and the second, the "copy," to the PAC for its records. EMILY's List has resisted that solution publicly, and Ellen Malcolm has estimated that such a revision in her organization's modus operandi would raise costs by 25 percent and cut contributions by 40 percent. Unquestionably this is a fallback option that would make greater demands on the loyalty and discipline of the members; it would also unquestionably increase the PAC's operating costs. Even by Malcolm's figures, however, it appears to be greatly preferable to extinction.

Wisconsin Bundles against the Freeze

The foregoing scenarios in congressional campaign finance are all still hypothetical, but PACs in one state have actually used bundling as adaptation. Some years ago Wisconsin enacted a two-stage limit on candidate receipts from political committees. No more than 45 percent of the spending limit for the office sought could be raised from nonparty committees,[19] and no more than a cumulative 65 percent could be raised from those sources plus political party committees. (Although the spending limits were imposed as a condition for the candidate's acceptance of public funding, they apply for this purpose to all candidates, whether or not they accept public money.) Candidates felt the constraints early on, but the impact became much more severe in 1986 when Wisconsin froze the previously indexed spending limits and thus froze the sums candidates could raise from sources other than themselves and other individuals.

Even before the freeze of 1986 some Wisconsin PACs had begun to experiment with bundling, but the 1986 legislation created a process for reporting conduit activity that, at the same time, explicitly legitimated it. Wisconsin conduits may accept earmarked contributions from donors, put the funds in their treasuries, and then ultimately take out all the funds marked for a candidate and forward those funds, duly bundled, to the candidate. They must provide a list of donors and the sums they gave to the candidate and to the Wisconsin Elections Board. Through all of this, the contributions remain those of individuals and thus are not subject to the 45 and 65 percent limits.[20]

Conduit contributions in Wisconsin have increased steadily since 1986. In 1987-88 they totaled $258,103 for all state legislative candidates, a figure 35 percent the size of PAC contributions to the same candidates. By 1991-92 the total was $679,601, a figure 97 percent of the PAC total. In the same cycle conduits funneled almost $1.1 million to all state candidates in Wisconsin. Although it is not easy to generalize about the 59 conduits registered in 1993, the largest single number represent business and professional associations, followed by those of large corporations, utilities, banks, and insurance companies. There are no conduits of labor unions.

Reports to the Wisconsin Elections Board document all of this. Not documented are the reported attempts at less structured bundling, especially cases in which the bundled funds do not enter the conduit's treasury. Beyond the traditional bundling, apparently, Wisconsin has seen other variants intended to preserve greater organizational initiative. For instance, through "pledge conduits," individuals pledge to make contributions later for candidates designated by the conduit; at least one has solicited checks with sums filled in but with the names of recipients to be added later by the conduit.[21] Both variants were plagued by problems; the pledge conduits by broken pledges, the incomplete checks by donor displeasure over the conduit's choice of recipient.

The Wisconsin evidence is tantalizing, if limited. It points in directions consistent with what we know about bundling and PAC adaptation to heightened regulation. The Wisconsin conduits are most common among associations of well-educated individuals and institutionalized networks. They are, moreover, overwhelmingly the adaptations of larger organizations with larger PACs. Interestingly, too, Wisconsin groups have opted for the conservative, legally sanctioned bundling option: the statutorily defined conduit. It is above board and clearly legal; it can also be used for payroll-deduction and dues-based contributions. But if that option were absent—and there have been a number of unsuccessful attempts recently to repeal the authorization of conduits—would Wisconsin PACs go back to the less formal, the legally less certain options? Even the uncongenial adaptation can be made congenial by the elimination of alternatives.

The Uncertainties of Adaptation

The law of unanticipated consequences appears to have jinxed many attempts to regulate or limit the flow of campaign money. The growth of PACs from 1974 to 1988—from 608 to 4,268—was certainly not anticipated by Congress when FECA passed in 1974. But by imposing stern new limits on individual contributions and much more generous ones on political committees, Congress created the incentives for a shift to PACs as an avenue for political action. Similarly, few foresaw the successful mixture of individual choice and organized group action that is the essence of bundling. The intense associational life and single-issue politics on which bundling rests had only begun to mature by the early 1970s.

The unanticipated consequences bemoaned by regulators are merely the adaptations of the regulated. From the point of view of the regulated, "unanticipated" consequences are merely adaptations to regulation that the legislature was not able to predict and head off. They are the norm in all regulation, whether of campaign finance or environmental hazards or television programming. As legislatures and administrative agencies introduce new rules, the regulated find the least costly ways of pursuing their goals under the new regulatory regime. Regulators then assess the patterns of adaptation and attempt to end the least desirable of them by various strategies of reregulation, such as closing "loopholes."

In the case of congressional campaign finance, contributors and candidates have had free rein to adapt since 1974 because the two houses of Congress and the president have been politically deadlocked over readjustments in the regulatory regime. There have been no legislative responses to the adaptations of PACs since the 1974 legislation. Moreover, the regulatory system was relaxed by the Supreme Court's 1976 decision in *Buckley v. Valeo*, in which the Court created new adaptive opportunities—notably independent spending on campaigns for federal office—that the Congress could not have anticipated.

Beyond all of this, however, lie two fundamental reasons why in campaign finance the legislators have had such troubles in anticipating adaptation and why the major actors have found it so easy to adapt creatively. First, money is a fluid, flexible, mobile resource; it is easily transferable in a way that, say, volunteered labor is not. It is not easy to contain or channel, and it flows to points of least restraint in the system. Second, there is a flourishing market for campaign money. Moneyed contributors believe their contributions yield important access and influence or that it *might* do so. In the media-based campaigns of today, candidates need those contributions badly. So the incentives for adapting rather than abdicating are very great.

Despite the adaptive freedom they enjoy, most PACs operate according to traditional forms that date back to long before 1974: the PAC collects money from individuals who accept the PAC's interests—usually the interests of a parent organization— and who cede to the PAC control over how the money will be spent. No successful amendments to FECA have threatened that basic form of organization; indeed the FEC buttressed it in 1975 by ruling that parent organizations could pay the administrative and overhead expenses of their PACs.[22] And with the form so comfortable, there has been little innovation with it. The stability in the organizational forms and operating strategies of PACs testifies to a basic fact about political organizations: they adapt when they must, but otherwise they are conservative and slow to innovate.

Although few PACs have changed their organizational form, some have altered their strategy and tactics. Some had their fling at independent spending. In the late 1970s it appeared that several nonlabor PACs were poised to adopt the expanded PAC role that characterized the labor PACs almost from their beginning: programs of political education, candidate endorsement, and voter registration and turnout drives. Ultimately they did not do so, largely because they discovered how difficult it was to defeat congressional incumbents. Instead they gradually increased their support for incumbent candidates. In 1992, for example, 75 percent of all the contributions all PACs made to House candidates went to incumbents seeking reelection; in the less competitive politics of 1990, it was 80 percent. As a response to the electoral success of incumbents, therefore, many PACs abandoned campaign finance as electoral politics in favor of campaign finance as part of the politics of legislative access.

Innovation, then, may be either organizational or strategic, and so also may adaptation. Because strategic adaptation is the easier and more readily reversible of the adaptive alternatives, PACs have usually thought in those terms. Hence the early promises that changes in the regulation of PACs would be met by greater independent spending by PACs. The shift to greater independent spending was one PACs could make without any fundamental changes in the basic operating model. But the forays by association PACs in the 1980s showed that the practice risked tensions, even fractures within the organizations. Moreover, the strategic aspects of independent spending—its unpopularity, even dysfunction in campaign politics—worked against it increasingly. That PACs are talking about bundling and networking options as adaptations in 1993—adaptations that would alter the very nature and organization of PACs—suggests that they have run out of the less drastic strategic options.

Adaptations often change those who adapt and their relationships. If some form of bundling or networking proves to be a common response to future regulation, many PACs will be profoundly changed. Those changes will have at least two important consequences. First of all, PACs will function more ideologically and less pragmatically than they have in the past. They will support more challengers and only those incumbents who are congenial on issue grounds. Their donors will demand as much for designating them as the recipients of their funds. Second, PACs may become less useful to many parent organizations because they will find it increasingly difficult to do what many parent organizations want—to pursue the legislative strategies of access that support the parent's lobbying program.

Ultimately, the question of PAC adaptation to regulation depends on the nature of the underlying group and its politics. Bundling is most feasible in PACs that bring together highly politicized and motivated individuals to support a focused issue or set of issues. It is probably also feasible among groups with well-established networks in which the individuals share common interests and are bound together by shared experiences and a mutual confidence born of joint activities. In the first case, that of EMILY's List and CLW, commitment to an issue binds the actors together. In the second, that of large national membership groups, the bond of shared interest and experience is the key.

Conversely, one may ask what it is about the group life of labor unions and corporations that has disposed them so little to bundling. Is it lower levels of information and involvement among their donors, and thus their inability to exercise the disciplined independence that bundling presumes? Is it the greater reluctance of these PACs to surrender the central control and the flexibility it offers? In labor's case, is it simply because the average contributions to labor PACs are too small to make bundling feasible? Whatever the reasons, it is possible that even these PACs may adapt bundling to their group goals and imperatives. One adapts to the adaptive options if the stakes and incentives are great enough.

Notes

I want, first of all, to express my gratitude to my research assistant, Peter Gronvall, for his invaluable help in preparing this article.

Some of the sources for the research here have been the traditional scholarly ones, and they are noted in the endnotes. But since the topic is a contemporary one, and a speculative one, I have relied more than ordinarily on interviews and national newspaper and periodical sources.

For information on EMILY's List I also depended on interviews with Eleanor Lewis and on materials published by the List. For information on the Council for a Livable World, interviews with John Isaacs and the Council's materials were equally helpful. I also drew on the knowledge of Lynn Shapiro of WISH List and Brad Considine of Sundstrand. For current trends and developments among PACs more generally, my conversations with Peter Kennerdell, Peter Shafer, Steven Stockmeyer, and Edward Zuckerman were very useful. Gail Shea of the Wisconsin Elections Board was an important informant about conduits in that state. Needless to say, I am grateful for the time and expertise of all these people.

Data on the movement of campaign funds for Congress come from the Federal Election Commission except where noted to the contrary. On Wisconsin conduits they come from the Wisconsin Elections Board.

1. "Soft money" is money that cannot be accepted and used under FECA either because of its source (direct contributions from labor unions or corporations are prohibited) or its amount (contributions may not exceed the act's limit of $1,000 per candidate per election or $20,000 per year to national party committees). Soft money cannot be used to support presidential or congressional candidates. It may be used to support candidates for state and local office, because state law, not FECA, applies to such elections. Soft money may also be used for party building and voter mobilization under amendments to FECA passed in 1979.

2. The Supreme Court struck down all limits on all spending, by candidates and noncandidates alike, in campaigns for federal office in *Buckley v. Valeo*, 424 U.S. 1 (1976). In the same case it upheld the constitutionality of limits on contributions to candidates, as opposed to spending on the campaign itself. These holdings were based on the Court's decision to cover all of the activities with the protections of the First Amendment and its reckoning that limits on contributions were less restrictive of political freedom.

3. I have treated PACs and their strategies much more fully in *Inside Campaign Finance: Myths and Realities* (New Haven: Yale University Press, 1992), especially chaps. 2 and 4.

4. Since its heady days in the early 1980s, NCPAC has declined to the point that it reported independent spending of only $6,394 in the 1990 congressional elections. In that year it also reported a debt of almost $3.9 million. Even in the early days, its reported independent spending included much more than the usual outlays for campaigning. Most nonconnected PACs that make independent expenditures must raise their funds by expensive direct-mail solicitations, and because those solicitations usually contain messages of support for certain candidates, PACs typically report them as independent expenditures. Many PACs may spend just 10 to 20 percent of their reported independent expenditures on the stuff of campaigns per se: media ads, billboards, or mailings to voters.

5. One other limit applies to individual contributors. Individuals may contribute no more than $25,000 per calendar year to candidates, PACs, or party committees involved in federal elections.

6. Although EMILY's List does not disclose the amounts it bundles for individual candidates, it does list every check it bundles in voluminous reports to the FEC, even though it is not required to report the names and sums of individual contributions of less than $200. A very enterprising journalist or academic could compute the candidate subtotals by spending days with microfilm and calculator, but so far, to the best of my knowledge, no one has.

7. 11 CFR chap. 1, sec. 110.6. The word "bundling" does not appear in this section of the *Code of Federal Regulations*, which bears the title "Earmarked contributions." The chief definition of a "conduit or intermediary" is simple: "any person who receives and forwards an earmarked contribution to a candidate or a candidate's authorized committee."

8. See note 7. Most bundling performed by individuals differs significantly from the bundling carried out by PACs. Most individual bundlers arrange an occasion and bring contributors together, but they do not accept the checks and forward them. The checks generally go to the candidate or the candidate's representative or committee. Of the minority of individuals who do actually bundle, many are not aware of their obligation to report to the FEC as a conduit.

9. S. 3 (102d Cong., 2d sess.), section 401, to amend 2 U.S.C. 441a(a)(8).

10. March 10, 1993.

11. *New York Times*, March 30, 1993.

12. The bill the House passed later in 1993 repeated the exemption for bundling PACs with no parent organization. As of July 1, 1994, the two separate bills had not even moved to a conference committee. In view of the great difference between them on a number of points, the chances of a single bill emerging from the Congress in 1994 did not appear to be good.

13. S. 3, section 401. The section provides that the term, "contributions made or arranged to be made," includes contributions made "in a manner that identifies directly or indirectly to the candidate ... the person who arranged the making of the contributions or the person on whose behalf such person was acting."

14. S. 3, section 102.

15. 424 U.S. 1 (1976).

16. Those who would eliminate PAC activity in federal elections sometimes talk of abolishing PACs and sometimes of prohibiting their contributions. While strictly speaking the two are not the same, the intention, and probably the consequences, are very similar. I use the two terms synonymously.
17. Such groups are most often called "501(c)(3) or (4)" groups after the sections of the Internal Revenue Code that give them tax-exempt status. Subsection 3, for example, describes nonprofit educational foundations; it also prescribes that they not try to influence legislation or participate in any political campaigns.
18. Reform legislation in recent years has featured attempts to make independent spending more difficult, or at least less advantageous. Both the 1992 bill the Congress passed and the Senate's bill in 1993 would have compensated a candidate who was adversely affected by an independent expenditure (that is, one urging his or her defeat or the election of the candidate's opponent). Under S. 3, for instance, such a candidate would have received publicly funded vouchers for radio or TV time in the amount of any independent expenditure of more than $10,000.
19. For reasons not easy to fathom, candidates must also include the public funding they receive in the 45 percent.
20. A bundling system in which earmarked funds were held in the treasury or bank account of the conduit would be legal under federal law in 1993. The proposed legislation of 1992 and S. 3 of 1993, however, would no longer consider such contributions as individual contributions.
21. The major scholarly piece on the Wisconsin conduits is Don M. Millis, "The Best Laid Schemes of Mice and Men: Campaign Finance Reform Gone Awry," 1989 *Wisconsin Law Review* 1465-93. It contains the relevant statutory citations, some empirical history, and long arguments on the unconstitutionality of the receipt limits on committee contributions.
22. FEC Advisory Opinion 1975-23 (December 3, 1975) is usually referred to as the SunPAC opinion because it was sought by the Sun Oil company on behalf of its PAC.

III. GROUPS IN THE
POLICY-MAKING PROCESS

9

Choosing to Advertise: How Interests Decide

Burdett A. Loomis and Eric Sexton

In general we know little about how organized interests make decisions on how to employ their resources. Decisions to commit resources are often made under conditions of great uncertainty and high stress. Results are difficult to predict, and ordinarily group leaders cannot determine the impact of their actions. Still, interests commit significant resources, even if they have little confidence in their ability to influence outcomes—of elections, information campaigns, or policy efforts.

This chapter examines a highly specialized outlet for interest group spending: advertising in the *Congressional Quarterly Weekly Report* and *National Journal,* two Washington "trade journals" that are well read on Capitol Hill and within the executive branch. Burdett Loomis and Eric Sexton sort through the types of advertisements and appeals. Somewhat surprisingly, advocacy advertising does not dominate; instead, marketing to the public sector accounts for most of the placements. As advertising is increasingly used as a lobbying tool, especially in the health-care debate, this research opens a window onto the patterns of its use.

The *New Yorker* advertisement, if it was indeed an advertisement, was gorgeous, though more than a bit mysterious. Mottled by clouds, the dark blue-turning-to-black evening sky spread across the two pages at the magazine's center. The photograph was striking, yet there was something missing—no product, no brand name, nothing. After thirty seconds or so, lurking in a patch of purple, the single word "Lockheed" emerged. Okay. It was an ad for the defense/aerospace contractor. The "Where's Waldo"-like search continued. Tucked between a couple of clouds was the minute image of a plane. That was that. Lockheed had paid tens of thousands of dollars to place an advertisement in the upscale magazine, even though the corporation was not promoting any product that any reader would conceivably purchase. The presentation made the initial, obscure ad campaign for the Infiniti automobile seem straightforward, even obvious, by comparison.

The image-oriented Lockheed ad directs us toward the core of the problem this chapter addresses: Why do interests commit substantial resources to an endeavor that will have little immediate or measurable pay-off? A public relations consultant or marketing expert might have no prob-lem answering this question. Indeed, emphasizing the positive, if nebulous, benefits of an enhanced corporate identity is an article of faith among many business advisers.[1] For those of us who approach corpora-tions as interests, however, two related questions remain: (1) how to gauge impact and, perhaps more important, (2) how to understand the internal processes of resource allocation.

In particular, we focus our attention here on paid advertisements directed at political elites. Although there are numerous outlets for such communications, two of the publications that provide extremely concen-trated readerships of national policy makers are *Congressional Quarterly Weekly Report* and *National Journal*. Why advertise in these specialized weeklies? Will a key subcommittee staff director or assistant secretary for weapons procurement have an epiphany when leafing through the arid pages of these inside-the-beltway trade magazines?

Decision Making by Organized Interests

We do not know a lot about the internal processes through which interests make important decisions. For example, despite strong theory on the dynamics of group membership, little analysis has been performed to discover when group leaders (or group "entrepreneurs") change the organization's mix of incentives as they seek to recruit or retain members (although Christopher Bosso's work on environmental groups stands as an exception).[2] Likewise, in the ten years following Jack Walker's finding that patrons were crucial to many groups' survival, only recently have we gleaned insights into how and why patrons fund particular interests.[3]

Although detailed information on how groups allocate resources is limited, there are some good pictures of overall trends[4] and some de-tailed case studies, especially on the relatively open Common Cause organization.[5] Schlozman and Tierney observe that groups have tended to do "more of the same" and that resources tend to dictate the capac-ity to act. Thus, "an organization with plenty of money ... can hire well known lobbyists, mount expensive public relations campaigns, [and] mobilize members at the grass roots...."[6] The key word here is "can." Among interest groups with great resources, some choose to lobby extensively, form political action committees (PACs), and mount exten-sive public relations campaigns, while others consciously eschew these tactics.

Group decision makers would like to think themselves rational in their commitment of resources, but both the Schlozman-Tierney data and interviews with elites demonstrate that the ability to target efforts effec-tively is extremely difficult. Organized interests compensate for uncer-tainty by engaging in increasing numbers of activities,[7] even though assessing impact is problematic at best; one veteran lobbyist described it as "a blind man searching for a black cat in the coal bin at midnight."[8]

Although our research will eventually encompass decision making by all kinds of interests, our decision to examine advertising choices has led to an initial emphasis on the business community. This short-term strategy arises from the finding (see below) that the vast majority of advertising aimed at policy elites comes from business interests.

Public Policy and the Rise of Business Involvement

Although it is debatable how much unity the American business community exhibits,[9] in general corporate interests have grown more organized and activist over the past thirty years. As David Vogel summarizes:

> [C]ompared to the situation less than two decades ago [circa 1970], businesses in the United States have become much more capable of defending and asserting their interests in Washington. Large corporations have become extremely sophisticated at dealing with both the public and government: they closely monitor political and social trends, and for many firms government relations has become an integral part of corporate strategy.[10]

Vogel concludes that business will remain heavily involved in public policy. The reach of government is great, and the stakes are extraordinarily high.

Although the variation in participation among business interests is substantial, the trend toward action is unmistakable. Organizations like the Business Roundtable have brought many chief executive officers to Washington to meet with top policy makers, thus gaining access that their regular lobbyists might not obtain. More generally, individual corporations have become increasingly active—not supplanting the actions of trade associations, but supplementing these efforts.[11] Through the 1970s and 1980s, the number of business lobbyists and lawyer/lobbyists representing corporations grew steadily. Vogel reports that, all told, well over ninety thousand lawyers, lobbyists, trade association personnel, public relations specialists, and public affairs consultants ply their trades in Washington.[12] The representation business has boomed, fueled in large part by the private sector.

Decision Making by Interests

Although decisions to allocate resources have not received much attention, there are some partial exceptions. Political action committee (PAC) choices are easily accessible and available for statistical analysis; political scientists have flocked toward the study of PAC contributions.[13]

And there have been some nascent attempts to unravel the relationships between interest groups and their patrons (see Chapters 4 and 5 of this volume).

PAC Contributions

Given their alleged influence in American politics, the simple assertion that many, and perhaps most, PAC contributions are wasted may come as a surprise. But it can scarcely be otherwise. Operating funds often consume huge chunks of PAC monies, especially for independent or "nonconnected" (in the parlance of the Federal Election Commission) organizations. PACs may back losing candidates or contribute to those candidates who will support their interests in any event. They may seek to obtain access that they would have regardless. Still, a nagging uncertainty remains: What will happen if we don't give? So give they do. For the most part PAC staff calculate who gets what.[14] For example, the manager of a business PAC concluded that a $250 contribution to key Energy and Commerce subcommittee chair Henry Waxman (D-Calif.) was worthwhile to help gain access, but that a $1,000 donation to Sen. Edward Kennedy (D-Mass.) was too expensive.[15]

The conventional wisdom is that PAC donations help ensure access[16] and that this can be measured, within rough limits. Still, much of the key activity occurs in informal conversations among legislators or in obscure subcommittee meetings.[17] The findings on PACs' impact on votes are mixed, and certainly there is no smoking gun that demonstrates effectiveness. In sum, much PAC giving comes from a defensive posture reflecting a perceived need to participate, rather than the hope that a contribution will lead to a specific favorable result.

Patrons and Public Interest Groups

A very different kind of decision takes place among public interest organizations, whose leaders often solicit large gifts or contracts from patrons such as foundations, corporations, individuals, or the government. Public interest groups seek to retain their own identity, yet they often must bend to the current winds of patron preferences.[18] On the one hand, foundations and other patrons usually have an issue orientation or an ideological bent. On the other, they are in the business of "making a determination about how they give away [their] money," as one group executive put it.[19] Given broad agreement on policy direction, foundations and groups must locate some common ground where both patron and interest will be satisfied that their purposes are being met.

Public interest groups calculate how much autonomy they can relinquish in exchange for sorely needed funds. As noted in Chapter 4, the American Civil Liberties Union has fielded criticism for accepting

$500,000 from Philip Morris; critics contended that the donation compromised the organization. ACLU leaders have argued that the relationship is "old news" and that its policies are not affected at all by the grant. Out of the glare of publicity, interest group executives regularly make this sort of judgment call; likewise, corporate officials engage in similar calculations to assess the potential impact of providing grants. Anthony Nownes observes that corporate giving, while relying on informal contacts and exchanges of ideas, "tends to be more 'bottom-line' oriented [than foundation giving and] trendier.... Because it is designed to draw good 'PR,' it may shift quickly from issue to issue and group to group." [20]

In short, businesses and other large-scale interests seek to invest in candidates (through PACs) and public interest groups (through grants). Their internal decision practices, while understudied, generally reflect a mix of rational calculation and personal networking. And in both instances, either predicting the impact or assessing the ultimate results is no simple matter.

Advocacy Advertising: A Specialized Decision

> At last, business is going on the offensive in the marketplace of ideas.... It is presenting its case directly to the public in an effort to raise awareness, inform, illuminate, and build support.... In the new activism of business, advocacy-issue advertising has become a potent vehicle of communication. Companies are adopting it to make themselves heard on a broad range of social, economic, and legislative issues.
> —Henry Gray, former CEO, United Technologies Corporation[21]

To the extent that political scientists think about policy-related advertising at all, their attention is most likely directed toward specific presentations—ranging from Mobil Oil's advocacy advertisements on the op-ed page of the *New York Times* to the NRA's more image-oriented campaign to show how "just folks" make up their membership.[22] Without any question, advocacy advertising increased over the 1970s, although exact amounts and changes are difficult to pin down.[23] Still, despite a long history of such advertising, dating back at least to a 1908 American Telephone and Telegraph campaign, the term "advocacy" gained currency only in the mid-1970s as Mobil and various other corporations and trade associations took their messages to the public.

In his pioneering (and sympathetic) study of advocacy advertising, Sethi observes that "business considers its access to the public communication space limited." [24] Hence it pays to have its message delivered to various audiences. Herbert Schmertz, the driving force behind the long-term Mobil campaign, argued that "from time to time our ads might be directed toward one person—the president of the United States, for example—or toward a small group—say the members of a congressional committee," but that ordinarily the audience was a much broader range of interested individuals who would read the weekly *Times* advertisement.[25]

Central to advocacy advertising is the notion that products are not being pushed directly. Rather, some public policy goal or corporate point of view is expressed, which may or may not have a clear connection to the corporation's immediate interests. For example, in 1981 the drug firm, SmithKline, purchased a double-page spread to discuss a potential cutoff of strategic foreign minerals as one in an extensive series of ads that presented various policy experts expounding on a host of issues.[26]

Ordinarily, there is a corporate/trade association axe to grind, although the tone is usually restrained and civilized, given the desire to be heard as a legitimate voice within a continuing debate. The question of audience remains a thorny one for advocacy advertisers. The choice of publication provides many clues in that specialized trade publications, the business press, news magazines, opinion journals, and newspapers all offer distinct "demographics." Still, the effectiveness of advocacy advertising remains difficult to gauge, even when a specific policy goal is at stake.

Pure advocacy advertising remains a weapon in the corporate arsenal, as the debate over health care has demonstrated, but an increasing share of policy-related ad expenditures goes for broad marketing efforts that offer, at most, a much-restrained advocacy voice. Moreover, in an era of corporate belt-tightening, advocacy ads may seem a luxury to some firms. All the more reason to examine the decision to advertise in expensive, low-circulation trade journals like *Congressional Quarterly Weekly Report* and *National Journal*.

Advertising in the Executive/Legislative "Trade Press"

In the highly competitive world of elite advertising, a number of vehicles offer great penetration of the Washington policy-making population. For all elites, *The Wall Street Journal* offers the most to potential advertisers in that it reaches the largest number of "issue-oriented opinion leaders" and is the publication most often cited by this group as being influential.[27] Within Washington, *The Washington Post* is the best bet, with almost all principals and staff in both the executive branch and the Congress reading it daily.[28] Although the *Journal* and the *Post* provide broad, timely exposure, they are exceedingly expensive alternatives, especially when one's audience is concentrated within the Congress and the top levels of the executive branch.

To reach senior staff and principals in Washington policy making, the two key periodicals are undoubtedly *Congressional Quarterly Weekly Report* (CQ) and *National Journal* (NJ), also a weekly. (*Roll Call*, too, has a significant presence, at least on Capitol Hill.) CQ and NJ compete against and complement each other. Their competition comes largely in a battle for the attention of extraordinarily busy individuals, most of whom face a flood of information. At the same time, CQ and NJ have carved out complementary niches in the Washington policy environment. The former stands out as a key research tool; in a sense CQ has become Congress's publication of record, whose reporters are acutely aware of their responsibility to "get it right." Although there is an increasingly analytic bent to CQ, it remains focused more on past actions than future possibilities. NJ, to the contrary, seeks to be more anticipatory, as it lays out the current agendas and scenarios of various policy communities. NJ does not take the place of a trade journal that covers a particular policy area, but it might well explain the state of affairs within that subfield to an extended audience of nonspecialist activists and decision makers.

Established in 1969, NJ has long accepted advertisements, whereas CQ began accepting them only in 1990, after forty-four years without advertising. It remains, on the whole, a bit more restrained in its pursuit of ads. For example, CQ lists each issue's contents on the back cover, thus eliminating a potentially lucrative ad space. Moreover, NJ averaged a little more than 7.5 paid advertisements per issue in 1991-1993, while CQ lagged at 5 paid ads. Still, the publications do feature much the same kind of—and often literally the same—advertisements, and competition is intense to sell this specialized type of space.

The cost of advertising in these publications is not cheap. In 1993 CQ charged $9,400 for a single full-page, four-color ad (with a ten percent premium for an inside cover position). NJ's 1993 rate for a similar ad amounted to $8,300, with a twenty percent premium for the most coveted locations. Although there are volume discounts and cheaper rates for less color (e.g., for a black-and-white ad run six times in a nonpremium space, CQ would charge $6,400 for each insertion, and NJ $5,800), the rates are enough to give pause to executives choosing among tools of influence. For example, thirteen four-color, well-placed ads would cost $115,000 to $120,000 in each of these magazines—the equivalent of twenty-three or twenty-four maximum ($5,000) PAC contributions to a congressional campaign or the annual salary of a full-time lobbyist.

Advertising Patterns

The data here come from a coding of the advertisements appearing in CQ and NJ for 1991 through 1993. We coded every advertisement from two issues per month from each publication. All were full-page presentations; neither journal accepts fractional ads. Our data reflect the content of 898 advertisements purchased by a wide range of interests.[29]

Advertising Patterns: More Voices for the "Heavenly Chorus"

What follows is a set of brief descriptions of the advertising patterns within CQ and NJ for 1991-1993. Before asking questions about why

Table 9-1   Advertisers in *Congressional Quarterly Weekly Report* and *National Journal*, by Sector, 1991-1993

Sector	Number of advertisements	Percentage of total
Aerospace/defense	280	31.2%
Finance/insurance/banking	138	15.4
Telecommunications	117	13.0
Publishing	46	5.1
Pharmaceutical manufacturers	28	3.1
Automotive	26	2.9
Electronics	26	2.9
Nuclear power	18	2.0
Others	219	24.4
[Health care[a]]	[82]	[9.1]

Note: Advertisements for publications and services offered by CQ and NJ are omitted from this and all subsequent tables. N=898.

[a] Combines health insurers, pharmaceutical companies, medical professionals, health organizations, and medical suppliers.

interests advertise in such publications, we will lay out the relevant trends. We had anticipated that the "heavenly chorus" of advertisers would be tilted in a corporate/upper-class direction.[30] This proved to be the case; even so, we were surprised by the almost complete lack of "cause" advertising from ordinarily vocal groups. A few ads by Planned Parenthood and prolife organizations, for example, were great exceptions.

Likewise, we expected substantial attention to be directed at specific policy decisions, but we were unprepared for the degree of emphasis on given, well-defined decisions, as opposed to attempts to define alternatives or to affect a general policy agenda.[31] Much of the advertising constitutes marketing to the government of specific products—often weapons systems. There is also a substantial amount of general image advertising, most often for corporations, although some other interests (e.g., a Washington-area public radio station) combine marketing with image polishing.

Types of Advertisers

For even the most casual reader of CQ or NJ, it can come as no shock that the defense/aerospace, telecommunications, finance, and health industries, broadly defined, dominate this particular kind of elite communication (Table 9-1). Each of these sectors depends heavily on federal policies, and key interests have deep pockets to finance their advertising.

Although this analysis will be fleshed out in greater detail, there should be no confusion at all about the nature of the advertising sector by

Table 9-2   Advertising by Specific Interests: The Top 15

Advertiser	Number of advertisements
McDonnell Douglas (aviation/defense)	64
Merrill Lynch (financial services)	38
Lockheed (aviation/defense)	32
Grumman (defense)	27
Bell-Boeing Partnership (aviation/defense)[a]	27
General Dynamics (defense/aerospace)	24
Regional Bells (telecommunications)	22
Health Insurance Association of America	22
Ameritech (communications)	21
Freddie Mac (financial)	19
Hughes (aviation/electronics)	19
Lockh'd/Boeing/Gen. Dyn./Pratt & Whitney (defense)[a]	18
U.S. Council on Energy Awareness (nuclear power)	18
Hitachi (electronics)	18
Pharmaceutical Manufacturers' Association	18

[a] Including various partnerships, Boeing's ads combine to a total of 60; Lockheed's add to 50.

sector. What we are seeing is not pluralism at work; rather, the monied voices are weighing in. Lockheed and McDonnell Douglas may disagree over specific weapons systems, but the defense/aerospace sector as a whole speaks with a single voice in promoting its products for the post-Cold War era.

In none of these sectors does a countervailing commercial force appear. Medium-sized insurers may make a different health-reform argument than the drug industry, but there are no advocates, say, for a single-payer system to be found on the advertising pages of CQ or NJ during 1991-1993.

There was a smattering of advocacy advertising by "cause" groups—twenty-one instances by organizations like the Union of Concerned Scientists, the National Right to Life Committee, and Planned Parenthood. But advertisements by such groups with no direct economic interests stand out as real exceptions; weeks can go by without the audience of NJ or CQ coming across a presentation that does not reflect mainstream corporate or trade association thinking.

Advertising by Specific Interests

Nothing in the list of the most frequent advertisers contradicts the findings by sector (Table 9-1). McDonnell Douglas is the most aggressive individual advertiser, with its presentations appearing in 44 percent of the issues sampled (64 of 144; see Table 9-2). As with those of Boeing and

Lockheed, McDonnell Douglas's ads aim at the government market and combine dramatic visuals with self-congratulatory texts. The other top advertisers offer a similar commitment to a government-elite advertising strategy, although the particulars of the campaigns vary. For the most part, aerospace/defense/aviation ads follow the McDonnell Douglas model, while the financial and health placements provide more text and fewer visuals. (After all, an expanded individual retirement account does not take off from a carrier deck or ride the space shuttle.)

One modest pattern does emerge here. Even though some health/drug corporations (Pfizer, Baxter) have recently begun to advertise in these magazines, most of this sector's advertising has been purchased by trade associations. In contrast, the aerospace/defense industry is almost exclusively represented by individual companies with specific, often competing, products. At the same time, competition goes hand in hand with cooperation, as many advertisements promote items produced by multicompany partnerships (for example, the X-30 experimental aircraft team). Even when pursuing a speculative, future policy like the X-30, the defense/aerospace industry does not operate through a trade association; its coalitions are defined by products, not overall interests.

Types of Advertisements

More than any other aspect of our study, the question of classifying types of advertisements proved the most difficult. We divided advertisements into five types: government marketing, private marketing, general policy, specific legislation, and public service. The two-page spreads purchased by Aetna illustrate some of the coding problems. These ads are dominated by visual effects, yet they often focus their brief texts in very effective ways. NJ/CQ readers see these ads in other publications (*The New Yorker*) and react to them as public policy makers and as potential private Aetna clients. In addition, Aetna often provides a kernel of general policy thought in its presentations. We chose to code the Aetna ads as public service on some occasions, private marketing on others, and government marketing on another. The overlapping messages all contributed to the Aetna corporate image, but individually they were difficult to characterize.

Most advertisements focused their messages on specific products, policies, or legislation. Almost half the ads sought either to market a product to the government or advocate passage of specific legislation (Table 9-3). The specificity is striking; nothing is more pointed than an ad for an F-18 fighter or a V-22 Osprey (the controversial vertical take-off aircraft). At the same time, the repetitive nature of many ads, including those for the V-22, burnished the overall image of the corporation—or the partnership, in the case of Bell-Boeing Osprey.

General policy advocacy is emphasized in about one-fifth (21.8 per-

Table 9-3   Types of Advertisements

Type	Number of advertisements	Percentage of total
Government marketing	341	38.0%
General policy	196	21.8
Private marketing	146	16.3
Public service	135	15.0
Specific legislation	80	8.9

Note: N=898.

cent) of all ads, and the public service category makes up the remainder (15 percent). Still, specific messages are the order of the day. When private marketing ads are added to those promoting government marketing and specific legislation, almost two-thirds of the advertisements are accounted for. The elite policy journals do serve as vehicles for specific policy information, but most often in the form of marketing messages rather than in presentations directed at pending legislation. The defense industry pushes its products, but does not lobby directly for more spending, at least in these pages.

Still, there are a substantial number of classic advocacy advertisements, which make up more than 17 percent of the total (154 of 898) and include virtually all those in the specific-legislation category, plus some with a general policy message. These range from a handful of prolife ads to several pointed campaigns that focus on particular policies or legislation. Given the nature of the advertisers, most of the advocacy messages echo the preferences of well-funded interests such as the nuclear power industry, the railroads, and health insurers. And much of the advocacy comes through in muted tones. Although the railroads' trade association did mount a brief, well-focused 1991 campaign to discredit truckers' requests for longer trailers and three-trailer rigs, such a consistent, concentrated effort is noteworthy as an exception to most messages. More common were the tactics of the cable television industry. Because cable reregulation was hotly contested during the 102d Congress, we expected that cable organizations might have embarked upon a tough-minded advocacy campaign.[32] The industry did indeed advertise a good deal, but almost all of its presence (nine placements) highlighted its C-SPAN sponsorship—a service near and dear to most legislators' hearts. More generally, given the high levels of information within congressional and executive offices, sharply worded advocacy presentations might have little impact, especially when issues have been thoroughly aired. Efforts in a lower key—featuring balanced information or strong visuals—may find a more receptive audience. This may be why, when specific information is presented, it most often comes

Table 9-4   Advertising by Policy Stage

Type	Number of advertisements	Percentage of total
Agenda stage	140	23.6%
Alternative proposal stage	130	21.9
Specific decision stage	324	54.5

Note: Of the 898 advertisements in our sample, 304 did not refer to any policy position. Most public service ads followed this pattern. N=594.

through in visually attractive presentations, rather than dense, text-based advocacy ads.

Advertising by Policy Stage

In his work on agenda setting, John Kingdon distinguishes among stages in policy development, beginning with relatively broad agendas, continuing with more focused policy alternatives, and ending in specific decisions.[33] Setting aside those ads not oriented to the policy process, such as public service placements, we separated the remainder according to their place in the policy process. A majority of the ads that could be classified into one of the policy stages focus on specific decisions, even though Table 9-3 showed that there were more than twice as many "general policy" ads (21.8 percent of all) than "specific legislation" messages (8.9 percent). Why this seeming contradiction?

First, more than a third of all the ads (304 of 898) could not be placed into any policy stage at all; these included most public service and private marketing presentations (Table 9-4). Second, most government marketing ads emphasize particular products or programs, many of which already exist. These ads encourage lawmakers to continue funding items that have worked well in the past, such as McDonnell Douglas's "battle-proven" pair of cruise missiles, which are "used by 20 nations worldwide," or to adopt new programs or systems already in the policy pipeline.

Although traditional advocacy ads do account for a fair number (80) of the specific-decision stage presentations, government marketing ads are much more numerous (244, or 75 percent). In short, advertisers (corporations and their ad agencies) run relatively traditional, product-oriented campaigns, rather than emphasizing advocacy efforts.

Why Advertise? Catering to Pols and Policy Wonks

Committing substantial funds to advertise in these "congressional trade magazines" reflects a combination of decision elements. The immediate calculation of readership numbers cannot be comforting to a corporate advertising director. CQ had a "qualified" subscription base of 9,863 in December 1992; NJ's was 5,971.[34] Based on location within the publication and the number of issues in which the ad was to run, an advertiser would expect to pay $1-$2 per qualified subscriber for its placement; that's the bad news. The good news is two-fold. First, each copy of these elite journals is read by several individuals. NJ claims that each issue is perused by 6.3 readers beyond the initial subscriber. In addition, these readers spend a substantial amount of time with each issue; CQ cites research showing that almost half (46 percent) of its subscribers spend more than an hour with each issue. NJ claims that subscribers spend an astounding average of seventy-one minutes with each issue. Even more important than the pass-along readership and the extended scrutiny given the magazines are the institutional positions of subscribers. The cornerstone of the value provided by CQ and NJ is their entree into the offices of movers and shakers—both on Capitol Hill and within the executive branch, as well as within the mainstream media.

Equally important, no matter how expensive, CQ/NJ advertising often represents a minuscule amount of a corporation's overall investment in Washington or of its total advertising budget. For Boeing, McDonnell Douglas, or Aetna, "trade journal" advertising is a small part of a much broader corporate image strategy. Although advertising and public relations generally overlap quite a bit, they seem especially intertwined in the Washington environment, where so much information is aimed at so many targets.

Robert Wallace, CQ's advertising director, sees much of the advertising as "a vital part of the legislative process." His counterpart at NJ, Linda Cheesman, takes a somewhat less policy-driven perspective.[35] She sees NJ ads as keeping a corporation or interest at the "top of mind" of key decision makers—who might conceivably set up a conference, ask for advice, or issue an invitation to a hearing. Both Wallace and Cheesman observe that their magazines can provide a constancy of presence within congressional and (especially) executive offices that lobbyists cannot offer. The Clinton administration has proved resistant to some corporate efforts at gaining access, and these policy journals offer an alternative avenue. In addition, with substantial legislative turnover in 1992, one government relations staffer observed that "you really need an entree. Ads are alternatives to meeting with all these new members."

Although from the outside CQ and NJ appear to cover similar ground, at least two major differences stand out in the sales literature they provide to prospective advertisers and in conversations with advertising executives. First, CQ is more a recorder of events; it cites research that 69 percent of its subscribers keep their issues for a year or longer, and 81 percent refer back to previous issues. NJ emphasizes its ability to lead opinion; included in its packet was a raft of press clippings citing the magazine as a source.

Second, CQ focuses more narrowly on the Congress than NJ, and much of its policy reporting comes from a congressional perspective. NJ, by contrast, emphasizes its broad reach across Washington. Its introductory letter offers the comparison: "Other Washington publications primarily target Congress. Savvy advertisers recognize the considerable influence of the Executive Office of the President, federal agencies and the Cabinet in the policy formulating process."

After leafing through dozens of CQs and NJs, we found ourselves surprised by the extent to which the advertisements did not seem directed at elite policy makers and politicians. The policy messages presented in the highly visual ads were often no more sophisticated than those that could be found in *Newsweek*. Occasionally one finds the exception—the Hughes Corporation on science developments or Merrill Lynch on finance policy. The question remains, however: Why were more advertisements not more sophisticated in their approach to this elite policy audience?

CQ's Wallace argues that many ads had previously been approved within a stratified corporate environment, so that CQ received the same ad that might be placed in, say, *Business Week*, with its own elite audience. Although CQ might be appreciated for its readership, that was not enough to move most interests to shape a new ad.

From a more traditional advertising perspective, NJ's Cheesman put a different spin on highly visual, repetitive corporate ads. She emphasized the desirability for repetition and retention—with policy elites not being much different in many ways than other readers. If key aides or principals maintained a "top of mind" reference to a firm, that could well be more valuable than communicating a specific, sophisticated message.

Merrill Lynch

Although a few interests did generate sophisticated, reasonably complex messages, no firm was more noteworthy than Merrill Lynch, which used a consistent, text-dominant format to put forward a range of policy messages that related to its multiple financial missions. In particular, the firm emphasized a need for greater savings and legislation to increase eligibility for individual retirement accounts (IRAs).

Rather than using previous ad copy, Merrill Lynch emphasized the role of its Washington government relations personnel. Working through a single member of the firm's Corporate Advertising Department, they discuss the issues they wish to address in their next ad. Once the subject and direction of the ad are decided, the agency is brought in. Often the agency's role is limited to creating an illustration and headline for the copy written by the government relations staff and/or their advertising department contact. Other times the agency is given background materi-

"Welcome back to Washington."

The second session of the 103rd Congress will be marked by difficult and challenging debates on numerous issues.

The Administration's health-care reform proposal, which is aimed at restructuring about one-seventh of the U.S. economy, is one of the most far-reaching and ambitious domestic policy initiatives ever proposed.

Budget reforms and further deficit reduction efforts will also be debated as will a number of important international trade issues, including China MFN and legislation to implement the recently completed GATT agreement.

Also, we hope Congress will begin to explore ways to encourage more saving and investment

and deal with our saving crisis.

The debates on these and other issues will be watched from Washington to Wall Street, to Main Street, and to other streets throughout the world.

 **Merrill Lynch**

A tradition of trust.

Merrill Lynch, Government Relations Office, 1800 K Street, N.W., Suite 620, Washington, D.C. 20007 (202) 965-5575
© 1994 Merrill Lynch & Co., Inc.

als and a clear statement of Merrill Lynch's position on the issue involved. In either case, the entire process rarely takes more than three or four days. Figure 9-1 is a typical ad. The Merrill Lynch staff was extremely clear about its targeted audience:

> Regardless of where our ads appear, Congress is our constituency. We focus on "in-house" publications such as CQ, NJ, and *Roll Call*. It's an "inside baseball" approach. We want members and staffers to say, "We know what's on your mind."

This targeted process, while efficient, would scarcely seem exceptional. Yet it was highly unusual among most interests, which did not seek to craft individual messages for the elite audience of CQ and NJ. Merrill Lynch stood as an outlier by systematically tying its government affairs staff in Washington to its ad agency's efforts, with timely reactions to the magazines' deadlines. On another dimension, however, Merrill Lynch did typify heavy advocacy advertisers in that its chief executive officer stood solidly behind its message-oriented approach. Such top-level support is often critical for a corporation to advocate any substantial policy position.

The V-22 Osprey

If Merrill Lynch reflected one end of the advertising spectrum, the efforts on behalf of the V-22 Osprey aircraft represented the other. Resisted by the Reagan and Bush Administrations, unwanted by the armed services save the Marine Corps, the V-22 gained much of its support from congressional allies who saw jobs in this huge weapons system. The Bell Helicopter-Boeing partnership ("The Tiltrotor Team") put forward, time and time again, a visual image of the aircraft taking off, accompanied by a modest text, much of which listed the wide array of missions the plane might fulfill (Figure 9-2).

The V-22 campaign exemplifies the "top of mind" reasoning in deciding to advertise. No new information is conveyed. Rather, the same points are made in the same ways—much as Nike or Reebok might seek to establish high name recognition. The focus is on a single decision—to produce the highly suspect vertical take-off aircraft. With the stakes so high, a corporation may view hundreds of thousands of dollars in advertising as a truly modest expenditure.

In addition, the advertising campaign for such a large and tenuous project may well be directed as much within the corporate structure as toward Washington elites. As one lobbyist pointed out, "Lots of money is spent externally for internal corporate reasons—to cover your ass. The defense boys are the best in the world at that—of course they live and die on a few contracts."

The Thorny Question of Effectiveness

The impact of advertising in these trade journals is exceedingly difficult to assess. Ordinary measures, such as those based on sales or surveys,

04 DEC. 90, 2120Z; BEGAN SHIPBOARD TESTS.

The V-22 Osprey – the multimission, vertical-lift aircraft represents American technology at its absolute best. And the National Aeronautic Association apparently agrees. Because it awarded the V-22 the most prestigious Collier Trophy for greatest achievement in aeronautics in the past year. Never before has one aircraft held so much promise. Had so much versatility. With so little compromise. In fact, the V-22 meets or exceeds 32 multiservice mission requirements. And on December 7, 1990, it successfully completed initial Navy shipboard compatibility tests in the Atlantic Ocean. Let's keep our edge. Let's produce the V-22.

BELL BOEING

The ▼ Tiltrotor Team
A JOINT SERVICE PROGRAM
© 1991 Bell® Helicopter Textron Inc./Boeing Helicopters.

are inappropriate, given small audiences and the lack of ordinary sales figures. NJ's Cheesman sees two ways of roughly estimating effectiveness. First, given a specific goal, was it accomplished? Granted that no cause-effect relationship can possibly be established, success casts a glow over everything that one does, much like victorious political candidates' "congratulation-rationalization" assessments of their own performances.[36] Goals may include more than winning or losing, however. As one public relations firm's vice-president noted, "Other clients may have different goals. Tobacco firms, for example, have essentially been buying time for the past twenty years."

Second, Cheesman argues that anecdotal evidence can provide meaningful indicators of impact. "If you hear your position articulated by someone else, it's an indication of some effect," she states. Various advertising professionals agree. One noted that "In talking to staffers, we know that the ads are read.... We've had stuff show up in the *Congressional Record*—not attributed, often just a fragment, but sometimes a whole sentence." And a trade association representative notes, "You get [a sense of impact] by monitoring C-SPAN. Suddenly you'll hear a familiar phrase."

CQ's Wallace is somewhat more skeptical; he observes that impact is almost impossible to gauge and that some advertising agencies enjoy doing elite policy ads precisely because of this difficulty. Their clients cannot hold them directly accountable for effectiveness, and the agencies can argue that the ads have established a certain presence without having to demonstrate a specific impact.

More broadly, much of the corporate advertising in CQ and NJ may fall more under the heading of public relations than ordinary advertising. Indeed, the decision to advertise often relates directly to the CEO's approach to public relations. For example, Robert H. Hood, the president of Douglas Aircraft Co. (of McDonnell Douglas) concludes that "the way public relations can have the most value is to make it an integral component of the management team—that means being in the room when key decisions are made and strategies developed."[37] Measured by its expenditures and regular presence, no firm made policy journal advertisements more a part of an overall strategy than did McDonnell Douglas.

Rather than making a case-by-case assessment of individual ads, a firm with an integrated public relations strategy may simply fold advertising decisions into its overall philosophy. Again, the commitment of a CEO is central. As one veteran oil industry lobbyist commented,

> Given the strong political orientation of our CEO [to be a national-level player], there are two levels of political activity ... the "megaframe" perspective on big issues like the budget, free trade, and health. And then there are whole sets of policies where the company is more explicit in its interests. Our goal is to build a sense of comfort within the Administration ... to provide information and imply "be involved."

Interests' Internal Decisions and Advertising for Elites

The stakes of public policy making are frequently astronomical, given a federal budget of more than $1.5 trillion in annual outlays. In addition, shaping or adapting to regulatory policies can require millions, even billions, in corporate expenditures. And broad health-care reforms mean the potential disruption of one-seventh of the economy. It is thus scarcely a curiosity that Merrill Lynch and McDonnell Douglas annually spend roughly $200,000 each on advertising in the trade journals of Congress and the executive branch. The more relevant question may be why more interests do not pursue similar strategies. Two basic reasons emerge, one simple, the other more complex. First, many interests do not possess adequate resources to advertise regularly, if at all. The "heavenly chorus" of advertisers in elite policy journals sings with a monied accent.[38]

More complex are the internal decision-making processes that lead to systematic advertising campaigns. Many lobbyists, advertising executives, association representatives, and public relations specialists report that, even in the 1990s, many CEOs shy away from Washington politics, especially when it involves taking a public position. The product-based advertising of the defense industry presents few problems, but anything smacking of a policy message requires active support from the top levels of the trade association, corporation, or interest group. CEO backing will usually carry the day in a corporation, but trade associations and membership groups present more complex situations. One staff member of the American Association of Retired Persons observed that the very size of the organization (33 million members) dictated a laborious process for clearing ads, even on a crucial issue like health care: "The ads have to go through a lot of different checkpoints—the legislative people, legal, the CEO—and the ads [thus] tend to be cautious."

Conversely, the nuclear power industry has adopted a much more aggressive strategy. As a top U.S. Council for Energy Awareness official put it,

> Our membership of 400 nuclear clients, including utilities, corporations, universities, and medical facilities, has turned over the whole job to us. We're paid as experts; there's not a whole lot of discussion. We tell our industry what we should be doing.

If this seems an extreme position, it has won the day because the nuclear energy campaign, emphasizing clean air and energy choices, has apparently had a substantial effect on public opinion.

In sum, most advertising directed at policy elites can be best understood as one component of the broad public relations strategies of those interests that can afford them. The commitment of a CEO explains much of the decision, as well as the stakes of individual policy choices, such as weapons procurement. Moreover, marketing efforts outweigh advocacy presentations, and most interests do not choose a medium that, in the end, serves more as a complement to traditional lobbying than as a substitute for it.[39]

Notes

1. See, among many others, James G. Gray, Jr., *Managing the Corporate Image* (Westport, Conn.: Quorum Books, 1986).
2. Mancur Olson, Jr., *The Logic of Collective Action* (New York: Schocken, 1971), Terry M. Moe, *The Organization of Interests* (Chicago: University of Chicago Press, 1980), and John Mark Hansen, "The Political Economy of Group Membership," *American Political Science Review* 79 (March 1985): 79-96. Christopher J. Bosso, "Adaptation and Change in the Environmental Movement," in *Interest Group Politics*, 3d ed., ed. Allan J. Cigler and Burdett A. Loomis (Washington: CQ Press, 1991): 151-176. For more on the notion of groups as entrepreneurs, see chaps. 1-5 of this volume.
3. Jack Walker, Jr., "The Origins and Maintenance of Interest Groups in America," *American Political Science Review* 77 (June 1983): 390-406; Anthony Nownes, "The Other Exchange: Public Interest Group Entrepreneurs and Patron," Ph.D. dissertation, University of Kansas, 1993.
4. In particular, see Kay Lehman Schlozman and John T. Tierney, *Organized Interests and American Democracy* (New York: Harper and Row, 1986).
5. Andrew S. McFarland, *Common Cause: Lobbying in the Public Interest* (Chatham, N.J.: Chatham House, 1984), and Lawrence Rothenberg, *Linking Citizens to Government* (New York: Cambridge University Press, 1992) and "Agenda-Setting at Common Cause," *Interest Group Politics*, 3d ed., ed. Cigler and Loomis, 131-149.
6. Schlozman and Tierney, *Organized Interests and American Democracy*, 161, and Burdett A. Loomis, "A New Era: Groups and the Grass Roots," in *Interest Group Politics*, ed. Allan J. Cigler and Burdett A. Loomis (Washington: CQ Press, 1983), 169-190.
7. Ibid., 150, 155.
8. Cited in Loomis, "New Era," 184.
9. Jeffrey M. Berry, *The Interest Group Society*, 2d ed. (Glenview, Ill.: Scott Foresman Little Brown, 1989), 216ff.
10. David Vogel, *Fluctuating Fortunes* (New York: Basic, 1989), 296.
11. Schlozman and Tierney, *Organized Interests and American Democracy*, 287.
12. Vogel, *Fluctuating Fortunes*, 198.
13. There is a huge and growing literature here. See Chapters 7 and 8 of this volume, and, more generally, Frank Sorauf, *Inside Campaign Finance* (New Haven: Yale University Press, 1992).
14. Berry, *The Interest Group Society*, 137.
15. Dan Clawson, Alan Neustadl, and Denise Scott, *Money Talks* (New York: Basic, 1992), 123.
16. Ibid.
17. Richard L. Hall and Frank W. Wayman, "Buying Time: Moneyed Interests and the Mobilization of Bias in Congressional Committees," *American Political Science Review* 84 (September, 1990): 797-820.
18. Nownes, "The Other Exchange."
19. Ibid., 111.
20. Ibid., 166.
21. Introduction to S. Prakash Sethi, *Handbook of Advocacy Advertising* (Cambridge, Mass.: Ballinger, 1987), ix.

22. Sethi, *Handbook of Advocacy Advertising*, 43.
23. Ibid., 21.
24. Ibid., 18.
25. Herbert Schmertz, *Good-Bye to the Low Profile* (Boston: Little Brown, 1986), 136.
26. Sethi, *Handbook of Advocacy Advertising*, 176-177.
27. Erdos & Morgan/MPG survey, 1992, cited in CQ's media kit for prospective advertisers.
28. Ibid.
29. Coding categories include name of interest (e.g., Boeing); type of interest (e.g., aerospace firm); ad subject (e.g., V-22 Osprey); ad category (e.g., government marketing); policy stage (either agenda, alternative, or specific decision); location (e.g., inside front); and ad character (e.g., combines text and visuals). Beyond the 898 paid ads, an additional 188 promoted in-house publications, seminars, and services of Congressional Quarterly Inc. or the *National Journal*. Indeed, Congressional Quarterly Inc. and *National Journal* were the leading advertisers in their respective publications. Almost a fourth of all CQ's ads (115 of 472, or 24.4 percent) represented self-marketing. Even with more modest ancillary publications and services, NJ devoted 73 of its 614 advertisements (12.3 percent) to self-marketing—far more pages than any paying client purchased. Both these publications use their self-marketing to bolster their own claims to influence. In particular, Congressional Quarterly Inc. employs the *Weekly Report* to push products, such as the daily *Congressional Monitor*, spun off its tremendous overhead of reporting and data compilation. In addition, CQ offers seminars that often feature many of the very policy-making figures that its ads target; these seminars use some CQ staff, but also rely heavily on outside experts in legislative procedures, budgeting, regulation, electoral interpretation, and lobbying. In sum, Congressional Quarterly Inc. is a force within the Washington community far beyond the reach of its lead publication.
30. Kay Lehman Schlozman, "What Accent the Heavenly Chorus? Political Equality and the American Pressure System," *Journal of Politics* 46 (1984): 1006-1032.
31. John Kingdon, *Agendas, Alternatives, and Public Policies* (Boston: Little Brown, 1984).
32. The cable industry was certainly capable of playing hardball; the Wichita cable operation ran hundreds of editorials blasting local Rep. Dan Glickman (D-Kans.), who won both the right of response and the election.
33. Kingdon, *Agendas, Alternatives, and Public Policies*, 206ff.
34. BPA International figures, which are the standard benchmarks for publications.
35. Statements attributed to individuals, whether or not the individuals are identified, are drawn from personal interviews and roundtable discussions. We are particularly indebted to CQ's Robert Wallace for organizing a roundtable discussion among several advertisers.
36. John Kingdon, in *Candidates for Office* (New York: Random House, 1968), argues that victorious candidates congratulate themselves on winning strategies, whereas losers rationalize their defeats. Neither winners nor losers actually know what works.
37. Dana Winokur and Robert W. Kinkead, "How Public Relations Fits into Corporate Strategy," *Public Relations Journal* (May, 1993): 16-17.
38. There are modest exceptions, of course. When CQ published a special health-care supplement in September 1993, several interests anted up the funds for a one-time purchase of advertising space in a publication that was explicitly designed to serve as a reference work for the forthcoming debate on health-care reform. These included the American Osteopathic Association, the Council for Responsible Nutrition, the American Academy of Physician Assistants, and the Paralyzed Veterans of America.

39. Indeed, various advertising professionals noted that lobbyists liked having ad reprints available to leave with staffers as tangible reminders of positions that their interests had taken publicly.

10

Campaigning for the Court:
Interest Group Participation in the
Bork and Thomas Confirmation Processes

Christine DeGregorio and Jack E. Rossotti

From the onset of the Reagan administration in 1981, the politics of federal judicial appointments have become increasingly, although not universally, contentious. The Reagan Justice Department explicitly sought conservative Supreme Court Justices and federal judges; appointments also came overwhelmingly from the ranks of white males. The Bush administration continued this general trend, if in a somewhat muted way. Still, most appointments raised few objections, and even a tough-minded, controversial conservative such as Antonin Scalia won unanimous confirmation to the Supreme Court from the Senate.

Quite different, however, were the bruising Supreme Court confirmation battles over Federal Court of Appeals judges Robert Bork and Clarence Thomas in 1987 and 1991, respectively. The interest group politicking over these nominations was unprecedented. The first battle left a new verb in the American political lexicon: for conservatives, to be "Borked" came to signify an ambush by hostile interests.

In this article, Jack Rossotti and Christine DeGregorio provide a somewhat more dispassionate analysis of interest group actions on the Bork and Thomas nominations. They carefully compare two bitter, highly publicized battles over that most valuable of presidential appointments—a lifetime position on the highest court in the land.

B y the mid-1980s the proliferation of interest groups in American politics had become a well-established phenomenon. Not only had advocacy groups, both conservative and liberal, become well entrenched in the legislative process, but these same groups had also penetrated executive policy making.[1] The one area where interest groups still had a relatively modest impact on policy was in judicial politics. While the judiciary was

The authors wish to acknowledge in particular the valuable assistance provided by Nancy Broff (Alliance for Justice), Brent Bozell (Conservative Victory Committee), Tom Jipping (Coalitions for America), and Bob Bingaman (NARAL). We also wish to thank Laura Natelson of The American University for her valuable assistance in the preparation of this manuscript.

not totally free of interest group activity, it experienced less outside pressure than did the legislative and executive branches.[2]

Two landmark events, the confirmation processes of Robert H. Bork and Clarence Thomas to the United States Supreme Court, in 1987 and 1991 respectively, may have permanently changed this condition. During these two events, hundreds of interest groups, conservative and liberal, engaged in campaign-style attempts to confirm or defeat the nominees.

This article analyzes the array of tactics that organizations employed in seeking to shape the membership of the Supreme Court. To this end we examine how organizational resources, attitudes, and conflict shape the promotional character of the debate. Our evidence is drawn from interviews with 109 participants representing one hundred advocacy groups that took the lead in promoting their organizations' wishes concerning the confirmations.[3]

Historical Perspective

Although interest group activism in judicial nominations has increased, it is by no means unprecedented. Definitive evidence shows that advocacy organizations were major players in the confirmation processes of Louis Brandeis in 1916 and John J. Parker in 1930. In the Brandeis case, organized labor worked mightily on his behalf, and Jewish organizations contributed to a smaller degree. Brandeis was opposed by a collection of business groups, including the American Bar Association and some Wall Street law firms. The latter hired a full-time lobbyist in Washington.[4]

The unsuccessful Parker nomination involved even greater interest group activity. At the forefront of the opposition were organized labor and the National Association for the Advancement of Colored People (NAACP). Caldeira and Wright have called the NAACP's campaign against Parker "one of the most sophisticated and best organized political operations of the twentieth century," involving grassroots activity, Washington lobbying, and public exposure through the media.[5]

More recently, advocacy groups were active in Richard M. Nixon's failed nominations of Clement Haynsworth (1969) and G. Harrold Carswell (1970). In the Haynsworth case, interest group activity was largely limited to the opposition. Leading the groups against Haynsworth were labor and civil rights organizations, "the same coalition which defeated the Court nomination of Parker in 1930."[6] The AFL-CIO, the NAACP, the International Union of Electrical, Radio, and Machine Workers and the Textile Workers Union of America were the most notable of these.[7] The Americans for Democratic Action, the Leadership Conference on Civil Rights, and the Urban League also participated.[8]

Maltese's case study of the process reveals that the White House operated almost by itself in supporting Haynsworth.[9] Among the tactics the administration used were a mass mailing to three thousand editors, publishers, and broadcasters, personal phone calls to editors and broadcasters, and public appearances by administration officials. The White House also used state groups and prominent individuals to put pressure on senators. Still, "no major organized groups lobbied for the nomination." [10]

The Carswell nomination immediately followed the unsuccessful Haynsworth nomination. A *Congressional Quarterly* analysis of the process revealed that the well-organized opposition to Carswell came both from individuals and groups. Predictably the AFL-CIO and the NAACP were out front in opposing Carswell. However, the Leadership Conference on Civil Rights and the National Organization for Women were also part of the anti-Carswell forces, as were individual judges, law school deans, and law school professors.

In sum, the trend is toward more involvement in the Supreme Court confirmation process by an increasingly diverse array of advocacy groups. Combined with the overall growth of these organizations in the 1960s and beyond, it should come as no surprise that the Bork and Thomas confirmations became so hotly contested.

The Bork Nomination in Context

In the spring of 1987, immediately prior to Bork's nomination, the Supreme Court was almost evenly divided between liberal and conservative justices. Many commentators inside and outside the federal government agreed on the dividing lines. By most accounts, the four liberals included Justices William J. Brennan Jr., Thurgood Marshall, Harry A. Blackmun, and John P. Stevens III. The four conservatives included Justices William H. Rehnquist, Antonin Scalia, Sandra Day O'Connor, and Byron R. White. When issues split the Court evenly it was Justice Lewis F. Powell Jr. who typically provided the decisive swing vote.[11] This combination of judicial temperaments, together with the tendency of the Supreme Court to encroach into legislative business,[12] made for a politically explosive situation when Justice Powell submitted his resignation in June 1987. Liberals and conservatives alike viewed the appointment of Powell's replacement as one likely to have major ramifications for the subsequent decisions of the Court.

The decisions the liberals had embraced and the conservatives abhorred since the days of the Warren Court (1953-1969) pertained to civil liberties, the role of the federal courts, and the power of the states versus the federal government. Coinciding with this expansionist orientation of the Court, the number and diversity of citizen-based interest groups rose to new heights. The first wave of growth occurred among liberal groups during the 1960s and 1970s, partly in response to government expansion associated with the programs of the Great Society. During the 1980s many conservative groups sprang up, in part to protect society from what they perceived to be an erosion of basic family values.¹³

The uncertainty surrounding the outcome of this confirmation intensified when the Democratic party regained its Senate majority following the 1986 elections. The three previous Reagan nominees had won confirmation easily, with only one generating any opposition within the Republican-controlled Senate (1981-1986).¹⁴

Furthermore, having come to the federal judicial system by way of academia,¹⁵ Judge Robert Bork had left a paper trail of opinions and law review articles. His extensive and often controversial record intensified the public's interest in the debate. Bork repeatedly criticized the activism of the Supreme Court during the post-1954 period. He maintained that the Constitution should be interpreted according to the 'doctrine of original intent,' an orientation that might have restricted many rights advanced by the Warren Court, including the right to privacy that guaranteed a women's ability to obtain an abortion.¹⁶

The Thomas Nomination in Context

By the time of the Thomas nomination the Supreme Court had changed markedly from its near-even philosophical division immediately preceding the Bork nomination. According to most Court observers, the high Court was firmly in the control of conservatives by the spring of 1991. Only three political liberals or moderates remained—Justices Marshall, Blackmun, and Stevens. Six justices usually sided with conservative opinion: Rehnquist, Scalia, O'Connor, White, David Souter, and Anthony J. Kennedy.¹⁷

For at least two reasons a different mood surrounded the Court. President Bush had just appointed Justice Souter, an apparently conservative justice, and there was no reason to believe the Thomas nomination would not follow suit. Moreover, no great ideological change was likely, even if another conservative seat was added. In their book on the Thomas nomination, Phelps and Winternitz observe:

> For the senators preparing for Thomas's confirmation the fundamental question no longer had anything to do with balancing the Supreme Court. The Republicans had already succeeded in packing it with conservatives. The question was where Thomas would come down in the new power struggle within the Court's right wing.¹⁸

While the atmosphere was initially less charged over Thomas, owing in part to the new status quo, Judge Thomas was controversial in his own right. His record, race, and age help account for the conflict he aroused. At the time of his nomination, Thomas was a judge on the United States Court of Appeals for the District of Columbia Circuit, nominated for that position by President Bush in 1990. Thomas had served previously as chair of the Equal Employment Opportunity Commission (EEOC) and as assistant secretary for civil rights in the Department of Education. While Thomas's brief tenure on the Court of Appeals may have been of limited utility in evaluating his nomination, his record at the EEOC was extensive and controversial. As chair, for example, he allegedly blocked numerous age-discrimination complaints from older workers and retirees. As Dan Schulder of the National Council of Senior Citizens pointed out, this alone was enough to arouse that group to come out early as an ardent foe of the nominee.[19]

Thomas had clearly benefited from federal affirmative action policies, particularly as applied at Yale Law School.[20] In his tenure as senior executive and judge, however, he renounced these interventions and instead embraced self-help and empowerment approaches. Black and Hispanic organizations were particularly perplexed over how to proceed. Despite their desire for an African American on the Court, they were fearful that he might undermine movement on major issues central to their groups' agenda.[21] Some opponents attributed their boards' ultimate decision to get involved to Thomas's disinclination to use government intervention as a means of increasing the numbers of women and minorities in the workplace.

Working sometimes in his favor and sometimes against him was the candidate's race. As an African American and a staunch conservative, he created a wedge in certain segments of the minority interest group community. Although several polls showed that a majority of African Americans in the United States supported confirmation,[22] several activists in the anti-Thomas camp reported that their organizations were split over how to proceed. Hesitation among these governing boards delayed the groups' entries into the process; this factor may have contributed to the initial success of the nominee's proponents. Nor could some of the groups rely on a cohesive following when they finally went public with their opposition to the nominee.[23]

Thomas's age also motivated both supporting and opposing advocacy groups. Only forty-three at the time of his nomination, he would probably remain on the Court for a long time, perhaps four decades. When added to his apparently conservative ideology, Thomas's youth aroused intense fear on the part of some and hope on the part of others. Each side saw a reason to get involved.

Finally, controversy raged in the latter stages of the confirmation process in response to allegations that Judge Thomas had sexually harassed university professor Anita Hill.[24] We omit this facet of the interest group struggle from our analysis for two reasons. First, we focus on what is typical of advocacy campaigns to understand customary practices. Second, the media extravaganza that arose to address these specific charges did not prevent Thomas from being confirmed by the Senate, although the final margin may have been narrowed.[25]

The Cases Compared

The Bork and Thomas confirmation processes differ along several dimensions: (1) the cohesiveness of membership opinion for or against the nominee within the organizations involved; (2) the aggressiveness with which the White House promoted each candidate; (3) the extent to which the appointee might change the Court's decisions; (4) the readiness, solidarity, and motivation with which the two sides embraced their task; and (5) the partisan composition of the Senate.

Rank-and-file members within the pressure groups interested in the nominations held substantially different opinions toward Bork and Thomas. Bork supporters and opponents were clear about their positions; group leaders and followers experienced no intragroup conflict over what stand to take. As noted, such clarity did not exist within the ranks of organized interests over Judge Thomas. We will analyze how intragroup conflict over whether to support or oppose Thomas affected the ability of the opposition to rally its troops.

Second, as pressure groups prepared to do battle over Bork, they found the Reagan administration remarkably passive. Fed either by overconfidence[26] or fear that their involvement would serve as a lightning rod to the opposition,[27] the president and his surrogates demonstrated little initial enthusiasm for their nominee. They launched no media campaign, nor did they make many visits to Capitol Hill.[28] Determined not to repeat the mistake of 1987, the Bush White House took an active role from the outset in defending Thomas.[29] The difference in the way the two administrations approached these cases may have affected the aggressiveness of some interest groups.

Third, the consequences the two confirmations would have on the decisions of the Court differed greatly. Recall that after Justice Powell's resignation in 1987, the Court was evenly split between political liberals and conservatives. The addition of one reliably conservative justice would doubtless shift some court decisions on important issues such as privacy and civil rights. By 1991, the Court was already solidly controlled by conservatives, and Thomas's presence would not have the far-reaching ideological consequences that would likely have occurred with Bork.[30]

Fourth, the camp that was most highly motivated differed in the two cases. With Bork, it was the opponents who were most motivated by their cause. The Democrats had just regained control of the Senate in the 1986 elections and wanted to use the Bork nomination to inflict a defeat on the conservatives' judicial and social agenda.[31] With Thomas, the roles were reversed, as the proponents of the nomination sought a cause. Conservative groups had raised money for an ideological battle, and the Thomas nomination became that cause.[32]

Lastly, between 1987 and 1991 the Democrats had gained two more Senate seats to raise their majority to 56-44. Thomas' supporters had a significant uphill battle to piece together a winning coalition. However, this problem was somewhat offset by the inability of some of the leading Democratic senators to speak out against Thomas as they had against Bork. Anticipating character attacks against Thomas, conservatives produced a television ad attacking three Democratic senators for being involved in their own personal scandals.[33] One of the sponsors of the ad, Brent Bozell of the Conservative Victory Committee, told us that the ad "neutralized the leadership on the Left."

Interest Group Politics: Strategies and Tactics

Organized interests typically employ many approaches when pursuing a legislative objective. They may lobby officials, hold strategy sessions with key players, inspire their members, coordinate their efforts with other groups, or reach out to the media with promotional ads and editorials.[34] Scholars attribute the choice of tactics primarily to the resources the groups have to commit to a political struggle and to the level of conflict the outcome arouses.[35]

Key resources include any number of items that help an organized group build support for its cause. Money, staff, active members (volunteer supporters), timely information, personal credibility (of members and staff), organizational credibility, and personal rapport (for example, trust) are particularly valuable to an advocacy group.[36] These and other resources open doors on Capitol Hill. And in the words of one interest group scholar, "access begets influence, and unequal access begets unequal influence."[37]

Still, group leaders expend resources differently, depending on their availability and appropriateness for action. This is where the political context comes into play, and two factors are especially important here. The elective nature of lawmakers' jobs makes them particularly cautious when the public is aroused and interested in their decisions (a condition known as public salience). Also, when issues are controversial, interest group leaders need to be careful not to worsen matters by increasing resistance to their aims.[38] Because a high degree of public interest existed in both of these confirmation battles, we cannot evaluate how the presence or absence of public salience affected interest group politics. That intragroup divisions emerged in one instance and not in the other, however, presents a splendid opportunity for observing the effects of conflict on advocacy.

In the following sections we examine how contextual features that distinguish these events (for example, intragroup conflict and the role of the administration), the groups' position toward the outcome (for example, supporting or opposing the nominee), and organizational resources (for example, staff and members) affect three spheres of interest group activity.

Interest group tactics involve three different groups of participants: individuals internal to the group, those from other organizations, and individuals unaffiliated with any organized effort. In the first sphere, professional staff members and committed volunteers (often high-profile directors from the groups' policy-making boards) pressure senators by lobbying them directly and testifying in public hearings. Also, group leaders prompt letter-writing campaigns by reaching out to known partisans already affiliated with the organization. This strengthens the group's hand because officeholders are receptive to appeals from their constituents, particularly when the organizations can demonstrate widespread confidence in their position.[39] Of all the activities we consider, these should be most frequently employed because they entail a minimum amount of coordination and the least risk of arousing unforeseen opposition to one's cause.

The second sphere of activity, the coalition approach, occurs when one organized group reaches out to other organized groups for the purposes of coordinating resources and sharing information. The coalition members may or may not be political allies from previous promotional endeavors. This activity, although appealing when the division of labor provides valuable economies of scale, may be costly to an organization's own interests. (See Chapter 11.) This is particularly true when the search for common ground among coalition partners undermines the peace and stability group leaders have worked to achieve within their own organization.

The third and final sphere of activity entails applying pressure on Senate insiders by arousing mass opinion through campaign-style techniques. To be effective this approach requires an attentive citizenry, a condition that existed in both controversies that we study. Of all the activities described, this is the only one that involves unorganized individuals. Because the public strategy can arouse friends and foes alike, this approach is particularly dangerous when support for one's cause is tenuous or unknown. The Bork and Thomas controversies provide an excellent test of such a risky course of action.

Tactics, Contexts, and Cases

In an effort to piece together a comprehensive picture of what interest groups do to influence confirmation politics, either directly or indirectly, we listed a variety of techniques and invited the participants in the study to rate them according to their perceived usefulness in molding Senate opinion. The activities presented in the rows of Table 10-1 are clustered into three spheres of influence, according to our theoretical interests.

As expected, some tactics are reported to have been employed with greater frequency than others, and the hierarchy roughly conforms to our

Table 10-1 Priority Tactics as Employed by Advocates in the Bork and Thomas Confirmation Processes

Tactics	Total (N=109)	Bork priority (N=59)	Thomas priority (N=50)
Internal Group Activities			
1. Lobbying Senate	65.0%	59.3%	72.0%
2. Holding strategy sessions with members of Congress or staff	13.0	13.6	12.0
3. Preparing witnesses	13.0	10.2	16.0
4. Reaching out to group members	40.4	57.6	16.0[a]
5. Coordinating internal group efforts	33.9	33.9	34.0
Intergroup Activities			
1. Coordinating activities with other groups	44.4	42.4	46.0
2. Participating in strategy sessions with other groups	30.0	37.3	22.0[a]
External Group Activities			
1. Writing op-ed pieces, appearing on talk shows, etc.	20.0	20.3	20.0
2. Conducting polls or other research towards building mass appeal	4.6	6.8	2.0
3. Networking to keep presence in media	18.3	22.0	14.0

Note: Respondents assigned each activity a value: "1" through "4" indicating first, second, third, and fourth priority rating, respectively. These are collapsed into two columns labeled "priority" above. The tactics that were employed but not ranked as a priority and the tactics that were not employed at all make up the unreported balance in each cell.

The row percentages do not sum to 100 because the figures in each column reflect only the proportion of participants who assigned the activity a priority rating: overall, in the case of Bork, or the case of Thomas, respectively.

[a] $p < .05$.

theoretical hunches. As evidence of this, the only activities to appeal to more than 50 percent of the participants are in the top third of the table (see the column labeled "total"). The activities endorsed by more than one-third of the participants fall in the middle tier of approaches, and those receiving the least support fall into the final sphere of activity.

When the data are broken down by cases, we find that the groups behaved similarly from one debate to the next. Although the participants in the Thomas fight place a higher priority on direct lobbying of the Senate than did those in the Bork fight, this is the tactic of choice in both cases (72 and 59 percent, respectively). Moreover, with only two exceptions, the frequencies are remarkably consistent across the board.

The exceptions—"reaching out to group members" and "participating in strategy sessions with other groups"—are very convincing ($p < .01$). And because they both involve outreach of one sort or another, we return to the circumstances that surrounded the events to explore why these discrepancies occurred. According to the respondents, the case for (or against) Bork was clear. His record could only be interpreted one way, and it was good news for conservatives and bad news for liberals. Group organizers could reach out to their members and their organizational allies with little fear of eroding their base. By contrast, the argument for (against) Thomas was ambiguous. His record was not as extensive as Bork's, and some group advocates had difficulty anticipating how Thomas would rule as a justice. His race also raised problems for some organizations. Members of La Raza, for example, had been hoping that an Hispanic would be nominated.[40] Leaders of the NAACP faced dissension from members who feared Thomas might undermine some hard-won civil rights advances. Indeed, the division in many segments of the black community was substantial. As one writer put it:

> For the nation's black leaders, it has been a fractious summer of internal wrangling since President Bush nominated a black conservative to the Supreme Court. From that moment, the core of civil rights officials, ministers, and lawyers usually regarded as the barometer of African-American sentiment no longer was a monolith. Black leaders have suffered an unprecedented spasm of disunity as they face an apparent gulf between the black establishment and the ordinary black citizen over the nomination of federal Judge Clarence Thomas.[41]

Under conditions like this, it is no wonder that participants in the Thomas debate rank outreach tactics lower in effectiveness. According to Bob Bingaman of the National Abortion Rights Action League (NARAL), the opposition failed in its effort to block Thomas's confirmation because members of African-American organizations were insufficiently united and vocal in calling for the nominee's defeat.

Tactics and Positions

Does support for or opposition to a candidate affect group tactics? Looking at the evidence, some important similarities and dissimilarities stand out (Table 10-2). First, the only activities that receive consistent, and sometimes remarkably high, favor by opposition forces are those that rely exclusively on the groups' internal resources (staff and members). The opposition forces in both struggles see little advantage in influencing senators by first reaching the mass electorate through published editorials and talk shows.

Some findings are particularly noteworthy. Opponents in the Thomas case, compared to opponents in the Bork case, place markedly less importance on three activities. These include: "reaching out to group members," "participating in strategy sessions with other groups," and "appealing to unorganized citizens through the mass media." The pro-Bork and pro-Thomas groups differ from one another only in their regard

Table 10-2 Selected Tactics by Case and Position Toward Nominee

	Bork		Thomas	
Tactics	Supporting priority (N=30)	Opposing priority (N=29)	Supporting priority (N=25)	Opposing priority (N=25)
Internal Group Activities				
Lobbying Senate	51.7%	66.7%	64.0%	80.0%
Reaching out to group members	51.7	63.3	4.0[b]	28.0[a,c]
Coordinating internal group efforts	31.0	36.7	20.0	48.0[a]
Intergroup Activities				
Coordinating activities with other groups	48.3	36.7	40.0	52.0
Holding strategy sessions with other groups	27.6	46.7	28.0	16.0[a]
External Group Activities				
Writing op-ed pieces, appearing on talk shows, etc.	24.1	16.7	32.0	8.0[a,c]

Notes: The activities included in this table received priority status from 20 percent or more of the participating groups. Respondents assigned each activity a value: "1" through "4" indicating first, second, third, and fourth priority rating, respectively. These are collapsed into the columns labeled "priority" above. The tactics that were employed but not ranked as a priority and the tactics that were not employed at all make up the unreported balance in each cell.

[a] Opponents in the Bork case differ significantly from opponents in the Thomas case. p < .05.
[b] Supporters in the Bork case differ significantly from supporters in the Thomas case. p < .05.
[c] Supporters and opponents within a specified case differ significantly. p < .05.

for reaching out to rank-and-file members. As before it is the Thomas participants who discount this activity.

Lastly, Table 10-2 demonstrates when and how the adversaries varied their tactics in particular contexts. There are no marked differences in the choice of tactics of the belligerents in the Bork controversy. Such uniformity is not present among the parties to the second debate, however. Thomas's opponents embrace two tactics more than do his supporters—"reaching out to group members" and "coordinating internal group efforts." And when it comes to public outreach via op-ed pieces and talk shows, Thomas's supporters are considerably more enthusiastic than are his opponents (32 and 8 percent respectively).

Tactics and Resources

The evidence demonstrates that interest group leaders vary their organizations' tactics according to the challenges they face in their political environments. But resources (for example, staff and members) also

Table 10-3   Mean Level of Organizational Resources by Case and
Position Toward the Nominee

		Bork		Thomas	
Resources	Total (N=109)	Supporting (N=29)	Opposing (N=25)	Supporting (N=25)	Opposing (N=25)
Paid staff	44.3	13.1	36.0[c]	33.0	91.4[a,c]
Individual members (in thousands)	351.8	316.0	422.0	137.0	525.5
Active members (in percent)	31.3	38.8	28.2	34.3	26.8
Resources committed to this campaign (in percent)	17.9	29.1	21.4	5.7[b]	11.11

Note: One extraordinarily large organization with staff and membership twice the size of other organizations participating in the Thomas study was deleted from this analysis.
[a] Opponents in the Bork case differ significantly from opponents in the Thomas case. p < .05.
[b] Supporters in the Bork case differ significantly from supporters in the Thomas case. p < .05.
[c] Supporters and opponents within a specified case differ significantly. p < .10.

figure into the groups' appraisals of tactics. In particular, we want to know if these political skirmishes were fought on a roughly even playing field. To address this issue we must answer two questions. Are the groups that took opposing positions toward the nominees organizationally richer, poorer, or on a par with their adversaries who supported confirmation? Second, is there any connection between resources such as staff strength or membership size and the choice of tactics? We review three measures of organizational strength: paid staff, total membership, and active members (in percentages). We then examine the resources committed to specific fights (in percentages).[42]

The groups involved in the Bork and Thomas confirmation fights have an average of 44 paid staff members and 352,000 members (Table 10-3). At any one time the respondents count on the active involvement of only about 31 percent of their members. In the Bork and Thomas fights the average (annualized) commitment of overall organizational resources was about 18 percent. (Some groups committed full-time attention to the issue for as long as four months. Thirty-three percent, therefore, represents the maximum of the range.)

The differences in organizational resources that reach conventional levels of statistical significance (p < .05) are of two types. Either the opponents or the supporters differ among themselves from one event to the next, or the adversaries in the same contest report substantially different resources. The Thomas opponents enjoyed more paid personnel than those who opposed Bork. Faced with this show of force, Thomas's backers report making one-fifth the organizational commitment made by Bork's supporters, further exaggerating the disparity between the contestants. Although we cannot definitively explain this difference in commitment, the modest show of force by Thomas supporters fits with the increased commitment of the administration, something the group leaders could not help but sense. Looking at it another way, Bork's supporters may have steeled themselves for a tough fight knowing that President Reagan and his subordinates were relatively inattentive to their nominee. Ironically, those record-high levels of commitment coincide with White House urgings that pro-Bork groups maintain a low profile so as not to arouse the opposition.

In both confirmation battles the opposition forces report having many more paid staffers than those supporting the nominee. While this gap was immense in the Thomas struggle and may have serious implications for group politics, the statistical test of significance ($p < .10$) raises doubts about its stability. In terms of members, the opposing forces are again somewhat larger than the supporting forces, but there is great variation among the allies on each side. Lastly, the contestants in each of the confirmation battles were roughly similar in their shares of active members and overall organizational commitments.

When we aggregate the participants into two camps—those who assign priority status to a tactic and those who do not (data not shown)—there is a positive and significant relationship between the groups' appraisal of "lobbying the Senate" and their supply of staff (in the Bork case only). In the Thomas fight two positive relationships emerge, although one is more pronounced than the other. The groups that place a high priority on "networking to keep a presence in the media" have large numbers of members relative to those who do not see this as a priority. And to a lesser degree the large membership groups are the ones that place a high value on "coordinating internal group efforts."

Taking the last point first, we do not know for certain if group leaders paid more attention to internal coordination because of their groups' numbers alone, or because Thomas aroused intragroup conflicts that leaders needed to quell. Both explanations are plausible. The positive relationship between an organization's membership and contacts with the media is intriguing because it seems counterintuitive. A naive observer might speculate that organizations with the fewest members would have the greatest incentive to reach out to the unorganized masses through the media. Instead, we find evidence for an alternative explanation: Apparently, the more members one has the more media outlets one can pursue (local, regional, and national).

Taken together, the results uncover a kind of balancing act. When a specific resource is found to have some bearing on a particular activity (say, membership size and networking), the resource is distributed fairly evenly among the competing groups. When a resource is most unevenly distributed between competitors, such as paid staff in the Thomas fight, it has little bearing on the choice of tactics. Indeed the strongest indication that resources affect tactics is the relationship between staff and lobbying, a phenomenon observed only in the Bork campaign.

Coalition Politics

When groups combine forces, they usually forfeit a piece of their organizational agenda[43] and in some instances a large measure of their recognition. Still, officeholders appreciate when traditional adversaries within the interest group community bury their differences and provide Congress with a workable solution. The passage of the Clean Air Act of 1992 is a case in point. After twelve years of haggling, clean air advocates got together with business and industry representatives to provide a solution that most legislators could defend with their respective constituencies.[44]

The up or down nature of the confirmation process and the short time horizon in which senators must come to judgment pose different challenges to officeholders and advocates. Rather than reducing conflict and reconciling differences over judicial appointments, coalitions that form over judicial appointments seem to expand the conflict, raise public awareness, and put senators on alert. With this in mind, we address two questions about intergroup coalitions. Under what circumstances do groups work with other groups? And what do the coalition partners share that may account for their willingness to join forces?

Contrary to journalistic reports that describe the opposing forces as better organized than the supporting forces over Bork [45] and vice versa over Thomas, we find that the adversaries in both events joined informal coalitions at a very high rate. Table 10-4 presents information on the subset of players who joined coalitions to support or defend Judge Thomas. Comparable quantitative data are not available on the groups that fought over Judge Bork.[46] In the following paragraphs, therefore, we draw primarily from the qualitative statements that the Thomas participants used to explain their scores.

The pro-Thomas coalition was orchestrated by five major players: Coalitions for America, the Family Research Council, Concerned Women for America, the Christian Coalition, and the Traditional Values Coalition. The anti-Thomas coalition was primarily directed by the Leadership Conference on Civil Rights, the Alliance for Justice, NARAL, and People for the American Way. Both sides emphasized the importance of coalition work.[47]

This was a grassroots coalition effort. It [the confirmation] succeeded only because it was a coordinated effort. (Tom Jipping, Coalitions for America) The anti-Thomas effort would not have gotten

Table 10-4   Information Shared Among Coalition Partners by
Position Toward the Thomas Confirmation

Information on	Total (N=46)	Pro-Thomas (N=22)	Anti-Thomas (N=24)
Thomas's record	89.1%	86.4%	91.7%
Strategies (brainstorming)	78.3	72.7	83.3
Coordination of effort	73.9	68.2	79.2
Senate committee members (Judiciary)	73.9	68.2	79.2
Senate committee staff (Judiciary)	71.7	68.2	75.0
Media contacts	45.7	45.5	45.8
Polls on public opinion	44.4	40.5	47.8
Research on crafting messages	43.2	31.8	54.5[a]

[a] $p < .05$.

to first base without the coalition. (Charlotte Flynn, The Gray
Panthers)

Beyond speculating on the connection between coalition work and
the ultimate outcome, the participants described what they shared with
their organizational allies. Much coalition behavior involves sharing information; the sharing varies according to the type of knowledge transferred. Sharing materials on the nominee's record, which is done routinely, has an educational flavor and involves essentially public—if not
widely known—information. In the case of Bork, whose writings were
extensive and technical, the task of assembling what became known as
the "Book of Bork" required considerable expertise and time. The
groups that were ill-equipped for the task counted on their allies for the
analysis.

Groups also regularly joined together to "brainstorm" about strategies. This give and take is qualitatively different from the mere transfer of
facts. NARAL's Bingaman describes how comprehensive such strategic
planning can be. As he put it, the anti-Thomas forces had a four-part plan
that included targets inside and outside the Washington beltway. Initially
the groups focused on shoring up friendly senators who would logically
oppose Thomas. Then the coalition went after undecided senators, particularly southern Democrats and prochoice Republicans. Next, the coalition laid out a grassroots effort with various organizations using their affiliates to engage in postcard and telephone campaigns to senators. Finally,
efforts were made to meet with editorial boards of local newspapers.

Coordination extends beyond planning. Three activities in Table 10-
4 attract strong endorsements from participants: coordinating group efforts (73.9 percent) and sharing information about Senate insiders—Judiciary Committee members (73.9 percent) and staff (71.7 percent). This

makes sense, in that groups often specialize in narrow issue niches.⁴⁶
Some participants knew the players on the Judiciary Committee from
previous advocacy campaigns, whereas others did not. Together, groups
share their knowledge of who's who in Congress and target senators for
appeals from key individuals and interests. The coordination of information and tactics often go hand in hand. As Schulder of the National Council of Senior Citizens noted, "The anti-Thomas coalition helped by sharing information on senators. These discussions led to strategic decisions
about tactics—who would do grassroots work with a given senator." But
not all coalitions look the same. Brent Bozell of the Conservative Victory
Committee stated: "The groups in the pro-Thomas coalition took different tacks. The coalition lobbied the Senate and stayed exclusively inside
the beltway, while the Conservative Victory Committee went outside."
     Through coalition work the groups capitalized on their strengths—
inside knowledge of Judiciary Committee members, well-placed members, and staff expertise. Through specialization, the participants also
maximized the resources of any one group. This was particularly important to the supporting forces who commented on their relative shortage of
resources. According to Laurie Tryfiates of Concerned Women for America, "The conservative groups did not have the resources that the other
side had. We needed a coalition effort."
     The three types of information that fewer than 50 percent of the
groups share pertain to the media, either knowledge of whom to contact
(45.7 percent), or data on public opinion (44.4 percent) or messages (43.2
percent). This is reasonable, in view of the fact these activities command
the least attention of the groups (Table 10-1).
     A second major finding lies in the similarities in both sides' views
of sharing information (Table 10-4). Although the anti-Thomas groups
report slightly higher reliance on almost all modes of sharing information, only one activity is viewed substantially differently by the two
sides. The opposition forces shared research on crafting messages more
often (54.5 percent) than did the supporting forces (31.8 percent). In
that pro-Thomas groups disagreed among themselves over the use of
negative ads, they may have avoided collaborating on the content of
promotional material because to do so would create unwanted conflict
among allies. For example, Bozell and the Conservative Victory Committee favored an aggressive posture because of the closeness of the vote,
but other groups resisted that approach, preferring positive messages
and tactics.⁴⁹
     In most cases a group's position toward the nominee does little to
explain why it chooses to cooperate with other interests and share valuable information. What, then, of organizational resources? The only such
resource that varies substantially in terms of coalition work is one that has
offered no explanatory insights thus far. Now we find that the groups with
large shares of "active members" are the ones that engage in "coordinat-

ing group efforts" and "sharing information on members of the Judiciary Committee."

These patterns reflect the importance that legislators accord appeals from community leaders in their own constituencies. The organizations that capitalize on sharing information on senators and coordinating their efforts with other groups are those with large shares of active members who will vigorously make such targeted appeals.

Conclusions

The confirmations of Judges Bork and Thomas ended differently, one in defeat and one in victory. There are many explanations for these results that have little to do with the power and organization of the competing groups.[50] The partisan balance in the Senate, the president's term in office, the force with which the administration pursues its nominee, and the record and style of the nominees themselves are just a few of the ingredients that could tip the decision one way or another. We thus side-stepped the question of the precise degree of influence interest groups might have on the confirmation process and tackled a more manageable one about the nature of organized promotional politics.

Using evidence from interviews with 109 participants who led the causes for and against two candidates for the high court, we identified an array of tactics, differentiated between high priority and nonpriority items, and examined the extent to which these appraisals varied with the groups' resources, their positions toward the nominees, and the challenges they faced in the political environment.

Several lessons came to the fore. First, after classifying interest group tactics according to who takes part in the initiatives, we found that some practices were more widely accepted than others. As we expected, group leaders placed the highest priority on the tactics that involved their own members and staff. To a moderate degree they favored activities that entailed working with members and staff of other advocacy organizations. Apparently the economies of scale brought on by coalition work more often than not outweigh the organizational drawbacks. The promotional practices that commanded the least appeal were those that entailed reaching out to unorganized citizens in the mass public.

Second, we found that resources, contexts, and tactics changed appreciably from one confirmation to the next. And although resources alone seldom dictate diverging views toward tactics, dissimilar contexts do. Substantial variations in interest group practices correspond with differences in the way the two presidents pursued their nominees and the level of intragroup conflict each event aroused.

Third, the most valuable lesson that comes from comparing the promotional behavior of interest groups over time is perhaps the importance of sequencing. By all accounts, the failure to confirm a conservative judge to the Supreme Court in 1987 galvanized support for another such judge in 1991.[51] Even before Clarence Thomas's name was announced, conservative organizations were planning their campaign. Not only were the losers in the Bork controversy more determined to win, but also they adjusted their behavior according to what had and had not worked for them before.[52] In particular, Thomas's supporters decided to wage a more public and, at times, a more negative campaign than they had ever done in the past.

Our final observation is about the future. The escalating struggles over judicial nominations, culminating with the Bork and Thomas confirmation battles, lead us to believe that highly contentious public campaigns, although not inevitable in Supreme Court confirmations, are likely to return to the political landscape with some regularity. The logical question is, when will the next one occur?

We have seen that it takes special circumstances to generate a situation resembling that of the Bork and Thomas confirmations. Most likely, anyone perceived by the president's opposition party as being excessively partisan and anyone seen as politicizing the law can expect treatment similar to that received by judges Bork and Thomas. A recent warning of this type has already sounded. As we go to press, Justice Harry A. Blackmun has announced his retirement. Writing in a newspaper column about Blackmun's possible replacement, Tom Jipping, one of the leaders of pro-Thomas coalition, observed: "If [President] Clinton chooses someone to replace Justice Blackmun who lacks clear and unimpeachable credentials on crime and who will legislate from the bench, he can expect vigorous opposition."[53]

Notes

1. Burdett A. Loomis and Allan J. Cigler, "Introduction: The Changing Nature of Interest Group Politics," in *Interest Group Politics*, ed. Allan J. Cigler and Burdett A. Loomis (Washington, D.C.: CQ Press, 1986), 1-26.

2. For a considerable time interest groups such as the American Civil Liberties Union have been active in filing friend of the Court briefs in important Supreme Court cases. See Gregory Caldeira and John R. Wright, "Interest Groups and Agenda Setting in the Supreme Court of the United States," *American Political Science Review*, 82 (1988): 1109-27. See also, Lee Epstein and C. K. Rowland, "Interest Groups in the Courts," *American Political Science Review*, 85 (1991): 205-217.

3. Our evidence on interest group politics comes from two independent studies, one conducted in 1990 (Bork) and the other conducted in 1992 and 1993 (Thomas). In each case, the investigators drew a random sample of organizations from a larger population of groups as identified in a variety of published sources. Groups were categorized as small or large depending on how they measured up in terms of reaching or exceeding median levels of three resources—paid staff, membership, and budget. Deborah M. Burek and Karen E. Kolk, *Encyclopedia of Associations*, 2d ed. (Detroit, Mich.: Gale Research, 1990). The fifty-nine groups that participated

in the first study represent 78 percent of the targeted sample, whereas the fifty groups that participated in the second study represent 68 percent of the targeted sample. In each case the nonresponse rate stems from one of two sources. Either the individuals could not be located or they refused to participate. The lists of organizations that comprise each sample are presented in Appendices 1 and 2.

4. Caldeira and Wright, "Lobbying for Justice."
5. Ibid.
6. Ibid., 337.
7. *Congressional Quarterly Almanac* (Washington, D.C.: CQ Books, 1969), 1076-1077.
8. Warren Weaver, "Rights and Labor Leaders Oppose Court Nomination," *New York Times*, August 19, 1969, 27.
9. John Anthony Maltese, "The Selling of Clement Haynsworth: Politics and the Confirmation of Supreme Court Justices," *Judicature* 72, 6 (April-May 1989): 338.
10. *Congressional Quarterly Almanac* (Washington, D.C.: CQ Press, 1969), 1077.
11. See Lawrence H. Tribe, *God Save This Honorable Court.* (New York: Random House, 1985); Ethan Bronner, *Battle for Justice: How the Bork Nomination Shook America* (New York: W.W. Norton, 1989); Michael Pertschuk and Wendy Schaetzel, *The People Rising: The Campaign Against the Bork Nomination* (New York: Thunder's Mouth Press, 1989).
12. Bronner, *Battle for Justice*; David O'Brien, *Storm Center: The Supreme Court on American Politics*, 2d ed. (New York: W.W. Norton, 1990).
13. Loomis and Cigler, "Introduction: The Changing Nature of Interest Group Politics"; Jeffrey M. Berry, *The Interest Group Society.* 2d ed. (Boston: Little, Brown, 1989).
14. Justice O'Connor was confirmed by a 99-0 vote (1981); Justice Rehnquist was elevated to the position of Chief Justice by a 65-33 vote (1986); Justice Antonin Scalia was confirmed by a 98-0 margin (1986).
15. From 1962 to 1975 and 1977 to 1981, Judge Robert Bork was a member of the faculty at Yale Law School; from 1982 to 1988 he was a judge on the United States Court of Appeals for the District of Columbia Circuit. During this period he built up an extensive publication record on a wide variety of legal issues. One article, in particular, was often cited during the debate; in a 1971 issue of the *Indiana Law Journal* he attacked the Supreme Court's decision to create a constitutional right to privacy.
16. *Roe v. Wade*, 410 U.S. 113 (1973). Bork, Robert H., *The Tempting of America: The Political Seduction of the Law* (New York: Erie Press, 1990).
17. Justice Kennedy was the ultimate recipient of the seat that Ronald Reagan intended to go to Judge Bork.
18. Timothy Phelps and Helen Winternitz, *Capitol Games: Clarence Thomas, Anita Hill, and the Story of a Supreme Court Nomination* (New York: Hyperion, 1992), 163.
19. Schulder also noted, "Many thousands of claims under the ADEA [Age Discrimination and Employment Act] lapsed for lack of processing and investigation by the ADEA staff under Thomas' leadership." In response, Congress passed a special law extending the time to pursue claims of older workers under the ADEA.
20. Phelps and Winternitz, *Capitol Games.*
21. Phelps and Winternitz, *Capitol Games*; Thomas was nominated to replace Justice Thurgood Marshall, who in 1991 was the only African-American member of the Court.
22. Paul Bedard, "Bush Stresses Black Support" *Washington Times*, October 15, 1991, A1.
23. Ronald Taylor, "Thomas Shatters Black Consensus," *Washington Times*, August 28, 1991, A1; Ruth Marcus, "Group That Helped Defeat Bork Opposes Thomas," *Washington Post*, July 20, 1991, A5.
24. Phelps and Winternitz, *Capitol Games.*

25. When the topic came up in our interviews, the respondents reported that they had been ready for character attacks in advance of Hill's charges. One of the leaders of the pro-Thomas effort, Tom Jipping of Coalitions for America, planned for character attacks, believing that the anti-Thomas groups could not defeat the candidate on the merits. His organization prepared a strategy that took issues and character into consideration.

26. Patrick McGuigan and Dawn H. Weyrich, *Ninth Justice: The Fight for Bork* (Lanham, Md.: University Press of America, 1990).

27. Bronner, *Battle for Justice.*

28. McGuigan and Weyrich, *Ninth Justice.*

29. Phelps and Winternitz, *Capitol Games.*

30. Ibid., 163.

31. Ibid., 26.

32. Ibid., 142.

33. The three senators were Edward Kennedy (D-Mass.), Joseph Biden (D-Del.), chair of the Senate Judiciary Committee, and Alan Cranston (D-Calif.).

34. Two accounts of the value interest group representatives place on these activities can be found in Kay Schlozman and John Tierney, *Organized Interests and American Democracy* (New York: Harper and Row, 1986); and Jack Walker, *Mobilization of Interest Groups* (Ann Arbor: University of Michigan Press, 1991).

35. Christine DeGregorio and Jack E. Rossotti, "Resources, Attitudes and Strategies: Interest Group Participation in the Bork Confirmation Process," *American Review of Politics*, 15 (Spring 1994); and Walker, *Mobilizing Interest Groups.*

36. Christine DeGregorio, *Networks of Champions: Leadership, Access, and Advocacy in the U.S. House of Representatives*, in preparation.

37. John T. Tierney, "Organized Interests and the Nation's Capitol," in *The Politics of Interests*, ed. Mark P. Petracca (Boulder, Colo.: Westview Press, 1992), 204.

38. On the first point see, for example: John F. Manley, "Congressional Staff and Public Policy Making: The Joint Committee on Internal Revenue Taxation," *Journal of Politics*, 30 (1968): 1046-1067; Morris P. Fiorina, *Representatives, Roll Calls, and Constituencies.* (Lexington, Mass.: Lexington Books, 1974). On the second point see, for example: Jeffrey H. Birnbaum and Alan S. Murray, *Showdown at Gucci Gulch: Lawmakers, Lobbyists and the Unlikely Triumph of Tax Reform* (New York: Basic Books, 1987); and Diana Evans, "Lobbying the Committees: Interest Groups and the House Public Works and Transportation Committee," *Interest Group Politics*, ed. Allan J. Cigler and Burdett A. Loomis, (Washington, D.C.: CQ Press, 1991).

39. Scott Ainsworth, "Regulating Lobbyists and Interest Group Influence," *Journal of Politics* 55 (February 1993): 41-56.

40. According to Charles Kamasaki of the National Council of La Raza, "We did not want to oppose Thomas because he was not Hispanic, but we thought an Hispanic justice was appropriate. The political calculus was difficult ... the White House said, in effect, 'if you think you will get an Hispanic justice next time by defeating Thomas you are wrong.'"

41. Ronald A. Taylor "Thomas Shatters Black Consensus," *Washington Times*, August 28, 1991, A1.

42. Early in the interview, after the respondent had established that the group was intimately involved in the confirmation process, the interviewer asked, "How much of your organization's overall resources went into the (named nominee) fight? The question came next, followed by the subsequent question on resources. The question read, "Thus far you have described the activities that absorbed resources—the expenditure side of the budget, so to speak. Now I want to know about the group's resources from an income perspective." Three of the

items listed for the interviewees' comment were: total membership, active membership (as a percent of the whole), and paid staff.

43. In a 1988 seminar with students from The American University's Washington Semester Program, Althea Simmons of the national office of the NAACP described the delicate balance between her organization and the National Abortion Rights Action League. By her account, the liaison worked because the groups focused on their mutual distaste for Bork's conservative political philosophy and not on abortion rights.

44. Richard Cohen, *Washington At Work* (New York: Macmillan, 1992).

45. Pertschuk and Schaetzel, *The People Rising*.

46. With one exception, the instrument remained unchanged from one study to the next. Only in the Thomas study were closed-ended questions used to provide systematic, easily comparable evidence on how they worked with their coalition partners.

47. Not everyone we interviewed agreed with this sentiment. Mark Allison of the National Jewish Coalition provides the minority view. "Individual groups had more success than the pro-Thomas coalition. Our group had more success working on its own; for example, being able to have one-on-one meetings with senators on the Judiciary Committee. Packing the room with groups diminishes that effectiveness."

48. William P. Browne, "Organized Interests and Their Issue Niches: A Search for Pluralism in a Policy Domain," *Journal of Politics* 52 (May 1990): 477-509.

49. For more on this question see Phelps and Winternitz, *Capitol Games*, 143.

50. Even some participants who invested energy in championing their cause concede that interest groups may not be decisive in these outcomes. John Motley of the National Federation of Independent Business provides a comment representing this view. "The [Thomas] confirmation was not decided by interest group politics. If Republican senators did not support the nomination, that would have been a direct challenge to the president. Senators reached a decision on whether or not to support Thomas on their own."

51. Justice David Souter was confirmed between the Bork and Thomas nominations in 1990. Souter generated little opposition in part because his positions on controversial issues were largely unknown. Therefore, it was not until the far more controversial Thomas nomination that a full-scale mobilization of interest groups occurred.

52. Peter Senge *The Fifth Discipline: The Art and Practice of the Learning Organization* (New York: Doubleday, 1990).

53. Jipping, Thomas L., "The Lessons of Rosemary Barkett," *Washington Times*, April 20, 1994, A19.

Selected Bibliography

Ainsworth, Scott. "Regulating Lobbyists and Interest Group Influence," *Journal of Politics* 55 (February 1993): 41-56.

Bedard, Paul. "Bush stresses black support," *Washington Times*, October 15, 1991, A1.

Berry, Jeffrey. *The Interest Group Society* 2nd ed. Boston: Little, Brown and Co., 1989.

Birnbaum, Jeffrey H. and Alan S. Murray, *Showdown at Gucci Gulch: Lawmakers, Lobbyists and the Unlikely Triumph of Tax Reform*. New York: Basic Books, 1987.

Bork, Robert H. *The Tempting of America: The Political Seduction of the Law*. New York: The Erie Press, 1990.

Bronner, Ethan. *Battle for Justice: How the Bork Nomination Shook America*. New York: W. W. Norton and Co., 1989.

Browne, William P. "Organized Interests and Their Issue Niches: A Search for Pluralism in a Policy Domain," *Journal of Politics* 52 (May 1990): 477-509.

Burek, Deborah M. and Karen E. Kolk. *Encyclopedia of Associations.* 2nd ed. Detroit, Michigan: Gale Research, Inc., 1990.

Caldeira, Gregory and John R. Wright. "Interest Groups and Agenda Setting in the Supreme Court of the United States," *American Political Science Review* 82 (1988): 1109-1127.

Caldeira, Gregory and John R. Wright. "Lobbying for Justice: Organized Interests Before the Senate, 1916-1990," *Newsletter of Political Organizations and Parties* 10:2 (1991): 5-6.

Congressional Quarterly Almanac. Washington, D.C.: Congressional Quarterly Press, 1969.

DeGregorio, Christine. *Networks of Champions: Leadership, Access, and Advocacy in the U.S. House of Representatives,* book manuscript in progress.

DeGregorio, Christine and Jack E. Rossotti. "Resources, Attitudes and Strategies: Interest Group Participation in the Bork Confirmation Process," *American Review of Politics* 15 (Spring 1994).

Epstein, Lee and C.K. Rowland. "Interest Groups in the Courts," *American Political Science Review* 85 (1991): 205-217.

Evans, Diana. "Lobbying the Committee: Interest Groups and the House Public Works and Transportation Committee," ed. Allan J. Cigler and Burdett A. Loomis, *Interest Group Politics.* 3rd ed. Washington, D.C.: Congressional Quarterly Press, 1991.

Fiorina, Morris P. *Representatives, Roll Calls, and Constituencies.* Lexington, Mass.: Lexington Books, 1974.

Gaillard, Ralph Jr. "Clarence Thomas: Pros and Cons," *Washington Post,* September 9, 1991, A13.

Jipping, Thomas L. "The Lessons of Rosemary Barkett," *Washington Times,* April 20, 1994, A19.

Loomis, Burdett A. and Allan J. Cigler. "Introduction: The Changing Nature of Interest Group Politics," in *Interest Group Politics,* ed. Allan J. Cigler and Burdett A. Loomis. Washington, D.C.: Congressional Quarterly Press, 1986.

Maltese, John Anthony. "The Selling of Clement Haynsworth: Politics and the Confirmation of Supreme Court Justices," *Judicature* 72:6 (April-May 1989).

Manley, John F. "Congressional Staff and Public Policy Making: The Joint Committee on Internal Revenue Taxation," *Journal of Politics* 30 (1968): 1046-1067.

Marcus, Ruth. "Group That Helped Defeat Bork Opposes Thomas," *Washington Post,* July 20, 1991, A5.

McGuigan, Patrick and Dawn H. Weyrich. *Ninth Justice: The Fight for Bork.* Lanham, Maryland: University Press of America, Inc., 1990.

O'Brien, David. *Storm Center: The Supreme Court on American Politics.* 2nd ed. New Jersey: W.W. Norton and Co., Inc., 1990).

Pertschuk, Michael and Wendy Schaetzel. *The People Rising: The Campaign Against the Bork Nomination.* New Jersey: Thunder's Mouth Press, 1989.

Phelps, Timothy and Helen Winternitz. *Capitol Games: Clarence Thomas, Anita Hill, and the Story of a Supreme Court Nomination.* New York: Hyperion, 1992.

Schlozman, Kay and John Tierney. *Organized Interests and American Democracy.* New Jersey: Harper and Row, 1986.

Senge, Peter. *The Fifth Discipline: The Art and Practice of the Learning Organization.* New York: Doubleday, 1990.

Taylor, Ronald. "Thomas Shatters Black Consensus," *Washington Times,* August 28, 1991, A1.

Tierney, John T. "Organized Interests and the Nation's Capitol," in *The Politics of Interests,* ed. Mark P. Petracca. Boulder, Colorado: Westview Press, Inc, 1992.

Tribe, Lawrence H. *God Save This Honorable Court*. New York: Random House, 1985.
Walker, Jack. *Mobilization of Interest Groups*. Michigan: University of Michigan Press, 1991.
Weaver, Warren. "Rights and Labor Leaders Oppose Court Nomination," *New York Times*, August 19, 1969, 27.

Appendix One
Sample of Interest Groups

Pro-Bork	Anti-Bork
Ad Hoc Committee in Defense of Life	Alliance for Justice
American Conservative Union	American Civil Liberties Union
American Farm Bureau Federation	American Federation of State, County,
American Legislative Enchange Council	and Municipal Employees
Americans for Tax Reform	Americans for Religious Liberty
Center for Judicial Studies	Center for Population Options
Christian Action Council	Citizen Action
Christian Voice	Communications Workers of America
Coalitions for America	Epilepsy Foundation of America
College Republican National Committee	Federally Employed Women
Concerned Women for America	Federation of Women Lawyers
Conservative Leadership PAC	Friends of the Earth
Council for National Policy, Inc.	International Association of Machinists
(CNP, Inc.)	Mexican-American Women's National
Federal Criminal Investigators Association	Association
Fraternal Order of Police	National Abortion Rights Action League
Free the Court	National Association of Social Workers
International Association of Chiefs of	Associations
Police	National Coalition to Abolish the Death
International Narcotics Enforcement	Penalty
Officers Association	National Conference of Women's Bar
Moral Majority	Associations
National District Attorneys Association	National Council of La Raza
National Jewish Coalition	National Gay and Lesbian Task Force
National Law Enforcement Council	National Lawyer's Guild
National Republican Heritage Group's	National Urban League
Council	National Women's Health Network
National Sheriffs' Association	9 to 5, National Association of Working
National Troopers' Association	Women
Renaissance Women	People for the American Way
Victims Assistance Legal Organization	Rainbow Lobby
We the People	Sane/Freeze
	Sierra Club
	United States Student Association
	YWCA/USA

Note: Two names have been omitted in deference to the respondents' requests for complete anonymity.

Appendix Two
Sample of Interest Groups

Pro-Thomas	Anti-Thomas
American Road and Transportation Builders Association	AFL-CIO
Americans for Tax Reform	American Association for Affirmative Action
Aqudath Israel of America	American Federation of Teachers
The Associated General Contractors of America	Americans for Democratic Action
Association of Christian Schools International	Equal Rights Advocates
Association of Retired Americans	The Gray Panthers
Citizens for Educational Freedom	Human Rights Campaign Fund
Coalitions for America	National Abortion Rights Action League
Concerned Women for America	National Association of Commissions for Women
Congress of Racial Equality	National Black Caucus of State Legislators
Conservative Caucus	
Conservative Victory Committee	National Conference of Black Lawyers
International Narcotic Enforcement Officers Association	National Council of Churches
	National Council of Jewish Women
National Black Nurses Association	National Council of La Raza
National Deputy Sheriffs Association	National Council of Senior Citizens
National District Attorneys Association	National Federation of Business and Professional Women's Clubs
National Federation of Independent Business	National Lawyers Guild
National Jewish Coalition	Older Women's League
National Small Business United	People for the American Way
National Tax Limitation Committee	Service Employees International Union
Seniors Coalition	United Church of Christ
Students for America	United Auto Workers
Traditional Values Coalition	Women's Employed Institute
U.S. Business and Industry Council	
U.S. Chamber of Commerce	

Note: Two names have been omitted in deference to the respondents' requests for complete anonymity.

11

Rounding Up the Usual Suspects:
Forging Interest Group Coalitions in Washington
Kevin Hula

As the number and variety of interest groups have grown over the past thirty years, so too have the incentives for groups to act in concert. Groups benefit by joining alliances that imply extensive support and hone the essential messages they deliver to policy makers. Legislators and bureaucrats often encourage interests to form coalitions to iron out intergroup differences and speak with a single voice on a given subject.

There are risks in joining coalitions. An interest may find itself in a minority position, with its issue preferences submerged under those of other groups. Or it may not receive credit for whatever success the coalition achieves. Group leaders must continually evaluate the trade-offs between autonomy and the potential for enhanced influence.

Although the politics of coalition formation among interests is important, political scientists have spent much less time attempting to understand these unions than they have in sorting out why individuals do or do not join membership groups. In large part this state of affairs derives from the theory of group formation articulated initially by Mancur Olson and subsequently refined by dozens of researchers. In this article, Kevin Hula applies an Olson-style framework to groups as they decide whether or not to join a coalition and what level of resources to commit to coalition activities. Drawing from an extensive set of interviews with Washington representatives (lobbyists), Hula discovers that the notions of selective and collective benefits that have helped untangle individual membership choices can help us understand coalition formation as well. Groups join coalitions for various reasons—not just to affect the issue of the moment.

In the hothouse world of Washington politics, Hula argues, coalitions serve the interests both of their member groups and of the policy makers they hope to influence.

The research reported in this chapter was made possible through the generous support of the Brookings Institution. The helpful comments of Patrick Asea, John Bader, Frank Baumgartner, Jeff Berry, William Browne, Kevin Carey, Mo Fiorina, Ann Lin, Burdett Loomis, Mark Peterson, Wendy Schiller, Elizabeth Schneirov, and Susan Hula on earlier drafts are gratefully acknowledged.

L obbying "is no longer somebody coming with a bag full of money and laying it on a member's desk or relying on personal contacts to have the member do you a favor—if it ever was," explains Coretech lobbyist Stuart Eizenstat. "The difficulty of passing legislation has increased exponentially. To make a common cause with people who would not be your traditional allies is important."[1]

Although many interest group representatives share Stuart Eizenstat's assessment of the importance of political coalitions, few scholars and analysts have attempted to apply the vast literature on interest-group formation to explain coalitions of those groups. This is somewhat surprising, because a cursory glance at the legislative history of almost any bill is likely to reveal a detailed description of the coalitions that supported or opposed the legislation. This chapter focuses on the incentives for and the character of an interest group's participation in political coalitions—defined as groups of organizations united by a common political goal.[2] I argue that the incentives a particular group responds to in joining a coalition strongly influence the ultimate role the group will play in the coalition structure.

In the first half of the chapter I examine several of the key reasons organizations participate in coalitions. Since Mancur Olson and Robert Salisbury wrote their seminal works on collective action and exchange theory, respectively, political scientists have stressed the need for interest group founders—or "entrepreneurs"—to offer selective benefits to potential group members to induce them to join the group rather than remaining outside as "free riders." According to Olson, a rational actor will choose to free ride unless induced by other means to join a group pursuing a collective good.[3] I follow this general approach, but with a proviso. The incentives to which organizations respond when they join political coalitions are somewhat different from the benefits interest group entrepreneurs offer to overcome the free rider problem.

Subsequently, I argue that understanding whether a group joins a coalition for *strategic reasons* or *selective benefits* also helps determine whether it will become a "core member," a "player," or a "peripheral member" of that coalition. The distribution of goals, priorities, and resources across members of a coalition helps determine its organizational structure.

The data presented here were collected in ninety-five in-depth interviews with Washington representatives of corporations, associations, unions, and other organizations that actively lobbied the 101st Congress on transportation or education issues. The resulting sample contains organizations that are active in each policy sphere, but which need not be primarily identified with that particular sphere.[4]

Incentives and Strategy in Coalition Participation

Although it might seem intuitively obvious that groups join policy-oriented lobbying coalitions to pursue strategic policy goals, the vast literature on collective action suggests that this may not always be true. Most of the work done since Mancur Olson published *The Logic of Collective Action* in 1965 has focused on the origin and maintenance of interest groups, the free-rider problem, and the selective benefits offered by interest group entrepreneurs to potential members who agree to join the organization. Selective benefits have been considered generally in three broad categories: material, solidary, and expressive or purposive.[5]

Does coalition formation among organizations represent the same collective action phenomenon as forming an interest group of individuals or firms? In many ways it does, but the origins of coalitions and interest groups differ in intriguing ways.

Similar incentives are at work in both cases. An organization's Washington representative might join a political coalition for many reasons, but three stand out. Organizations often join coalitions for strategic, policy-oriented reasons, reasons that Peter B. Clark and James Q. Wilson would call "purposive" and Salisbury would label "expressive." These organizations hope to shape public policy outcomes through their coalition membership. Sometimes organizations join coalitions to obtain selective benefits that they would not otherwise have had, such as information or timely intelligence about the policy process. Still other groups join coalitions purely as a symbolic gesture, for example, to convince their own members that they are working on an issue or to demonstrate solidarity with another organization. In these cases, cultivating an appearance rather than actually obtaining specific policy outcomes is the primary goal. Any coalition probably contains members who have joined for each of these reasons.

Strategic Incentives for Participation

Some organizations are motivated to participate in coalitions by strategic policy concerns. Given a range of political options, they select coalition strategies because they view them as the most effective way to shape policy outcomes. Although some organizations will always choose to be free riders, it is not necessarily irrational for Washington representatives to join coalitions in pursuit of policy goals. Furthermore, from an institutional standpoint, politically active organizations have been pushed increasingly towards coalition strategy by developments in government and in the interest group system. In fact, the use of coalition strategies is self-reinforcing: As more organizations pursue coalition strategies, participation in coalitions may become more important in shaping favorable outcomes.

The Free Rider Question. Is it irrational for strategically minded groups not to try to free ride on the collective action of other groups? The fact that some organizations join coalitions to lobby for strategic legislative goals can be explained partially by Olson's small-group principle. If the number of potential coalition members on a given issue is limited, the decision of one group to participate or not to participate can have a measurable impact. The motivation to free ride is reduced when nonparticipation measurably reduces the likelihood that the collective good will be achieved. Furthermore, the presence or absence of a given group is likely to be noticed in a small universe of organizations, and the potential exists for the application of coercive sanctions by other coalition members to discourage free riding. At the least, there may be a strong element of peer pressure.

Relying only on the small-group principle to explain coalition formation misses many of the unique characteristics observed in this form of collective action. The differences between the potential individual members of interest groups and the potential members of coalitions are significant. Whereas the potential member of a coalition is, at least formally, an organization, the actual member is usually a staffer employed by the organization. This creates an important qualitative difference between the task confronting an interest group entrepreneur, who must mobilize potentially apolitical individuals, and the role of a coalition broker, who brings paid Washington representatives into a coalition. In the first case, the free rider problem grows from the potential member's reluctance to expend any resources for political action. In the second case, the already politically active representative is offered an opportunity to *reduce* his or her resource expenditure on that issue and to increase the likelihood of policy success through a specific strategy, namely a coalition.

Furthermore, the free rider principle itself was developed to explain why individuals or organizations do not cooperate to achieve collective goods. But most of the legislative goals pursued by coalitions are not pure collective goods. The issue is not so much whether a given policy will be enacted or defeated, but how the issue will be defined and how benefits will be distributed. The rational group recognizes that opportunities to shape that policy are closely tied to membership in the coalition (see below).

Institutional Imperatives. How do external, institutional conditions affect interest group strategies? Scholars such as Samuel Huntington, Hugh Heclo, and Daniel McCool have argued that the rapid growth in the number of interests represented in Washington, increasing policy complexity, and the increasing growth and decentralization of government have created an increasingly atomistic interest group system.[6] Burdett Loomis and William Browne have argued that the atomization of the interest group system has had the surprising effect of pushing groups *toward* coalition strategies.[7] Jeffrey M. Berry suggests that the coalition is a form of conflict management that has grown in importance since the fall of "subgovernments," or institutionalized relationships among interest groups, agencies, and congressional committees.[8] In fact, Washington representatives who join coalitions for strategic, legislative reasons frequently cite changes in government and the growth of organizational representation in Washington as key institutional explanations for the growth of coalitions.

Within the federal government, the number of institutional access points for organizations interested in a given policy has increased dramatically over the last twenty years. More members of Congress and their staffs have been brought into play at early stages of the legislative process as subcommittees have grown in number and as committees have expanded in jurisdiction through multiple referrals of bills.[9] Organizations find it necessary to present their case to more political actors than ever before. Because even the largest individual groups find it difficult to reach all of the relevant congressional players, collective strategies may be necessary if groups wish to present their case in all the appropriate forums. A hallmark of coalition strategies is that membership enables the workload to be spread out. As Berry notes, "One interest group may have only two lobbyists; ten interest groups with the same number of lobbyists can provide twenty operatives for the coming battle."[10]

The second key institutional motivation for groups to join coalitions grows out of the explosive increase in the number of organizations active in Washington over the last three decades. The number of public-interest groups representing consumers, environmental concerns, and welfare interests expanded dramatically, as did the number of groups with foreign policy agendas and the number of business and trade associations active in Washington.[11] This growth in organized interests has created a paradox: the creation of more groups has meant less clout for any of them.[12]

As each new group joins the Washington melee, governmental capacity to process external demands is reduced. Groups are pressured to work out their differences before approaching Congress, rather than requiring Congress to sort out a seemingly infinite number of differences among groups. Congressional staffers, the Office of Public Liaison in the White House, and individual agencies all initiate coalitions to encourage groups to work out what Douglas Costain and Anne Costain label "predigested policies" outside governmental institutions.[13]

The growth in the number of interests represented in politics has been paralleled by increasing public criticism of "special interest groups" over the last twenty years. Public and campaign rhetoric creates a more hostile political climate for organized interests and generates another incentive for collective action. In order to avoid stigmatization as "special interest groups," individual organizations advocating particular policy outcomes turn to coalition strategies in an attempt to demonstrate varied support for their positions. A union leader stated:

> The more diverse you can make your coalition, the better.... [It looks like] good government—you know, broadly held ideals, a broad array of citizens with perceived wide varying interests, all interested in this issue.

This emphasis on public perception and on the rhetoric of public criticism is something different from a mere "weight in numbers" approach to politics. Some coalitions are consciously structured to provide tactical cover for members of Congress who fear being linked by the public to "special interest group politics." As one lobbyist put it:

> [Y]ou get to sign a zillion names: all those members of the coalition who represent all those people in the organizations.... [O]n education, you're speaking for not just a hundred associations, but a hundred associations that represent every single facet of education from the janitors in the buildings to the principals to the supes to the school board members to the state superintendents to the governors.... And how that translates—I mean, guys up on the Hill aren't stupid. They know. But what they have to do is generate [a good story]—to find one day in the *Congressional Record* William Ford[14] saying, "A hundred zillion organizations and people all agree that Chapter I has to be increased" or "Head Start has to be increased." That plays well. It's a game, but it does the job. That's my feeling on the value of coalitions.

The Opportunity to Shape the Issue. One of the first stages of coalition formation is the development of an explicit policy goal around which groups can rally. The goal may be vague, such as preventing tax increases or supporting increased funding for education, but it must be clear enough that organizations can identify themselves as being for or against it. This general policy goal is the common ground all organizations share, although early on there is substantial flexibility around the edges as the members work towards a more rigorous self-definition. As the representative of a professional association explained,

> What you want is a set of principles. You know, "I will support any legislation that has the following principles in it." And those principles are the driving issue. Otherwise you can't work out something that multiple organizations can support.

In the case of proactive coalitions—those that are formed to seek a change in the status quo—the general policy stance becomes more formalized as details are added and the coalition's platform is fleshed out. A large, proactive coalition's platform often profoundly influences the terms of the ensuing policy debate; therefore, there is a strong incentive for sympathetic organizations to join the coalition in order to influence that platform with their own particular policy goals before the chorus begins to sing it in public. A teachers' union representative put it this way: "We prefer to be in the coalition early. When you see things forming, you want to be in it before the concrete sets."

The more inclusive the coalition, the more difficulty individual organizations outside the coalition have in shaping the issues with which the coalition is dealing. This is particularly true when the coalition contains divergent interests that are trying to work out differences outside the legislative arena and "prepackage" a compromise position.[15] There is a powerful incentive to join coalitions in order to have a voice within them, even when groups seek collective goods. Collective or "public" goods carry private as well as public benefits, and joining a coalition can be a strategy for seeking a favorable distribution of those benefits. It is, in part, a matter of perspective. Education funding, for example, is considered a collective good by the society at large, but for the representative of a school system, a college, a university, or a research group, the funds quickly become a private good that someone else may be chosen to administer.

Consider the Committee for Education Funding (CEF), the best known coalition in the education policy arena. With its ninety-five members, CEF lobbies for higher funding levels across the board for educational programs. While education funding is hailed by the coalition as a public good, groups that join CEF do so not to increase overall funding, but to ensure inclusion of and advocacy for their particular programs in CEF publications, lobbying, and testimony. By organizing and speaking with a common voice, CEF can define the public debate in terms of overall government funding for education while making a case for each member's specific programs. A CEF member described the logic of the coalition this way:

> [CEF] is necessitated by our opponents who would take various organizations in the education arena and divide and conquer them, so to speak; in other words, put so much money on the table and say "You [could] have this if X higher ed organization weren't also going after it." [This] would turn the education organizations against themselves. In order to get past that, we look at a full range of the kinds of funding needs that CEF members have, pool it all together, and we all go to bat for each other.

Putting it mildly, CEF members are loath to think of losing the exposure they gain for their programs through membership in the coalition.

Efficacy of Coalition Strategies. None of these policy-related incentives would be particularly important in the decision calculus of organizational leaders if those leaders did not believe that coalitions were an effective solution for the institutional and issue-shaping challenges they faced. To examine their opinions of coalitions, I presented Washington representatives with an extensive series of statements about coalition membership and asked them to respond to each on a five-point scale ranging from strong agreement to strong disagreement. Three of these statements dealt with efficacy, and the responses are recorded in Table 11-1. Organizational representatives showed an overwhelming belief in the efficacy of coalitions for pursuing legislative goals.

An overwhelming majority of the organizational leaders surveyed noted the central importance of coalition strategies in Washington. In fact, approximately 80 percent of both the education and transportation samples agreed with the statement "Coalitions are the way to be effective in politics."

Of course, as noted, coalition membership can be useful for several reasons. For groups that are strategically motivated, the key issue is the final outcome of a public policy debate. Fully three quarters of the respondents stated that belonging to a coalition helped them to control the outcome of an issue.

Organizations that do not join a coalition often find that they cannot help determine how an issue is translated into policy. More organizations in both samples agreed than disagreed with the statement: "If our organization does not join a coalition, we may lose our ability to shape the outcome of the issue." A majority of the transportation sample agreed with that statement, as did 40.8 percent of the education sample. Still, approximately 38 percent of the respondents in each sample disagreed. Coalition building is not a strategy for all issues or all organizations.[16]

Although these responses do not show why particular groups join specific coalitions, they do demonstrate an overwhelming sense of the efficacy of coalition strategies.

Information as a Selective Benefit

Coalitions, like interest groups, can offer membership incentives not directly related to specific public policy goals. For those groups not joining political coalitions to obtain a policy outcome, *information* is the single most important selective benefit. Information is a difficult benefit to categorize. In some cases it appears to be a material benefit with monetary value; in others the information exchange is laden with solidary benefits. In any event, joining coalitions for information is a common phenomenon.[17]

Information benefits are particularly important as incentives for smaller groups with limited staff and resources. As one overworked staff member for school officials noted,

> if you are not a part of the loop, it shuts you out of things you may need to be aware of. And there's so much to know. There's no way you can keep up with just the *Federal Register* and the *Congressional Record* unless you have a big staff or a lot of lawyers.

This lobbyist's situation is scarcely unique. In fact, one-third of the transportation and education organizations in my sample had only one professional with governmental relations duties on staff. In several cases that

Table 11-1 Reported Efficacy of Coalition Strategies

	Sample	Percent agree (cumulative)	Percent agree strongly	Percent agree somewhat	Percent neither agree nor disagree	Percent disagree somewhat	Percent disagree strongly	
Coalitions are the way to be effective in politics	transportation	81.3	43.8	37.5	10.4	6.3	2.1	N=48
	education	79.6	38.8	40.8	16.3	2.0	2.0	N=49
Being a member of a coalition helps an organization to control the outcome of an issue	transportation	75.0	35.4	39.6	8.3	14.6	2.1	N=48
	education	77.6	24.5	53.1	12.2	8.2	2.0	N=49
If our organization does not join a coalition, we may lose our ability to shape the outcome of the issue	transportation	55.5	11.1	44.4	6.7	31.1	6.7	N=45
	education	40.8	12.2	28.6	20.4	28.6	10.2	N=49

person also served as executive director. A full 56 percent of the transportation groups and 51 percent of the education organizations had two or fewer professionals assigned to government relations.

In addition to monitoring the introduction of bills and proposed regulations, small staffs without significant contacts on Capitol Hill may find it nearly impossible to monitor activities in the relevant subcommittees, follow legislation between hearings and markups, and maintain contact with relevant congressional staff. For these groups, coalitions are a lifeline of information, scuttlebutt, and rumors about developments in the policy process. Coalition partners often function as an early warning system on issues that a representative had not been following. As one education lobbyist noted:

> It's very important [to be in a coalition], because people tend to talk about things that I might only have a tangential interest in or might not think [are] important, and it's very important for information sharing. Saves you about a dozen phone calls when you can have a regular meeting where people can bring those kinds of things to the table.

Group Maintenance and the Symbolic Benefits of Coalition Membership

One way leaders maintain their group membership is by showing members that the Washington staff is busy. Photographs of organizational leaders testifying before a congressional committee or subcommittee frequently grace the front pages of their newsletters. Participation in a coalition can represent a low-cost trophy that group leaders can deliver to the membership to demonstrate activity on issues they may view as secondary, if not downright unimportant. The investment is small—perhaps no more than attending an hour-long meeting each month.

The phenomenon is not restricted to membership associations. Corporate lobbyists are sometimes instructed by headquarters to be active on issues, whether or not there is a "window of opportunity."[18] A Washington corporate representative in the trucking industry noted that she sometimes joins coalitions

> [b]ecause it's seen as the thing to do, perhaps by corporate headquarters. *They* may say, "This is an issue that's important to us." But *we* can't spend a lot of time on it, so we're going to give it nominal support. We want to show [headquarters] that this is an "important" issue.

Participating in a coalition demonstrates activity, even when the representatives do not expect a positive policy return.

Joining a coalition as a purely symbolic action can satisfy group members or a corporate hierarchy because of a "principal-agent" problem.[19] Most group members and many corporate executives located outside of Washington do not have the political experience and information necessary to adequately interpret and supervise the activities of their Washington representatives. For the Washington representatives, corporate misconceptions about the legislative process can be a frustrating burden, as was the case with a former auto industry lobbyist who stressed that Detroit was out of touch with the political realities of Washington:

> There is a certain mentality within a corporation that says "lay out our objective for the year." It's very difficult to do that in a political environment.... [T]hey were used to goals; you know, by the end of the month you're going to have this done.... You know how many hours it takes to produce a car. You have a timeline. Or you've got production goals for the year. Congress doesn't work like that.... And that's what a lot of times in the private sector people lose sight of when they're trying to do government relations.... You can demand something when you're in a corporation; you can set goals, and you can fire people. Congress doesn't work that way, and government doesn't work that way, really. [Corporations] don't understand the fluid element that's involved.

Credit claiming for symbolic participation in coalitions occurs not only in large coalitions but also in small activities such as joint letter signing. The extreme form of this symbolic activity can be seen when groups volunteer to endorse joint projects or letters without knowing the substantive content. The director of government affairs for a relatively arcane branch of higher education related this example:

> One of the other associations knows that [Rep. William] Ford wants the Hawkins-Stafford recommendations. So he called me and said, "Are you doing this?" I said, "Yes, I'm doing it." And he said, "Can I sign on?" I mean, he doesn't even know what I'm doing, but he doesn't want to spend the time doing it, because it's not important to him, but he wants to be part of the game. So he called and said "I assume you're doing this. Unless it's something that we can't live with, I want to just tell you I will sign on to what you're going to recommend." Two other associations have done that as well. So there are three that just out of the blue called me, and it's because no one else does this, really.

These groups did not sign the letter to achieve a policy goal; they did it so they could tell their members they had worked on the project and show the relevant committee staff they were active in the policy area.

Symbolic participation also occurs in cases where an organization joins a coalition for reasons such as paying back a debt, doing a favor for another group, or setting an example for other organizations.

Coalition Structure and Membership Asymmetry

Clearly, groups join coalitions for different reasons, some of them apparently only tangentially related to strategic public policy goals. This

Figure 11-1   Coalition Membership and Structure

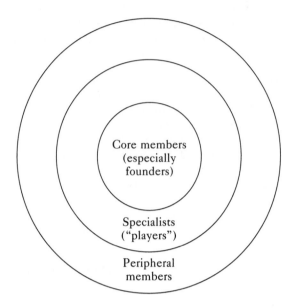

Core members
(especially
founders)

Specialists
("players")

Peripheral
members

results in an asymmetry among the goals of members, which in turn affects how coalitions are organized.

The incentives that induce a group to join a coalition also help determine the position it will occupy within the larger group. In every coalition, the constituent groups shoulder different degrees of responsibility. The amount of responsibility a group assumes is closely correlated with the reasons it joined in the first place. In short, a group's goals, priorities, and resources together determine the position a group holds in a coalition and the role it plays.

Coalition members can be divided roughly into three concentric groups: coalition core groups, coalition players, and peripheral groups (Figure 11-1).

The *coalition core* consists primarily of the founders and other resource-rich groups that band together to achieve broad strategic policy goals. Core members are notable for their willingness to expend significant resources to promote overall legislative victory. The members of the ring closest to the core can be thought of as *players*. Players tend to be specialists who join a coalition for tactical reasons; these groups are highly interested in shaping specific provisions of the legislation in question. Characterized by their desire to hone the issues, these players will spend a fairly high level of resources to achieve their specific policy goals. The third body of members are *peripheral groups* that tag along with the rest of the coalition for nonpolicy incentives such as information or group main-

Figure 11-2   Coalition Members, Their Goals, and Their Resources

	Core member	Specialist or "player"	Peripheral or "tag-along"
Issue importance	high	high (specific)	low (peripheral)
Organization's goal	overall strategic victory	issue honing	coalition byproducts
Degree and type of resources brought by an organization	high level: • money • reputation • expertise • membership	enough to buy a place at the negotiating table • expertise • reputation • membership • money	a name: • perhaps a prestigious name • perhaps just another name for the list
Time commitment (work level)	high level for overall goal	high level for specific goals	low level across the board

tenance benefits. While generally supporting coalition goals, these groups are not willing to expend significant resources for a coalition victory. Rather, membership in the coalition is an end in itself. A summary of these relationships between coalition members and their goals, resources, and coalition positions is shown in Figure 11-2.

The asymmetry in organizational goals and resources that groups bring to a coalition has practical implications. The distribution of goals and resources across groups in a coalition determines the structure of that coalition. Core members and players believe that they can affect policy outcomes, and they join the coalition to achieve policy goals. Core members are intent on final legislative outcomes and a broad strategic approach to those outcomes. This is certainly the case for the founding members, who must be willing to finance the bulk of the coalition's expenses in the early stages. Coalition founders, or brokers, to use Loomis's term, are at the heart of the core group.[20]

As Loomis points out, coalitions do not simply emerge. Rather, they are assembled by an individual or small group of individuals who play a role more similar to a broker than to a group entrepreneur. The broker provides the initial stimulus and capital to organize the coalition. At a minimum this includes hosting, chairing, or co-chairing the coalition, as well as providing clerical support for organizational tasks. Founders want more groups to join their coalitions for strategic reasons; they believe coalition size and diversity increases the likelihood of eventual policy success. Because of the critical role brokers play in organizing a coalition, they are likely to play a continuing, core role in coalition leadership for some time.

Although the Anne Wexlers and other professional coalition brokers of Washington may receive the lion's share of the notoriety, they start a minority of the coalitions. Most cooperative political efforts among groups are started by organizational staff lobbyists. More coalitions are initiated by large organizations than by small ones. Not surprisingly, most coalitions are begun by groups with a strong, broad interest in a particular legislative issue within their policy domain.[21] Reputation, centrality of the issue to the group's self identification, and political resources all weigh heavily in enhancing the likelihood that a given organization can successfully found a coalition.

Core membership is not limited to the brokers of a coalition. Other groups may become core members if they have a strong commitment to overall goals and devote time, energy, and other resources to the coalition's work. Because of their size, reputation, and resources, some groups are almost automatic core members if they participate actively within the coalition. A representative of one of the two major teachers' unions noted:

> We try not to [dominate coalitions], *try* not to, especially try not to foster or feed that kind of thing. But, by and large, in many coalitions, if we are opposed to something, it may influence [others]. If we're for something, it may influence others.

In many coalitions the core is defined explicitly for functional reasons. If a coalition becomes too large and diverse for consensual agenda setting and logistical control, core members create a leadership committee to carry out these functions. As the director of governmental relations for a children's lobby put it,

> [You need to] form a nucleus of your coalition. The Children First coalition has got some sixty groups in it. Well, that's too big to plan the agenda. But we're trying right now to [form] what we call sort of an executive committee or ... working group, that will meet more often than the larger group, talk about some issues, and spread the work out, too. So we're trying to again pull in the education and business leaders and groups here into that so we can get the word out, get interesting agendas, and then share in the responsibilities of putting together a program.

Like core members, players also join coalitions to pursue policy goals. They, too, desire eventual policy successes, but they may have more limited goals. Because a proactive coalition's position may strongly influence the terms of debate on an issue, strategically motivated groups with specialized but related interests often seek to be included in the coalition's platform. If they were not included, they could do little to shape the coalition's position and therefore would be less likely to obtain a favorable policy outcome.

Despite their limited interests, players often bring specialized expertise to the coalition that core members may lack. This expertise on specific points of the legislation is their key source of political capital within the coalition. Because players may not hold great sway in the overall legislative battle as individual groups, their narrow focus and expertise are used primarily in shaping the coalition's agenda and honing its position on the points that are relevant to them. When asked whether their membership really made any difference in a coalition, the manager of federal affairs for a professional association said:

> [I]n terms of *what the coalition is saying* to the Hill or the administration, then I would say yes. One can be effective within the coalition without necessarily being able to judge how effective the coalition is in the overall outcome of the issue. Being a member of the coalition can help you to shape the position of a coalition.

None of this is to suggest that players do not expend resources outside the coalition. They do. However, their lobbying efforts in the legislative arena, as within the coalition, tend to focus on their specific piece of the issue or legislation, rather than the package as a whole.

Salisbury and his collaborators reported that the most important relationships between organizations are found within the same policy sphere and frequently among groups that are functionally most similar.[22] It follows that founders and core members generally emerge from the same policy domain, whereas other players or specialists may come from other domains. Furthermore, organizations that are core members of one coalition within a single issue domain are likely to be core members of others. When shown a draft of Figure 11-1, the manager of federal relations for a professional association of scientists confirmed these observations and pointed out an important difference between specialists, hired outside lobbyists, and core members in long-term coalitions:

> [The specialists are involved] just to make sure their view was taken into consideration when this group was developing its position. I find in my experience these people would tend to be more the folks that are the lobbyists-for-hire types, the folks that have specific clients—not part of an association or a society, but ... they've got multiple clients with multiple interests.... Now sometimes they're in here if it's something that's very fundamental to their interests.... But they don't tend to be in this long-term core.... I mean we [in the core] have a long-term concern about these issues, not just exactly what is the funding in this particular year.... [T]hey are on a case by case basis. They have a contract. We have the luxury, if you will, of taking a longer-term view and a bigger-picture view.

In fact, if players are unable to integrate or to piggy-back their particular interests into the broader coalition platform, they are likely to leave the coalition.

Peripheral groups, or "tag-alongs," are in some respects the most interesting type of coalition member. Peripheral members have neither a compelling commitment to the legislation in question nor a willingness to exert much effort to achieve the coalition's policy goal. They join to receive selective benefits available to coalition members such as information or the benefits of symbolic participation for their members. This does not escape the attention of core members.

> I would say that maybe 10 percent of them do [the work]. The rest of them are just there for information gathering.... Just because someone joins a coalition doesn't mean they're going to do much. A lot of them just do it for information, or, you know, someone at their company [says] "Oh, you have to get involved in this issue." Well, okay, I'm involved—I went to a coalition meeting.

Peripheral groups are not necessarily resource-poor or apolitical. Even the largest politically active organizations sometimes act in a peripheral capacity. Because of the reputation, resources, and perceived clout of some organizations within an issue domain, coalition brokers see their membership, even if inactive, as critical to the success of the coalition. Particularly on obscure issues in which the desired organization might not be interested, the broker's job becomes much more difficult. One lobbyist notes:

> I can occasionally drag along the NEA, and I can occasionally drag along one of the principals' organizations, but it really is not the main focus for them, and so, because it is not of great interest to them, one of two things happens. They either say, "Oh.... I just can't be bothered with it" or they say, "All right, as a favor, use our name on the letter with you." But it's more a courtesy than getting them involved and having them marshal their memberships....

A lobbyist for one of the two major teachers' unions described the other side of the relationship: "The perception is that if we're not going to play, that it will affect the outcome. We are sought after to be on coalitions."

Where smaller organizations may seek inclusion in coalitions as peripheral members for benefits such as information, the "big guns" of an issue domain do not respond to those incentives. They are probably the best sources of intelligence in a coalition and do not join for that benefit. Rather, the major group often lends its name to coalitions as a favor, without any expectation of active participation.

Individual organizations thus bring very different goals, levels of interest, and resources to a coalition, and yet the asymmetries in membership are generally acceptable to all concerned. An exchange is taking place: On the one hand, the coalition has the benefit of a group's name to present to Congress and can claim additional diversity in the coalition's membership. From a health and education lobbyist:

Some [of the coalition members] are not even headquartered here, so they kind of keep in touch by mail. But they're also very effective as a name to lend to a list. If you have three hundred associations on a list, that's a pretty strong message.

On the other hand, the member organization, even if inactive in the legislative arena, has gained a source of information or a symbolic activity to report to its membership. Furthermore, the group may have developed contacts and potential allies for issues of higher priority in the future. Coalition leaders need to be able to differentiate between groups that are willing to work for policy goals and those that are just "warming seats." From a medical association lobbyist:

You know, some people belong to larger coalitions because they want to learn something, and have some information to carry forward. Others will give you their time and effort on Capitol Hill. I think you have to look at both of those.... And then you have to evaluate who's in there for the "Yeah, this is going to be a high priority for me, too" or "I'm in here because it's a medium or low priority for me, and I just want to make sure that I'm up on the issues."

Yet not a single group leader suggested that the tag-alongs were not welcome in the coalition. While their contribution might have been merely to add another signature to joint letters, that was a welcome addition. Some respondents who see themselves as core members of coalitions expressed frustration that more groups were not willing to commit more time and energy to the coalition's broad legislative goals, but even these individuals did not suggest that the peripheral groups should be expelled. On another issue, their own group might be on the periphery.

In spite of the asymmetry between the goals of core members, players, and peripheral members, the relationship is symbiotic. Each organization can seek its own benefits, so long as it does not infringe on the legislative interests of other coalition members. A frequent broker of coalitions in the education field noted that in forming and maintaining a coalition, he dealt with

those organizations that we know pretty well can deliver; those organizations that talk a good game but don't deliver; those that can count votes; those that influence votes; and those that think they can, but can't. I guess you really learn to separate the real deliverers from those who want to be deliverers—and in a coalition, try not to shut down any of them.

"Not shutting down any of them" means not cutting off the flow of coalition membership incentives to any of the members.

Conclusion

The literature on collective action has emphasized the provision of selective benefits to potential members in exchange for their participation in a group. In a related vein, I have suggested that the benefits sought by organizations joining a coalition are similar, but not identical, to those sought by individuals joining a group. What is more important, however, the goals, priorities, and resources that an organization brings to the coalition will determine the ultimate role it will play in that coalition.

Strategically motivated Washington representatives perceive coalitions as an effective instrument for influencing public policy. By helping to pool resources in pursuit of a common legislative goal, strategic coalitions help organizations face the challenges brought on by institutional changes in the government and in the increasingly complicated universe of interest groups.

Not all coalition members are motivated by strategic policy concerns. Washington representatives from some organizations join political coalitions primarily to receive selective benefits such as information and intelligence or to demonstrate symbolic action to their membership or their corporate superiors.

Examining coalition benefits is useful not only to explain why groups join a coalition, but also to define the roles they will play once they are members. Groups that join a coalition for broad strategic goals are generally willing to commit time and effort to carrying the coalition's platform into battle. They are the core members, the leaders of the coalition. Organizations that join coalitions for more narrow strategic goals are unlikely to become core members, but these specialists are still important players. Because of their specific priorities, they focus on tactically shaping the coalition platform to include their particular interests. Their external lobbying on behalf of the coalition focuses on their piece of the coalition platform as well. These specialists are willing to commit time and resources to the coalition as long as it continues to emphasize their particular goal. Organizations that join a coalition for symbolic reasons or solely in order to gain benefits such as information are generally unwilling to expend significant resources to further the coalition goal. Although they support the goal in principle, coalition membership is an end in itself, and they will remain on the periphery of the coalition, welcome all the same.

Notes

1. Quoted in Jeffrey H. Birnbaum, *The Lobbyists: How Influence Peddlers Get Their Way in Washington* (New York: Times Books, 1992).
2. Coalitions that coordinate and undertake joint political action may be distinguished from the myriad other groups that function solely as information clearinghouses or social gatherings for Washington organizational representatives. Political coalitions may spin off from the latter groups, of course.

3. If individuals can enjoy the collective benefits of group action without joining the group, they will ordinarily choose to remain outside the group as free riders. "Entrepreneurs" must offer selective benefits to overcome the problem incurred when the group is pursuing collective goods which nonmembers could enjoy without joining. Mancur Olson, *The Logic of Collective Action* (Cambridge: Harvard University Press, 1965); Robert H. Salisbury, "An Exchange Theory of Interest Groups," *Midwest Journal of Political Science* 13 (February 1969): 1-32.

4. For example, in the sample of organizations lobbying in the transportation domain, there are not only groups and firms representing "planes, trains, and automobiles," but also energy producers and safety advocates. Similarly, the education sample included trade unions interested in job training and computer manufacturers promoting the development of a technologically literate work force. Transportation-related interviews were conducted from January through July of 1992, and education-related interviews were conducted from October 1992 through March 1993. Since most of the interviews were conducted under an implicit guarantee of anonymity, respondents are generally identified in the text only by the type of organization they represent and their position.

5. Peter B. Clark and James Q. Wilson, "Incentive Systems: A Theory of Organizations," *Administrative Science Quarterly* 6, 2 (September 1961): 219-266; and James Q. Wilson, *Political Organizations* (New York: Basic Books, 1973). Clark and Wilson use the term "purposive" rather than "expressive." Salisbury develops the concept of expressive benefits in "Exchange Theory."

6. Samuel Huntington, "The Democratic Distemper," *Public Interest* 10 (Fall 1975): 9-38; Hugh Heclo, "Issue Networks and the Executive Establishment," in *The New American Political System*, 1st ed., ed. Anthony King (Washington, D.C.: American Enterprise Institute, 1978); Daniel McCool, "Subgovernments and the Impact of Policy Fragmentation and Accommodation," *Policy Studies Review* 8, 4 (Winter 1989): 264-287.

7. Burdett A. Loomis, "Coalitions of Interests: Building Bridges in the Balkanized State," in *Interest Group Politics*, 2d ed., ed. Allan J. Cigler and Burdett A. Loomis (Washington, D.C.: CQ Press, 1986); William P. Browne, *Private Interests, Public Policy, and American Agriculture* (Lawrence: University Press of Kansas, 1988).

8. Jeffrey M. Berry, "Subgovernments, Issue Networks, and Political Conflict," in *Remaking American Politics*, ed. Richard A. Harris and Sidney M. Milkis (Boulder, Colo.: Westview, 1989).

9. Steven S. Smith and Christopher J. Deering, *Committees in Congress*, 2d ed. (Washington, D.C.: CQ Press, 1990).

10. Jeffrey M. Berry, *The Interest Group Society*, 2d ed. (Glenview, Ill.: Scott, Foresman, 1989), 165.

11. Jack L. Walker, "The Origins and Maintenance of Interest Groups in America," *American Political Science Review* 77 (June 1983): 390-406; Kay Lehman Schlozman and John T. Tierney, *Organized Interests and American Democracy* (New York: Harper and Row, 1986); Thomas E. Mann, *A Question of Balance: The President, the Congress, and Foreign Policy* (Washington: Brookings, 1990).

12. Robert H. Salisbury, "The Paradox of Interest Groups in Washington—More Groups, Less Clout," in *The New American Political System*, 2d ed., ed. Anthony King (Washington, D.C.: American Enterprise Institute, 1990).

13. Douglas W. Costain and Anne N. Costain, "Interest Groups as Policy Aggregators in the Legislative Process," *Polity* 14, 2 (Winter 1981): 249-272. See also Schlozman and Tierney, *Organized Interests*, 307; Christopher J. Bosso, *Pesticides and Politics: The Life Cycle of a Public Issue* (Pittsburgh, Pa.: University of Pittsburgh Press, 1987), 233.

14. Ford (D-Mich.) is the chairman of the House Committee on Education and Labor, as well as chairman of the Subcommittee on Postsecondary Education and Training.

15. In the extreme case, absence from an inclusive coalition preparing a legislative package could leave nonmember groups in the position of unrecognized interests in corporatist societies, where groups not formally recognized by the state are excluded from negotiations. For brief reviews of the literature on interest groups and corporatism, see Ruth Berins Collier and David Collier, "Inducements versus Constraints: Disaggregating 'Corporatism,'" *American Political Science Review* 73 (December 1979): 967-986; Leo Panitch, "Recent Theorizations of Corporatism: Reflections on a Growth Industry," *British Journal of Sociology* 31 (1980): 159-187.

16. The large number of "neither agree nor disagree" responses among education groups on question three is particularly high because of the number of groups who differentiated between appropriations and authorization in that policy domain. The modal response for this group ran along the lines of "I agree *and* disagree. For appropriations, it's very important for us to be in CEF; but for authorizations, we can act more on our own." It should be noted that CEF takes no positions on authorization issues.

17. This is not surprising, in view of research demonstrating the importance of information gathering and communications among Washington group representatives. See Robert H. Salisbury, John P. Heinz, Edward O. Laumann, and Robert L. Nelson, "Who Works With Whom? Interest Group Alliances and Opposition," *American Political Science Review* 81, 4 (December 1987): 1217-1234; Edward O. Laumann and David Knoke, *The Organizational State* (Madison: University of Wisconsin Press, 1987); John P. Heinz, Edward O. Laumann, Robert H. Salisbury, and Robert L. Nelson, "Inner Circles or Hollow Cores? Elite Networks in National Policy Systems," *Journal of Politics* 52, 2 (May 1990): 356-390.

18. For a lucid discussion of "windows of opportunity" in the policy process, see John W. Kingdon, *Agendas, Alternatives, and Public Policy* (Boston: Little, Brown, 1984).

19. The principal-agent theory explains some organizational behaviors as the outgrowth of asymmetries in information between organizations (the principals) and their agents. In large organizations, agents have a broad latitude of discretion because of inadequate possibilities for supervision by the principal. Thus, agents have broad opportunities to "shirk" responsibilities. See Stephen A. Ross, "The Economic Theory of Agency: The Principal's Problem," *American Economic Review* 63, 2 (May 1973): 134-139; Carl Shapiro and Joseph E. Stiglitz, "Equilibrium Unemployment as a Worker Discipline Device," *American Economic Review* 74, 3 (June 1984): 433-444. The decision organizational representatives make to participate symbolically in a strategic coalition rather than to lobby actively on an issue amounts to a sophisticated form of "shirking."

20. Loomis, "Coalitions of Interests."

21. A "policy domain" can be thought of as the political landscape surrounding a set of related issues, such as transportation or education. It includes individuals, institutions, and events. For detailed examinations of several domains, see Edward O. Laumann and David Knoke, *The Organizational State* (Madison: University of Wisconsin Press, 1987); and John P. Heinz, Edward O. Laumann, Robert L. Nelson, and Robert H. Salisbury, *The Hollow Core: Private Interests in National Policy Making* (Cambridge: Harvard University Press, 1993).

22. Salisbury, Heinz, Laumann, and Nelson, "Who Works with Whom?"

12

Consumer Groups and Coalition Politics on Capitol Hill

Loree Bykerk and Ardith Maney

Consumer groups have a long history in American politics, but only occasionally have they proved to be effective agents of change. Consumers are difficult to organize, in that the incentive to "free ride" is tremendous. Consumers Union gains members not by its success in pushing for safer cars or truth in advertising, but by offering an extremely valuable selective benefit, *Consumer Reports*, to its members. In a related vein, activist and organizer Ralph Nader makes claims to represent broad consumer interests, even though his myriad organizations enjoy relatively modest memberships.

In this article, Loree Bykerk and Ardith Maney explore the ways in which consumer groups seek to press their cases through a wide range of policy subsystems. Although they find a consumer network, they also note that consumer groups must operate on the home turf of many well-entrenched interests. To address the problem of being a marginal player in a complex issue network, consumer groups often seek to build coalitions that link them to more mainstream interests in the subsystem. In so doing the consumer groups obtain information and access while the other interests gain the broad support of the consumer movement. Still, consumer groups must fight to become more than window-dressing within the coalitions they join.

C onsumers and their advocates have brought a wide range of issues to the public agenda. Among these are food and drug safety, labeling and product content disclosure, banking and credit regulations, deceptive and anticompetitive practices, energy costs, housing availability, auto safety, and access to health care—to name just a few. Consumer concerns also extend to the behavior of producers in the public arena in areas such as accountability to stockholders, openness to consumer inquiries, disclosure of investments, and dealings with public officials. In this chapter we examine consumer coalitions to test competing claims about who allies with whom, why, and to what ends.

Consumer Politics Then and Now

Waves of consumer activism occurred during the major reform periods of the past century. In the Progressive Era, the administrations of Theodore Roosevelt and Woodrow Wilson developed new instruments for regulating financial institutions in the form of the Federal Reserve Board and the Federal Trade Commission. Health and safety issues were addressed with pure food and drug legislation. Activism at the federal level was mirrored at state and local levels with laws regulating transportation and insurance and protecting workers' wages, hours, and working conditions. Although courts ultimately struck down most of the attempts to protect workers, Progressives succeeded in arguing that some industries were public utilities and that the public had an ongoing interest in their operation.

Consumers were also part of President Franklin Delano Roosevelt's broad New Deal coalition. New techniques of government interaction with the private sector were designed and new agencies were created to carry them out. Some new agencies, like the Agricultural Adjustment Administration, were dissolved as the crisis eased, whereas others, such as the Federal Deposit Insurance Corporation and the Securities and Exchange Commission, remain active today. Another legacy of the New Deal and World War II was the appointment of agency-based consumer representatives.

The most recent reform wave began in the early 1960s and continued until the mid 1970s. Auto safety, deceptive credit practices, energy costs, product liability, legal services, funeral industry practices, the effects of smoking and tobacco use, television content, nutrition, and laxity by regulatory agencies were parts of an extensive domestic policy agenda. New laws were passed and new agencies created to enforce them, including the National Transportation Safety Board and the Consumer Product Safety Commission. New consumer groups were founded and old ones rejuvenated with the appearance of a new breed of consumer policy entrepreneurs who institutionalized their activities into a network of watchdog groups. Media attention focused on consumer issues, and prominent politicians capitalized on the wave of interest. This was the "golden age" of consumer protection policy in the United States. President Jimmy Carter appointed numerous public interest activists to prominent positions in his administration, but he could not persuade Congress to create an Agency for Consumer Advocacy—a goal long sought by consumer activists. The failure of the consumer agency bill in 1978 is an important benchmark in consumer protection policy.

By the late 1970s, business had reacted to the public interest reform wave and entered the national political environment in unprecedented fashion. Trade, professional, and peak business associations were refurbished and numerous individual corporations established their own

Washington presence. Public-opinion lobbying, grass-roots lobbying, and direct lobbying of Congress, staff, the White House, administrative agencies, and the courts became the order of business. More subtle efforts to turn the tide included funding think tanks, university centers, and professorships for the study of American business, and publishing periodicals to disseminate free-market ideas.[1]

As candidate and president, Ronald Reagan pledged to deregulate business and free private sector producers from interference by government or so-called public-interest advocates. The Reagan presidency struck powerful blows against consumer protection in its efforts to abolish or gut the Consumer Product Safety Commission, the Federal Trade Commission, the National Highway Traffic Safety Administration, the Environmental Protection Agency, the Occupational Safety and Health Administration, the Legal Services Corporation, and the Freedom of Information Act. Although these institutions survived, the Reagan counterreform accomplished as much as zealous appointees, budget and personnel cuts, and a chokehold on the regulatory process could be expected to do.

Pluralism?

The larger debate about consumer protection turns on the influence of private interests on American public policy. Since James Madison expressed concern about the influence of "factions," scholars have asked how a market economy and popular sovereignty can coexist. At present, the debate is defined on one side by Charles Lindblom's arguments that the market is a prison, and that producers use the political system more effectively than do other contestants and are able to keep certain fundamental questions off the agenda entirely.[2] Neopluralists such as Andrew McFarland, Jeffrey Berry, and David Vogel take the other side of the debate. They acknowledge that producer interests are powerful but argue that countervailing influences in government, among producers, and from organized public interest groups keep the system balanced.[3]

The roles and impacts of consumer groups are difficult to trace in the interest group literature. Most recent accounts of public interest group activity mention consumers but focus on governmental reform organizations or environmental organizations.[4] Our research has revealed that consumer protection activity before congressional panels peaked in the mid-1970s and then stabilized in the Carter and Reagan years at the level of the early 1970s.[5] Consumer groups and their issues eventually became institutionalized as part of the congressional agenda rather than disappearing altogether, as scholarly neglect might have implied.

The Consumer Federation of America (CFA), Consumers Union (CU), and groups associated with Ralph Nader appear most frequently to represent consumer voices on Capitol Hill. They are joined on occasion by many more specialized groups—some of which become regular allies. Bankcard Holders of America, the Center for Auto Safety, the Center for Science in the Public Interest, the Community Nutrition Institute, the National Insurance Consumer Organization, and Public Voice for Food and Health Policy typify the specialized organizations that bring their expertise forward on select consumer topics.

Other organizations that represent a segment of consumers, such as the elderly or those concerned with health or the environment, supply allies to the core consumer groups. Many of these allies are prominent organizations, including the American Association of Retired Persons; the National Women's Health Network; and, on environmental issues, the Environmental Defense Fund, the Natural Resources Defense Council, and the Sierra Club. Organized labor is another frequent participant in consumer-oriented coalitions. The American Federation of Labor-Congress of Industrial Organizations (AFL-CIO) is most often the labor voice, but individual unions, such as the International Ladies Garment Workers Union, are also active. By and large, the consumer movement gains a great deal from its linkages to prominent groups, for whom consumerism is but one of many concerns. What this behavior contributes to the larger issues of pluralism is a question to which we return in the concluding section.

From Subgovernments to Networks

Since the early 1980s, organized interests have increasingly used coalition building as a strategy.[6] Research on coalition behavior yields varying answers to the questions of how coalitions come into being and why they are increasingly prevalent. On the question of what groups come to be included in a coalition, scholars most often note clusters of organizations with similar views. However, because "politics makes strange bedfellows," some of the most powerful coalitions arise among organizations that usually find themselves on opposite sides of issues.

Increasing reliance on coalitions occurs as issue areas shift from "subgovernment" toward network relationships.[7] Subgovernments are made up of influential individuals from a committee or subcommittee of Congress, administrators from an agency or bureau of the executive branch, and representatives of the relevant organized interests. The three groups make up the "iron triangle" of subgovernment politics. Largely impervious to outside information, influence, or accountability, these individuals negotiate policy among themselves. Within such issue areas as agriculture or veterans' affairs, policies were stable and predictable as long as policy making by subgovernments persisted.

By the late 1970s, many of the conditions facilitating subgovernments had begun to change. Congress experienced high levels of membership turnover, subcommittees proliferated, seniority became less powerful, staff numbers increased, decision-making environments became increasingly open to outside scrutiny, and more members sought to act as "policy entrepreneurs." Growth in budget deficits, an expansion of the policy agenda, and an explosion in the number and variety of interests represented in Washington, including more citizens' groups, also contributed to deterioration of subgovernments and the rise of policy (or issue) networks.[8]

Compared to subgovernments, policy networks are large, inclusive, permeable, fluid, and defined by expertise rather than official position or material interest. Members may come from official legislative or executive positions or staff, state or local governments or their staff, think tanks, academia, interest groups, the media, or the corporate sector. Participants often move in and out of networks and have varying degrees of dependence on the others.

Still subject to debate among scholars is whether the current environment for policy making is genuinely competitive. Although the more densely populated policy network would seem to have increased the likelihood of competition among contenders, some scholars argue that specialization has countered competition. Groups are said to search for a narrow niche within which their expertise can be recognized and influential. Emerging interests may avoid challenging entrenched interests on a widespread scale, choosing instead to concentrate on gaining accommodation for their narrow concern.[9]

Thus, although the new environment may include more interests, it may not facilitate the resolution of long-standing conflicts. Research to date concludes that those looking for competition, compromise, countervailing power, and pluralist outcomes may find instead expanded complexity, informed skepticism, continuing dissension, and lack of closure.[10]

Other research has focused on major policy arenas that correspond to economic sectors such as agriculture, labor, health, and energy. Historically, each of these arenas has been characterized by subgovernments that have expanded recently to look more like policy networks. Other scholars have paid little attention to what may be called "externality groups," those organizations that sprang up in reaction to "business as usual." These groups, representing consumers, environmentalists, women, and others, show up on the fringes of traditional interest group politics.[11]

How do subgovernments and networks look from the vantage point of those on the fringes? An examination of consumer group activity may provide some answers to how, why, and with whom groups coalesce to influence policy making and its environment.

Consumerism and Increasing Group Activity: They Never Had It So Good

In a subgovernment environment, issues of concern to a particular interest would be addressed by a small, stable set of congressional com-

Table 12-1 House and Senate Consumer Protection Hearings, 1970-1980, by Committee

House committees		Senate committees	
Aging	2	Aging	8
Agriculture	7	Agriculture	5
Appropriations	**65**	**Appropriations**	**56**
Banking	**36**	**Banking**	**44**
District of Columbia	5	**Commerce**	**61**
Education & Labor	5	Energy & Natural Resources	4
Foreign Affairs	1	Environment & Public Works	5
Government Operations	**41**	Finance	1
Interior	1	**Government Affairs**	**22**
Interstate & Foreign Commerce	**83**	**Judiciary**	**36**
Judiciary	7	**Labor & Human Resources**	**28**
Merchant Marine	1	**Small Business**	**14**
Post Office	4	Veterans	3
Public Works & Transportation	1	Nutrition & Human Needs	8
Science, Space & Technology	1		
Small Business	**16**		
Ways & Means	9		

Source: Congressional Information Service.

mittees. Records of committee hearings provide a reliable indication of who seeks to be active on a given topic. Research on consumer protection in the late 1960s detected activity by five committees in the House and six in the Senate.[12] Hearings in the 1970s classified by the Congressional Information Service as consumer protection-related are displayed in Table 12-1. The committees holding the most hearings are shown in bold face.

Although consumer interests might have been able to form fairly close and stable relationships with members and staff of the House Interstate and Foreign Commerce Committee, their attempts to keep things cozy would have been thwarted by the substantial attention of other House and Senate committees that also held consumer protection hearings. In addition, congressional attention expanded between 1970 and 1980 to the point that only five House committees and four Senate committees did *not* hold consumer protection hearings. By 1980 there were no cozy triangles for consumer policies. The congressional angle of the "consumer triangle" was highly visible and crowded with legislators and committees.

Nor did the quiet, almost invisible nature of subgovernment relationships between members of Congress and private interests apply on consumer policies. The public political value of consumer issues contributed to many early legislative victories for consumer interests. Congressional issue entrepreneurs such as senators Philip Hart (D-Mich.), Paul Douglas

(D-Ill.), Gaylord Nelson (D-Wis.), William Proxmire (D-Wis.), and Abraham Ribicoff (D-Conn.), and representatives John Moss (D-Calif.) and Benjamin Rosenthal (D-N.Y.), successfully sought favorable media attention and political credit for consumer hearings and legislation.[13]

The subgovernment model does no better in explaining executive branch actions. Consumer interests did try to gain their "own" agency; indeed, in the 1970s they conducted a vigorous but futile effort to establish an Agency for Consumer Advocacy as an interdepartmental watchdog and advocate. Legislation to create a consumer agency passed either the House or Senate five times in seven years, but ultimately went down to defeat in 1978. The intensity of this battle demonstrated both how important such a focal point was for consumer interests and how dangerous its opponents thought it might become.[14]

Consider how dispersed executive branch responsibility for consumer issues was at that time. If we scan the hearings held during 1976 and 1977, the peak years of House activity on consumer protection, for executive branch agency involvement, we find a wide range of agencies touched by consumer issues (Table 12-2). To be sure, there is the predictable activity of consumer affairs offices within major departments and agencies such as Health, Education, and Welfare, Housing and Urban Development, the National Highway Traffic Safety Administration, the Food and Drug Administration, and the Federal Trade Commission. Dominating the data, however, is a long list of agencies making single appearances. Single appearances require some attention from organized advocates but do not permit the development of close working relationships.

The hearing records hint at yet another aspect of the executive role in a subgovernment: state government agencies also show up at consumer protection hearings. At 1976-77 hearings, thirteen state agencies and two national associations of state policy makers appeared to testify about evidence of problems or about how states were responding to a specific problem. Because states have responsibilities for enforcing consumer protection standards, the growth of a subgovernmental relationship involving a small, stable set of federal executive personnel is less likely. In sum, consumer interests did not forge close subgovernment relationships with either the legislative or executive branches of government in the 1970s.

Consumer interest representation did expand in the late 1970s and 1980s, in terms both of the number of groups with a Washington presence and the range of topics that commanded their attention. The National Consumers League (founded in 1899) and CU (founded in 1936) were joined in 1967 by the CFA and in 1971 by Ralph Nader's Public Citizen, along with its related groups (Health Research Group, Congress Watch, the Media Access Project), and the Center for Science in the Public Interest. By 1981, the roster of consumer groups included Bankcard Holders of America, Citizens for Tax Justice, the Child Nutrition Forum, and the

Table 12-2   Agencies Subject to Consumer Protection Hearings
before the House, 1976-1977

Appeared in four hearings	Appeared in one hearing
National Highway Traffic Safety Administration	Civil Aeronautics Board
	Department of Agriculture
Federal Trade Commission Bureau of Consumer Protection	Department of Transportation
	Federal Deposit Insurance Corporation
Food and Drug Administration	Federal Trade Commission Bureau of Competition
Housing and Urban Development	Health, Education & Welfare
	National Institute for Environmental & Health Sciences
Appeared in three hearings	National Institute for Occupational Safety & Health
Comptroller of the Currency	Housing & Urban Development
Federal Energy Administration	Office of Consumer Affairs & Regulatory Functions
Federal Reserve System Board	
Health, Education & Welfare Office of Consumer Affairs	National Bureau of Standards
	National Cancer Institute
Appeared in two hearings	Nuclear Regulatory Commission
Consumer Product Safety Commission	Presidential Assistant for Consumer Affairs
Energy Research and Development Agency	Securities & Exchange Commission
Federal Power Commission	Securities Investor Protection Corporation
Federal Trade Commission	United States Postal Service

Source: Congressional Information Service.

National Insurance Consumer Organization, among others. In all, forty-three groups were formed between 1967 and 1985, including seven in 1971 alone.[15]

The organized consumer community thus became more specialized as well as more highly populated; the number and breadth of issues emphasized by these organizations expanded the scope of consumer protection as a policy idea. Fed by a more inclusive view of politics and by the increasingly well-organized resources of Ralph Nader and others, consumer issues grew to encompass not only safe drugs and autos but also open government, transportation deregulation, and access to health care.[16]

The Consumer Network

Although there is no generally accepted way to map a policy network, several principles of networks emerge consistently.

Networks have unclear or "sloppy" boundaries.
Some groups are more central because their involvement is more general, whereas others have more specialized interests and thus are more peripheral.
Sectors or clusters of groups that express common concerns and ex-

change information with greater frequency can be distinguished.[17]

Figure 12-1 sketches out the consumer policy network as it evolved from the early 1970s through the Reagan-Bush era. The CFA, CU, and Nader's Public Citizen are the three generalist organizations at the heart of the network. They monitor consumer issues, broadly defined, articulate positions, and generally offer a formal presence. Among the generalist groups, CU focuses especially on products and services, whereas CFA attends to state-federal relations, regulation, and macroeconomic and redistributive issues like housing and taxation. Public Citizen is more likely to emphasize government process issues such as openness, ethics, and accountability, and it serves as a communications center for the separately identified groups that operate under its umbrella. Other, specialized groups take on a wide range of issues, including nutrition, smoking, government reform, insurance, banking, housing, energy, trade, taxation, and the media. These are clustered in the figure according to the similarity of their concerns and the frequency with which they communicate.

Think tanks and organizations of state or local officials approach federal policy with resource bases and goals that frequently differ from those of other organized interests. To the extent they are regarded as more intellectual or as motivated by official obligations they can constitute a buffer or bridge between consumer groups and their policy "competitors." For this reason they are shown in a ring in the figure. The ring is not meant to suggest that the consumer network is bounded by these organizations. In fact, it may be useful to visualize the ring as operating in a space not congruent with but in a different dimension than the other organizations, more like an angled orbit.

Organizations usually opposed to consumer group positions are placed furthest from the center but are clustered in the same way as their competitors in the core. Most of the opponent organizations are trade and professional groups, although a few are peak business associations such as the U.S. Chamber of Commerce and Business Roundtable. Also evident are a few consumer groups, such as Consumers for World Trade and Consumer Alert, that usually align themselves with producer interests. Note that there is no organized opposition to the government reform advocates such as Public Citizen, Congress Watch, and Common Cause. There are no "bad government" groups, but opposition, often intense, does arise from those interests most advantaged by the status quo.

The nature of a consumer interest cannot always be inferred from a cluster on a network map. Careful analysis of policy proposals is required to understand how various initiatives advantage or disadvantage consumer interests. The complexity of consumer policy encourages public interest advocates, spokespersons for producers, government officials,

Figure 12-1   Consumer Policy Network

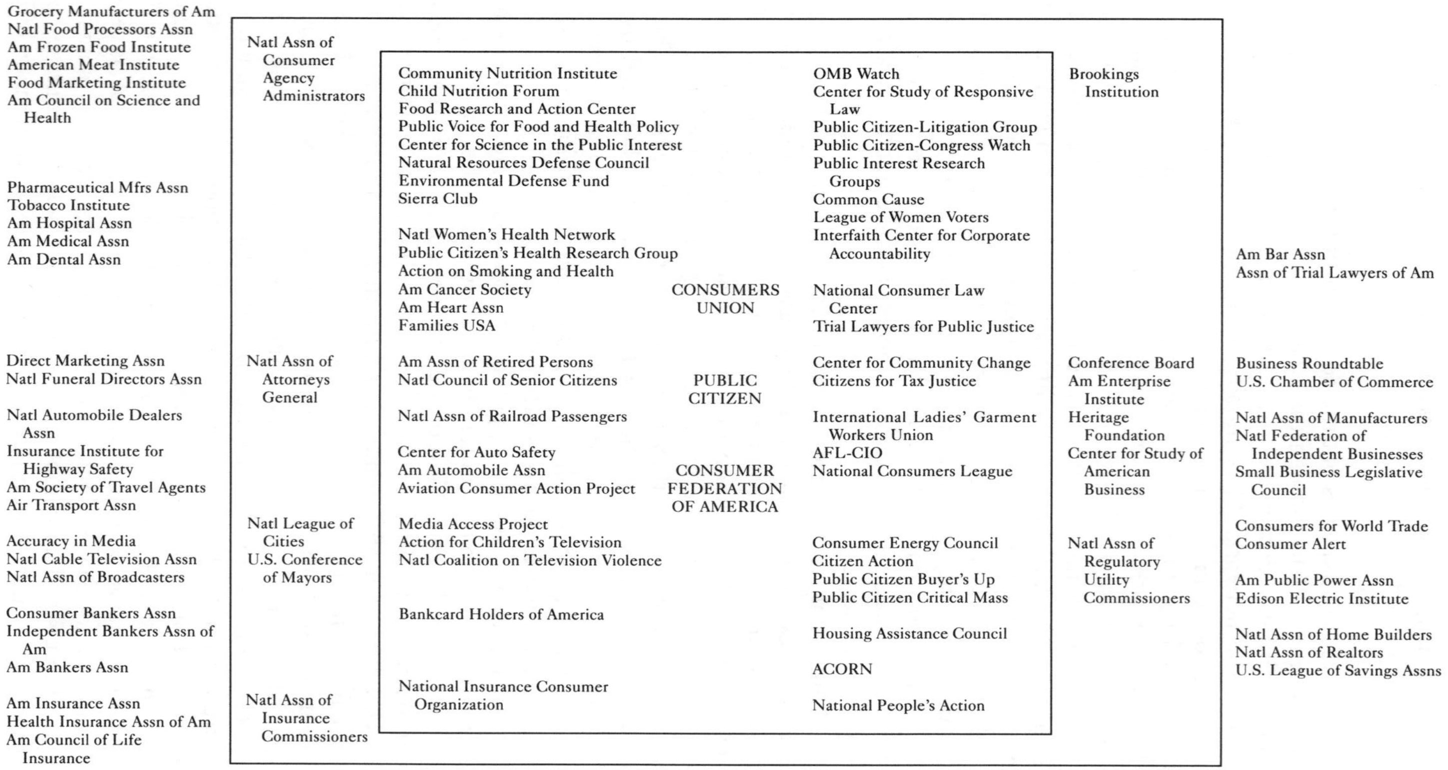

Grocery Manufacturers of Am
Natl Food Processors Assn
Am Frozen Food Institute
American Meat Institute
Food Marketing Institute
Am Council on Science and Health

Pharmaceutical Mfrs Assn
Tobacco Institute
Am Hospital Assn
Am Medical Assn
Am Dental Assn

Direct Marketing Assn
Natl Funeral Directors Assn

Natl Automobile Dealers Assn
Insurance Institute for Highway Safety
Am Society of Travel Agents
Air Transport Assn

Accuracy in Media
Natl Cable Television Assn
Natl Assn of Broadcasters

Consumer Bankers Assn
Independent Bankers Assn of Am
Am Bankers Assn

Am Insurance Assn
Health Insurance Assn of Am
Am Council of Life Insurance

Natl Assn of Consumer Agency Administrators

Natl Assn of Attorneys General

Natl League of Cities
U.S. Conference of Mayors

Natl Assn of Insurance Commissioners

Community Nutrition Institute
Child Nutrition Forum
Food Research and Action Center
Public Voice for Food and Health Policy
Center for Science in the Public Interest
Natural Resources Defense Council
Environmental Defense Fund
Sierra Club

Natl Women's Health Network
Public Citizen's Health Research Group
Action on Smoking and Health
Am Cancer Society
Am Heart Assn
Families USA

Am Assn of Retired Persons
Natl Council of Senior Citizens

Natl Assn of Railroad Passengers

Center for Auto Safety
Am Automobile Assn
Aviation Consumer Action Project

Media Access Project
Action for Children's Television
Natl Coalition on Television Violence

Bankcard Holders of America

National Insurance Consumer Organization

CONSUMERS UNION

PUBLIC CITIZEN

CONSUMER FEDERATION OF AMERICA

OMB Watch
Center for Study of Responsive Law
Public Citizen-Litigation Group
Public Citizen-Congress Watch
Public Interest Research Groups
Common Cause
League of Women Voters
Interfaith Center for Corporate Accountability

National Consumer Law Center
Trial Lawyers for Public Justice

Center for Community Change
Citizens for Tax Justice

International Ladies' Garment Workers Union
AFL-CIO
National Consumers League

Consumer Energy Council
Citizen Action
Public Citizen Buyer's Up
Public Citizen Critical Mass

Housing Assistance Council

ACORN

National People's Action

Brookings Institution

Conference Board
Am Enterprise Institute
Heritage Foundation
Center for Study of American Business

Natl Assn of Regulatory Utility Commissioners

Am Bar Assn
Assn of Trial Lawyers of Am

Business Roundtable
U.S. Chamber of Commerce
Natl Assn of Manufacturers
Natl Federation of Independent Businesses
Small Business Legislative Council

Consumers for World Trade
Consumer Alert
Am Public Power Assn
Edison Electric Institute

Natl Assn of Home Builders
Natl Assn of Realtors
U.S. League of Savings Assns

and other experts all to claim, sometimes persuasively, that they are working in the best interest of consumers.

Examining the institutional paths along which consumer issues are carried, we find that consumer groups contend in an environment structured more by production categories and interests than by consumption categories and interests. This assessment is reaffirmed by examining data on the committees and agencies where relevant issues are decided. More often than not, consumer advocates must play on the "home court" of the producers—committees and agencies defined by food production, health care delivery, transportation provision, banking, and so forth. This suggests that producers rather than consumers are more likely to gain from the process by which issues are defined, expertise is sought and delivered, and policy options are assessed.

Coalition Behavior

A principal adaptation to the complexity of a network environment is for organizations to coalesce to accomplish their goals. Some coalitions form through arrangements made by consultants from law and public relations firms who work for some or all of the groups involved. These facilitators are often in a position to observe the common interests at stake, to have contact with at least some of the various organizations who are potential allies, and to have a financial interest in bringing a coalition together. Brokers offer flexibility, speed, and access that individual organizations may lack; they can organize as broad or narrow a set of interests as the issue requires.[18]

The Role of Brokers in Consumer Coalitions

To test whether groups in the consumer network are formed in this fashion, we compiled a list of twenty of the organizations appearing most often before Congress on consumer protection issues.[19] Persons registered as representing these organizations were traced through their listings in the 1984 and 1988 editions of *Washington Representatives*.[20]

Three patterns stand out. First, consumer groups rarely use outside consultants to complement their own staff. In 1984 only six consumer organizations listed consultants. Ralph Nader consulted for three of these: Public Citizen, Center for Study of Responsive Law, and Telecommunication Research and Action Center. Jay Angoff consulted for Public Citizen Congress Watch and Public Citizen Tax Reform Research Group. T. B. Smith consulted for the Community Nutrition Institute while serving on the staff of Public Voice for Food and Health Policy (which broke off from Community Nutrition Institute).

In 1984 consultants for just two of the consumer groups were positioned to broker among organizations that were not already familiar allies. The Consumer Energy Council retained James Feldesman, an attorney,

whose firm's clients included an array of farmworker and migrant programs, some television stations, and the YMCA. The National Women's
Health Network retained two consultants with some outside ties. By
1988, however, the consumer groups had dropped all consultants.

Second, and by contrast, well-positioned brokers do appear in the
data, ordinarily working for groups like the National Association of
Realtors, which listed one consultant who also represented the Business
Roundtable, Sony, Westinghouse, CBS, the National Football League,
and Metropolitan Life. Likewise, in addition to its twenty registered staff
lobbyists, the Edison Electric Institute (the electric power industry's
trade group) retained seven consulting firms, including O'Connor and
Hannan, whose forty-nine clients range from manufacturers to advertisers
to insurers.

Organized labor allies do provide consumer groups with the kind of
connections that producers can afford. The AFL-CIO retained four and
later five consultants, one of whose 1984 clients included an air transport
company, car rental firms, trucking interests, and hotels. In 1988 one
consulting firm listed clients in manufacturing, insurance, tobacco, banking, and chemicals, in addition to its labor connections. But these wide-
ranging consulting arrangements were exceptions; most of the clients
listed by firms retained by the AFL-CIO were other labor organizations.
One can envision opportunities here for brokering alliances, but they
would reach from labor to manufacturers or service industries rather than
to consumers.

Third, notable changes can be seen over time. By 1988, the core
consumer organizations were even less likely than before to retain anyone
whereas the trade and professional organizations retained more consultants and also listed more staff as lobbyists. Turnover among the consultants employed by the associations is high; for example, among the five
firms retained by the American Insurance Association in 1988, only two
had ties with them in 1984. By comparison, there was less turnover among
the consumer groups' staff.

In short, there is some potential for consumer coalitions to be arranged by consultants from labor allies, but it is relatively unlikely to
occur as compared to the opportunities for brokering among the producer
organizations. Among consumer organizations, alliances are usually arranged by staffers who are familiar with each other. Although this pool of
individuals is larger than it was in the 1970s, it remains relatively small
within the expanding Washington community of interests and representatives.

Why, Who, and with Whom

Coalitions frequently come together as their members seek to extend
their resources in an environment of large numbers of organized interests
and fragmentation of formal decision-making power. In the case of the

Table 12-3 Washington Representation of Frequent Consumer
Participants

Type of group	1984			1988		
	N	Staff	Retained	N	Staff	Retained
Consumer	13	28	7	14	24	0
Allies	2	26	5	2	37	6
Intergovernmental lobby	3	4	3	2	7	0
Producers	10	167	23	10	218	22
Totals	28	225	38	28	286	28

Source: Washington Representatives 1984, 1988; groups are listed in note 19.

consumer network, the primary reason for the greater complexity is
not the opening up of a traditional subgovernment, but growth in the
number of highly specialized groups and an expanded definition of subjects considered relevant to consumer protection. Both of these trends
have produced greater needs for coalition building among consumer
groups.

In fact, central to understanding why consumer organizations participate in coalitions is their poverty of resources, which differentiates them
from their usual opponents (Table 12-3). Even if consumer groups join
organized labor and the elderly and intergovernmental lobbyists do not
oppose them, they face disproportionate odds. Not only do they usually
have to play on the producers' home court, but their traveling squad all
fits in a van rather than a bus.

The data also suggest that the frail coalition behavior observed by
other scholars may be motivated less by reluctance to devote resources to
a collective-action problem than by an inability to do so.[21] Joining a coalition as an extension of your group's monitoring effort, to say that you are
taking a position even if that amounts only to a staff decision communi-
cated by way of a few articles in newsletters, is a reasonable strategy when
competing against a formidable foe. Most consumer groups must choose
their full-fledged battles carefully; coalitions allow them both to conduct
major campaigns and to "show the flag," while not committing many
scarce resources. Indeed, when groups are acutely aware of their resource
disadvantage, we expect them to actively seek out coalition partners. This
contrasts with the behavior of business interests, which usually do not
have to worry greatly about extending modest resources.

The actions of consumer organizations support the explanation that
groups join coalitions to compensate for their relative dearth of resources.
What, then, can they bring to coalitions, aside from the symbolic association with individual consumers? Most notably, they come to the table

with inside-the-beltway savvy gained from years of surviving against difficult odds and lobbying effectively on tight budgets.

Our recent research reveals numerous examples of coalition behavior upon which we can draw to answer the question, "Who allies with whom?" [22] Coalitions of usual allies are the norm. They have come together on campaign finance reform, pesticide policy, banking reform, trade policy, and creation of a consumer advocacy agency. For example, Public Citizen, Common Cause, and the League of Women Voters combined on campaign finance reform, while allies from organized labor and the elderly joined core consumer groups on banking reform and a consumer agency. Over the years, coalitions tend to form and reform, bringing together different sets of partners within the same universe of groups. (For more on coalitions as round-ups of the "usual suspects" see Chapter 11 in this volume.)

Two additional observations merit mention. First, consumer coalitions often include a combination of at least one generalist group and some of the more specialized groups. Exemplifying this pattern are the alliance between CFA and Public Voice for Food and Health Policy on pesticide policy and the trade policy coalition of the CFA, Public Citizen, the Community Nutrition Institute, the Public Voice for Food and Health Policy, the Center for Science in the Public Interest, and assorted environmental organizations. Specialized groups tend to take the lead on issues where they have recognized expertise; generalists are more likely to lead on multifaceted issues where no single specialized organization is clearly in the vanguard. Such complex issues often require difficult strategic and resource questions about which battles to choose and what risks to take. Generalist groups are more likely to have the necessary resources as well as the experience that allows for a coherent weighing of the costs and benefits of involvement.

Second, there are notable effects of long-standing ties among the set of organizations established by Ralph Nader and his followers. The linkages among the groups that operate under the Public Citizen umbrella are apparent, but there is also a larger set of organizations that have matured with some ties to Nader. He may have assisted in the development of an organization, or its staff may have had earlier experience working with Public Citizen or as one of Nader's Raiders. These organizations include the Aviation Consumer Action Project, the Center for Auto Safety, the Center for Study of Responsive Law, the National Insurance Consumer Organization, the Telecommunication Research and Action Center, the Public Interest Research Groups, and Citizens for Tax Justice.

Adversary Coalitions and Pluralist Competition

What does consumer coalition behavior contribute to the larger questions of politics? Does consumer group behavior shed light on whether the American political system is able to settle conflict constructively with decisions that are reasonably fair? Consumer network activists have to use direct, competitive confrontations in order to raise issues to salience. By the very nature of their position, consumer advocates cannot afford to be conflict-averse; they must confront the behavior of those who provide goods and services.[23] While much of that encounter may turn on relatively narrow product or service issues, it may also extend to broader issues of fundamental fairness.

Within that context, consumer groups on occasion join coalitions that include not just the usual allies, but also those who are ordinarily adversaries. The adversary coalitions combine competition and compromise. They are valuable because they offer real possibilities for resolving thorny issues, in part because they include members whose interests are ordinarily at odds. If that conflict can be surmounted, the resolution the coalition proposes has a greater chance of acceptance by formal decision makers, who must take notice of an alliance of strange bedfellows.

Consumer groups—being reluctant compromisers—have often fostered a purist image, acting as though they would "rather have the issue than the legislation." [24] Group leaders recognize the risks to consumer organizations' independence and integrity when they work with business. Leaders must be particularly cautious to guarantee that outcomes will offer sufficient benefits for consumers to justify whatever gains business receives. When consumer groups enter into a coalition with producers, their leaders want to send the message that it is a worthy settlement, a win-win proposition.

Endorsement by more than the usual allies is also positive for conflict-averse decision makers, who can interpret the range of support as constructive. Adversary coalitions tend to form when decision makers appear likely to act on a contested issue; at such times it is worthwhile to devote resources to a coalition. Finally, adversary coalitions are more apt to form if potential allies are not simultaneously battling each other on another issue or in a different forum.

Adversary coalitions can be very influential. For example, the broadcaster-consumer alliance proved formidable in the late 1980s and early 1990s politics of cable television reregulation. (On this issue there were two other major coalitions—one bringing together the cable television and motion picture industries, and one centered within the telephone industry.) The consumer-broadcaster coalition also included labor, satellite dish and wireless cable interests, and local governments. Specific organizations included the CFA, CU, Public Citizen, the Media Access Project, the AFL-CIO, the National Association of Broadcasters, the Association of Independent Television Stations, the Satellite Broadcasting and Communications Association, the Wireless Cable Association, the U.S. Conference of Mayors, and the National League of Cities.[25]

The coalition came together incrementally during years of lone, unsuccessful efforts on the part of each of the members to address cable company abuses in a deregulated environment. The separate parties came to recognize their common interest in reimposing some measure of regulation on cable providers and the common benefits that an alliance might produce. Moreover, the only way they could succeed in their individual desires was to proceed as a coalition.[26] Consumers wanted rate relief, service improvements, long-run competition among providers, and improved customer complaint processes. Broadcasters sought must-carry rules (for local stations), some compensation for their signals, and long-run assurances that they would not be closed out of a marketplace increasingly dominated by what they described as anticompetitive deals between cable providers and affiliated programmers. Local governments desired rate moderation and service improvements, and a measure of control over cable companies.

Within the other coalitions, the cable owners' basic position was to defend the deregulated market in which they had flourished since 1984; the motion picture industry sought additional revenues for its films or, failing that, the denial of greater returns to broadcasters. The telephone companies wanted to enter the video programming and delivery business.[27]

Of particular interest is how the adversary coalition behaved. Broadcasters provided most of the support for an expensive advertising campaign that defended "free TV"; consumer groups supplied extensive data on rates and service; and the cities reported on customer complaints and abuses.[28] Broadcasters made political action committee contributions, but these represented only a fraction of cable interests' contributions.[29] Each of the coalition partners had contacts with different members of Congress; the consumer groups, and particularly the CFA, took the lead in speaking to the print media. These groups could agree on an elevated public interest argument that defended the value of common media, accessible to most consumers, rather than a two-class system with cable available only to wealthier subscribers.

The coalition was able to compromise on an operational approach of having the Federal Communications Commission regulate the price of basic cable service, monitor other rates, set uniform customer service and equipment standards, require streamlined consumer complaint processes, and increase competition by requiring cable companies to deal fairly with other providers (e.g., satellite dish companies). Consumer groups also were relieved to have the telephone industry closed out of the cable business because of the risks of monopoly and subtle cross-subsidization among customers of the sort that occurred historically between long-distance and local telephone services. Broadcasters got the right to charge cable operators for using their programs or require them to transmit their signals for free.[30] The interest of local officials in regaining control over cable operators was not satisfied, although it is intriguing to speculate that

cable interests might have chosen that as a compromise if they had anticipated that Congress would override President Bush's veto of the final
legislation.

In these respects, this case supports findings that coalitions allow
groups to extend their monitoring network, forge an extended set of contacts among policy makers, and approach policy makers as a broad interest. Coalition members compromised among themselves in order to
present decision makers with a united front and increase the likelihood
that the issue would be decided in their favor.

The victorious adversary coalition probably could not have succeeded without the persistence of Rep. Edward J. Markey (D-Mass.),
chair of the House Energy and Commerce Subcommittee on Telecommunication and Finance. On the other hand, it is doubtful that without
the coalition's formation the legislation would have achieved the notable
status of being the only successful override of President Bush's thirty-six
vetoes and of instituting the only significant reregulation of an industry
since the Reagan-Bush era began. The alliance of consumer groups and
the broadcast industry brought together the power of good ideas, defensible to viewers-constituents, and the lobbying influence derived in part
from the broadcasters' great financial resources. By rounding up more
than the usual suspects, the consumer/broadcasting coalition provided
excellent cover for decision makers and thus achieved closure on a difficult, complex, high-stakes issue.

Other adversary coalitions have been visible recently on consumer
policy issues such as airline deregulation, Medicaid extension, and interstate bank branching.[31] The coalition supporting airline deregulation in
the late 1970s included Nader's Transportation Consumer Action Project,
Common Cause, and Americans for Democratic Action, along with the
National Association of Manufacturers, the National Federation of Independent Businesses, and the American Conservative Union. The Children's Defense Fund allied with the Health Insurance Association of
America, the U.S. Chamber of Commerce, the National Association of
Manufacturers, the American Medical Association, and the American
Hospital Association to extend Medicaid coverage to impoverished children under the age of eighteen. This latter grouping suggests that there
are ample opportunities for complex adversary coalitions to develop in
health care as policy makers wrestle with reform proposals. Indeed, they
may be essential for any major legislation to move forward.

Summary: Consumers and Coalitions

The performance of coalitions emerging from a broad consumer network provides a useful corrective to mainstream accounts of the behavior
of organized political interests. Previous research on coalitions often neglected consumer organizations and other public interest groups. Al-

though consumer interests coalesce to adapt to diffused decision-making power and multiple organized interests, their environment differs from that of most other interests, especially those in the business sector.

Historically, consumer groups have not belonged to a specific subgovernment; rather, in the 1970s they began to intervene within many separate subgovernments, often through testimony at congressional hearings or through attention to various executive branch agencies. Thus, as broad, loose issue networks have supplanted subgovernments, consumer groups have easily adapted. In fact, while consumer interests remain active across many issue areas, they also operate within their own network, populated by three generalist organizations, many specialized groups, some continuing allies, and various regular adversaries. At the same time, because the institutional paths of policy are structured more along lines of production than consumption, consumer groups usually have to compete on the home court of producer interests.

Analysis of coalition behavior within this network reveals that consumer coalitions are unlikely to be arranged by consultants, especially when compared to the producer interests they usually oppose. Still, the small number of representatives of consumer interests does facilitate familiarity, so that coalitions can be arranged with relative ease. Most consumer coalitions occur among allied groups seeking to stretch their resources, but it may be more fruitful to study adversary coalitions for their contributions to constructive management of conflict. The adversary coalition active in cable television reregulation illustrates what can be accomplished when more than the usual allies come together.

The presence of competition, compromise, and change, however, is not enough to establish the countervailing power associated with pluralism. A cynic might assert that when consumer groups are prominently featured in an adversary coalition they are being used as window dressing to mask the narrow self-interest of other interests. Although that did not appear to be the case with cable reregulation, the resource disadvantages of consumer groups lead to legitimate questions of differential impact on policy formation.

Consumer advocates are not in an equal bargaining position with producer interests. They do not have access to members of Congress through campaign contributions or producers' constituency ties. They do, however, have the ability to raise consumer considerations to an audible level, and their support provides heightened levels of legitimacy for a proposal. Thus, consumer interests may actually be more influential when they combine with their usual adversaries to lend, albeit cautiously, the mantle of the public interest to the coalition's position.

Notes

1. David Vogel, *Fluctuating Fortunes: The Political Power of Business in America* (New York: Basic Books, 1989).

2. Charles E. Lindblom, "The Market as Prison," *Journal of Politics* 44 (May 1982): 324-336; Charles E. Lindblom, *Politics and Markets* (New York: Basic Books, 1977).

3. Andrew McFarland, "Interest Groups and Theories of Power in America," *British Journal of Political Science* 17 (April 1988): 129-147; Jeffrey Berry, *The Interest Group Society*, 2d ed. (Glenview, Ill: Scott, Foresman/Little Brown, 1989); Vogel, *Fluctuating Fortunes*.

4. On governmental reform organizations, see Andrew McFarland, *Common Cause* (Chatham, N.J.: Chatham House, 1984). On environmental organizations, see Michael W. McCann, *Taking Reform Seriously: Perspectives on Public Interest Liberalism* (Ithaca, N.Y.: Cornell University Press, 1986); and Vogel, *Fluctuating Fortunes*.

5. Loree Bykerk and Ardith Maney, "Where Have All the Consumers Gone?" *Political Science Quarterly* 106, 4 (Winter 1991): 677-694.

6. Jeffrey M. Berry, *The Interest Group Society* (Boston: Little, Brown and Company, 1984), 202-205; Burdett A. Loomis, "Coalitions of Interests: Building Bridges in the Balkanized State," in *Interest Group Politics*, 2d ed., ed. Allan J. Cigler and Burdett A. Loomis (Washington, D.C.: CQ Press, 1986), 258-273; Kay Lehman Schlozman and John T. Tierney, *Organized Interests and American Democracy* (New York: Harper and Row, 1986), 306-307; Robert H. Salisbury, *Interests and Institutions: Substance and Structure in American Politics* (Pittsburgh: University of Pittsburgh Press, 1992), 339-361.

7. Schlozman and Tierney, *Organized Interests*, 276-277; Allan J. Cigler and Burdett A. Loomis, "Organized Interests and the Search for Certainty," in *Interest Group Politics*, 3d ed., ed. Allan J. Cigler and Burdett A. Loomis (Washington, D.C.: CQ Press, 1991), 388-389; Ardith Maney and Loree Bykerk, *Consumer Politics: Protecting Public Interests on Capitol Hill* (Westport, Conn.: Greenwood Press, 1994).

8. Hugh Heclo, "Issue Networks and the Executive Establishment," in *The New American Political System*, ed. Anthony King (Washington, D.C.: American Enterprise Institute, 1978), 87-124. We prefer the term policy network to issue network. Policy implies a wider, more durable set of concerns and connections than issue, thus better describing how Washington actually works. It is not inconsistent with the intent of Heclo's original formulation.

9. William P. Browne, "Issue Niches and the Limits of Interest Group Influence," in *Interest Group Politics*, 3d ed., ed. Allan J. Cigler and Burdett A. Loomis (Washington, D.C.: CQ Press, 1991), 352-355; Robert H. Salisbury, "Putting Interests Back into Interest Groups," in *Interest Group Politics*, 3d ed., ed. Cigler and Loomis, 381.

10. Heclo, "Issue Networks."

11. Robert H. Salisbury, John P. Heinz, Edward O. Laumann, and Robert L. Nelson, "Who Works with Whom? Interest Group Alliances and Opposition," *American Political Science Review* 81 (December 1987): 1217-1220; William P. Browne, "Organized Interests and Their Issue Niches: A Search for Pluralism in a Policy Domain," *Journal of Politics* 52 (May 1990): 493; Schlozman and Tierney, *Organized Interests*, 285.

12. Mark V. Nadel, *The Politics of Consumer Protection* (Indianapolis: Bobbs-Merrill Educational Publishing, 1971), 117-120.

13. Michael Pertschuk, *Revolt Against Regulation: The Rise and Pause of the Consumer Movement* (Berkeley: University of California Press, 1982), 20-23.

14. Mark Green, "Why the Consumer Bill Went Down," *The Nation*, February 25, 1978, 198-201.

15. Loree Bykerk and Ardith Maney, "Where Have All the Consumers Gone?" (Paper

delivered at the annual meeting of the Midwest Political Science Association, Chicago, April 13-15, 1989). Included are consumer organizations appearing two or more times before House consumer protection hearings from 1977 to 1987 as indexed by Congressional Information Service. The groups are: Accuracy in Media, ACORN, Action for Children's Television, Action on Smoking and Health, American Council on Science and Health, Aviation Consumer Action Project, Bankcard Holders of America, Center for Auto Safety, Center for Community Change, Center for Science in the Public Interest, Center for Study of Responsive Law, Child Nutrition Forum, Citizen Action, Citizens for Tax Justice, Community Nutrition Institute, Consumer Alert, Consumer Energy Council of America, Consumer Federation of America, Consumers for World Trade, Consumers Union, Families USA, Food Research and Action Center, Housing Assistance Council, Insurance Institute for Highway Safety, Interfaith Center on Corporate Responsibility, International Organization of Consumers Unions, Media Access Project, National Association of Railroad Passengers, National Coalition Against Misuse of Pesticides, National Coalition on Television Violence, National Consumer Law Center, National Consumers League, National Heart Savers Association, National Insurance Consumer Organization, National People's Action, National Women's Health Network, OMB Watch, Public Citizen, Public Citizen: Buyer's Up, Congress Watch, Critical Mass, Health Research Group, Litigation Group, Public Interest Research Group, Public Voice for Food and Health Policy, Telecommunication Research and Action Center, Trial Lawyers for Public Justice.

16. Bykerk and Maney, "Where Have All the Consumers Gone?" 677-693; Maney and Bykerk, *Consumer Politics*.

17. Edward O. Laumann and David Knoke, *The Organizational State* (Madison: University of Wisconsin Press, 1987), 38; Berry, *The Interest Group Society*, 2d ed., 186-192; David Knoke, *Political Networks: The Structural Perspective* (Cambridge: Cambridge University Press, 1990), 235-240; Bernd Marin and Renate Mayntz, eds., *Policy Networks: Empirical Evidence and Theoretical Considerations* (Boulder, Colo.: Westview Press, 1991).

18. Loomis, "Coalitions," 270-272; Salisbury, *Interests and Institutions*, 351-354.

19. Bykerk and Maney, "Where Have All the Consumers Gone?" Consumer groups were oversampled to compensate for the ten producer organizations among the twenty appearing most frequently. The organizations, in order of their frequency of appearance, include Consumers Union, Consumer Federation of America, American Bankers Association, American Association of Retired Persons, AFL-CIO, Public Citizen Congress Watch, National Consumers League, National Association of State Regulatory Utility Commissioners, American Medical Association, Public Interest Research Group, National Association of Attorneys General, National Association of Insurance Commissioners, Chamber of Commerce, National Association of Home Builders, National Association of Realtors, U.S. League of Savings Associations, American Dental Association, Small Business Legislative Council, American Insurance Association, Edison Electric Institute. Oversample of core consumer groups: National Consumer Law Center, Aviation Consumer Action Project, Consumer Energy Council of America, National People's Action, Bankcard Holders of America, Center for Auto Safety, Center for Science in the Public Interest, Community Nutrition Institute, National Insurance Consumer Organization, Public Citizen Health Research Group, Public Voice for Food and Health Policy, National Women's Health Network.

20. Arthur C. Close, ed., *Washington Representatives 1984*, 8th ed. (Washington, D.C.: Columbia Books, 1984); Close et al., eds., *Washington Representatives 1988*, 12th ed. (Washington, D.C.: Columbia Books, 1988). These years were long enough into the decade for groups to have adapted to the environment and were prime times to take advantage of presidential election year opportunities. That is, if these groups

were going to "buy into" consulting assistance, these years should have been the years to do so.

21. Browne, "Organized Interests and Their Issue Niches," 494-496; Browne, "Issue Niches," 352-354.

22. Maney and Bykerk, *Consumer Politics*.

23. David C. King and Jack L. Walker, Jr., "An Ecology of Interest Groups in America," in *Mobilizing Interest Groups in America: Patrons, Professions, and Social Movements*, ed. Joel D. Aberbach, Frank R. Baumgartner, Thomas L. Gais, David C. King, Mark A. Peterson, and Kim Lane Scheppele (Ann Arbor: University of Michigan Press, 1991), 66-67.

24. The quotation is from a House of Representatives staff member experienced in consumer protection issues (telephone interview by Loree Bykerk, August 2, 1993). Support for the ideas expressed in the quotation was provided by another House of Representatives staff member experienced in consumer protection issues (telephone interview by Loree Bykerk, August 24, 1993) and by Mark V. Nadel of the General Accounting Office (personal interview with Loree Bykerk, July 26, 1993).

25. Mike Mills, "Cable Industry Insists The Price Is Right," *Congressional Quarterly Weekly Report*, March 30, 1991, 790-792; Mike Mills, "Senate Action on Cable Bill Provokes Clash of Titans," *Congressional Quarterly Weekly Report*, January 11, 1992, 47-51; Mike Mills, "Markey's Cable Re-Regulation Bill Survives Democrats' Defections," *Congressional Quarterly Weekly Report*, April 11, 1992, 943-944.

26. Bradley Stillman, Consumer Federation of America legislative liaison, Washington, D.C., March 25, 1993; telephone interview by Loree Bykerk.

27. Paul Farhi, "Keeping an Eye on Cable TV," *Washington Post National Weekly Edition*, February 10-16, 1992, 6-8.

28. Mike Mills, "Media Groups Try Paying Way To a Favorable Cable Bill," *Congressional Quarterly Weekly Report*, May 30, 1992, 1523-1529.

29. Beth Donovan, "Big Donations from Cable, Hollywood Shouted at Lawmakers to Oppose Bill," *Congressional Quarterly Weekly Report*, September 19, 1992, 2798-2799.

30. Mike Mills, "Scarred by Media War, Cable Bill Wins Solid Vote From House," *Congressional Quarterly Weekly Report*, September 19, 1992, 2796-2801; Mills, "Cable TV Regulation," *Congressional Quarterly Weekly Report*, October 31, 1992, 3518-3521.

31. Maney and Bykerk, *Consumer Politics*.

13

Organized Interests, Grassroots Confidants, and Congress

William P. Browne

The agriculture sector is often singled out as a policy area in which interest groups exercise inordinate power. For much of this century powerful peak associations like the American Farm Bureau and commodity organizations like the National Corn Growers Association were viewed by members of Congress as speaking for farm interests.

In this chapter, William Browne argues that changes in the political environment have made legislators distrustful of taking their cues on agriculture issues from the national agriculture groups. Particularly influential have been (1) the multiplication of groups having an interest in agriculture and (2) the congressional reforms of the 1970s, which, by weakening committee powers, made it easier for legislators to look after specific interests in their districts. Legislators increasingly find that farm groups are internally divided and that group policy positions do not reflect the interests of their own agricultural constituents.

Using interviews with members of Congress and their staffs, Browne finds that most legislators have come to rely upon district "confidants," individual constituents whom legislative offices have come to trust as sources of reliable information about district opinion. In identifying such confidants, congressional offices often deliberatively avoid constituents who are leaders or activists in national farm groups, believing that such constituents are too likely to repeat or reflect policy directives from group headquarters. In Browne's view, "Members of Congress pursue issues on behalf of constituents, battle national interest groups to do so, and win."

This project was funded principally by the Ford Foundation through the Rural Economic Policy Program of the Aspen Institute. Other financial and facility support was provided by the Economic Research Service, U.S. Department of Agriculture; the E.M. Dirksen Congressional Leadership Research Center; the National Center for Food and Agricultural Policy at Resources for the Future; and Central Michigan University, Research Professor Program and Institute for Social and Behavioral Studies. Allan Cigler and Burdett Loomis deserve thanks for suggesting revision of an earlier draft of this chapter.

One of the truisms of political science is that, for Congress, constituents matter. This chapter goes beyond that generalization to argue that constituents matter more than anyone else to members of the modern Congress. The point is important because grassroots constituents and organized groups often represent the same interests from distinctly different points of view. What constituents and group leaders want from public policy often varies, particularly because organized groups need to balance regional differences and argue from a national policy perspective. Constituents, on the other hand, reside and do business in very specific places. Thus, they represent their own locales, the particular problems apparent there, and public-policy issues that seem a great deal like pork-barrel demands.

This conflict between constituent interests and organized group interests has been largely ignored by scholars of interest groups and Congress. The scholarly neglect of geographically fragmented interests may be due to the recency of the phenomenon, both in terms of its political possibilities and its wide scope.

Three historical factors make it easier today than it was two decades ago for constituent interests to emerge and be pursued separately from the goals of organized Washington lobbies. First, contemporary communications technologies have developed to the point that messages about public policies now move back and forth between the district and Washington with minimal delivery problems for constituents, group leaders, and congressional staff.[1] Constituents can easily articulate demands. Members and staff just as easily can stir up the home folks with their own messages.

Second, the relatively recent proliferation of interest groups has been accompanied by a greater emphasis on using grassroots sentiments in lobbying.[2] Mobilization of the grassroots by group leaders generates interest back home, causing constituents to think, but not necessarily about what group leaders are emphasizing. They are much more likely to think in strictly local terms.

Third, the Congress has changed in past years due to the procedural reforms of the 1970s.[3] Members have greater latitude to pursue more issues that they know less about, but they have large and capable staffs to help them. Committees, in contrast, are less able than they once were to ignore the policy proposals of rank-and-file members of Congress.

Why Congress Values Private Interests Differently over Time

Lobbying is often said to provide valuable information to policy makers.[4] In agriculture, interest groups supplanted political parties in influence in the 1920s once they had gained a competitive advantage over the parties. Groups were better able to rally members of Congress behind specific policies.[5] Farm interest groups had two advantages over parties at that time. First, group leaders had greater knowledge of the specifics of farm problems than did party leaders—in those days, agricultural policy was farm policy and little else. Second, group leaders had the organizational means for knowing what troubled farmers and for telling them what government was or was not doing about their problems. The combination of these two factors led important members of Congress to listen to interest groups in order to relate better to farm constituents.

From the 1920s, interest groups came to be important in the reelection of members of Congress from farm states. Lobbyists explained the problems that troubled the agricultural sector, the ways in which farmers were responding, and the electoral implications for legislators who ignored farm demands. Organized groups also had other important information to offer. They played on the other motives of legislators, who had more to do in Congress than simply seek reelection.[6] Groups developed and argued on behalf of public policies designed to protect the farm sector. To farm-state members of Congress, this looked awfully similar to making good policy. Groups offered information on how farm-state legislators could amass their collective political power, form congressional coalitions, and pass bills that presidents would be reluctant to veto. Interest groups, in that sense, helped particular members of Congress turn information into strategy. One important consequence was the emergence of powerful congressional leaders from farming areas.[7]

Despite this informational assistance, members of Congress and their staffs at some point lost much of their faith in the contribution of interest groups. This appears to be the case at any rate in this now multipurpose policy domain, where groups first gained independent influence over parties and pioneered modern lobbying techniques.[8] In the postreform Congress—characterized by greater decentralization and more autonomy for rank-and-file members—agriculture committees and their members are no longer the only ones who devote time and attention to farm policy, food and nutrition, agroenvironmental issues, food and fiber trade, agroresearch, and rural policies. Rank-and-file members with no special knowledge or concern for farming routinely intervene in what often seem to be more socially important agricultural policies than those affecting farmers. A recent study showed that more than 90 percent of members of Congress sought to include one or more of their favored issues in some form of agricultural legislation. Although most congressional offices did so on just one or two issues over a two-to-three-year period, they were successful 70 percent of the time.

This successful involvement of so many members of Congress in what had long been seen as an isolated, even exclusive, domain of public policy making has created considerable problems for House and Senate agriculture committees.[9] Initiatives brought forward by the congressional rank and file are most often intended to reward district or state constituents who are disadvantaged by existing agricultural policies or by local producer, agribusiness, or consumer problems. Thus, the committees face burgeoning policy demands on increasingly narrow yet diverse issues. This politics of home places has created intense interests among members eager to win something of personal and district importance from the committees responsible for agricultural policy. Such members really care about winning, and they use their leverage accordingly. If they do not get what they want from the committee, they threaten to oppose pending agricultural legislation, especially the omnibus farm bills that must be renewed every four to five years.

This behavior stems from reforms of congressional procedures in the 1970s. Since the reforms, Congress has opened up to the increased participation of its members and become much more individualistic. The reforms stripped considerable authority from the committees and their chairs. Some authority was transferred to subcommittees, where smaller sets of legislators develop policy without much coordination by the whole committee. Some was allocated to party caucuses, whose members focus on policy directions. Some power went to the leadership to counter committee control of bills. Along the way, congressional norms of deference to the autonomy of the committees also were lost.[10] It is now much easier for members to follow district influences in agricultural policy than it was in the prereform Congress. Of course, the agriculture committees of today have become much more accommodating to rank-and-file members.

The Declining Importance of Group Information

Why did postreform congressional circumstances compromise the credibility of interest groups as purveyors of information? What altered the competitive advantage that such groups had held over other information sources? As one veteran agriculture committee member stated, "I find that I just don't need lobbyists anymore, not like I once did. They're just not as useful to my problems." The declining usefulness of interest group information results in part from the multiplication of groups and organized policy views. A congressional staff director explained, "There are now so many interest groups around that you always wonder and ask who they represent. Every year, I get more cynical about interest groups and why I should listen to them."[11]

Many agricultural interest groups have seen their influence erode as members of Congress come to perceive a split between group and constituent interests. Indeed, many organizations have been disadvantaged because of problems with their own grassroots. As groups compete with each other for attention, they have turned increasingly to bringing constituents in to see their representatives in Congress. Dragging a carefully selected group supporter to Washington, however, usually fails to make group politics look truly representative of district politics.

Traditional farm groups such as the American Farm Bureau Federation (AFBF) and the National Corn Growers Association (NCGA) now face great disagreements within the ranks of their supporters over the exact content of legislative proposals. Modern production agriculture is especially place-specific and highly susceptible to home-style politics. Crops vary from region to region with cost advantages built into specific types of highly variable soil and weather patterns. As farming has become more technology-intensive and specialized by commodity, these differences create greater inequalities over time within all major crops.

For example, some corn-belt states have better growing conditions than others, and even within a state such as Iowa, corn growers in one congressional district have lower costs of production and higher yields than their neighbors in another. This makes it particularly hard for a group such as AFBF to lobby for farm policies that cover all crops and livestock from what their nationally distributed supporters see as a fair perspective.[12] It also makes it very difficult for a more narrowly focused group like NCGA—even with its strong Midwest membership—to lobby for a national corn price support program. Not all supporters will see any specific program as fair. Within the membership ranks of both farm groups and the Congress, consensus over policy is accordingly rare. Disagreements, and therefore district-inspired deals in an accommodating Congress, are common. Meanwhile, disadvantaged interest group factions bombard congressional offices with their complaints about inequities in group-proposed public policies.

Farm groups face internal problems that exaggerate these conditions. Policy conferences at the national, state, and local levels often fail to resolve differences among farmers. Such meetings may actually worsen conflict. A member of Congress explained, "What comes out of a national conference, even with their lobbyists' advice about representing all regional producers, screws somebody.... Most of the farmers (who) come out of policy making sessions are (very angry)." The conflict is all the more intense, and therefore more likely to reach Congress, because relatively few group members go to the policy meetings. Many members join the group not for its advocacy activities, but for insurance or marketing assistance. Debates over policy, as a consequence, usually involve group activists who want some form of the program under consideration, but almost certainly not the same form.[13] Some members may even believe that farm commodity programs are no longer needed in a modern agricultural sector.[14] Such divided opinions eventually get to Washington, of course, where they erode congressional faith in national lobbying initiatives.

Agribusiness groups face other, though similar, problems. Most trade associations in agriculture are made up of relatively large firms engaged in multiple activities, from new product research to manufacturing and sales.[15] As a result, they typically belong to several groups that assist the firm's personnel with business problems. In addition, most agribusiness trade associations are made up of a small number of firms. A typical agribusiness association may count twenty supporters, many of whom are competing with one another in the marketplace. No one in Congress, therefore, expects them to agree with any frequency on more than the broad outlines of public policy. Agribusiness trade associations, for these reasons, are seldom intense lobbying interests. Individual firms do their most important lobbying on their own, using trade associations more to monitor Washington events than to build consensus within the industry.

This fragmentation means that members of Congress gain no holistic view of what agribusiness leaders want from public policy or how they can be kept happy. Firms speak for themselves one at a time on specific issues that affect their market shares, and they do so largely through their own local House and Senate members. Their policy demands are kept narrow in order to be less difficult to negotiate.[16] As one corporate lobbyist explained, "This is really mini-politics. It's about solving unique business problems, but it does little to help a congressman understand the mood of even a part of the public."

Surprisingly, public interest groups in agriculture do little more than agribusiness firms in communicating the public policy wants of the electorate to Congress. Public interest groups in agriculture have gained distinct identities as reform-minded, better-government organizations that challenge the status quo on behalf of a sound environment, good health, and the quality of rural life.[17] Yet despite gaining substantial publicity, they do little to link even the interested citizenry to the issues on which public interest lobbyists work. According to members of Congress and their staffs, public interest lobbyists pursue issues and policies that are in keeping with their supporters' values but not reflective of discrete wants. Unlike farm groups, public interest groups neither generate nor mobilize much momentum behind specific government programs. Citizens, for example, value clean water but are hard pressed to comment on nitrate contamination in wells or agrichemical runoff in lakes and rivers unless these problems occur in their own local environs. As an environmental lobbyist complained, "Our dues-payers just don't know the problems or the programs from a stakeholder perspective."

Public interest groups concerned with agriculture have several disadvantages in speaking for citizens in terms that members of Congress can use. First, the numerous groups are often divided among themselves on public policy preferences, which makes it hard to supply the public with consistent messages. As a lobbyist observed, "We fight and send competing signals to the electorate." Second, many of the groups lack mass memberships and derive their revenues from grants and financial patrons.[18] Such organizations do little to use district and state intermediaries to reach members of Congress.

Third, almost none of the groups build public policy support through democratically styled, grassroots processes. Although the farm groups experience problems from such meetings and exercises, and public interest groups understandably avoid them, such avoidance leaves the latter at a disadvantage. Specifically, it fails to generate cadres of local activists who identify strongly with groups such as the National Wildlife Federation and their public policy agendas. As one environmental leader explained, "No, I don't have grassroots activists who can help me out. And, yes, that hurts." He meant that public interest groups have even a more difficult time than farm groups in being able to mobilize knowledgeable and agreeable home folks to come to Washington or to buttonhole congressional members at home on behalf of the group's national position. Grassroots environmentalists and other public-minded activists tend to see greater salience in local issues, such as quality-of-life hazards and environmental problems in their own back yards.[19]

In the area of public-interest policy, as in that of farm policy, interest groups fail to give Congress clear information as to what appeals to the interested electorate. Congress lacks clearly defined signals about what moves voters, how political power can be gained through agroenvironmental issues, or what might form the basis for popularly inspired congressional coalitions. In short, quite unlike the situation in the 1920s, a diverse array of agricultural interest groups now confronts the common problem of supplying information that congressional members can use.

Competition between Constituents and Groups

Do their problems in communicating unambiguous messages actually disadvantage various nationally organized interest groups? Members of Congress and their staffs indicate that they do. Two sets of data from congressional interviews conducted in 1991 and 1993 show that groups suffer disadvantages that constituents do not.[20]

Who Matters Most?

The first data set indicates that, on recent agricultural issues, constituents were the source members of Congress relied on most for their information. This was true of legislators considering whether or not to initiate issues from their own offices and of office staff deciding how to react to issues proposed by other members of Congress. Table 13-1 shows that constituents were the most important source of ideas for 78 percent of all members, whereas interest groups were ranked first by just 15 percent. Seven percent of members relied first on agency personnel, policy professionals, or media sources.

Interest groups were by far the most important nonconstituent information source for Congress. Respondents in 54 percent of congres-

Table 13-1   Ranking of Most Important Information Source by Congressional Offices

Type of information source	Number of selections	
Constituents	87	(78.0%)
Organized interest representatives	17	(15.0)
Agency officials	4	(3.4)
Other policy professionals	2	(1.8)
Media sources	2	(1.8)
Total choices	112	(100.0)

sional offices rated lobbyists as second in importance overall. Nonetheless, the entire noncongressional Washington policy community took a decidedly secondary position to the folks back home. A senior staff director explained, "Even if we want an issue that gets us on network news, the information that makes news overwhelmingly comes from constituents who feel comfortable walking into their own member's office."

Members of Congress do not follow just any ideas that their constituents bring to their offices. By and large, members' home work truly and rationally reflects their Washington work.[21] That merger of home and Washington politics is reflected in four additional dimensions of the information-use patterns cited by members and their staffs. Seventy-six percent of congressional offices followed constituent advice first in *selecting* issues for their policy initiatives. On the more complex matter of *determining the content* of the members' issue initiatives, which frequently involved lobbyists in drafting legislative language, 58 percent of congressional offices were still most likely to use constituent information.

Information from constituents also was more *trusted* than that from any source within the Washington policy community. That claim was made by 73 percent of congressional members. As one said, "These are the only people I know who have no track record of putting a spin on things. They're brutally honest and see problems first hand." This sort of appraisal led those in 68 percent of the member offices to mobilize, or seek out, information from constituents on pending issues. In comparison, 56 percent of offices sought information from lobbyists, and only 22 percent looked to anyone else in the Washington policy community.

Clearly, at least in modern agricultural policy making, constituent information comes first. It comes first for members of Congress on the committees that dealt with these issues as well as those not on one of the committees.

Because congressional offices consistently ranked interest groups well above agency experts, policy consultants, and the media, it appears that lobbyists have a deserved reputation for superior access and influence among Washington policy players. Yet they look less potent than those whom members know from their districts and states.

Conflict between Home and Washington

The comparative potency of constituents also emerged in conflicts members encountered over their issue initiatives. Such conflicts were frequent, forcing legislators to consider two or more competing demands on 44 percent of all issues. The amount of conflict seemed to us particularly high because agricultural interest groups have a reputation for reconciling their differences before going to Congress.[22]

On closer examination, it appeared that conflict over which issues members of Congress should pursue occurred much more often between constituents and groups having similar interests than between constituents and groups with competing interests (Table 13-2). Most conflicts (90 percent) involved constituents disagreeing with the Washington policy community outside Congress. Typical disagreements facing a congressional office included local environmental activists disagreeing with the Sierra Club, or dairy farmers in conflict with the National Milk Producers Association.[23] Such intra-interest contests between home places and a national lobby accounted for 57 percent of all conflicts over issue initiatives.

Members and their staffs rarely were party to conflict between constituent supporters of inherently competing groups such as the American Agriculture Movement and the American Farm Bureau Federation or Greenpeace and Ducks Unlimited. Legislators often choose to avoid such battles. In the words of one member, "I just won't wade into an issue where district interests are hotly divided, say between new agribusiness products and consumer opposition to their use."

However, members were quite willing to initiate issues on which district constituents disagreed with competing national interests or others in the Washington policy community. One-third of all the reported conflicts were of those types. "Hell yes!" was a common but not really surprising response, "Always stand up for the guys at home. You can't stay around if you represent some phony group in Washington or administrators trying to control your district." In fact, this member and his colleagues did just that, siding with constituents in 91 percent of their disagreements with Washington policy players.

Such conflicts—and the attendant choice of home over Washington—did not negate the chances of congressional members succeeding on their chosen issues. In fact, offices were slightly more likely to win on contested issues than on agricultural issues as a whole. This suggests quite strongly that constituent information matters most not only to individual members, but also to Congress as a whole, as policy is brought together from the numerous issues of many legislators. Members of Congress select issues popular with the home folks, resist policy positions

Table 13-2 Reported Incidents of Competing Demands on Issue
Initiatives of Congressional Offices

Sources of important conflicts	Number of incidents	
Constituents and groups of the same interest	82	(57.0%)
Constituents and groups of competing interests	35	(24.5)
Constituents and agency officials, policy professionals, or the media	12	(8.5)
Between groups of competing interests	9	(6.5)
Groups and agency officials, policy professionals, or the media	5	(3.5)
Total reported conflicts	143	(100.0)

with which their constituents vocally disagree, and succeed when they
represent coherent points of view from their districts. But who articulates
district interests and why do congressional members listen to them?

Informants and Confidants

Members of Congress and their office staffs described in our 1991-
1993 interviews five characteristics of the district "informants" they listened to on farm issues. Those characteristics were:

Independent views,
Active involvement in state and community events,
Influence as a local opinion leader,
Status as a large-scale producer, and
User of modern farm technologies.

As a veteran staff member explained, "We want to know how national policies play out locally among major agribusiness people who produce most of our district crops and generate most of the cash receipts. We
want to know about the viability of our district's farm sector. That is not, I
repeat, the information you get from a national farm organization."

Similar considerations apply to constituent informants on other agricultural issues. On food and fiber trade issues, congressional offices listened to those with headquarters or plants in the district and with experience in trade. Nutrition, agroresearch, and rural issues also were
influenced by knowledgeable, practical, and locally directed informants.
Members of Congress sought local activists with local government experience or experience in managing outreach programs, technical facilities,
and large herds and fields. "It's simple," explained one representative,
"I'm looking for stakeholders who, regardless of issue, know precisely
how things operate and get done."

Even on agroenvironmental issues, where the Washington policy field is crowded, congressional emphasis was on the informant's experience, independence, and commitment to peculiarly local problems. A member of Congress summarized, "We rely on local opinions because that's where the strong source of (policy) demand lies. I mean local well-water contamination, river and bay degradation, or something like Love Canal. You know how it is, the local landscape engenders powerful interests from a select number of truly perceptive yet normal people."

These attitudes mean that members of Congress and their staffs seldom worried about whether their constituent informants joined nationally prominent groups or not. Most legislators assumed that their farm informants belonged to several interest groups, including nonfarm groups. The same was true for local business leaders, environmental activists, and informants on other issues. A legislative assistant explained why: "People who are politically active join groups, lots of them. But that's not why we look to these specific individuals for information."

Quite the reverse was true. Almost all congressional office enterprises avoided informants who were leaders or intense activists in nationally organized groups.[24] Such constituents were too likely to internalize most of the policy appeals they received from group headquarters: "After they get stroked from Washington, the inveterate joiners believe what they read and not what they see or experience." The collective opinion in Congress is that interest groups can capture the strongly committed supporter. After a barrage of magazines, newsletters, appeals in the mail, electronic communications from Washington, and direct meetings and conferences, group supporters come to be seen in Congress as having a greater stake in the organizations they join than in district conditions. A senator emphasized the point, "I want to know what some independent son-of-a-bitch thinks. Why? That's the person who knows state problems and will be listened to by others. Nobody else cares what the county Farm Bureau and Audubon Society chairmen think when they mouth off about issues that the average farmer or citizen can't relate to at all."

When structuring their issue choices, legislators and their staffs seek to understand the effects public policy will have back home. To avoid negative policy consequences that may create animosity in the district, congressional office enterprises want to know and understand the background of those they rely on as informants. Members of Congress emphasized that point in our interviews, referring several times to their valued "district confidants." Congressional staffs, in particular, spoke of maintaining lists of confidants in various policy areas whom they knew to be good sources of information about local conditions and problems. Both legislators and staffs repeatedly contacted such individuals, often calling them from Washington and seeking them out at home. Offices also tested their confidants, judging previous information and opinions as sound or not and comparing the backgrounds of similar complainants from home.

"I often ask," said one legislative assistant, "is this guy still with it? It may be that a former employee just found her or him an easy call to make." From an informational perspective, confidants play a unique political role. Members of Congress do not use them to further democracy, promote political participation within the district, represent the views of most residents, count local voter preferences on a wide range of issues, or encourage equality of interests. Their purpose is far simpler: to help members of Congress avoid the interest-specific problems in the district that might come from pursuing or following policies advocated by nationally organized interest groups.

Choosing and Maintaining District Confidants

Although neglected by scholars, the identification, testing, and retention of district confidants are important to a thorough understanding of the representation of local interests. As noted above, not all voices in the district are heard, nor do members of Congress intend that they should be heard. Each congressional office is content with a selective view as long as that view meets the member's needs.

Although no systematic data on district confidants exists, members of Congress and their staffs did talk extensively with me about confidants in our interviews. Thus it is possible to generalize about the origins of confidants, why members trust them, and how offices are organized to use them effectively.

Finding Confidants

Some confidants are simply born or, more precisely, raised with congressional members. Over the course of their lives, many legislators remain close to a select few whose opinions were long ago found useful, especially in the initial decision to run for office. Some are childhood friends, others are college pals, and some began their careers with the future member of Congress. A member explained, "There are three people who I've known from back home since before I was in public office. I like them and trust them, but most importantly I know that they know the district." Each of these confidants provides information on one or more issues, with some overlap among them. Not surprisingly, legislative staffs saw these individuals as the most potent noncongressional influence on their members. As one administrative assistant noted, "These are the guys who get (the member) in a locked room and talk things over. When they're done, a decision is made that leaves even me out of the loop." Born confidants are in frequent contact with congressional members back home.

A second type of confidant is self-created. These are individuals in the district who first cultivate either the member or someone from the office. Usually they start by repeatedly writing, calling, and sending materials on a single area of policy that is important to the district. Frequently they show up at the member's public appearances during swings through the district to meet with constituents. Rarely does their status extend to more than one issue. "What I like about these people," said a staffer, "is that they show up to talk turkey on one program." After some time communicating with the office, self-created confidants begin to get staff requests for their opinions and observations. But Washington-to-district requests only come after the confidant gains trust as a reliable source. Most staff members initially regard all constituents with some reservations. The staffer quoted above continued, "After I figured out that this guy knew more about feedgrains than an agricultural economist, I knew we had a jewel. Sometimes I call him just to let him know what's going on [in Congress]."

These self-created informants provide feedback that, in a legislative director's words, "goes into our office brew, the big pot of ideas that we sort through in deciding what [the member] should do on every important issue." That is to say, each self-creating confidant remains one among many information sources. Other district confidants are very likely to address the same issues and have their opinions judged as part of the mix. "Lesson number one," warned a legislative assistant, "Never trust the view of just one guy. That's not to say we don't, but we try to look for reinforcing information."

Seldom are self-created confidants socially involved with members or their office staffs. Not infrequently, however, they actively support members as candidates and make political donations to show their goodwill. In return for their support, they are often appointed to the district and state advisory groups that most members of Congress create on locally important policy areas. Confidants, along with other politically balanced selections, are added to advisory committees on farming, local government, the environment, business and trade, and myriad other subjects.

The third type of district confidant is created by the congressional office. These people share most of the same characteristics as self-creators: knowledge about a single policy area, contact with the office a few times each year, one of several informants on each pending issue, and—occasionally—impersonal political support of the congressional member. Confidants of either type need not think of themselves as influential, but many of them do. As one district activist argued, "My congressman listens to me a lot more than to the National Milk Producers Association."

The difference between self-created and office-created confidants is that the latter have been sought out to fill a void. While they may have written letters to the office or previously met with the member, office-created confidants are solicited. Members and, especially, their staffs look for them. They pull out constituent letters, read district newspapers, listen for sensible comments made at the plethora of local meetings they attend, and just ask around about who understands specific district problems. "What you're always searching for," concluded a member, "is someone who can give you some guidance about avoiding local problems. You'll go to great lengths to get that kind of information." For that reason of scarcity, office-created confidants appear to be the most frequent of the three types.

Testing and Keeping Confidants

Not surprisingly, some confidants remain influential over time, even when one member replaces another in a district. But other confidants come and go: "They die, get disinterested, go broke, or just burn out." In other instances, offices quit paying attention. "After a while," explained a legislative assistant, "some locals will start to make incessant demands, things you can't do. They think that they own you so you stop listening."

Because change is likely and information uncertain, local confidants are subject to continued testing, increasingly so as their opinions take on more weight to the member. Most testing goes on easily since the information from one constituent informant is judged for reliability against that of others. Advisory committee meetings are particularly useful for that purpose: "There are several environmentally concerned people in a room and you can judge the soundness of their ideas against one another."

Other tests take on elaborately comic proportions. Staff in one congressional office explained that they requested an analysis of a district farmer's financial records to see if that confidant held reliable opinions. A U.S. Department of Agriculture economist confirmed the request: "What they wanted to know was how typical this farm was of large regional units as well as national producers of the same crop." In another instance, a farm interest group was called about a state farmer. A lobbyist explained, "They wanted to know if he was active in our group. When I said he wasn't and suggested an alternate choice, they said thanks. Later I found out that the person they inquired about was chairing their farm advisory committee." A legislative assistant corroborated the story: "We wanted somebody who wasn't in bed with a Washington Beltway view."

Usually, however, the testing and retention of district confidants is handled quite simply and logically. Collectively, several members of Congress and their staffs helped reduce the strategies of organizing their offices and working with confidants to five points. The following are their rules.

First, there exist several informants in each district for each issue, but only a few will stand out. The standouts must be kept responsive to the congressional office. Second, confidants should be encouraged to keep talking about conditions that are both immediate and local. Members should show them the public policy gains from their efforts. Third, the accuracy of confidant remarks must be judged against the practical problems of the district and not against the demands of national groups. The difference should be explained to those who contact the office. Fourth, offices should determine whether confidants carry information back to the district as well as from the district. Both should be encouraged. Finally, members should make it known that district communications are easily arranged. A district confidant should never be allowed to doubt that providing information is a manageable task that has its rewards in congressional access and public policy making.

As these rules indicate, and as the numerous and successful issue initiatives of congressional members suggest, district interests are given considerable prominence in the modern Congress. Indeed, district networking seems at least as much a part of the policy process for members of Congress as networking with lobbyists and others from the Washington policy community.

Constituent Interests and Congressional Interests

That grassroots constituents and organized groups represent the same interest from different points of view is hardly unique to agriculture. Competing views have complicated Common Cause's efforts to decide which issues to advocate: campaign reform or banning MX missiles. As Lawrence Rothenberg observed of that organization: "The sheer difficulties of inducing individuals to join and be involved and the subsequent pitfalls in trying to channel the resulting energies into political influence sometimes seem staggering."[25]

Upon reflection, that should not be surprising. There exists no particularly good reason to believe that organized groups are indeed real and cohesive interests rather than organizations of individuals with potentially conflicting views. Each interest group may well represent a particular point of view in the policy process, but the scholarly literature is resplendent with evidence that not all of those with that view join the group, and not all who join the group share that view.[26] These are generic problems of interest group politics. It is reasonable to suppose that members of Congress and their staffs are aware of the problems and seek to identify those interests that really matter to their congressional enterprises.

As members of Congress turn to their districts, favorable home-style images are nicely advanced by representing and even mobilizing local constituents in national policy making. Well staffed offices in the post-reform Congress appear quite capable of obtaining the cooperation of today's weaker committees. Congressional offices employ capable personnel in the districts, routinely follow constituent problems, frequently send members and other staff back home, regularly attend various district events, raise about half of their campaign funds locally, and face reelection in those places every two or six years. Quite obviously, as a result, constituent interests must mesh well with the interests of congressional members.

This means that political interests in Washington are often defined by constituents who communicate effectively with key members of Congress. That is clearly the case with numerous issues of agricultural policy, from farms to the environment. Members of Congress pursue issues on behalf of constituents, battle national interest groups to do so, and win. District informants and confidants provide them much of the capacity to succeed. Do district confidants have this effect, or similar ones, on the interest politics of the rest of American government? The division between constituents and interest groups, it seems, needs considerably more study.

Notes

1. Richard C. Fenno, *Home Style: House Members in Their Districts* (Boston: Little, Brown, 1978); John R. Johannes, "Individual Outputs: Legislators and Constituency Service," in *Congressional Politics*, ed. Christopher J. Deering (Chicago: Dorsey, 1989), 90-110.
2. Jeffrey M. Berry, *The Interest Group Society*, 2d ed. (Glenview, Ill.: Scott, Foresman/Little, Brown, 1989), 99-116.
3. Kenneth A. Shepsle, "The Changing Textbook Congress," in *Can the Government Govern?* ed. John E. Chubb and Paul E. Peterson (Washington, D.C.: Brookings Institution, 1989), 238-266.
4. The classic analysis of lobbying as a communications process is Lester W. Milbrath, *The Washington Lobbyists* (Chicago: Rand McNally, 1963).
5. John Mark Hansen, *Gaining Access: Congress and the Farm Lobby, 1919-1981* (Chicago: University of Chicago Press, 1991).
6. Richard C. Fenno identifies the interplay of electoral, good policy, and personal power goals in *Congressmen in Committees* (Boston: Little, Brown, 1973), 1-14.
7. Hansen, *Gaining Access*. Speaker of the House Thomas Foley and Senate minority leader Robert Dole are the best current examples of powerful leaders who moved up in Congress through their success on the agriculture committees.
8. William P. Browne, *Private Interests, Public Policy, and American Agriculture* (Lawrence: University Press of Kansas, 1988); Hansen, *Gaining Access*.
9. On the problems of these committees, see William P. Browne, "Agricultural Policy Can't Accommodate All Who Want In," *Choices* 4 (First Quarter 1989): 9-11; William P. Browne and Won K. Paik, "Beyond the Domain: Recasting Network Politics in the Postreform Congress," *American Journal of Political Science* 37 (November 1993): 1054-1078.
10. Steven S. Smith, *Call to Order: Floor Politics in the House and Senate* (Washington, D.C.: Brookings Institution, 1989); David W. Rohde, *Parties and Leaders in the Postreform House* (Chicago: University of Chicago Press, 1991); Barbara Sinclair, *The Transformation of the U.S. Senate* (Baltimore: Johns Hopkins University Press, 1989).
11. The quotes in this chapter and the data discussed in a later section were obtained in the course of interviews with 54 members of Congress and 133 members of their staffs between 1991 and 1993. For that study, see William P. Browne, *Cultivating Congress: Constituents, Issues and Interests in Agricultural Policymaking* (Lawrence: University of Kansas Press, forthcoming).

12. Browne, *Private Interests, Public Policy, and American Agriculture*, 89-108.
13. Robert H. Salisbury, "An Exchange Theory of Interest Groups," *Midwest Journal of Political Science* 13 (February 1969): 1-32.
14. William P. Browne, "Organized Interests and Their Issue Niches: A Search for Pluralism in a Policy Domain," *Journal of Politics* 52 (May 1990), 477-509; and Browne, "Issue Niches and the Limits of Interest Group Influence," in *Interest Group Politics*, 3d ed., ed. Allan J. Cigler and Burdett A. Loomis (Washington, D.C.: CQ Press, 1991), 366-370.
15. Browne, *Private Interests*, 109-129.
16. David Vogel, *Fluctuating Fortunes: The Political Power of Business in America* (New York: Basic Books, 1989).
17. Don F. Hadwiger, *The Politics of Agricultural Research* (Lincoln: University of Nebraska Press, 1982); Browne, *Private Interests*, 130-149.
18. Jeffrey M. Berry, *Lobbying for the People* (Princeton, N.J.: Princeton University Press, 1977).
19. Daniel A. Mazmanian and David Morell, "The 'NIMBY' Syndrome: Facility Siting and the Failure of Democratic Discourse," in *Environmental Policy in the 1990s*, 2d ed., ed. Norman J. Vig and Michael E. Kraft (Washington, D.C.: CQ Press, 1991), 233-249.
20. The data in this chapter come from a 1991 study of the offices of 113 randomly sampled members of the U.S. Congress. Interviews were held in 1991 with 48 members and 107 staff personnel. In 1992-1993, 6 more members and 26 more staff from the same offices were interviewed. For the questions and more analysis, see Browne and Paik, "Beyond the Domain," 1066-1070.
21. See Morris P. Fiorina and David W. Rohde, eds., *Home Style and Washington Work: Studies of Congressional Politics* (Ann Arbor: University of Michigan Press, 1989); and Carl E. Van Horn, "Congressional Policymaking: Cloakroom Politics and Policy," in *Congressional Politics*, 220-235.
22. Browne, "Organized Interests."
23. Christopher J. Bosso, "Adaptation and Change in the Environmental Movement," in *Interest Group Politics*, 3d ed., 151-176; and Bosso, "After the Movement: Environmental Activism in the 1990s," in *Environmental Policy in the 1990s*, 31-50.
24. A small number of legislators preferred the reverse, hoping to capture the loyalties of group leaders as they rose through organizational ranks.
25. Lawrence S. Rothenberg, *Linking Citizens to Government: Interest Group Politics at Common Cause* (New York: Cambridge University Press, 1992), 266.
26. Only those with a commonly held interest really group together or network as a unit. This is the important point of Arthur F. Bentley, *The Process of Government* (Chicago: University of Chicago Press, 1980). See also Robert H. Salisbury, "Putting Interests Back in Interest Groups," in *Interest Group Politics*, 3d ed., 371-384. Studies that show interest fragmentation within a group go back to Arthur Kornhauser, Harold L. Sheppard, and Albert J. Mayer, *When Labor Votes: A Study of Auto Workers* (New York: University Books, 1956).

14

Deregulation and Interest Group Influence

Lawrence S. Rothenberg

When we consider the policy-making process in the United States, most of our attention is directed at the Congress, the president, and, on occasion, the Supreme Court. In the twentieth century, however, the greatest growth in policy-making authority has come through regulation, often by independent federal and state agencies. Organized interests of every stripe understand this, of course, and their representatives devote untold hours to affecting regulatory rulings. Despite its importance, regulation has not attracted much attention from interest group scholars, although many studies of bureaucratic politics have closely examined the role of interests in regulatory decision making.

In this article Lawrence Rothenberg explores the dismantling of motor carrier regulation that began in the 1970s. Motor carrier regulation was a policy with a long record of failure, but it was strongly supported by key transportation interests that benefited from the crazy-quilt patterns of routes and rates that had grown up since the 1930s. In a longitudinal analysis of the forces leading to the Motor Carrier Act of 1980, Rothenberg illustrates how the context of policy making can either reinforce or challenge group-based power. In particular, the attitude of the president can have a great impact on this context and on the likelihood of change.

During the 1970s, group theories that emphasized the predominance of interest groups in the making of bureaucratic policy were at the height of their popularity.[1] Generally, these theories hold that agencies reflect the wishes of the groups in their external environment. Thus, when the distribution of such organizations is heterogeneous, the resulting policy may be fairly balanced, but when the environment is dominated by a single well-organized group, policy may be highly skewed. Under such circumstances, agencies are said to be *captured*. Indeed, many proponents of group theories maintained that agencies were commonly

The results of the present research derive from a larger project entitled *Regulation, Organizations, and Politics: Motor Freight Policy at the Interstate Commerce Commission* (Ann Arbor: University of Michigan Press, forthcoming). Thanks to all those who agreed to be interviewed (anonymously) and to the Nixon Project, the Gerald R. Ford Library, and the Jimmy Carter Library.

created in response to the actions and wishes of the producer groups they were to regulate, and, once established, that they continued to operate in the interest of those organizations.

To advocates of such perspectives, the regulation of the motor freight industry by the Interstate Commerce Commission (ICC) epitomized agency capture by special interests.[2] Critics saw trucking policy as a reflection of a stable and mutually beneficial set of relationships among members of Congress, interest groups, and regulators and had little doubt that this state of affairs would persist for many years.

Yet, in the late 1970s, motor carrier regulation began to be dismantled. Initially, the ICC itself moved to reduce governmental restraints by lowering barriers to entering the industry and attacking the cartelistic rate-setting process that had kept prices artificially high.[3] Ultimately, Congress passed and President Jimmy Carter signed the Motor Carrier Act of 1980, which incorporated the bulk of the commission-sponsored changes.

The deregulation of the trucking industry forces us to ask: What are the limits of interest group influence? Explaining motor carrier reform and the roles that organizations played requires an understanding of ICC deregulation in the late 1970s and of its failure during the previous three decades.[4] Transportation deregulation was not a new idea upon which political decision makers suddenly seized.[5] As Thomas Gale Moore put it, "Virtually from the date the Motor Carrier Act [of 1935] was passed, economists have criticized the idea of regulating such an inherently competitive industry."[6] Thus, examining motor freight reform must extend beyond a discussion of how a particular bill became law and incorporate an analysis of regulation.

The motor carrier case is far from an isolated example. The telecommunications, railroad, airline, and banking industries also moved toward free market systems between 1975 and 1985. What distinguishes the case of trucking is a matter of degree: In no other instance is the failure of vested interests to get their way more pronounced. Although voters were less aware of motor freight regulation, both business and labor had a greater stake in preserving the regulatory status quo in the trucking industry than did their counterparts in many other industries.

Even though public opinion had become disenchanted with government programs generally and economic regulation specifically by the mid-1970s, political decision makers generally agreed that the average citizen did not associate the motor carrier system with costly government regulation. Connections were far easier to draw for the other industries mentioned because citizens dealt with them directly as part of their everyday lives.

At the same time, motor carriers' high levels of profitability made them—and their trade association, the American Trucking Association (ATA)—ardent supporters of the regulatory regime. Governmental control of trucking companies lacked the negative side effects that it had for owners in other industries. Analogously, the principal union representing motor carrier employees, the International Brotherhood of Teamsters (IBT), was far more successful in getting a piece of the pie for itself than were the unions in most other regulated industries, where increased job security had not been accompanied by higher wages.[7]

In short, while voters remained passive, truckers and their employees had enormous incentives for maintaining motor freight regulation and, accordingly, the ATA and the IBT fought furiously, if futilely, to sustain the status quo. Coming to grips with the remarkable sequence of events leading to the Motor Carrier Act of 1980 promises important insights into our understanding of interest groups and the limits of their influence.

An Overview of Regulation

A broad-brush picture of trucking policy before reform suggests a stable and mutually beneficial set of relationships among members of Congress, regulated motor common carriers and their employees, and the regulators themselves. The Motor Carrier Act of 1935, which added trucking regulation to the ICC's existing responsibilities for regulating railroads, provided little guidance on how truckers should be policed. Nevertheless, the key elements that defined the status quo at the time of deregulation can be readily summarized:[8]

Although citizens were disinterested, the regulated truckers promoted group goals by (1) employing their political advantages (large numbers, wide geographic distribution, and strong political organization) to cultivate ICC staff and commissioners; (2) acting as effective watchdogs over the day-to-day operations of the agency; and (3) wielding influence over members of Congress and, occasionally, the White House or the judiciary. The Teamsters played a subsidiary role, rarely active at the ICC but sometimes assisting with the Congress or the White House. The railroads, lacking the truckers' political advantages to be politically effective, were dominated by the motor carriers.

Members of Congress, in turn, generally supported the status quo and remained interested largely in parochial concerns such as placating constituents angry about their treatment by moving companies.

Presidential administrations, while voicing unhappiness over the nature of policy, were preoccupied with other issues. They devoted modest resources to altering the system and achieved incremental change toward opening up the regulatory regime.

The courts intervened at the behest of the ICC's "regulatees" only
when the agency undeniably violated procedural rules or grossly
overstepped its boundaries.

The commission remained wedded to the status quo, even though
commissioners of marginal quality chosen for idiosyncratic reasons (whom I call "wild cards") were increasingly selected to
run the agency in conjunction with a veteran staff of declining
quality.

If a reason for the downfall of motor freight regulation is to be found,
then it should be because of some fundamental change in one or more of
these key elements. Already, deviation in the behavior of the principal
organizations themselves has been rejected as an explanation. The ATA
and the IBT were more formidable operations than ever, and they had
every desire to perpetuate the status quo. Thus, the conditions necessary
for organizations to flourish must have been altered in a manner to which
the ATA and the IBT could not easily adapt. From whence, then, did the
motivation for change come, and what means proved successful in
circumventing the processes of organizational influence available to the
ATA and the IBT?

The Structure of Interactions

The key to reform was that the presidential administrations of Gerald Ford and, especially, Jimmy Carter undermined the processes that
were crucial for the common carriers' effectiveness. These presidents
were spurred to attack the ICC's regulation of truckers because, for understandable reasons, they were willing to designate motor freight reform
a top priority for the first time. The economy was struggling and, although
citizens cared little about motor freight reform per se, the general ideological climate toward economic regulation was negative.

In focusing on motor freight deregulation, the Ford and Carter administrations searched for procedural loopholes in the laws and prece-
dents that governed the commission to alter the status quo in a manner
that put the legislature, the ATA, and the IBT in disadvantageous positions. Specifically, both presidents chose to undercut Congress, and implicitly the ATA and the IBT, by directing policy administratively. This
was accomplished mainly by creatively employing delegated authority,
which had been poorly exploited by earlier administrations because the
political costs were too great. Although the ICC was the key arena in
which reform was administered, the responsibility rested primarily with
the chief executive.

In particular, the chief executive went around the ATA and IBT by
redefining the roles of ICC commissioner and chairman. To accomplish
this, the president changed the incentives offered to appointees so that

they would favor change and abandoned a precedent set by Richard Nixon (during whose administration a permanent chair was first established) that commissioners favored by regulated interests would occupy the ICC chairmanship. Presidents Ford and Carter took advantage of the same appointment system that others had claimed formed the underpinning of regulatory capture. Such actions satisfied two key prerequisites for presidential control: (1) they fell within the current statutory mandate so that they would survive judicial scrutiny, even if all of the resulting policy did not, and (2) they sought no budgetary authorization—indeed, budget cuts only promised to accelerate the rate of reform by reducing regulatory enforcement.

In steering policy administratively, chief executives altered the circumstances of motor carrier regulation and interest group influence. Maintenance of most of the essential elements of regulation at the commission traditionally had required only legislative inaction. Legislators had reaped political benefits in the form of interest group and agency support and an ability to claim credit with their constituents for the casework they performed. Executive proposals to change policy had been allowed to languish, providing a disincentive to propose such legislation except for symbolic purposes.

By changing the status quo administratively, the president forced lawmakers into the position of having to legislate, and face the risk of a veto, if they wished to return to the prior state of affairs. On the other hand, without legislative action, it appeared probable that the executive would push the political process further in the direction of deregulation.

By taking action, Presidents Ford and Carter moved from a disadvantageous position to an advantageous one relative to members of Congress and their organized supporters. This rather abstract discussion will be more concretely illustrated by examining the details of motor freight reform.

The Increasing Salience of Regulatory Reform

Through the 1960s presidents had given regulatory reform low priority. The situation started to change with the advent of "stagflation"—the combination of stagnant economic conditions and rapid inflation that came to characterize the economy in the late 1960s. Economic issues again moved to the forefront of American political concerns.[9] One solution proposed to presidents beginning with Nixon was liberalization of economic regulation generally and of trucking regulation specifically. This cure could be touted as an example of administration responsiveness to the burgeoning consumer movement, which had been critical of regulatory agencies such as the ICC.[10] Unlike legislators, who were slow to make the connection between overregulation and economic stagnation, presidents linked the two together almost as soon as inflation became a thorny political problem. However, Nixon's ties to the IBT and the truckers led him to withdraw support for reform as the 1972 election approached.

Ford's ascension to the presidency in 1974, with inflation raging at an annual rate of 12 percent, buoyed the hopes of the proponents of deregulation. The new administration lacked Nixon's connections to the truckers and the Teamsters and appeared to attach sufficient importance to solving the nation's economic woes that it was willing to forgo the political benefits of strong alliances with them.[11] In November 1975, Ford sent a proposal to Capitol Hill—labeled the Motor Carrier Reform Act—that called for drastically easing restrictions on entering the industry. Like other trucking reform bills before it, this one encountered congressional and interest group hostility and failed to escape committee. The ATA's and IBT's ability to block action in Congress rendered Ford's legislative strategy ineffective.

Although two presidents had placed increasing importance on reform, little headway was made on the legislative front during the first half of the decade. No constituency for change existed to counteract the well-established opposition. As one observer wryly put it, "A funny thing happened on the way to the slaughterhouse."[12] What would it take to circumvent voter indifference, group opposition, and congressional intransigence?

Administrative Changes at the ICC: 1971-1976

While attention was still focused largely on legislative reform initiatives, movement was brewing on another front: at the ICC itself. Although the magnitude of change should not be exaggerated, the attitudes of several officials responsible for trucking policy were evolving. Proponents of reform won some limited victories at the commission, setting the stage for more dramatic upheaval in the years to come.

Behind this modest movement at the ICC lay changes in the system for appointing commissioners. From the standpoint of the supporters of regulation, the selection process started breaking down in two ways. First, some of the wild card appointees, whom organized interests assumed could always be induced to support the status quo, began favoring at least some reforms. Although they certainly were not ideologues, these commissioners started to take some of the executive branch's criticisms seriously, either for pragmatic reasons—presidential reappointment was required every seven years—or simply because they became convinced that some change was necessary. Second, Ford appointed several commissioners who, from the beginning, supported a degree of regulatory reform.

By themselves, the wild card appointees receptive to reform were not a major threat to regulatory interests. At the end of the Nixon administration, only three of the ICC's ten commissioners (there was one vacancy) might have been supportive of any significant change. The ICC was still wedded to regulation. One Johnson appointee (Virginia Mae Brown) and two Nixon nominees (Robert Gresham and A. Daniel O'Neal) could be categorized as somewhat willing to liberalize the status quo. All three eventually became part of the majority supporting regulatory reform in the late 1970s. (Nixon appointee Charles Clapp would be somewhat of a centrist in these battles.) Brown and Gresham, in particular, seemed concerned with job security and modified their views as they saw the tides turning. O'Neal was different. When he came to the ICC, many believed that he wanted to shake things up at the agency, possibly to advance his political career in Washington state. However, it is unclear whether he was truly committed to reform or was just a maverick. Only as the deregulation movement gained steam did his commitment appear to deepen.

Whatever their motivations, this threesome constituted an unstable minority in the face of a majority committed to regulation. It is important not to exaggerate the degree to which these commissioners favored deregulation and the extent to which they could have moved the agency away from its basic policies before the reform movement began gaining strength through presidential management.

With the advent of the Ford presidency and the increasing salience of trucking regulation in the 1970s, efforts at administratively centered reform increased. Gerald Ford's first step was to seek to alter the composition of the commission. Upon assuming office, he added two well-qualified commissioners who were committed to change. Robert J. Corber was appointed in 1975 and Betty Jo Christian in 1976. Although Corber was not a "deregulator" he favored reform. Appointed to serve the remainder of an unexpired term, Corber resigned near the end of the Ford administration because he believed that Carter would desire a more fervent deregulator. Christian became a strong ally of O'Neal's during the Carter years when administrative deregulation began in earnest. She would eventually be offered (and decline) reappointment in 1979. Slowly, the composition of the commission, although not the majority on most crucial issues, had begun to shift.

Both Ford nominations reflected "a change in philosophy" by the chief executive.[13] The president was no longer willing to select nominees solely on the basis of parochial political criteria. Introducing a new breed of commissioners at the ICC facilitated the administration's efforts to engineer the reform process by undermining a key means by which organized interests controlled the policy process.

As ICC support for reform strengthened, proponents of change began to win a few administrative victories. The commission made it easier for truckers to reduce their rates without strong opposition and expanded unregulated zones around metropolitan areas.[14] Nevertheless, such blows for reform remained sporadic. The balance of power on the Ford commission still favored regulation. In addition, progressive forces faced a major obstacle in chairman George Stafford; it was clear that far-reaching change would require breaking Nixon's covenant regarding the nature of the ICC chairmanship. Stafford would have to be replaced with a dynamic reformer.

By 1975, Ford had resolved to find a new chair. However, the administration's first three choices for the job all declined it.[15] Finally, Ford nominated Warren Rudman, a former New Hampshire attorney general and later U.S. senator, to replace a retiring commissioner (Kenneth Tuggle) and to chair the ICC.

Many, extrapolating from a long history of conflict-free nominations, assumed that Rudman's appointment would sail through the Senate. However, the common understanding that Rudman shared Ford's views on reform, along with some other unrelated political concerns, prompted hostility behind the scenes. The Commerce Committee refused to hold hearings before the election, and Rudman bitterly withdrew his name from consideration.[16] With the election fast approaching, Ford's subsequent nomination to the commission, Richard Quick (who was not announced as the president's choice for ICC chair), was ignored as well.

As Ford left office, he could claim some administrative victories at the ICC. He could point to a minority bloc favoring reform, but internal opposition to reform was still too strong to permit the executive to attack the basis of trucking regulation. Efforts to change the balance through appointments requiring congressional (and, implicitly, organizational) approval had run into a roadblock; the agency remained proregulation. The impact of administrative changes continued to be marginal.

The Carter Years: Successful Deregulation through Administration

Jimmy Carter entered the White House determined to bring about economic deregulation.[17] Indeed, shortly after his election, in a March 1977 "town meeting" in Clinton, Massachusetts, Carter made a public proclamation that he would reform all transportation regulation. Why did the new administration succeed where its predecessor had failed?

The answer lies in certain advantages Carter had over Ford and in Carter's choice of strategy. Carter was privileged in two respects compared to Ford. First, he took office with several commissioners in place who were at least potentially receptive toward his policies. The other was that Carter served for a full term, which gave him the requisite time to formulate and execute a plan to build a solid majority for deregulation at the ICC that could undercut organizational influence.

The White House perceived three options: (1) to propose legislation mandating significant deregulation, (2) to encourage ICC reforms backed by a congressional resolution, or (3) to rely exclusively upon the commission. After considerable debate, the president chose the third alternative.[18] Unlike Ford's unsuccessful efforts to shove reform down congressional throats, Carter eschewed an immediate legislative solution, which in any event appeared unfeasible. Instead, he opted for the deceptively simple strategy of short-circuiting the fundamental conditions for group influence.

Carter encouraged the commission to use the means at its disposal to change the status quo. He focused on a key element necessary for motor carrier success that was open to executive manipulation but relatively unsusceptible to being blocked by the regulated motor carriers. His plan of attack required an aggressive, committed chair to spearhead the reform effort. It also required fostering proreform sentiment on the commission through new appointments (an option that could not be used because of congressional opposition), conversion of existing members, or failure to replace hostile members (who could be encouraged to leave). The legislative solution was postponed until June 1979, two and a half years into the president's term, by which time policy had been qualitatively changed. With trucking reform already in place, members of Congress and their group allies were forced to act in the public spotlight with the threat of a veto and the specific promise of more dramatic administrative reform hanging over their heads. The political difficulties of tightening the government's grip on the market once it had been loosened were much greater than those of resisting reform in the first place.

The new administration's first order of business was to oust Stafford as chair. Initially, Carter ran into problems analogous to those his predecessor had experienced. Senators acting at the behest of the regulated trucking industry and their unionized employees made it abundantly clear that Carter's choice for the chairmanship, Sam Hall Flint, had no chance of confirmation. It appeared virtually impossible for the administration to obtain Senate approval to appoint any mutually acceptable new commissioner as chair.

Having unsuccessfully tested the waters, the Carter administration switched gears and named O'Neal chair—on the condition that he advance White House policy toward motor carrier regulation. By choosing a leader from the ICC's current membership, the senatorial confrontations and delays that prevented Ford from replacing Stafford were sidestepped, since no approval was required. (Similarly, O'Neal could be removed as chair without approval.) The ATA, the IBT, and their congressional allies had been thwarted. Much to their consternation, O'Neal proved to be a forceful, reform-oriented chairman.

O'Neal acted to overhaul the commission in its structure, personnel, and substance. He quickly moved to undercut proregulation commissioners by changing the ICC's decision-making structure and worked to stimulate proreform sentiment by courting existing staff and bringing more sympathetic people into the agency.[19]

Thus, a variety of mechanisms provided an institutional foundation for pushing the ICC toward reform. Although Congress had proved to be an impediment for a president bent on energizing the commission through his appointment powers, the legislature could not, without the extraordinary step of revoking presidential authority to appoint a chair, prevent the chairman from employing his authority over agency structure and staff appointments.

In June 1977 O'Neal appointed a task force to develop ways of easing the burdens of trucking regulation. One month later, the task force submitted thirty-nine recommendations, which were sternly criticized by the ATA and the Teamsters. The task force took particular care to advocate changes that did not require new legislation or budgetary increases and consequently limited the ability of interest groups and their congressional allies to circumvent the commission's efforts. Within a year, the ICC had adopted a third of the recommendations and was close to supporting twenty-three of the remaining twenty-six. Meanwhile, O'Neal had produced even more far-reaching proposals.[20] Teamster president Frank Fitzsimmons was so incensed that, in early 1979, he wrote to Carter to demand O'Neal's removal in light of the chairman's "unmistakable anti-labor and anti-worker bias."[21]

Perhaps the Carter administration's most critical decision, however, was to adopt the task force's recommendation to reduce the number of commissioners from eleven to seven (the number of commissioners actually shrank to six by the end of 1979, although it would increase again to nine when it fit Carter's needs). Although the law provided that commissioners could serve past the expiration of their terms until their successors were chosen and approved, the administration found a way around the statutory constraints:

> It announced its refusal to name new commissioners when slots on the ICC became vacant. This had the effect of preventing members of Congress and their allies from demanding the appointment of a new cohort of proregulation commissioners.
> It declared a policy of not reappointing commissioners who adopted proregulatory stances. This gave commissioners three choices: (1) quit as soon as a good job offer was received rather than waiting to be thrown out at a potentially inopportune time or suffer the indignity of an unpleasant battle; (2) continue to advocate a proregulatory stance and hope that the president would not be able to get a replacement approved; or (3) adopt the Carter program and hope to be rewarded with job security.

In response to the administration's stance, some commissioners hostile to deregulation exited (Alfred McFarland, Dale Hardin) and a few others hung on and continued to voice their opposition (Rupert Murphy until August 1978, Stafford). Others, often more recent appointees without proven track records, moved toward the proreform camp. Brown, most notably, continued to serve for almost two years after her term expired; she had an understanding with the White House that her continued tenure at the ICC was contingent upon her voting with the reformers. (Her hopes of eventually being renominated were never realized.) Gresham also fell in step with the White House even though his appointment ran until 1981. Gradually, the balance of power within the commission shifted, and a stable majority favoring deregulation emerged. While reform might have come a few months earlier if new commissioners had been successfully appointed, the administration effectively excluded Congress, the ATA, and the IBT by relying on attrition and not naming a single new commissioner for nearly three years. Carter used the same appointment system that had been an intricate part of the stability of motor carrier regulation to undo it. The commissioners' malleability, which the ATA and the motor carriers had previously exploited, made them unlikely to stick together and preserve trucking regulation on principle.[22]

With the gradual evolution of a proreform majority, the commission tackled the task of stripping away forty years of regulation. At first, with the proreform majority only beginning to take hold, O'Neal and the ICC moved slowly. Only a few tentative steps were taken in 1977.[23] But by 1978, as the majority in favor of deregulation solidified, the pace of reform quickened. The commission's initial efforts centered on removing restrictions to entry into the trucking industry. Its overall impact was phenomenal. From 1975 to 1979, the number of applications for entry increased 700 percent, and the number approved grew by more than 800 percent.[24] Nor were the commissioners prepared to rest on their laurels: Additional proposals to open the market further were already in the works.

Congressional and Group Response to Administrative Change

By this time, the ATA and the IBT had set off fire alarms in legislative districts far and wide. Neither they nor Congress was prepared to watch passively as the ICC dismantled motor freight regulation. Although legislative sentiment toward deregulation had long been negative, the opposition of the ATA and the union to changes at the ICC brought added pressure to bear on representatives. Both groups mounted vigorous campaigns in reaction to the commission's rapidly advancing reform program and in anticipation of future legislation. They simultaneously mobilized their forces in the hinterlands and lobbied actively in Washington. Although proponents of deregulation did not lack group support, they were no match for the ATA/IBT alliance.

Many, reassured by the reform movement's numerous failures in Congress, still believed that there was little chance that the legislature would pass a reform bill. This included the Teamsters themselves. The union's legislative counsel, Bartley O'Hara, publicly predicted as late as July 1978 that trucking deregulation was "the one issue that the man standing on the loading dock understands. I don't think they [the Carter administration] will meet with much success if they choose the legislative route."[25] Privately, IBT officials allegedly promised Senate committee staffers that anyone who voted for a reform bill would not be reelected.[26]

Such confidence was undoubtedly reinforced by the positioning of congressional opposition in key committee posts.[27] In the Senate, Commerce Committee chairman Howard Cannon (D-Nev.) was a strong proponent of the regulatory system. Although in uncertain health, Warren Magnuson (D-Wash.), Appropriations Committee chairman and senior Commerce Committee member, was an ally of the truckers and the Teamsters and would eventually seek to amend the reform legislation on the Senate floor. Budget Committee chairman Ernest Hollings (D-S.C.), also a key Commerce Committee member, was another capable Senate leader who opposed motor carrier reform and was a strong ATA ally. In the House, Public Works and Transportation Committee chairman Harold Johnson (D-Calif.) and Subcommittee on Surface Transportation chairman James Howard (D-N.J.) distinctly disapproved of trucking reform.

More generally, there had been no major changes in the committee system and, correspondingly, no reason to think that members of the relevant committees would suddenly turn against the motor carriers. The limited support for deregulation was largely among representatives who were not members of the authorizing committees.[28] The lack of enthusiasm for deregulation among the members of the Commerce and Public Works committees is underlined by the failure of either entity to hold hearings on trucking deregulation before a bill was introduced in June 1979. The only congressional investigation originated from an unlikely source: the Senate Judiciary Committee's Antitrust and Monopoly Subcommittee.[29] Those hearings—conducted in October 1977 to the chagrin of Cannon, the Teamsters, and the ATA—reflected the efforts of subcommittee chairman Ted Kennedy (D-Mass.) and appeared propelled by his presidential aspirations. After leading the fight for airline deregulation, Kennedy felt he could get similar visibility by turning toward the trucking industry. ("[H]is political people tell him it's the best thing he has going," said one Carter administration domestic policy staff member.[30])

Interviewees suggested that perhaps the only other key senator who stood out as favorably inclined toward reform was Robert Packwood (R-Oreg.), the ranking Republican on the Senate Commerce Committee, who would help to escort the eventual legislation through the Senate labyrinth.

In the first half of 1980, many analysts were certain that representatives' electoral aspirations would sideline efforts to free the motor carrier industry from governmental controls. Those holding this viewpoint ignored what was unfolding at the ICC. Maneuvering there had qualitatively changed the context in which reform was being considered. Carter had found a way around the ATA and the IBT. Those organizations and their congressional allies might not have been clamoring for change, but if they wished to preserve regulation, they had to act, either by informally persuading the commission to abandon reform or by passing legislation. Their ability to implement either of these strategies was limited, however.

On the one hand, convincing the ICC to drop its efforts required an enforcement mechanism. But Congress and its interest group allies lacked an effective punishment or an enticing reward for recalcitrant regulators. On the other hand, legislation to restrict the commission's discretion—the favored solution of both organized labor and the trucking industry—was sure to elicit presidential threats of a veto and had the possibility of exacting political costs for the legislators as the general election approached. Although some administration officials were willing to compromise, Carter was unyielding. To many analysts' continuing surprise, the president held firm to his support for deregulation even after the Teamsters accepted a wage package that fell within the administration's inflation guidelines. Indeed, the union believed that it had cut a deal, exchanging wage concessions for postponement of deregulation legislation, but members of the Carter administration refused to go along. (Carter officials had been prepared to introduce their reform legislation on May 17, the day after Teamster balloting on the wage accord was completed, but introduction was deferred because of scheduling difficulties.[31]) Teamster leaders, feeling that they had been duped, were irate.

All that was left for the ATA, the IBT, and their congressional allies was persuasion or capitulation. At first, the proponents of regulation attempted the former by going straight to the commissioners. In a meeting with O'Neal in December 1978, Representatives Johnson and Howard, long-time allies of the ATA, asked the ICC chairman to end the commission's reformist edicts, arguing that the agency had usurped congressional authority. Predictably, given the contingent nature of his chairmanship, O'Neal declined their request. Cannon was less subtle. In an October 1979 speech (presumably at the behest of the IBT) he publicly condemned the commission, proclaiming: "We are mad as hell, and we're not going to take it anymore. The Congress does not expect any independent agencies to act in 'novel' ways to achieve their own special goals."[32] But the ICC stuck to its guns.

The proregulation advocates were now on the defensive. In June 1979 forces within the Carter administration agreed that the time was ripe for reform legislation and, with five senators, introduced the Trucking Competition and Safety Act. The administration also nominated three new ICC commissioners—Thomas Trantum, Marcus Alexis, and Darius Gaskins—and the Senate approved them. (When O'Neal left the agency at the end of the year, Gaskins assumed the chairmanship.) They would be followed by Reginald Gilliam in the spring of 1980, bringing the total number of commissioners (with Brown's departure) to nine.

Why, it might be asked, did the Senate go along with those appointments, and why did the ATA and the IBT not mount strong campaigns to defeat them? Simply put, it was commonly recognized that opposition would have proved fruitless in changing policy. If the administration were struggling to gain a sympathetic majority on the commission to implement reform, it would have been worthwhile for the Congress, the IBT, and the ATA to challenge the nominations. As interviewees made clear, the ICC's firm majority for deregulation and reform made it pointless to oppose the nominations. Even the ATA and IBT realized that only statutory action would save them now.

The shift in mood is illustrated well by Commerce chairman Cannon's metamorphosis. Trucking interests were extremely encouraged when the Commerce Committee wrested jurisdiction over trucking legislation from Kennedy and the Judiciary Committee. But although Cannon's initial reaction to reform legislation was unenthusiastic, his opposition eventually softened. With the failure of efforts to persuade the ICC, the only alternative left for proponents of regulation such as Cannon was to agree to legislation and try to get the best deal possible from what had become a disadvantageous bargaining position.

In a meeting with the commissioners, Cannon capitulated. The senator requested a moratorium on further administrative deregulation in exchange for his personal pledge that legislation would be passed by June 1, 1980. The commissioners consented, but they stressed that they would revive their reform efforts if legislation had not been passed by that date.

Meanwhile, the ATA and the Teamsters were gearing up for one last fight. They were skillfully organized, extremely well funded, and, especially in the case of the ATA, politically savvy. In response to the announcement of the administration's proposal, ATA president Bennett Whitlock accused the president of succumbing "to political pressures from Senator Kennedy [Carter's competitor for the presidential nomination] by accepting his radical approach to trucking deregulation."[33] By the fall of 1979, the ATA had raised $2 million to fight deregulation; it hired the high-profile Washington public relations firm of Hill and Knowlton; and group representatives began contacting legislators personally. In addition, an extensive grassroots campaign ensured that every representative was contacted by at least one district trucking concern.[34] The IBT, aware that large numbers of union jobs were at stake, also mobilized strongly and became involved on a daily basis in the fight to preserve regulation. Trucking deregulation generated more White House mail than any other issue at the time, and that mail was overwhelmingly against reform.[35]

It was abundantly clear to these groups that blocking legislation would only leave them with an increasingly market-oriented ICC. Therefore, they prepared their own bill which provided for some liberalization but prohibited the ICC from going further in opening up the motor carrier system. The ATA's and the IBT's hopes—briefly bolstered by the ICC's moratorium on reform—were quickly dashed. Given the amount of control over the commission that had already been lost by proregulation forces, their bargaining position was simply too weak. Their moderate alternative was unacceptable to the administration, and it was clear that two-thirds of the House and Senate were not going to support a bill that would be denounced as endorsing regulation, big business, and the Teamsters.

As the June 1980 deadline and the prospect of renewed ICC administrative rulings approached, the legislative bottleneck began to break up. Because Carter had made it clear that he would veto unacceptable legislation and would turn administrative deregulation loose, the legislation would have to embody the great majority of the ICC's administrative changes. Without numerous prods and veto threats from the White House, the legislation would probably have been far weaker; indeed there might well have been no legislation at all.[36] Legislative support for reform reflected the unenthusiastic response of members of Congress to environmental factors that had limited their choices. Ultimately, Cannon and Packwood agreed on legislation that was acceptable to the forces favoring deregulation.

Even with this accord, the bill almost fell by the wayside several times. Indeed, many observers thought that trucking deregulation would be buried in committee as time ran out for the Ninety-Sixth Congress and the 1980 election approached. Packwood had trouble getting even ten of the nineteen Republicans on the Senate Commerce Committee to go along with crucial sections of the bill so that it would pass in the committee, although once he mobilized the requisite Republican support the legislation was approved by a margin of seventy to twenty on the Senate floor.[37]

The House was even more recalcitrant than the Senate. Here the ATA and the Teamsters tried, once again, to back more favorable legislation. But the White House countered that their bill was unacceptable and repeated its veto pledge. The ATA/IBT legislation was withdrawn, and the Cannon/Packwood proposal was substituted. After renewed veto threats and an effective White House lobbying campaign, a final attempt to weaken the legislation substantially failed by just three votes (189-192). The House passed the Senate bill on June 20 by a vote of 367 to 13. Eleven days later Carter signed the Motor Carrier Act of 1980 into law, confidently declaring that "I know I can count on the Commission to take prompt and effective action to bring to the public the benefits of greater competition, greater productivity, and lower prices that this law will provide."[38]

Naturally, all of the parties involved—including reluctant members of Congress, the ATA, and the Teamsters (who, nonetheless, remained especially angry)—attempted to claim what little credit might be had for legislation with such low visibility and diffuse benefits. Perhaps the most ironic case was that of Senator Cannon, who attempted to portray himself as a deregulator. The Nevada senator's ties to the IBT were so close that they became the subject of a legal investigation in February 1980.

By largely codifying prior ICC actions, the legislation assured the proponents of deregulation that their hard-won changes would not be overruled by future commissions or the judiciary.[39] In return, group and congressional proponents of regulation were given a few concessions, although none has had much long-lasting effect. The legislation also provided one final consolation for supporters of trucking regulation. Although unable to have language prohibiting future reforms put into the law, they hoped that the Motor Carrier Act would satisfy the president and the commission while preventing further damage.

Group Influence and Deregulation

After World War II, a consensus emerged that the ICC had been captured by organized interests. The commission was routinely cited as the quintessential example of an agency dominated by those it purported to regulate. As a broad description of commission policy, this perspective is understandable. However, it glosses over the nature of the system underpinning policy stability and change. Once the president had undermined key features of the system organized interests were unable to stop deregulation.

The alliance among regulators, legislators, and interest groups had worked well because successive presidents had been unwilling to take the steps necessary to manage the political process. Without any significant change in the interest group system, the regulatory system unraveled once presidents Ford and Carter assigned a high priority to reducing economic regulation and, for the purpose of deregulation, took advantage of conditions that had previously perpetuated the status quo.

Although the groups holding the greatest stake in regulation amassed and mobilized immense resources and made no obvious mistakes, their fight against deregulation proved futile. These associations slowed the reform process, dictated the method of its implementation, and rendered the ultimate result somewhat less comprehensive than it would have been otherwise, but they could not prevent it from occurring. By appointing a chairman committed to reform and declining to replace hostile commissioners, Jimmy Carter left the ATA and IBT with few sanctions to use against uncooperative agency decision makers. The influence of these two groups—which had been conditioned on the chief executive staying out of the regulatory fray—largely broke down when the chief executive chose a strategy designed to circumvent the ATA and IBT.

At a more general level, this analysis of the reform process indicates that students of political and regulatory behavior must pay careful attention to the conditions underlying the political influence of organizations. It is imperative to focus on the process through which influence is exercised and the conditions under which it operates if the forces that underlie policy are to be thoroughly appreciated.

Because this analysis has used a temporal, rather than a cross-sectional, approach, it may seem a bit idiosyncratic. For example, the president's ability to reduce the number of ICC commissioners may strike one as unique. However, the broader points that this investigation makes for explaining reform and conceptualizing organizational influence should be generic.

Notes

1. Well-known examples of these theories include: George J. Stigler, "The Theory of Economic Regulation," *Bell Journal of Economics and Management Science* 2 (Spring 1971): 3-21; Richard A. Posner, "Theories of Economic Regulation," *Bell Journal of Economics and Management Science* 5 (Autumn 1974): 335-358; Sam Peltzman, "Toward a More General Theory of Regulation," *Journal of Law and Economics* 19 (August 1976): 211-240; and Gary S. Becker, "A Theory of Competition among Pressure Groups for Political Influence," *Quarterly Journal of Economics* 98 (August 1983): 371-400.
2. The idea of agency capture was originally applied to the ICC. See Samuel P. Huntington, "The Marasmus of the ICC: The Commission, the Railroads, and the Public Interest," *Yale Law Journal* 61 (April 1953): 467-509.
3. On the ICC's actions, see Edward J. Schack and Bruce M. Kasson, "Recent Decisions of the Interstate Commerce Commission," *Transportation Law Journal* 10 (Summer 1978): 1-14; and Fritz R. Kahn "Motor Carrier Regulatory Reform—Fait Accompli," *Transportation Journal* 19 (Winter 1979): 5-11.
4. See Barry Weingast, "The Congressional-Bureaucratic System: A Principal-Agent Perspective with Applications to the SEC," *Public Choice* 44 (1984): 147-192.
5. On the potential importance of new ideas, see Martha Derthick and Paul Quirk, *The Politics of Deregulation* (Washington, D.C.: Brookings Institution Press, 1985); Dorothy Robyn, *Braking the Special Interests* (Chicago: University of Chicago Press, 1987); and Paul Quirk, "Deregulation and the Politics of Ideas in Congress," in *Beyond Self-Interest*, ed. Jane J. Mansbridge (Chicago: University of Chicago Press, 1990).
6. Thomas Gale Moore, "Deregulating Transportation: Tracking the Progress," *Regulation* 4 (March/April 1978): 41.
7. See Wallace Hendricks, "Regulation and Labor Earnings," *Bell Journal of Economics and Management Science* 8 (Autumn 1977): 483-496.
8. Further details can be found in Rothenberg, *Regulation, Organizations, and Politics: Motor Freight Policy at the Interstate Commerce Commission* (Ann Arbor: University of Michigan Press, forthcoming).
9. See, for example, *The Gallup Report: Political, Social, and Economic Trends*, report no. 229 (Princeton, N.J.: George Gallup and Associates, 1984).
10. See Seymour Martin Lipset and William Schneider, *The Confidence Gap: Business,*

316   Rothenberg

Labor, and Government in the Public Mind (New York: Free Press, 1983).

11. See Paul W. MacAvoy and John W. Snow, eds., *Regulation of Entry and Pricing in Truck Transportation: Ford Administration Papers on Regulatory Reform* (Washington, D.C.: American Enterprise Institute, 1977).

12. Don Byrne, "Congress Passes Air, Highway, Rail Aid Bills, Shows Need for Unified Committee," *Traffic World*, January 5, 1976, 18.

13. Thomas Gale Moore, "Deregulating Rail and Truck Transportation," Hoover Institution Working Paper no. E-84-5 (Stanford, Calif.: Hoover Institution), 4.

14. See Ex Parte no. 297, *Rate Bureau Investigation*, 349 I.C.C. 811 (1975), 351 I.C.C. 437 (1976), and Ex Parte no. MC-37, *Commercial Zones and Terminal Areas* (1976). For a discussion of the second decision, which, to the author's knowledge, was not published, see *Ninety-first Annual Report of the Interstate Commerce Commission* (Washington, D.C.: Government Printing Office).

15. "Two Names Are Added to 'Prospect List' for ICC Chairmanship," *Traffic World*, November 20, 1975, 18.

16. "Rudman Decides against Remaining a Candidate for Appointment," *Traffic World*, June 21, 1976, 12.

17. See Lawrence J. White, *Reforming Regulation: Processes and Problems* (Englewood Cliffs, N.J.: Prentice-Hall, 1981), and Robyn, *Braking the Special Interests*.

18. The options were detailed in an early 1978 staff "options" paper. See Robert M. Butler, "Deregulation of Trucking Industry Is Foreseen as Goal of White House," *Traffic World*, December 12, 1977, 21-22; and Irwin B. Arieff, "Truck Deregulation Faces Tough Battle in Congress," *Congressional Quarterly Weekly Report*, July 29, 1978, 1975-1979.

19. See Gary J. Edles, "The Strategy of Regulatory Change," *ICC Practitioners' Journal* 49 (December 1982): 626-637; and Derthick and Quirk, *The Politics of Deregulation*.

20. See Ernest Holsendolph, "ICC Chief Proposes a Series of Changes," *New York Times*, July 31, 1977, 17; American Enterprise Institute, *Major Regulatory Initiatives during 1978* (Washington, D.C.: American Enterprise Institute, 1978).

21. Frank Fitzsimmons, "Letter to Jimmy Carter," Domestic Policy Staff Files: Neustadt (Atlanta, Ga.: Jimmy Carter Library, January 16, 1979).

22. See Paul Stephen Dempsey, "Erosion of the Regulatory Process in Transportation—The Winds of Change," *ICC Practitioners' Journal* 47 (June 1980): 303-320.

23. See Ex Parte no. 55 (Sub-No. 25), *Revision of Application Procedures, Federal Register* 42, 62486 (December 1, 1977).

24. See the ICC's annual reports for the years 1976-1980, Interstate Commerce Commission, *Annual Report of the Interstate Commerce Commission* (Washington, D.C.: U.S. Government Printing Office, 1977-1981); see also Thomas Gale Moore, "Rail and Truck Reform—The Record So Far," *Regulation* 9 (November/December 1983): 33-41.

25. See Irwin B. Arieff, "Trucking Deregulation Runs into Jurisdictional Dispute, Mixed Signals from Carter," *Congressional Quarterly Weekly Report*, February 3, 1979, 216-217.

26. Richard Neustadt, "Administratively Confidential Memorandum: Rick Neustadt for Stu Eizenstat," Domestic Policy Staff Files: Neustadt (Atlanta, Ga.: Jimmy Carter Library, January 30, 1980).

27. But see Derthick and Quirk, *The Politics of Deregulation*.

28. Richard E. Cohen, "Will Carter Be Able to Apply the Brakes to Deregulation?" *National Journal*, May 14, 1977, 748-753.

29. See U.S. Congress, Senate, Committee on the Judiciary, Subcommittee on Antitrust and Monopoly, *Federal Restraints on Competition in the Trucking Industry: Antitrust Immunity and Economic Regulation* (Washington, D.C.: U.S. Government Printing Office, 1980).

30. Mary Schuman, "Memorandum for Stu Eizenstat," Domestic Policy Staff Files: Neustadt (Atlanta, Ga.: Jimmy Carter Library, January 10, 1979).
31. Walter Mondale, Brock Adams, Griffin Bell, Fred Kahn, Charles Schultze, Esther Peterson, and Stu Eizenstat, "Memorandum for the President: Recommendation on Trucking Deregulation," Presidential Handwriting File (Atlanta, Ga.: Jimmy Carter Library, March 15, 1979).
32. Ernest Holsendolph, "Senator Criticizes Moves to Ease U.S. Regulation," *New York Times*, October 23, 1979, 12.
33. Judy Sarasohn, "Carter Proposes Trucking Deregulation," *Congressional Quarterly Weekly Report*, June 23, 1979, 1278.
34. See Marcus Alexis, "The Applied Theory of Regulation: Political Economy at the Interstate Commerce Commission," *Public Choice* 39 (1982): 5-27.
35. Allan Butchman, "Memorandum for White House Task Force on Motor Carrier Reform," Domestic Policy Staff Files: Neustadt (Atlanta, Ga.: Jimmy Carter Library, April 6, 1979).
36. See Marcus Alexis, "The Applied Theory of Regulation," and "The Political Economy of Federal Regulation of Surface Transportation," in *The Political Economy of Deregulation: Interest Groups in the Regulatory Process*, ed. Roger G. Noll and Bruce M. Owen (Washington, D.C.: American Enterprise Institute, 1983).
37. On ATA lobbying in the Senate, see John P. Frendreis and Richard W. Waterman, "PAC Contributions and Legislative Behavior: Senate Voting on Trucking Deregulation," *Social Science Quarterly* 66 (June 1985): 401-412.
38. *Public Papers of the Presidents of the United States: Jimmy Carter, 1980-1981, Book 2: May 24 to September 26, 1980* (Washington, D.C.: U.S. Government Printing Office, 1982), 1267.
39. For a detailed analysis, see Donald V. Harper, "The Federal Motor Carrier Act of 1980: Review and Analysis," *Transportation Journal* 20 (Fall 1980): 5-33; and James F. Hayden, "Teamsters, Truckers, and the ICC: A Political and Economic Analysis of Motor Carrier Deregulation," *Harvard Journal of Legislation* 17 (December 1980): 123-151.

15

Centralizing Regulatory Control and Interest Group Access: The Quayle Council on Competitiveness

Jeffrey M. Berry and Kent E. Portney

Interest groups have long understood the necessity of working closely with the executive branch as well as with the legislature, recognizing that the staff of federal agencies and departments often have considerable discretion in the implementation of policies. Resourceful and well-organized groups may develop close ties with bureaucrats that transcend even changes in presidential administrations; in the process successful groups become "clients" of an agency, worthy of special treatment and access.

Not surprisingly, relations between officials and interest groups may pose serious problems for presidents who wish to see that the agencies of the executive branch operate in a manner consistent with administration goals. Recent presidents have attempted to develop administrative procedures for controlling interest group access to the executive branch and for reviewing bureaucratic discretion in responding to interest group pressures.

In this article Jeffrey Berry and Kent Portney describe and evaluate an attempt by the Bush administration to combine centralized regulatory control with a means of centralizing interest group access. Vice President Dan Quayle was assigned the task of chairing the President's Council on Competitiveness, created in response to the president's concerns that certain agencies were overregulating business interests and thereby sabotaging the administration's goals of freeing business from excessive and costly regulation.

The authors conclude that although the Council experienced some notable successes it had great difficulty in disrupting the pattern of "strategic accommodation" that occurs in the rule-making process. Mobilization by liberal advocacy groups, supported by press opinion and Democrats in Congress, made it difficult for the Bush administration to move rule making too far in a conservative direction.

An earlier version of this essay was delivered at the annual meeting of the American Political Science Association, September 1993, Washington, D.C. We would like to thank Allan Cigler, Joan Lucco, Ronald Moe, and Joseph Pika for their comments on that paper.

How do presidents take control of the executive branch? Despite the imposing powers of their office, the sheer breadth of the executive branch and the substantial authority vested in the departments and agencies of government make it difficult for presidents to exert their will in a consistent and coherent fashion. Part of the problem presidents face is that departments and agencies have well-organized and resourceful clientele groups with which to contend. These groups have their constituents' interests at heart, not the president's. Administrators cannot simply ignore their client groups, even when those organizations are opposed to the president's agenda.

Recent presidents have used various means to enhance their control over parts of the executive branch, including efforts aimed at overseeing the rule-making process. By centralizing control over the content of regulations, presidents can achieve greater congruence between their own goals and the actions of departments and agencies. Recent presidents have also organized the White House in different ways in an attempt to structure interest group access in the most advantageous manner. Principally, they have centralized interest group access to help them mobilize support and to reach out to constituencies important to their electoral coalition.

The Bush administration combined, for the first time, centralized regulatory control with a means of centralizing interest group access. The President's Council on Competitiveness, chaired by Vice President Dan Quayle, was established after the president became frustrated with what he regarded as excessive regulation by his own administration. The Quayle Council, as it became known, reviewed regulations before they were issued in their final form and frequently sent them back to the issuing agencies with instructions to change them to be less burdensome to the affected industries. The Quayle Council staff was small and could take up only a modest number of cases at any one time. It usually selected its cases after hearing an appeal from industry representatives who believed that agency regulations were excessive.

For example, when the Department of Housing and Urban Development (HUD) issued regulations designed to make apartments more accessible to the disabled, the National Association of Home Builders objected, asserting that the rules would add too much to construction costs. Industry representatives appealed to the Quayle Council, which pressured HUD to redo the regulations. The new rules were more sympathetic to the industry, and lobbyists for the home builders claimed that hundreds of millions of dollars would be saved each year in aggregate building costs.[1]

Because actions by the Quayle Council could reduce regulatory costs so significantly, access to it was highly prized among Washington lobbyists. Detailed examination of the Bush administration's experience in combining centralized regulatory review with centralized interest group access provides a unique perspective on how presidents organize the White House to achieve their goals and on how Americans are represented in the administrative rule-making process. The means by which interest group access is facilitated or inhibited directly affect how effectively different constituencies are represented before policy makers.

The Quayle Council is a difficult research subject because it purposely avoided leaving any paper trail. As a Council staffer told the *Washington Post*, its operations were designed to leave "no fingerprints."[2] Consequently, there are no Quayle Council documents. Instead, data have been gathered from congressional hearings, journalistic coverage of the Council, publications issued by advocacy groups, and interviews that we conducted with people knowledgeable about the Council.

The Politicized Presidency

The desire for control of the federal rule-making process may be seen as a logical and perhaps inevitable extension of the evolution of the modern presidency.[3] Terry Moe suggests that a key feature of the modern presidency is the process of achieving "congruence" between the institutional structures of the presidency and the ambitions and resources of the president. As Moe puts it,

> If presidents are dissatisfied with the institutional arrangements they inherit, then they will initiate changes to the extent they have the resources to do so. These changes subsequently have feedback effects on the president ... which may then prompt further adjustments ... until congruence is realized.[4]

To Moe, the drive for presidential control stems from an effort to achieve this high degree of congruence. Modern presidents are faced with extremely high expectations and a crucial need to accomplish their major goals, but they are severely constrained by the limited constitutional powers of their office, the external environment (Congress, interest groups, and the general public), and the complexity of the executive branch itself.

One consequence of the high expectations in the context of severe constraints is that presidents develop an ever-increasing need for more information and technical competence in the executive branch. They fulfill this need not by seeking the professional competence of career bureaucrats who are neutral with respect to the president's political objectives, but rather by institutionalizing "responsive competence." As a politician, the president "is not interested in efficiency or effectiveness or coordination per se."[5] Rather, he wants an institutional system that is technically competent and responsive to his needs as a political leader.

According to Moe, the pursuit of responsive competence has two results. First, it contributes to the increasing centralization of the institutional presidency in the White House. More and more of the tasks required to achieve a president's policy and political goals are moved into the White House so that they are not diluted by the less-responsive permanent bureaucracy. The second consequence of the need for responsive competence is the "increasing politicization of the institutional system,"[6] whereby the president increasingly uses his executive powers, especially that of appointment, to encourage personal loyalty and build ideological or programmatic support for his agenda.

Presidential Control of the Rule-Making Process

Within the context of the politicization of the presidency, it is not surprising that presidents from Gerald Ford to George Bush turned their attention to the regulatory functions of the bureaucracy. Although the Nixon presidency provoked controversy with its efforts to manage the bureaucracy through a domineering White House staff, its efforts were not aimed at rule making per se.[7] Presidential efforts to control the rule-making process can be traced to Gerald Ford's creation of the Council on Wage and Price Stability (COWPS) in 1974. Although the stated justification for COWPS was a desire to develop neutral competence in rule making, the political motivation for the measure was unveiled when James C. Miller III, assistant director of COWPS, wrote that the intent of the council was to find a way "to avoid the tendency for agencies to serve special constituent interests, often at greater cost to the general public."[8] COWPS was not terribly successful at influencing the rule-making process, largely because it had little ammunition. Although Inflation Impact Statements were made part of the formal rule-making process, agencies were not required to respond to or comply with COWPS recommendations.[9]

Presidential control over rule making was strengthened in 1978 when President Carter created the Regulatory Analysis Review Group (RARG), which consisted of representatives from seventeen executive branch agencies and the Council of Economic Advisors, and the Regulatory Council, which was composed of representatives from thirty-six executive branch and independent regulatory agencies. Focusing on a small number of regulations whose annual economic impact was estimated to be at least $100 million, the Carter reforms gave the White House greater firepower. The two organizations provided guidelines that required federal agencies to prepare and publish extensive analyses of proposed regulations in the *Federal Register*, to review existing regulations to identify those which were no longer needed, and to provide more time and opportunity for "the public" to participate in rule making by extending the period of time people had to comment on newly proposed rules. RARG and the Regulatory Council, much like COWPS, sought to strengthen the means by which the White House could guide and coordinate the review of rules without necessarily exerting any overt control over them.[10]

The effort to institutionalize presidential control over the regulatory process advanced significantly in 1981. First, in January, President Reagan announced the creation of the Task Force on Regulatory Relief. The task force, headed by Vice President George Bush, consisted of seven cabinet-level officials. James Miller served as the executive director. Second, Reagan issued Executive Order 12291 delegating to OMB responsibility for reviewing agency rules before they were formally proposed. And third, the Reagan administration used the recently enacted Paperwork Reduction Act to authorize the newly created Office of Information and Regulatory Affairs (OIRA) within OMB to serve as the principal agency for exercising centralized review.[11]

The formal powers of the task force were not greatly expanded from previous efforts to exert presidential control over the rule-making process. The stated goals of the task force were to review major proposals by regulatory agencies, especially those with significant policy implications or where there was disagreement among agencies; to assess regulations already on the books; and to reduce the burden of regulations on business and society.[12]

The goals of the task force closely resembled those of the Carter administration's Regulatory Council.[13] Yet the development of informal powers through coordination with OIRA ensured that this was an effort with a difference. Centralized review of rule making was accomplished by making the regulatory review delegated to OMB subject to the supervision of the task force, by intentionally intermingling the task force's staff with that of the White House and of OMB, and by expanding the authority under which OMB could perform regulatory review.

Although OMB had been a key player in earlier efforts to provide guidance to regulatory agencies, its role was enhanced by the formation of OIRA. OIRA was legislatively charged with reducing the burdens of gathering information in federal agencies and with improving the management of federal agency information. The Reagan administration imaginatively used OIRA's broad paperwork clearance mandate to provide a vehicle for systematically reviewing agency regulatory proposals and for changing the content of those that did not conform to White House goals.[14] The work of the task force and OIRA soon became one and the same. As OIRA administrator Christopher DeMuth commented before the Senate Governmental Affairs Committee in 1982, "Our responsibilities under the Paperwork Reduction Act and Executive Order 12291 are completely intertwined, both in terms of staff and use of funds."[15]

In addition, according to Miller, what gave this initiative real teeth was having it headed by the vice president: "If it were just OMB versus the agencies it would be a loggerhead, it would be horizontal."[16] With the vice president in charge, the task force assumed a preeminent position. As Howard Ball notes,

The agency head, or bureau chief, in a dispute regarding a proposed regulation ... does not confront another department head; he or she has to confront the vice-president. There was, from the very beginning of the task force's life, a very basic political fact of life quite different from the regulatory control programs developed by Ford and Carter—buck the task force and you are bucking the vice-president and the White House.[17]

The intent was clearly to exercise centralized scrutiny over the regulatory agencies. Viewed through Terry Moe's lens, the Reagan administration was greatly dissatisfied with the institutional arrangements for regulatory review it inherited. Thus it sought changes in institutional arrangements and incentives by mobilizing available resources, including those of the vice president and OMB. Even after the task force ceased operations in 1983, the institutionalization of its tasks in OMB created a rather stable system of regulatory review that persisted for five more years.

Formation of the Quayle Council

The history of the Council on Competitiveness is not as clear-cut as that of its predecessors, mainly because it was not established through executive order or any other formal act. The first mention of the Council was made by President Bush in his February 1989 State of the Union address, when he announced that "I've asked Vice President Quayle to chair a new Task Force on Competitiveness."[18] In April the vice president's office released a "Fact Sheet" reporting the establishment of the Council on Competitiveness as of March 31. But it was not until June 15 of the following year that the White House issued a statement saying that "the President today designated the Council on Competitiveness ... to exercise the same authority over regulatory issues as did the Task Force on Regulatory Relief."[19]

According to several accounts, the president established the Council after hearing complaints about new regulations being produced by agencies that he ostensibly controlled. As a story in the *National Journal* has it,

The White House's renewed assault on regulations came after Bush had heard criticisms from friends in the business community that his Administration was reversing what he had accomplished as Vice President by issuing lots of "extraneous regulations," said Wayne Valis, who, as a member of the Reagan White House staff, had worked with Bush in the early 1980s on the regulatory reform effort. So upset was Bush about tales of burgeoning regulations that over the 1989 Christmas holidays, he directed a top aide to track Valis down—finally contacting him as he was riding a camel in Egypt—to set up a meeting to discuss how the earlier effort on regulatory relief had worked.[20]

A high-ranking Quayle Council staffer told the history this way:

> I think it was an article in the *Wall Street Journal* on regulating by
> the Bush administration. Bush sent a note to [OMB Director Richard]
> Darman saying, "Are we re-regulating? Let's not let the regulatory
> creeps get in charge." But Darman more or less sat on it. Then there
> was a later article that pissed off the President, and that got the thing
> rolling.[21]

The Quayle Council, then, would appear to have been born from the president's recognition that inherited institutional arrangements for controlling regulation had deteriorated. The events that followed represented an effort to mobilize resources and create incentives for the purpose of recreating the congruence between institutional structures, incentives, and resources that had existed before. Perhaps because the political environment had changed, so too had institutional arrangements and incentives.

Allan Hubbard, a Harvard-trained lawyer and successful Indiana businessman who was serving as Quayle's deputy chief of staff, was appointed as the Council's executive director. David McIntosh, a young lawyer out of the University of Chicago, was made deputy director.[22] According to White House statements, the Quayle Council was given very much the same charge as that given to Reagan's Task Force on Regulatory Relief. The vice president's April fact sheet stated that

> [t]he Council will review issues ... with the same authorities over
> the matters it reviews that were given to the Presidential Task Force
> on Regulatory Relief over regulatory issues in Executive Order No.
> 12291 (February 17, 1981) and No. 12498 (January 4, 1985).

Thus, at the start, the Bush administration sought simply to resurrect the arrangements made by the previous administration. But it was clear by early 1991 that the Council, working closely with OIRA, was intervening directly in the rule-making process. Members of Congress began to hear complaints about "interference" from the Council and OIRA on worker safety standards, environmental regulations, and other issues. Congressional examination and media accounts began to build a picture of a Council that was exercising political control over rule making by serving as a gatekeeper, providing special access for some interests, mostly business, while excluding others. In a relatively short time, the Quayle Council and OIRA became the institutional locus of Moe's "responsive competence" when it came to matters of federal regulation.

Helping Quayle and Bush

In addition to being an extension of the movement toward centralized White House control of the executive branch, the Council on Competitiveness was a critical part of a strategy to rehabilitate Vice President Dan Quayle. As soon as he was selected as George Bush's running mate at the 1988 GOP convention, Quayle became a lightning rod for criticism. The youthful Indiana senator was portrayed in the media as a lightweight who had relied for advancement on family connections rather than hard work, and whose family had pulled strings to keep him out of the war in Vietnam. He became a serious liability for candidate Bush and during the campaign was largely relegated to stroking the party faithful in GOP backwaters. Matters did not improve after the election; few politicians in recent American history have been treated as savagely or as unfairly as Quayle.[23] He became the butt of endless jokes on late-night television, and political observers began to wonder if he would be on the ticket in 1992. Quayle's dismal standing with the public, following Walter Mondale's expansion and enhancement of the vice presidency, meant that something had to be done.

President Bush's frustrations extended far beyond the expanding scope of federal regulation. During the second year of his term, the economy began to soften, and the administration seemed to lack focus or a clear agenda. The president's public disapproval ratings rose significantly, and he was whipsawed in negotiations with congressional Democrats over the budget. The abandonment of his "no new taxes" pledge was severely damaging. Domestic policy stalled after the 1990 congressional elections, and the president's chief of staff, John Sununu, reportedly said after the 1990 congressional elections, "Frankly, this President doesn't need another single piece of legislation.... In fact, if Congress wants to come together, adjourn, and leave, it's all right with us."[24]

It is within this environment of an administration stuck in first gear and an economy beginning to slide that the Quayle Council starts to gather momentum. For the Vice President it became an idea shop where conservative proposals could be incubated. For the President, it was a tool to fight the slumping economy and to re-energize his administration. Refusing to stimulate the economy the way that Democrats would (with spending programs), and hemmed in by a deficit that made a tax cut unfeasible, trying to free up capital for business through regulatory relief became one of his few strategies.

Centralizing Interest Group Access

The logic of centralizing control over administrative rule making within the Executive Office of the President is unmistakable. The president has strong incentives to keep agencies in line with the larger policy goals of the administration. He has the resources to accomplish this with a strong and capable White House staff whose loyalty is to the president and not to agency client groups. He also has a large and technically competent OMB staff to assist him. But institutional mechanisms to accomplish centralized regulatory control are not simple. As discussed below, firm gatekeeping procedures are needed to prevent the White House from being overwhelmed by the avalanche of regulations that pour out of Washington each day. Still, it is feasible to control rule making if the focus is limited to regulations with large economic impact or precedent-setting implications. These are exactly the kind of regulations that the Quayle Council singled out for attention.

But what of the logic of centralizing access to the White House? The Quayle Council departed from earlier institutional approaches to centralizing White House control over agencies in its open door policy toward aggrieved business groups. OMB officials in charge of the Reagan administration's review of agency rules also met frequently with lobbyists, but their efforts were not dependent on interest groups bringing cases before them. Although members of the Quayle Council may have believed that they were simply taking the Reagan approach a step farther, that step had enormous symbolic importance. Meeting with interest group leaders to listen to their complaints became the basis of operation for the Quayle Council, which conducted no review of proposed agency regulations. Even though OIRA was still reviewing significant regulations within OMB, the Quayle Council's autonomy and its effort to promote the vice president as an independent and effective advocate within the administration meant that it had to have a case-selection method that fit both its political objectives and its sparse staff structure.

Was the Quayle Council's institutionalization of interest group access to the White House an inevitable extension of the broader centralization of White House control over the executive branch? Is control over interest group access a logical consequence of control over administrative rule making?

At first glance the centralization of interest group access does seem analogous to the centralization of White House control over agencies. The roots of both phenomena can be traced to the Nixon administration, for example. Although earlier presidents had made use of individual staffers to reach out to different interest groups, the Nixon White House organized and broadened this activity through the creation of the Office of Public Liaison (OPL). Early in the Nixon administration an extensive effort was undertaken by the White House to mobilize and coordinate the lobbying of interest groups on critical issues such as the nomination of G. Harrold Carswell to the Supreme Court and congressional initiatives designed to stop the war in Vietnam. Staffers were given responsibilities for various constituencies such as Catholics, Jews, blacks, business, and consumers. These White House staffers acted in a liaison capacity, giving specific interests a contact in the White House whom they could lobby and who could keep them informed of administration plans. The two functions—mobilization and liaison—were brought together with the establishment of OPL.[25]

The OPL continued under Gerald Ford, but Jimmy Carter deemphasized interest group relations because of his disdain for conventional Washington politics. Faced, finally, with the need for help from interest groups to get his legislation passed, Carter eventually resuscitated an active interest group outreach effort. The Reagan White House utilized its OPL from the outset; it functioned similarly to the Nixon-Ford operation, mobilizing support for the president's program and providing liaison to particular constituencies. But OPL declined again under Bush. Writing about the OPL during the middle of Bush's term Joseph Pika noted, "The Bush operation has been low key and has maintained low visibility."[26]

Ultimately, the similarities between the centralization of regulatory control and the centralization of interest group access are quite limited. For one thing, the centralization of regulatory control has moved much further along. The White House has used OPL as it has suited its needs, but until the establishment of the Quayle Council interest group access remained no more institutionalized than it had been under President Nixon. One reason for this is that the president has had little incentive to do more than what the OPL was designed to do under the Nixon administration. Contrary to the logic of enhancing White House control over administrative rule making, the president and his aides have neither the incentives nor the resources to try to build a structure institutionalizing enhanced interest group access. There are many reasons for this.

To begin with, centralizing regulatory control and centralizing interest group access are contradictory impulses. *A primary virtue of institutionalizing White House control over rule making is to diminish interest group influence.* Presidents often become dissatisfied with the behavior of administrative agencies because they inevitably try to reach agreements with their client groups. With so many interest groups actively lobbying and with legislators so willing to intervene in agency rule making, agency administrators need to reach accommodation so they can get things done. Presidents are understandably less interested in moving any particular regulation out the door. If they are to establish ideological coherence over their administration's rule making, they must find ways of decreasing interest group influence. By moving control of rule making to the White House, presidents make it more difficult for interest groups to influence regulations, unless, of course, they facilitate interest group access to the White House as well.

A second reason why greater institutionalization of interest group access may be counterproductive for presidents is that it threatens the White House with overload. Every new presidential office is a bridge over which more policy issues can enter the White House.[27] With tens of thousands of lobbyists in Washington, making the White House a centralized locus for lobbying has obvious dangers. Could not case selection, as with centralized control over rule making, solve this problem? As a practical matter, the only way the White House can keep from being inundated by interest group requests is to make access difficult. Mechanisms must be created that give the White House firm control over the type and quantity of interest group advocacy.

The OPL is actually well designed to accomplish this gatekeeping function. Small, with no policy-making responsibilities, its goal is to keep in touch with valued constituencies so that they can be activated when needed. In return, a limited number of top lobbyists for these groups have someone in the White House who will return their phone calls. The OPL is not, of course, the only point of access for interest groups.[28] Organizations of critical importance to the White House will have access to the president's personal staff or other key officials. Often, however, despite these multiple points of access, interest groups have a difficult time gaining the opportunity to lobby the White House. Mark Peterson's study of White House-interest group relations during the Reagan era measured the frequency of interaction between a sample of Washington lobbies and any part of the Executive Office of the President. Only 11 percent of the sample reported "frequent" interactions with the White House, and just 8 percent said they had frequent and "normally" cooperative relations.[29]

A third reason why presidents have limited interest in centralizing interest group relations in the White House is that in the culture of American politics lobbying is an odious activity.[30] Interest groups suggest the privilege of money and traditional Washington politics, precisely the things that presidential candidates like to campaign against. Indeed, a study based on interviews with presidential staffers during the Carter and Reagan years reveals that the public liaison office is the least respected unit in the White House.[31] This surely has to do with OPL's lack of clout as well as the nature of its clientele, but it also is a clear indication of the low priority the White House traditionally places on centralized interest group access.

How the Quayle Council Operated

The Quayle Council aimed to remove excessive regulation and cut back on litigation. But knowing the goals tells little about what the Quayle Council did right and what it did wrong. To understand this requires some knowledge of how the Council actually operated. An examination of two issues—the Council's relations with OMB and how it selected its cases—provides a glimpse of the Council's operations.

Council Relations with OMB

As with the Task Force on Regulatory Relief before it, the Council relied on OIRA in OMB to perform much of the routine review and screening of regulations. OIRA would raise a flag when it spotted regulations with an estimated impact of at least $100 million. According to one Council staffer, it would also flag those which involved expansion of regulatory authority, questions of property rights or federalism, and others that met the guidelines set out by the Council.

Before the Quayle Council was created, OIRA operated more or less as it had under the Reagan administration. As one lobbyist remarked,

> OIRA never stopped doing what it had been doing. There was never a lapse in it being a funnel for [review of] all "significant" regulations. The Quayle Council could count on OIRA staffers to do the grunt work, and they could then do the juicy things.

What was different, however, was that OIRA had been leaderless since October 1989, and apparently OMB director Richard Darman was not particularly enthusiastic about regulatory oversight.[32] According to one administration conservative, Darman perceived that Bush's appointees were not as staunch in their free-market orientation as President Reagan's appointees had been and that accomplishing regulatory review objectives would be too politically costly in that environment. According to one Council staffer, Darman "didn't want to invest his political capital in this. He wanted OIRA to do its work and leave him alone. He was afraid that [regulatory review] would get in the way of getting the budget passed."

The consequence was that there was no one with authority in OMB to carry the deregulatory banner. With the creation of the Council on Competitiveness, this changed. Not only did the Council take up that banner, but it reinvigorated and empowered OIRA's earlier regulatory review mission. Once the Council got going, the position of OIRA director became superfluous. In a sense, the Council served that capacity, using the OIRA staff as its own.

Case Selection

True to its intent, the Council did indeed focus on many important regulations, especially those being developed by the Environmental Protection Agency (EPA), the Occupational Safety and Health Administration (OSHA), and the departments of Transportation, Labor, and Health and Human Services. Beyond that it is not entirely clear how or on what basis the Council decided to take up specific issues or regulations. The Council's official policy was that it would meet with any individual or company wishing to raise a regulatory issue. Linking the Council's actions to the campaign activities of the vice president, David Broder and Bob Woodward declared that the Council's agenda was largely set by the business community.

> Word quickly spread throughout the business community that the Competitiveness Council was ready and able to help on regulatory matters, and its agenda filled up. In almost every city he visits as a

campaigner, Quayle holds closed-door round tables with business people who have made sizeable contributions to the local or national GOP. [Quayle Council Executive Director Allan] Hubbard who has the title of deputy vice presidential chief of staff often travels with Quayle and sits in on these sessions.[33]

The motivations of the businesses and lobbyists who sought assistance through the Quayle Council were undoubtedly varied, but a significant number of requests to the Council consisted of appeals of decisions made by the regulatory agencies. The Council's own policies, as noted below, almost guaranteed that the issues the Council took up would be those in which a business or industry had lost a battle involving the development of agency rules.

The Council obviously did not take up every case brought to it by members of the business community. There does not appear to have been any sort of complex process or set of criteria used to determine which issues the Council would take up and which it would ignore or refer elsewhere. The Council's actions ranged far across the regulatory landscape, including intervention on regulations to control formaldehyde; regulations stemming from the 1990 Clean Air Act regarding permitting, incineration, recycling, and radioactive emissions; the FDA drug approval process; safety labeling for toys; nursing home reform; savings and loan operations; and new rules to protect wetlands.[34] In one of its most ambitious efforts, the Council intervened to ask the EPA to make more than one hundred probusiness changes to Clean Air Act regulations.[35] These were not polite written requests—the Council was very forceful in its oversight of EPA. According to communications from EPA's assistant administrator for air and radiation, during 1991 Allan Hubbard attended at least nineteen meetings, and other Quayle Council staff at least thirty meetings, with EPA staff over issues of pending air pollution rules.[36]

The Council was designed from the outset to get involved in broad issues of policy and economic impact rather than to do casework, a feature that clearly made sense given the desire to create maximal impact with very limited resources and a staff of only six to eight professionals. In one of its few public documents, the Council announced that its purpose was to address "broad policy questions in upcoming regulations and revisions of existing regulations that have a broad and general effect—not applications of regulatory programs to individual persons."[37] In practice, there were many attempts by company officials, interest group lobbyists, and members of Congress to get the Council to take up a specific company's cause. But the Council's philosophy, said one staffer, was to resist such entreaties:

> We had an unwillingness to deal with any single company's problems.... There was a lot of Hill correspondence, from both parties. There was a lot of "Could you help this company?" We explained that

we didn't do casework. But then we started to get correspondence aimed at broader rules: "There is this hearing at OSHA and the rule they are considering could hurt all dry cleaners in my state. Could you look into it?" That kind of thing. We welcomed this.

The operational rules of the Council discouraged casework requests. When contacted by business executives, the Council purportedly required that they provide evidence that they had already dealt with the regulatory agencies in question and sometimes referred people back to those agencies for further action.

Perhaps the most significant dilemma encountered by the Council was that its policies with respect to casework created the impression that it was ignoring a significant portion of a traditionally Republican constituency—small and medium-sized businesses. The tilt toward big business spurred speculation about the connection between campaign contributions and Council actions. A review of ninety-six petitions to the Council selected at random in a study conducted by the *Legal Times* suggested that there was a substantial bias in favor of large, and against small and medium-sized, companies:

> [The Quayle Council] ignores pleas from small businesses, granting access instead to well-endowed companies and associations. Those small firms that do get in the door rarely get results.... Only a quarter of the [96] companies ... were able to meet with council staffers.... Of the 24 advocates who succeeded in gaining direct access to council officials, 13 were from individual companies. Ten of them were Fortune 500 companies.[38]

There was also a tendency for the Council to select cases with high visibility and importance to specific constituencies about which it seems to have cared a great deal. One lobbyist suggested:

> What the Quayle Council did was pick targets that were important to special constituencies. For example, there was one matter involving recoupment fees for R&D for defense contractors. The money was only $150 million, not much overall, but it made a whole lot of defense contractors happy.

However, what appears to have been a bias in favor of large or special corporations or their associations seems to be consistent with the Council's desire to focus on issues with significant impact or importance. There is little question that the regulations and issues with which the Council dealt, such as those of OSHA and EPA, were broad ones typically affecting more than one company. And the revisions that the Council pushed on agencies were sometimes very beneficial to small business, as in the case of the final Clean Air regulations. Yet the Council's case-selection pattern helped create the perception that the Council was responsive only to large special interests rather than to a broader constituency, a perception that it was never able to shake.

The Attack Against Strategic Accommodation

The efforts of the Quayle Council went beyond giving business groups better access and lightening the government's regulatory hand. Its actions also were an assault against the structural problems that have induced successive presidents to centralize regulatory control. In a deliberate and forceful manner the Quayle Council attacked the tendency of agencies to seek "strategic accommodation" with their interest group clientele.

Regardless of an administration's ideology, agency heads find it difficult to run their organizations without some attempts to satisfy opposition interest groups. Although administrators often would like to exclude opposition groups from agency policy making, they are not always able to do this. Compromise is frequently the key to getting things done in the near term, whereas taking on opposition groups is sure to promote conflict and delay in the short run without any guarantee of superior long-term results.

The propensity of administrators to seek accommodation with interest groups is hardly a new phenomenon, but the explosion in the numbers of interest groups active in any single policy area has made such accommodation more difficult to achieve. In an issue network made up of many different kinds of interest groups representing diverse constituencies, administrators will find competing factions vying for agency favor. The relationship between the many groups within a network is complex and ever-changing as new coalitions are quickly formed and just as quickly disband.[39] In Washington, today, agency heads look toward their dense interest group environments as sources of uncertainty, complexity, and conflict.[40]

The pressures pushing administrators toward strategic accommodation have four principal sources. First, of course, is the advocacy of opposition groups. Conservative administrators in the Reagan-Bush years found the liberal advocacy groups to be much more resourceful and enduring than they expected. Despite a concerted effort to "defund the Left" by the Reagan administration, liberal citizen groups actually thrived during the 1980s. The liberal groups proved to be especially adept at finding new sources of funding as the government funds they received were reduced or eliminated.[41] For many Americans on the liberal side of the ideological spectrum, citizen groups made a better "loyal opposition" than did the Democratic party. (Likewise, many conservative groups found that the election of Bill Clinton catalyzed a revival in membership and donations.)

Legal action by opposition groups is an important counterweight to ideologically based regulators. The power of liberal citizen groups and labor unions to fight conservative administrators was greatly enhanced by the work of staff lawyers with expertise in specific policy areas. These staff lawyers frequently used litigation to tie up proposed rules they claimed violated congressional intent or due process, or to force action when an agency was refusing to issue new rules ostensibly mandated by law.

A second force pushing administrators toward strategic accommodation is the Congress. Obviously Democrats in Congress were concerned about how Republican administrators were interpreting congressional intent when they wrote regulations. Administrators, of course, have a strong incentive to stay on good terms with committee and subcommittee chairs, even those of the opposition party. Interest group influence is also felt through the Congress as lobbyists encourage sympathetic legislators to intervene in agency rule making.

Agency administrators expect the intervention of powerful members of Congress, and it is difficult to ignore their entreaties. Congressional committees also have substantial weapons to fight agency administrators who are antagonistic to the preferences of the majority on the committee. When a committee anticipates that an administrator may write regulations in a way the committee would not like, it can make the statute highly specific so as to minimize agency discretion. Language can be added in legislative reports to spell out exactly what is meant by the wording of the statute.[42] It is not always possible to anticipate what regulations will need to be written, but Congress can always rewrite regulations it does not like when it reauthorizes an agency or has another reason to amend an existing law.[43] Congressional oversight has also become much more aggressive in recent years as the growth in committee staffs has facilitated closer scrutiny of agency actions.[44]

Third, agency administrators often seek accommodation with opponents because of what might be termed "internal pressures" or pressures from "friendly sources." Interest groups that generally support the agency may find it preferable to have a compromise rule written than to have to deal with the uncertainty of court action or the possibility of contradictory regulations at the state level. In a case involving the regulation of formaldehyde use in industrial processes, the Formaldehyde Institute (an organization representing industry) decided on its own to negotiate with the unions representing industry employees even though OMB was continuing to resist publication of any new rule restricting use of the chemical.

Agency administrators may seek strategic accommodation because of their own desire for accomplishment. They want to be able to claim that they have fixed problems and gotten programs to work right. This tendency will vary, of course, with the ideological orientation and intensity of the administration. During the Bush era administrators tended to be less ideological and more willing to compromise than the "Reaganauts" who preceded them. Agency heads like Gerald Scannell at OSHA and William

Reilly at EPA wanted to be seen as fair-minded administrators who could get new regulations and new policies up and running. Bush administration regulators also were more willing than their predecessors to listen to the civil-service staff in their agencies. As one Quayle Council member complained, "The appointees often came in without an agenda or plan for the agency. As a result they got a lot of their ideas from agency staff [who] were not free-market oriented. These staff members put forth a lot of reregulatory proposals." The Quayle staffers were right in their perception: Regulation writing increased significantly after Bush took over from Reagan.[45]

The Bush administration also wanted things both ways. The president wanted to be the "environmental president" as well as a probusiness president, with the result that EPA played good cop to the Quayle Council's bad cop. Liberal critics of the Quayle Council as well as members of the administration regarded Bush as sincere in his desire to be the environmental president. As one liberal lobbyist put it, "There was a kind of schizophrenia in the administration.... He was going to be the kinder, gentler, president. But he also wanted to keep business happy."

Fourth, and finally, administrators are pushed toward strategic accommodation because of the difficulty of making policy in dense environments. As "iron triangles" among interest groups, regulators, and key members of congressional committees were transformed into "issue networks," and as agency and congressional committee jurisdictions began to overlap more and more, policy making became increasingly complicated. The complexity of some policy issues and administrative processes creates substantial incentives for administrators to play the role of facilitator in addition to their role as advocate for the president. One of the most controversial actions of the Quayle Council was its intervention overturning a delicately wrought compromise among four federal agencies over the definition of what constitutes a wetland. The four agencies, in turn, were being pressured by a variety of competing interest groups. The compromise had been engineered by EPA's Reilly, the administration's point man on the wetlands issue.[46] What choice did he have but to negotiate among the conflicting parties?

Both formal and informal mechanisms have emerged to deal with the problem of policy making in dense environments. One such development is the increasing use of negotiated regulations, or "reg-negs." A reg-neg is a regulation written by interest group adversaries which the agency then adopts as its own.[47] Whatever the variation, institutional arrangements for mediation or negotiation sanction the role of interest groups in the policy-making process.

This sanctioning of policy making by a balanced system of interest groups is troubling to critics who believe that government would work better if the role of interest groups were reduced.[48] From the Quayle Council's perspective, strategic accommodation permitted the wrong kinds of groups to participate. The Council's attack on strategic accommodation was based on a majoritarian philosophy that views cooperative rule making as a perversion of the democratic process. Its efforts also were an attack on the lassitude of the Bush administration and the willingness of many administrators to break bread with the enemy. As one Council staffer put it, the president and many of his aides "had made peace with [the] calculus of power in Washington." Quayle, Hubbard, and McIntosh wanted to disrupt strategic accommodation by forcing administrators to consider a new factor: the possibility that the vice president and the Council might embarrass them by forcing them to withdraw proposed regulations.

The Opposition Mobilizes

As the Quayle Council grew as a center of conservative activism within the administration, the critics' voices became more shrill. Liberal advocacy groups, Democrats in Congress, and many respected media outlets assailed the Council. Although each of the critics had distinct motivations for taking on the vice president's regulatory watchdogs, their collective efforts worked to damage the Council's credibility. The motivation of liberal public interest groups was to restore strategic accommodation so as not to be excluded from agency rule making. Democrats in Congress were upset at what they saw as a usurpation of power by the Bush administration as well as by the success of the Council in pulling rule making in a more conservative direction. For newspapers, the story was one of the Bush administration cozying up to big business lobbies.

Liberal Advocacy Groups

For liberal advocacy groups, saving strategic accommodation was a serious issue. If agency administrators were unwilling to talk to them, their job would become considerably more difficult. Influencing regulations in the absence of a liberal administration or strategic accommodation by a conservative one meant relying on expensive litigation or getting Congress to act on their behalf, which was slow and unreliable. More broadly, the lack of strategic accommodation marginalized the liberal groups, making them "adversaries" rather than "players."

The fight against the Quayle Council was led by two small groups, OMB Watch and Public Citizen's Congress Watch, a Ralph Nader organization. With modest resources but a great deal of determination, Christine Triano of OMB Watch and Nancy Watzman of Public Citizen became the leaders of the anti-Quayle crusade. Known around Washington as the most knowledgeable people about the Council, they were a good source of information for the media. Watzman and Triano were responsible for five monographs on the Quayle Council and Bush's regulatory moratorium in 1992. Their central arguments against the Council were that it was imposing its nonexpert judgment in "scientific and technical matters better left to agency experts"; that it operated in secret and violated administrative law by ignoring the procedures set to ensure fair and objective regulation writing; and that its actions were undermining the health and safety of American consumers and workers. They also tried to document a link between campaign finance contributions and actions of the Council and joined in the attack against Allan Hubbard for an alleged conflict of interest arising from his stock holdings in a public utility affected by regulations under the Clean Air Act. Watzman and Triano were unrelenting: they distributed fact sheets, wrote op-ed pieces, provided information to people on the Hill, and were a human on-line database for those interested in the Quayle Council.[49]

OMB Watch and Public Citizen were not the only interest group critics of the Quayle Council. Labor unions, too, were vocal because of the Council's effort to revise OSHA regulations. Environmental groups were outspoken critics because of the Council's treatment of EPA. A coalition of thirty interest groups eventually formed to support efforts in Congress to shut down the Council.[50] The American Heart Association, the American Cancer Society, and the American Lung Association wrote to President Bush complaining that the Quayle Council was weakening standards intended to improve the nation's health.[51] Meanwhile, the perception among small businesses that they were being ignored persisted. A steady stream of groups visited Capitol Hill to ask sympathetic legislators to do something about the Council on Competitiveness.

Congress

The Congress had its own reasons to be upset with the Quayle Council. The White House unit had changed the process by which regulations were written, imposing itself as a superregulatory agency that stood apart from the administrative processes specified under the Administrative Procedure Act. Members of Congress believed that the authority to write regulations was a grant of power from the Congress to an administrative agency; when an agency was given a mandate to write regulations it was bound by congressional intent as it formulated rules. The Quayle Council seemingly thumbed its nose at Congress, giving short shrift to congressional intent and the provisions of the Administrative Procedure Act that govern rule making.[52] The important questions of separation of powers and administrative law inevitably comingled with partisan differences on Capitol Hill. Republicans who would have been critical of a similar operation in a Democratic administration defended the Quayle Council. Democrats were surely provoked by their policy differences with the administration as well as by their concerns about process.

Congressional Democrats had thrown down a marker before the

Quayle Council was even up and running. Led by Sen. John Glenn (D-Ohio), chairman of the Governmental Affairs Committee, a group of legislators made an unsuccessful attempt to write into law procedures that would open OIRA's activities to public scrutiny. Frustrated with the Reagan administration's use of regulatory review, Democrats wanted to prevent the Bush administration from centralizing control over rule making in the same manner. As the Quayle Council began to have an effect on the regulatory process, the Democrats became increasingly insistent that it was a "rogue operation" working outside the laws governing rule making. Rep. Henry Waxman (D-Calif.) told the *Washington Post* that "the Council on Competitiveness has usurped power, holds secret meetings with industry groups, and violates administrative procedures on public hearings and public access to information on decision-making." [53]

Democratic anger over the Quayle Council led to a serious effort to cut off funding for the unit. The House voted—largely along party lines—to terminate funding for the Council.[54] The Senate did not include a similar provision and the conference dropped the House provision. The message, however, was unmistakable: The Quayle Council would have to clean up its act.

The Press

It is easy to summarize press reaction to the Council on Competitiveness: It was virulent. News stories rarely cast the Council in a favorable light, and most focused on the controversy it aroused. Virtually no coverage portrayed the Council uncovering ill-advised regulations or making policy more sensible and cost-effective by forcing an agency to revise some rules.

Critical editorials focused on the Council's warm relations with big-business lobbies, its lack of technical expertise on the issues it dealt with, its secrecy, Allan Hubbard's alleged conflict of interest, and the substance of the policies that the Council wanted to pursue. The *Seattle Post-Intelligencer* called the Council a "goofy idea." [55] The *Los Angeles Times* asked Congress to "investigate reports that the council is trying to sabotage the Clean Air Act of 1990." [56] The *Atlanta Constitution* warned that the "Council will fight hard to keep in the dark its tawdry mission: helping businesses to circumvent government regulations designed to protect the rest of us." [57] In its habitually succinct manner, *USA Today* said bluntly, "Vice President Quayle should abandon his back-door attempt to subvert environmental laws." [58] For reporters the story line was "good government." Not surprisingly, reporters found the secretive dealings between the Quayle Council and business lobbyists to be unsavory.

Some voices supported the Council. The *Wall Street Journal* noted with more than a little irony that "It wasn't so long ago that Vice-President Dan Quayle was said to be Washington's village idiot. All of a sudden he's become its scheming Rasputin. This can only mean he's begun to accomplish something."[59] Yet the negative image of the Council led Republicans to let the body fend for itself. President Bush was largely silent. Although they supported the Council, few congressional Republicans saw much to be gained by speaking out on the Council's behalf. Business lobbyists who dealt with the Council were not in a very good position to defend it: their claims of the Council's effectiveness would be a tacit admission of big-business influence at the highest reaches of government. A press aide on the Council's staff defended it against the flood of accusations, but the Council's public relations were insignificant and ineffective.

Despite the political invective, the debate among liberal lobbyists, members of Congress, the media, and the Council on Competitiveness did at times deal with the substantive issues of separation of powers and administrative law. Nevertheless, the debate about the appropriate role of centralized regulatory review was colored by many fictions. On the liberal side, the main fiction was that the normal rule-making process was a technical, largely nonpolitical process that followed the dictates of the Administrative Procedure Act. Civil servants with scientific expertise in the subject gather data, read the written comments submitted to the agency, and then, after routine review by their political superiors, publish the finalized regulations in the *Federal Register*. The liberals' claim that the creation of the Quayle Council introduced politics into the rule-making process calls to mind the police chief in *Casablanca* who professes to be shocked to learn that there is gambling going on in Rick's Cafe.

The Quayle Council's main fiction was that it followed a fair and open process, and that those affected by regulatory decisions influenced by the Council had satisfactory redress. One Council staffer claimed that "we had a policy to meet with whoever asked for a meeting." Responding to criticism, the vice president wrote in the *Washington Post* that "the Council stands with the worker, the consumer, and the businessman against unelected, selfish and increasingly powerful special interests."[60] Even allowing for the normal rhetorical license that must be granted to high government officials, the Quayle Council's public stance about its regulatory-review process strained credulity. The Council was not open to meeting with anyone who wanted to meet with it, and groups representing workers and consumers were anything but welcome. And to those who felt aggrieved because of the Quayle Council's process, the Council's suggested remedy was more than a little disingenuous. Allan Hubbard defended the Council by declaring that "whenever a regulation is issued that someone thinks is inconsistent with a statute, all they have to do is to take it to court, and the court will adjudicate the matter."[61] Conservatives usually do not propose ways of lengthening the policy-making process.

The vice president and his staffers suffered from a certain blindness about the process the Council used in reviewing agency regulations. It

340 Berry and Portney

was unrealistic for them to believe that they could follow a process that openly relied on meetings with big business lobbyists, excluded other groups, kept no records, treated congressional Democrats with contempt, and generated a tidal wave of bad publicity, and expect to maintain the unit's political viability.

More than anything else it was the use of pleadings from big business lobbyists that discredited the Council. The public image that practice created was poisonous. Council staffers hoped they would be seen as government officials trying to work through complex regulatory problems with those directly affected by them. Instead they were seen by most as engaging in traditional Washington politics and dispensing favors to the privileged few. The Council's problems were compounded by its failure to apply a coherent and systematic philosophy of economic regulation or to rely on any particular tool of regulatory analysis. As a result, the staff convinced few beyond the conservative faithful that they were doing anything but fixing problems for interest groups with which they sympathized. The staff resented this "fixer" image; they held a sincere belief that their work was not troubleshooting for interest groups, but repairing the damage that overregulation was doing to the economy. They avoided casework and stuck to issues that were precedent setting or that involved significant sums of money.

After the House voted to cut the Council's funding, the Council staff came to realize that the process had to be changed. One member of the staff said that their plans for Bush's second term included reaching out to their interest group adversaries, "to invite them in." In other words, the Council was making plans for its own strategic accommodation.

Ideal Systems

This analysis of the Council on Competitiveness leads to three evaluative questions. First, did the Quayle Council achieve the goals set for it? Second, what can we conclude from the experience of the Quayle Council about future efforts to centralize regulatory review? And finally, what does the Quayle Council teach us about the best way to organize White House-interest group relations? These last two questions are really questions about ideal systems: How should future presidents and their aides proceed in building structures to review regulations and manage interest group access?

The Council's Success

Evaluating the success of the Quayle Council is not easy. There are no accepted standards by which to judge it, no comprehensive database, and only very general policy goals articulated by the vice president and his staffers. The Council's avowed intent was to make the American economy more competitive by reducing the inefficiencies imposed by regulation. Even if "more competitive" could be defined and operationalized, it would be unfair to hold the Council to this criterion. It existed for too short a time and had too few resources to exert the kind of influence that would make our economy more competitive in the world marketplace.

It is fair, however, to judge the Quayle Council's level of success in three areas. First, did the Council's efforts change the way regulations were written in the Bush administration? Clearly, President Bush and Vice President Quayle were interested in getting their agency heads to think more critically about the economic impact of the rules they were writing. We have little doubt that the Council had an impact on the way regulations were written, although that impact has not been, and perhaps cannot be, measured. Significantly, the vice president was willing to spend time and political capital within the administration to give muscle to the Council. Although they met resistance at some agencies, Council staffers found other agencies, such as Commerce, Treasury, and Transportation, very cooperative in reviewing regulations that came under scrutiny. In short, agency heads knew that they could not ignore the Council on Competitiveness.

Second, was the Quayle Council successful in institutionalizing a new way of matching presidential resources and incentives with a structure for carrying out administration goals? At the beginning of this paper we described the evolution of centralized regulatory control in the White House. Over time presidents have tried to increase their control over administrative rule making and have used different administrative arrangements to enhance their influence. The Council on Competitiveness offered a new approach, but it is an approach unlikely to be followed by future presidents. As presidents and their aides think about how to centralize regulatory review, they are likely to regard the Quayle Council model as a failure. Its interest group base, the conflict with Congress that it generated, and the open fights that emerged between it and EPA make it an unattractive design. The Clinton administration disbanded the Council immediately upon taking office but has taken some initial steps toward establishing White House oversight of rule making and has given Vice President Al Gore a leading role. The vice president can intervene in agency rule making, but in direct contrast to the Quayle Council he can only do so at the request of an agency. He cannot intervene at the behest of an interest group and any actions he takes are to be made public.[62]

A final question to ask about the Quayle Council was whether it contributed to a political rehabilitation of the vice president. Whatever the value of centralizing regulatory review, a clear part of the Council's agenda was to give the vice president a more important role in the administration and to convey the impression that he was a man of substance and intelligence. The verdict here is split. Among political elites Quayle did help himself. Over time his reputation for effectiveness and influence grew, and he became increasingly popular with the conservative wing of the Republican party. The Competitiveness Council was seen as a source of conservative policy initiatives as well as a backbone for an administration whose conservative credentials were suspect. With the broader public, the Competitiveness Council did nothing to erase the image of Quayle as a lightweight who was unfit to take over the job of president of the United States. During his last two years in office, while the Quayle Council was active, Quayle's favorability rating in the Gallup Poll dropped.[63]

Organizing Regulatory Review

Our overall conclusion about the Bush administration's attempt at centralizing regulatory review can be stated simply: The Council on Competitiveness was the wrong means to the right end. It is foolish of presidents *not* to institute some form of regulatory review. President Bush and OMB director Darman made a serious error by deemphasizing OIRA review of agency rule making. The strong forces pushing agency administrators toward strategic accommodation make it necessary for presidents to exert control over the rule-making process. A president wants to lead the executive branch in a particular direction, but the broad themes he sounds in outlining that direction will not be sufficient guidance to agency administrators. Presidents need ways of enforcing discipline on administrators, both in terms of budgets and policy. It is easy for agency heads, enveloped in a conflictual environment, to rationalize that they are doing the president's bidding by finding a compromise on a pending rule.

How can presidents best enhance the goals of their administration through centralized regulatory review? How can their resources be used to build institutions and processes that will bring greater White House control over the content of regulations? We think presidents would be wise to follow these three principles in designing their review process:

Regulatory Review Should be Centralized in OMB. The appropriate place for White House review of regulations is the Office of Management and Budget. OIRA or some other office in OMB is the best choice for centralized review because adequate staff are available and because Congress will likely give OMB more leeway for regulatory oversight than it will allow the president's personal staff. Presidents prefer the political responsiveness of their own staff to the neutral competence of career bureaucrats. With guidance from political appointees, however, OMB staffers can provide the appropriate data and analysis along with enhanced credibility for regulatory review.[64] Moreover, it is difficult for the president (or vice president) to command the resources necessary to staff a new unit large enough to systematically review all significant agency regulations.

Critics of centralized regulatory review are quite right in arguing that such review is a means of "politicizing" the administrative process. That is precisely what is so valuable about it: Regulatory oversight by the

White House appropriately gives the president's electoral coalition greater say in regulatory policy. But if White House review is simply a means of letting dissatisfied interest groups reargue a case they have just lost before Congress or an agency, or if it is used as an excuse to flout congressional intent or ignore the Administrative Procedure Act, then the case for centralized oversight is seriously weakened.

Regulatory Review Should not Be Driven by Interest Group Appeals. Using regulatory review to promote the will of the majority is justifiable; using it to satisfy interest group complaints discredits it. Such a process also invites congressional retribution. It is not possible to muzzle interest groups or to keep them from lobbying on regulatory matters. This lobbying, however, should be channeled toward departments and agencies. As we argue below, there are substantial incentives for the president to minimize interest group access to the White House.

Regulatory Review Should Be Systematic and Analytical. The Quayle Council was damaged by its inability to develop a coherent and defensible set of cost-benefit criteria. Justifying its intervention on the grounds that it was preventing the overregulation of business was a satisfactory explanation to staunch Republicans. To more dispassionate observers, the Council's review of regulations lacked rigor. The savings to industry that it claimed seemed to be derived from calculations that were more than a little suspect. Centralized regulatory review will gain legitimacy from systematic, rigorously applied cost-benefit criteria.

A strong component of regulatory review should be the clearance of agency proposals before formal rule making begins. This was part of the original design of centralized regulatory review implemented by the Reagan White House. Ideally, White House preferences should be expressed as guidelines to administrators, who should retain some flexibility in achieving those goals in the drafting process. Publicly rebuking agency heads by telling them to rewrite regulations they have already developed, as the Quayle Council did with EPA head Reilly, should be avoided.

Building a regulatory review system with these three attributes would not come without costs. The greatest assets of the Quayle Council—the active involvement of the Vice President and the ideological zeal of Hubbard, McIntosh, and other staffers—could be lost in a system that is overly reliant on OMB. This is why it is crucial that effective political leadership be a part of any structure for overseeing administrative rule making. Inevitably, there will be trade-offs between political responsiveness and universal credibility.

Structuring Interest Group Relations

If centralizing interest group access should not be a goal of presidents, how should they structure their relations with advocacy organizations? In Moe's language, what institutional structure is congruent with the president's incentives and resources? We suggest that congruence will be approached when the relationship between the White House and advocacy groups is structured in accord with three guiding principles:

Interest Groups Must Be Easily and Immediately Accessible for Mobilizing and Informing Their Members. The greatest value interest groups present to the White House is that they can help to mobilize public opinion on behalf of the president's agenda. In an era when publicly selling his program is one of the most important requirements of the president's job, interest groups represent a valuable resource that can be utilized to the White House's benefit. The ideal structure for the White House is somewhat analogous to the data on the hard disk of a computer: Interest groups should be instantly available with just a few keystrokes but should otherwise remain dormant, waiting to be called upon. But how does the White House build a structure in which the interest groups remain on disk rather than becoming active on their own accord and overloading the institution with more demands than the president and his aides can handle? The next two principles provide part of the answer.

The White House Should Keep Interest Groups in a Marginalized Position. This may seem counterintuitive. Should not the White House try to maintain and expand its supporting coalition by doing its best to make various constituencies feel highly valued by the president? For the White House interest group relations are a two-level game. To rank-and-file members of or identifiers with an interest group, the White House does want to communicate that it regards that constituency as something special. At another level, the White House wants Washington-based lobbyists for the same groups to feel highly privileged if allowed a small amount of access to the White House. To prevent overload, but to give interest groups some incentive to cooperate, the White House must allow the *chance* of access. This is why the OPL is structured not as a policy-making body but as one that offers lobbyists the possibility that their pleas will be passed on to higher-level White House staffers who have the power to do something on their behalf. The White House is able to get away with this because its relationship with any given interest group is clearly asymmetric: What the White House can do for any individual interest group is much, much greater than what that interest group can do for the White House.

Interest Groups Should Not Be Led to Believe That Agency Decisions Can Be Appealed to the White House. This is the corollary of the principle that centralized regulatory review should not operate on the basis of interest group appeals. If the White House is seen as an appeals court in the rulemaking process, the authority of agencies is weakened, creating incentives for groups that support the administration to harden their bargaining position with the agency writing the rules. To keep groups marginalized, the White House must make them believe that it is not likely to intervene on their behalf when they do not get the regulations they prefer.

Notes

1. Bob Davis, "Home Builders Used Quayle Council to Help Ease Disabled-Access Rules," *Wall Street Journal*, June 30, 1992.

2. David S. Broder and Bob Woodward, "Quayle's Quest: Curb Rules, Leave 'No Fingerprints,'" *Washington Post*, January 9, 1992.

3. For a review of presidential efforts to gain control over rule-making processes, see *Regulatory Review Sunshine Act*, 102d Cong., 2d sess., 1992, S. Rep. 102-256. Also see Howard Ball, *Controlling Regulatory Sprawl: Presidential Strategies from Nixon to Reagan* (Westport, Conn.: Greenwood Press, 1984).

4. Terry M. Moe, "The Politicized Presidency," in *The New Direction in American Politics*, ed. John E. Chubb and Paul E. Peterson (Washington, D.C.: Brookings, 1985), 238.

5. Ibid., 239.

6. Ibid., 245.

7. Richard P. Nathan, *The Plot That Failed* (New York: John Wiley, 1975).

8. Quoted in Howard Ball, "Presidential Control of the Federal Bureaucracy," in *Federal Administrative Agencies: Essays on Power and Politics*, ed. Howard Ball (Englewood Cliffs, N.J.: Prentice-Hall, 1984), 217.

9. Ibid.

10. *Regulatory Review Sunshine Act*, 13.

11. On the impact of the Reagan administration on the national bureaucracy, see Peter M. Benda and Charles H. Levine, "Reagan and the Bureaucracy," in *The Reagan Legacy*, ed. Charles O. Jones (Chatham, N.J.: Chatham House, 1988), 102-142; and Elizabeth Sanders, "The Presidency and the Bureaucratic State," in *The Presidency and the Political System*, 3d ed., ed. Michael Nelson (Washington, D.C.: Congressional Quarterly, 1990), 409-442.

12. Ball, *Federal Administrative Agencies*, 219.

13. *Regulatory Review Sunshine Act*, 13.

14. Ibid., 16.

15. *Paperwork Reduction Amendments of 1984*, S. Rep. 98-576, 98th Cong., 2d sess. (1984), 6, 8.

16. Quoted in Ball, *Federal Administrative Agencies*, 219.

17. Ibid., 220.

18. *Regulatory Review Sunshine Act*, 20.

19. Ibid.

20. Kirk Victor, "Quayle's Quiet Coup," *National Journal*, July 6, 1991, 1677.

21. All unattributed quotations come from personal interviews conducted with the understanding that the speaker would not be identified.

22. In 1992 McIntosh succeeded Hubbard as executive director of the Council. He had spent a few years in private practice and served at the Justice Department and the White House. Keith Schneider, "Administration's Regulation Slayer has Achieved a Perilous Prominence," *New York Times*, June 30, 1992.

23. Two major studies of Quayle have found him to be capable and politically astute. See Richard F. Fenno, Jr., *The Making of a Senator: Dan Quayle* (Washington, D.C.: CQ Books, 1989; and David S. Broder and Bob Woodward, *The Man Who Would be President: Dan Quayle* (New York: Simon and Schuster, 1992). Broder and Woodward's work first ran as a series in the *Washington Post* between January 5 and January 12, 1992.

24. Sidney Blumenthal, "All the President's Wars," *New Yorker*, December 28, 1992, and January 4, 1993, 68-69.

25. Joseph A. Pika, "Opening Doors for Kindred Souls: The White House Office of Public Liaison," in *Interest Group Politics*, 3d ed., ed. Allan J. Cigler and Burdett

Loomis (Washington, D.C.: CQ Books, 1991), 287-290.

26. Ibid., 294.

27. Stephen Hess, *Organizing the Presidency* (Washington, D.C.: Brookings Institution, 1976).

28. See Mark Peterson, "The Presidency and Organized Interests: White House Patterns of Interest Group Liaison," *American Political Science Review* 86 (September 1992): 612-625.

29. Peterson, "The Presidency and Organized Interest Groups," 617-618.

30. On Americans' perception of lobbying, see Alan Rosenthal, *The Third House* (Washington, D.C.: CQ Books, 1993), 7-8.

31. John H. Kessel, "The Structures of the Reagan White House," *American Journal of Political Science* 27 (May 1984): 231-258.

32. The vacancy at OIRA became prolonged because of two events. First, Congress did not act on the nomination of James F. Blumstein, largely because of concern over renewal of the Paperwork Reduction Act and the Bush administration's use of the act to authorize regulatory intervention. As one Democratic staffer noted, "If the bill doesn't pass, Mr. Blumstein doesn't get confirmed." *Congressional Quarterly Weekly Report*, October 27, 1990, 3602. Second, the nominee, when finally given the opportunity to testify at his confirmation hearing, gave a less than stellar performance. As one lobbyist put it, "It was a bumbling congressional hearing. This guy [Blumstein] came to Washington, put his foot in his mouth, went back to Tennessee, and was never heard from again."

33. Broder and Woodward, "Quayle's Quest."

34. Taken from the October 24, 1991, testimony of David Doniger, then an attorney for the Natural Resources Defense Council, before the Senate Committee on Government Operations, in *Regulatory Review Sunshine Act*, 22.

35. Michael Duffy, "Need Friends in High Places?" *Time*, November 4, 1991, 25.

36. This figure comes from correspondence between William G. Rosenberg of EPA and Rep. Henry Waxman, December 9, 1991, cited in Nancy Watzman and Michael Waldman, *The Quayle Council on Competitiveness: The Campaign Finance Connection* (Washington, D.C.: Public Citizen's Congress Watch, 1992), 15.

37. Daniel Issac, "They Can't Compete," *Legal Times*, September 7, 1992, 19.

38. Ibid., 1, 18-20.

39. John P. Heinz, Edward O. Laumann, Robert L. Nelson, and Robert H. Salisbury, *The Hollow Core* (Cambridge, Mass.: Harvard University Press, 1993).

40. Jeffrey M. Berry, "Subgovernments, Issue Networks, and Political Conflict," in *Remaking American Politics*, ed. Richard A. Harris and Sidney M. Milkis (Boulder, Colo.: Westview, 1989), 239-260.

41. Michael S. Greve, "Why Defunding the Left Failed," *Public Interest* 89 (Fall 1987): 91-106; and Mark A. Peterson and Jack L. Walker, "Interest Group Responses to Partisan Change," in *Interest Group Politics*, 2d ed., ed. Allan J. Cigler and Burdett A. Loomis (Washington, D.C.: CQ Books, 1986), 162-182.

42. Legislative reports are documents accompanying legislation sent to the floor of the House or Senate. They are crucial guides to legislative intent.

43. Jeffrey M. Berry, *Feeding Hungry People* (New Brunswick, N.J.: Rutgers University Press, 1984).

44. Joel D. Aberbach, *Keeping a Watchful Eye* (Washington, D.C.: Brookings Institution, 1990).

45. Jonathan Rauch, "The Regulatory President," *National Journal*, November 30, 1991, 2902-2906.

46. Christine Triano and Nancy Watzman, *All the Vice President's Men: How the Quayle Council on Competitiveness Secretly Undermines Health, Safety and Environmental Programs* (Washington, D.C.: OMB Watch and Public Citizen's Congress Watch, 1991), 9-11.

47. Jeffrey M. Berry, "Citizen Groups and the Changing Nature of Interest Group Politics in America," *Annals of the American Academy of Political and Social Sciences* 528 (July 1993): 30-41.

48. Steven Kelman, "Adversary and Cooperationist Institutions for Conflict Resolution in Public Policymaking," *Journal of Policy Analysis and Management* 11 (1992): 195.

49. Triano and Watzman, *All the Vice-President's Men*; Christine Triano and Nancy Watzman, *Conflict of Interest on the Council on Competitiveness* (Washington, D.C.: OMB Watch and Public Citizen's Congress Watch, 1991); Watzman and Waldman, *The Quayle Council on Competitiveness: The Campaign Finance Connection*; Nancy Watzman and Christine Triano, *The Hidden Story: What Bush and Quayle Don't Say About the Regulatory Moratorium* (Washington, D.C.: Public Citizen and OMB Watch, 1992); and Nancy Watzman and Christine Triano, *Voodoo Accounting: The Toll of President Bush's Regulatory Moratorium; January-August 1992* (Washington, D.C.: Public Citizen's Congress Watch and OMB Watch, 1992).

50. Kelly Richmond, "Coalition Takes on Quayle's Council on Competitiveness," *Boston Globe*, June 24, 1992.

51. "Complaint About Quayle's Council," *San Francisco Chronicle*, August 21, 1992.

52. The debate on the constitutional issues underlying the conflict over centralized administrative review is detailed in *Presidential Control of Agency Rulemaking*, Report prepared for the House Committee on Energy and Commerce, 97th Cong., 1st sess. (1981).

53. Woodward and Broder, "Quayle's Quest."

54. Kenneth J. Cooper, "Divided House Bars Funds for Quayle," *Washington Post*, July 2, 1992.

55. "Empty Economic Policy," *Seattle Post-Intelligencer*, January 23, 1992.

56. "Competitiveness Council, or Hit Squad?", *Los Angeles Times*, November 24, 1991.

57. "A Look into Mr. Quayle's Council," *Atlanta Constitution*, December 2, 1991.

58. "Go Easy on Trashing Vital Federal Regulations," *USA Today*, April 29, 1992.

59. "Shooting Quayle," *Wall Street Journal*, November 25, 1991.

60. Dan Quayle, "Protecting America's Greatness," *Washington Post*, December 8, 1991.

61. Victor, "Quayle's Quiet Coup," 1676.

62. Executive Order, "Regulatory Planning and Review," the White House, September 30, 1993; "Memorandum for the Administrator, Office of Information and Regulatory Affairs," the White House, September 30, 1993; and Bob Davis, "Clinton Orders New Regulatory Process in Effort to Reduce Influence-Peddling," *Wall Street Journal*, October 1, 1993.

63. This seems to have little to do with the Competitiveness Council but rather reflects the decline in the fortunes of the Bush administration, as well as the misfortunes of Quayle himself. See "Quayle and his Predecessors," *American Enterprise* 2 (May/June 1991): 99; and *Gallup Poll Monthly* (January 1993): 10.

64. Francis E. Rourke, "Responsiveness and Neutral Competence in American Bureaucracy," *Public Administration Review* 52 (November/December 1992): 539-546.

16

The Japanese Lobby in Washington: How Different Is It?

Ronald J. Hrebenar and Clive S. Thomas

Americans have long viewed organized political interests with disquiet. Although we recognize their inevitability in a free society, we nevertheless tend to suspect their motivations. Particularly troublesome have been foreign lobbies, which have tried to influence both domestic and foreign policy in Washington on behalf of other nations, at times seemingly at the expense of the national interest of the United States. Of all the foreign lobbies, that of Japan has commanded the most attention, particularly in recent years, as Americans have strived to compete effectively with the nation's chief trade rival.

In this chapter Ronald Hrebenar and Clive Thomas describe the growth and development of the Japan lobby as a domestic political force, starting with its beginnings prior to World War II. In their view, the Japan lobby is difficult to understand because it has so many actors and focuses, ranging from cultural organizations that aim to create favorable attitudes toward the Japanese in the minds of U.S. citizens to professional economic organizations and direct lobbying operations that represent Japanese business interests in the United States. They suggest that one of the major reasons for the success of the Japan lobby is that the Japanese have been very skillful in cultivating "intellectual America" by making donations and grants to U.S. universities, foundations, and charitable institutions and by magnifying the voices of Americans already favorably oriented toward Japanese culture. In the policy process much of the success of the Japan lobby is due not to the use of Japanese personnel but to the skillful employment of an "insider" lobby of former government officials, professional Washington lobbyists, super-lawyers, and political consultants whose services the Japan lobby has purchased.

The authors conclude that although Japan's lobbying efforts are extensive—reflecting their economic stake in their relationship with the United States—those efforts do not differ markedly from the lobbying efforts of other nations such as Canada and Great Britain. The problem is rather that "there appear to be few in Washington whose services cannot be rented if not purchased."

W hen Michael Crichton's novel *Rising Sun* was released as a motion picture in the summer of 1993, there was considerable reaction from Japanese Americans, native Japanese, Asian Americans, and even non-Japanese Americans. On the *New York Times* op-ed page Roger M. Pang wrote:

> The Asians are the villains.... Mr. Crichton's larger purpose is to present a dark vision of Japan's economic ambitions.... [T]he book portrays the Japanese as hard-edged exploiters of an increasingly vulnerable America.[1]

Pang's comments echo the concerns of many Japanese regarding the stereotypes many Americans hold about contemporary Japan, concerns that extend to cultural misunderstandings, economic difficulties, and political confusions. The Japanese government and many individual Japanese are also convinced that many Americans simply do not understand enough about Japanese culture to appreciate differences in behavior in the two societies. They are also convinced that many Americans, including some of the nation's top political and business leaders, blame Japan for the inability of the United States to compete in recent years and for American political problems in various parts of the world. A *New York Times*-CBS News-Tokyo Broadcasting poll of July 6, 1993, supported these conclusions. Covering Japanese and American attitudes toward each other, the poll found that nearly two-thirds of Japanese polled described their country's relations with the United States as "unfriendly." This was the highest such negative Japanese response ever recorded in these polls.[2]

For all of the above reasons, Japanese organizations have spent billions of dollars in recent years to influence American attitudes toward Japan, Japanese culture, Japanese politics, and Japanese business and its practices. In his 1990 book, *Agents of Influence*, Pat Choate dubbed these efforts "the Japan Lobby."[3]

The Origins of the Japan Lobby: Prewar and Postwar Versions

The earliest manifestation of the Japan lobby, as Mindy Kotler has noted, was largely comprised of American missionaries of the late nineteenth and early twentieth centuries who served in Japan and returned to the United States to plead the case of Japan as a potential Asian, Christian ally. The central thrust of the advocate missionaries was the goal of educating Americans on the unique nature of Japan and the creation of an American model for Japanese political development. The missionary advocates sought a Christian Japan, urged the end of anti-Japanese immigration laws, and defended Japanese expansionary activities in Asia.[4]

In the years preceding World War II, the Japanese government and a few American corporate interests that did business with Japan lobbied for

Japanese interests in the United States. One lawyer, James Lee Kaufman, represented nearly all of the American businesses operating in prewar Japan. Of course, all of this lobbying ceased with the onset of war in 1941.[5]

The postwar Japan lobby focused on the threat of communism to Japan and to American interests in the Pacific. American businessmen sought to rebuild Japan as a potential market for American products.[6] One early organization typifies the early pro-Japan American advocacy groups, the American Council on Japan (ACJ). The ACJ sought to bring Japan into the American mutual security system and promoted the role of American business in the reconstruction of Japan. One of its leaders was Harry F. Kern, the foreign editor of *Newsweek* magazine. (Kotler argues that *Newsweek* was seeking a Japan focus to compete with *Time* and the latter's focus on China.[7])

Harry Kern capitalized on his two-nation political access by opening up his own consulting firm, Foreign Reports, in the mid-1950s. He developed a list of Japanese clients, to which several Arab companies were added. Soon after, Mike Masaoka, long-time spokesman of the Japanese American Citizens League in Washington, D.C., opened up a consulting-lobbying operation for Japanese interests. Although Masaoka was a pioneer in representing Japanese trade interests, he defended his work as a "duty to U.S.-Japan relations" and an attempt to "keep Japan on America's side."[8] William Tanaka, a Japanese-American lawyer, opened the first law firm to represent Japanese business interests in the District of Columbia. Kotler designates Tanaka as the first Japanese "hired gun" who detached emotional concerns from the task of representing Japan.

Japan also sought to employ lobbyists who were not of Japanese extraction to represent its interests. One of the first "celebrities" hired was 1948 GOP presidential nominee Thomas E. Dewey, enlisted in 1959 to lobby against restrictions on Japanese cotton products. The Japan External Trade Organization (JETRO), a spinoff of the Ministry of International Trade and Industry (MITI), paid Dewey $500,000 over five years.[9]

The Japanese continued to Americanize their lobbying efforts during the 1950s as various textile conflicts dominated trade discussions between the two nations. Various "front organizations" were created to achieve an American look. Mike Masaoka created the American Textile Importers Association, which was composed entirely of American companies whose interests paralleled those of the Japanese textile manufacturers. Washington, D.C., lawyers Nelson Stitt and Noel Hemmendinger founded another front organization, the U.S.-Japan Trade Council, which played a significant role in Japanese lobbying over the last three decades. Stitt and Hemmendinger were the first of a flood of U.S. government officials who would leave government service to represent Japanese interests.

The U.S.-Japan Trade Council used its annual budget of $300,000, most of which was provided by the Japanese Ministry of Foreign Affairs through its Japan Trade Promotion Office in New York City, to produce "intellectually respectable" and useful information for Washington opinion makers. The Japanese did not admit to controlling the U.S.-Japan Trade Council until the Department of Justice filed suit in 1976. The organization changed its name to the Japan Economic Institute and today openly acknowledges its funding from the Ministry of Foreign Affairs.

The next step in the growth of the Japan lobby came with the passage of the 1975 Trade Act, [10] which forced the Japanese (and others) to organize to deal with a more complex American trade-policy environment. The Japanese aggressively pursued American trade experts to represent Japan's side in the debates. One of the most important U.S. experts to sign on with the Japanese was Harold Malmgren, who had served as deputy special trade representative for President Ford and was one of the drafters of the Trade Act. Malmgren, one of the first expert lobbyists not to be a lawyer, successfully kept tariffs from being imposed on Japanese television sets in 1978. He received $300,000 for his three months of work on the case. Malmgren continues to work for the Japanese on trade issues but now functions as an information and communication conduit between Japan and the United States.

From the early 1960s, Japanese interests began to hire American advisers to teach them about American politics and how to influence American public policy. One of the most important of these teacher-advisers was Richard V. Allen, who later served as Richard Nixon's chief adviser on foreign policy and national security in the 1968 presidential campaign. After a stint on the National Security Council, Allen became deputy assistant to the president for international trade and economic policy. In 1980, Allen was Ronald Reagan's foreign policy and national security adviser during the presidential campaign. In the 1980 campaign the *Wall Street Journal* revealed that Allen had written in 1970 to a powerful Japanese political leader criticizing Japanese lobbying efforts and urging the Japanese to create an American-led lobbying machine. [11]

The Three Parts of the Japan Lobby

Although few organizations are pure examples of a particular type of lobby, one can divide them into three major subcategories: cultural, economic, and political. The Japan lobby comprises all three of these strains.

Japan's Cultural Lobby

Japan's cultural lobby centers on several large organizations headquartered in New York City. [12] These include the Japan Foundation, the Japan Society, and the United States-Japan Foundation. Two of these organizations—the foundations—essentially operate as funding sources for many other, largely American organizations that affect American attitudes toward Japan.

The Japan Foundation. The Japan Foundation—or *Kokusai Koryu Kikin*—is perhaps the best known of the Japanese cultural organizations in the United States. Founded as a special body of the Ministry of Foreign Affairs in October 1972, its aim is to deepen other nations' understanding of Japan, to promote better mutual understanding among nations, and to encourage friendship and goodwill.[13] Funded by the Japanese government and the Japanese private sector, its program budget had grown to Y15.74 billion by 1992. That same year it had a staff of 199 and fifteen overseas offices. New programs had been instituted, such as the Japanese Language Institute (July 1989), the ASEAN Cultural Center (1990), and the Center for Global Partnership (CGP, April 1991). The Japan Foundation had become the core organization of Japan's international cultural-exchange activities.

To accomplish its goals, the Japan Foundation promotes Japanese studies abroad by providing grants to organizations and offering financial assistance to researchers. It also supports Japanese-language education overseas (including salary assistance for full-time Japanese language instructors), student study tours, Japanese speech contests, the translation and publishing of Japanese materials, and the broadcasting of Japanese language educational television programs. All together, the Japan Foundation in 1992-1993 granted more than $2.9 million to 35 individuals and 236 institutions in the United States.

The Japan Foundation established the CGP for the specific purpose of improving relations between the United States and Japan. Offices were established in Tokyo and New York City. Among the issues the CGP placed on its initial agenda were world economics, disarmament, environmental and economic development, and various urban problems such as education and immigration. In fiscal year 1991, the CGP provided assistance to twenty-two projects in Japan and the United States. Among the major study grants were:

• Asia Pacific Association of Japan: "U.S.-Japan Dialogue on Japan: U.S. Regional Crisis Management and the UN"
• Brookings Institution: "Integrating the World Economy: The Next Steps"
• Council on Foreign Relations: "Redefining the U.S.-Japan Relationship"
• Japan Institute of International Affairs: "Japan-U.S. Environmental Center"

The CGP has also established other very significant projects in the general area of improving American understanding of Japan. It has assisted the Roper Center for Public Opinion Research at the University of Connecticut in the collection of Japanese public opinion polls. It also initiated and financed the establishment of the Japan Documentation Center within the Library of Congress for the purpose of improving U.S.

access to the latest information and publications on contemporary Japan. An important part of this new library is a collection of Japanese government publications and the published studies of Japanese think tanks.

However, perhaps the most important new project of the CGP is the establishment of the Abe Fellowships, named after the late Japanese foreign minister. The Abe Fellowship is awarded to academic researchers and specialists who "work to promote political research through mutual exchange between Japanese and U.S. specialists." The program is administered by the CGP, the U.S. Social Science Research Council, and the American Council of Learned Societies. In fiscal year (FY) 1991, fifteen U.S. and Japanese scholars were awarded fellowships, including Professor Robert Gilpin of Princeton University for a study entitled "Transformation of the Global Political Economy."

The CGP also administers a set of programs for promoting "mutual understanding on the regional and grassroots level." These public outreach programs promote public understanding of problems faced by both Japan and the United States and the raising of public awareness on global issues. They are targeted at educators, students, and other citizens.

Finally, the CGP makes substantial donations to several American universities to support the establishment or expansion of Japanese studies centers and programs. In FY 1991, these included Columbia University's Center for Japanese Economy and Business, Monterey Institute of International Studies' Center for East Asian Studies, Bowling Green State University, the Hoover Institute, Reischauer Institute of Japanese Studies at Harvard University and the Harvard University Center for International Affairs, San Diego State University, University of Chicago Center for East Asian Studies, and the University of Hawaii.

Japan-United States Friendship Commission. Perhaps the most unusual of the Japanese cultural organizations is the Japan-United States Friendship Commission (JUSFC), an independent agency of the U.S. government "dedicated to promoting mutual understanding and cooperation between the United States and Japan." It administers grant programs in support of Japanese studies in the United States, policy oriented research, public affairs and education, American studies in Japan, and the arts. The JUSFC was established by Congress in 1975 to administer a trust fund formed from part of the Japanese government's repayment for U.S. facilities built in Okinawa and later returned to Japan and for postwar American assistance to Japan. Annual income from the fund amounts to about $34 million. JUSFC is administered by a commission of U.S. officials including members of the Senate and House, representatives from the Department of State and the Department of Education, and the chairs of the national endowments for the arts and for the humanities.

A major part of JUSFC's budget goes into training the next generation of American Japanese scholars. To further this goal, programs have been started to provide for graduate student fellowships, graduate school faculty and curriculum development, library support, faculty research, language training, and general programs of public education. In general, the Commission seeks to fund very focused, collaborative research projects. Recent research has been funded through the Social Science Research Council and the University of California-Berkeley.

The Japan Society. The Japan Society uses grants from various foundations and from Japanese and American corporations to expand American understanding of Japan. Founded in 1907, the Society is the oldest Japanese cultural advocate in the United States. With a full-time staff of sixty, eight thousand individual members, and four thousand corporate members, it is also the largest. Cyrus Vance, the Society's 1992 chairman, noted in the organization's 1990-1991 report:

> As an organization devoted to enlightened and mutually enriching relations between the United States and Japan, the Japan Society had its work cut out for it this past year.... I sense real urgency about the danger of the negative trend characterizing mutual attitudes. We seem to be drifting rather mindlessly toward thinking of each other in adversarial terms.... This kind of challenge brings out the best in the Japan Society, its members and supporters.

The heart of the Japan Society's effort to promote mutual understanding is the U.S.-Japan Program which, with a staff of ten and three major orientations—corporate, public policy, and outreach/education, provides forums for discussion of the political, economic, business, and social issues that affect the two countries, as well as educational programs that promote cross-cultural understanding.

In 1990-1991, the Society held more than a hundred discussion meetings, conferences, and exchanges to foster better understanding between Japan and the United States. The New York City Japan Society schedules corporate meetings two or three times a month and holds business conferences two or three times a year.

The Japan Society's MacEachron Policy Forum has focused on security issues, women, the environment, and health care in Japan. In 1993-1994, it added to that list the issue of aging. That same year, the Forum sponsored twenty-seven luncheon discussion meetings featuring speakers such as Robert Reich, professor of political economy at Harvard University and later President Clinton's secretary of labor; Michael Boskin, chair of President Bush's Council of Economic Advisers; Koji Kakizawa, chair of the committee on foreign affairs in the lower house of the Japanese legislature; and former deputy prime minister Miyazawa. In the Distinguished Lecturer Program, Henry Kissinger spoke to more than four hundred guests.

The Society's outreach/education program sent sixteen experts on U.S.-Japan relations on speaking tours of thirty-four American cities. These caravans are usually made up of three-person teams consisting of a journalist, an academic, and a businessman who travel for ten days, meeting with groups and holding discussions with local Japan Society chapters.[14]

The Japan Society runs an extensive exchange program with three important subprograms. The U.S.-Japan Leadership Program sends eight to ten midcareer professionals to Japan for three to six months of basic orientation to Japanese society. In recent years, the exchangees have included several individuals who later moved into key positions in the Clinton administration, including HHS chief Donna Shalala. The 1990-1991 fellows included lawyers, academics, the staff director of a U.S. House subcommittee, the chief economic correspondent for *U.S. News and World Report*, and Juan Williams, a *Washington Post* staff writer.

In the Business Fellowships program, MBA students spend six weeks working for a Japanese corporation in Japan. The U.S.-Japan Parliamentary Exchange Program sends six to eight members of the Japanese Diet and an equal number of members of the U.S. Congress abroad for ten-day orientations to the other's country. The Japan Society tries to seek out members of Congress who are particularly aggressive toward Japan or active on trade issues.

The Japanese Economic Lobby

The Japanese economic lobby is composed of several types of professional organizations that fit together nicely to represent Japanese business interests. One part generates a tidal wave of general economic data and specific subsector analyses; another provides think-tank advocacy for Japanese economic policies; and others represent specific industries through trade associations.[15]

The Japan Economic Institute of America. Located in Washington, D.C., the Japan Economic Institute of America (JEIA)—the reconstituted and legitimized successor of the previously discussed U.S.-Japan Trade Council—is the primary source in the United States for economic and business data on Japan. JEIA is a unit of the Japanese Ministry of Foreign Affairs, which largely funds its operations. Those operations include hosting a series of seminars on Japan, with an emphasis on business and trade issues. However, its major contribution to the understanding of Japan lies in its three publications: the *Japan Economics Report* (weekly); the *Japan-U.S. Business Report* (monthly); and the *Japan Economic Survey* (monthly). JEIA also issues periodic reports on Japan. In recent years, these have covered Japanese fiscal policy, budgetary process, defense, trade competition, education, banking, foreign affairs, industrial policy, labor, political reform, U.S.-Japan trade relations, health policy, and the status of women. For those seeking detailed and current information on Japan, these publications are among the best in the world. The current president of JEIA is Arthur Alexander. With a doctorate in economics from Johns Hopkins

University, Alexander came from The Rand Corporation to head JEIA's staff of seven.

Other Organizations and Operations in the Economic Arena. C. Fred Bergsten is the head of a powerhouse that has had a profound effect on U.S.-Japanese economic relationships. Located in Washington, D.C., the Institute for International Economics (IIE) derives part of its research funding from Japanese sources. The organization is cited frequently in the *New York Times* and the *Washington Post.* Whenever a story is published on U.S. trade problems or Japanese economics, C. Fred Bergsten of the IIE seems to appear "to put the issue into proper perspective." Bergsten is also a favorite expert source of Hobart Rowen, the chief economics writer of the *Washington Post* and nationally syndicated columnist.

Information has always been the primary objective of Japanese organizations—inside and outside Japan—and Japan has developed a formidable information gathering network. The Japanese are voracious accumulators and consumers of information of all kinds: political, social, and economic. Much of the money the Japan lobby spends in the United States is allocated for the collection and interpretation of such information. The Japanese government, in particular, through its fifteen consulates in the United States, is a major collector of all types of hard data and opinion.[16] Complementing the consular operations of the Ministry of Foreign Affairs is the JETRO program of the Ministry of International Trade and Industry (MITI). The JETRO program not only promotes Japanese business, but also conducts so-called soft-side propaganda campaigns that use the provision of information as their vehicle.

Akio Morita, the head of Sony Corporation, founded a group of 160 Japanese companies with major investments in the United States. Originally named the Council for Better Investment in the United States, the group was renamed the Council for Better Corporate Citizenship in 1989. Now led by the powerful Japanese business association Keidanren, the Council's goal is to defeat adverse policies in the United States on both the state and federal levels.[17]

Japan's Political Lobby

Choate faults the Japan lobby for its recruitment of high-level American governmental officials to work for Japanese interests. The list of prominent Americans who have lobbied or consulted for Japan in recent years is indeed impressive:

- William Colby, director of central intelligence in the Reagan administration
- Richard Allen, President Reagan's National Security Adviser
- Frank Fahrenkopf, former chair of the Republican National Committee

- Robert Strauss, former chair of the Democratic National Committee
- Stanton Anderson, former deputy assistant secretary of state
- Stuart Eizenstat, former White House domestic policy chief
- Henry Kissinger, former secretary of state
- Ron Brown, former chair of the Democratic National Committee and President Clinton's secretary of commerce

The above is only a small sample of the prominent Americans who work for Japanese interests. As Holstein comments, the longer list reads "like a who's who of Washington's toughest, savviest political operators."[18] Brother International Corporation has used Hogan & Hartson to represent its interests; Fujisawa USA hired Hill and Knowlton. Toyota Motor Sales USA has its own lobbyist, Mary Khim. Toyota's major rival, Nissan, pulled a major coup in 1991 when it engaged Tim MacCarthy, the lobbyist for the Motor Vehicle Manufacturing Association of the United States, to direct Nissan North America's governmental and industry affairs. Pointing to the fact that Nissan has the largest automobile manufacturing plant in the United States, MacCarthy argues that "We're a good American company."[19]

Because of the importance of trade issues in the U.S.-Japan relationship, the Office of the U.S. Trade Representative has become a training ground for Japanese lobbyists. Several years of service in the federal government produce the experience and connections required to secure a lucrative position with a Japanese corporation or an American law firm representing Japanese interests.[20] As U.S. Trade Representative in 1977-1979, Robert Strauss met frequently with Japanese governmental and corporate leaders. In 1990, he and his company arranged the merger of Matsushita Electric Corporation and MCA, the Hollywood media giant. Strauss is described as a lawyer-lobbyist "who can do everything."[21]

Evaluating the Japan Lobbies: Stakes, Strategy, Spending

Pat Choate's 1990 book, *Agents of Influence: How Japan's Lobbyists in the United States Manipulate America's Political and Economic System*, created a torrid debate in American, and Japanese, policy circles.

> Japan's campaign for America serves one very important purpose: to influence the outcome of political decisions in Washington, D.C., that directly affect Japanese corporate and economic interests, decisions where every day hundreds of millions of dollars—and cumulatively billions of dollars—are on the line.[22]

Choate argued that Japan had constructed a powerhouse lobby in the United States that had effectively championed Japanese interests, sometimes to the detriment of American industry and labor.[23] Choate later argued that the Japanese "lobbying corps constituted virtually a bipartisan shadow government."[24]

Clearly, the stakes Japan has in continuing good relations with the United States are enormous. The potential for difficulty with Congress, the various executive branch departments and agencies, and even in the states is also enormous. In this section we will assess the methods and the scale of Japanese lobbying efforts against the stakes Japan has in its trading relationship with the United States. The key question will be that of the commensurability of stakes, strategy, and spending.

Choate's Critique

Choate argues that fundamental political differences between Japan and the United States contribute to the success of the Japan lobby. Among these differences are the following:

- America allows its top governmental officials to become the lobbyists of foreign nations.
- America allows its politicians and parties to accept money from organizations controlled by foreigners.
- America allows foreign interests to stage-manage grassroots political campaigns among its people.
- America allows foreign nations to influence its policy proposal process by investing in "think tanks."
- America allows foreign nations to manipulate the curricula taught in its elementary schools, high schools, and colleges.[25]

The amounts spent by the Japan lobby, charges Choate, are huge.

Japan is running an ongoing political campaign in America as if it were a third major party. It is spending at least $100 million each year to hire hundreds of Washington, D.C. lobbyists, super-lawyers, former high-ranking public officials, public relations specialists, political advisers— even former presidents. It is spending another $300 million each year to shape American public opinion through its nationwide local political network.[26]

The Japanese, like other foreign interests, have tended to choose former government insiders as lobbyists, at least until recently. Although the services of such individuals typically do not come cheap, there is considerable evidence to indicate that the Japanese believe they are getting their money's worth. William Holstein, the Japan correspondent for *Business Week*, writes of the business of "managing the Americans" in his book, *The Japanese Power Game*. As an illustration, Holstein relates a political joke going the rounds in Tokyo in 1990: "Washington is just as easy a place to do business as Jakarta. You can get anything done for a price."[27]

In 1993, Japanese interests hired more than 125 American law firms, economic consultants, and public relations firms.[28] As a case in point, Howard Baker, former U.S. senator and White House chief of staff under Ronald Reagan, wrote a very favorable article for the Spring 1992 issue of the prestigious journal, *Foreign Affairs*. The article analyzed U.S.-Japanese economic relations and recommended closer economic and political links between the two nations. It never mentioned that Howard Baker had been and continued to be a lobbyist and lawyer for Japanese corporations. Baker's law firm had helped negotiate the Matsushita takeover of the Hollywood media powerhouse MCA in 1990; for its work in the transaction Baker's firm earned more than $1.6 million. When William Hyland, the editor of *Foreign Affairs*, was asked if he had known about Baker's relationship with Japan before the article was accepted for publication, he responded: "I had no idea that Baker was a lobbyist when the article was submitted. If I had known, I would have had to think twice [about publishing it]." Hyland noted that Baker's first draft had been too mild in its treatment of Japan; it was revised to make the analysis more critical.[29]

One of Tokyo's problems is trouble may occur at so many points in the policy-making process. Expert help to deal with these potential trouble points often is very specialized. Take, for example, two of the major lobbying firms representing foreign interests in Washington, D.C.: Black, Manafort, Stone & Kelly and Neill & Co. The *forte* of Black, Manafort had been its long-term relationship with the Republican White House. However, Black, Manafort has had almost no access with the Democratic Congress. Neill & Co. has had great congressional access, but, until Bill Clinton's election in 1992, had little executive branch access.[30]

The Japan lobby has been particularly effective in dealing with Congress and especially congressional staff. This tactic began in a serious manner in the early 1980s. In 1984, a major Japanese research institute published a study of the significance of congressional staff in the policy-making process. The study received a great deal of informed attention in Japan and was republished in summary forms in influential Japanese media sources. The Japanese Embassy in Washington now assigns four officials to become experts on congressional staff members, and the Japan lobby in general spends a great deal of money wining and dining congressional staff in parties with the ambassador and many smaller lunches. Key staffers are offered expense-paid fact-finding trips to Japan. Noting that many other nations have picked up this tactic from the Japanese, Choate argues that much of the opposition to ethics reform legislation comes from congressional staff members who worry about not being eligible for jobs with foreign lobbies after their government service is finished.[31]

In Good Company

Media reporting of the huge expenditures of the Japan lobby make it appear as though only the Japanese are spending big money to influence

American public policy. There is much evidence, however, to indicate that the Japanese are not the only big spenders in the foreign lobbying game. The Kuwaiti government in 1990-1991 reportedly spent millions of dollars on lobbying and public relations to secure American support for the Gulf War. The substantial Kuwaiti account was only a small part of the billings of Hill and Knowlton's Washington, D.C. office—an estimated $38 million in 1990.[32] The same year, Hong Kong trading companies paid R. Marc Nuttle, the former executive director of the Republican National Congressional Campaign Committee, $200,000 to lobby on the renewal of China's favored trading status.[33]

Even the poorest, least developed nations have spent millions of dollars lobbying Washington. Kenya and Zaire pay $1 million a year to secure the lobbying services of Black, Manafort. Liberia pays about half that amount to Neill & Co. Solo lobbyist Bruce Cameron charges Third World nations such as Mozambique and Guatemala a minimum of $100,000 a year for lobbying services.

Among developed nations, Japan's reported expenditures, although high, are not wholly incommensurate with their economic relationship with the United States. The Canadian lobby spent about $22.7 million in 1992, compared to $60 million for Japan, $13 million for Germany, $12.8 million for France, and $11 million for Mexico.[34] Estimates of the lobbying expenditures of various nations vary depending on what is counted and how. One source suggests that in 1989 the Japanese were spending $45 million a year on public relations, $140 million on corporate philanthropy, and $30 million on academic research grants.[35] Like all estimates of lobbying expenditures heard and repeated in Washington these numbers are largely fiction, but they give some idea of the relative effort of various nations. Choate estimates the annual expenditures of the Japan lobby at $400 million, a figure he contrasts with the $402 million reported to have been paid by all foreign interests to their U.S. registered lobbyists in 1987.[36]

Mitchell's study of direct foreign investments and political action committees (PACs) found that in proportion to their economic stake in America the Swiss and Canadians were politically overrepresented in the United States compared to the Japanese. The companies in which the Japanese have invested were found to have a much smaller share of foreign money than was the case with Canadian and Swiss companies in this country.[37] When ownership was combined with PAC spending for 1987-1988, British companies emerged as the largest foreign participants in American politics; Japanese companies ranked sixth. With regard to their representation by lobbyists in Washington, Mitchell found that Japanese companies were not disproportionately engaged; indeed, they were outweighed by the British and Canadians. Only when parent firms were included did the Japanese firms hire more Washington representatives than any other nation.

It is interesting that the Japan lobby makes less frequent use of PACs than do other foreign interests seeking influence in the United States. Federal law prohibits foreign-owned firms from making political contributions in U.S. elections, but a Federal Election Commission ruling cleared the way for U.S. subsidiaries of foreign corporations to set up PACs provided the PAC officers and contributors were U.S. citizens. In 1986, ninety-two such PACs were identified in a *National Journal* article; three years later, the total was 118 PACs, which collectively contributed $2.8 million to federal candidates in the 1987-1988 election cycle, about 5 percent of all corporate PAC contributions during that cycle.[38] Of the ten largest foreign-owned corporate PACs contributing to congressional candidates during the 1987-1988 election cycle, not one was Japanese.[39] The top-ranked foreign-owned PACs were formed by corporations owned by British, Dutch, Swiss, Canadian, Saudi, Hong Kong, German, and Kuwaiti interests. Of the aforementioned 118 PACs run by corporations owned by foreign interests, only twelve had Japanese ties.[40] Mitchell reports that the dozen Japanese PACs gave $370,000 to federal candidates in 1987-1988.[41]

Robert Morse, executive vice-president of the Economic Strategy Institute, a Washington think tank formed by Japan critic Clyde Prestowitz, argues that if PACs owned by foreign interests were restricted in reform legislation, it would not reduce the influence of the Japan lobby very much:

> The Japanese prefer indirection: They don't like head-on types of things. The Japanese prefer to increase their political influence by hiring well connected lobbyists and by, increasingly, making donations to U.S. foundations, educational and charitable institutions.[42]

The Stakes for Japan: High by Any Measure

The stakes of the game for the Japanese are, by nearly any measure, enormous. The Japanese-American bilateral economic relationship is perhaps the most important in the world. The two economies have developed a complementary pattern in many sectors, but there are many areas of continuing conflict in areas such as automobiles, machinery, electronics, and computers. The agenda for U.S.-Japanese relations includes a wide range of issues: the U.S.-Japan trade deficit of more than $50 billion a year; structural impediments that prevent the opening of the Japanese market to American and other imports; and the restructuring of the U.S.-Japan security relationship.

What then is a proportionate lobbying program for a nation as involved as Japan is with the United States? Choate himself argues that the $400 million Japan spends annually in the United States on lobbying and lobbying support activities is trivial when compared to the $50 billion annual trade surplus Japan enjoys with America. When compared to the huge investments Japan has in the United States, Choate argues the lobbying costs "would be a bargain at ten times the price."[43]

Growing Ties with Intellectual America

As suggested earlier, various ministries of the Japanese government, such as the Ministry of Education and Ministry of Foreign Affairs, have tried to shape American public opinion by educational programs for the schools, media programs for home viewing, cultural events in various communities and higher education settings, and several programs which bring Americans to Japan. The Ministry of Finance maintains an informal council of economic advisers that includes more than one hundred of the world's top trade experts—fifty-two are American. Chalmers Johnson has estimated that more than 80 percent of all American studies programs on Japan are financed by the Japanese. Choate, who believes the 80 percent figure is low, calls this tactic "shaping the marketplace of ideas."[44]

Japan has funneled tens of millions of dollars to a relative handful of elite universities to assist in the establishment or expansion of major Japan studies programs or centers. Universities such as Harvard, Yale, Berkeley, Washington (St. Louis), Michigan, and others compete regularly for renewal of existing grants or for new funds from organizations such as the Japan Foundation or a growing number of Japanese organized corporate foundations. These corporate foundations include those established by Toyota, Honda, Nissan, Mitsui, and other major Japanese corporations with operations in the United States. Other academics are cultivated through programs of sponsored language study, teaching, and research in Japan. Programs have been established to bring politicians, media personnel, school teachers, and government staff members on fact-finding trips to Japan.

The key to understanding the significance of the opinion-influencing efforts is to note that their primary goal is to magnify the voices of Americans who already support Japan. Supporters of Japan are assisted financially and offered forums for presenting pro-Japanese statements. Holstein cites the examples of Peter G. Peterson, Fred Bergsten, and Stephen Bosworth. Peterson, secretary of commerce in the Nixon administration, chairs the Blackstone Group, a New York-based investment bank that was a major player in multibillion dollar acquisitions in the United States by Sony, Bridgestone, and Mitsubishi. Nikko Securities invested $100 million in Blackstone and provided another $100 million for a fund Blackstone manages. Peterson also chairs the Council on Foreign Relations and the Institute for International Economics. The latter organization, of which Bergsten is president, received $280,000 of its $3.6 million 1988 budget from Japanese sources, including the U.S. Japan Foundation, which is chaired by Stephen Bosworth, a former ambassador. Holstein asserts that through speeches and articles Peterson supports the position that the United States needs the capital that Japan provides and should not change its policies toward Japanese investment. Peterson, Bergsten, and Bosworth were all supporters of free trade long before their Japanese connections began, but all three have been of great assistance to Japanese efforts to mold public opinion.[45]

Choate and John Judis fault the "think-tank contractors" of the Japan lobby such as the Brookings Institution, the American Enterprise Institute, the Institute for International Economics, the Reischauer Center for East Asian Studies, and the Center for Strategic and International Studies (CSIS) because they accept funding from Japanese firms and foundations. Hobart Rowen, the *Washington Post*'s chief economic correspondent, counters that such critics approve only those think tanks that oppose free-trade policies (such as the Economic Policy Institute and the Free Congress Federation). "Choate's simplistic assumption would seem to be that anything Japanese is evil," writes Rowen, "therefore, any association with Japan or Japanese companies is a taint."[46]

The think tanks and universities that accept Japanese funds routinely deny that Japanese money dictates in any way the conclusions of their studies of U.S.-Japan issues. Writing in *The New Republic* after John Judis's article, "The Japanese Megaphone," appeared in the January 22, 1990, issue, Fred Bergsten argued that no funder of his organization's research had ever tried to influence it and that his organization would immediately reject both the attempt and the funds if any ever tried. In the same issue, CSIS president David M. Abshire asserted that CSIS never consults the donors of any of its five endowed chairs in the process of selecting incumbents; instead, donors are informed of the selections only after the fact. The chairman of the Electronics Industry Association wrote to deny that it was a front group for the Japanese. Finally, Elliot L. Richardson noted that although he was a partner in a firm that offered legal counsel to Japanese clients, he did not have any Japanese clients at that time. He did note that he was the chairman of the Hitachi Foundation and the Japan-America Society of Washington, but asserted that neither organization sought to influence governmental policy.[47]

Despite these protests, one must assume that responsible researchers are at least somewhat aware of the possibility of difficulty in renewing or attracting grants if their efforts became too critical of Japan or Japanese policies. Nevertheless, there is no evidence to indicate that opponents of Japanese interests have been induced to switch sides and become intellectual advocates of Japan. The absence of such evidence constitutes a serious weakness in the cases of Choate, Holstein, and others who assert that Japanese money has "purchased" policies that would not otherwise have been adopted.

The Japan Lobby: Some Final Thoughts

The reaction to Choate's *Agents of Influence* was strong indeed. The Japanese and their well-paid representatives took offense to being singled-out as "an evil force" when many other nations were behaving similarly.[48] Hiroshi Hirabashi, the economic minister at the Japanese Embassy in Washington complained: "Why are they pointing mainly at the Japanese and not the British, not the Dutch, not the Canadians, not the Koreans?"[49] Many Americans used Choate's arguments to reaffirm their belief that America was "losing the war on a variety of fronts" to the Japanese, who were not playing the game fairly.

Two basic themes seem to account for most of the American emotion on the question: long-term American bias against Japan and the refusal of many Americans to attribute the recent economic difficulties of the United States to their own actions. After all, it is easier to blame someone else for one's difficulties after a long run of tremendous successes, and the Japanese make perfect targets, especially now that the Soviet threat has receded. The Japan lobby has become a symbol of 150 years of distrust and misunderstanding between Japan and the United States.

In fact, however, Japan's lobbying efforts appear to be commensurate to the stakes it holds in its relations with the United States. Meanwhile, the Japan lobby has shifted its emphasis away from the use of expensive lobbyists toward the utilization of American organizations and Japanese subsidiaries to get its message to American political leaders.

The fact that Japan's lobbying efforts are commensurate with its stake in the United States does not mean foreign lobbying in this country is not a problem. Although he was perhaps unfair in singling out Japan, Choate has shown clearly how foreign interests can buy access to our nation's policy makers and opinion leaders. Japan is not the only nation that has come to understand Jessie Unruh's classic observation that "money is the mother's milk of politics." Many nations appear to understand that there appear to be few in Washington whose services cannot be rented if not purchased.

Notes

1. Roger M. Pang, "Rising Sun Is Old Business: Asians Are Still the 'Bad Guys,'" *New York Times*, August 8, 1993.
2. "Sixty-Four Percent of Japanese Say U.S. Relations Are Unfriendly," *New York Times*, July 6, 1993.
3. Pat Choate, *Agents of Influence: How Japan's Lobbyists in the United States Manipulate America's Political and Economic System* (New York: Knopf, 1990).
4. This discussion on the history of the Japan Lobby and the role of the U.S.-Japan Economic Institute draws extensively from Mindy Kotler's, "Making Friends: A History of Japan's Lobby in Washington, D.C.," *Venture Japan* 2, 2 (1990).
5. For a study of the prewar Japan Lobby, see Jonathan G. Utley, "Diplomacy in a

Democracy: The United States and Japan, 1937-1941," *World Affairs* 139, 2 (Fall 1976): 130-140.

6. The early history of the Japan Lobby in its early postwar form can be found in Howard Schonberger, "The Japan Lobby in American Diplomacy: 1947-1952," *Pacific Historical Review* 46, 3 (August 1977): 327-359. For more on this period, see Russell Warren Howe and Sarah Hays Trott, *The Power Peddlers: How Lobbyists Mold America's Foreign Policy* (Garden City, N.Y.: Doubleday, 1977), 29-100.

7. Kotler, "Making Friends," 58.

8. Ibid., 58.

9. "Pat Choate vs. Komori Yoshihisa" (in Japanese), *Bungeishunju* 68 (November 1990): 268-278.

10. Kotler, "Making Friends," 59.

11. Choate, *Agents*, 69.

12. Ron Hrebenar interviewed the major Japanese cultural foundations and societies in New York City in early June 1993. The same month, Hrebenar conducted interviews in Washington, D.C., with several of the Japanese economic organizations.

13. The Japan Foundation Law, Article 1, passed by the Diet on June 1, 1972.

14. Japan Societies are now located in Seattle, Portland, San Francisco, Los Angeles, Denver, Houston, Chicago, St. Louis, Indianapolis, Birmingham, Boston, New York, Washington, D.C., Pittsburgh, Richmond, Atlanta, Tampa, and Miami.

15. The U.S.-Japan Trade Council was perhaps the best example of the Japan Lobby's use of front groups to promote Japanese interests. Choate notes that after this bad experience, the Japanese joined hundreds of real U.S. trade associations and public interest groups such as the Consumers for World Trade, a Washington, D.C.-based advocate of open-door U.S. trade policies. Other prominent Japanese-dominated trade associations include the International Electronic Manufacturers and Consumers of America, the Pro-Trade Group, and the Japan Automobile Manufacturers Association.

16. Japan has more consulates in the United States than any other nation has ever had. Choate, *Agents*, 222.

17. William J. Holstein, *The Japanese Power Game: What It Means for America* (New York: Scribner's, 1990), 234.

18. Ibid., 223.

19. *National Journal*, May 25, 1991, 1243.

20. Holstein, *Japanese Power Game*, 223.

21. *National Journal*, June 29, 1991.

22. Choate, *Agents*, xi.

23. "Pat Choate vs. Komori Yoshihisa," 268-278. Choate offers four case studies to illustrate his claim of damage to U.S. industry and labor: the 1989 tariff on light trucks; the 1987 Toshiba Machinery-Soviet submarine propellers case; the failure of the United States to open up the Japanese domestic market to American rice imports; and Japan's reluctance to open up Japanese domestic construction projects to American participation. It is interesting to note that two of these case studies involve American failures to penetrate Japanese markets and are not the usual issues one thinks about when the Japan Lobby in the United States is discussed. However, the Toshiba case has been explored by others and does make a useful case study on the extent and success of the Japanese lobby. *Agents*, 4.

24. *National Journal*, May 25, 1991, 1939. Other commentators opposed Choate's view. Yoshihisa Komori argued in a 1980 book that while Japan had indeed spent many millions of dollars in various lobbying and public relations activities, the nation had not gotten fair value for such expenditures. Indeed, Komori argued, despite all these efforts, the interests of Japan and its various interests, corporate and otherwise, had declined in recent years. Yoshihisa Komori, *The Japan Lobby* (in Japa-

nese) (Tokyo: publisher unknown, 1980); Tomohito Shinoda, *America Giyai o Lobbi Suru* (Tokyo: Japan Times, 1989).

25. Choate, *Agents*, xi.

26. Ibid., xviii. Estimates of the lobbying expenditures of Japan and other nations vary.

27. Holstein, *Japanese Power Game*, 221. Japanese politics and the Japanese style of lobbying in Tokyo are also probably the most expensive in the world. See Hirose Machisada, "Pressure Groups in Japanese Politics" (in Japanese), *Jurisuto*, special issue no. 35 (Summer 1984): 52-56.

28. *New York Times*, November 2, 1993.

29. "Japan Article: A Question of Partiality," *Washington Post*, May 13, 1992. After Baker left the White House in 1988, he made at least three trips to Japan, including a visit in 1992 to attend a meeting of the U.S.-Japan Leadership Council, an organization of businessmen and politicians seeking to promote closer ties between Japan and the United States.

30. *National Journal*, August 4, 1990, 1885.

31. Choate, *Agents*, 75.

32. *National Journal*, May 18, 1991, 1189.

33. *National Journal*, June 15, 1991, 1385.

34. *New York Times*, November 2, 1993.

35. Clyde H. Farnsworth, "Japan's Loud Voice in Washington," *New York Times*, December 10, 1989. As is the case with American domestic lobbying expenses, reported numbers are merely a small fraction of the real amounts. Ronald J. Hrebenar and Ruth K. Scott, *Interest Group Politics in America* (Englewood Cliffs, N.J.: Prentice Hall, 1990), 167.

36. Choate, *Agents*, 45.

37. Neil J. Mitchell, "The Global Polity: Foreign Direct Investment and Political Action Committees" (Paper presented at the 1992 Annual Meeting of the Western Political Science Association, San Francisco, March 19-21, 1992).

38. *National Journal*, August 11, 1990, 1938.

39. Ibid.

40. Ibid., 1935.

41. Mitchell, "The Global Polity."

42. *National Journal*, August 11, 1990, 1938.

43. Choate, *Agents*, 39. Japanese cultural lobbying, too, must be placed into a comparative perspective to evaluate the proportionality of Japanese efforts to influence American attitudes regarding Japan. Two other nations have long operated extensive cultural lobbying efforts similar to those of The Japan Foundation. The United Kingdom's British Council and Germany's Goethe Institute are those nations' equivalents of the Japan Foundations. Both have much longer histories than the Japan Foundation's, far larger budgets, bigger organizations, and larger staffs.

44. Choate, *Agents*, 187, 228. Choate argues that Japan has carefully cultivated its ties with "intellectual America" so as to be able to guide the academic and scholarly side of the policy-making process. Holstein discusses the "surprisingly sophisticated perception game to shape the way Americans think about trade, investment, technology, military relations, and other issues of keen importance to Japan." Holstein, *Japanese Power Game*, 228.

45. Holstein, *Japanese Power Game*, 230.

46. Hobart Rowen, "Choate's View," *Washington Post*, September 9, 1990.

47. *New Republic* (letters to editor), February 26, 1990.

48. Yoshi Tsurumi, "U.S.-Japanese Relations: From Brinkmanship to Statesmanship," *World Policy Journal* 7, 1 (Winter 1989-90): 1-34.

49. "Critic Turns Up Heat on Japan," *Washington Post*, August 31, 1990.

17

All Politics Are Global: Interest Groups and the Making of Foreign Policy

Eric M. Uslaner

When we think of interest groups in American politics, most of us conjure up images of the National Rifle Association, Common Cause, or a host of political action committees. Such images are apt, of course, but in recent years groups with various kinds of international ties have become increasingly prominent in American politics. These links are expressed in several forms. Foreign governments may lobby, often through paid Washington representatives. Other nations may mount much broader campaigns, as Ronald Hrebenar and Clive Thomas discuss in Chapter 16. Increasingly, foreign corporations bring their weight to bear in American politics, sometimes in conjunction with their home governments, but often not. After all, many companies have interests that transcend national boundaries.

In this chapter, Eric Uslaner uses ethnic groupings as a lens through which to view American foreign policy making. Increasingly, he argues, decision making on foreign policies has come to resemble the discord typical of domestic policy making. Although he touches on many ethnic/racial groupings, Uslaner pays special attention to disparities in domestic interest group support for Israel and the Arab nations, carefully laying out the many reasons for the long-term success of pro-Israeli groups. He sees the growing contentiousness of foreign policy making as potentially dangerous, especially as conflict takes place within the already fragmented context of American politics. Concluding his essay, Uslaner worries that in an era of expensive, highly visible foreign policy lobbying, "Causes that have heretofore enjoyed widespread and bipartisan support among the public ... might become objects of great conflict. The very groups that spawned this [lobbying] effort might ultimately regret such tactics."

The support of the General Research Board, University of Maryland-College Park, is gratefully acknowledged, as is the assistance of Nalini Verma, Fred Augustyn, Rodger Payne, and Galen Wilkenson. The comments of Allan J. Cigler, Burdett A. Loomis, and George H. Quester are greatly appreciated.

Interest groups are the stuff of domestic policy making. Americans are used to speaking of diverse constituencies: butchers, bakers, candlestick makers, and so on. Members of Congress talk about their districts in terms of these interests. In the words of former Speaker Thomas P. O'Neill, "All politics is local." On foreign policy, we don't often think of a variety of interests within the United States. We see the world as "us" against "them." Especially in international crises, when the stakes are clear and our entire way of life might be threatened, the nation must speak with one voice, not many. There simply doesn't seem room for interest groups. Yet interest groups have long been active on foreign policy. Group activity has grown increasingly important in recent years as the world has become more interdependent. The new mantra has become "All politics is global." [1] Why has foreign policy been different from domestic policy and how have things changed?

Foreign Policy and Domestic Policy

Interest groups have traditionally been less active on foreign policy than on domestic issues. First, the stakes are much higher in foreign policy. The entire world could be destroyed by nuclear weapons as a result of a decision that might take only minutes to make. Second, foreign policy decisions are often irreversible. Relations between nations change slowly. Unpopular domestic policies can be altered much more easily. Third, relations with foreign nations are not entirely within the control of American policy makers. Both domestic pressures and the attitude of the Chinese government precluded the establishment of diplomatic relations for more than three decades after the United States decided in 1949 not to recognize the regime. It was not until 1972 that President Richard Nixon visited China and 1979 that Beijing and Washington agreed to exchange ambassadors.

Fourth, foreign policy decisions, particularly in crises, need to be made quickly. During the Cuban missile crisis in 1962, President John F. Kennedy had to set national policy in just a few weeks as the threat of a nuclear confrontation with the Soviet Union loomed over the world. Domestic issues rarely get resolved so rapidly; government provision of medical care to the elderly remained just an interesting proposal on the legislative agenda for more than half a century. Expertise on foreign policy is much more centralized than on domestic policy. The goals of all Americans are posited to be the same: at the very least, the survival of a democratic way of life against a hostile power that is not committed to individual freedoms. If the nation does not speak with a single voice, our adversaries might think that we lack the resolve to defend ourselves.

Fifth, foreign policy issues are of less concern to most Americans than domestic policy. Citizens find events in the international arena far more remote than domestic affairs. Many members of Congress seek to highlight their role in domestic policy and to play down any interest they have in foreign policy. One member of the Senate Foreign Relations Committee said of his assignments:

> It's a political liability.... You have no constituency. In my reelection campaign last fall, the main thing they used against me was that because of my interest in foreign relations, I was more interested in what happened to the people of Abyssinia and Afghanistan than in what happened to the good people of my state.[2]

Only a small share—less than a quarter—of members of the House of Representatives consider themselves activists on foreign policy.[3] Most Americans are content to let the president make foreign policy and give virtually unchallenged support to the chief executive as long as crises do not appear to get out of hand.

Congress generally follows the president's lead, rarely overturning presidential initiatives in foreign policy. Partisan divisions have not traditionally disrupted international affairs the same way they affect most domestic issues.[4] Bickering over priorities is supposed to stop "at the water's edge," at each of the great oceans that long isolated the United States from the world's problems. Conflict over domestic policies was natural. On foreign policy there was but one interest—the national interest—behind which all Americans should—and generally did—unite.[5]

Groups that oppose a national consensus will be viewed with suspicion, especially if they could profit from a change in policy. Many Americans conjure up a diabolical picture of how private interests affect international politics for their own advantage, such as the 1970 attempt by International Telephone and Telegraph to rig an election in Chile to prevent the election of a Marxist president. Americans, always suspicious of the power of big oil, became even more hostile when the multinational energy giants tried to tilt U.S. foreign policy away from Israel and toward the Arabs following the 1967 and 1973 Middle East wars. Americans have ambivalent attitudes toward interest groups generally; a 1988 poll showed that 72 percent of Americans believed that big business had too much influence on American policy and 47 percent felt similarly about labor. A 1991 survey found that almost 60 percent of Americans believe that corporations do *not* strike a fair balance between profits and the public interest; 80 percent hold that business has too much power and 65 percent believe that business makes too much profit.[6] Groups with ties to foreign interests, whether they are primarily domestic or foreign, are viewed with particular suspicion.

Interest Groups and Foreign Policy

There has been a sharp rise in the number of groups participating in foreign policy since the 1970s, even as there are no firm numbers as to how many new actors there are. Why is foreign policy a more appropriate arena for interest group politics now than even 20 years ago? The principal reason is that in an interdependent world the traditional barriers between foreign and domestic politics have broken down. Most policies are now "intermestic."[7] The dramatic increase in oil prices in 1973-1974 (and again in 1979) changed our perception of energy policy. Before 1973, energy decisions were made strictly according to the domestic politics of specific fuels. Thereafter our attention shifted to the producing nations. President Jimmy Carter forbade grain sales to the Soviet Union following the nation's invasion of Afghanistan in 1979; Ronald Reagan made the unpopular embargo an issue in the 1980 elections and reversed the policy after his election. Domestic economic groups expanded their horizons to foreign policy as their international market share grew.

Foreign interests joined domestic ones in pressing their case. Foreign governments are among the new lobbyists. West Germany, Canada, France, Arab countries, Japan, China, and Mexico have mounted extensive efforts to sway American policies. These countries hire distinguished Americans who have served in the cabinet, in the Congress, and even in the vice presidency.[8] Japan alone spent up to $60 million in 1989 on lobbying, four times as much as in 1984. The government of Kuwait reportedly spent $10 million to drum up support for the Gulf War in 1990. Mexico hired at least 33 former U.S. government officials, including former Senator and Trade Representative Bill Brock, in a $28 million lobbying effort on behalf of the proposed North American Free Trade Agreement (NAFTA).[9]

A second reason is the decline of consensus on foreign policy. The Vietnam War changed the way Americans react to foreign policy. Support of the president's policies was no longer automatic. Various ideological interest groups sprang up to challenge some of the key assumptions behind our involvement in the war. The post-World War II era of bipartisanship in foreign policy had come to an end. From 1968 onward, parties increasingly took divergent stands on foreign policy in their platforms and in their votes on the floor of the House and Senate.[10]

The waning of a cohesive sense of national purpose gave rise to a greater number of interest groups on both foreign and domestic policy. The political universe expanded greatly from the late 1960s onward, as previously unheard voices—those of citizens groups—entered the fray. Interest groups concerned with foreign policy and national security most resembled organizations focusing on civil rights and civil liberties. Many were free of the taint of special interests seeking to profit from lobbying. Interest groups focusing on foreign policy were about equally divided between for-profit and not-for-profit organizations. Citizen groups in the 1980s were more interested in foreign policy than in any other issue area.[11]

These new interest groups came from sectors not traditionally associated with foreign policy. Church groups, which played an important role in war protest, branched out into concerns for nuclear disarmament, the conflicts in El Salvador and Nicaragua (some churches gave sanctuary to refugees from these countries), the ending of apartheid in South Africa, the establishment of a Palestinian state, and the Gulf War. Secular organizations formed for each of these policy areas as well. The New Christian Right chimed in on behalf of NAFTA, while several environmental organizations, most notably the Sierra Club, succeeded in 1993 in blocking Congressional consideration of the accord until the Environmental Protection Agency prepared an environmental impact statement.[12] On energy, the environment, and agriculture, groups reflecting a dizzying array of complexity made policy formation on these intermestic issues very difficult.[13]

Some lobbying, especially that by churches and ethnic groups, is considered quite legitimate: two-thirds of Americans believe it is legitimate for churches to engage in political activity.[14] Why are some types of group activity acceptable and other types held in disdain? The answer is little different from a distinction on domestic policy noted by E. E. Schattschneider between the National Association of Manufacturers (an umbrella organization of major firms) and the American League to Abolish Capital Punishment: "the members of the [latter] obviously do not expect to be hanged."[15] While economic interests expect to gain something for themselves from lobbying, neither religious nor ethnic groups do. The United States is a nation of immigrants and many Americans have strong bonds with the countries of their heritage.

The rise of foreign policy interest groups is also tied to the more general increasing salience in foreign policy. The percentage of Americans who claim to be "very interested" in news stories about foreign policy has risen dramatically and now is about equal to the percentage claiming to be concerned with local and national news. In recent elections—1992 excepted—candidate preference has been shaped by foreign policy issues as well as domestic concerns.[16] Finally, lobbying on foreign policy has spread for a very straightforward reason: It works.

Ethnic Groups in Foreign Policy

Among the most prominent lobbies on foreign policy are those representing ethnic groups in the United States and their ties to the home country. Mohammed E. Ahrari has suggested four conditions for ethnic group success on foreign policy. First, the group must press for a policy in line with American strategic interests. Second, the group must be assimilated into American society, yet retain enough identification with the "old country" so that its foreign policy issue motivates people to take some political action. Groups that stand outside the mainstream of American life, Arab Americans for a complex of reasons discussed below and Mexicans because many are not citizens, cannot mobilize for political action.

Yet something more is required: a high level of political activity. Fourth, groups should be politically unified.[17] To Ahrari's list we add several additional criteria. The group's policies should be backed by the larger public. The group should be sufficiently numerous to wield political influence. Finally, the group must be seen as pursuing a legitimate interest. Speaking on behalf of one's ethnic group is acceptable so long as others do not think you have divided loyalties or somehow will profit from your lobbying efforts.

American Jews are distinctive in their ability to affect foreign policy. They have established the most prominent and best-endowed lobby in Washington by fulfilling each of the conditions for an influential group. In recent years, some conditions have not been met and the pro-Israel lobby is no longer the dominant force it once was. Its rival in Washington, the pro-Arab lobby, has remained weak because it has failed to meet any of the conditions.

The Israeli and Arab Lobbies

The best-organized, best-funded, and most successful of the ethnic lobbies, indeed perhaps of all foreign policy lobbies, represents the interests of Israel. Jews, who dominate the pro-Israel lobby, comprise 2.7 percent of the American population. However, they are strongly motivated and highly organized in support of Israel. They seek to provide U.S. financial aid (both economic and military) to Israel and to deny it to those Arab nations in a state of war with Israel. And they have been very successful indeed: the lobby, since its inception in 1951, is believed to have lost on only four key decisions. In 1978 it failed to prevent the sale of F-15 fighter planes to Saudi Arabia and Egypt; in 1981 and 1986 it could not block arms sales to the Saudis;[18] and in 1991 it could not overcome President George Bush's opposition to loan guarantees to resettle Soviet Jews so long as Israel continued to build settlements in the West Bank and Gaza Strip. In 1992, when a new Israeli government pledged to stop the settlements, the loan guarantees went forward, though not through the efforts of the pro-Israel lobby.

Israel receives the largest amount of foreign aid from the United States, more than $3 billion a year. Only Egypt even approaches the Israeli aid figure. In 1985 Israel and the United States signed a free-trade pact that completely eliminates all tariff barriers between them by 1995. Israel annually benefits from large tax-exempt contributions from the American Jewish community, including some $500 million in direct charitable grants and a similar amount from the sale of Israeli government bonds.[19] No other foreign nation is so favored.

The Israeli lobby combines one organization devoted entirely to the cause of that country and a wide-ranging network of Jewish groups that provide support. The American Israel Public Affairs Committee (AIPAC), founded in 1951, has a staff of 150, an annual budget of $15 million, and 55,000 members. It operates out of offices one block away from Capitol Hill as well as in other major cities.[20] The success of the Israeli lobby has been attributed to its political acumen. Sanford Ungar stated:

> In a moment of perceived crisis, it can put a carefully researched, well-documented statement of its views on the desk of every Senator and Congressman and appropriate committee staff within four hours of a decision to do so.[21]

The organization's close ties to many congressional staffers keep it well informed about issues affecting Israel on Capitol Hill. Its lobbying connections are so thorough that one observer maintained, "A mystique has grown up around the lobby to the point where it is viewed with admiration, envy, and sometimes, anger."[22] Activists can readily mobilize the network of Jewish organizations across the country to put pro-Israel pressure on members of Congress in their constituencies, even in areas with small Jewish populations. Even though liberals (and Democrats) tend to be somewhat more sympathetic to Israel than conservatives (and Republicans), the lobbyists are careful to maintain bipartisan support. AIPAC works together with other interest groups, particularly organized labor.[23] It blocked proposed arms sales to Jordan and Saudi Arabia in the late 1980s. In 1986 Secretary of State Shultz reportedly asked AIPAC what kind of arms and aid package the Reagan administration could get passed.[24] Among its recent activities was the organization of 1,500 "citizen lobbyists," armed with individualized computer printouts of their legislators' backgrounds, pressing for additional aid to Israel because of the damage it incurred in the Gulf War.[25]

The Arab lobbying effort has been singularly unsuccessful. There were no major Arab organizations operating at all before 1972, and a Washington presence did not begin until 1978. The oldest Arab group, the National Association of Arab Americans (NAAA) claims 13,000 members, a mailing list of 80,000 names, most of whom are inactive, and a $500,000 annual budget funding a staff of 25.[26] The NAAA seeks closer ties between the United States and the Arab world in political, military, and economic arenas. Despite its support for a weakening of the United States-Israel bond and creation of a Palestinian state, it recognizes the right of Israel to exist. A rival organization, the American Lebanese League, is harshly critical of the NAAA and views it as essentially anti-American.[27] Two newer organizations are the Arab American Anti-Discrimination Committee, with 25,000 members, which fights negative stereotypes of Arab Americans, and the Arab-American Committee. Only the NAAA lobbies in Washington; the AADC and the AAC are split by the personal animosities between the groups' founders.[28]

There have been some efforts to get American businesses with interests in the Middle East, especially oil companies, to do more lobbying and fund raising for the Arab cause, but they have not yielded much success to date. One analysis concludes: "Most Arab embassies throw impressive parties, but have little day-to-day contact with Congress, according to lawmakers and aides. Israel, by comparison, has a staff of congressional relations counselors who keep in touch with Capitol Hill."[29] Unlike AIPAC, the NAAA makes no pretense of being free from "mother country" direct influence. For example, advertisers in the business survey published by the NAAA are primarily Arab governments, the Palestine Liberation Organization (PLO), and firms doing business in the Persian Gulf. The Arab uprising in the West Bank and Gaza that began in 1987 has energized the Arab-American community. NAAA now maintains a grassroots network organized by congressional district, patterned directly after AIPAC.[30]

A second major Arab organization, the American-Arab Anti-Discrimination Committee, was founded in 1980 on the model of the B'nai B'rith Anti-Defamation League, established some 50 years ago to combat discrimination against Jews. It does not lobby on legislation.

The heart of the difficulty of Arab-American lobbying efforts is found in the existence of another group, the American Lebanese League, which claims ten thousand members and seeks a democratic and pro-Western Lebanon. It represents Christian forces in Lebanon, which have little in common with the Muslims and Druze of that country. Even a past president of NAAA admits the central hindrance to Arab lobbying in the United States:

> We can't represent the Arabs the way the Jewish lobby can represent Israel. The Israeli government has one policy to state, whereas we couldn't represent "the Arabs" even if we wanted to. They're as different as the Libyans and the Saudis are different, or as divided as the Christian and Moslem Lebanese.[31]

Inter-Arab divisiveness thus accounts for some, but not all, of the difficulties that these lobbying organizations confront.

Public opinion plays a much larger role. Americans have for a long time taken a much more sympathetic view toward Israel than toward the Arabs. Most polls show that Americans favor the Israeli position by better than a 3-1 margin. Occasionally, as during the Israeli invasion of Lebanon or the 1985 TWA hostage crisis, public support for Israel drops sharply, but it has generally rebounded. Even as the Arab uprising in the Israeli-occupied territories has sapped public support for Israel, there has been no appreciable increase in support for the Arab cause.[32]

The roots of the friendship between the United States and Israel include factors such as: (1) a common biblical heritage (most Arabs are Muslim, an unfamiliar religion to most Americans); (2) a shared European value system (most Arabs take their values from Islam, which is often sharply critical of the moral tenor of the West); (3) the democratic nature of Israel's political system (most Arab nations are monarchies or dictator-ships); (4) Israel's role as an ally of the United States (most Arab countries have been seen as either unreliable friends or within the Soviet sphere of influence); and (5) the sympathy Americans extend toward Jews as vic-tims (Arabs are portrayed as terrorists or exploiters of the American econ-omy through their oil weapon).[33] The close connection of Arab-American lobbying efforts to the Middle East does not help to overcome such diffi-culties.

The smaller Arab-American population, two million to three million compared with almost six million Jews, further limits the political clout of Arab Americans. Even more critical, however, is the much greater politi-cal mobilization of American Jews, particularly in support of Israel. Jews have a very high rate of participation in politics, Arab Americans a rather low rate. Jews also are among the most generous campaign contributors in American politics: 60 percent of individual contributions to President Bill Clinton's 1992 campaign came from Jewish donors.[34] Arab Americans have not been very active in politics. Only a hundred thousand belong to any Arab-American organization compared to two million Jews who are active in Jewish causes. Many Arab Americans, especially the older, na-tive-born, shun politics. They are divided politically, with younger and more liberal Arab Americans voting Democratic and raising $750,000 for Jesse Jackson's 1988 race for the presidency. Older, more conservative Arab Americans identify with Republicans for their support for traditional social values. Democratic identifiers sometimes find their support unre-quited: Arab Americans complained that the 1984 Democratic nominee returned their campaign contributions.[35]

While Arab groups are divided among themselves and have no com-mon frame of reference, American Jews are united behind support of Israel. A 1982 survey of American Jews showed that 94 percent considered themselves either pro-Israel or very pro-Israel. Two-thirds often discuss Israel with friends and, by a 3-1 margin, reject the notion that support for Israel conflicts with one's attachment to the United States. Three-quar-ters of American Jews argue that they should not vote for a candidate who is unfriendly to Israel, and a third would be willing to contribute money to political candidates who supported Israel.[36]

Overall, the pro-Israel lobby prior to the late 1980s met all of the conditions identified as critical for a group to be successful. The Arab-American lobby met none (see Table 17-1). Jews were well assimilated, had a high level of political activity, were homogeneous in their support of Israel, and had the support of public opinion. Israel was seen as a strategic asset by the American public and particularly by decision makers. Activity on behalf of Israel was perceived as legitimate by the American public; backers of AIPAC and other organizations did not stand to gain from their lobbying. They had to contribute their own money to participate. While not numerous in comparison to many other groups, American Jews and

Table 17-1 Conditions for Foreign Policy Success by Ethnic Interest
Groups: Pro-Israel and Arab-American Groups

Conditions	Pro-Israel groups before 1987	Arab Americans	Pro-Israel groups after 1987
Group goals conform to U.S. strategic interests	+	−	·
Group well assimilated	+	−	+
High level of political activity	+	−	+
Group internally homogeneous	+	−	·
Group has support of public opinion	+	−	·
Group numerous with political clout	+	−	+
Group tactics legitimate	+	−	·

+Condition met positively
−Condition not met (met negatively)
· Condition partially met

other supporters of Israel were concentrated in key states that were important to presidential candidates (New York, California, Pennsylvania).
Although Jews largely supported Democratic candidates, they were more
likely than most other groups to shift their votes from one election to the
next. In 1980, when they distrusted Jimmy Carter, they gave him just 42
percent of their vote; in 1992, when they distrusted George Bush, they
gave his Democratic rival Bill Clinton almost twice Carter's percentage.

Arab Americans met none of the conditions. Until the Gulf War, few
Americans saw any Arab nation except Egypt as a strategic ally of the
United States; even after the war, many Americans harbored doubts about
the reliability of most Arab nations as military partners. Many Arab Americans are not well assimilated into American society and politics; the community is neither homogeneous with respect to Middle East politics nor
politically active. Arab Americans are more numerous than some other
groups, but they are not strategically situated in states with large numbers
of electoral votes. American public opinion has never been favorable to
the Arab (or Palestinian) cause. The financing of Arab-American organizations by Middle Eastern interests and the active pursuit of changes in U.S.
policy by economic interests have served to weaken the legitimacy of the
Arab-American cause.

In 1987 the pro-Israel groups began to lose some of their clout. The

Palestinian uprising against Israeli control of the West Bank and Gaza (the *intifada*) raised international consciousness about the Palestinian cause. The often-harsh Israeli attempts to quell it led to a drop in American public support for the Jewish state. They also led to conflicts within the Jewish community as to what Israel ought to do. One survey found that up to three-quarters of the leaders of major Jewish organizations favored direct talks between Israel and the PLO and similar shares backed some type of Palestinian homeland or state.[37]

AIPAC, on the other hand, became increasingly linked to the more hawkish right-wing government in Israel, which rejected the idea of "land for peace." When President Bush decided to withhold the $10 billion in loan guarantees for Israel, AIPAC decided to fight. Israel's opposition leader, Yitzhak Rabin, criticized AIPAC for interfering with the direct Washington-Jerusalem relationship. Bush also challenged the lobby, dramatically portraying himself as a lone statesman fighting "powerful political forces." Many more dovish Jewish organizations chose not to fight the president. AIPAC was battered in 1992-93 when: (1) Rabin became prime minister promising to seek peace with the Palestinians and reiterating his criticism of the lobby; (2) the organization was accused of harassing Jewish peace groups and Arab-American activists; and (3) the top officers of the organization were forced to resign for a variety of sins ranging from boasting about influence with the Clinton administration to uttering slurs against ultra-orthodox Jews and Israeli politicians. The collapse of AIPAC's governing structure reflected deeper tensions about the organization's loss of clout rather than simply a series of unrelated incidents.[38]

Some military leaders, politicians, and citizens no longer see Israel as an important strategic asset. In the Gulf War Bush saw Israel's treatment of the *intifada* as a barrier to cooperation with Arab states, reportedly calling Israel an "unruly partner and a nuisance." With the demise of the Soviet Union, Israel no longer was a strategic bulwark against countries allied with a hostile power.[39] Public opinion did not tilt toward the Arabs, but it became less supportive of Israel than it was in the 1970s and 1980s. By 1988 the public was almost equally divided over whether pro-Israel groups had too much influence or the right amount over U.S. foreign policy. Leading politicians, including the president, were willing to challenge AIPAC's role.[40] AIPAC's clout fell further in 1992 when several of its leaders, including director Tom Dine, were forced to resign in internal power struggles over the direction of the organization.

The pro-Israel lobby was wounded, but not mortally. While the Arab Americans failed to meet any of the conditions in Table 17-1, even after 1987 the worst pro-Israel groups scored was a neutral rating. One senator who called AIPAC "ruthless" nevertheless admitted that "there's no countervailing sentiment."

The Arab-American community has become more politically active in recent years. It was active in raising funds for Jesse Jackson's races for the presidency in 1984 and 1988. Two NAAA leaders report that Arab Americans were the only ethnic group to provide Republican volunteers in every state for Reagan and that no ethnic group provided more volunteers than Arab Americans for the president's reelection campaign.[41] Arab Americans were highly visible in Jackson's 1988 campaign and unsuccessfully pressed the Democratic party to go on record in favor of a Palestinian state. Yet, James Zogby, head of the Arab-American Anti-Discrimination Committee, admitted, "We don't make policy."[42]

The American Jewish community has become more heterogeneous about what Israel's strategy should be toward the Palestinians, but as the Gulf War indicated, if the fundamental interests of the Jewish state are at stake, the community closes ranks. When they perceive an American president as hostile to their interests—as they did with Bush—they form a cohesive voting bloc.

The few Arab Americans in Congress do not identify with their cause and do not caucus on Middle Eastern issues.[43] The only Arab-American senator, former Majority Leader George Mitchell (D-Maine), is a Lebanese Christian who received substantial support from pro-Israel political action committees. In contrast, Jewish members of Congress seek out committee assignments that focus on the Middle East. As of 1994, 20 percent of the members of the House Foreign Affairs Committee and 40 percent of that body's subcommittee on the Middle East were Jewish. The ranking minority member and the second- and third-ranking Democrats are Jewish.

Other Ethnic Interest Groups

No foreign policy interest group, and certainly no ethnic group, has the reputation for influence that the pro-Israel forces have. Even a weakened AIPAC still sets the pace—for two reasons. First, AIPAC is the model for most other successful groups. Second, other ethnic groups have been more divided over the best course of action for their countries of concern. The ethnic lobby that was poised to capture the role of "king of the Hill" from AIPAC, the Cuban American National Foundation (CANF), has been wrought with its own conflicts.

Latinos

Latinos now constitute almost 9 percent of all Americans, up from 6.4 percent in 1980. Yet they have little unity. Mexican Americans constitute 60 percent of all Latinos, but many are not American citizens and even those who are have ambivalent feelings toward Mexico. Until recently Mexican leaders did not encourage intervention by Mexican Americans.[44]

The next largest group is Puerto Ricans. Yet they too are divided over the status of Puerto Rico, some favoring statehood, others continuation of the commonwealth status, and some independence. A 1985 meeting of the National Congress for Puerto Rican Rights could not reach a resolution over the issue of coordinating strategies with other Hispanic groups. Some Puerto Ricans resent other Latinos because on average Puerto Ricans earn less although they have had American citizenship longer.[45] Mexican Americans and Puerto Ricans are generally less well off than many other Americans. They overwhelmingly identify with the Democratic party.[46] For countries such as El Salvador and Nicaragua where American policy is more controversial, foreign policy lobbies are dominated by religious organizations, such as the Washington Office on Latin America, with few ties to the indigenous communities. These organizations largely focus on human rights issues. Some have influence on Capitol Hill, but their lobbying activities tend to concentrate more on legislators who are already committed to their cause.[47]

The third largest group, Cuban Americans, are much better off financially and vote heavily for Republican candidates. Cubans comprise just 5.3 percent of Latinos, yet they have established the second most potent ethnic lobby in the country. A small part of their success stems from modeling CANF upon AIPAC. Cuban Americans are generally strongly anticommunist. They helped to fund Lt. Col. Oliver L. North's legal expenses during the Iran-Contra affair and a lobbying effort to force Cuban troops from the African nation of Angola.[48]

CANF's leader, Jorge Mas Canosa, "may be the most significant individual lobbyist in the country."[49] The foundation lobbied successfully in 1990 for TV Marti, a direct broadcast station aimed at Cuba from the United States that has been effectively jammed by the Cuban government. State Department officials privately state that CANF has been responsible for maintaining the American hard line against Fidel Castro's regime. The federal government funds a resettlement program for Cuban refugees that CANF runs. Mas stood close to Bush when he signed the Cuban Democracy Act, strengthening sanctions against the Castro regime. CANF has 100 directors, each of whom contribute $10,000. It claims 50,000 donors. CANF contributed to fifty-six congressional campaigns in 1988 and to forty-eight in 1990, focusing largely on members of the House Foreign Affairs Committee. Overall, its Free Cuba Political Action Committee contributed $670,000 to congressional candidates from 1982 to 1992 and more than $1 million to presidential candidates in 1992 alone.[50] All three Cuban-American representatives—two Republicans from Florida and a New Jersey Democrat—serve on the House Foreign Relations Committee, compared to just one other Latino member.

Yet CANF may have been proven too partisan for its own good. While it has backed some Democrats in Congress, its partisanship has been overwhelmingly Republican. It believed that it held power over both parties and in early 1993 blocked a black Cuban-American nominee of the Clinton administration for the post of chief policy maker on Latin

America. That tilted the administration toward a more moderate line on Cuba. Clinton invited 100 Cuban Americans to the White House for Cuban Independence Day, slighting CANF office holders. A new, more moderate Cuban-American group, Cambio Cubano (Cuban Change), was founded, and the administration appeared more sympathetic to it when it did little to stop Congress from slashing funding in half for Radio Marti and from abolishing TV Marti.[51]

The fragmentation of the Latino community limits the unity and effectiveness (especially on foreign policy issues) of the Hispanic Caucus in the House of Representatives.[52] Not only is there tension among different groups of Latinos, but leaders of the Mexican-American and Puerto Rican communities appear to be out of step ideologically with their more conservative constituencies.[53] Mexican Americans and Puerto Ricans are both numerous and concentrated in key states—Texas and California for the former and the Northeast for the latter—but they have low rates of participation. While Latin America is important strategically to the United States, it is not terribly salient to most non-Latinos. Latinos are not well integrated into American political culture: Most Mexican Americans and Puerto Ricans born in the continental United States identify themselves with their place of origin (usually their parents' place of birth) much more than as Americans; even native-born Cuban Americans are equally divided.[54] Cuban Americans are more united in their attitudes, very active politically, and constitute a powerful bloc in one of the nation's fastest growing states. They account for up to 10 percent of the Republican vote in Florida and have elected a Cuban-American mayor of Miami. They have great political legitimacy and a compelling target in Castro's regime. Yet they have had limited success in isolating Castro and none at all in provoking direct confrontation with him. Americans may not like Castro, but they have not believed that his demise was imminent. Nor does Castro's rule appear very salient.[55] The demise of the Soviet Union reduced the strategic threat of Cuba and opened up new opportunities for alternative Cuban-American views; the election of a Democratic president the CANF opposed further weakened the clout of conservative forces within the community.

Greeks and Turks

Greek Americans were long considered second in power to the pro-Israel lobby. The American Hellenic Institute Public Affairs Committee (AHIPAC) is consciously modeled after AIPAC; the two groups have often worked together. AHIPAC lobbied successfully for an arms embargo on Turkey after its 1974 invasion of Cyprus and has pressed for a balance in foreign aid between the two states. The two million Greek Americans are very politically active and loyal to the Democratic party. In 1988 they raised more than 15 percent of Greek-American Michael Dukakis's early campaign funds. In contrast, the Turkish-American community of 180,000 is not well organized. Recently it has employed a Washington public relations firm to lobby the government, but Turkish Americans do not lobby. As one member of Congress stated, "I don't have any Turkish restaurants in my district."[56] Overall, Greek Americans in 1988 were advantaged over Turkish Americans on virtually every condition. They were more assimilated into American life, more active politically, more homogeneous and numerous, and—to the extent they were Christian rather than Muslim—had public opinion on their side. Each group claims strategic importance and, since the demands of each could be met through foreign aid, there was no fundamental clash. Greek-American influence has waned as American foreign policy has shifted emphasis from Greece and Turkey to other trouble spots, especially after the fall of the Soviet Union limited the strategic value of both Greece and Turkey to the United States. In turn, the economic integration of Europe made both countries turn toward their own continent.

Eastern Europeans

Eastern Europeans have a long history of political activism in the United States. There are eight million Polish Americans and almost a million Lithuanians, Latvians, and Estonians. Several midwestern states have large concentrations of eastern Europeans, and both major political parties have recognized the importance of these groups by establishing divisions dealing with their affairs. Congress enacted a law in 1959 denoting the third week of July as Captive Nations Week, to be observed until the Soviet Union withdrew from eastern Europe and the Baltic states.

These ethnic groups have little impact on foreign policy. They are not united among themselves and many worry that emphasizing their ethnicity would only stir negative emotions among other Americans. The lobbies are all understaffed and underfunded. They also pressed the government to sacrifice détente with the Soviet Union, a policy at odds with that of presidents of both parties. Especially as the policies initiated by Mikhail Gorbachev led to greater freedom within the Soviet Union and the liberation of eastern Europe, Bush did not want to jeopardize this new openness. The United States never accepted Soviet occupation of the Baltic states but refused to grant them recognition in 1989 and 1990 when Lithuania, Latvia, and Estonia declared independence. The ethnic lobbies favored such recognition, but the general public did not. After Lithuania, Latvia, and Estonia gained independence in 1991 the long-time alliances in the Baltic-American community came apart as each ethnic group fought for a share of the decreasing American foreign-aid pie.[57] Neither the president nor Congress was willing to take any side in the many ethnic tensions emerging in eastern Europe, even as the small lobby of the 70,000 Albanian Americans pressed for a resolution attacking discrimination against Albanians in the former Yugoslavia.[58] One of the least numerous groups in the United States, Muslims from Bosnia-Hercegovina, established the most unusual alliance in recent years. Muslim, Jewish, and Christian groups united to press the United States to intervene militarily to protect the Bosnian Muslims from attacks by Serbs and Croatians.[59]

Baltic Americans were never homogeneous, numerous enough, or sufficiently active to overcome the U.S. government belief that a united Soviet Union was more strategically important than a set of independent nations. When independence appeared imminent, public opinion among Americans failed Baltic Americans: 31 percent favored immediate recognition in March, 1990, compared to 41 percent who favored bolstering Soviet leader Mikhail Gorbachev.[60]

African Americans

African Americans, like Latinos, traditionally have been more concerned with domestic economic issues than with foreign policy concerns. Most black Americans cannot trace their roots to a specific African country. Until the 1960s, black participation in politics was restricted, both by law and by socioeconomic status. There were few blacks in Congress, especially on the foreign policy committees, or in the Foreign Service. Blacks contribute little money to campaigns and electorally they have been strongly tied to the Democratic party, thus cutting off lobbying activities to Republican presidents and legislators. Black activity on foreign policy heightened over the issue of the ending of the apartheid system of racial separation in South Africa. The Congressional Black Caucus and TransAfrica, a lobbying organization that in 1993 expanded its role to become a think tank dealing with foreign policy issues, are the two most prominent actors.

The South African issue united the black community. Whites also strongly opposed the South African regime. They responded in public opinion polls that giving black South Africans freedom was more important than keeping the country as a stable ally.[61] President Ronald Reagan ultimately agreed in 1985 to accept sanctions against the South African government; he was pushed in that direction by the weight of public opinion, a mobilized black community, and a supportive Congress. The Congressional Black Caucus, now with thirty-nine members, has taken firm stands on South Africa, sending U.S. troops to Somalia, and lifting the ban on Haitian immigrants infected with the AIDS virus. Four of the forty-five members of the House Foreign Affairs Committee are blacks; blacks have increasingly held key positions on foreign policy in the executive branch; and they are now more united on wider issues of Africa than ever before.[62] While blacks are well assimilated into American politics and becoming more powerful, their overall level of activity remains lower than whites.[63] Their influence is further limited by the low salience of Africa and other black nations, especially as strategic concerns, to most Americans.

Asian Americans

Given the impressive lobbying efforts of Japan and Taiwan and the size of the Asian population—10 percent of the California population—one might expect considerable power from this group. Yet they have not participated in politics in large numbers. Many recent immigrants are preoccupied with economic issues and eschew politics. They came from cultures without democratic traditions and have not placed adaptation at the top of their agenda. Older Japanese and other Asians who faced discrimination in earlier periods (especially during World War II) shy away from politics, in contrast to blacks, who have used politics to gain civil rights. The Asian-American community, like the Hispanic community, is very diverse and there are few common bonds among Koreans, Indochinese, Japanese, and Chinese. There are tensions between Japanese Americans and Chinese Americans stemming from Japan's occupation of China during World War II. Vietnamese immigrants bear grudges against Cambodians, while Hindus and Moslems from South Asia have long-standing quarrels.[64]

Many recent Asian-American immigrants still see themselves as "guests" in a strange land and are reluctant to get involved in politics. Others simply want to be left alone by the government, believing that self-reliance is the best course. Asian Americans constitute three percent of the population but one percent of the electorate. Those who do vote are among the most loyal Republican blocs in the population. They are attracted by the strong anticommunist positions of the GOP, as well as the party's emphasis on family values. Japanese Americans are an exception. They are overwhelmingly Democratic and have high rates of participation. Three of the five Asian Americans in Congress are of Japanese ancestry and all are Democrats. Only one Asian American, a nonvoting delegate from American Samoa, serves on the House Foreign Affairs Committee. Rep. Jay Kim (R-Calif.), the first Korean American elected to Congress, said: "I have no special agenda for Asian-Americans."[65]

The Electoral Connection in Foreign Policy

Most lobbyists concentrate on legislation in Washington, but tactics have been shifting increasingly toward the electoral arena. Interest groups use political action committees to channel contributions to candidates for Congress. If a sound presentation doesn't convince a legislator to accede to one's cause, the argument runs, perhaps a campaign contribution might.

Former senator Charles McC. Mathias, Jr. (R-Md.), worried that such tactics might make it difficult for the nation to speak with one voice on foreign policy:

> Factions among us lead the nation toward excessive foreign attachments or animosities. Even if the groups were balanced—if Turkish-Americans equaled Greek-Americans or Arab-Americans equaled Jewish-Americans—the result would not necessarily be a sound, cohesive foreign policy because the national interest is not simply the sum of our special interests and attachments.... [E]thnic politics, carried as they often have been to excess, have proven harmful to the national interest.[66]

The strategies of pro-Israel groups usually have focused on placing intense constituency pressure on legislators who make either anti-Israel or pro-Arab statements. The most notable efforts occurred in Illinois in 1982 and 1984. Rep. Paul Findley (R) and Sen. Charles Percy (R), who chaired the Foreign Relations Committee, were strong critics of Israel. Jewish sources raised $685,000 to defeat Findley in 1982 and $322,000 to beat Percy two years later; a California donor contributed more than $1 million in "uncoordinated expenditures" against Percy. That same year pro-Israeli groups targeted Sen. Jesse Helms (R-N.C.), an even more strident critic of Israel, who upon reelection dramatically shifted to a pro-Israel position.

Pro-Israel political action committee (PAC) contributions rose from $2,450 in 1976 to $8.7 million in 1990—a higher figure than that for the largest domestic PAC, that of the realtors. Virtually every senator and most members of the House have received support from the more than eighty pro-Israel PACs. Senate Foreign Relations Committee members received $1.2 million from pro-Israel groups in 1990, more than twice as much from the second largest ideological PAC and 40 percent of *all* ideological political action committee contributions. Pro-Israel PACs have, like others, concentrated on incumbents; they also favor Democrats by more than two-to-one. Arab Americans are far behind: In 1986, they contributed just $70,000 to congressional candidates compared to $4.6 million from pro-Israel groups.[67]

The imbalance of resources between pro-Israel and pro-Arab groups is not the major reason for concern about the potential for campaign contributions to influence foreign policy. The nature of interest group participation in foreign policy may well change because of the heavy spending. What should the role of money in American politics be? Is political support to be given to the highest bidder? Even though ethnic lobbies do not stand to benefit financially from a foreign policy that suits their preferences, many Americans are simply so skeptical of the role of money in politics that they will worry that something is not right. Support for foreign policy initiatives might be open to the influence of campaign contributions. The victorious group might be viewed with suspicion by the larger public, much as large corporations are. The strategy of influencing policy by shaping the membership of Congress may thus backfire. The public and members of Congress may strongly disapprove of winning policy debates by threats.

Purely domestic issues have traditionally divided our parties, while foreign policy has been bipartisan. A strident electoral campaign by a foreign policy interest group might disrupt this pattern. Jewish groups give far more money to Democratic candidates than to Republicans. Might this endanger support for Israel among Republicans? Pro-Israeli groups recognized this problem in 1985 and 1986 when they gave 60 percent of their contributions to Republicans. This attracted the support of many Christian Right supporters in Congress, who disagree with American Jews on most other issues, especially prayer in schools. It did not prevent the emergence of partisanship on the Middle East. Secretary of State James Baker reportedly justified the Bush administration's strong criticism of Israel by noting that "[Jews] don't vote for us anyway."[68]

Some observers see this strategy as leading to a situation in which concern for Israel's security will be the only issue for American Jews; this will ultimately make political alliances between members of Congress and pro-Israeli forces into little more than contests for campaign contributions (not unlike some domestic political issues) rather than bonds based on long-term philosophical commitments.[69] As unsettling as this is for the Middle East, the problem is more widespread and even more ominous. Pro-Israel groups do not seek financial rewards for their campaign contributions. Nevertheless, such tactics might backfire. On the one hand, 61 percent of Americans believe it is acceptable for American Jews to contribute money to Israel. On the other, almost as many Americans hold that Israel has too much power in America as those who believe it has too little.[70]

Other PACs financed by foreign money, including American subsidiaries of Japanese firms and foreign car dealers, have more direct economic stakes and have used their clout to shape tax law in at least one state. As long as the money is raised exclusively in the United States, such practices are legal. As such strategies prove effective, they will become more widespread.

The bipartisan nature of our foreign policy is threatened by making international politics too much like domestic issues. We can afford to be contentious at home. The stakes are much greater abroad. Already Soviet leaders complain that negotiating with American presidents is difficult because our leaders cannot ensure that agreements reached will be approved by Congress. These problems could only increase if foreign policy issues became important in election campaigns marked by heavy expenditures and threats. What the correct policy ought to be becomes less important than which group can yell the loudest, and the volume is af-

fected by the purchasing power of television advertising. Causes that
have heretofore enjoyed widespread, bipartisan support among the public, such as support for Israel, might become objects of great conflict. The
very groups that spawned this effort might ultimately regret such tactics.

Notes

1. "All Politics Is Global," *Wall Street Journal*, November 25, 1992, A12; E. J. Dionne, "All Politics Is Now Global," *Washington Post*, July 13, 1993, A15.
2. Richard F. Fenno, Jr., *Congressmen in Committees* (Boston: Little, Brown, 1973), 141.
3. Eileen Burgin, "Representatives' Decisions on Participation in Foreign Policy Decisions," *Legislative Studies Quarterly* 16 (December 1991): 521-546.
4. See Aage R. Clausen, *How Congressmen Decide* (New York: St. Martin's Press, 1973).
5. Stephen Krasner, *Defending the National Interest* (Princeton: Princeton University Press, 1978).
6. Seymour Martin Lipset and William Schneider, *The Confidence Gap* (New York: Macmillan, 1983); CBS News Poll press release, October 23, 1988; and Times-Mirror Center for People and The Press, *The People, The Press, and Politics on the Eve of '92*, December 4, 1991 (Washington, D.C.: Times-Mirror Center for The People and The Press).
7. Bayless Manning, "The Congress, the Executive, and Intermestic Affairs: Three Proposals," *Foreign Affairs* (January 1977): 306-324.
8. David Osborne, "Lobbying for Japan, Inc.," *New York Times Magazine*, December 4, 1983, 133-139; and Robert Sherrill, review of Steven Emerson, *The American House of Saud*, *Washington Post Book World*, May 5, 1985, 4.
9. Clyde H. Farnsworth, "Japan's Loud Voice in Washington," *New York Times*, December 10, 1989, F1, F6; and Center for Public Integrity, *The Trading Game: Inside Lobbying for the North American Free Trade Agreement* (Washington, D.C.: Center for Public Integrity).
10. James M. McCormick, *American Foreign Policy and Process*, 2d ed. (Itasca, Ill.: F. E. Peacock, 1992), 441-444; and McCormick and Eugene R. Wittkopf, "Bipartisanship, Partisanship, and Ideology in Congressional-Executive Foreign Policy Relations, 1947-1988," *Journal of Politics* 52 (November 1990): 1077-1100.
11. Jack L. Walker, *Mobilizing Interest Groups in America* (Ann Arbor: University of Michigan Press, 1991), 63, 71.
12. David S. Broder, "Christian Coalition, Shifting Tactics, To Lobby Against Clinton Budget," *Washington Post*, July 18, 1993, A7; and Peter Behr, "NAFTA Pact Jeopardized by Court," *Washington Post*, July 1, 1993, A1, A4.
13. On energy, see Eric M. Uslaner, *Shale Barrel Politics: Energy Politics and Legislative Leadership* (Stanford: Stanford University Press, 1989), esp. chaps. 5 and 6. On the three policy areas, see John Spanier and Eric M. Uslaner, *American Foreign Policy Making and the Democratic Dilemmas*, 6th ed. (New York: Macmillan, 1994), chap. 9.
14. Sixty-four percent uphold the right of religious organizations to endorse candidates. See Marjorie Hyer, "Tolerance Shows in Voter Poll," *Washington Post*, February 13, 1988, E18.
15. E. E. Schattschneider, *The Semisovereign People* (New York: Holt, Rinehart and Winston, 1960), 26.
16. John E. Rielly, *American Public Opinion and U.S. Foreign Policy* (Chicago: Chicago Council on Foreign Relations, 1991), 7-8; John H. Aldrich, John L. Sullivan, and Eugene Borgida, "Foreign Affairs and Issue Voting," *American Political Science Review* 83 (January 1989): 123-142; Martin P. Wattenberg, *The Rise of Candidate-Centered Politics: Presidential Elections of the 1980s* (Cambridge: Harvard University

Press, 1991), 112-147; and Spanier and Uslaner, *American Foreign Policy Making and the Democratic Dilemmas*, chap. 6.

17. Mohammed E. Ahrari, "Conclusion," in *Ethnic Groups and Foreign Policy*, ed. Mohammed E. Ahrari (New York: Greenwood Press, 1987), 155-158.

18. Thomas M. Franck and Edward Weisband, *Foreign Policy by Congress* (New York: Oxford University Press, 1979), 186; and Ben Bradlee, Jr., "Israel's Lobby," *Boston Globe Magazine*, April 29, 1984, 64.

19. Cheryl A. Rubenberg, "The Middle East Lobbies," *The Link* 17 (January-March 1984): 4.

20. Thomas L. Friedman, "A Pro-Israel Lobby Gives Itself a Headache," *New York Times*, November 8, 1992, E18.

21. Sanford J. Ungar, "Washington: Jewish and Arab Lobbyists," *Atlantic*, March 1978, 10.

22. Bradlee, "Israel's Lobby," 64.

23. Robert H. Trice, "Congress and the Arab-Israeli Conflict: Support for Israel in the U.S. Senate, 1970-1973," *Political Science Quarterly* 92 (Fall 1977): 443-463; and Robert Pear with Richard L. Berke, "Pro-Israel Group Exerts Quiet Might as It Rallies Supporters in Congress," *New York Times*, July 7, 1987, A8.

24. Hedrick Smith, *The Power Game: How Washington Works* (New York: Random House, 1988), 222-228.

25. Lloyd Grove, "On the March for Israel," *Washington Post*, June 13, 1991, D10.

26. Bill Keller, "Supporters of Israel, Arabs Vie for Friends in Congress, at White House," *Congressional Quarterly Weekly Report*, August 25, 1981, 1527-1528; and David A. Dickson, "Pressure Politics and the Congressional Foreign Policy Process" (Paper presented at the annual meeting of the American Political Science Association, San Francisco, August-September 1990).

27. Keller, "Supporters of Israel," 1528.

28. Nora Boustany, "Arab-American Lobby Is Struggling," *Washington Post*, April 6, 1990, A10.

29. Keller, "Supporters of Israel," 1528.

30. Rubenberg, "The Middle East Lobbies"; Keller, "Supporters Vie"; Steven L. Spiegel, *The Other Arab-Israeli Conflict* (Chicago: University of Chicago Press, 1985), 8; and David J. Saad and G. Neal Lendenmann, "Arab American Grievances," *Foreign Policy* (Fall 1985): 22.

31. Quoted in Spiegel, *The Other Arab-Israeli Conflict*, 8.

32. Spanier and Uslaner, *American Foreign Policy Making*, chap. 7.

33. Keller, "Supporters Vie," 1523.

34. Thomas L. Friedman, "Jewish Criticism on Clinton Picks," *New York Times*, January 5, 1993, A11.

35. Boustany, "Arab-American Lobby Is Struggling"; and Maralee Schwartz, "Parties Are Paying Greater Attention to Arab-Americans," *Washington Post*, January 20, 1992, A10; Mae Ghalwash, "Arab Americans Face Voting Quandary," *Washington Post*, November 1, 1992, A12-A13; Peter Steinfels, "Despite Role on World Stage, Muslims Turn to the Personal," *New York Times*, May 7, 1993, A1, A13; and Robert A. Trice, *Interest Groups and the Foreign Policy Process* (Beverly Hills, Calif.: Sage Publications, 1976), 54-55.

36. Leon Hadar, "What Israel Means to U.S. Jewry," *Jerusalem Post*, international edition, June 19-25, 1982, 11; Bradlee, "Israel's Lobby," 8.

37. Peter Steinfels, "Survey of U.S. Jewish Leaders Finds Overwhelming Support for Israeli-P.L.O. Talks," *New York Times*, February 10, 1991, 11.

38. Thomas L. Friedman, "Uneasy Debate for Jews in U.S. on Loan Guarantees," *New York Times*, March 2, 1992, A1, A6; Friedman, "Israeli Loan Deal Is Linked by Baker to a Building Halt," *New York Times*, February 25, 1992, A1, A6; Robert Friedman, "The Wobbly Israel Lobby," *Washington Post*, November 1, 1992, C1,

C4; and Robert S. Greenberger, "Head of Largest Pro-Israel Lobby Quits under Pressure in Flap Over Book Quote," *Wall Street Journal*, June 29, 1993, A4.
39. John M. Goshko, "Persian Gulf Crisis Drives U.S.-Israeli Relations to Historic Ebb," *Washington Post*, October 27, 1990, A20; Clyde Haberman, "Israelis Worry If World's New Epoch Will Find Them Shunted Aside by U.S.," *New York Times*, August 3, 1992, A8.
40. Spanier and Uslaner, *American Foreign Policy Making and the Democratic Dilemmas*, chap. 7; and CBS News press release, October 23, 1988.
41. "Arab Americans Take an Increased Political Role," *New York Times*, November 4, 1984, 74; and Saad and Lendenmann, "Arab American Grievances," 22.
42. Grove, "On the Move for Israel," D10; and Boustany, "Arab-American Lobby Is Struggling."
43. Ungar, "Jewish and Arab Lobbyists," 12.
44. Robert Reinhold, "Mexico Leaders Look North of the Border," *New York Times*, December 8, 1989, A1, A28.
45. Rodolfo O. de la Garza, "Chicanos and U.S. Foreign Policy: The Future of Chicano-Mexican Relations," *Western Political Quarterly* 23 (December 1980): 571-572; and Jesus Rangel, "Puerto Rican Need Discussed at Home," *New York Times*, June 3, 1985, B18.
46. Barbara Vobejda, "Asians, Hispanics Giving Nation More Diversity," *Washington Post*, June 12, 1992, A3; and Bernard Weinraub, "Wooing Cuban-Americans in G.O.P.," *New York Times*, May 22, 1987, A14.
47. Bill Keller, "Interest Groups Focus on El Salvador Policy," *Congressional Quarterly Weekly Report*, April 24, 1982, 895-900.
48. Robert S. Greenberger, "Right-Wing Groups Join in Capitol Hill Crusade to Help Savimbi's Anti-Communists in Angola," *Wall Street Journal*, November 25, 1985, 58.
49. John Newhouse, "Socialism or Death," *The New Yorker*, April 27, 1992, 77.
50. Newhouse, "Socialism or Death," 76-81; Lee Hockstadter and William Booth, "Cuban Exiles Split on Life After Castro," *Washington Post*, March 10, 1992, A1, A14; Peter H. Stone, "Cuban Clout," *National Journal*, February 20, 1993, 449; and Larry Rohter, "A Rising Cuban-American Leader: Statesman to Some, Bully to Others," *New York Times*, October 29, 1992, A18.
51. John M. Goshko, "Controversy Erupts on Latin America Post," *Washington Post*, January 23, 1993, A4; and Larry Rohter, "Moderate Cuban Voices Rise in U.S.," *New York Times*, June 27, 1993, A16.
52. David Rampe, "Power Panel in the Making: The Hispanic Caucus," *New York Times*, September 30, 1988, B5.
53. Robert Suro, "Hispanic Pragmatism Seen in Survey," *New York Times*, December 15, 1992, A20.
54. David Gonzalez, "What's the Problem with 'Hispanic'? Just Ask a 'Latino,'" *New York Times*, November 15, 1992, E6.
55. NBC News press release, October 4, 1991; and Yankelovich, Clancy, Shulman press release, September 10, 1992, which reported that only 37 percent of Americans believed that it mattered whether Castro remained in power (57 percent said it did not).
56. Thomas M. Franck and Edward Weisband, *Foreign Policy by Congress* (New York: Oxford University Press, 1979), 191-193.
57. Isabel Wilkerson, "A Battle Is Over for Baltic-Americans," *New York Times*, September 3, 1991, A9.
58. "The Albanians," *New York Times*, August 24, 1987, A14.
59. Amy E. Schwartz, "Brought Together by Bosnia," *Washington Post*, May 14, 1993, A31.
60. CBS News press release, April 5, 1990.

61. Kenneth Longmyer, "Black American Demands," *Foreign Policy* (Fall, 1985): 3-18; Michael Beaubien, "Making Waves in Foreign Policy," *Black Enterprise*, April 1982, 37-42; and David Hoffman, "Americans Back S. Africa's Blacks," *Washington Post*, September 25, 1985.

62. Milton D. Morris, "African-Americans and the New World Order," *The Washington Quarterly* 15 (Autumn 1992): 19; and Keith B. Richburg, "Americans Bring an Agenda Out of Africa," *Washington Post*, May 30, 1993, A39.

63. Sidney Verba et al., "Citizen Activity: Who Participates? What Do They Say?", *American Political Science Review* 87 (June 1993): 306.

64. Stanley Karnow, "Apathetic Asian-Americans?", *Washington Post*, November 29, 1992, C2.

65. Sonal Gandhi, "Asian American Political Behavior" (Student paper, Department of Government and Politics, University of Maryland, 1992); Karnow, "Apathetic Asian-Americans?"; and "Asian-Americans in Politics? Rarely," *New York Times*, June 3, 1993, A16.

66. Charles McC. Mathias, Jr., "Ethnic Groups and Foreign Policy," *Foreign Affairs* 59 (Summer 1981): 981.

67. Charles R. Babcock, "Israel's Backers Maximize Political Clout," *Washington Post*, September 26, 1991, A21; Barbara Levick-Segnatelli, "The Washington Political Action Committee: One Man Can Make a Difference," in *Risky Business*, ed. Robert Biersack, Paul Hernnson, and Clyde Wilcox (Armonk, N.Y.: M. E. Sharpe, 1994); Edward Roeder, "Pro-Israel Groups Know Money Talks in Congress," *Washington Times*, September 18, 1991, A7; and Richard H. Curtiss, *Stealth PACs* (Washington, D.C.: American Educational Trust, 1990).

68. Robert Kuttner, "Unholy Alliance," *The New Republic*, May 26, 1986, 19-25; Robert S. Greenberger, "Pro-Israel Lobby Faces Political Tug of War: Conservative Leadership vs. Liberal Constituents," *Wall Street Journal*, December 20, 1988, A16; and Haberman, "Israelis Worry."

69. See Robert Kuttner, "Unholy Alliance"; and Paul Taylor, "Pro-Israel PACs Giving More to GOP," *Washington Post*, November 4, 1985, A1, A11.

70. Hyer, "Tolerance Shows in Voter Poll"; and CBS News press release, October 23, 1988.

IV. CONCLUSION

18

Contemporary Interest Group Politics: More Than "More of the Same"

Allan J. Cigler and Burdett A. Loomis

With the growing reach of government and the rising stakes of policy decisions, organized interests have increasingly sought to reduce the uncertainty inherent in the policy-making process.[1] In many instances they have succeeded, often by creating insular policy niches that protect them from change.[2] Some groups have moved beyond attempts to influence government to engage in direct action such as abortion-clinic harassment or eco-terrorism. Still, uncertainty abounds, whether in international trade, national health care reform, or in restructuring the American military in the still dangerous post-Cold War world.

Writing in 1983, Schlozman and Tierney concluded that interest groups—although increasing in number—had not transformed their techniques of influence. The amounts of Washington activity by organized interests had changed in the 1970s and early 1980s, but the end result was "more of the same": more testimony before Congress, more communication with the media, more coalition-building, more grassroots campaigns, and so on.[3] Based as it was on an extensive analysis of group actions, and buttressed by two other large-scale studies in the 1980s, this "more of the same" conclusion was sound.[4]

More recently, however, the highly public decision to ratify the North American Free Trade Agreement (NAFTA), recent budget battles, and, especially, the intense health care politicking of 1993-1994 have made the "more of the same" interpretation of group activity less and less persuasive. Changes in the behavior of organized interests and in their relations with key policy makers may reveal a new era of interest group politics, one that is defined by three distinct but related developments.

First, more of the same kind of activity becomes, at some point, something categorically different. For example, as a host of interests, ranging from tobacco companies to health insurers to drug companies, greatly expand their visibility in the national media, a qualitative change may occur in the way these entities seek to affect policies. A certain amount of advocacy advertising has long existed, but the politics of NAFTA, health care, tobacco regulation, and abortion have led to substantial increase in the use of this tactic—and public relations tactics in general—to the point that these actions are no longer just more of the same.

Second, new tactics and relationships have emerged, accompanied by significant changes in the policy-making environment that have required organized interests to make major adaptations in how they act. The impact of Ralph Nader is a case in point. Nader's grassroots, consumer-based lobbying techniques have been extensively copied by technically sophisticated corporate interests.[5]

Third, despite their range of activities, organized interests of all stripes may be losing their ability to affect important decisions. Political analyst Kevin Phillips argues that many key policy developments, from deficit reduction to interest rate manipulation to multinational corporate policies, are essentially immune from most lobbying efforts, however sophisticated.[6] At the same time, individual participation in politics—participation that bypasses organized groups—may be enhanced by technological leaps such as computer-based interactive television. Political parties have lost much of their importance as mediating institutions over the last thirty years; a similar fate might well befall any number of interest groups, despite the great adaptive skill that many have demonstrated since the 1960s.

In the following two sections, we will first scrutinize a key aspect of the changing politics of organized interests: the growing use, sophistication, and, perhaps, discounting of grassroots lobbying techniques. Then we will provide an extensive review of organized interests' mobilization in response to President Clinton's call for health care reform; if nowhere else, we should find interests engaging in much more than "more of the same" on this once-in-a-generation issue.

Finally, we will speculate on some implications of the new era of interest group politics. In particular, we will explore the convergence of interest group politics and the conduct of political campaigns for office. On major, highly visible issues, many actions by organized interests have come to resemble, more than anything else, a national electoral campaign. Policy making and politics merge more than ever, as interests campaign for legislators' votes, the president's blessing, and the public's approval. This is not to say that Washington lobbyists do not remain important. Rather, Washington-centered campaigns combine inside influence with numerous techniques that bring to bear various well-targeted outside, constituency-based pressures.

Grassroots, Astroturf, and Influence

Historically, Capitol Hill lobbying by well-paid representatives of various interests has been distinguished from grassroots efforts to mobilize constituencies—and key constituents—within members' districts. Textbooks on American politics often divide group efforts at influence into "insider" and "outsider" strategies and tactics. Emergent groups, those lacking the resources to hire expensive professional lobbyists, historically have relied most on mobilizing group constituents to contact legislators and other decision makers. Such grassroots lobbying brings to mind the confrontations of abortion politics, with large numbers of prolife and prochoice protesters flooding congressional offices, or the vision (from the 1970s) of farmers driving to Washington on their tractors to "discuss" farm commodity prices with their representatives and Agriculture Department officials.

Such mobilization has come not only from the politically disenfranchised, however. Labor insiders in Washington often lobbied through local officials, and grassroots campaigns have long been orchestrated from the "K Street Corridor" of capital lobbying firms. By the 1980s, well-heeled interests were running highly sophisticated, targeted operations that resembled nothing so much as campaigns for office.[7] Today grassroots lobbying, in some form, is a key tactic for many mainstream groups. For example, the American Society of Travel Agents sponsors an annual "march" in Washington to highlight the benefits of travel and tourism; in 1993 more than a thousand travel agents went to D.C. to oppose additional taxation of the industry in the Clinton budget plan.

What has changed most is the sheer magnitude, sophistication, and cost of grassroots politicking. The mass efforts of travel agents, abortion activists, and dozens of other groups are only the most visible tactics. Reflecting fundamental, organic changes in American politics, grassroots efforts by organized interests now rely heavily upon mass marketing, high technology, and public relations ploys reminiscent of modern political campaigns. Rather than endorsing candidates for office, however, groups urge their members to contact their individual legislators on upcoming votes. Veteran Washington journalist Hedrick Smith observes that such lobbying can sometimes produce an avalanche of communications. Smith cites the cases of

> the National Rifle Association generating three million telegrams in seventy-two hours and blanketing Capitol Hill with so many phone calls that members cannot make outgoing calls.... [and] the "grey lobby" dumping up to fifteen million postcards on [former Speaker] Jim Wright in one day to warn Congress not to tamper with Social Security cost-of-living adjustments.[8]

A growing number of interest groups have constructed elaborate and expensive electronic networks capable of directly connecting citizens to their representatives. The U.S. Chamber of Commerce, for example, has a phone bank that allows it to contact the group's 215,000 members. Those who answer have the option of pressing 1 on their touch-tone phones to send a personal mailgram or letter to their legislator, pressing 2 to direct a voice-mail message to the lawmaker, or pressing 3 to have a computer connect them immediately with their representative's office for a personal phone call.[9]

Unlike the well-heeled Chamber, most groups still contract out the direct-mail and phone-bank components of their grassroots operations, and, as with political consultants in the electoral arena, an ancillary industry has arisen to meet the demand for the new technology. One of the most successful of the new organized-interest consultants has been Jack Bonner, whose Washington firm prefers to work for conservative corporate interests. Although often accused of producing "astroturf" responses rather than legitimate grassroots sentiments, Bonner's firm has prospered; in the 1980s, the cards, letters, and calls generated by his efforts (1) helped protect funding for Northrop's stealth bomber, (2) assisted the Big Three auto makers in thwarting efforts to impose tougher fuel-mileage standards, and (3) enabled the banking industry to defeat a forced reduction in credit card interest rates. During the Clinton administration, the firm has experienced a bull market for its services as industries such as insurance and pharmaceuticals have attempted to mobilize grassroots opposition to the Clinton health care reform proposals.[10]

Service vendors have arisen on the left as well. One of the most successful has been the Clinton Group (which has no connection to the current administration). This firm uses an extensive computer phone bank to construct a list of likely supporters on a particular issue, and employs its "patch through" capacities to set in motion an onslaught of seemingly spontaneous phone calls to legislators. For example, if the National Organization for Women (NOW) opposes a Supreme Court nominee because of his abortion rights record,

> [t]he Clinton Group will take the membership rolls of the group and match names to phone numbers. It might also use its computer to cross-reference magazine subscriptions, data on personal purchasing habits, and precincts with particular voting and income profiles to come up with a bigger list of sympathetic people.
> At the company's phone bank in Louisville, Kentucky, a computer dials the numbers. When someone answers, an operator comes on the line and explains NOW's position, offering to transfer the caller, at no charge, to the White House switchboard or local member of Congress.[11]

Such astroturf mobilization of issue supporters is typically directed not just at lawmakers, but also at the broader attentive public, as public relations and lobbying become increasingly intertwined in the politics of influence. Often a group aims to redefine an issue so that its position is politically acceptable, as illustrated by the actions of the National Restaurant Association in the face of President Clinton's 1993 attempt to reduce the tax deduction for business meals.

The business-meal deduction is widely perceived as a "fat-cat" issue that benefits lobbyists and their corporate clients, as well as restaurant owners and the business community. The deduction enjoys little general public support. As a consequence, the National Restaurant Association, rather than expanding its formal lobbying efforts, chose to engage in an elaborate public relations campaign to present the proposed tax change as one that would affect the most vulnerable in society: women, minorities, first-time job holders, and the disabled. The organization's strategy included holding a Washington press conference where a waitress from a small Maryland town told reporters she feared losing her job if Congress approved the reduction in the business deduction. Subsequently, the same waitress appeared in a thirty-second commercial and claimed that the planned cuts in the business-meal deduction would endanger the jobs of 165,000 people (an apparently arbitrary figure). At the end of the advertisement, she invited viewers to call a toll-free telephone number, which was answered by professional telemarketers who would offer to connect callers to the offices of their senators.[12]

Notwithstanding the pleas of food-service workers, most sophisticated and expensive grassroots efforts serve the interests of elites. For example, much has been made of Japan's high-priced lobbying presence in Washington. According to Justice Department records, Japanese interests hired more than 125 law firms, economic consultants, and public relations companies between 1988 and 1992.[13] By the early 1990s the highly publicized Japanese corporate effort to use Washington insiders as "superlobbyists" had provoked a negative reaction in the American press; this caused Japanese interests to reconsider their strategy of directly influencing decisions in Washington. Much as domestic lobbyists have mobilized ordinary citizens as part of their influence campaigns, Japanese interests have developed their own, distinctive grassroots strategy by using American corporate executives to lobby in their behalf.[14] In 1993 the Toyota Motor Corporation successfully urged 119 of its American suppliers to contact decision makers to oppose import quotas and efforts to raise tariffs on minivans.[15] (See Chapter 16 for a close look at "the Japan lobby.")

Other foreign interests have followed the Japanese lead. In its efforts to retain most-favored-nation trading status, China has relied less on lobbyists and more on American business interests that would suffer financial losses if trade relations were downgraded. Boeing and its employees, beneficiaries of Chinese aircraft orders worth hundreds of millions of dollars, have been among China's strongest Washington defenders.

The grassroots tactics of capital interest groups have even been emulated by President Clinton, who in 1993 and 1994 showed a propensity to use the political party apparatus to marshal support for key parts of his policy agenda, notably his health care reform initiative. One element of Clinton's health care lobbying team, named the "Democratic Action Networks's National Health Care Campaign," is based in the Democratic National Committee, and has been in charge of orchestrating "a series of purportedly spontaneous grassroots movements" coordinated by regional directors across the country and supplemented by "liaisons for every interest group from ethnics to seniors."[16] Besides television advertisements and targeted mailings, the national party reached back to the 1992 presidential campaign to borrow another mobilization tactic. One element of the summer 1994 campaign on behalf of the president's proposal was a privately organized $2-million bus tour, the "Health Security Express." Proreform groups, particularly unions, consumer groups, senior citizens' organizations, and churches contributed roughly $20,000 per vehicle to launch the tour. The effort was to converge in Independence, Missouri, for a rally at the home of Harry Truman, who proposed a half a century ago that all Americans should be covered by health insurance.[17] The tour's aim was straightforward: to "generate enough grassroots pressure on members of Congress that ... they will hear 'the whisper of the guillotine' if they fail to act."[18] The bus tour's results proved somewhat disappointing, in that the caravans produced at least as much publicity for opponents of health care reform as for supporters.[19]

The consequences of the increasing use of grassroots tactics are difficult to determine, even roughly. The number of actors in the process obviously has expanded, and some might see this as helping the nation reach its democratic potential. Others, however, "fear that the rising tide of citizen voices is so fraught with manipulation that the decision-making process is in danger of being twisted, especially if most of the expressions on an issue conflict with true public opinion."[20]

Moreover, the increasing use of highly orchestrated grassroots lobbying may add to the difficulties decision makers have in arriving at acceptable compromises. Many interest groups have discovered that grassroots mobilization often works best when constituents are motivated by fear. As one activist put it, "nothing rouses the faithful like a simple message denouncing your archenemy as evil incarnate."[21] This scarcely increases the quality of policy debates. Rep. David R. Obey (D-Wis.), chair of the House Appropriations committee and a frequent target of mobilization efforts, sees grassroots politics as "a corruption of participatory democracy.... It means that those who are well-organized with special axes to grind will have an advantage over persons genuinely interested in the issues."[22] For better or for worse, the politics of grassroots mobilization, along with other efforts to reach the public, have become the norm, at least on highly visible and important national issues.

Health Care: Policy Complexity Meets Hyperpluralism

By 1994, the Clinton administration's effort to reform America's health care system had become the mother of all mobilization campaigns. "It's the largest mobilization since the establishment of Social Security," opined Frank Mankiewicz, public relations executive and former Kennedy administration aide, in September 1993.[23]

Mankiewicz was wrong; the activity levels of organized interests in the health care debate of 1993-94 have surpassed those of any such mobilization in American political history. The business community has rarely been more exercised; add to that the concerns of the medical sector (one-seventh of the economy) and the intense preferences of many citizens groups, such as the American Association of Retired Persons (AARP), and there is little question that more interests have become active on health care reform than on any other issue to have come before the federal government. The magnitude of the engagement reflects both the growth of organized interests and the extensive reach of the national government.

When tobacco companies, large corporations, major universities, the bishops of the Catholic Church, senior citizens' groups, and public interest organizations take an active role in health care policy making, all in response to a presidential initiative, few punches are pulled. The large-scale nature of the policy change virtually demands that all affected interests weigh in.[24] The stakes are high, and the window of opportunity to affect outcomes is relatively brief. Thus, in the struggle over health care reform, we find an extremely large number of interests engaging in an extremely large number of actions, across a host of American political institutions.

Although health care presents especially complex and far-reaching problems, the very difficulty of resolving its myriad issues provides an excellent opportunity to examine the contemporary nature of interest group politics. In this section, we will look at the interest groups in the health care universe to determine how those interests have mobilized in response to a policy challenge and what tactics they have employed in seeking to influence the outcomes of health care reform initiatives. To do this, we will rely on an organizing scheme that was first articulated in the previous edition of this book. Based in part on E. E. Schattschneider's notion that "the outcome of all conflict is determined by the scope of the contagion,"[25] we categorized group-related conflicts along two dimensions: (1) the scope of the conflict and (2) the number of people and interests affected by it (Table 18-1).

Historically, most health care policy conflicts have been narrowly defined, most often by professionals and, increasingly, by bureaucrats within the medical community. On occasion, there have been attempts to broaden the scope of conflict (for example, President Truman's call for universal coverage and the passage of Medicare in 1965), but physicians, other professionals, and health business interests have ordinarily dominated the issue area, whether in niche-specific decisions such as licensing requirements or in complex policy choices on hospital consolidation. With some important exceptions, such as AARP, consumers of medical care have not been well represented.

The 1992 presidential campaign succeeded in opening up health care issues far beyond the limited perspectives of the "middleman"

Table 18-1 Scope and Impact of Group-Related Conflict

Number of people and interests affected	Scope of conflict	
	Narrow	Broad
Few	Niche politics (e.g., weapons procurement)	Symbolic politics (e.g., flag-burning amendment)
Many	Policy community politics (e.g., banking)	Public confrontation politics (e.g., abortion)

groups that make up the policy community (see Chapter 1). The sheer number of organized interests in the health care debate has been astonishing; as early as 1992, reporter Robert Pear identified 741 health-related groups,[26] a figure so large that it suggests the extensive growth of countervailing interests *within* the health care sector. At least as important, however, has been the *entry of many other powerful interests into the health care arena.* In particular, the business community has become extremely active, although it has not spoken with a single voice. At least during 1993-94, and despite its inherently technical nature, much of health care policy making has taken on a "public confrontation" cast, in the terms of Table 18-1, as the scope of conflict has expanded greatly and the number of people affected has grown to encompass virtually everyone from high-tech surgeons to Haitian refugees. Given the complexity and importance of the issues of health care and its costs, it is no surprise that many groups have embarked upon highly emotional, symbolic campaigns that emphasize ill-defined notions of "choice" or "socialism" rather than more specific elements of the debate. At least during the 1993-94 period, health care reform has led to group activities on all policy fronts, often simultaneously.

Health Care Niches and Policy Communities

Like any complex policy debate, much of the health care discussion is arcane and limited. Highly specialized policies are often hammered out by relatively small numbers of interested parties, far from the glare of publicity that has surrounded more general decisions. These "issue niches" often involve highly technical choices that only a handful of interests care about or understand.[27] There are thousands of these in health policy, ranging from the intricacies of Medicaid billing to the role of optometrists under various possible plans.

Whereas niches admit relatively few participants and relatively little conflict, policy communities (composed of interest groups, bureaucratic units, professional organizations, congressional subcommittees and committees, and think tanks)[28] are open to participation from large numbers of interests. Health care encompasses too broad a collection of issues to host a single policy community; rather, several overlapping policy communities bring together large numbers of interests and other players. The extensive Medicare-based policy community includes hospitals, some physicians, the AARP, a House Ways and Means subcommittee, and many other actors, but ordinarily it would not attract much attention from obstetricians, medical researchers, and medical schools. Conversely, the medical education community is smaller, consisting of key players such as large universities, other major institutions, and "star" physicians. Ordinarily, these separate aggregations can work out policies without much outside attention, although not every interest may be accommodated. Faced with comprehensive changes, however, these and other policy communities, although continuing to be important in hammering out decisions, often lose control of the policy agenda.

Public Confrontation Politics and Symbolic Politics

When the "scope of the conflict," in Schattschneider's terminology,[29] is expanded, more political forces come into play, and organized interests must adapt accordingly, if grudgingly. In the case of health care reform, what most interests wanted was "ad hoc, particularistic legislative or regulatory relief that would restore their advantages vis a vis the others"—in other words, politics as usual within the health policy community.[30] But many groups came to agree with President Clinton that "additional fragmented correctives would not work and that only 'comprehensive' and 'fundamental' reform could hope to stabilize this fractious group universe."[31] The complexity of health care issues meant that many decisions would still be made within policy communities, but the fate of large-scale policy change moved beyond the control of policy specialists. A host of major interests became active in public confrontation politics, none more aggressively than the business community.

Employers have always paid some attention to the costs and mechanisms of providing health care, but President Clinton's proposal to require them to provide coverage to their workers propelled the business community—and especially smaller businesses—into the heart of the fray. Although the 610,000-member National Federation of Independent Businesses (NFIB) has pressed hard through its capital lobbying corps, it and other major organizations have relied on extensive grassroots efforts as well. For example, Rep. Mel Reynolds, a first-term Chicago Democrat, received a visit from the owners of eight "mom and pop" groceries from his district, accompanied by a tobacco lobbyist. The business owners contended that the high cigarette taxes proposed to help pay for health care would cut their sales and force layoffs.

"When constituents come in like that, it gives you a moment of pause to think," observed Rep. Reynolds, who remained a supporter of "sin taxes" to fund expanded health care.[32] As health care politics came to a head in 1994, the NFIB was prepared. With a sophisticated telelobbying system in place—much like that of the Chamber of Commerce—and 500,000 pieces of direct mail targeted at sixty-five members of Congress, NFIB continued its effective strategy of seamlessly combining inside and outside tactics.[33]

There is general agreement among most interests that American health care, especially in its coverage and financing, requires substantial modification. This "negative consensus" offers an important point of departure toward real change,[34] but it is inadequate to produce widespread agreement among interests. One effect of the negative consensus is that several key organizations have defined themselves by what they *oppose*. For example, the small businesses of the NFIB oppose requirements that employers must offer health insurance to their employees; the Catholic Church opposes requirements that abortions be a part of the health care package. Ironically, the more a single, well-publicized issue comes to dominate an organization's approach to a multifaceted set of proposals, the less influence that organization may wield, save on its central concern. Both the NFIB and the Catholic Church, for example, have called for many changes in the American health care system; both interests would like coverage to be extended to the working poor. But the NFIB cannot abide an employer mandate to provide insurance, and Catholic bishops have proven intractable in their unwillingness to approve any system that would provide abortions—even if Catholic physicians or medical facilities could opt not to participate.

Both the NFIB, with 1,500 businesses in an average congressional district, and the Catholic Church, with "Catholic Charities, the pro-life office, the social-justice groups, and the health-care providers all working together,"[35] offer striking examples of the power to mobilize grassroots support for a single, easily comprehensible position. The question remains, however, whether their success in thwarting meaningful employer mandates and mandatory abortion coverage means that they will sacrifice influence over other parts of the package, which may be ironed out in the more private arenas of committee rooms and executive offices, far from the glare of public confrontation politics.

Only occasionally do interest group politics venture into the realm of the purely symbolic—where the scope of the conflict is broad but relatively few individuals or interests are seriously affected. Symbols usually are most important in relations between leaders and group members, which then directly affect the abilities of groups to support moderate policies. "You get a polarization of debate generated by elites which ordinary citizens find neither affects their interests or addresses their concerns," observes Tom Mann.[36] Rather, rhetorical intensity, often including the demonization of governmental officials serves to bolster campaigns for new members and increased contributions.

In the health care debate, the notions of "choice" and "universal coverage" have occasioned symbolic exchanges. Although most citizens' choice of medical care is already limited by medical plans or cost considerations, and the Clinton plan provided for more choice than many other packages (especially those that gave insurance companies a major role in determining coverage), such considerations did not stop the Health Insurance Association of America (HIAA) from running its "Harry and Louise" series of television advertisements, which focused, misleadingly, on the question of choice under the Clinton proposals. Most public relations professionals concluded that those advertisements altered the nature of the debate over health care and succeeded in raising serious doubts about the Clinton plan.[37]

In a similar vein, the administration and some liberal groups enshrined the idea of universal coverage, despite a lack of agreement on what universality actually meant (98 percent coverage immediately? 95 percent in five years?). Both "choice" and "universal coverage" became symbols only loosely related to important, underlying concerns.

Using symbolic, emotionally charged issues to build membership rosters and take a readily identifiable position in the public debate often means that policy making takes a back seat. For example, in July 1994 the powerful American Medical Association, the AFL-CIO, and the AARP, with a total of 49 million members, touted their agreement on achieving universal coverage and assuring patient choice among physicians and plans.[38] As we ordinarily understand pluralistic politics, when these three groups can present a single set of principles, a basis for compromise and closure should exist. But in the face of the highly visibly HIAA television campaign and the sharp reactions among Clinton supporters to any compromises on universal coverage, the impact of these three large membership groups has been greatly reduced.

The Parallel Politics of Health Care

Because of its importance to the economy, to many professionals, to most politicians, and to virtually all citizens, the debate over health care reform has been conducted simultaneously in all of the four arenas of interest group politics (Table 18-1). Consider the case of a heart surgeon under contract with two HMOs and a major teaching hospital. Her specialist medical group will seek policy niches for protection from the effects of impending changes on highly technical issues, such as decisions on when to operate. Various organized interests, including the AMA, a surgical organization, the HMOs, and her hospital will represent her, sometimes in contradictory ways, within a number of overlapping health policy communities, and many of these groups engage vigorously in public confrontation politics in Washington. Finally, some of the interests will venture into symbolic politics, although these are more the province of consumers and insurance companies than of practitioners and health professionals.

In short, many organized interests in the health care debate believe they must fight a multifront war to protect themselves and reduce the tremendous uncertainty inherent in any major change. It is no wonder that public relations firms, advertising agencies, Washington insiders, direct mail specialists, and dozens of other purveyors of influence have prospered during the escalation of the health care wars. As of mid-1994, more than $100 million had been spent on health care lobbying and public relations efforts.[39] With new technologies, immense resources, and great visibility, health care interests have escalated their efforts far beyond merely doing "more of the same."

Conclusion: The Consequences of Lobbying as Campaigning

If, as we suggest, lobbying efforts on major political issues have come increasingly to look like national electoral campaigns, replete with slick advertisements, intense and extreme rhetoric, high-tech mobilization of supporters, and the expenditure of large sums of money, the short-term implications are not positive. Such efforts contribute to the fragmentation and disintegration of our political order, without enhancing its representative or deliberative aspects.[40] Many voices may be raised, but few are genuinely heard and evaluated in the plebiscitary environment that characterizes the debate over issues such as national health care. Because closure is so difficult to obtain, the policies that do emerge are more likely to be token than substantial and more symbolic than real, further disillusioning a citizenry already cynical and suspicious of politicians' lofty promises.

Over the long term, the increasing use of more public lobbying techniques does not serve the interests of elected politicians, who have already begun to adapt to these tactics. Like organized interests, officeholders seek to reduce uncertainty, especially in the electoral arena. Officials have traditionally granted access to organized interests in part because such interests have helped them reduce uncertainty by providing the human and material resources necessary for winning reelection. In addition, organized interests often provide "political intelligence" for officials seeking efficient ways to gather information about voters.[41] Interest groups have typically proved to be invaluable to legislators in understanding constituent issue positions and their rationales.

Still, it is often difficult for elected officials to understand what voters "really think" or to know whose opinions are actually being expressed in the information-rich Washington environment. The many sophisticated, highly orchestrated attempts by organized interests to communicate with lawmakers run the risk of being largely discounted by policy makers already overwhelmed with information the accuracy and reliability of which is often difficult to judge. In Chapter 13 of this volume, William Browne outlines one adaptive consequence of such overload: on agriculture policies at least, members of Congress have come to rely less on national interest groups and more on key local "confidants," whom they have learned to trust as both working farmers and barometers of district opinion.

Ironically, the growth of well-coordinated grassroots efforts by organized interests to influence public officials may ultimately lead to less influence for these groups. Elective politicians, a most sensitive breed, may well try to sniff out their own, independent sources of information on the political ramifications of major policy decisions.

Notes

1. Allan J. Cigler and Burdett A. Loomis, "Organized Interests and the Search for Certainty," in *Interest Group Politics*, 3d ed., ed. Allan J. Cigler and Burdett A. Loomis (Washington, D.C.: CQ Press, 1991), 385-398.
2. William P. Browne, "Organized Interests and Their Issue Niches: A Search for Pluralism in a Policy Domain," *Journal of Politics* 52 (May 1990): 477-509.
3. Kay Lehman Schlozman and John T. Tierney, "More of the Same: Washington Pressure Activity in a Decade of Change," *Journal of Politics* 45 (May 1983): 351-377, and *Organized Interests and American Democracy* (New York: Harper and Row, 1986), 155.
4. Jack L. Walker, Jr., *Mobilizing Interest Groups in America* (Ann Arbor: University of Michigan Press, 1991); Robert H. Salisbury, John P. Heinz, Edward O. Laumann, and Robert L. Nelson, "Who Works with Whom? Interest Group Alliances and Opposition," *American Political Science Review* 81 (December 1987): 1217-1234.
5. Peter H. Stone, "Learning from Nader," *National Journal*, June 11, 1994, 1342-1344.
6. Kevin Phillips, "Under the Influence: Just How Sick Is the System?", *Time*, June 13, 1994, and *Arrogant Capital: Washington, Wall Street and the Frustration of American Politics* (Boston: Little Brown, forthcoming).
7. Burdett A. Loomis, "A New Era: Groups and the Grass Roots," in *Interest Group Politics*, ed. Allan J. Cigler and Burdett A. Loomis (Washington, D.C.: CQ Press, 1983), 169-190; Hedrick Smith, *The Power Game* (New York: Random House, 1988), 240ff.
8. Smith, *The Power Game*, 240.
9. "Using Public Rage for Private Ends," *The Kansas City Star*, March 17, 1993, 1.
10. Ibid.
11. Ibid, 20.
12. Joel Brinkley, "Lobbying Rules of the 1990s Show the Most Vulnerable," *New York Times*, June 16, 1993.
13. Stephen Engelberg with Martin Tolchin, "Foreigners Find New Ally in U.S. Industry," *New York Times*, November 2, 1993.
14. Ibid.
15. Ibid.
16. "The Clinton Sales Campaign," *Newsweek*, November 8, 1993, 41-42.

17. "Harry and Louise to Have Company in Health Battle," *Lawrence* (Kansas) *Journal World*, July 7, 1994.
18. "The Clinton Sales Campaign," 41.
19. Catherine Manegold, "Health Care Bus: Lots of Miles, Not So Much Talk," *New York Times*, July 25, 1994, A7.
20. "Using Public Rage for Private Ends," 12.
21. W. John Moore, "Going to Extremes, Losing the Center," *National Journal*, June 6, 1994, 1395.
22. "Using Public Rage for Private Ends," 12.
23. Quoted in Clifford Krauss, "Lobbyists of Every Stripe on Health Care Proposal," *The New York Times*, September 24, 1993, A1.
24. On agenda change, see Frank R. Baumgartner and Bryan D. Jones, *Agendas and Instability in American Politics* (Chicago: University of Chicago, 1993), chap. 1.
25. E. E. Schattschneider, *The Semi-Sovereign People* (New York: Holt, Rinehart, and Winston, 1960), 2.
26. Robert Pear, "Conflicting Aims in Health Lobby Stall Legislation," *New York Times*, March 18, 1992, 2A.
27. See William P. Browne, "Issue Niches and the Limits of Interest Group Influence," in *Interest Group Politics*, 3d ed., ed. Allan J. Cigler and Burdett A. Loomis (Washington, D.C.: CQ Press, 1991), 345-370.
28. For an extensive discussion of such politics, see James A. Thurber, "Dynamics of Policy Subsystems in American Politics," in *Interest Group Politics*, 3d ed., ed. Allan J. Cigler and Burdett A. Loomis (Washington, D.C.: CQ Press, 1991), 319-344.
29. Schattschneider, *The Semi-Sovereign People*, 2.
30. Lawrence D. Brown, "National Health Reform: An Idea Whose Political Time Has Come?," *PS: Political Science and Politics* 27, 2 (June 1994): 200.
31. Ibid., 200.
32. Krauss, "Lobbyists of Every Stripe," A1.
33. Reported on PBS's "Nightly Business Report," July 19, 1994.
34. Theodore Marmor, quoting Paul Starr, in "The Politics of Universal Health Insurance: Lessons from Past Administrations?," *PS: Political Science and Politics* 27, 2 (June 1994): 194.
35. Rev. Michael Place, quoted in Peter Steinfels, "Bishops Mobilize against Abortion in Health Plans," *New York Times*, July 13, 1994, A7.
36. Quoted in Moore, "Going to Extremes, Losing the Center," 1395.
37. Based on presentations at a Congressional Quarterly professional seminar on "Issue Campaigns and the Clinton Administration," held in Washington, D.C., July 7, 1994.
38. Advertisement, *New York Times*, July 21, 1994, A7. The content of the advertisement was duly noted in a news story on the next page.
39. Neil A. Lewis, "Vast Sums Spent to Sway Health Plan," *New York Times*, July 22, 1994. The story relies on an extensive report by the Center for Public Integrity.
40. Robert Dahl, *The New American Political (Dis)Order* (Berkeley, Calif.: Institute of Governmental Studies Press, 1994).
41. John Mark Hansen, *Gaining Access* (Chicago: University of Chicago Press, 1991), 16.

Index

Exchange theory, 80, 81, 82, 90, 91
Executive branch
 consumer issues, 265
 interest organizations and, 319, 320-321, 327-329, 343-344
 intergovernmental organizations and, 147
 Japanese lobbies and, 360
 presidency, 320-325, 326-329, 343-344
 regulation and, 302-304, 305, 306-307, 314, 322-329, 341, 342-343
Executive Office of the President, 326, 329
Executive Order 12291, 323, 325
Executive Order 12498, 325
Exxon, 120, 121
Exxon Valdez, 120

FACE. *See* For a Cleaner Environment
Fahrenkopf, Frank, 357
Family Research Council, 60, 228
Family values, 217-218
Family Voice monthly publication, 59
Farmers. *See* Agriculture sector
FCC. *See* Federal Communications Commission
FDA. *See* Food and Drug Administration
FDIC. *See* Federal Deposit Insurance Corporation
FEC. *See* Federal Election Commission
FECA. *See* Federal Election Campaign Act of 1971
Federal Communications Commission (FCC), 274
Federal Deposit Insurance Corporation (FDIC), 260
Federal Election Campaign Act of 1971 (FECA), 156, 157-158, 176, 181, 183, 185, 187, 190n1
Federal Election Commission (FEC), 155, 156, 157, 176, 179, 181, 188, 196, 362
Federal Grants and Contracts Weekly publication, 84

Federal Register, 84, 322, 339
Federal Reserve Board, 260
Federal Trade Commission (FTC), 260, 265
 funding of citizens' organizations, 14
 insurance investigations, 27
 physicians' business affairs, 27
 Reagan administration, 261
Feldesman, James, 269-270
Feminist movement, 65
FIA. *See* Freedom of Information Act
Financial sector, 200-201, 202, 260, 272, 275, 300
Findley, Paul, 386
Fitzsimmons, Frank, 308
Flint, Sam Hall, 307
Flynn, Charlotte, 228-229
Focus. *See* Focus on the Family
Focus on the Family (Focus), 59, 62
FOE. *See* Friends of the Earth
Foley, Thomas, 163, 296n7
Food and Drug Administration (FDA)
 consumer issues, 265
 Council on Competitiveness, 331
 funding of citizens' organizations, 14
 Health Research Group, 34
 infant formulas, 38
 legislative mandate, 50n20
Food Research and Action Center (FRAC), 92
For a Cleaner Environment (FACE), 35, 40, 45
Ford, 121
Ford Foundation, 109, 118
Ford, Gerald, 302, 304, 305, 324, 328, 352
Ford, William, 244, 249
Foreign Affairs, 360
Foreign interest organizations, 349, 360-362. *See also* Ethnic/racial issues and organizations; Japanese lobbies; individual countries by name
 effects of, 365, 369, 371
 elections and, 385-388
 expansion of, 371, 372-373
 foreign policy and, 373-374, 385
 methods of, 397

Media
conservative vs. liberal sources of information, 71
consumer issues, 260
Council on Competitiveness, 336, 338-340
Hill, Anita and, 219
interest organization politics, 223*t*, 224, 225, 227, 230
intergovernmental groups and, 143
radio, 71
radio and TV Marti, 381, 382
role of, 20
television, 46, 71
victim organizations, 33, 40, 45-46, 48
Medicaid/Medicare, 275, 399. *See also* Health care reform; Health care sector
Medical establishment, 42, 43
Medical organizations, 34. *See also* individual organizations by name
Mennonites, 62
Merrill Lynch, 201*t*, 206-208, 211
Metropolitan Life, 270
Mexican Americans, 380, 381, 382. *See also* Ethnic/racial issues and organizations
Mexico, 361, 372, 373
Mica, Dan, 38
Middleman organizations, 13
Mikkelsen, Edwin J., 45
Mikulski, Barbara, 178
Milbrath, Lester, 25
Miller, James C., III, 322, 323
Ministry of International Trade and Industry (MITI). *See* Japan
Minority issues, 19, 219. *See also* Ethnic/racial issues and organizations
Mitchell, George, 380
Mitchell, Neil J., 361, 362
Mitchell, Robert C., 113, 114, 116, 125
MITI (Ministry of International Trade and Industry). *See* Japan
Mitsubishi, 363
Mitsui, 363
Miyazawa, Kiichi, 355
Mobil Oil, 197-198

Modern Maturity magazine, 12. *See also* American Association of Retired Persons
Moe, Terry M., 2, 9, 41, 321, 324, 343-344
Mondale, Walter, 163, 326
Monterey Institute of International Studies, 354
Moore, Demi, 123
Moore, Thomas Gale, 300
Moral Majority, 15, 56
Morita, Akio, 357
Morse, Robert, 362
Moss, John, 264-265
Mothers Against Drunk Driving (MADD), 51*n*29
Motion picture industry, 273, 274
Motley, John, 235*n*50
Motor Carrier Act of 1935, 300, 301
Motor Carrier Act of 1980, 299, 300, 301, 312-314
Motor Carrier Reform Act, 304
Motor freight industry, 299, 300-315. *See also* Transportation industry
Motor Vehicle Manufacturing Association of the United States, 358
Mott, Stewart, 23
Mozambique, 361
Murphy, Rupert, 308
Muslims, 384

NAAA. *See* National Association of Arab Americans
NAACP. *See* National Association for the Advancement of Colored People
NACo. *See* National Association of Counties
Nader, Ralph
consumer groups and, 259, 261, 265, 269, 272, 394
Health Research Group, 34
as a policy entrepreneur, 39, 45, 259
Nader's Raiders, 272
NAFTA. *See* North American Free Trade Agreement
NAM. *See* National Association of Manufacturers

Protestantism, 55-56, 58, 61, 63, 64
Proxmire, William, 264-265
Prudential, 13
Public Affairs Council (PAC), 183-184
Public Citizen, 265, 267, 269, 272, 273.
 See also Nader, Ralph
Public Citizen Congress Watch, 265,
 267, 336-337
Public Citizen Health Research
 Group, 34, 265
Public Citizen Media Access Project,
 265, 273
Public Citizen Tax Reform Research
 Group, 269
Public interest organizations. *See also*
 Citizens' organizations; Environmental organizations
 agendas, 87, 88-89, 97
 agriculture sector and, 286-287
 benefits, 78, 80, 82, 90-91, 95-96
 Congress and, 287
 definitions of, 98n18, 132
 development and formation of, 80-
 81, 82t
 entrepreneurs and leaders, 78, 80-
 82, 85-88, 93-96, 97, 196
 expansion of, 77, 78, 138
 "free-riders," 78
 government funding, 93-94
 intergovernmental organizations
 and, 138, 143
 membership, 81, 94-96
 networks, 85-87, 92, 94, 95
 radical groups, 118, 127
 revenues, 107
 role of, 78, 79, 81-82
 sponsorship and patronage, 78-80,
 81, 82, 83-97, 196-197
 staffing, 106
Public Interest Research Groups, 272
Public opinion, 19, 25, 243-244. *See
 also* United States
Public policies. *See* Policies, public
Public Voice for Food and Health Policy, 262, 269, 272. *See also* Community Nutrition Institute
Publishing sector, 200-201

Puerto Rico, 380-381, 382. *See also*
 Ethnic/racial issues and orga-
 nizations
Putting People First (PPF), 22

Quayle Council. *See* Council on Competitiveness
Quayle, Dan, 115, 325-326, 327, 330-
 331, 336, 339, 341-342, 345n23. *See
 also* Council on Competitiveness
Quick, Richard, 306
Quinn, Marie, 38

Rabin, Yitzak, 379
Racial issues. *See* Ethnic/racial issues
 and organizations
Radio Marti, 382
Railroad industry, 203, 300
Rainforest Action Network (RAN),
 128
RAN. *See* Rainforest Action Network
RARG. *See* Regulatory Analysis Review Group
Rational man theory, 8-9
Reagan, Ronald
 assassination attempt, 31n69
 Citizens for the Republic, 59
 consumer issues, 261
 deregulation, 261
 environmental organizations, 114
 funding of citizens' organizations,
 14-15
 growth of government, 11
 interest group organizations, 328,
 380
 intergovernmental organizations,
 137, 138, 139, 140, 146
 political action committee, 163
 regulatory issues, 323-324, 327, 338
 religious organizations and, 69, 70t
 South Africa and, 384
 Soviet grain sales, 372
 Supreme Court nominations, 215,
 218, 220, 227
Redford, Robert, 123
Reed, Ralph, 60
Reformed churches, 62, 64

Reforms, 188. *See also* Health care reform
  banking, 272
  business issues, 7
  campaign finance, 1, 3, 10, 158, 168-171, 181-183, 184-188, 192*n*18, 192*n*20, 272
  congressional, 284
  ethics, 360
  governmental, 267
  intergovernmental organizations and, 150
  lobbies, 26-27
  motor freight industry, 300, 302, 304-315
  political action committees, 3, 159, 162, 163, 181-190
  regulatory, 322-324
  religious organizations and, 56-57, 63
"Reg-negs" (negotiated regulations). *See* Policies, public
Regulations. *See also* Council on Competitiveness; Office of Information and Regulatory Affairs; Regulatory review
  cable television industry, 274, 275
  Congress and, 337
  litigation and, 333-334, 336
  motor freight industry, 299, 300-301, 303-315
  overview of, 301-303
  presidency and, 326-329, 342-343
  reforms, 322-324
  strategic accommodation, 335-337, 342
Regulatory Analysis Review Group (RARG), 322
Regulatory Council, 322, 323
Regulatory review, 341, 342-343. *See also* Council on Competitiveness; Executive branch; Office of Information and Regulatory Affairs
Rehnquist, William H., 217, 218, 233*n*14
Reich, Robert, 355
Reid, Harry, 43
Reilly, William, 120, 334-335, 343

Reischauer Center for East Asian Studies, 364
Reischauer Institute of Japanese Studies, 354
Religious organizations. *See also* Christian Left; Christian Right; individual denominations by name
  agendas and issues, 66-70
  church and religious beliefs, 62-63
  coalitions, 57, 62
  contemporary activism, 55, 57-58
  denominational patterns, 57-58, 61-63
  development and growth of, 56-59
  foreign policy and, 372-373, 381, 384
  ideological patterns, 55, 58, 61-63
  politics and, 63-66, 70-73
  power of, 58-59
  profile of organizations, 59-61
  resistance to, 58
  role of clergy, 72
Rendell, Ed, 149
Republican Party. *See also* Political parties
  Arab Americans and, 377, 380
  campaign finance reform, 171
  Council on Competitiveness, 337, 339
  environmental organizations, 102
  intergovernmental organizations, 141, 148
  Israel/Jews and, 375, 387
  Latinos and, 381-382
  New Deal coalition, 17
  1992 platform, 60
  political action committees, 161-162, 163, 164, 165, 168, 181
  Quayle, Dan and, 342
  religious organizations, 56-57, 68-69, 74
  Thomas, Clarence and, 235*n*50
Research, 25, 43, 44
Resource Conservation and Recovery Act, 43
Revenue Act of 1971, 156
Revenue sharing. *See* Economic issues
Reynolds, Mel, 401-402
Ribicoff, Abraham, 264-265